THEATRES OF INDIA
A CONCISE COMPANION

edited by
ANANDA LAL

OXFORD
UNIVERSITY PRESS

OXFORD
UNIVERSITY PRESS

YMCA Library Building, Jai Singh Road, New Delhi 110 001

Oxford University Press is a department of the University of Oxford.
It furthers the University's objective of excellence in research, scholarship,
and education by publishing worldwide in

Oxford   New York
Auckland   Cape Town   Dar es Salaam   Hong Kong   Karachi
Kuala Lumpur   Madrid   Melbourne   Mexico City   Nairobi
New Delhi   Shanghai   Taipei   Toronto

With offices in
Argentina   Austria   Brazil   Chile   Czech Republic   France   Greece
Guatemala   Hungary   Italy   Japan   Poland   Portugal   Singapore
South Korea   Switzerland   Thailand   Turkey   Ukraine   Vietnam

Oxford is a registered trade mark of Oxford University Press
in the UK and in certain other countries.

Published in India
by Oxford University Press, New Delhi

ISBN-13: 978-0-19-569917-3
ISBN-10: 0-19-569917-3

Typeset in AGaramond 11.5/13.9
by Eleven Arts, Keshav Puram, Delhi 110 035
Printed in India by Gopsons Papers Ltd., Noida
Published by Oxford University Press
YMCA Library Building, Jai Singh Road, New Delhi 110 001

Contents

Introduction

The Oxford Companion to Indian Theatre appeared as a hardback in 2004. When Oxford University Press, India, proposed an affordable edition last year, so that this pioneering and well-received reference work could reach a much wider audience, we had to weigh two important considerations. First, for pricing reasons, we could not possibly retain the full text of 563 large-format pages. Second, to update the 700-odd entries would have taken at least a couple of years, along with the responsibility of adding new entries to cover contemporary theatre adequately.

Given these constraints of space and time, we decided to limit the scope of the present project to two parts: the long overviews of Indian theatres by language in Part I, and the general surveys of specific forms, genres, and traditions in Part II. Thus, more than one-third of the material concerns urban, and the rest rural, theatre—a fair representation of the art as I see it. Most of the essays in Part I have been revised and brought up to date, through corrections as well as addenda dealing with recent developments, sometimes written by new contributors as the original authors have, sadly, exited from the great theatre of life. Two completely fresh articles were commissioned, on Mizo theatre and women's theatre, since research now exists in these previously uncharted areas.

We had to leave out, however, virtually all the biographical entries in the original volume, so as to keep this book to a manageable size. There are two exceptions to this principle; for obvious reasons, the two world-famous names synonymous with Indian classicism and modernism respectively: Kalidasa and

Rabindranath Tagore. Similarly, the two preeminent institutions that have historically shaped contemporary Indian theatre retain their places—the Indian People's Theatre Association and the National School of Drama—one non-governmental, the other state-subsidized. Both have become major and influential traditions in their own right. All other groups and companies that had separate entries in the *Companion* have regrettably lost their independent spaces here.

CONVENTIONS

Dates. Cultural factors related to theatre create complications in dating. Apart from perhaps two or three linguistic regions where the sense of history has developed better, all Indian urban stage traditions reveal blithe unconcern about chronology. Nobody cared to write down the date of a premiere. As a result, huge anomalies arose in later, secondary literature. Since a theatre resource, by commonly accepted standards, is expected to provide the year of first production rather than publication, this handicap posed major difficulties. Often, where no consensus emerged, the year of a play's first edition has been printed. But even this cannot be considered sacrosanct, since no Indian calendars correspond to the Gregorian, and sometimes no copy of the play survives. Inevitably, I expect readers to point out errors, but request them to send me copies of supporting primary evidence or documentation unambiguously substantiating cause for change.

Leave alone the Indian countryside, even in the cosmopolitan megalopolises facts are hard to come by. Until recently, dates of birth were not registered, and remembered only by such temporal signposts as 'the day the big cyclone hit our town' or 'the full-moon night in Paush the year that electricity arrived' (which could fall in two Christian years, as the month of Paush straddles December–January). Furthermore, many Indians habitually decreased their children's ages officially, so that when they grew up they could have an extra few years to apply for jobs, which normally carried an age bar. I know of one famous director actually born four years before the 'official' year printed here.

Names. Spellings of names also raise difficulties. In Bengali, Rabindranath Tagore is actually Rabindranath Thakur. Yet in English he chose to sign and publish in the Anglicized form of Tagore and became a world celebrity under that name. I have tried to respect the English spellings that people used for themselves, to the best of our knowledge. I do not believe that anyone has the right (as has occasionally happened in academic publications of late) to alter an individual's legal personal choice just to suit methodological conformity. Why should Badal Sircar have to turn into 'Badal Sarkar' or Bohurupee metamorphose into 'Bahurupi', when they preferred to spell their names in English in particular ways? In all other instances, of course, we have transliterated the Indian names into English.

Places. Similarly, for place names I use the official versions sanctioned by the Survey of India. This means that you will find Varanasi here rather than Benares, Ahmadabad rather than Ahmedabad, Thrissur rather than Trichur, Guwahati rather than Gauhati, and so on. I have allowed three exceptions on account of the long history of associations with them: Bombay/Mumbai, Calcutta/Kolkata, and Madras/Chennai appear as alternates, depending on the context. In fact, while editing the *Companion*, I discovered that my built-in spellcheck programme did not underline Bombay, Calcutta, and Madras, proving their currency in world culture, whereas it questioned all other Indian spellings. I should add the rider that, owing to the frequency with which new districts are carved out of old ones in India, it could happen that a village might no longer be located in the district specified in the text.

Transliteration. The transliteration of Indian names, titles, and words into English creates enormous problems. A scientific system of diacritical marks has gained universal approval for Sanskrit–English transcription, and it is often extrapolated on to modern Indian tongues descended from Sanskrit, but it cannot be enforced on languages like Kashmiri, Sindhi, and Urdu (scripts derived from Arabic), or Manipuri (from Tibeto-Burman). While one can still apply such a system—modified, if necessary—when dealing with one language, it becomes virtually impossible to impose it on a book handling over twenty languages without either generating internal contradictions or—an important consideration—having to use so many diacritics that reading becomes a strain on the eyes. For the benefit of sceptical scholars, let me illustrate a few such contradictions:

1. The standard Sanskritic *c* and *ch* seem quite inappropriate in all modern Indian languages when these letters actually indicate the sounds *ch* and *chh* respectively, whereas the force of tradition and consensus compels us to retain them for Sanskrit–English transliteration.

2. In Bengali and Oriya, *b* is indistinguishable from the stand-alone *v* both phonetically and scriptorially; for example *bhaba* is the accurate English transcription, but non-native speakers will not recognize the word unless it is rendered as *bhava*.

3. The *r* with a dot under it conventionally represents the liquid Sanskritic vowel in most Indian languages; but in transliteration from Assamese, Bengali, Hindi, and Punjabi, it can also be read as the retroflex flap, the rolled version of *d* with a dot under it—a separate consonantal character.

Because no diacritical system can satisfy these many cross-linguistic discrepancies, I decided to drop the marks altogether.

Some newfangled transliterating practices avoiding diacritics have come into vogue, if anything, more unsatisfactory. In southern India, the soft *t* is rendered as *th* (Seetha, Therukoothu) and hard *t* as *d* (Koodiyattam), perhaps justifiable because the Dravidian mother language, Tamil, has a truncated alphabet of thirty-odd letters, compared to the average of forty-five in others. The trouble is that this confuses readers nationally, accustomed to the standard spelling of Sita or the Sanskritic transcription of Terukkuttu and Kutiyattam. Others in northern and western India, including the world of Hindi films, have taken to double vowels to measure length: *aa* as in *kathaa*, *ee* as in *leelaa*, *oo* as in *poojaa*. They do not realize that this is untenable since it does not accommodate the elongated *e* (pronounced as in 'grey') and *o* (as in 'grow')—vowels separate from the short *e* and *o*, and present in Gujarati, Marathi, and all four Dravidian languages. Besides, the far-too-common recurrence of the sound *aa* in Indian languages makes *aa* look very awkward in English, if spelt consistently, hence repeatedly. Indeed, even advocates of double vowels wrongly spell *leelaa* as *leela* and *poojaa* as *pooja*, perhaps subconsciously aware of this visual gawkiness. In any case, the English character *a* suffices for the diverse sounds in 'bat', 'war', and 'car'.

By the logic of the highest common factor, therefore, I adopted the method of Sanskrit–English transliteration without the diacritical marks, permitted modifications for every language when I thought it essential (for instance *w* as an alternate for *v*; or *f*, *q*, and *z* in words of Persian-

Arabic origin), but maintained consistency within the language on the basis of spelling, not pronunciation. The purpose is to enable the maximum number of English readers—which includes Indians—familiar with India to recognize vocabulary, rather than confound them with spellings that may be more faithful to regional pronunciation but end up obscuring the word's meaning to outsiders.

Vocabulary. One must resort to indigenous terms frequently in this kind of reference work. Fortunately, the English language has expanded at such a rate that many Indian words have entered household English dictionaries, which may even surprise Indians. If my standard lexicon, the one-volume *Concise Oxford Dictionary* (eleventh edition, 2004), included Indian vocabulary that I used—such as baksheesh, begum, bhakti, cowrie, darshan, dharmashala, dholak, diwan, ghazal, kumkum, kurta, mandala, namaskar, paisa, panchayat, pukka, purdah, rishi, sahib, salwar, sarangi, satrap, sloka, tantric, or tulsi—I treated them as English words, neither italicized, nor explained or translated. All other Indian words are italicized, with a normally literal translation or meaning in parentheses following their first occurrence in an entry.

Titles of plays. Similarly, dramatic titles are given literal translations within inverted commas, except when they constitute proper names or English words. However, if the play exists in English translation in book form, that translated title has been preferred after the original title, and italicized to distinguish it from the usual procedure. (Sometimes, I have kept the literal translation as an aid to greater clarity.) Likewise, in the case of Indian films that have designated alternate English titles, these are placed in italics following the originals. Since Indian scripts do not employ capitalization, separate words in play titles have not been capitalized unless they are proper nouns, to make it easier for the reader to differentiate them.

Cross-references. References to other entries are very simply identified, with an asterisk preceding a headword at its first appearance in the text of an entry. In Part I, each one of the concise histories of theatre in the different languages marks, with asterisks, all other entries relevant to theatre in that particular language.

Bibliographies. The bibliographies are of two kinds, but refer only to books in English. Since this volume is meant for the ordinary reader, published material in other languages has been excluded, as has periodical literature in English (whether articles or plays), for reasons of limited availability. Instead, I have attempted to catalogue all books and monographs ever printed in English on Indian theatre, regardless of quality, because they comprise a comparatively small corpus anyway. The general bibliography at the end contains items of broad or national scope, including anthologies of plays and names of relevant journals. Books of more specific interest are cited in reading lists appended to the appropriate entries.

For their help in the proof-reading of this edition, I thank my former student and lead actor Rohini Chaki, editorial assistant on this project, and my present student and lighting designer, Arnab Banerji, both of whom have promised to pursue doctoral studies in theatre and boost the relatively small body of scholarship on Indian theatre. I had dedicated *The Oxford Companion to Indian Theatre* to my daughter and her generation; I re-dedicate this edition to them, the standard-bearers of future Indian theatre.

November 2008   ANANDA LAL
Kolkata

Key to Initials

ABP	Anand B. Patil
AK	Anuradha Kapur
AKV	Akshara K.V.
AL	Ananda Lal
AR	Ashish Rajadhyaksha
BD	Birendranath Datta
CA	C. Annamalai
DB	Devajit Bandyopadhyay
DNP	Dhirendra Nath Pattanaik
GP	Goverdhan Panchal
HB	Hasmukh Baradi
HKD	Hemant Kumar Das
IBR	Indra Bahadur Rai
JM	Javed Malick
JP	Jiwan Pani
KAP	K. Ayyappa Paniker
KDT	Kamalesh Datta Tripathi
KG	Kalyani Ghose
KJ	Kirti Jain
KKB	Kulada Kumar Bhattacharjee
KNP	Kavalam Narayana Panikkar
KR	Kironmoy Raha
KSNP	K.S. Narayana Pillai

KU	Kamlesh Uppal
LA	Lokendra Arambam
LK	Laltluangliana Khiangte
MNS	M. Nagabhushana Sarma
MP	Maya Pandit
MS	Makhanlal Saraf
NA	Nissar Allana
NJ	Nemichandra Jain
NMSC	Neelam Man Singh Chowdhry
PA	Param Abichandani
PAg	Pratibha Agrawal
PCR	Purna Chandra Rao
RJ	Ramdeo Jha
RS	Ranbir Sinh
SD	Sudhanva Deshpande
SG	Shanta Gokhale
SI	Sameera Iyengar
SK	Sunil Kothari
SKD	Sisir Kumar Das
SM	Swapan Majumdar
SS	Shafi Shauq
TM	Tutun Mukherjee
TSG	Tejwant Singh Gill
VA	V. Arasu
VP	V. Padma
VS	Venkat Swaminathan
VVP	Vayala Vasudevan Pillai
ZC	Zarin Chaudhuri

Contributors

ANANDA LAL is Professor of English, Jadavpur University, Kolkata. He taught previously in the Department of Comparative Literature at the same university. He also directs and translates, and is theatre critic of *The Telegraph*, Kolkata. His books include *Rabindranath Tagore: Three Plays*, *Rasa*, *Shakespeare on the Calcutta Stage*, and (on CD) *The Voice of Rabindranath Tagore*. He has contributed entries on Indian theatre to the *Oxford Encyclopedia of Theatre and Performance*, *Microsoft Encarta Encyclopedia* (on CD), *Companion to Twentieth Century Theatre* (Continuum), *Encyclopedia of Postcolonial Literatures in English* (Routledge), and *Critical Survey of Drama* (Salem).

PARAM ABICHANDANI, Sindhi fictionist, critic, and translator, formerly worked with the national television network, Doordarshan, in New Delhi. He contributed on Sindhi literature to Sahitya Akademi's reference works, and was editor for its *Encyclopedia of Indian Literature* project.

PRATIBHA AGRAWAL is founder-director of Natya Shodh Sansthan, Kolkata. Active in Hindi theatre for fifty years as actress, director, and translator, she has written monographs on Master Fida Hussain, Mohan Rakesh, and Habib Tanvir.

NISSAR ALLANA, a stage designer by profession, is Director of the Dramatic Art and Design Academy, and the production company Theatre and Television Associates, both in New Delhi. He has designed sets and lights for theatre, lighting for *son-et-lumières*, and art direction for television. He has published several articles on scenography.

C. ANNAMALAI works as Relationship Marketing Officer for the BBC
World Service, Chennai. He is also a freelance journalist and theatre critic,
trained at Koothu-p-pattarai in Chennai.

LOKENDRA ARAMBAM is President, Forum for Laboratory Theatres of
Manipur, Imphal. A Manipuri cultural figure, director, and scholar, he
headed Aryan Theatre, Imphal, and the Audiovisual Research Centre of
Manipur University, Canchipur.

V. ARASU is Professor in the Department of Tamil Literature, University
of Madras, a theatre researcher, and critic. A specialist in traditional and
contemporary performance, he edits *Kattiyam*, a theatre journal in Tamil.
He has published widely, including a collection of Tamil essays on theatre
and media.

DEVAJIT BANDYOPADHYAY is a musicologist and singer, with a special
interest in theatre music. He lives in Kolkata, researches and directs concerts
of theatre songs, and has written many essays in Bengali on music.

HASMUKH BARADI is a Gujarati playwright, teacher, broadcaster, and
television producer. Director of the Theatre and Media Training Centre,
Ahmadabad, and editor of the theatre quarterly *Natak*, he is author of
History of Gujarati Theatre and four textbooks on theatre.

KULADA KUMAR BHATTACHARJEE, Assamese critic, director, and producer
of theatre, cinema, television, and radio, was former President, Short Film
Makers Association of Eastern India.

ZARIN CHAUDHURI, Kolkata-based actress and director of English theatre,
is founder of The Action Players, the only company of deaf actors in India.

NEELAM MAN SINGH CHOWDHRY teaches drama at the Department
of Indian Theatre, Punjab University, Chandigarh. She is director of the
Punjabi theatre group The Company, which has performed all over India
and participated at major international festivals.

HEMANT KUMAR DAS retired as Principal of a government college in
Cuttack. He taught Oriya for thirty years, specializing in Oriya drama. He
has written over sixty plays, books of fiction, and criticism in Oriya and
English, including *Baishnab Pani* and a dictionary of Oriya theatre.

SISIR KUMAR DAS, Bengali dramatist, poet, critic, and translator, was
Tagore Professor in the Department of Modern Indian Languages,
University of Delhi. His books include two volumes of *A History of Indian*

Literature (1800–1910 and 1911–1956) and *The English Writings of Rabindranath Tagore.*

BIRENDRANATH DATTA is Professor and Advisor, Department of Traditional Culture and Art Forms, Tezpur University, and editor of *Anandam* (Journal of the Anundoram Borooah Institute of Language, Art and Culture). An Assamese writer, critic, composer, and musicologist, he is author of *A Handbook of Folklore Material of North-east India, Jyotiprasad Agarwala,* and *Traditional Performing Arts of North-east India.*

SUDHANVA DESHPANDE is an actor, director, and dramatist with Jana Natya Manch, New Delhi. He also writes on theatre and cinema, and teaches at the A.J.K. Mass Communication Research Centre in Jamia Millia Islamia, New Delhi.

KALYANI GHOSE is a publisher, researcher, translator, and critic of Bengali arts and culture, with a special interest in folk forms. She lives in Kolkata and contributes in Bengali and English to several journals and periodicals.

TEJWANT SINGH GILL retired as Professor of English from Guru Nanak Dev University, Amritsar. A critic in Punjabi and English, he has several books and translations to his name.

SHANTA GOKHALE is a writer, columnist, translator, and theatre critic living in Mumbai. Her original publications include a novel and a play in Marathi, and a history in English of Marathi theatre, titled *Playwright at the Centre: Marathi Drama from 1843 to the Present.*

SAMEERA IYENGAR is a member of the Prithvi Festival team, organizing its prestigious annual theatre festival in Mumbai, and was associated with *Seagull Theatre Quarterly,* where her articles have been published. She is working on a critical documentation of the Chennai-based theatre project Voicing Silence.

KIRTI JAIN is Professor at the National School of Drama, New Delhi. She headed it from 1988 to 1995, and also worked as Producer at the national television network, Doordarshan. A founder-trustee of the Natarang Pratishthan theatre archive, she has organized workshops, festivals, and conferences there, and documented the creative processes of eminent directors. She has contributed articles on Indian theatre to several Hindi and English publications, and directs in Hindi.

NEMICHANDRA JAIN was Chairman of Natarang Pratishthan, New Delhi, and editor of the Hindi theatre quarterly *Natarang.* A poet, critic, and translator, he wrote the books *Indian Theatre* and *Asides*. He headed the Centre for Cultivation of Arts in Jawaharlal Nehru University, New Delhi (1976–82), and served as Director of the National School of Drama (1960–62) and Joint Secretary of the Indian People's Theatre Association (1948–50).

RAMDEO JHA was Professor of Maithili, L.N. Mishra Mithila University, Darbhanga, and Joint Secretary of the All India Maithili Sahitya Parishad (1957–59). He also wrote fiction, drama, and criticism in Maithili.

AKSHARA K.V. teaches and directs at Ninasam, Heggodu, Karnataka. He studied theatre at the National School of Drama, New Delhi, and the Workshop Theatre, University of Leeds, UK. He has written several books on theatre, and two award-winning plays, all in Kannada.

ANURADHA KAPUR is Professor of Acting and Direction at the National School of Drama, New Delhi, which she currently heads. She has written extensively on theatre, including the book *Actors, Pilgrims, Kings and Gods: The Ramlila at Ramnagar*, and has taught and directed productions in India and abroad.

LALTLUANGLIANA KHIANGTE is Professor of Mizo Language and Literature at Mizoram University, Aizawl. An important Mizo playwright, he has also written books in Mizo on dramatic theory and, in English, *Mizo Drama*.

SUNIL KOTHARI is Visiting Professor in Dance at the School of Arts and Aesthetics, Jawaharlal Nehru University, New Delhi, after retiring as Professor from Rabindra Bharati University, Kolkata. A renowned dance critic, he has published several books, including *Bharata Natyam*, *Kathak*, *Odissi*, *Kuchipudi*, *New Directions in Indian Dance*, and *Chhau Dances of India*.

SWAPAN MAJUMDAR is director of Rabindra-Bhavana (Centre for Tagore Studies and Research), Visva-Bharati, Santiniketan, after retiring as Professor of Comparative Literature, Jadavpur University, Kolkata. He has written widely on Bengali theatre and literature.

JAVED MALICK is Reader in the Department of English, Khalsa College, New Delhi, and a theatre critic and commentator. His publications include *Toward a Theatre of the Oppressed—Dramaturgy of John Arden and Margaretta D'Arcy*, an edition of Beckett's *Waiting for Godot*, and *A Critical Companion to Dario Fo's 'The Accidental Death of an Anarchist'*.

TUTUN MUKHERJEE is Professor and Head of the Centre for Comparative Literature, and Joint Professor in the Theatre Department at the University of Hyderabad. She has research interests in translation, women's writing, theatre, and film studies, and has edited the anthology *Staging Resistance*.

V. PADMA works under the pseudonym of A. Mangai in Tamil theatre, as a performer, director, and writer. She teaches English in Stella Maris College, Chennai, and previously taught in Manonmaniam Sundaranar University, Tirunelveli. Her Tamil essays on women's theatre have appeared in one volume, and she has also published articles in English.

GOVERDHAN PANCHAL was an artist, designer, and authority on traditional Indian theatre architecture and Gujarati folk forms. His books include *Bhavai and its Typical Aharya* and *The Theatres of Bharata*.

MAYA PANDIT is Professor at the Central Institute of English and Foreign Languages, Hyderabad. She has been involved in Marathi theatre for twenty years as an actor, writer, translator, and critic. She has also translated Marathi plays into English.

JIWAN PANI was an authority on Indian puppetry, masks, and folk performance, especially of Orissa. His many publications include *World of Other Faces: Indian Masks, Living Dolls: Story of Indian Puppets*, and *Purulia Chhau*.

K. AYYAPPA PANIKER was an eminent Malayalam poet and scholar of art, literature, and theatre. Former Professor and Head, Institute of English, Kerala University, he was also Chief Editor of the *Encyclopedia of Indian Literature* and author of *A Short History of Malayalam Literature*.

KAVALAM NARAYANA PANIKKAR, award-winning poet, playwright, and director in Malayalam and Sanskrit, heads the Sopanam Institute of Performing Arts and Research, Thiruvananthapuram. He previously served as Secretary of the Kerala Sangeetha Nataka Akademi.

ANAND B. PATIL is Professor of English, Goa University, and author of fiction and criticism in Marathi, and of the book *Western Influence on Marathi Drama.*

DHIRENDRA NATH PATTANAIK, leading scholar on Orissa's traditional performing arts and former Secretary of the Orissa Sangeet Natak Akademi, lives in Cuttack.

K.S. NARAYANA PILLAI served as Editor in the State Institute of Languages, Thiruvananthapuram, and Professor of Malayalam in Christian College, Marthandam. His publications include two plays, a monograph on K.N. Panikkar, and books on theatre and of literary criticism.

VAYALA VASUDEVAN PILLAI is Director of the Centre for Performing Arts, University of Kerala, Thiruvananthapuram, and former Director of the School of Drama, Calicut University, Thrissur. A noted theatre director, he has also written a history of Malayalam drama.

KIRONMOY RAHA called himself an 'observer' of Bengali theatre over six decades. He wrote for many periodicals on performance, authored the books *Bengali Theatre* and *Bengali Cinema,* and translated Bengali drama and fiction into English.

INDRA BAHADUR RAI retired as Professor of English from St Joseph's College, Darjiling. He has written fiction and criticism in Nepali.

ASHISH RAJADHYAKSHA is Senior Fellow at the Centre for the Study of Culture and Society, Bangalore. A leading scholar of Indian film, he co-authored the *Encyclopaedia of Indian Cinema.*

PURNA CHANDRA RAO, Telugu theatre activist, dramatist, critic, and cultural commentator, is founder of the Ethnic Arts Centre in Secunderabad.

MAKHANLAL SARAF is a director and actor based in Jammu. He has written books on Kashmiri theatre, produced radio drama for All India Radio in Srinagar, and scripted and directed for television.

M. NAGABHUSHANA SARMA served Osmania University, Hyderabad, and the University of Hyderabad as Professor of Theatre and Dean, Faculty of Performing Arts. A director, playwright, and actor, he directs in English and Telugu, writes plays in Telugu, and translates from English and Hindi. His monographs in English include *Bellary Raghava*, *Folk Performing Arts of Andhra Pradesh*, and *Tolu Bommalata*. His Telugu books cover cultural history, theatre criticism, and folklore studies.

SHAFI SHAUQ is Professor, Department of Kashmiri, University of Kashmir, Srinagar. An author in Kashmiri, English, Hindi, and Urdu, he writes criticism, scripts films, and translates. He has published a history of Kashmiri literature.

RANBIR SINH, dramatist and historian of Parsi theatre, lives in Jaipur. He has served as Vice-President, National Committee of the Indian People's Theatre Association, Cultural Advisor to the Government of Mauritius, Vice-Chairman of the Rajasthan Sangeet Natak Akademi, and Executive Secretary of Bharatiya Natya Sangh.

VENKAT SWAMINATHAN is a senior critic and commentator on arts and literature, especially Tamil culture. He has ten volumes of writings in Tamil and English to his credit. A contributor to Sahitya Akademi's *Encyclopedia of Indian Literature*, he has also scripted for Tamil films and television serials. Employed for the major part of his life in north India, he has now returned to Tamil Nadu.

KAMALESH DATTA TRIPATHI, leading scholar of Sanskrit theatre, retired as Professor from the Department of Religious and Agamic Studies, Banaras Hindu University, Varanasi. He is the author, among other monographs, of *Sanskrit Theatre*.

KAMLESH UPPAL retired as Professor of Dramatics from Punjabi University, Patiala. A polyglot scholar, she has written on Hindi, Punjabi, English, and Russian literature, including the monograph *Generative Impact of Absurdism on Punjabi Theatre*.

REGIONAL THEATRES

a

ASSAMESE THEATRE

Assamese theatre (in the eastern state of Assam) goes back many centuries
to extant devotional forms such as *Ankiya Nat/Bhaona, composed by
Vaishnava reformers like Sankaradeva (1449–1568) and Madhavadeva
(1489–1596), staged in community halls termed *nam-ghar*, as well as other
traditional performatory modes such as *Bhaoriya, *Dhuliya, and Oja-Pali.
Theatre of a Western mould, with proscenium stage and Anglo-European
dramatic structure, made its first appearance in 1875 at Guwahati, forty-
nine years after the British annexation of Assam. English education and
exposure to *Bengali theatre during higher studies at Calcutta inspired new-
generation Assamese in the late nineteenth century to launch theatre in
their own language, which became instantly popular and in no time swayed
all of Assam.

Initially, performances were held on temporarily erected stages. But
permanent structures came up in the 1890s and by the second decade of the
twentieth century, all the district and subdivisional towns, including a few
semi-urban places, had at least one theatre. However, it was neither daily,
nor weekly, nor even monthly fare. Usually plays were performed during
festivals or important occasions or just for the pleasure of putting up a show.
Till this day, apart from the recent touring repertory companies known as
*Bhramyaman Mancha ('mobile theatre'), no group performs daily or

weekly on a regular basis, though a few made unsuccessful attempts previously. Yet shows take place almost daily in the cultural capital, Guwahati, by one group or the other.

Although proscenium theatre arrived in 1875, modern playwriting commenced eighteen years earlier. The first play, Gunabhiram Barua's *Ram-Nabami* ('Ram and Nabami') on widow remarriage, was written in 1857. The next, *Kania kirtan* ('Kirtan to Opium', 1861), was a satire on opium addiction by Hemchandra Barua. Rudra Ram Bordoloi wrote a social farce, *Bongal-bongalani* ('Bengali Couple', 1871–2), satirizing lascivious concubines and promiscuous women who married non-Assamese outsiders. However, there is no documentation whether these texts were staged. Neither is it known for certain with which play Assamese theatre raised its curtain.

The first *mythological drama, *Sita haran* ('Stealing of Sita') by Rama Kanta Chaudhury, came in 1875. With two exceptions, all ten or twelve plays written later in the nineteenth century belonged to this genre. The presumption that the first staged Assamese drama was mythological may stand confirmed by a gazette notification of four shows of *Ramabhishek* ('Rama's Coronation'), from 15 May 1875, though this earliest available record does not mention if it was the first-ever production. Bhaona, the most popular traditional Assamese form of that time, drew its plots from mythological sources like the *Mahabharata*, *Ramayana*, and the Puranas. It was perhaps natural in the transition from traditional theatre to the new variety to retain the content. Mythological drama dominated till about 1920, though it survived till the 1940s, as in the spectacular plays of the prolific Atulchandra Hazarika (1903–86).

Early Assamese drama of this age was in blank verse modelled on the Bengali *amitrakshar* metre, containing fourteen syllables in each line. Later playwrights broke these constraints by adopting the *gairish* metre, a kind of free blank verse popularized by the Bengali actor-manager Girish Ghosh. Benudhar Rajkhowa introduced prose dialogue in his *Duryodhanar urubhanga* ('Duryodhana's Broken Thigh', 1903).

*Historical drama appeared alongside the mythological from the beginning of the twentieth century with *Jaymati* (1900) by Padmanath Gohain Barooah (1871–1946), as Indian nationalism and the struggle against British colonialism grew in strength. Emotions ran high; courage, valour, and glories of the past were recreated to arouse patriotism. Such plays dominated after 1920, a supremacy that remained intact till just after Independence in 1947. *Maniram Dewan*, *Lachit Barphukan* (both by Prabin Phukan), and

Piyali Phukan (collectively by four members of Nagaon Shilpi Samaj in the town of Nagaon), written and staged immediately before and after Independence, earned phenomenal popularity.

The source of most historical drama was the Ahom period of Assamese history, which provided many heroes and martyrs—men and women. Among them, two were particularly revered, on whom several works have been written: Jaymati and Lachit Barphukan. Jaymati, an Ahom princess, chose torture and death rather than disclose the whereabouts of her fugitive husband. Lachit Barphukan, a successful Ahom general, twice defeated the Mughal army between 1667 and 1671. His heroics and patriotism are legendary.

The much-revered Assamese cultural icon, Jyoti Prasad Agarwala (1903–51), moved from romanticism to realism, and for the first time made a conscious approach to theatre production in *Shonit Kunwari* ('Princess of Shonitpur', 1924). Before him, attending to actors' speech seemed the manager's only concern. After him, a few performers like Mitradev Mahanta Adhikar (1894–1982) showed similar awareness, but by and large the existence of a concrete production plan correlating and coordinating all departments of theatre was evident only from the 1960s with the arrival of a number of persons formally trained in theatre arts.

Within a few years after Independence, historical drama became scarce and made room for social consciousness. The era of modernist social drama may be counted from 1950. Social plays were written before 1947, as early as Benudhar Rajkhowa's *Seuti-Kiran* ('Seuti and Kiran', 1894), but the number was very small; most concentrated on reform and national awakening against foreign rule, while other aspects of life remained almost untouched. After Independence, playwrights extended their horizons into political problems, class struggle, the caste system, conflict between generations, erosion of values, communal tensions, enmity between tribals and non-tribals, unemployment, disintegration of the joint family, hopes and frustrations of the middle class, and individual psychological conflicts.

After *Kania kirtan* and *Bongal-bongalani*, the first light social play or farce had been *Litikai* ('Servant', 1890) by the respected author Lakshminath Bezbaroa (1868–1938). It was followed by a number of similar comedies, particularly in the 1930s. Such scripts are written even today, especially in one act, but the number is not large. However, one-act drama holds an important position in Assamese theatre. From the mid-1950s, writers as well as performers felt attracted to it. It became so popular that, during the 1960s, it overshadowed full-length plays. Many one-act competitions used to be held all over Assam, and there were dramatists who specialized in writing short scripts.

Until 1949, men portrayed female characters. There were a few attempts to cast women in the 1930s—by Braja Natha Sarma in his short-lived, commercial Kohinoor Opera Party; by the playwright, actor, director, scholar Satya Prasad Barua (1919–2001) in his Sundar Sevi Sangha (Guwahati); and by Rohini Barua in Dibrugarh. But the trendsetters had to wait till 1948 when All India Radio launched twin stations at Guwahati and Shillong. Since radio drama required women for female roles, these readers grew used to acting along with men, hence facilitating their appearance on stage. By that time Assamese society also had grown liberal enough to accept, in fact to demand, actresses performing alongside men.

In the early days theatres were lit by candles; later, by hanging rows of kerosene lamps, gaslight, or pressure lamps of the brand name Petromax, producing a very bright light. When portable power generators became available, they were pressed into service. Electricity came to Assam in the 1920s, but only in a few important towns. The process of electrification in the state started only after 1947.

Before 1930, stage decor meant rolled-up painted screens and drapes. Afterwards, flats were used along with painted screens. There were a few attempts at realism by using three-dimensional set pieces. However, realistic *scenography made a permanent entry only in the late 1940s, replacing painted backdrops. Stylized sets, even bare stages, have served as theatre designs of late. Costumes were usually hired from agencies that specialized in renting them out. But this practice was more or less abandoned after the 1950s, when mythological and historical plays gave way to realistic social drama, and costumes started to be specially designed for each production.

The idiom in the first phase after Independence was naturalism. Gradually, as contact was established with neo-modern playwrights from the rest of India as well as classics by Ibsen, Chekhov, Gogol, Gorky, Sartre, Camus, Brecht, Beckett, and Ionesco, novelty in form and content became distinctly visible, as in the avant-garde anti-realistic work of Arun Sarma (1931–), the leading contemporary dramatist. The interface of theatre with cinema also created some star performers, notably Phani Sarma (1910–70), who had great physical presence, and creative experimental directors like Dulal Roy (1943–).

Folk and traditional forms inspired many recent plays, most important among them *Jarouroua parja* ('Impoverished Subjects'), a Marxist

Bhagirathi and Baharul Islam in Arun Sarma's *Parashuram*, directed by Bhagirathi Islam and Parag Sarma (Seagull, Guwahati, 1998)

interpretation of the historic revolution by one of the five Vaishnava sects in Assam. Karuna Deka and Ramani Deka produced *Sang* ('Clown') and *Suna suna sabhasad* ('Listen, Gentleman') in Dhuliya style. Gunakar Dev Goswami adopted Bhaona in *Jerenga* (2000) and *Birangana* (2003). Robijita Gogoi's Jirsang Theatre used the Karbi language and folksongs for *Rangpharpe Rangbe* (2001) and *Thong Nokbe* (2002), on the two most popular rebels in Karbi history. She also pioneered installations in Assamese theatre. Several of Jyoti Prasad Agarwala's plays were staged in Bodo and Nepali languages. Attention to tribal languages like Bodo and Karbi is a development in the new millennium.   KKB

Satya Prasad Barua, *Assamese Theatre* (Guwahati: Padma Prakash, 1996); S. Bharali, *Tragic Outlook in Assamese Drama* (Delhi: Shree, 1980); Harichandra Bhattacharyya, *Origin and Development of the Assamese Drama and the Stage* (Gauhati: Baruah Agency, 1964); Birendranath Datta (ed.), *Traditional Performing Arts of North-east India* (Guwahati: Assam Academy, 1990); Pranati Sharma Goswami, *Female Characters in Modern Assamese Drama: 1857–1977* (New Delhi: B R, 2004); Dhaneswar Kalita, *Traditional Performances of South Kamrup* (New Delhi: Gian, 1991); Pona Mahanta, *Western Influence on Modern Assamese Drama* (Delhi: Mittal, 1985).

b

BENGALI THEATRE

Theatre in the Bengali language occurs in Bangladesh and the present eastern Indian states of West Bengal and Tripura. The age-old folk forms, *Jatra in particular, as well as *Alkap, *Bahurupi, *Chhau, *Gambhira, *Kabigan, Kathakata, *Palagan, Panchali, and *Putul Nach, have been popular for centuries in the vast countryside and growing townships. Proscenium theatre originated and developed in Calcutta which, by the end of the eighteenth century, grew into a bustling town of commerce and diverse activities, the seat of governance and most important city of the expanding British empire in the East. The colonists introduced *English theatre for the entertainment of the increasing number of British administrators, traders, soldiers, and a motley crowd of many bents and motives. The shows were at first exclusively for the English and Europeans; later, Indians were also allowed. The plays included those by Shakespeare, Oliver Goldsmith, and many now-insignificant authors who had proved popular in London.

As a matter of historical interest, *Kalpanik sambadal* ('Imaginary Transformation'), a Bengali translation of an English play titled *The Disguise*, was staged with Bengali actors and actresses by Herasim Lebedeff, a Russian musician, linguist, tireless traveller, and possible adventurer, at the 'Bengally Theatre' in 1795 and repeated in 1796. Laudable as the endeavour was, it does not appear to have influenced subsequent events.

By the 1830s a large and fast-growing class of affluent Bengali merchants, landholders, moneylenders, rentiers, and professionals settled in Calcutta. English opened for them a window through which blew a fresh wind of occidental ideas and learning. These and the institutional frameworks of government and education turned into their role models and they became ardent admirers of English literature and drama. The early patrons of theatre, the enlightened Bengali aristocracy, built stages in their palatial homes and gardens and put up shows strictly for invited audiences. The first such venture came in 1831 and a second in 1835. Since no original Bengali drama existed, mostly Sanskrit classics in translation were performed. The first original Bengali play, *Kulina-kulasarbaswa* ('All about a Kulin Clan') by Ramnarayan Tarkaratna (1822–86), criticizing the Brahman practice of polygamy, was staged in 1857. The emergence of a few notable dramatists partly removed the absence of original writing: the contemporaries Michael Madhusudan Dutt (1824–73) and Dinabandhu Mitra (1830–73) gave Bengali theatre much-needed sustenance in the 1860s.

Meanwhile the new, loosely-called middle class, comprising lawyers, doctors, writers, educationists, traders, the salariat, and people of other vocations, developed lively and many-sided interests including English drama, which they admired and aspired to copy in their enthusiasm to have a Bengali stage. The English models did not make it a wholly alien implant: Bengali theatre in its infancy could not shed Jatra's subterranean or even overt influence. Outwardly, though, the English-educated gentry derided and held Jatra in contempt. At the same time, the private theatres of the wealthy provided an incentive for amateur theatres started by this stage-struck middle class in that part of north Calcutta where the Bengalis mostly lived. The amateur theatres depended on the patronage of the well-to-do, but in turn helped feed the rising demand for public theatres where the common citizen could enter.

The desire grew widespread and articulate enough for some active amateurs and other enthusiasts to form an association to meet the demand. They called it the National Theatre, hired part of a zamindar's mansion at forty rupees per month, built a stage and makeshift auditorium, and put up Mitra's anti-British *Nildarpan* ('Indigo Mirror') for the public on 7 December 1872. The response was overwhelming. One show a week was scheduled, a few of which were held before National Theatre split up. The acclaim and popularity that attended the maiden venture prompted others to start public theatres at hired sites and temporary structures. They soon felt the need for permanent playhouses. The first, Bengal Theatre, was built with the flimsiest of materials, a mud structure, and a tarpaulin sheet as roof. It opened on 16 August 1873 with Dutt's romantic *Sharmishtha* and deserves mention for another reason. It was the first (after Lebedeff) to engage women for female roles, which men had so far played. A storm of protest erupted, as the actresses were from the red-light district and thus considered corrupting agents. However, the protest was short-lived and other companies followed suit.

Other permanent venues came up in the same locality, the prominent among them being the Great National Theatre and Star Theatre. The former caused a furore in 1876 by successively staging political farces by Upendranath Das (1848/9–95), leading to the imposition of the *Dramatic Performances Act. The Star opened in 1883 with a play by Girish Chandra Ghosh (1844–1912), who wrote any number of scripts to feed the theatre, acted in them and other productions, produced and managed, taught and recruited, and became the foremost personality in Bengali commercial theatre for nearly the first four decades of its history. The building of permanent playhouses indicated two developments. One, the growth in theatre's popularity among the educated middle class, reflected a significant change in the structure of Bengali society. Theatre no longer needed the patronage of the rich; the public provided it. A sizeable section among them discussed the merits and demerits of acting and other aspects of production with knowledge and discernment.

The other development was an increase in the number of plays. Many dramatists emerged, while the dramatization of novels (Bankimchandra Chatterjee's in particular) and a few long narrative poems became a fruitful source. Most of the new playwrights, however, showed little understanding of the nature and craft of drama. Jyotirindranath Tagore (1849–1925) was one exception. Although the majority of his plays were translated, mostly from Sanskrit classics, he rid them of Sanskritic diction and phraseology, thus making them known to Bengalis at large. He also adapted a few comedies of his favourite, Molière, changing names and locales to make them sound like Bengali plays. Others like the farceur Amritalal Basu (1853–1929), Manomohan Basu, Rajkrishna Ray, and above all Girish Ghosh (in religious works like *Bilwamangal Thakur*, 1886, and social works like *Praphulla*, 1889) added to Bengali dramatic literature. Rabindranath *Tagore also began writing his unique plays in the 1880s.

Still, the corpus was not large enough to meet the growing demand for entertainment. The companies staged scripts by indifferent authors. Except for the Tagores, they all wrote for the theatre of the day, which had to cater to the preferences and prejudices of the public, who thronged playhouses to experience vicarious emotions, momentary sensations, broad clowning, and histrionic exposition, and see the dances and hear the songs accompanying the plays. One notices a proliferation of productions with religious themes, quasi-historical figures or heroic stories from the Hindu epics, operatic pieces in the genre known as *Gitabhinay, or comedies and satires depicting facets of current social modes. In most one sees the incorporation in a veiled manner of Jatra ingredients—high-pitched delivery of lines, melodramatic flourishes, profusion of songs, crude humour.

The educated class did not acknowledge or accept the influence. It wanted theatre to follow the English mould not only in terms of painted backdrops and wings, but also in copying Elizabethan dramatic structure and the surprising amount that it had learnt about acting styles and manner of presentation in English theatre. The owners, producers, managers, and actors knew better. They realized that the first thing was to draw people to the box office; that however much they emulated the British, unless the fare served met the tastes of the larger public who never outgrew the hold of Jatra, the theatre could not survive. The contrary pulls of English theatre and Jatra presented a big hurdle. The effort was to yoke them into a form that the audience liked. Bengali theatre succeeded in doing so primarily because of Girish Ghosh, who fused the ill-fitting combination into a distinct entity that answered to the Bengali genius and became the standard for many decades.

Among many others who contributed in the early days, the comedian and composer Ardhendu Mustafi (1850–1908) rivalled Ghosh in dedication, thespian talent, and popularity; Binodini Dasi (c. 1863– 1941), the foremost actress, rose to the top within a short time; Amritalal Basu, Manomohan Basu, Sukumari Dutta, Amritalal Mitra were by all accounts first-rate actors and

Binodini Dasi acting a male role in Upendranath Das's *Sarat-Sarojini* (Calcutta, originally 1874)

actresses who swayed theatregoers to ecstatic joy, hearty laughter, and cathartic sorrow. The plays gave them ample scope, written with an eye to the star system and the grand style that they associated with British performers of whom they had a store of information. The first three decades formed a period of exciting growth. Weekly shows increased; their appeal is reflected by the lively coverage in Bengali and English newspapers. However, by the closing years of the nineteenth century and the opening years of the twentieth, the average member of the audience had begun to weary of the fare and the hamming.

A reprieve came when the young Amarendra Dutta (1876–1916) took over the old Star Theatre to launch his Classic Theatre, which soon became the most popular company. Still, his innovations failed to lift Bengali theatre from the rut into which it had fallen. Two important and versatile playwrights, Dwijendra Lal Roy (1863–1913) and Kshirod Prasad Vidyavinod (1863–1927), appeared but their works received appreciation from spectators and readers much later. Increased critical awareness among theatre lovers intensified into harsh attacks. The intelligentsia moved away, the public became unenthusiastic. Intrigues, squabbles, mismanagement, and financial disorder compounded the decline.

Girish Ghosh's death symbolized the end of a long chapter in Bengali theatre history. Some able performers like Surendra Ghosh (his son), the actor-manager-dramatist Aparesh Mukhopadhyay (1875–1934) and Tara Sundari (his leading lady) kept going but the years, on the whole, were bleak and barren. Theatre remained unchanged whereas the theatregoer had changed.

Theatre, dying on its feet, was rescued from that fate by Sisir Bhaduri (1889–1959), a college lecturer of English who gave up his job and became a professional actor in 1921. By 1925 he had won acclaim as a naturalistic actor and director from the learned and elite, and tumultuous praise from public and press. He gave Bengali theatre respectability and prestige, establishing and sustaining its claim as a pursuit for artists and intellectuals. While

Krishna and Draupadi in Aparesh Mukhopadhyay's *Karnarjun* (Art Theatre, Calcutta, 1923)

he rejuvenated it and obviously influenced others, a host of realistic performers not belonging to his troupe, like Ahindra Choudhury (1895–1974), Nirmalendu Lahiri, Naresh Mitra, Durgadas Banerjee, and Sarajubala Devi (1912–94), made their mark in the changed perceptions of the playgoer.

By the mid-1930s, signs resurfaced that theatre had once again entered the doldrums. Despite the debuts of many excellent actors and actresses like Chhabi Biswas, Bhumen Ray, and Santi Gupta, improved technology largely contributed by Satu Sen (1902–78), and more playhouses, the drama seemed oblivious to the reality of changing socio-economic and historical conditions. The rise of cinema resulted in the defection of talent from theatre, though some stars like Molina Devi (1917–77) maintained parallel careers in both professions. In 1942 there arose nationalistic turmoil and 1943 saw the horrendous Bengal famine, when millions died. A few competent playwrights like Sachin Sengupta (1893–1961), Tulsi Lahiri (1897–1959), Manmatha Ray (1899–1988), and Bidhayak Bhattacharya (1907–86) sensed the situation and wrote serious drama reflecting the transformed mores and sentiments. But, on the whole, theatre did not react to the cataclysmic changes nor mirror the anguish, anger, and aspirations of the people. No one seemed to know how to arrest the steady slide.

The remedy, to drop the deadweight of the past, came from outside the established theatre when the Bengal unit of the *Indian People's Theatre Association (IPTA) impressively staged Nabanna ('New Harvest') by Bijon Bhattacharya (1915–78) in 1944. The play about the starving peasantry articulated the prevailing mood. The production, shorn of painted scenes, any but the barest of props, and acted by mostly inexperienced amateurs without make-up, created a sensation. It was enthusiastically received in Calcutta and elsewhere, performed under makeshift arrangements. Sadly, IPTA's pioneering role was short-lived. Many members left, irked by diktats on matters of art. They formed troupes of their own, classified as *group theatre, which generated the 'new drama movement'. These remained a minority phenomenon for many years—as the professional theatre, which staged a comeback during the 1950s purveying escapist entertainment, ate into part of their audience—but they gradually assumed leadership of Bengali theatre.

The new movement emphasized depiction of the lives of the exploited and downtrodden. Although many groups veered away from this exclusive preoccupation and began exploring new avenues, it does not mean that

Sombhu Mitra as Jaysingha and Tripti Mitra as Gunabati in Rabindranath Tagore's *Bisarjan*, directed by Sombhu Mitra (Bohurupee, Calcutta, 1961)

they denied theatre's social purpose and responsibility. Indeed, commitment to socio-political causes remained and remains an important feature of Bengali theatre. A few of the groups formed in the late 1940s, after India's independence. The number rose in the 1950s and 1960s to a hundred or more, of which only some prominent ones are mentioned here to indicate broadly the contours of this professedly progressive and technically non-professional theatre.

Monoranjan Bhattacharya and Sombhu Mitra (1915–97), the sources of inspiration behind the group Bohurupee, built its foundation firmly enough for it to be active even now. Mitra was without question the supreme actor-director of contemporary Bengali theatre. Of Bohurupee's many achievements under his lead, the most exciting were the magnificent productions of several of Rabindranath Tagore's major plays, considered till then unstageable. The group also had actors of high calibre, including Gangapada Basu, Amar Ganguly, lead actress Tripti Mitra (1925–89), current director Kumar Roy (1926–), and singer Sabitabrata Dutta (1934–95), and two of the trailblazing technicians in post-Independence Indian theatre—set designer Khaled Choudhury (1919–) and lighting designer Tapas Sen (1924–2006).

Like Mitra, Utpal Dutt (1929–93) departed from IPTA but did not give up his Marxist beliefs. He formed the Little Theatre Group (LTG, subsequently People's Little Theatre). It held the lease of the old playhouse Minerva for nearly ten years, where it produced one spectacular revolutionary play after another, revealing Dutt's enormous talents as actor, director, and dramatist. Besides his inspiring leadership, it featured a number of able performers like his wife Sova Sen (1923–), Sekhar Chatterjee (1924–90), and Satya Bandopadhyay (1933–2006). Sen, also with IPTA before she joined the LTG, was a gifted and versatile actress possessing uncommon managerial ability, whose boundless capacity for work contributed largely to the group's success.

Nandikar shot into prominence with its 1961 adaptation of Pirandello's *Six Characters in Search of an Author*. It rapidly won repute for the excellence of its productions and the performances of its members, specially the remarkable actress Keya Chakrabarti and actor Rudraprasad Sengupta (1936–). The personality behind its growing popularity was its founder and leader, the exceptionally fine actor-director, Ajitesh Bandopadhyay (1933–83). No group relied more on foreign drama for material, notably the unforgettable adaptations of Chekhov's *Cherry Orchard* and Pirandello's *Henry IV* and translation of Anouilh's *Antigone*. Nandikar took on lease in 1969 a new playhouse, Rangana, where its adaptations of Brecht's *Threepenny Opera* and *Good Person of Setzuan* drew large crowds. Despite Chakrabarti's untimely death and Bandopadhyay's departure, it continued to stage a variety of plays under Sengupta's stewardship and, recently, original musicals directed by Gautam Halder. It hosts a prestigious annual national theatre festival.

Theatre Workshop was formed in 1966 with Bibhash Chakraborty (1937–) as director and leading man, and an impressive acting team including Ashok Mukhopadhyay and Maya Ghosh. It made its mark with intense productions of works by new dramatists: the political allegory *Rajrakta* ('Royal Blood', 1971) by Mohit Chattopadhyaya (1934–) and the moving rural story *Chakbhanga madhu* ('Honey Fresh from the Hive', 1972) by Manoj Mitra (1938–). Chakraborty left the troupe in 1985 to form Anya Theatre, which produced *Madhab Malanchi-kainya* ('Madhab and the Girl Malanchi', 1988), a delightful east-Bengali fairy tale full of colour, music, and flights of fancy. The group Chetana won a following for Arun Mukherjee's physical acting in his plays like the mock mythological *Marich sambad* (*Mareech, the Legend*, 1973) and *Jagannath* (adapted from Lu Xun's *The True Story of Ah Q*, 1977).

The group theatres mostly performed at the newly built Academy of Fine Arts; only a couple consciously devised alternative venues. Souvanik in 1960 built Mukta Angan, an improvised auditorium with tin sheets as roof, having no pretension to elegance or comfort. Nevertheless it contributed significantly with experimental plays, for instance premiering

Badal Sircar in *Bhoma*, written and directed by him (Satabdi, Calcutta, 1976)

Evam Indrajit (1965) by Badal Sircar (1925–), and by renting out Mukta Angan at affordable rates. Another distinctive group, Theatre Centre, was formed in 1954 by Tarun Roy (1928–88), whose productions shunned wild-eyed, modish experiments, yet had a freshness about them. He aimed at a middle-of-the-road theatre that was needed but, despite a few attempts like the successful adaptations of foreign works by film star Soumitra Chatterjee (1935–), had failed to take off. Roy converted part of his residence into a cosy and small intimate hall, the only one of its kind for Bengali theatre.

When Sircar published the strikingly original, absurdist *Evam Indrajit* on identity crisis in a magazine in 1965, he partly alleviated the chronic paucity of worthwhile Bengali drama. He continued writing equally powerful plays and was soon acknowledged as the most outstanding contemporary dramatist. Subsequently he became disillusioned with the proscenium, and propounded and launched what he called the *Third Theatre. Many of his disciples took this movement outside Kolkata, like Probir Guha in Khardah, while a few extended it into *theatre for development, like the Augusto Boal-influenced Jana Sanskriti troupe in Madhyamgram. A decentralization of proscenium group theatre into district towns has also taken place, creating a flourishing theatre culture in places like Kalyani and Baharampur.

Other eminent authors included Manoj Mitra, who heads Sundaram and has turned director of his recent complex, layered plays subtly blending humour with pathos; Mohit Chattopadhyaya, whose simple yet profound latter-day work has found its best interpreter in actor-director Dwijen Bandyopadhyay; and Debasis Majumdar, who shows considerable dexterity in conveying his despairing views of the breakdown in individual and social values. While substantial original playwriting continues to appear, the lack of superior literary and theatrical craftsmanship, perhaps because the entire state still has only one university department of theatre, remains a concern. Periodically, critics also complain about a dependence on foreign drama, mostly adapted, some translated, some recreated retaining only the storyline or theme.

During the 1980s it became clear that the new drama movement's passion was spent, and Bengali theatre had to do some soul-searching. A few tentative observations may be made to pinpoint reasons. The widespread and violent political turbulence in West Bengal, from the late 1960s to the early 1970s, proved unsettling both for the players and public, but fomented stimulating theatre. Stability came afterwards and state patronage grew under the Left Front government, widening the opportunities and facilities for groups. Quantitatively their productions increased but the quality, and cutting edge of radical theatre, was missing as ideological complacence and lack of imagination set in. Finally, the invasion of video and television had its well-known deleterious effects by luring audiences away. Bengali theatre did not attract spectators in the droves it had been accustomed to, but remained vibrant, with possibly the largest number of active troupes and new productions in Indian theatre.   KR

In the 1990s, the unlamented euthanasia of the comatose commercial theatre, caused partly by the mass defection of its votaries to multi-channel television, left a small vacuum that a few practitioners like Meghnad Bhattacharya filled with popular mainstream productions featuring moral messages. However, the media boom is of further interest because the cornucopia of channels fell back on experienced group-theatre actors to populate their interminable soaps and serials. Not only did many stage performers suddenly discover a lucrative income that persuaded some to leave theatre for good, rendering several talented groups defunct, but, ironically yet happily for theatre today, their visibility on screen makes their onstage appearances appealing to viewers, who enter auditoriums to see their favourite TV stars live.

At the turn of the century, troupes led by women, often galvanized by gender issues, figure prominently in the resurgent theatre. Sima Mukhopadhyay, a dramatist, director, and actress, best represents this movement that began a decade earlier, her own plays invariably dealing with subjects that male writers tend to bypass. In a fairly long career, Sohag Sen has directed in a spectrum of forms and styles. Saoli Mitra, daughter of Sombhu and Tripti Mitra, won fame for her solo contemporized interpretations of epic heroines, then deliberately rejected the hallowed temple of group theatre, the Academy of Fine Arts, in an attempt to establish an alternative space.

Younger men followed in her footsteps to ensure for themselves greater freedom to perform and flexibility in performances. Notable such directors with marked drawing power at present include Suman Mukhopadhyay, who displays a strikingly physical, optical, imaginative approach to conceptualizing texts, and Kaushik Sen, who has a penchant for staging poetical drama sensitively. The most consistent and prolific playwright of this generation is Bratya Basu, who also directs and acts, writing with highly unorthodox and radical ideas about themes and language.

The chance entry of visual artist Sanchayan Ghosh into Bengali theatre gave its relatively prosaic set décor a shot in the arm; his abstract designs and innovative use of diverse materials to construct them bestow on many productions a touch of aesthetic class that has challenged other designers to think likewise. Finally, one must notice the increasing activity in *children's theatre and theatre in education, as major groups like Nandikar encourage outreach projects in schools and underprivileged sections, which bode well for the future, if only these trained juniors get the rare opportunity to pursue theatre formally at the college level.   AL

Brajendra Nath Banerjee, *Bengali Stage: 1795–1873* (Calcutta: Ranjan, 1943); Utpal K. Banerjee (ed.), *Bengali Theatre: 200 Years* (New Delhi: Publications Division, Ministry of Information and Broadcasting, 1999); Himani Bannerji, *The Mirror of Class: Essays on Bengali Theatre* (Calcutta: Papyrus, 1998); Rustom Bharucha, *Rehearsals of Revolution: The Political Theater of Bengal* (Honolulu: University of Hawaii, 1983); Nemai Ghosh, *Dramatic Moments: Theatre in Calcutta since the 60s* (Calcutta: Seagull, 2000); P. Guha-Thakurta, *The Bengali Drama: Its Origin and Development* (London: Kegan Paul, Trench, Trubner, 1930); Sushil Kumar Mukherjee, *The Story of the Calcutta Theatres: 1753–1980* (Calcutta: K.P. Bagchi, 1982); Kuntal Mukhopadhyay, *Theatre and Politics: A Study of Group Theatre Movement of Bengal* (Calcutta: Bibhasa, 1999); Kironmoy Raha, *Bengali Theatre* (New Delhi: National Book Trust, 1993).

d

DOGRI THEATRE

The Dogri language is spoken in Jammu and adjacent southern districts of Jammu and Kashmir state, and in adjoining areas of Punjab and Himachal Pradesh. Its rich and varied performances of ethnic folklore revolved around the Baghtan, a clan of actors and singers who frequently arrived from the Sialkot region (now in Pakistan) with a repertoire of *Ramlila and *Raslila, narratives inherently rhythmic in movement. Patronage at the Dogra royal court caused Baghtan shows to accelerate in the temple city of Jammu and reach other towns like Punch, Ramnagar (Udhampur district), and Basoli (Kathua district).

In 1898, Maharaja Pratap Singh called upon the Victoria Company, Bombay, to perform at a family ceremony in the Green Hall of his palace in Jammu. This event inspired proscenium theatre in Dogri. The Sanatan Dharam Natak Samaj came up in 1914, its focal point of activities the Dewan Mandir at Kachi Chawni, Jammu, where a playhouse still exists. The Hindi film star, Om Prakash, and singer-actor K.L. Saigal are just two famous names to have emerged from this cultural organization, which staged numerous mythological and moralistic plays. Friends Club (1920–1) copied the *Parsi theatre in such productions as *Dard de jiga* ('Bleeding Heart') and *Mohabbat ke phul* ('Flowers of Love'). For the coronation of Maharaja Hari Singh in 1925–6, many troupes presented command performances, including local folk groups, Baghtan from Sialkot, Suraj Vijay Company and Amateur Dramatic Club from Bombay, and Madan Theatres from Calcutta.

The thread of modern Dogri theatre can be picked up with the staging of Vishwanath Khajuria's social satire *Achut* ('Untouchable', 1935), directed by him at the Middle School, Ramnagar, followed by D.C. Prashant's *Devaka janam* ('Birth of the Gods'). The Dogri Sanastha, formed in 1944 under Dinubhai Pant and Ramnath Shastri, both literary personalities, proved a boost for theatre. After the Dogra regime collapsed in 1947 with the dawn of Indian democracy, the Dogri psyche sagged but for Shastri's *Bawa Jitto*, produced at the Kisan (farmers') Conference at Tikri in Jammu, 1948. Khajuria and Prashant also separately dramatized this folktale about the fifteenth-century heroic martyr. A *children's theatre developed when Narender Khajuria began to write plays for performance by children.

As the Sanatan Dharam Natak Samaj continued its pursuits and the Jammu and Kashmir Academy of Art, Culture and Languages was established in 1958, the Dogra cultural identity re-emerged. New groups appeared, besides the revival of Friends Club in 1965. Dewan Mandir and

Ramnath Shastri's *Bawa Jitto* directed by Balwant Thakur (Natrang, Jammu, 1987)

the Dogri Sanastha became the hub of activity. Financial assistance from the Academy sustained most groups and supported multilingual theatre festivals, still in vogue. Important original plays in the 1970s included those by the eminent Dogri author Narsingh Dev Jamwal (1931–), Madan Mohan Sharma, and Puran Singh. During the 1980s, Dogri theatre earned recognition beyond Jammu and Kashmir through young artistic directors like Balwant Thakur, who heads the popular group Natrang.   MS

Shivanath, *History of Dogri Literature* (New Delhi: Sahitya Akademi, 1977).

e

ENGLISH THEATRE

The British colonizers built the earliest proscenium-arch auditoria in India, for the theatrical entertainment of their trading garrisons in the major seaports. The Playhouse in Calcutta, said to have received help from English actor-manager David Garrick, came up in 1753. The Bombay Theatre, modelled after London's Drury Lane, dates to 1776. British residents staged amateur performances at such halls of popular plays by Shakespeare and Congreve, later Sheridan and Goldsmith. Soon, it became common for companies and individuals from England, travelling to or from Australia and New Zealand, to present shows during halts in Calcutta or Bombay for the expatriate community.

Even before Macaulay declared English the educational medium for chosen Indians in 1835, the Rev. Krishna Mohan Banerjea (1813–85) wrote the first play in English by an Indian: *The Persecuted, or Dramatic Scenes Illustrative of the Present State of Hindoo Society in Calcutta* (1831)—a dramatized debate on the conflict between orthodox Hindu custom and new Western ideas. Native students under the new system understandably looked to English literature for inspiration. Study of Shakespeare led to a spurt not only of translations and emulations of his work in the Indian languages, but also stagings in English of scenes and, often, full plays by Shakespeare, particularly among Indian collegians. Since only men studied in those days, they enacted women's roles too. Rarely, British and Indian actors participated in the same production; a version of *Othello* in 1848 set the Calcutta press agog with its 'real unpainted nigger Othello', a Bengali gentleman.

Gradually, major Indian dramatists fluent in English emerged. Although Michael Madhusudan Dutt and Rabindranath *Tagore wrote in Bengali, they translated several of their plays into English—Dutt's rendering of *Sharmishtha* (*Sermista*, 1859) ranks among the earliest Indian cases of self-translation, which some theorists now classify as original literature. A student's English translation of Tagore's *Dakghar* (*The Post Office*, 1913) was produced by the famed Abbey Theatre, Dublin, even before Tagore won the Nobel Prize; in fact, it qualifies as the world premiere of that play, which did not appear on the Bengali stage until 1917. Indians sent to England for higher studies began to perform there in English, as amateurs. Niranjan Pal (1889–1959), son of the nationalist Bepin Pal, started the Indian Players in London, producing his own scripts like *The Goddess* (1924), revived in Calcutta after he returned in 1929.

Another bilingual author, T.P. Kailasam (1884–1946), who lived six years in England, applied his two languages discretely. Professing that 'the delineation of ideal characters requires a language which should not be very near', he composed Shakespearean-style English drama on the *Mahabharata*, but used spoken idiom for his Kannada plays on contemporary themes. He recited his works extempore, and the stage directions in his six English plays (including *The Purpose*, 1944; *Karna*, 1946; *Keechaka*, 1949) reveal a strong theatrical sense unlike many closet English dramatists in India. Among the latter, who used the form more to tell a story through dialogue than as theatrical offerings, Sri Aurobindo (1872–1950) and Harindranath Chattopadhyaya (1898–1990) left a large dramatic corpus chiefly on mythical or religious subjects.

After Independence, Indians have published as many as 200-plus plays in English, though most remain unperformed; many are not even performable. The absence of stage opportunities deprived the writers of means to learn the craft. The fourteen plays by Joseph Lobo-Prabhu (1906–?) dealt with social reform, but reduced any effectiveness by providing glib solutions. However, the 1950s injected some vigour into English-language theatre through the efforts of Shakespeareana, a touring company from England run by Geoffrey Kendal (1909–98) and his wife Laura (1908–91), whose productions of Shakespearean and other classics barnstorming through Indian cities and towns influenced such young enthusiasts as Utpal Dutt, later to become a famous Bengali director.

In the 1960s, the unsung socio-political work of Asif Currimbhoy (1928–94) brought power, passion, and complexity to original Indian-English drama in at least a dozen important plays on topical matters, but offended conservatives, which led to a ban on *The Doldrummers* (1961). A similar fate befell *A Touch of Brightness* (1965), set in a Bombay brothel by Partap Sharma (1939–), who has written four other plays. Chosen by the likes of Kenneth Tynan and George Devine from among 150 other plays for the first Commonwealth Arts Festival in London, and directed by Alyque Padamsee (1931–), it raised the hackles of India's image-makers, who proscribed it.

Among English-language troupes, the Theatre Group (Bombay), led by the first major Indian director in English, Ebrahim Alkazi (1925–), and later by Padamsee, is the most long-lived and accomplished. It staged original plays by Gieve Patel (1940–); Gurcharan Das (1943–), whose dance-drama *Mira* had premiered at La Mama, off-off-Broadway, in 1970; and the freshest and most promising Indian-English dramatist, Mahesh Dattani (1958–). The Madras Players, who produced Girish Karnad's self-translated plays and held a competition for new scripts jointly with the daily *The Hindu*, and Delhi's Yatrik also encouraged original playwriting, a policy followed in recent years by Lillete Dubey's Prime Time Theatre. The annual *Deccan Herald* theatre festival in Bangalore gave a boost to English drama by such local authors as Dattani and Poile Sengupta. The Sahitya Akademi Award to Dattani for *'Final Solutions' and Other Plays* (1994) finally gave Indian-English drama respectability.

Other dramatists with substantial output include the poet Nissim Ezekiel (1924–2004), whose five plays show the result of working with Alkazi, his mentor, in the Theatre Group; Dina Mehta (1928–), who won a worldwide BBC radio drama competition for *Brides Are Not for Burning* (1979), on dowry-related bride-burning; the prolific Madras-based Leo Fredericks (1932–), specializing in television drama with often exotic situations; and Manjula Padmanabhan (1953–) from Delhi, who has written highly provocative scripts on social mores, such as *Harvest*, awarded the international Onassis Prize in 1997. Padmanabhan revealed an activist's anguished conscience in *Hidden Fires* (2003), five riveting monologues on the Bombay communal riots of 1992. Most Indian-English drama, whether original or translated, has been published by Writers Workshop, Calcutta, and the theatre journal *Enact*, Delhi (1967–82).

Mahesh Dattani's *On a Muggy Night in Mumbai*, directed by Lillete Dubey, centre (Prime Time Theatre, Mumbai, 1998)

A commercial English-language stage became possible in Bombay after Adi Marzban (1914–87) directed his comedy *Ah! Norman* (1972, adapted from *Norman, Is That You?* by Ron Clark and Sam Bobrick), a milestone hit logging up hundreds of performances. Before long, indigenous English theatre came to mean bedroom farces and slick revues in this vein, exemplified by Bharat Dabholkar's *Bottoms Up* series, full of double entendres. Dabholkar and his imitators use a lingo mixing Hindi and English, dubbed 'Hinglish', commonly seen in advertising copy nowadays. Although the audience for English theatre, largely comprising the elite metropolitan minority, is expanding, it relates more to these Hinglish so-called 'laugh riots' than to serious theatre. While Indians have accepted English as one more Indian tongue, nowhere except in Mumbai (and perhaps Delhi) is English theatre commercially viable; amateur groups, rather than risk untried Indian dramatists, still rely heavily on a Western repertoire to attract playgoers.   SG

S. Krishna Bhatta, *Indian English Drama: A Critical Study* (New Delhi: Sterling, 1987); Jaydipsinh Dodiya and K.V. Surendran, *Indian English Drama: Critical Perspectives* (New Delhi: Sarup, 2000); C.L. Khatri and Kumar Chandradeep (eds), *Indian Drama in English: An Anthology of Recent Criticism* (Jaipur: Book Enclave, 2006); M.K. Naik and S. Mokashi-Punekar (eds), *Perspectives on Indian Drama in English* (Madras: Oxford University Press, 1977); P. Bayappa Reddy, *Studies in Indian Writing in English with a Focus on Indian English Drama* (New Delhi: Prestige, 1990).

g

GUJARATI THEATRE

The westernmost state of Gujarat had a rich tradition of writing and performing Sanskrit plays till the fourteenth century, when a folksinger of religious narratives, Asaita Thakar, launched a participatory form called *Bhavai using mythological and historical themes and characters, creating awareness among audiences on social issues. Said to have written about 360 veshas (literally 'dress') or acts, he performed them all over Gujarati-speaking western India with the help of his three sons.

This interactive tradition was ignored in the mid-nineteenth century by Bombay's theatre enthusiasts who, imitating the British masters, developed the later typical *Parsi theatre formula in proscenium-arch auditoria with curtains and drop-scenes. The first such auditorium, Grant Road Theatre, was built by Jagannath Sunkersett in 1846; the first Gujarati production there is normally regarded as *Rustam Zabuli and Sohrab* (1853). By 1868, thirty natak mandalis or troupes operated in Bombay (among them the Parsee Stage Players, Victoria, Elphinstone, Alfred, and Zoroastrian companies), owned mainly by Parsis led by Kaikhushro Kabraji (1842–1904), Dadabhai Patel (1840?–76), Cowasji Khatao (1857–1916), and Jehangir Khambata (1856–1916), which attracted middle- and upper middle-class Gujaratis and Parsis with mythological drama and clever Indianizations of Shakespeare's plays mingling Sanskrit and European dramaturgy. Hindu authors also contributed, like Ranchhodbhai Dave (1837–1923), who wrote original popular drama on mythological themes (*Harishchandra*, 1875) and preached social reform (*Lalita dukhdarshak*, 'Lalita's Manifold Sufferings', 1866), staged by the Gujarati Natak Mandali (founded 1878).

In Gujarat, three dramatist-managers embarked on a mission to initiate serious theatre: Dahyabhai Jhaveri (1867–1902), and the brothers Moolji and Vaghaji Asharam Oza (1850–97). They introduced elements new to the stage, like tableaux, social themes, and the traditional Garba dance. The Morbi Arya Subodh Natak Mandali and Wankaner Aryahit Vardhak Natak Mandali made a name in the Kathiawar peninsula as travelling repertories. But the style remained melodramatic, together with fashionable attire, painted two-dimensional backdrops, and music, which had already acquired a very important position in making theatre popular. Fresh air blew in when performers like Amrit Keshav Nayak (1877–1907), Bapulal Nayak (1879–1947), and the legendary female impersonator Jaishankar Sundari (1889–1975), with subtler understanding of the medium, rejected overacting.

Some pioneering plays written in the early twentieth century, such as the verse drama of Nanalal Dalpatram Kavi (1877–1946), never reached the stage. A few dramatists, feeling neglected, tried to assert themselves and formed their own companies to avoid exploitation by owners. They included Phoolchand Master (*Malti Madhav*, 'Malti and Madhav'; *Mudra Pratap*, 'Pratap's Ring'), Nrisinh Vibhakar (*Meghamalini*; *Madhu bansari*, 'Sweet Flute'), and Jaman (*Soneri jal*, 'Golden Net'). But, unconversant with theatre business, they finally had to give in to the managers, marking the final surrender of the dramatist for the next fifty

Jaishankar Sundari (left) and Bapulal Nayak in *Shirin Farhad* years. Slowly, the director's role was carved out by Bapulal Nayak, Mulchand Mama, and Muljibhai Khushalbhai Nayak (1893–1971), who directed great actors (Ashraf Khan, Anandji Kabutar) and actresses (Munnibai, Motibai) in plays by Raghunath Brahmbhatt (1892–1983), Prabhulal Dwivedi (1892–1962), Pragji Dossa (1907–97), Gaurishankar Vairati (*Virat nagri*, 'Virat City'), Parmanand Trapajkar (*Anarkali*), and Prafulla Desai (*Sarvodaya*, 'Development for All').

With cinema capturing audiences in the late 1920s, theatre showed two parallel trends, independent and misguidedly opposing each other. For the so-called 'old' professional theatre (better known as Parsi theatre outside Gujarat), this period was marked by money-investors owning or controlling companies, where each element (including the script) was hired and sold to the public. Writers like Brahmbhatt, Dwivedi, and Dossa; actors like Pransukh 'Eddie Polo', Mohan Lala, Ashraf Khan (1893–1962), and Chhagan 'Romeo'; directors like Master Kasam, Mulchand Mama, and Kasambhai Nathubhai Mir (1906–69) worked for such troupes as Desi Natak Samaj, which normally staged formulaic plays maintaining status quo, while renting their playhouses to exhibit films for profit. Performances continued to be caught in the sentimental rut, finally leading to the closure of many companies, and pushing the remainder to travel in small towns and villages for their sustenance.

On the other hand, between the Quit India movement (1942) and Independence (1947), barefoot folklore research by Zaverchand Meghani, poetry by Umashankar Joshi (1911–88) and Sundaram, novels by Pannalal Patel, and short stories by Chunilal Madia (1922–68) provided a realistic base to the portrayal of rural Gujarat; Joshi and Madia also composed one-act drama in the same style. Life in the state was generally full of the sense of sacrifice and hope. Quit India was followed by the Naval mutiny in Bombay, but the old Gujarati theatre remained blissfully unaffected. Instead, the so-called 'new' (amateur) theatre rose from the 1920s with missionary zeal, led by C.C. Mehta (1901–91) and K.M. Munshi (1887–1971) who, writing and producing original modernist plays, reflected realism under Western influence, as in Munshi's *Putra samovadi* ('Daughter like Son', 1929).

Individual actors and dramatists formed their own groups: the *Indian People's Theatre Association (IPTA, Bombay and Ahmadabad), Bharatiya Vidya Bhavan, Indian National Theatre, and Rangbhoomi (Bombay); Rangmandal, National Theatre, Rupak Sangh, and Natmandal (Ahmadabad); Rashtriya Kala Kendra (Surat). The decade after Independence also saw the launch of three educational institutions (Natya Vidya Mandir, Ahmadabad,

1949; M.S. University, Vadodara, 1950; Saurashtra Sangeet Natak Academy, Rajkot, 1956), the publication of short-lived theatre magazines (*Natak*, 'Drama'; *Nepathya*, 'Backstage'; *Gujarati natya*, 'Gujarati Theatre'), the centenary celebrations of Gujarati theatre in 1953, and the commencement of state drama competitions of the then bilingual Bombay State in 1955, helping the spread of theatre consciousness.

The most important productions of the time were by the educationist Jashwant Thaker (1915–90) and Sundari. Thaker had Mehta's biographical play *Narmad* (1937), on the revolutionary poet, enacted by IPTA in 1954, followed by Gunvantrai Acharya's *Allahbeli* ('Allah as Saviour', 1942), depicting the revolt by the Mer community of Saurashtra against colonial rule. Mehta had already raised the slogans that 'actors should be paid adequate remuneration' and 'troupes should have permanent performing places of their own'. His vision of the rise of 'new theatre' was well delineated in his play *Dhara Gurjari* ('Land of Gujarat', written 1944, staged 1955 by Thaker).

Meanwhile, after retiring, Sundari had come to Ahmadabad in 1948 and established the first theatre-training school in Gujarat and the experimental troupe Natmandal. He directed Ramanbhai Neelkanth's *Raino parvat* ('Mustard-seed to Mountain', 1913) in 1950, Rasiklal Parikh's *Mena Gurjari* ('Mena of Gujarat', 1953, assimilating elements of Bhavai and Beijing Opera, and incorporating the imaginary character of Rangli, the female counterpart of Bhavai's Ranglo, solely for actress Dina Pathak), and the classic comedy *Mithyabhiman* ('False Vanity', published in 1871 by Dalpatram, 1820–98) in 1955, introducing the Bhavai actor Pransukh Nayak (1910–89)—all important theatre events. Pathak (1923–2002) became the public image of the rejuvenated theatre. Natmandal's academic approach inspired Parikh to write *Sharvilak* (1957), based on the Sanskrit

Rasiklal Parikh's *Mena Gurjari*, directed by Jaishankar Sundari (Natmandal, Ahmadabad, 1953), with Dina Pathak (right)

Mricchakatika by Sudraka. Two other notable experiments in 1956 also used Bhavai: C.C. Mehta's *Hoholika* and actor-playwright Jayanti Patel's political satire *Neta abhineta* ('Leaders and Actors').

A beginning was thus made with the performance of original drama, but Bombay troupes soon turned to translations and adaptations, the most popular among them being *Rangilo rajja* ('Playful Fellow', 1954, by Dhansukhlal Mehta) and *Manuni masi* ('Manu's Aunt', 1951, from Brandon Thomas's *Charley's Aunt*). The annual state drama competitions encouraged the formation of many groups, which later produced translations and adaptations mainly imported from Piccadilly or Broadway, via the Marathi stage. While the 'old' stage had rarely taken translation seriously, the 'new' stage now also thrived on adaptations, commercial interests winning the upper hand after the initial zeal died down. Furthermore, the boxed action behind the proscenium arch with European conventions seemed to affect the live actor–audience relationship.

In the early 1960s, the Indian National Theatre, Bahuroopi, and Rangbhoomi in Bombay introduced many actors and managers like Vishnukumar Vyas, Pratap Oza, Madhukar Randeriya, Damu Zaveri, Lalu Shah, and Vanlata Mehta, while Rangmandal, Rupak Sangh, Darpana, and Javnika in Ahmadabad brought forward actors like Dhananjay Thaker, Kailash Pandya, Markand and Urmila Bhatt, Damini Mehta. Adi Marzban (1914–87) and Phiroz Antia were very active in Parsi comedies. However, the most popular were the actor-couple Pravin (1936–80) and Sarita Joshi (1941–) of Indian National Theatre, usually producing adapted Broadway hits, sometimes directing original drama such as Ramji Vania's *Moti veranan chokman* ('Pearls Scattered in the Yard', 1969) and Madhu Rye's *Kumarni agasi* (translated as *The Terrace*, 1972). Actor-director Kanti Madia also attracted full houses with his plays like *Ame barafna pankhi* ('We are Birds of Snow', 1974).

This period was marked by some good one-act drama from Jayanti Dalal (1909–70), Prabodh Joshi (1926–91), Shiv Kumar Joshi (1916–88), and Chunilal Madia. The brief one-act diversion imitated the European trend of absurdist theatre. There were notable sparks in writers like Labhshankar Thaker (1935–), Subhash Shah (*Ek undar ane Jadunath*, 'A Rat and God', 1966), and Adil Mansoori (*Hath pag*, 'Hands and Feet', 1970). This apparently rootless movement spread like wildfire, catching the imagination of young playwrights, but also died with the same speed when the Youth Festivals in the state were discontinued. Credit for an attitudinal change to the language of theatre should go to Madhu Rye (1942– , in

Koipan ek phulnun nam bolo to, 1968, or *Tell Me the Name of a Flower*), who also gathered some dramatists in an informal self-training group, Akanth Sabarmati, in 1972. Newer voices included Shrikant Shah (*Tirad*, 'Crack', 1972), Hasmukh Baradi (*Kalo kamlo*, 'Black Blanket', 1975), Raghuvir Chaudhari (*Sikandar Sani*, 1976), and Chinu Modi (*Navalsha Hirji*, 1977). The authors turned to performing as well: Rye and Labhshankar Thaker with Darpana, Subhash Shah and Modi at Hathisingh Visual Arts Centre, Baradi in Garage Studio Theatre. These efforts benefited their search for a modern theatre language.

The noticeable trend of the 1980s was towards stylization, especially in Thaker, Sitanshu Yashashchandra (1941–), and Baradi (*Janardan Joseph* and the verse drama *Jashumati*, both 1981), and a quest for elements fresh from performing traditions rooted in the soil. The rich heritage of folk expressions like Bhavai and musical dance forms like Ras-Garba, or storytellers like Man Bhatt, contributed. Kailash Pandya (1923–2007) and Janak Dave extensively used folk elements in their productions. Stylistically at the opposite pole, professional companies had commercially sold-out shows like Vinod Jani's *Prit piyu ne panetar* ('Love, Husband and Wedding Gown', 1963), which still runs after a record 7000 performances, and those of Arpan Theatre led by Ramesh Amin.

There are three distinct kinds of Gujarati theatre now. The commercial variety in Mumbai depends on Hindi films or Broadway adaptations for easy formulae laced with double-entendre dialogue, commissioned by agents for 'contract shows' to societies, ringing the death knell of the box office, which used to form an acid test for their (so-advertised) 'slick and efficient' performances. They sell mystery, tears, jokes, and even ideals in high-speed exchanges delivered by smartly costumed casts in fashionable decor, in scripts proudly imported from abroad or Marathi. However, alongside this activity, notable experiments were conducted by US-based actor-director Chandrakant Shah and others, for instance performing a series of successful 'Gandhi plays' that presented controversial aspects of the Mahatma's life.

The second category is the amateur activity, centred in the cities of Ahmadabad, Vadodara, Surat, Rajkot, and marginally in Mumbai (the Chhabildas experimental movement and Mahendra Joshi), where groups stage original plays or classics, following Stanislavskian Method acting or Brecht, Grotowski, and Peter Brook. New drama among these groups seems to have increased: the critic Vinod Adhvaryu evaluated the 1990s as the 'most notable decade of playwriting'; the poet-editor Niranjan Bhagat forecast that the 'Gujarati play is emerging'. Solo scripts were produced in

Mumbai and Gujarat on the lives of great writers like Narmad, Kalapi, and Kant. The longest-running troupe is the thirty-year-old Garage Studio Theatre, from which flowered a production, training and media centre with land and partial financial help from the government. A recent theatre movement among the young is led by writer-director Saumay Joshi, who has tackled themes of communal conflict and the sorrows of the common man.

The third category is developmental, socially relevant attempts by non-government organizations and committed troupes like Parivartan (Vadodara), Garage, Chetna, Awaj, and Nehru Foundation (Ahmadabad) who conduct workshops and perform thematic plays for awareness, inspired by Badal Sircar and Augusto Boal, in which the audience is allowed equal participation. *Third theatre's contribution is the emergence of *street theatre (Samvedan, Garage, and Lok Kala Manch in Ahmadabad, Parivartan in Vadodara) in efforts to take theatre to people at street corners, in middle-class housing colonies, or open public places. Hiren Gandhi and Swaroop Dhruv of Samvedan stage socially conscious plays with actors from the weaker sections of society.

The onslaught of television has affected the output of directors like Nimesh Desai and Bharat Dave, among others in Gujarat responsible for some very interesting productions in the 1990s. Actor-directors now find money and glamour in the electronic medium, not realizing that it cuts both ways: theatre loses and television does not benefit. Elsewhere, the four-decade-old theatre training facilities at the university level have not been very beneficial, nor the efforts to preserve Bhavai, although authentic performers like the female impersonator Chimanlal Naik (1925–) did conduct workshops. Furthermore, in the absence of even the semblance of research or serious theatre criticism, most remarkable works go unnoticed and writers get discouraged.

On the positive side, the efforts of scholar-designers Goverdhan Panchal (1913–96) and Mansukh Joshi (1922–2000) had a singular effect in creating the right theatre consciousness. Panchal researched and reconstructed classical traditions, while Joshi won respect for work on folk stagecraft. The Sangeet Natak Akademi scheme to encourage young directors discovered talents like Aditi Desai, Janak Rawal, Manvita Baradi, Prabhakar Dabhade, and P.S. Chari. National festivals organized by Rajendra Bhagat, almost every year, brought fresh air and glimpses of newer experiments in sister theatres. One-act competitions over the past fifteen years by the Indian National Theatre and *Gujarat Samachar* also raised interest among young people.

Tame ana thi Ramtata,
directed by Manvita
Baradi and Janak Rawal
(Sangeet Natak Akademi,
Ahmadabad, 1993)

Still, an overview does make one feel that no great drama in Mahatma Gandhi's state evolved from Gandhian non-violence or satyagraha. The empty-bellied remained miles away from the thick walls of theatre halls in urban centres. Similarly, the division of the country, recurrent communal disharmony, long shadows of rising fundamentalism, child labour, class exploitation have not inspired any notable Gujarati dramatic expression. The road to relevant and vibrant theatre is long: revival of the box office; better actor–audience relationship reflecting local and culture-specific themes; close ties between writers and troupes for stageable plays; groups owning their performance spaces; useful and meaningful theatre research; insightful criticism; reach of theatre to a wider audience which faces the all-out onslaught of media and 'open skies'; and the emergence of directors who do not just direct actors, but theatre as a whole.   HB

Hasmukh Baradi, *History of Gujarati Theatre* (New Delhi: National Book Trust, 2003); S.D. Desai, *Happenings: Theatre in Gujarat in the Eighties* (Gandhinagar: Gujarat Sahitya Akademi, 1990); S.D. Desai, *More Happenings: Gujarati Theatre Today (1990–99)* (Gandhinagar: Gujarat Sahitya Akademi, 2002).

h

HINDI THEATRE

Although theatre in Hindi has a tradition spanning more than four centuries, in many ways it represents the continuity of *Sanskrit theatre in various literary languages or spoken dialects of a large part of northern India, comprising the present states of Uttar Pradesh, Bihar, Jharkhand, Madhya Pradesh, Chhattisgarh, Rajasthan, Haryana, Himachal Pradesh, and Uttarakhand. This geographical spread and diversity of Hindi linguistic structures naturally found expression in equally varied theatrical narratives like *Ramlila (in the Avadhi tongue), *Raslila (in Brajbhasha), *Bhagat, *Nautanki/Sangit/*Swang, and *Naqal (all in Haryanvi or Khariboli mixed with Brajbhasha), *Bidesiya (Bhojpuri), *Mach (Malvi), *Nacha and *Pandavani (Chhattisgarhi), *Khyal (Rajasthani), and *Karyala (Himachali mixed with Khariboli).

These forms or, more appropriately, *natya*s (theatres) incorporated many elements from Sanskrit dramaturgy: its aesthetic of *rasa*, sources for themes and stories like the *Mahabharata*, *Ramayana*, and *Bhagavata*, theatrical approaches, conventions, and practices like the *purvaranga* (preliminaries), *kakshya vibhaga* (stage zones or locales), and treatment of time and space, and roles like the *sutradhara* (director-manager) and *vidushaka* (jester). Yet they were very different, a kind of evolution and extension in a changed socio-cultural context. As these *natya*s used the common people's spoken or literary idiom, theatre ceased to be an elite preserve and acquired wide popular patronage. It came out of the royal courts and their *mandapa*s (halls) and began to be staged in village squares or fields, town marketplaces, temple grounds, or other suitable outdoor locations, before large audiences.

Each *natya* has its specific character in its choice of themes, style of presentation, staging methods, quantum and use of speech, music, and dance, or nature of performance space. But they share some features with traditional forms in other parts of the country. First, unlike Sanskrit theatre, most have no literary drama or scripts. Instead, uninhibitedly theatrical, they employ memorized or written synopses of familiar mythological or historical episodes, legends, and tales, improvised by the performers with the help of poetry, song, dance, and mime. Second, some like the Ramlila, Raslila, and Bhagat were inspired by or closely related to the Bhakti religious movement that swept India in the fourteenth to seventeenth centuries. Later, especially in the eighteenth and nineteenth centuries, many others—Nautanki, Swang, Bidesiya, Mach, Nacha, Naqal, Karyala—with entirely secular (socio-political or economic)

A Swang performance in Haryana, 1971

themes came into existence or became popular. Even the devotional theatres, with predominantly ritualistic, spiritual content and tone, always had built-in provisions for reference to or comment on contemporary social reality.

As theatrical expressions, these *natyas* are actor- or singer-generated; the performer provides not only the flesh and blood to the narrative frame conceived by the producer, but also imbues it with vitality and meaning by his improvisations. For this purpose, the *natyas* adopted and reinvented the *sutradhara* and *vidushaka* to carry out crucial functions. The *sutradhar* now selects the story and prepares its scenario from existing versions, using the exquisite narrative or lyrical poetry and song available in the dialect. He trains the actors in singing, dancing, and miming, through constant practice. On stage, he controls the rhythm of the performance, sings most of the songs or narrates, links the action, and, if required, plays minor roles. In a sense, he is dramatist and director rolled into one. The *vidushak*, on the other hand, is a foil appearing at any point in the show, providing not only humour and wit but also commentary, frequently relating distant mythological situations or characters to contemporary life.

These theatres use music and dance along with words as a total language of communication, enriching the performances aesthetically, making them imaginative, absorbing, multi-level experiences. They fulfil an important function as vehicles of the social and cultural values of society, as well as sources of art and entertainment catering to all sections, so closely associated with the life of the people that in spite of many ups and downs they survive to this day.

Meanwhile, court poets or devotees continued to write plays on the pattern of Sanskrit drama. We may mention *Hanuman-nataka* ('Hanuman's Play', *c.* 1623) by Hridayaram, *Govind hulas* ('Govind's Delight') by Rup Goswami (1643–1713), *Karunabharana* ('Ornament of Compassion', *c.* 1715) by Krishnajivan Lacchiram, *Pradyumna vijay* ('Pradyumna's Victory', *c.* 1807) by Ganesh, *Ananda Raghunandan* ('Raghunandan's Joy') by Viswanath Singhju Deva (1789–1854), and *Nahusha* (*c.* 1851) by Giridhardasa Gopalchandra. All were, more or less, literary exercises and staged, if at all, only for family members or courtiers of the ruling prince to whom the poet-playwright was attached, or by the ruler himself as in the case of *Ananda Raghunandan*. A notable instance of this tradition was *Indarsabha* ('Indra's Court', 1853) by Amanat (1817–59), inspired by the Nawab of Avadh, Wajid Ali Shah (1823–87), who performed in its production at his court in Lucknow. *Indarsabha*, popular ever since, fused episodes based on medieval Islamic romances with Hindu mythology, music and dance styles of the region, and Hindi with Urdu languages.

In the nineteenth century, theatre began changing rapidly in an unexpected and unprecedented manner, particularly in the coastal cities of Calcutta, Bombay, and Madras, where the English had set up their commercial, administrative, and military strongholds. With the consolidation of British colonial rule across India and introduction of a new education policy to create a supportive middle class for administrative and commercial purposes, several elements of European and British culture entered, including theatre. This new art based on conflict and catharsis, with strong emotional situations of violence, passion, and sensation, in contrast to the traditional theatre of *rasa* and equilibrium, captured the attention and imagination of the urban population, especially the aristocracy, which had access to English education and lifestyle.

This trend reached the Hindi region by the mid-nineteenth century in two streams. The commercial *Parsi theatre based in and around Bombay toured all over the country, particularly north India, staging plays not just in Gujarati but Urdu-Hindi or Hindustani, as it was sometimes called. Primarily a money-making, entertainment-oriented theatre, imitative of the Victorian English companies which came to India to satisfy the colonial soldiers, administrators, and businessmen, it took its stories of heroic characters from the popular legends and romances of Europe, central Asia, and, eventually, Hindu mythology. It also enacted bowdlerized Shakespeare and crude interludes from comedies and farces by Molière and other Western authors. Spectacular scene changes, breathtaking fight sequences, colourful and glamorous costumes, split-second timing and humour, suspenseful and melodramatic treatment of love and valour in a highly theatrical mix of prose, verse, and song were presented on makeshift and, later, permanent proscenium stages. This style lasted about a hundred years, famous dramatists including Ahsan (fl. 1897–1905), Talib (1855–1922), Betab (1872–1945), Agha Hashr Kashmiri (1879–1935), and Radheshyam Kathavachak (1890–1963). It had no physical, social, or cultural roots in the Hindi belt but, because of its rampant commercialism, adversely affected the serious non-professional Hindi theatre, the second and more important stream of West-influenced theatre.

The pioneer poet-playwright from Varanasi, Bharatendu Harishchandra (1850–85), began this movement by founding an amateur group with his literary associates, writing, staging, and acting in his own and other plays, occasionally also travelling to nearby towns in Uttar Pradesh and Bihar with the productions. The first such drama was *Janaki mangal* ('Janaki's Marriage', 1867), written by one of his associates, Sitala Prasad Tripathi, and produced in Varanasi. Bharatendu explored skilfully and with creative insight various forms, not only of the Hindi region, but also Bengali, Sanskrit, and the newly introduced Shakespearean model. His play that has abided best, *Andher nagari* ('City of Darkness', 1881), is a musical farce that uncannily perceives the all-pervading degeneration of society—religious orders, native and foreign rulers, judiciary, bureaucracy—ultimately affecting the ordinary citizen. No less significant was his creation and mastery of an expressive Hindi dramatic prose.

However, this strong, promising start for modern Hindi theatre could not be sustained. After Bharatendu's premature death, the resourceful Parsi companies periodically visiting Hindi towns swamped the indigenous theatre. Despite sporadic efforts in urban literary centres, including revivals of Bharatendu's works, or formation of groups like the Bharatendu Natak Mandali and Kasi Nagari Natak Mandali in Varanasi, and the Ramlila Natak Mandali by nationalist actor-playwright Madhav Shukla (1881–1943) in Allahabad, hardly any regular or continuous dramatic or theatrical activity emerged anywhere, commercial or otherwise.

The next breakthrough, though partial, came with the appearance in Varanasi of Jaishankar Prasad (1890–1937), seniormost author among the trio of the new romantic school of Hindi poetry in the first quarter of the twentieth century. He wrote about a dozen plays, which established him as a major Indian dramatist and made Hindi drama a significant mode of creative expression. They explored basic human dilemmas through situations and characters from India's glorious past, also echoing the nationalist freedom struggle. Although structurally loose, with too many scenes and subplots, and traces of the contrived Parsi stagecraft, the plays show fascinating and complex men and women in conflict with their social environment as well as themselves. The language has a literary imprint, more lyrical than dramatic, but musical and evocative of inner and socio-political turmoil. Regrettably, in the absence of serious theatre groups, the texts could not be properly tried out on stage. They remained confined to students of literature, their distinctive and relevant theatre potential revealed much later in the 1970s and 1980s, in successful productions by imaginative directors.

With the advent of cinema in the 1930s, the Parsi companies one by one jettisoned theatre and joined the film bandwagon. Consequently, even the occasional theatrical experience they provided to Hindi audiences became increasingly scarce. Attempts to set up troupes by theatre enthusiasts in some towns failed, but infrequent dramatic activity in educational institutions and literary organizations, together with the newly arrived radio, encouraged one-act drama. Prasad's literary success also led to considerable playwriting by authors like Hari Krishna Premi (1908–74), Vrindaban Lal Verma, Govind Vallabh Pant, Seth Govind Das, and Ram Kumar Varma (1904–90). They generally followed the Parsi structure of melodramatic action, contrived situations, and sentimental characterization, but based their plots on mythological and historical episodes with direct or indirect patriotic overtones, on social evils, or, occasionally, on personal relations. Laxminarayan Mishra (1903–87), an exception, wrote a number of realistic works influenced by Ibsen and Shaw. Although some of these dramatic exercises found place in university curricula, they had little creative quality either as literature or theatre. Very few were performed.

In the 1940s, two developments unexpectedly infused life into Hindi theatre. The launching of the *Indian People's Theatre Association (IPTA) in 1943 by the Communist Party of India resulted in the writing and staging of new plays with a direct and immediate political and social message. An all-India multilingual cultural movement initially based in Calcutta and Bombay, besides some rural pockets of Communist influence, it soon spread to towns in the entire Hindi-speaking area. IPTA did not produce Hindi drama of importance, but unquestionably stimulated wide, sustained interest in theatre and attracted or inspired activists and talented practitioners like the famous actor Balraj Sahni (1913–73) and Habib Tanvir (1923–). It also gave unprecedented respectability to theatre in the socially conservative Hindi community. It lost its leading place by the end of the decade, but continued to function in many states. Meanwhile Prithvi Theatres, a professional travelling company started by the redoubtable film star Prithviraj Kapoor (1906–72) in 1944, emulated the Parsi model but staged clean and purposeful Hindi plays with a rare dedication and competence. In its hectic existence of about sixteen years, it moved thousands all over north India with its performances and, like IPTA, generated interest in theatre.

After Independence, creative energy spilled over all aspects of life in India. In the artistic field, particularly, it expressed itself in myriad individual and institutional forms. Hindi drama suddenly came of age. Apart from the realistic, light, and racy plays of Upendra Nath Ashk (1910–96), Jagdish Chandra Mathur (1917–78) wrote the complex *Konarka* (1950), which attracted theatre people everywhere. Dharamvir Bharati

(1926–97) composed his famous verse drama *Andha yug* (*Blind Age*, 1954) on the aftermath of the *Mahabharata* war, powerfully echoing post-World War II agonies. It drew some of the most talented Hindi directors, was translated into several Indian languages and English, and came to be regarded as a modern classic. Another outstanding playwright, Mohan Rakesh (1925–72), debuted with *Ashadh ka ek din* (*One Day in Ashadha*, 1958). Based on controversial events in the life of *Kalidasa, it examined the dilemmas of an artist in relation to his love, social commitment, creative urges, and consequent loneliness. Realistic in style but with language full of irony and deep resonances, it remains Rakesh's most significant achievement, widely translated and repeatedly staged. These two plays gave Hindi drama a high all-India profile.

Dharamvir Bharati's *Andha yug* revived by Ebrahim Alkazi at the Purana Qila (National School of Drama Repertory Company, New Delhi, 1974)

The explosion in playwriting was inevitably connected with the emergence of dedicated groups and directors like Anamika and the inventive Shyamanand Jalan (1934–) in Calcutta, Satyavrata Sinha's Prayag Rangmanch in Allahabad, Theatre Unit and the provocative Satyadev Dubey (1936–) in Bombay, and Habib Tanvir's Naya Theatre in Delhi. Tanvir produced in 1954 his musical drama, *Agra bazar* ('Bazaar in Agra'), based on the life of the popular eighteenth-century Urdu poet Nazir Akbarabadi, which became an instant hit and continued to run into the late 1990s. Tanvir evolved as one of the finest Indian directors, a trendsetter in many ways.

Official policies and their implementation strengthened this creative exuberance. The Government of India set up three autonomous bodies for literature and arts in New Delhi. The one for the performing arts, Sangeet Natak Akademi (SNA), established in 1953, began work almost immediately. In 1956 it organized a national drama seminar, which recommended the foundation of a *National School of Drama (NSD) in Delhi. The medium of instruction was to be primarily Hindi (the national language) or English whenever necessary, and performances only in Hindi—a momentous decision of far-reaching consequences for Hindi theatre, which became evident soon after the NSD started in 1959. In its forty years of existence, the NSD has produced around 600 directors, actors, designers, and technicians, a large number of them Hindi-speaking or choosing to work in Hindi. Its roster of star graduates includes such versatile performers as Om Shivpuri, Manohar Singh (1942–2002), Uttara Baokar (1944–), Surekha Sikri (1945–), and Naseeruddin Shah (1950–).

In the 1960s, Hindi theatre registered phenomenal advances with the NSD. The eminent Bombay director Ebrahim Alkazi (1925–), who had so far worked in English, joined the NSD in 1962 as Director and began staging original Hindi drama as well as Sophocles' *Oedipus Rex* (1964), Shakespeare's *King Lear* (1964), and Molière's *The Miser* (1965) in Hindi translation, with unusual artistry and professionalism. Another tremendously popular NSD production was the musical *Jasma Odan* (1968), a traditional *Bhavai play imaginatively recreated by Shanta Gandhi. The NSD also formed the nucleus of a repertory company, which became its full-fledged performing wing from the mid-1970s. Ever since, its productions continued to provide high-quality theatre in Hindi not only to Delhi audiences, but also toured different centres of the country.

During this period, new groups came up in several cities: Darpana in Kanpur, Allahabad Artists Association in Allahabad, Rupantar in Gorakhpur, Kala Sangam in Patna. In Delhi, Dishantar, formed in 1967 by NSD alumni, presented excellent productions over ten years, including the 1969 premiere of Rakesh's *Adhe-adhure*, directed by Om Shivpuri. This drama, depicting the breakdown of a lower middle-class family with a working woman as the central character, is one of the finest and most frequently performed modern Hindi plays, translated into many languages. Another Delhi group founded in 1967, Abhiyan led by Rajinder Nath (1934–), specialized in translating outstanding Indian drama (Bengali plays by Badal Sircar, Mohit Chattopadhyaya, Debasis Majumdar, Marathi plays by Vijay Tendulkar, Satish Alekar, G.P. Deshpande), besides original Hindi works like *Curfew* (1971) by Lakshmi Narayan Lal (1927–87) and Bhisham Sahni's *Hanush* (1977). It staged two or three productions every year and, though some ran for up to 100 shows, it deliberately refused to turn professional.

The 1960s were also notable for new performance spaces. After the decline of Parsi theatre, most auditoria in India were converted into cinema houses. In the Hindi region, the situation was even bleaker: no theatre halls survived in the major towns. Delhi during the 1950s had only three places for theatre. Sapru House, moderately equipped, with a small stage and approximately 600 seats, was attached to a research institution and meant for functions of various kinds, hosting the first SNA-sponsored National Drama Festival of over twenty productions in 1954. The other two, the YMCA's 150-seater Constantia Hall and the 550-seat Fine Arts Theatre, became the hub of new theatre activities. However, the nationwide Tagore centenary celebrations in 1961 came as a boon and reasonably equipped playhouses named after Rabindranath *Tagore came up in nearly all the state capitals, such as Lucknow, Jaipur, Bhopal, Patna, and Chandigarh.

In Delhi, the multipurpose Mavalankar Hall, with a capacity of 800 and other facilities, and the open-air Triveni Kala Sangam were erected. Alkazi created two venues on NSD's Rabindra Bhavan campus, a sixty-seat studio theatre and the 250-seat open-air Meghdoot Theatre, and explored the possibilities of outdoor historical sites like the ruins of Ferozeshah Kotla, Talkatora Garden, and, later, the Purana Qila fort. During the 1970s three more halls came up: the well-equipped Kamani Auditorium (capacity 600, with a wide, deep stage) of the Bharatiya Kala Kendra Trust and the Shri Ram Centre (a main stage for 600 spectators and a flexible 200-seat basement theatre) built by the Indian National Theatre Trust. The construction of Prithvi Theatre in Bombay, Kala Mandir in Calcutta, Sur Sadan in Agra, Sangit Samiti Hall in Allahabad, Nagari Rangasala in Varanasi, and Bharat Bhavan in Bhopal gave Hindi theatre further boost.

Surendra Verma's *Surya ki antim kiran se surya ki pahli kiran tak*, directed by Ram Gopal Bajaj (National School of Drama Repertory Company, New Delhi, 1974)

More playwrights, like Mudra Rakshasa, Mani Madhukar, Surendra Verma (1941–), Sarveshwar Dayal Saxena, Shankar Shesh, Nand Kishore Acharya, Nag Bodas, Rameshwar Prem, Swadesh Deepak, Asghar Wajahat; and directors, like B.M. Shah (1933–98), Ram Gopal Bajaj (1940–), Mohan Maharishi (1940–), Bhanu Bharti (1947–), Ranjit Kapoor, Dinesh Thakur, Satish Anand, Harish Bhatia, Girish Rastogi, Anil Bhowmik, Alakh Nandan, appeared in the 1970s. Yet the ever-growing number of theatre enthusiasts, amateur groups, trained directors, actors, and technicians led to a demand for new scripts that could not be met. As a result, they turned to drama from other languages; significant or popular, old or new, plays in Marathi, Bengali, Kannada, Gujarati, English, were translated and staged. Suddenly the Hindi repertoire expanded vastly, not only providing variety of content, form, and style but also greater opportunity and experience, raising the overall level of Hindi theatre. Hardly any Indian play of merit exists which has not been performed in Hindi. While this process gave an all-India coverage and national image to other Indian dramatists, it adversely affected original Hindi playwriting. Hindi directors and groups prefer to do translations of successful plays from elsewhere rather than pick up an untried Hindi script. But, undoubtedly, Hindi became a clearing house for Indian drama, as famous Indian plays were often retranslated into other languages from the Hindi translation instead of the original.

In yet another sense, Hindi theatre evolved a national character. A large number of its eminent directors came from non-Hindi regions: Alkazi from Bombay, Bansi Kaul (1934–) from Srinagar, Usha Ganguli (1945–) from Calcutta, Amal Allana (1947–) from Bombay, M.K. Raina (1948–) from Srinagar, Feisal Alkazi from Bombay. Moreover, many from other Indian languages and other nations created acclaimed and popular productions in Hindi: K.N. Panikkar, B.V. Karanth, Vijaya Mehta, Shanta Gandhi, Prasanna, Ratan Thiyam, Fritz Bennewitz (from Germany), Richard Schechner (from the US). Designers included Roshen Alkazi (1923–2007, costume), M.S. Sathyu (1930– , *scenography), Ashok Srivastava (1931– , make-up), and G.N. Dasgupta (1936–2001, lighting). This manifested in an unmatched diversity of style, idiom, and artistic vision, particularly remarkable in the absence of any regular commercial or professional Hindi theatre and the almost endemic shortage of spectators, as also of charismatic performers.

Habib Tanvir (left) in *Charandas Chor*, written and directed by him (Naya Theatre, originally 1975)

During the 1970s, a wave swept Indian theatre that partly originated in Hindi theatre: the desire to break from Western moulds and find indigenous models, leading playwrights, directors, and actors to folk or traditional forms, practices, and methods. An active interest arose in Sanskrit drama, Bharata's *Natyasastra*, and the exploration of ways to present them for modern audiences. Habib Tanvir had started the process with *Agra bazar* and *Mitti ki gadi* ('Clay Cart', 1958, adapted from Sudraka's *Mricchakatika* and acted by a mixed rural-urban cast), subsequently strengthened after the encounter he and Indian theatre people had with Brecht. He wrote his masterpiece, *Charandas Chor* (1975), followed by *Bahadur Kalarin* ('Heroic Kalarin', 1978) and a number of productions rooted in the folk traditions of Chhattisgarh, even of Sanskrit classics; he filled his entire company with Chhattisgarhi performers. Gandhi's *Jasma Odan*, Madhukar's *Ras-gandharva* ('Celestial Pleasure', 1973) and *Khela Polampur ka* ('Khyal of Polampur', 1975) in Khyal style, Saxena's *Bakri* ('She-goat', 1973) and Mudra Rakshasa's *Ala afsar* ('Senior Officer', 1977) in Nautanki idiom also opened new directions for an authentic indigenous theatre. The exercise revealed the great vitality and theatricality of traditional forms and their rural practitioners.

In the 1980s, professional or semi-professional repertories came up in different cities. In Delhi, apart from the NSD and Naya Theatre, the Shri Ram Centre Repertory Company, Sahitya Kala Parishad Rangmandal, and Little Theatre Group Repertory appeared. A more significant effort was the Madhya Pradesh Rangmandal in Bhopal, with B.V. Karanth as founder-director. Fully funded by the state government, it staged a variety of plays including an acclaimed production of Prasad's *Skandgupta* in 1984, and Sanskrit and Western classics, some in regional dialects. It toured extensively in Madhya Pradesh, besides most other Hindi centres. Among other troupes, Rang Vidushak in Bhopal, Padatik and Rangakarmee in Calcutta, Ank in Mumbai, Bhartendu Natya Akademi Rangmandal in Lucknow, and Asmita in Delhi deserve mention. Committed theatre groups operate in almost every major town in the Hindi belt, despite a talent drain towards the media and advertising.

Another phenomenon of some consequence was the emergence of women playwrights Mridula Garg, Mrinal Pande, and Kusum Kumar, and scripter-directors Tripurari Sharma, Kirti Jain, Anuradha Kapur, Anamika Haksar, and Nadira Zaheer Babbar. In a language where even in the 1960s it proved very difficult to get women to act in theatre, this marked a major advance. Among Indian languages, Hindi theatre has possibly the largest number of active women writers and directors. They took great risks, brought new vision and style with passionate and courageous political stands, unconventional and evocative images, more collaborative production processes, hence more varied and subjective expression, and often explored untapped sources for their narrative structures.

The search for fresh material frequently prompted scriptwriters to dramatize fiction such as the outstanding work of Premchand, Hazari Prasad Dwivedi, Phanishwar Nath Renu, Srilal Shukla, Krishna Sobti, and Mannu Bhandari. This quest took an innovative turn with *kahani ka rangmanch* ('the stage of stories'), invented by director D.R. Ankur, in which moving and perceptive short stories by authors like Ajneya and Nirmal Verma were presented verbatim, including descriptive or reflective passages, without any dramatization of the text. These attempts created a theatre at once challenging for the performer and exciting for the viewer. Ambitious recent efforts include Amal Allana's capturing Garcia Marquez' magic realism in *Erendira* (2004) and Abhilash Pillai's energetic presentation of Salman Rushdie's *Midnight's Children* (2005) using multimedia.

Contemporary Hindi theatre remains bedevilled by two major challenges. The absence of geographical and cultural focus due to its vast regional base with many-layered and diverse social structures makes it very difficult to define its roots and where it belongs. And the multiplicity of sub-languages or dialects means that it has to constantly negotiate not only between Hindi and Urdu/Hindustani, but also among many highly expressive spoken tongues, some with a rich literary or cultural past, like Brajbhasha, Avadhi, Bhojpuri, Maithili, Bundelkhandi, Malvi, Rajasthani, and Chhattisgarhi. A few claim independent histories of their own (see *Maithili theatre and *Rajasthani theatre), in spite of a constant and inevitable overlap of spectators and practitioners.

At the turn of the twenty-first century, the media explosion nibbles away at already meagre theatre audiences and existing or emerging talent, while seasoned theatre performers like Amrish Puri (1932–2005), Om Puri, or Ashish Vidyarthi moved to mainstream cinema and television. On the other hand, some observers claim that more actors and viewers are returning to theatre as disgust and disillusionment with the crude stereotypes on the large or small screen grow, while despite problems of all kinds, new professional or semi-professional companies are being formed by young people with imaginative ideas. The rising number of theatre festivals, often running to full houses, also indicates a growing audience keen to experience alternate sources of entertainment.   NJ

Solo performance is another trend that has emerged due to shortage of funds, and actors not having time to work with a team. It could also be the result of actors asserting their presence to make an independent statement without a director's intervention. Either way, it has given individuals the freedom and space to explore and extend their skills in related genres, as with Naseeruddin Shah's straight storytelling, or Maya Rao's intense and abstract *Kathakali-inspired dance-theatre of Manto's *Khol do* ('Open Up', 1997).

One must admit that in the present process of breaking the linearity of the grand narrative the biggest casualty has been original, orthodox dramatic literature in Hindi. While earlier the vacuum in the repertoire was filled by translations and adaptations of plays from the West and other Indian languages, today the directors themselves devise performance texts that rely on a variety of sources. Mohan Maharishi has used Einstein's life and the theory of relativity; Kirti Jain, interviews with Partition survivors; Anuradha Kapur, the autobiography of Gujarati female impersonator Jaishankar Sundari to examine gender representation; Anamika Haksar, the history of the *Dramatic Performances Act and a Tamil epic. The independent dramatist has gone missing.

Nevertheless, the outlook in Hindi theatre seems positive, definitely a site where much experimentation in content and form takes place. At the level of the visual language, space and design has been redefined, Alkazi's tradition of exploring found places carried on, as well as conventional venues deployed unconventionally. Compared to most other regions, Hindi theatre has become regularly innovative in scenography, attempting to enrich the meaning of the text through design elements including the new media. Directors have actively collaborated with painters, architects, and video designers to create a novel artistic vocabulary on stage.   KJ

J.P. Mishra, *Shakespeare's Impact on Hindi Literature* (New Delhi: Munshiram Manoharlal, 1970); Birendra Narayana, *Hindi Drama and Stage* (New Delhi: Bansal, 1981).

k

KANNADA THEATRE

The south-western state of Karnataka possesses a rich and ancient heritage of performatory forms in the Kannada language, a few dating perhaps to the twelfth century. For reasons of availability, *Yakshagana is the folk tradition most commonly associated with Karnataka by outsiders, but it is by no means a homogeneous entity: popular regional variants include the *Bayalata and *Sannata styles of the north, while *Talamaddale is a generic variant. The range of theatrical diversity in rural parts of the state also encompasses *puppetry, two branches of which fall under the term *Gombeyata; various forms of ritual *possession incorporating worship, such as *Bhutaradhane and *Karaga; and devotional narratives by and for specific religious sects, as in Kamsale and Viragase.

The history of modern Kannada theatre begins around the last quarter of the nineteenth century. The British administration had by then penetrated fairly deep into present-day Karnataka, the material infrastructure for Kannada printing and publishing had been established, and modern educational institutions had begun functioning across the region. All these, in turn, influenced the development of Kannada literature, the period 1880–1920 often being termed the 'Kannada Renaissance'. There were other factors, too. During these decades, and even until as late as 1956, Kannada-speaking areas lay scattered in the erstwhile provinces of Bombay, Hyderabad, Mysore, and Madras. Hence Kannada was open to influences from other Indian languages as well. At the same time, there was a strong popular desire for the unification of all Kannada-speaking regions under one Kannada identity. These several factors often confronted one another, leading gradually to a process of assimilation and forming the basis for a fine balance between rootedness and openness.

The manner in which modernity made its entry into Kannada theatre in the nineteenth century constitutes a highly interesting story. Surveys so far have missed this vital aspect, believing that the 1880s mark the beginning since new theatre companies and a new dramaturgy were formed at that time. On the contrary, closer examination reveals that modernity had seeped into Kannada theatre even earlier, when Yakshagana troupes began to travel outside their traditional geographical domain in the first half of the nineteenth century and, a little later, north Karnataka evolved new forms of Sannata depicting contemporary themes. In fact, recent research indicates that a Shakespearean plot had sneaked into a Yakshagana *prasanga* (script) much before Shakespeare had been translated or adapted. Later, when the new groups emerged, these modernized folk-theatre forms came to have a mutually influential relationship with them; hence one cannot be very certain whether modernism entered Kannada theatre from the bottom or from the top, with the threshold so indistinguishable.

The two main developments in the 1870s and 1880s—the establishment of new troupes and the formulation of a new kind of dramaturgy—need separate attention. The first was mainly due to influences from Maharashtra. Beginning in 1860, Marathi and *Parsi theatre companies from that state travelled across Karnataka several times, and the centres that they visited later became those where the first Kannada troupes were formed. The Kritapura Nataka Mandali was founded in Gadag (Dharwad district) in 1877, and the Halasagi Company near Belgaum around the same time. In the south, the Chamarajendra Karnataka Nataka Sabha commenced in Mysore in 1879 under the patronage of the royal court, and in 1881 another troupe, the Rajadhani Nataka Mandali, came up in the same place. These pioneers played a dual role culturally. They set up a new performance system based on the models of Parsi and *Marathi theatre; simultaneously, they competed against them in order to evolve a Kannada identity of their own. Therefore they chose a middle path—organizationally, between a commercially viable professionalism and an amateurish local support base, and artistically, between the spectacular musicals of the imported theatres and the earthy folk idioms of the native traditions. The clear distinction between the professional and the amateur, in fact, cropped up only after the turn of the century when *Company Nataka became prominent in Karnataka.

Parallel to these searches there developed a search for a new kind of drama, carried out in several directions: translating and/or adapting Shakespeare and Western plays on the one hand, and classical Sanskrit drama on the other; restructuring the folk and traditional narratives; and writing contemporary social drama. Two path-breaking plays in the 1880s illustrate this variegated quest in an idiomatic way. *Iggappa Hegade vivaha prahasana* ('Iggappa Hegade's Farcical Nuptials', 1887) explored a social problem and employed the dialect of the Havyaka Brahman community of Uttar Kannad district. *Sangya-Balya* ('Sangya and Balya'), orally composed and performed in north Karnataka around the same time, also narrated a contemporary story—in all probability, a real-life incident—but applied the song-dance-dialogue pattern of earlier Sannata forms. These trends of reshaping traditional narratives and composing social drama continued in the works of Santakavi (1856–1920) and Kerur Vasudevacharya (1866–1921).

The adaptations of Shakespearean and Sanskrit drama, too, show a similar pattern. Some of the important ones—*Ramavarma Lilavati* ('Ramavarma and Lilavati', from *Romeo and Juliet*), *Pramilarjuniya* ('Pramila and Arjuna', from *A Midsummer Night's Dream*), and *Raghavendra Rao nataka* ('The Drama of Raghavendra Rao', from *Othello*)—are significant not so much for their ability to faithfully capture Shakespeare as for the way the writers adapted his plots and structural elements to their own contexts. Likewise, two pioneering translations of *Kalidasa's *Sakuntala* by Churamuri Sheshagiri Rao (1869) and Basavappa Shastri (1880) represent contrasting possibilities. The former employed traditional metres and dialects of north Karnataka, and the latter the complex metres and diction of old Kannada. These diverse and amorphous explorations began to acquire a crystallized form by the turn of the century. On the one hand, strong professional theatre arose and on the other, a variety of amateur experiments started.

Company Nataka, a collective term encompassing a few hundred companies which sprouted all over Karnataka between 1900 and 1950, was basically a Kannada version of the Parsi commercial theatre. The more prominent troupes travelled the length and breadth of the state. Their distinct theatrical idiom with painted curtains, appealing songs, melodramatic acting, and mesmerizing special effects reigned supreme over the popular imagination of Karnataka till the advent of films. The

Kadasiddeshwara Sangita Nataka Mandali (also known as Konnur Company, founded 1901) and the Mahalakshmi Prasadika Nataka Mandali (also known as Shirahatti Company, founded 1903) mark the rise of Company Nataka in north Karnataka. Together, they introduced several innovations: importing the technique of transferring scenery, using dynamos to generate electricity, and introducing women to enact female roles. In south Karnataka, A.V. Varadachar (1869–1926) established the Ratnavali Theatrical Company in 1904. He refined the mode of singing and brought conflict into characterization, replacing the prevalent stereotyped renderings. Eventually these innovations were picked up by other companies, and through them evolved the magic formula of Company Theatre.

One troupe which exploited this formula to its fullest was the legendary Gubbi Channabasaveswara Nataka Sangha. It began in 1884 as a rural amateur group, but a glorious chapter opened in its history when the actor-director Gubbi Veeranna (1890–1972) took over its reins in 1917. The achievements of the Gubbi Company were twofold. It toured extensively, becoming famous even in parts of Andhra Pradesh and Tamil Nadu. Also, it utilized the entire repertoire available in the genre: spectacle, special effects, folk interludes, and modes of characterization. Its stars, like M.V. Subbaiya Naidu (1895–1962), B. Jayamma (1915–88), and R. Nagarathnamma (1926– , who later led an all-female troupe), drew huge audiences. This remarkable range as well as its great outreach turned it into a household name by the 1940s.

Other companies, after 1915, could never hope to surpass or even match the Gubbi troupe. Instead they tried to focus on, and specialize in, specific aspects of performance. For instance, the Dattatreya Sangita Nataka Mandali preferred to concentrate on prose plays and acting, under the strong influence of its head, Garuda Sadasivarao (1879–1956), and leading female impersonator, Balappa Yenagi (1914–). The Halageri Company devoted itself to comedy, and Vamanrao Master (1883–1935) made stage music his speciality. Down south, the Amba Prasadita Nataka Mandali and Mohammed Peer's troupes stressed acting, while the Hirannaiah Mitra Mandali relied on farce and witty speech.

The combined impact of all these companies, though, sustained the momentum of the movement at least up to Independence. It also gave birth to a large number of playwrights—Bellave Narahari Sastri (1882–1951), who wrote for Gubbi Veeranna, Kandagal Hanumantha Rao, and B. Puttaswamaiah the more important among them. As elsewhere in India, the

Kota Shivarama Karanth's *Abhimanyu* (Yakshagana Kendra, Udupi, 1974)

decline began with the arrival of cinema. The companies started closing down during the 1930s and 1940s, and the slide accelerated in the post-Independence years. Only a few managed to survive the crisis, but could never regain the popular appeal of previous decades.

At the turn of the century, as Company Nataka had continued to gather strength, non-commercial theatre activity, too, had begun to carve a niche for itself. However, amateur theatre in Karnataka never became an organized and unified movement because it was divided into the rural groups that imitated the Company Nataka within their limited capacities, and the urban amateurs who opposed that idiom and attempted an alternative theatre of their own. The Bharata Kalottejaka Sangita Samsthe (founded 1904) of Dharwad and the Amateur Dramatic Association (ADA, founded 1909) of Bangalore were two prominent amateur troupes of the period. They presented 'literary plays' to their limited memberships, and conducted theatre festivals and competitions as well. Their performances were not free from Company influences; for example, the well-known ADA actor Bellary Raghava (1880–1946), as available documents suggest, could not do much beyond improving upon and refining the Company acting style, despite his high intentions.

After 1915, however, the amateur theatre underwent a transformation. New playwrights emerged, and so did many new troupes, notable among them the Literary Dramatic Association of Mysore and Vasudeva Vinodini Natya Sabha of Bagalkot (Bijapur district). Concurrently, new theatre practitioners began to appear, too. T.P. Kailasam (1884–1946) contributed much to amateur drama in Bangalore, the iconic K. Shivarama Karanth (1902–99) made several experiments in Dakshin Kannad and, later, the prolific Sriranga (Adya Rangacharya, 1904–84) involved himself deeply in the amateur movement in north Karnataka while Parwathavani (1911–94) wrote entertaining comedies. Though they differed widely in concepts, they launched a common attack on the Company Nataka genre, specially its artificiality and anachronism. These factors effected a transition from epic to social plays, from painted curtains to suggested scenery, from rhetoric to everyday speech, and from melodrama to broad realism.

It was no fortuitous coincidence that the first major harvest of modern Kannada drama should appear at this precise juncture. If recent theatrical developments were one cause, the other significant impetus came from literature. By 1920 the Navodaya (renaissance) movement in Kannada had produced major authors, chiefly novelists and poets who also wrote plays, more as closet drama than as theatre pieces. The most important were B.M. Sri (Srikantiah, 1884–1946), who tried to bring the tragic mode of the West into Kannada drama; the classicist D.R. Bendre (1896–1981), who invoked Indian poetics; Srinivasa (Masti Venkatesa Iyengar, 1891–1986), who composed epic, historical, and social plays but with a unique touch of realism in characterization; and Kuvempu (K.V. Puttappa, 1904–94), who chiefly reworked epic plots. Another trend of the period was operatic theatre, whose pioneers included Pu. Ti. Na. (P.T. Narasimhachar, 1905–98) and K. Shivarama Karanth.

Apart from these 'literary' authors who wrote mostly between 1920 and 1930, four major writers concentrated mainly on drama and went on to make substantial contributions. They were Samsa (Sami Venkatadri Iyer, 1898–1939) and T.P. Kailasam from the south, and Sriranga and G.B. Joshi (1904–93) from the north. Samsa's plays are mostly about the kings of medieval Mysore and, like other historical dramatists of the time in India, he used history to counter colonial rule. But the great artist that he was, he never upheld a simplistic, nationalistic approach. Kailasam followed a different path, emphasizing the actual present and depicting the rising middle class of the old Mysore region, as well as interrogating their 'progressiveness' with an extraordinary strength for wit and farce. Sriranga, too, was a bitter critic of the hypocrisies of his society, but the style he employed could broadly and more appropriately be termed social realism.

Joshi, though he wrote many of his plays after 1950, began in the 1930s and essentially belongs to the same period. He captured with a rare poetic realism the shock that feudal families in north Karnataka encountered on entering the modern age.

Kannada theatre reached a turning point by the 1950s. On the one hand, Company Nataka had exhausted itself but the amateur movement had not yet achieved the professionalism that could enable it to make an impact outside its limited circles. Moreover, while opposing the Company mode for its excesses of theatricality, the amateur experiment itself remained an impoverished theatre of speech. Therefore, a process of assimilation was urgently needed for the art to survive. Sriranga, the first to sense this problem, not only wrote about it but also tried to find ways out of the situation. In the late 1950s, under the banner of Natya Sangha, he organized a series of theatre workshops, the first of their kind in Karnataka. Through these, an informal training for amateurs was begun and a new interest kindled in theatre as a medium.

At this moment, the arrival of B.V. Karanth (1929–2002) worked as a catalyst for the spread of amateur theatre. From 1967, he began directing plays in Bangalore and also travelled to several parts of Karnataka, working with children and many groups. The festival of plays he directed in Bangalore in 1972 served as a milestone. Through them, he evolved a new idiom that assimilated the best of Company Nataka, folk performance, and the *National School of Drama model of modern theatre. This early 1970s euphoria generated a large number of actors (like G.V. Shivananda and C.R. Simha), technicians (like V. Ramamurthy, 1935–), as well as active groups (Benaka and Rangasampada in Bangalore, Samatento in Mysore, the path-breaking Ninasam in rural Heggodu) who intensified the momentum of the amateur movement.

While the Karanth brand of theatre became increasingly popular, a reaction against it also appeared. It came from the new political awareness of the decade and was directed against indiscriminate use of folk elements, against stressing theatricality at the expense of content, and against theatre eventually turning into purposeless entertainment. Samudaya, a leftist group formed in the mid-1970s, became the advocate of this reaction and organized alternative work. Founder-member Prasanna (1951–) directed several plays over the next few years marking a departure from the Karanth mode towards a committed as well as medium-conscious theatre. Samudaya also conducted state-wide *jathas* (literally, 'processions') performing *street theatre and progressive cultural activities. Although this did not lead to the development of an explicit political theatre in Karnataka, it did effect a definite shift

B.V. Karanth (right) in Chandrasekhar Kambar's *Jokumaraswami*, directed by him (Pratima Nataka Ranga, Bangalore, 1972)

discernible by the 1980s: theatre became much more aware of content, new activists from lower castes and classes participated, and the amateur movement gained both an idea of theatricality as well as a sense of purpose.

Post-Independence Kannada drama shares many of these concerns. During the 1950s the Navya ('new', or modernist) movement developed in Kannada literature and its impact was also felt in drama. Older playwrights like Sriranga and Joshi changed their course from realism to a variety of post-realistic approaches, leading to a series of new works and trends in the 1960s. One such vogue was that of absurdist drama, practised by writers like Chandrashekhar Patil (1939–), N. Ratna, and Chandrakantha Kusnoor. Although short-lived, it certainly anticipated a turning point, which came quickly; three important playwrights appeared in that same decade: P. Lankesh (1935–2000), Girish Karnad (1938–), and Chandrasekhar Kambar (1938–). Together, they consolidated and crystallized all the modernist issues in well-structured plays that were not only picked up by Kannada theatre but also became renowned outside Karnataka.

Lankesh wrote short plays evolving a new dramaturgy comparable to that of the absurdist and angry theatres of contemporary Europe. Karnad began with *Yayati* (1961), where he fused existential concerns into a mythological episode. The crest of the wave is represented by Karnad's *Tughlaq* (1964) and Lankesh's *Sankranti* ('Transformation', 1972), both

Ninasam's production of *Sangya-Balya*, directed by K. V. Subbanna (Heggodu, 1993)

based on history but reflecting contemporary society, both essentially modernist in their themes but using the prevalent modes of Kannada theatre for their expression. During the 1970s another shift took place, towards incorporating folk and traditional elements. Karnad's *Hayavadana* (1971) began this trend and Kambar, who had written modernist short plays previously, joined in with *Rishyashringa* (1970, staged 1973) and *Jokumaraswami* (1972). Later, this fad became immensely popular with many dramatists who tried out various blends of the folk formula, which soon led to mechanical and merely ornamental dramaturgy and, in turn, an inevitable reaction against it quickly followed.

In demarcating and defining the general course of theatre since the 1980s, two tendencies are clear. The first can be termed as a drive towards decentralization. Amateur groups in rural Karnataka began to assert their identities in the 1960s and 1970s, a process further consolidated since 1980; a large number of these troupes, in towns like Mangalore, Udupi, Dharwad, Davangere, and smaller places like Sullia, Ilkal, Manchikeri, and Heggodu, do significant theatre work. Second, Kannada theatre moved toward a new professionalism. In 1980, the Ninasam Theatre Institute under K.V. Subbanna (1932–2005) initiated a one-year theatre course and, later in the decade, two professional companies (Ninasam Tirugata and Rangayana, in Mysore) started operations. Directors involved in these activities include the nationally-recognized B. Jayashree (1950–), C.G. Krishnaswamy, C.R. Jambe, Jayatirtha Joshi, S. Raghunandan, C. Basavalingaiah, Iqbal Ahmed, and B. Suresh. In recent years, two more groups began touring Karnataka with new productions every year: Shivasanchara of Sanehalli and

Kinnara Mela, led by K.G. Krishna Murthy, which focuses on *children's theatre performed on school campuses.

There were shifts in Kannada drama as well during the same period. The established generation of Karnad, Kambar, and Lankesh wrote new plays, often departing from earlier methods, while talented younger dramatists like H.S. Shiva Prakash (1954–) examined the present in the light of the past. A trend of late is the appropriation of any material as theatrical 'text'. Now one rarely hears of a lack of original Kannada plays; instead, directors use all sorts of available texts, drawing mainly from the rich repertoire of Kannada poetry and short stories, from the ninth-century poet Pampa to contemporary authors like Devanur Mahadeva and Vaidehi. The fact that many of the resulting scripts are not literary adaptations but theatrical renderings seems to have made an impact on the notions of drama in Kannada recently, redefining the concept of playwriting. A notable new dramatist is Vivek Shanbhag, who explores the multinational corporate ethos and its transnational diasporic existence.

There is also a marked feeling that the audience is returning to theatre, after a lull when it was perceived that television had snatched spectators away. A new venue in Bangalore has come up, Rangashankara, boasting of a well-equipped intimate stage, that has been attracting a large number of people with its yearly fare of festivals. Within this apparently hopeful scenario, the active young directors include Nataraj Honnavalli, Channakeshava, Jeevanram Sullia, and Pramod Shiggaon.   AKV

K.D. Kurtkoti (ed.), *The Tradition of Kannada Theatre* (Bangalore: IBH Prakashana, 1986); H.K. Ranganatn, *The Karnatak Theatre* (Dharwar: Karnatak University, 1960).

KASHMIRI THEATRE

Drama was an integral part of Kashmiri culture in ancient times and, as historical records like the *Nilamata Purana* and Kalhana's *Rajatarangini* (twelfth century) reveal, had already attained its glory when these texts were written. This idea is further anchored by considering theorists and aestheticians such as Abhinavagupta (tenth century), said to have lived in Kashmir, the northernmost part of India. Royal palaces were the main centres of theatrical activity, where literary connoisseurs were always present to point out merits and flaws. This golden age of drama in Kashmir lasted 1500 years—from the beginning of the Christian era to the fifteenth century—but very little of the dramatic literature has descended to us, and that too only in Sanskrit. Yet we know that theatre was inseparably associated with royal glamour: Lal Ded versified in the fourteenth century about *tsamari chhetri rath simhasan / ahlad netyras tuli-pryenkh* ('feathery canopies, chariots, throne, / pleasurable theatre, and cushioned swings').

There also existed a performatory tradition in the vernacular (old Kashmiri) which, unlike the elite drama, was based on the spontaneous folk imitation of elemental life—birth, calamities, death, rebirth—in connection with celebrations and festivals of sowing, reaping, and threshing. The *Nilamata Purana* advised that the descendants of Kasyapa should mark occasions with song, dance, and music, and that a public performance (*preksha*) was a form of religious obligation. Thus in the earliest form of Kashmiri theatre, the unschooled and naive Lagun ('imitation'), any person could mimic for mere entertainment a king, a sadhu, a soldier, a bridegroom, or other respectable social figures. The function of this primitive burlesque was only to provoke mirth. Although as a natural mimetic activity, Lagun did not require professional training, certain people called *kelak* ('buffoons') attained a special prowess in it and adopted it as their profession. A couplet by the poet Nur-ud-Din (*c.* 1400) goes, *Kyiliky gari gari resh lagan, / yithi pethir lagan manz rangan* ('The ascetics of today, like actors, go from door to door, / And perform as if they are on the stage floor'). Equipped with simple musical instruments like a drum, *dahri* (a rod with iron rings), or *surnay* (*swarnai*, a pipe), such folk performers wandered from house to house, exhibited their skill, and got their aliment from those whom they entertained. Some blithesome public entertainers who masqueraded as people of different vocations, mythical characters, or even animals and birds, were called *rangiryeviny* ('harlequins').

An improved form of Kashmiri folk theatre was the Pethir, a satirical comedy in which several actors exaggeratedly represented individuals, classes, or supernatural beings with the purpose of ridiculing human follies, frailties, and cruelties. Pethirs on social themes, with musical interludes and boisterous harlequins, are still known as *Bandi Pethir—a genre preserved through the efforts of Mohammad Subhan Bhagat (1927–93), himself born into a family of these performers. The impresario of a Pethir repertoire, called the *magun*, could assume more than one role, improvising dialogue and action on stage to make the audience laugh. A Pethir was performed in any open place where the audience could sit or stand in rings and have full view of the players from all sides. It relied mainly on dialogue and changes of costume to appeal to spectators. The task was particularly difficult for a *magun*: as Nur-ud-Din writes, *Pethir byon byon ti akoy magun* ('Characters are various while the *magun* is one'). Some Pethirs on religious and mystical themes have been preserved through folk memory; *Sivilegin* ('Siva's Marriage') and *Akanandun* are perhaps the most popular which can be traced in Kashmiri folk songs. *Sivilegin* is the dramatic representation of Parvati's birth, youth, and marriage to Siva. *Akanandun* is the story of man's complete submission to the will of God: a Brahman is given the boon of a son after much worship, but when the child grows into a handsome boy, the Brahman's surrender to God's will is tried when he is asked to kill his son and cook the flesh for the sadhu who had prayed for him.

Parallel to the Bandi Pethir, there flourished a tradition of devotional theatre that primarily aimed at conveying the message of truth and revealing the pleasure of leading a pious life. A repertoire of Hindu plays was always available to the performers and temple premises were the centres of these activities. However, no early manuscript of such drama is extant; among the preserved ones, *Satich kahvet* ('Touchstone of Truth') is the oldest accessible to readers. The author, Nandalal Kaul Nana (1877–1940), composed it on the life of Raja Harishchandra, in rhymed dialogue with lyrical interludes. It was first performed in 1932 at Raghunath Mandir, Srinagar. Inspired by its success, Tarachand Bismil (1904–48) also wrote a play on Harishchandra published under the title *Satich vath* ('Path of Truth') and staged by Krod Tirath Sabha Dramatic Club, Baramula. His other works include *Rama avatar*, *Akanandun*, and *Premich kahvet* ('Touchstone of Love'). Bismil was a good lyricist and his dialogue, free from archaisms, comes closer to natural discourse. The religious drama of Nilakantha Sharma (1881–1970), such as *Bilvamangala* and *Swapni Vasavadatta* ('Vision of Vasavadatta'), though derived from other sources, was also much admired.

The popularity of gramophones during the 1930s helped create a liking for the Rajpal Company's recorded dramatizations of traditional romances like *Shirin Khusrav* ('Shirin and Khusrav') and *Laila Majnun* ('Laila and

Majnun'). The scripts, by Ghulam Nabi Disoz (1916–41), were never staged but certainly stimulated other authors to write plays on secular themes. In 1938, *Grisy sund gari* ('A Peasant's House') by Mohi-ud-Din Hajani (1917–93) was a definitive departure from tradition, the first drama to depict the socio-economic conditions of the peasantry, through the misery of a family living in the grip of the feudal system. It also featured humour and satire in dialogue free from the deliberate artifice of poetic prose, which was a convention in Kashmiri drama. Abdul Satar Aasi (died 1950) authored the realistic *Vidhva* ('Widow'), staged by the Natak Vibhag; Prem Nath Pardesi (1906–55) the plays *Qudus Gojari* and *Bati har* ('Food Feud'). However, the scanty drama of the fourth and fifth decades, written under the influence of the new political awakening and the predominant social realism in Urdu literature, was essentially readerly in character, as people's theatre was still an ill-defined idea, despite the availability of versatile actors like Jagan Nath Saqui (1898–1973).

With the establishment after India's independence of a body of writers named the Jammu and Kashmir Cultural Front (later Congress), theatre received serious attention. Several plays were composed and staged to strengthen the Front's political viewpoint. However, it did not receive any encouraging response from the common masses, its desired audience. The historical programme of 'Land to the Tiller' had been successfully implemented, centuries-old feudalism was being abolished by the new government and, as such, the revolutionary anti-establishment message of the 'progressives' was an anachronism. In 1950, a new repertory, Kala Kendra, emerged but after presenting two plays on the socialistic pattern, *Tabiri khab* ('Interpretation of the Dream') and *Son gam* ('Our Village'), it returned to the old religious and romantic drama like *Krishnajanam* ('Krishna's Birth', 1952) and *Habba Khatun* (1956). The Sri Pratap College Dramatic Club appealed to a wide audience with its thoughtful productions, which also deviated from the revolutionary theatre. The important playwrights of the day, Dina Nath Nadim (1916–88) and Amin Kamil (1924–), won acclaim for their operas.

The founding of the Jammu and Kashmir Academy of Art, Culture and Languages (JKAACL) in 1958 initiated a new wave of enthusiasm for non-propagandist theatre, and several amateur clubs emerged in the capital, Srinagar, and other towns. Nav Rang Dramatic Club (1964) attracted attention by performances of Makhan Lal Kaul's *Bari geyi yimbirzal* ('Withered Narcissus', 1964) and *Mayi menzi tshay* ('Shadows in Love',

1969), and *Lal bi drayas lolarey* ('Lal in Love's Quest', 1972) by Moti Lal Kemmu (1933–). Rangmanch (1967) was perhaps the most popular theatre of the time, staging the collaborative comedies of Pushkar Bhan (1925–) and Som Nath Sadhu (1935–82), and the metatheatre of Hari Krishan Kaul (1934–). In Anantnag, the Valley's second largest town, the Royal Theatre (1967) gained great popularity through the activities of Firdous Gul, M.R. Noushad, Bashir Dada, and Zahid Mukhtar. Other significant productions in the early 1970s included Bansi Nirdosh's *Bas akh tamah* ('Just One Desire'), Ghulam Rasool Santosh's *Akanandun*,

Bansi Nirdosh's *Bas akh tamah* (Srinagar, 1973)

and *Badshah* ('Emperor') by Avtar Krishan Rahbar (1933–). Even in Delhi, several plays were presented by the Kashmiri Samity, a cultural organization of Kashmiri Pandits; for instance, *Ziy gabar* ('Two Sons', 1966) by Prem Nath Dhar (1914–) was an unforgettable performance.

In 1974, eighteen repertories working in the Valley set up an association called the Kashmir Theatre Federation under the able guidance of Ali Mohammad Lone (1926–87), Pran Kishore, Som Nath Zutshi, Bansi Mattoo, M.L. Kharoo, Moti Lal Kemmu, and Makhanlal Saraf. This led to some memorable presentations during that decade—a glorious period in Kashmiri theatre—of plays by Kemmu, Pushkar Bhan, Som Nath Sadhu, Sajood Sailani (1936–), Farooq Masoodi (*College pethir*, 'College Play'), and Mohan Nirash (*Rati devy posh*, 'Bleeding Flowers'). Among the many young performers who achieved remarkable success in those years were actor-directors Shabir Mujahid (1955–) and Bashir Ahmad Qadri (1953–), and Nazir Josh (1953–), versatile comedian of the National Theatre (Badgam) and author of popular comic plays like *Timi goryi gayi* ('Gone Are the Days'),

Mwal ('Vagabonds'), and *Hazar dastan* ('Thousand Tales'). The contribution
of Pran Kishore and Ashok Jailkhani (as directors), Gayoor Hassan (for make-
up), Abdul Rashid (as set designer), and Abdul Ghani (for special effects)
cannot be ignored even in a brief excursus like the present one.

In the years that followed, more groups joined the Federation and
participated in various theatre festivals. Meanwhile, the drama clubs of
Nawakadal Girls' College, S.P. College, and M.A. Road Girls' College also
produced several plays, specially those of Shamla Mufti (1928–), which
aroused interest in theatre among college students. The government's Song
and Drama Division organized a dance-drama with exaggerated costumes
and effects, *Esyi esy ti esyi asav* ('We Were and Shall Be'), in the open
purlieus of Parbat Hill, which was much admired by audiences. The show
was presented daily for several weeks and people thronged the site to
watch it. In the 1980s, theatre received fresh impetus as the JKAACL
strived to reinvigorate the cultural movement by coordinating the activities
of all rural and urban troupes. Among these units the Kashmir Cultural
Society deserves special mention for staging successful plays by Abid
Bashir Qadri, Amin Shakir, and Bhushan Lal Bhushan, while Roshan
Cultural Organization produced a play by Tariq Umar Batsh. Kashmir
Valley Theatre featured Sheikh Mohammad Hanif (1960–), a talented
actor and rising theatre-activist who performed memorably in Bashir
Dada's *Fankar* ('Artist') and *Zalur* ('Spider'), Shamas-ud-Din Shamim's
Byegur bani ('Cracked Vessels'), and R.K. Braru's *Yahu* ('Yahoo', for
Navratan Natsar, 1982).

Theatre began to fade in the mid-1980s with the beginning of militant
politics in the state, and came to a standstill by the early 1990s. Since
theatrical activities are a cause as well as effect of freedom of expression,
they could not flourish during the bloody years without the Kashmiri
people's free participation. The last major event was a festival sponsored in
Tsaar (Badgam) by the JKAACL in 1989, an attempt to revive theatre that
could not stimulate any fresh movement as most of the professional actors,
producers, and directors had started fleeing the Valley. The famous Tagore
Hall was burnt down and all theatre groups closed under pressure. Only
radio drama, television serials, and *cinema kept the acting tradition alive.

After ten years' complete lull, an initiative was undertaken by the
*National School of Drama (NSD) in 2001 under the able supervision of
M.K. Raina, a Kashmiri who had made it big on the national stage. A series
of workshops that followed resulted in the re-emergence of groups,

especially in rural areas. *Su yi* ('He Will Come', 2005), adapted from
Beckett's *Waiting for Godot* by Arshid Mushtaq with two Bandi Pethir
clowns in the lead, attracted remarkable attention and was widely admired
for obliquely hinting at the 'disappearance' of hundreds of young men. It
inspired some theatre lovers to encourage local talent, especially those who
had found refuge in television, to create a friendly space for theatre in
Kashmir again. The efforts of the talented director Yasir Bashir Bhawani
adequately enthused school and college students.

In 2006 Raina directed two plays through the workshop in
collaboration with the NSD, JKAACL, and the Centre for Heritage and
Culture of Kashmir. Actors like Gul Reyaz, Shahid Lateef, Ovais, Ahmad
Tufail, Showket Usman, Umar Rahman Reshi, Nadeem Afzal, Rifat,
Marjina, Alamjan Irfan Dar, Sameer, and Zahid Ahmad Zargar formed the
new hope for Kashmiri theatre. The same year, Sangeet Natak Akademi and
the JKAACL organized a folk festival in Srinagar, where it was heartening to
note that the old repertories of folk drama like Kashmir Bhagat Theatre
(Akingam), Kashmir Bandi Theatre (Wahthor), National Bandi Theatre
(Wahthor), Folk Ruma Reshi Theatre (Rohmoo), Aziz Folk Theatre (Hiller
Arhama), Sultan Bhagat Theatre (Gundpora), Alamdaar Bhagat Theatre
(Muhripora), Gulmarg Luki Theatre (Palhalan), and Qazi Kashmir Theatre
(Bomie) had resurfaced with fresh vigour.   SS

J.L. Kaul, *Kashmiri Literature* (Mysore: University of Mysore, 1970).

KONKANI THEATRE

Konkani theatre (in the south-western state of Goa and on the coast of
Maharashtra) exhibits a motley picture of indigenous as well as alien generic
repertoires in a multi-lingual/cultural situation. A rich folk tradition of
*Dasavatar, *Lalit, Jagar, and Gavalankalo among Hindus, and *Tiatr, Phel
(Westernized from *khel* or 'play'), and even drama in English by Christians
complicate the scene. The retrieval in 1989 (from Kerala) of *Godde Ramayan*,

a medieval Konkani folk play in Malayalam script, and of manuscripts in Roman script from archives in Portugal, demonstrates how theatre itself became a cultural battlefield.

The intermixture of Marathi and Konkani is well illustrated by the unique contribution of the Mochangadkar Dasavatari Mandali, a bilingual troupe. It is also interesting to study comparatively the rise of modern drama in British Bombay and Portuguese Goa. Portuguese rule was not favourable to the development of drama in Goa, yet the elite theatrical performances in Portuguese, Spanish, and French from the seventeenth to the nineteenth century in Goa paved the path for acculturation in the theatre. On the other hand, whatever was performed in the name of Tiatr in Konkani in the 1890s and later scripted in 'Romi' (Roman) by Goan migrants to Bombay, was imitative of the British colonial theatre.

Translations and adaptations of Western texts brought about the literary renaissance in Indian theatre, but this process started rather late in Konkani. When Shenoi Goembab (1877–1946) adapted *Moganche lagna* ('Love Marriage', 1931) from Molière's *A Doctor in Spite of Himself*, it marked the real beginning of modern Konkani drama. He had earlier adapted Shakespeare in 1914, Molière's *The Miser* as *Povananche taplne* ('Pot of Gold Coins', 1926), and based *Zilaba Rano* on the *Arabian Nights*. The plays of Ramchandra Naik (1893–1960) are also adaptations of European farces, except for *Chavathicha chandra* ('Fourth-day Moon', 1935), an original comic one-act drama that drew heavily on indigenous dialects and hybrid languages used in Goa. Among later full-length comedies, Pundalik Dande's *Tachi karamat* ('His Miracle', 1956), is a significant social satire.

Theatre is a public art, and its development owes much to spectators; but the number of Konkani speakers is limited and their tastes differ from region to region. Nevertheless, contemporary Konkani theatre has tried to keep abreast in experimentation by adapting mainly European plays. For example, Suresh Borkar turned to Albert Camus's *Caligula*; A.N. Mhambre freely adapted Eugene Ionesco's *The Bald Prima Donna*; Dilip Borkar's *Vargasatru* ('Class Enemy') is based on Ibsen's *An Enemy of the People*. His *Bharatebhar* ('High-tide Burden', 1982) depicts current educational problems. N. Shivadas's *Pisat* ('Manic-depressive', 1978) was a bold attempt at portraying psychological problems in women.

The twin processes of Westernization and Sanskritization gave rise to a tug of war in Konkani theatre too, but the latter force always remained weaker. The plays of Shantaram Hedo (1950–), mostly adaptations, demonstrate how oriental and occidental traditions of drama are juxtaposed.

He rendered Portuguese as well as Sanskrit plays into Konkani. His *Almaid Garre, Frier Louis D'Souz*, and *Madhalodut* ('Cloud Messenger', based on *Kalidasa's Meghaduta*) illustrate colonial culture contact in the theatre. These cross-cultural encounters were often mutually beneficial in vitalizing both Hindu and Christian theatrical activities. For example, *Boxttench thapott marinakai* ('Don't Slap without Reason', 1995) by Lambert Mascarenhas contains *cantara*s (chorus songs) just like a Christian Tiatr. It is also the only Indian play that depicts the Goan peasant's life from a nativistic point of view. Thus its structure is alien, but its language typically indigenous.

Tiatr artists singing *cantara*

Adaptations of renowned Indian plays have enriched recent Konkani drama. Prakash Thali (1945–), actor, director, and writer both in Marathi and Konkani, adapted *Sagina Mahato, Ajibpurchi kalpkatha* ('Fantastic Tale of a Strange City'), and other works in his collection titled *Tin kheti shannisurti* ('Three Wise Monkeys', 1987). *Historical drama is slowly developing in this comparatively young theatre, under Ramkrishna Juwarkar, known for such plays as *Bhagirathi* (1970), *Amache rajya* ('Our Rule', 1971), and *Anvalakhi* ('Strange Unknown', 1975).

Mumbai is the centre from where new dramatic trends usually spread all over Goa. Marathi plays (for instance by the Goa Hindu Association of Mumbai) are regularly staged in Goa, while the Saraswati Natya Mandal was founded by Konkani speakers in Mumbai. This interface still forms the link between Konkani theatre and theatre outside, revealing the continuing derivativeness of the former. The most original synthesis of popular and modern Goan theatrical traditions is exhibited in the dramatic works of the distinguished contemporary Konkani author, Pundalik Narayan Naik (1952–), focusing on social problems especially of the lower classes.   ABP

m

MAITHILI THEATRE

Maithili, spoken in the Mithila region of north Bihar state in eastern India, boasts of one of the oldest theatrical traditions in India, dating to the growth of *Kirtaniya in the fourteenth century. Hence it forms an important link between classical Sanskrit and regional forms. In the medieval period, Maithili theatre spread to Assam and Nepal, producing a huge corpus of Maithili drama. Siddhi Narasinghadeva (1620–57) and Bhupatindra Malla (1696–1722) were among the known playwrights in Nepal. At the end of the nineteenth century *Parsi theatre and *Ramlila reached Mithila, leading to the premature burial of Kirtaniya.

This created a vacuum in Maithili theatrical activity filled by Jivan Jha (1848–1912), who evolved a new genre by synthesizing Kirtaniya, Parsi, Ramlila, *Sanskrit theatre, and the theatrical renaissance in Bengal, but employing colloquial Maithili as the language. He wrote the first modern Maithili plays, *Sundarsanyoga* (1904) and *Narmada-sagar* (1906), based on social problems and premiered in Varanasi. However, Munsi Raghunandan Das (1860–1945) established modern Maithili theatre in Mithila. His *Maithili natak* ('Maithili Play', 1910) and *Dutangad-vyayoga* ('Dutangad's *Vyayoga*', 1932) were staged by commercial theatres like Umakant's Mithila Natak Company and other troupes. The mid-twentieth century was dominated by Ishanath Jha (1907–65), whose

Chini-ke-laddu ('Ball of Sugar', 1939) and *Ugna* (1957) charmed audiences for a long time.

No permanent playhouses existed in those days. Stages were made of bamboo and wooden platforms with curtains, castor-oil lamps for lighting, and a big bright brass disc as reflector. Regal dresses but simple make-up and the use of Maithili lyrics as fillers were the unusual features of the early modern phase. Having no access to microphones, actors delivered their dialogue in loud voices and took recourse to over-gesticulation and special sound effects. Harijee and Ramjatan Mishra were the most popular heroes.

After Independence, Maithili theatre spread to cities like Calcutta, Patna, and Delhi where migrant Maithili populations had congregated. In Calcutta, the Mithila Kala Kendra and Mithiyatrik under the stewardship of Prabodhnarayana Singh, Nachiketa, Gunanath Jha, and directors like Srikant, Dayanath, and Trilochan Jha achieved new heights. Since the 1950s Patna emerged as the mecca where groups like the Chetna Samiti (1953), Aripan (1982), and Bhangima (1987) even organized international Maithili drama festivals. In 1953, for the first time, Subhadra Jha, wife of dramatist Hari Mohan Jha, broke social taboos against women performing and acted on stage. This encouraged Kamla Choudhary, Lalita Jha, Premlata, and other progressive ladies to participate in theatre. Both in Calcutta and Patna, experiments were made in stagecraft by Sudhansu Sekhar Choudhary, Mahendra Malangia, and Arvind Akku.

Maithili theatre still has rural and urban divisions. Rural spectators prefer archetypical socio-historical or religious drama as well as fast-moving and grand spectacles. Performers can enter from within the audience according to need and musicians sit on the right flank of the stage. Urban theatre depends upon auditoriums, its literate viewers preferring psychological plays. Some groups like Jamghat, Navtarang, Tarjani, and Sankalplok created a new genre by fusing the modern and indigenous forms. Govind Jha, Somdev, and Ramdeo Jha reinforced this synthesis in their scripts. The Song and Drama Division of Darbhanga, Bihar, invented a style called 'Vidyapati ballad' after the great poet Vidyapati (1360–1440). Efforts to revive Kirtaniya have also been made.   RJ

Radhakrsna Choudhary, *A Survey of Maithili Literature* (Deoghar: Shanti Devi, 1976); Jayakanta Mishra, *A History of Maithili Literature* (Allahabad: Tirabhakti, 1949–50); Jayakanta Mishra, *History of Maithili Literature* (New Delhi: Sahitya Akademi, 1976).

MALAYALAM THEATRE

The southern state of Kerala can claim an ancient theatrical heritage, even though the dramatic literature in Malayalam (the language spoken there) is of recent origin. Its oldest extant genre, *Kutiyattam, fully established by the ninth century, may well represent the longest-surviving continuous theatrical tradition in the world. It is a system of staging classical Sanskrit plays, but not entirely *Sanskrit theatre in the strict sense because the enactment contains elaborate oral elucidation in Malayalam. Still, it was Kerala's first performing art based on written texts, and evidently served as a basic model of creative expression for all later forms in Malayalam. Yet it also differs significantly from them in being conventionally presented on raised stages within auditoriums known as *kuttampalam*, which used to be built within the premises of the major temples in central Kerala.

However, other indigenous but undatable traditions may be even older than Kutiyattam. Most are ritualistic in nature, centred on solo performances characterized by rhythmic movements and colourful costumes, often presenting gods or humans elevated to deified status. The best-developed and typical examples are *Teyyam of north Kerala and *Patayani of the south. In most of them, individuals assume the roles

A Teyyam performer

of gods as conceived and worshipped by the local communities. In others, the characters represented are valiant men who laid down their lives for noble causes in the course of heroic deeds or persons who became victims of social evils, their souls supposed to have risen to divinity after their demise. Similar but less refined folk enactment was generally known as *kolam* *Tullal, each representing a god or supernatural being revered by a particular community. The concept of god, the costume, *kolam* (mask), and performatory details differ from one Tullal to another.

Teyyam and Patayani are enacted as devotional rituals frequently connected with *kavus*, or temples to the goddess Kali. The performers belong to families that hold the hereditary duty or right to do these roles (also known as *kolams*). Each *kolam* has a specific costume of colourful dress material, ornaments made of objects obtained from nature, and an impressive crown (*muti*), often considerably high or broad. Pastes of different colours applied on the face function as *masks. The representation usually consists of an exhibition of the character's traits through facial expressions supported by make-up and gestures. In some cases, episodes of a narrative are also indicated through stylized body motion. The *kolams* perform spatial movements and rhythmic footwork in tune with the beating of drums and generally move along the streets around the place of worship, accompanied by the village folk who express their devotion by shouting aloud. Many approach the *kolams* as devotees and the *kolams* respond to their appeals for blessings. Thus the Teyyam artist's individual performance becomes part of a drama in which most of the villagers turn into active participants.

Other genres depict episodes and situations involving a number of characters, enacting mythological stories and ritualistic representations of natural phenomena or fertility cults, but dealing with definite themes developed in the course of the performance. Among those with a full-scale dramatic structure, *Mutiyettu is the most developed and powerful, presenting the conflict between Kali and the demon Darika. Thus theatricalization was and is widely accepted as a normal means of expressing spiritual concepts and devotion, evidenced not only by these forms but also lesser-known, localized ones like *Sanghakali, *Kotamuri, *Kurattiyattam, and *Tolpavakuttu (shadow puppetry). More secular folk theatre includes *Porattu Natakam and *Kakkarissa Kali. Christians, too, evolved a composite art called *Chavittunatakam by combining elements of the native and European traditions. They chose narratives from the history of Christian Europe and the actors performed rhythmic footwork in indigenous style.

The more sophisticated *Krishnattam and *Kathakali took their final shapes in the seventeenth and eighteenth centuries respectively, adopting the *Natyasastra concept of classical acting. Yet, like Kutiyattam, they seem indebted to Mutiyettu, Teyyam, and earlier traditions at least with regard to costumes and make-up. The esoteric Krishnattam remains confined to the Guruvayur temple in Malappuram district, while Kathakali became very popular in the eighteenth and nineteenth centuries, and a national cultural icon in the twentieth. It was also the first developed idiom of theatrical performance based on literary texts written in Malayalam. Even though Kathakali incorporated dance movements, these formed only an adjunct to the acting.

Proscenium theatre associated with Malayalam dramatic literature came into existence only in the second half of the nineteenth century. The first such play, *Kalidasa's *Abhijnana-Sakuntala* translated in 1882 by Kerala Varma, was staged by a troupe named Manomohanam Nataka Company, the first of its kind in Kerala. It appears to have been established along the lines of the commercial troupes from Tamil Nadu that used to tour Kerala regularly in those days. Naturally, the style of presentation and acting imitated that popularized by the Tamil companies. This production of *Sakuntala* under Thiruvattar Narayana Pillai was a stray event that did not result in the birth of a theatre. But the Tamil model influenced Kerala artists to such an extent that they organized troupes to perform similar plays in Malayalam, signifying the commencement of Malayalam theatre as we know it today.

The mode in which the plays inspired by the *Tamil theatre were written and staged is known as *Sangitanataka ('musical theatre'). It got this name from the fact that classical music formed an essential part of the productions. Even though the songs interrupted the narrative, they received prime importance and major actors were expected to be able singers. This quickly became the main attraction. The first and most successful plays in this style were T.C. Achyuta Menon's *Sangita Naishadham* ('Musical on Naishadha', 1892) and K.C. Kesava Pillai's *Sadarama* (1903). Their extraordinary appeal prompted others to compose and perform similar works. The influence of this model on the masses grew so strong that even generally realistic drama began to be produced with the addition of songs.

A literary development brought about a far-reaching change: the advent of prose farce. Amateur groups staging many such plays marked the birth of amateur theatre and the beginning of Western influence on proscenium theatre, which soon became dominant. A new kind of representation of life, broadly naturalistic even though exaggerated, crept in along with farce. C.V. Raman Pillai (1858–1922), author of *Kuruppillakkalari* ('Kalari without a Master', 1909) and *Pandatte Pachchan* (1918), introduced it, followed by E.V. Krishna Pillai (1894–1938) in *Koallapramanam* ('Spurious Document', 1931) and *BA Mayavi* ('Deceptive Graduate', 1934), and N.P. Chellappan Nair (1903–72) in *Pranaya-jambavan* ('Passionate Old Bear', 1938) and *Atom Bomb* (1946). They aimed at humorous or sarcastic criticism of social reality.

There were also a few attempts to produce plays based on Western concepts of comedy. Their staging became frequent and popular all over south Kerala and later in other areas, mainly on special occasions such as anniversaries of schools, colleges, libraries, associations, and local festivals. The performances took place on improvised stages with such scenery as could be easily arranged. The acting consisted of natural rendering of dialogue and emotion, though directorial planning, meaningful blocking, and creative action were absent. This branch of drama was enriched by M.G. Kesava Pillai, T.N. Gopinathan Nair, N.K. Achary, and the specialist in one-act plays, Omchery (N. Narayan Pillai, 1924–).

The amateur movement grew steadily. Very soon, serious romantic drama on historical personalities and events began to appear, notably on Velutampi Dalava and Raja Kesava Dasan, two heroes of the recent history of Travancore state. This was followed by dramatizations of historical novels. The second phase of amateur theatre featured gradual evolution brought about by the writing of various types of plays including dramatic literature adapted from the West, mostly romantic in nature. Some dealt with narratives drawn from realistic and historical sources. Others ranged from problems of human behaviour to experiences of contemporary life. But the variety was not reflected in the form or style of production, partly because the best works were really literary texts meant for reading, while stage-oriented scripts lacked organic unity, emphasizing scenes and techniques that appealed easily to the masses. The acting combined naturalism with overdramatic elements, tending to become melodramatic in the serious plays (melodrama dominated popular theatre). The few plays of literary merit that appeared on the amateur stage included the reputed works of the Kainikkara brothers (Padmanabha Pillai, 1898–1976, and Kumara Pillai, 1900–88), while Thikkurussi Sukumaran Nair (1916–96), later a film star, introduced the romantic trend.

Two important developments took place in the 1940s: realistic writing modelled after Ibsen, and drama protesting against social evils to bring about changes in social customs and structure (as by V.T. Bhattathirippadu). N. Krishna Pillai (1916–88) composed the first plays inspired by Ibsenism, followed by C.J. Thomas (1918–60) and C.N. Srikanthan Nair (1928–76), all hailed as excellent drama. Again, they proved successful only on the amateur stage, failing to attract ordinary viewers whose tastes had been moulded by the commercial theatre. Scripts that dealt with topical problems in such a way as to produce a strong emotional effect on the spectators, like those by the progressive S.L. Puram Sadanandan (1927–), were enthusiastically received. Drama that highlighted the problems of Nambudiri women or depicted landlords' exploitation of tenants and petty-wage earners was the first of this kind. Many of the latter type emerged as part of the revolutionary social movement in north Kerala. Although artistically imperfect, they created a new mode of amateur theatre.

Among those who wrote for the commercial theatre, Ponkunnam Varkey (1908–2004), who criticized the Church, the reformist P.J. Antony (1923–79), Thikkodiyan, C.L. Jose, P.R. Chandran, Chandran Pillai, and Kalandi Gopi at different times and in different ways aimed at recreating real life. Slowly, plays that combined semi-realistic depiction of society, melodramatic scenes, and entertaining elements like music, dance, and humour, began to appear on the professional stage. Thoppil Bhasi (1925–92) scripted *Ningalenne Communist akki* ('You Made Me a Communist', 1952) for the leftist Kerala Peoples Arts Club, and set the trend. Many companies copied its socialistic model, which became the popular form of theatre in Kerala. At the same time, dramatists like the provocative N.N. Pillai (1918–95), P.J. Antony, and the thematically-varied K.T. Mohamed (1929–2008), who started their own troupes and directed plays, attracted audiences by incorporating new Western ideas and techniques, and other innovations in their productions.

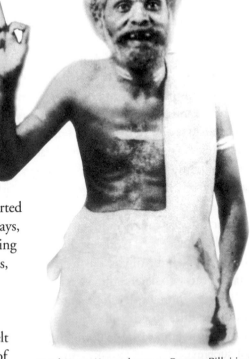

In spite of this, a number of playwrights and artists strongly felt the necessity of a newer concept of drama and theatre practice. C.J. Thomas and Srikanthan Nair

Kambissery Karunakaran as Paramu Pillai in Thoppil Bhasi's *Ningalenne Communist akki* (Kerala Peoples Arts Club, 1952)

made the first attempts in this direction. The former, in *Crime No. 27 of 1128* (1954), presented the central narrative in the form of an artistic enactment, the continuity of which is broken by discussions of the underlying facts by two persons who witness it. Thus the play repudiated the general practice of creating an illusion on stage. Srikanthan Nair wrote a trilogy in poetic idiom giving novel interpretations to different situations in the *Ramayana* story, which demanded an inventive style of production.

The Kalari (workshoop) movement followed, to evolve drama conceived as theatre, and to develop the skills of performers. Many authors, directors, and actors deeply interested in the integrated development of literature, theatre, and other arts actively participated in it, M. Govindan, M.V. Devan, K. Ayyappa Paniker, Srikanthan Nair, and G. Sankara Pillai prominent among them. A series of camps was organized in different parts of Kerala, pursuing the movement's objectives. New styles of acting and visual representation, as well as a system of training actors, potential directors, other artists, and technicians, were proposed. The experience led to the conviction that a play is not the naturalistic projection of a text, but an artwork composed in theatre language, consisting of gestures, movements, images, and varied employment of the voice, based on a total visualization by the director and realized through creative acting. Productions, of old and new plays, were at first ridiculed by those who believed in the sanctity of the text and in realistic presentation. Yet certain aspects of the new theory, at least those of stylization, soon reached the amateur stage.

The concept of *Tanatu Natakavedi or indigenous theatre sprang up in the course of the Kalari movement, mirroring similar ideas all over India. It aimed at developing new forms based on indigenous traditions. In the beginning the theory was very vague and its details left to be worked out in actual practice. But in time, various approaches were adopted and different models evolved. One was to shape distinctly modernist drama, but relying on socio-cultural images, theatrical devices, and modes of expression associated with the tradition. Another was to simply use an existing form like Kathakali to tell contemporary stories. Sankara Pillai (1930–89) and some others involved in the Kalari movement, and some trained at the Thrissur School of Drama, pursued the first path effectively and produced a number of memorable plays. The production of Pillai's *Karutta daivatte tedi* ('In Search of the Black God', 1980) was the best example. But repetitions of such experiments were not always successful.

A third approach was to discover the inherent aesthetic qualities and creative potential of traditional elements and adapt them to the requirements

G. Sankara Pillai's *Bharata vakyam*, directed by Vayala Vasudevan Pillai (School of Drama, Thrissur)

of contemporary theatre. Kavalam Narayana Panikkar (1928–), dramatist and director, who fruitfully developed this model in his own plays like *Daivattar* ('God-man', 1973), *Avanavan katampa* ('Self as the Obstacle', 1975), and *Pashu gayatri* ('Hymn to Cattle', 1986), as well as in his poetic, choreographed interpretations of the Sanskrit dramas of Bhasa, was acclaimed in Kerala and elsewhere for inspiring Indian theatre by his methods. Other directors who followed his example may not have met with similar success, yet the presentation of Sanskrit plays in Malayalam has been a praiseworthy phenomenon over the last 35 years. Besides Bhasa, Kalidasa, Kulasekhara, and Saktibhadra were some of the classical dramatists thus rediscovered.

Meanwhile, acting styles in the second half of the twentieth century ranged from the pioneering realism of C.I. Parameswaran Pillai (1898–1979) on the amateur stage and V.T. Aravindaksha Menon (1921–94) in professional theatre, to the larger-than-life villains and movie heroes of Kottarakkara Sridharan Nair (1922–86) and the chameleonic naturalism of Bharat Gopi (1937–2008). The School of Drama (Thrissur) contributed invaluably to the understanding and studying of theatre in Kerala. World theatre became part of this experience, which included the translating of major Western and Indian authors. Thus Malayalam theatre revealed an irreconcilable diversity as well as a meaningful search for identity.   KSNP

The seeds of the trends sown in the 1970s that germinated and budded in the 1980s are in full blossom now. Drab, bare realism was first replaced by a suggestive dramatic exposition. Vayala Vasudevan Pillai (*Tulasi vanam*, 'Tulsi Grove', 1977; *Agni*, 'Fire', 1982; *Kuchela gatha*, 'Kuchela's Song', 1988), T.M. Abraham (*Perunthachan*, 'Master Builder', 1979), R. Narendra Prasad (*Souparnika*, 1981; *Velliyazhcha*, 'Friday', 1988), and P. Balachandran (*Pavam Usman*, 'Poor Usman', 1987) belong to this category. There was an added strong critical analysis of social evils in the plays of P.M. Thaj (*Perumpara*, 'Big Drum'; *Ravunni*, both published 1984). K.J. Baby's controversial *Nadugadika* (1981) caused much political sensation and raised new questions about the concept of *street theatre. The new playwrights today draw much on Brechtian theory. K. Satchidanandan's *Sakthan Thampuran* (1983) and *Gandhi* (1995) are typical, *Kelu* (1998) by N. Sasidharan and E.P. Rajagopalan marks this style's zenith, and N. Prabhakaran's *Pulijanmam* ('Tiger's Life', 1987) is a representative work inspired by deep-rooted tradition and modern existential crisis.

*Children's theatre is catching up with national trends. Drama written especially for this audience had been successfully produced by Sankara Pillai and S. Ramanujam in the 1970s. Now, Rangaprabhath (Thiruvananthapuram), Rangachethana (Thrissur), Suhrud Natak Vedi (Vidhura), and Lokadharmi (Ernakulam) are some of the troupes giving training in the field and presenting plays for children.   VVP

G. Sankara Pillai (ed.), *The Theatre of the Earth Is Never Dead* (Trichur: Calicut University School of Drama, 1986); M.D. Raghavan, *Folk Plays and Dances of Kerala* (Trichur: Rama Varma Archaeological Society, 1947); Mallika Sarabhai (ed.), *Performing Arts of Kerala* (Ahmedabad: Mapin, 1994); G. Venu, *Puppetry and Lesser Known Dance Traditions of Kerala* (Irinjalakuda, Trichur: Natana Kairali, 1990).

MANIPURI THEATRE

The state of Manipur in extreme eastern India became a constituent part of the Indian Union in 1949 after British colonial rule from 1891 to 1947. A long stint of independence under the Ningthouja dynasty since the early Christian era helped develop its political and cultural features. The central trough-like valley supports two-thirds of the population, whose ethnic majority of Meiteis converted to Hinduism in the eighteenth century. The hills, with thirty-odd tribes of Naga and Kuki denominations, were progressively Christianized since the late nineteenth century. However, indigenous faiths and beliefs survived under the surface, having contributed to Manipuri artistic expression. The Meitei, who formed the nation in the fifteenth century, had encouraged the growth of theatre, while the hill tribes provided rich textures of music and dance.

The origins of Manipuri performance are traced to native primitive fertility-cults and ancestor-worship festivals, the *ritual forms perhaps established in the twelfth century. The celebratory rite of *Lai Haraoba received its formal shape with the monarch's participation, thereby assuming a politico-cultural significance later in the process of nation-making. Wari Liba, or the art of solo storytelling before the king or community, became institutionalized in the seventeenth century. Folk dances and music, collective enhancement of relations with ancestral spirits, and ritual control over clan principalities through cyclic festivals, with associated secular lessons for education and initiation of the young, developed into a national culture in the eighteenth century symbolizing the cosmos under the monarch as visible active principle.

Native followers of traditional religion resisted the massive Hindu conversion of the eighteenth century, leading to a division of beliefs. However, Manipur's devastation by the Burmese in the later half of the eighteenth century and subsequent liberation by the Vaishnava ruler Bhagyachandra (1763–98) gave him an opportunity to experiment with change. He effected a compromise between the dissenting faiths, manifested theatrically in the harmonious assimilation of both cultures in Manipuri *Ras Lila. The slow, soft, lyrical dance patterns healed the annihilating struggle within the self, and in turn became the precursor to a feverish explosion of performative genres conveying the new-found love, compassion, and synthesis. The many innovative minor forms, operas, and ritual performances in the Krishna cycle include the unique *children's theatre of *Sansenba and the twentieth-century *Gaura Lila, which produced such major practitioners as T. Kunjakishore (1891–1982).

Aristocratic ladies participated freely with commoners to celebrate Krishna's egalitarian and liberating actions. The converted took to representing his deeds with a sensuous delight in the fact that divinities could be conceived as mischievous children. Environmental performances simulating the Vrindavan forests, Govardhana hills, and mighty Jamuna river surcharged the polity with a spiritual abandon. As early as 1851, in the play *Kaliya daman* ('Vanquishing Kaliya'), Krishna's tryst with the serpent was enacted on a river, with Maharaja Chandrakirti's young son Kam Singh performing as Krishna.

The hierarchic hegemony of the noblemen also bred subtle subversions within the value systems of the feudal society, as slaves in the retinue gave vent to criticism with fun and humour. After release from periodic service to the monarch, these jesters roamed the countryside and the Phagi (clown play) arose in the mid-nineteenth century, developing into the itinerant *Shumang Lila of the early twentieth century. One specific variation, the folkloric *Moirang Parva, held sway for nearly the whole century.

After Manipur's defeat in the Anglo-Manipuri war of 1891, colonial influence undermined the old theatre. A new social order was introduced, based on British perceptions, with support from the existing aristocracy. English entered, along with modern literature and journals, and the semi-agrarian society was transformed with the incorporation of laissez-faire capital. Proscenium-arch theatre became the new performance aesthetic, imitating the latest happenings in cosmopolitan Calcutta. While Calcuttans looked toward Victorian London for artistic leadership, Imphal looked to the nearest imperial metropolis. The new leisured class took to models of historical and *mythological drama imported through the Bengali language, and the Friends Dramatic Union established in 1905 found Bengalis and Meiteis equally sharing responsibility for popularization of the new theatre.

The open *mandap* (pavilion)-style religious theatre of the nineteenth and early twentieth centuries, based on the Hindu epics, gradually changed into a closeted, fourth-wall representation of events, with wooden boxes in the front rows to welcome the colonial middle class. The royal presence in a collective theatre as life-giver, protector, and protagonist of rituals now shifted into the role of non-participating patron or individual witness. Proscenium stages on makeshift outhouses in residential localities increased in number, and the new materialism came into effect with ticketed shows introduced at the Manipur Dramatic Union in 1931. Sorokhaibam Lalit (1892–1955), the father figure of Manipuri proscenium theatre, ran the Manipur Dramatic Union as a strict disciplinarian. Two other pioneering troupes, Aryan Theatre (1935) and Rupmahal Theatre (1943), followed suit.

Elangbam Joychandra (1927–) began spreading the proscenium theatre movement in rural Manipur and Meitei-inhabited areas of neighbouring Assam with his professional National Touring Dramatic Party in 1949. Violence upon simple folk, their oppression and suffering constituted the subjects of his plays. Manipuri peasants know him well; 'Joy Drama' became the popular name for his group, the Manipur Artistes Touring Drama Party. Among rural activists, we must mention Elangbam Birkumar (1938–), blind from the age of thirty-one, who directs and acts for the Langmeidong Dramatic Union, founded in Langmeidong village, Thoubal district, in 1955.

Manipur's political integration with India in 1949 brought in the Nehruvian ethos, and melodramas on legendary folk love stories and poor-boy-rich-girl encounters attracted the national gaze after 1954, when Lalit's direction of *Haorang Leishang Saphabi* took Manipuri theatre into Jawaharlal Nehru's Indian mainstream of 'unity in diversity'. Maibam Ramcharan (1928–), prolific and popular dramatist of seventy-six plays and over twenty Shumang Lila scripts, capitalized on sentiment, romance, suffering, and family crisis. But the rapid urbanization, new economic norms, and decline in moral and community values ushered in modernist, critical social drama from the iconoclastic, prodigious G.C. Tongbra (1913–96) and the humanistic Arambam Somorendra (1935–2000). By the late 1960s, discontent against Indian rule and commercial exploitation by parasitic traders and outside agents led to the rise of youth power, search for identity, and resurgence of the indigenous spirit in artists like M. Biramangol (1908–79), as in his anti-Hindu *Sanamahi kolu yeikhaiba* ('Breaking Sanamahi's Iron Idol', 1965). In the wake of a separatist ideology, experimental theatre grew in the 1970s under directors like the

lyrical minimalist H. Kanhailal (1941–) in his self-composed masterpiece *Pebet* (1975).

Some creative individuals like Ratan Thiyam (1948–) initially transcended local and regional frontiers to seek greener pastures in New Delhi and attained meteoric success with colourful productions (*Chakravyuha*, 1984), while conventional commercial theatre posing as reformist continued to pander to non-cerebral tastes. At Aryan Theatre, Lokendra Arambam (1939–) developed 'theatre for resistance' to counter both modes, but the establishment appropriated him by featuring his *Macbeth—Stage of Blood* (1997), an environmental production on a lake, in the celebration of fifty years of Indian independence in London! The protest dramatist Khundrakpam Brajachand (1952–97) passed stinging comments on the decaying values of Manipuri society in plays combining humour with symbolism and existential anguish. Despite economic deprivation and socio-political marginalization, struggle and turmoil vitalized Manipuri theatre. Its exceptionally talented actors like Kanhailal's leading lady H. Sabitri (1946–) and Thiyam's hero R. Bhogen (1958–), strong in traditional training, won international acclaim in recent decades.

However, the prolonged armed conflict between India's security forces deployed for the protection of the nation-state and locals fighting for the 'restoration of Manipur's independence from Indian rule' has caused an

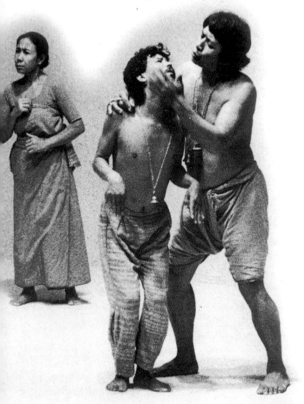

Pebet, written and directed by H. Kanhailal, with Heisnam Sabitri (on p. 79) as the mother (Kalakshetra, Imphal, 1975)

unprecedented cycle of violence lately. Civil society is up in extensive agitations to remove the Armed Forces Special Powers Act 1958, a draconian measure empowering the military, even to end an individual's life. Fear, resentment, distrust, withdrawal, and apathy fill the mood of innocent citizens who have no access to justice. Failure of governance by insidious public authorities and unresponsiveness to human suffering haunt their wounded psyche. In these conditions, theatre becomes fraught.

Extensive central patronage for cultural productions supporting the ideologies of assimilation and directed growth encouraged a race for more recognition and grants. Lack of introspection into the changed structure of social, economic, and political practices resulted in the development of performers, designers, and purveyors who satisfied the voyeuristic aesthetic hunger of the upper and middle classes in Indian metropolises rather than the disturbed masses at home. The artists who had been nationally and internationally celebrated in the last two or three decades of the twentieth century became magnificent objects of mainstream wonder, and their works, in the words of a visiting scholar Erin Mee, 'festival theatres of Manipur' circulating outside the native state.

Younger talent who succeeded Kanhailal and Thiyam immediately faced the trauma of doubt, anguish, and anxieties in their environment of conflict, but did not venture creatively into the real world of violence that marked daily life. The demands from the expectant centre for traditional products of another reality, and the compulsions of the present whose dynamics are beyond their imaginative insights, led them into composing in seclusion patterns of aesthetic imagery, in themselves beautiful, but not conveying authentic experience. Therefore, according to critics, the present theatre generation lacks the thrust and excitement of the erstwhile leaders. Nevertheless, in this period of crisis and ennui, we find some artists of inner energy and creativity like Lourembam Kishworjit (Paradise Theatre), Nongthombam Premchand (Aryan Theatre), H. Tomba (Kalakshetra), S. Jayanta from the *National School of Drama, and Thanilleima as a role model for women entering theatre.   LA

Birendranath Datta (ed.), *Traditional Performing Arts of North-east India* (Guwahati: Assam Academy, 1990); Ch. Manihar Singh, *History of Manipuri Literature* (New Delhi: Sahitya Akademi, 1996); *Theatre in Manipur Today* (Seagull Theatre Quarterly, Special Issue, June/September 1997).

MARATHI THEATRE

Although the western state of Maharashtra has a rich heritage of traditional Marathi-language forms like *Tamasha, *Lalit, *Bharud, Gondhal, Povada, and *Kalsutri Bahulya, its theatre history is generally conceded to have begun in 1843. In that year, Vishnudas Amrit Bhave (1819/24–1901), a talented puppeteer, poet, and storyteller in the service of Chintamanrao Patwardhan, Raja of Sangli in southern Maharashtra, staged a play called *Sita swayamvar* ('Sita's Choice of Groom') at the court. A year earlier, a *Yakshagana troupe from the Kannada-speaking region south of Sangli had performed there. The Raja had been impressed by the presentation of a mythological story, though he found the form crude. He therefore called upon Bhave to create a more refined version for the entertainment of the court.

Bhave rose to the challenge as a complete theatre man, adept at writing songs, composing music, making up his actors, and designing their costumes. The production proved an instant success, which gave him the confidence to do more plays. Pleased with his efforts, the Raja raised his salary by Rs 25 and promised to gift him enough land and money to keep his work and his troupe going. Its members, drawn from the lowest Brahman sub-caste in the court's employ, generally illiterate and relegated to the kitchens as cooks and water servers, were the only ones available to Bhave, since the higher-placed Brahmans looked down upon acting as disreputable.

His plays, which retold stories from the *Ramayana*, were called Ramavatari Khel ('Plays on Rama's Avatar'), a name analogous to Dasavatari Khel or *Dasavatar ('Ten Avatars'), the form depicting the lives of Vishnu's avatars and performed then as now in coastal Maharashtra and Goa. Bhave presented them against a red backdrop with a few wooden properties. The *sutradhara* (manager-director) assisted by a chorus of singers and musicians, sat on one side of the stage and sang two kinds of songs, those introducing each character as they entered and those describing the action that was to follow. As in all Marathi folk performances, Bhave's plays began with the god Ganapati and goddess Saraswati entering the stage to bless the show and the *vidushaka* (clown) engaging in repartee with the *sutradhara*. While the songs were formally composed and rehearsed, the speeches were sparse and left to the actors' improvisation, leading them to lean somewhat heavily on the *sutradhara's* prompting.

After the Raja's premature death in 1851, Bhave lost the patronage of the court. The heir gave him leave to travel with his productions to earn a living for himself and his troupe. At first Bhave toured nearby areas. In 1853 he set out for Pune and Bombay where his plays won much acclaim. His shows at the Grant Road Theatre in Bombay were the first ticketed performances in Marathi. Bhave thus became the father of the secular, professional, proscenium theatre in Maharashtra. The popularity of his plays spawned other touring troupes, which took their productions further afield to all Marathi-speaking areas. Music was the dominant feature. The other highlight was battle scenes. An integral part of all mythological stories, they provided ample scope for war cries, fireworks, and action, later condemned by the young university-educated audience as uncouth and crude.

The founding of the University of Bombay in 1857 and the spread of English education were responsible for this change in people's tastes. The new generation of writers was influenced by two distinct and separate dramatic traditions: the Shakespearean and the classical Sanskrit. The former model led to the composition of what became known as 'bookish' plays, so called because they were fully developed scripts, to be rehearsed and performed as written. Their authors, full of a new pride in their own heritage, turned from mythology to recent Indian history for their narrative material. They wished to arouse their audience's national consciousness by recapitulating their own heroes' brave deeds. These plays were in prose, with no place for songs.

The Sanskrit model, on the other hand, gave birth to *Sangitnatak, a genre of musical that Maharashtra proudly claims as its own. 'Annasaheb' B.P. Kirloskar (1843–85), a schoolteacher from Belgaum (in Karnataka), began by writing Bhave-style plays, but then adapted *Kalidasa's *Sakuntala* to invent Sangitnatak. He presented it first in his home town in an apparently incomplete form in 1875, and formally five years later, in Pune's Anandodbhava Theatre under the banner of his own company, the Kirloskar Natak Mandali. This troupe became the springboard for some of Maharashtra's finest acting-singing talents like Bhaurao Kolhatkar (1863–1901) and the charismatic female impersonator Bal Gandharva (1885/6–1967), and dramatists like Govind B. Deval (1855–1916) and Shripad K. Kolhatkar (1871–1934) who introduced social themes, before it finally folded up around 1935.

Kirloskar showed himself a consummate craftsman and a quintessential man of his time in modifying existing dramatic models in ways exactly suited to contemporary tastes and the prevalent sense of national selfhood. On the one hand, he converted the original Sanskrit slokas into songs, thereby making the adaptation more entertaining. On the other, he brought his work nearer to the concept of individuated character, a big step towards modern drama, by making his actors sing rather than have the *sutradhara* sing on their behalf. His use of culturally rooted melodies made his songs instantly acceptable. For instance, he drew eclectically from sources as diverse as traditional women's songs, folk songs, devotional Kirtan, ragas from the Carnatic and Hindustani systems, and Kannada stage songs. Another major difference with the Bhave style involved the formalizing of dialogues, which were now substantial in quantity and needed rehearsing. Reviews of Kirloskar's first play made a point of mentioning that his actors were better prepared than their predecessors.

Ironically, in making his actors sing, Kirloskar was, at one and the same time, innovating a new form of theatre and sowing the seed of its decay and death. For, in time, singing actors became such a valued resource that it soon ceased to matter if they could only sing and not act. Sangitnatak songs became the popular music of the day and, increasingly, sections of the audience went to the theatre exclusively to hear their favourite singers deliver the compositions, rather than to enjoy the production as a whole. The most illustrious singer-actors between 1911 and 1921, known as the golden age of Sangitnatak, were the elegantly mellifluous Bal Gandharva, who joined the Kirloskar Natak Mandali in 1905, and the vigorously energetic Keshavrao Bhonsle (1890–1921), who began playing lead for the Swadesh Hitachintak Mandali in 1902.

In 1908, Bhonsle formed the Lalitkaladarsha Natak Mandali, famous for such versatile actors as 'Nanasaheb' Gopal Phatak (1899–1974), 'Mama' Chintamani Pendse (1906–?), and 'Master' Dattaram Walwaikar (1913–84), and for painted scenery by the Painter brothers (Anandrao, died 1916, and Baburao, 1890–1954). It continued to produce Sangitnatak, albeit sporadically, well into the 1960s. Bal Gandharva in turn broke away from

Bal Gandharva (second from right) and Ganesh Bodas (second from left) in R.G. Gadkari's *Ekach pyala* (Gandharva Natak Mandali, Bombay, 1919)

the Kirloskar Mandali to form his Gandharva Natak Mandali with music director Govindrao Tembe (1881–1955) and leading man Ganesh Bodas (1880–1965) in 1913, later featuring music by 'Master' Krishnarao Phulambrikar (1898–1974).

Other impressive singer-actors included Dinanath Mangeshkar (1900–42), gifted with a comely appearance and a honeyed timbre, who joined the Kirloskar company after Bal Gandharva left and then departed with non-singing actor Chintamanrao Kolhatkar (1891–1959) to form the Balwant Natak Mandali; Ramchandra Ganesh Kundgolkar, known as Sawai Gandharva (1886–1952), who started acting in 1909 and founded his own Nutan Sangit Mandali in 1914; Vishnupant Aundhkar (c. 1893–1943), who formed the Samarth Natak Mandali starring the relatively realistic Keshavrao Date (1889–1971) and wrote his own plays; the female impersonator Vishnupant Pagnis (1892–1943); and the delicate-voiced Chhota Gandharva (1918–97).

During the eighteenth century, the old *dhrupad* tradition of Hindustani classical music had begun to give way gradually to the *khayal* form. By the mid-nineteenth century, singers from Maharashtra had gone north, to Gwalior and other places, to master this style. Their return at the turn of the century coincided with the predominance music had gained over drama in Sangitnatak, and the services of these and other vocalists and instrumentalists were much in demand for the training of singer-actors. The best-known gurus were Bhaskarbuwa Bakhle (1869–1922) and Ramkrishnabuwa Vaze (1871–1945). Later they were also entrusted with the job of composing melodies for stage songs.

Consequently, the traditional indigenous tunes used by the earliest dramatists like Kirloskar and Deval gave way to raga music in the plays of political allegorist K.P. Khadilkar (1872–1948) and social tragedian R.G. Gadkari (1885–1919). Actors began to present these raga-based songs elaborately while the dramatic action came to a standstill. The audience, intoxicated by the music, would call for encores to which the singers responded only too happily. By the 1930s, discriminating spectators regretted the transformation of Sangitnatak into a concert. The coming of talkies in that decade completed its downfall. One after the other, Natak Mandalis disbanded, unable to attract enough patronage to keep afloat. The playhouses that had witnessed so much opulence and public madness were taken over by cinema. Briefly, in the 1960s and 1970s, the dramatist Vidyadhar Gokhale, director Purushottam Darwhekar (1926–99), and composer Ram Marathe (1924–89) separately attempted to revive Sangitnatak.

Meanwhile, younger Marathi playwrights had discovered Ibsen, with whose social concerns and dramatic modes they felt greater affinity than with Shakespeare's. Deval had already written the first social play, *Sharada* (1899), dealing with the problem of poor parents marrying their young daughters off to old men. Maharashtra Natak Mandali, formed in 1904 by Govind, Yashwant, and Madhav Tipnis, and Trimbak Karkhanis, was dedicated to 'prose' drama of a high literary level, by playwrights like Khadilkar and N.C. Kelkar. But 'Mama' B.V. Warerkar (1883–1964) was the most serious and prolific of these dramatists. Lalitkaladarsha produced his *Satteche gulam* ('Slaves of Power', 1927) with realistic backdrops and props. Even his last play, *Bhumikanya Sita* ('Earth's Daughter Sita', 1958), created a furore because it reinterpreted the epic characters of Sita and Urmila, Lakshman's wife whom, he pointed out, Valmiki had totally neglected. The other influence on contemporary writers was Molière. 'Acharya' P.K. Atre (1898–1969), best known for his comedies of the 1930s, freely adapted Molière texts and was later inspired by Noel Coward.

S.V. Vartak's *Andhalyanchi shala* ('School for the Blind', 1933) produced by Natyamanwantar, a group of young men committed to a new, relevant theatre, was hailed as the first modern Marathi play. In it the Bombay audience saw theatre for the first time as a composite art, comprising text, performance, lighting, set, and music, and in Jyotsna Bhole (1914–2001), the first actress to come from a respectable family. However, cinema drew audiences away, and Natyamanwantar did not have the financial base to sustain experimentation. Later, the War years made

Chintamanrao Kolhatkar in M.G. Rangnekar's *Ashirvad* (Natyaniketan, Bombay, 1941)

stage activity even more difficult. M.G. Rangnekar (1907–95) and his company, Natyaniketan, dominated the 1940s, turning the Ibsenian influence into simplified and sentimental depictions of social problems, judiciously peppered with light songs kept within strict time limits to prevent breaks in narrative tension. His *Kulavadhu* ('Family Bride', 1942) ended in a scene that paralleled, albeit only superficially, the finale of Ibsen's *A Doll's House*. Thus was born the domestic drawing-room drama, located in the confines of the ubiquitous box set.

When Marathi theatre celebrated its centenary in 1943 all over the state, the festival of old and new plays organized in Bombay by the Mumbai Marathi Sahitya Sangh, a leading cultural society, drew thousands to the open-air stage erected for the purpose at Chowpatty and rekindled interest in theatre-going. In 1954, the Bharatiya Vidya Bhavan in Bombay, followed by the state government, inaugurated intercollegiate drama competitions that launched a movement. The subsequent wave of original drama combined with new Marathi and Gujarati plays sponsored by the Indian National Theatre to turn the tide away from the syrupy sentimentality of the mainstream theatre into a more raw realism expressed through intense low-key performance and imaginative use of lights, music, and sets. The first drama to deal with psychological aberration was *Vedyache ghar unhat* ('Madman's House out in the Heat', 1957) by Vasant Kanetkar (1922–2001), premiered in Pune.

Meanwhile Dalit theatre emerged outside Bombay, addressing the problems of oppressed lower castes. Scholars normally date it to M.B. Chitnis's *Yugyatra* ('Procession of an Age') on historical discrimination against Dalits, staged in Aurangabad (1955) and for an audience of 600,000 at a mass conversion to Buddhism in Nagpur (1956). The movement continues, with Datta Bhagat and Premanand Gajvi regarded as the prominent contemporary Dalit playwrights. Back in Bombay, the commercial mainstream flourished. A notable production to have a long and successful run was Atre's *To mi navhech* ('I'm Not Him', 1962), which told the story of a real-life con man who duped eight young women into marrying him and disappeared with their money. Its highlight was the revolving stage, specially constructed to allow quick cuts between the flashback of events and the courtroom, with necessary changes in the con man's costumes and make-up. Prabhakar Panshikar (1931–) acted the protagonist's role with virtuoso skill. The play still attracts full houses.

In the 1960s and 1970s, absurdist and Brechtian drama began influencing Marathi playwrights. The Hindi productions that Satyadev Dubey directed for Theatre Unit during these decades also had a lasting impact on Marathi theatre. Both he and director Vijaya Mehta (1934–), who made Rangayan, her theatre laboratory of the 1960s, so dynamic, had worked with the legendary Ebrahim Alkazi in the early 1950s. Alkazi's methods and principles to transform English-language theatre in Bombay became the context against or within which they located their own.

The big names that dominated the next thirty years found their feet during this period of experimentation. Among dramatists, Vijay Tendulkar (1928–2008) introduced with his crisp, incisive, understated style, rhythms and patterns of speech previously unknown to the Marathi stage. Mehta, Shreeram Lagoo (1927–), and Madhav Watve added to the effect of his plays with their natural acting. Other noted performers in this idiom included Dattatray Bhat (1921–84), Neelu Phule (1931–), Sulabha Deshpande (1937–), Bhakti Barve-Inamdar (1945–2001), and Mohan Agashe (1947–). Damu Kenkre (1928–) designed imaginatively naturalistic, symbolic, or, on occasion, abstract sets, generally comprising levels arranged for graphic and functional effect. The artistic *scenography of D.G. Godse (1914–92) and varied *music of Bhaskar Chandavarkar (1936–) contributed significantly to Mehta's productions. Lighting was moody or expressionistic, and has so remained. In infrastructure, the National Centre for the Performing Arts came up, housing five auditoriums, though not exclusively devoted to Marathi theatre.

A network was established during the 1970s for a free exchange among Hindi, Kannada, Bengali, and Marathi experimentalists. Maharashtra saw translations of Badal Sircar, Adya Rangacharya, Girish Karnad, and Mohan Rakesh, the dominant dramatic mode of which was non-realistic. In Marathi, too, this was the only time when major plays were written in other-than-realistic forms. Examples include Tendulkar's *Ghashiram Kotwal* (1972), and

Vijay Tendulkar's *Ghashiram Kotwal*, directed by Jabbar Patel, with Mohan Agashe (centre) as Nana Phadnavis (Theatre Academy, Pune, 1972)

some excellent works by C.T. Khanolkar (1930–76), Mahesh Elkunchwar (1939– , also famous for his naturalistic *Wada* domestic trilogy), Satish Alekar (1949–), and Achyut Vaze. The latter were mistakenly labelled absurdist for, though they adopted the non-sequiturs in speech, their angst was strictly middle-class, without any philosophical underpinning. These trends found supportive directors in Arvind Deshpande (1932–87), initiator of the intimate Chhabildas movement; Jabbar Patel (1942–), of Theatre Academy in Pune; and Amol Palekar (1944–), pioneer of theatre in open spaces.

Several plays appeared that aroused public wrath or had to battle with the censors. Tendulkar's *Gidhade* (*The Vultures*, 1970), *Sakharam Binder* (1972), *Ghashiram Kotwal*, and Elkunchwar's *Vasanakand* ('Period of Desire', 1974) were found offensive for their perceived caste biases or brutal outspokenness about social and sexual issues. G.P. Deshpande (1938–) gave post-Independence Marathi theatre its first consciously political play, *Uddhwasta dharmashala* ('Desolate Dharmashala', 1974). He remains the chief Marathi dramatist to use the stage for political issues and debates. The Emergency years (1976–8) were responsible for a stream of so-called political plays, which replaced the good–bad polarity of family drama with an equally facile opposition of corrupt politician against innocent commoner, in no way adding to political thought. Soon thereafter, both the experimental and mainstream stages returned to their steady preoccupation with interpersonal relationships and social or psychological problems.

However, the experimental movement became moribund in the mid-1980s. Younger writers and directors did not seem too interested in challenging the system or rebelling against middle-class values. A general exodus of talent took place from the experimental towards the mainstream theatre. The earlier generation of authors like Tendulkar and Kanetkar, and actors like Mehta and Lagoo had made the move in their own time, bringing to the mainstream a flexibility that the new theatre people could take full advantage of. Important mainstream dramatists included V.V. Shirwadkar (1912–99), P.L. Deshpande (1919–2000), Jaywant Dalvi (1925–94), Sai Paranjpye (1936–), and Ratnakar Matkari (1938–), whose most widely discussed plays focused on society or psychology, to which Marathi audiences respond warmly.

By the mid-1980s, the reign of Mumbai (Bombay) and Pune personalities was challenged by the arrival in Mumbai of trained writers, actors, and directors from other places, particularly the Drama Department of Aurangabad University in interior Maharashtra. The newcomers included playwrights

Ajit Dalvi and Prashant Dalvi, directors Waman Kendre and Chandrakant Kulkarni, and actors Sayaji Shinde and Nandu Madhav. Their mainstream productions were acclaimed for freshness of themes and directorial approach. In 1985, Pune's Theatre Academy identified twelve persons for a playwriting project, bringing to the fore Tushar Bhadre from Satara, Datta Bhagat from Nanded, and Makarand Sathe of Pune. Significant Mumbai dramatists now are Rajeev Naik and Shafaat Khan. Directors doing interesting work, in addition to the Aurangabad group, include Vijay Kenkre, Atul Pethe, Devendra Pem, and Santosh Pawar. Far too many talented performers exist to attempt an exhaustive list, but one should mention Kishore Kadam, Sanjay More, Prashant Damle, Vandana Gupte, Girish Oak, Sanjay Narvekar, Vijay Kadam, Nirmiti Sawant, Amruta Subhash, and Nikhil Ratnaparakhi.

No truly noteworthy experiments have occurred in set, sound, or lighting design since the mid-1980s. Since the audience that patronizes the urban professional play is largely middle- and lower middle-class, ticket rates cannot increase beyond a certain level. Consequently, the quality of technological inputs has remained more or less the same for two or three decades. Another reason for the design aspects not matching the writing and acting levels is the distrust the Marathi playgoer always had toward what he sees as 'gimmicks'. The bare script is what he holds aesthetically dear, unimpeded by anything likely to draw his attention away. The critic and the discriminating viewer, responding to an unexpressed and perhaps unrecognized streak of puritanism, think of the verbal content, which carries the moral lesson, as the 'real' play, and set, sound, and lighting as forms of dressing up.

Still, hit productions run for hundreds of shows, drawing full houses even in the afternoon. The phenomenal blockbuster of all times, now entered in the *Limca Book of Records*, is Devendra Pem's *All the Best* (1993), a lightweight but energetically acted comedy which completed 1000 performances by the end of 1995 and continues to go strong with three teams of actors to cater to the never-decreasing demand. Equally profitable have been its Gujarati and Hindi versions, running concurrently. Producer Mohan Wagh groomed it into a hit under the Chandralekha banner, one of the most professional and successful production houses in the business. Other notable mainstream companies are Suyog, Natyasampada, Kala Vaibhav, Shree Chintamani, and the Goa Hindu Association.

Theatre in the 1990s seemed lively and vigorous. Santosh Pawar took the mainstream by storm with his rambunctious comedy *Yadakadachit* ('Perhaps', 1999). There was an abundance of energy and talent in every area, the greater part of it directed toward the annual drama competitions held by the state and locally by all kinds of cultural bodies. The bad thing about competitions is that they encourage gimmicky, award-oriented work; the good thing is that they offer a platform to youth, allowing them to feel their way on the stage, helping them to decide whether they want to choose theatre as a profession. Many of the best artists on the mainstream and experimental stages have come from the competition circuit. However, the advent of multi-channel television has reduced theatre takings, not so much the result of a disinterested audience as the unavailability, particularly for the experimental stage, of actors with enough time to spare from lucrative television work. This development causes worry to those concerned with theatre art.

An encouraging trend occurred in the early years of the twenty-first century. Awishkar, the group founded in the 1970s by Arvind and Sulabha Deshpande, managed by Arun Kakade, turned a suburban municipal school hall in Mumbai into a small, minimally equipped space for off-mainstream theatre. Director Chetan Datar, in charge of programmes, selected and invited new plays from all over Maharashtra to participate in a mini-festival here every month. The venerable Mumbai Marathi Sahitya Sangh also started an off-mainstream wing under the guidance of actress Rekha Sabnis in a fully functional auditorium in south Mumbai, where productions state-wide are invited to perform regularly. Likewise, the Maharashtra Cultural Centre in Pune created a small theatre venue.

A new crop of young writers and directors, notably Paresh Mokashi, Sandesh Kulkarni, Sachin Kundalkar, Iravati Karnik, Girish Joshi, Vivek Bele, Mohit Takalkar, and Advait Dadarkar, explores contemporary issues. While the dominant mode remains realistic, Mokashi experiments with the theatres of music, fantasy, and ideas.   SG

Mahadev Apte, *Humour and Communication in Contemporary Marathi Theatre* (Pune: Linguistic Society of India, 1992); Shanta Gokhale, *Playwright at the Centre: Marathi Drama from 1843 to the Present* (Calcutta: Seagull, 2000); K. Narayan Kale, *Theatre in Maharashtra* (New Delhi: Maharashtra Information Centre, 1967); *The Marathi Theatre: 1843 to 1960* (Bombay: Marathi Natya Parishad, 1961); Dnyaneshwar Nadkarni, *New Directions in the Marathi Theatre* (New Delhi: Maharashtra Information Centre, 1967); Bapurao Naik, *Origin of the Marathi Theatre* (New Delhi: Maharashtra Information Centre, 1967); Anand Patil, *Western Influence on Marathi Drama* (Goa: Rajhans, 1993); Aroon Tikekar, *Marathi Theatre During the Last Two Decades* (Patiala: Department of Languages, 1982).

MIZO THEATRE

Mizo theatre (in the far eastern state of Mizoram) has ancient roots in annual ritual sacrifices to the gods and ceremonial dances celebrating victories in the hunt or against enemies, which enabled the heroes in their afterlife to enter Pialral (the Mizo paradise) ruled by the great dispenser Pawla. After the Christianization of Mizos, missionaries initiated drama at the Christmas festivities of 1912 held in a small thatch-roof theatre in Aizawl. The variety entertainment included seven humorous dialogues, such as between an Englishman and interpreter, a Christian and non-Christian, an old Englishman and old Muslim man. The most memorable item, *Borsap lem, leh thu chhia nei tu tu leh Rasi lem chang be* ('Superintendent's Court Scene between Magistrate and Interpreter'), was the first Mizo play proper, about a thief convicted of stealing a goat and bribing the interpreter.

The tradition of Christmas theatricals continued every year and spread to the villages. The church used them in its services too, to inculcate religious lessons, but withdrew after the spiritual revival of 1919. The immediate result was the emergence of secular drama, also influenced by the Puja plays of the Bengali community and amateur theatre in the army camp. The educationist Ch. Pasena (1893–1961) wrote and directed at a school in Aizawl, starting with *Heroda chawimawina* ('King Herod's Glory', 1925), a biblical tragedy. He dramatized two other stories from the Bible, *Fapa tlanbo* ('The Prodigal Son', 1927) and *Khualbuka mi a* ('Fool at the Inn', 1933), and composed three moralistic originals: *Tinreng daih khawl* ('Machine with a Brain', 1928) about a robot, *Ransa khawmpui* ('Animals' Conference', 1929) against the evil of drinking, and *Rorelna* ('Court', 1933) on the wages of sin for a bad boy. He helped produce *The Merchant of Venice* as *Sailoka* (1929), a grand success as the first Mizo Shakespearean drama.

In 1934, Chawngzika directed *Krista palai* ('Christ's Ambassador'), apparently the first script typed in Mizo, for the Aijal Theatre Performers, who sold tickets for the first time in Mizoram. Lalkailuia, the son of a village chief, based his plays on local folk tales and acted in the lead, dramatizing the popular love story of Tualvungi and Zawlpala in 1935. From 1937 to 1951, Rev. Samuel Davies, trained in theatre from London, directed and introduced modern techniques and stage technology in Aizawl. For the Gospel golden jubilee in 1944, he dramatized the coming of Christianity as *Thuhriltu* ('The

Herald'). He presented theatre jointly with Chawngzika, who adapted several biblical episodes for the stage, such as *The Royal Robes* (1948), *Christmas Spirit* (1949), and *The Star of Christmas* (1950). The dramatist and musician Lalzuithanga (1916–50) innovatively set a detective thriller, *The Black Corner of Aijal in 1999* (1940), in the future, and began a tragedy titled *The Horrible* (1941) with the protagonist's hanging, followed by his startling appearance as a ghost at the postmortem. Lalzuithanga performed the heroes' as well as comic roles in his productions.

By the end of World War II, nearly every Mizo village possessed a homegrown group of actors. Gradually, playwriting changed, to represent life more realistically, as in the works of the major contemporary dramatists Lalhmuaka (1915–2002), the first woman playwright Khawlkungi (1927–), Lalthangfala Sailo (1933–), Laltluangliana Khiangte (1961–), and Liansailova. After the printing of the first Mizo drama as late as 1962, over a hundred Mizo plays have been published.   LK

Laltluangliana Khiangte, *Mizo Drama* (New Delhi: Cosmo, 1993).

n

NEPALI THEATRE

Theatre in the Nepali language exists outside Nepal, in Nepali-speaking areas of India, mainly northern West Bengal and Sikkim states in eastern India.

The Kirata period of pre-recorded Nepali history produced the *Mundhum*, the Veda of the Tibeto-Burman Kiratas, which contains dramatic elements but makes no reference to plays or an actual stage. Some scholars, however, believe that the *Harisiddhi* play, still traditionally performed, had its inception during this time. The Licchavi period (third–ninth centuries) was notable for *Sanskrit theatre produced in the *mandapikas* (pavilions) adjacent to temples. Record has it that a *Ramayana* play of those days was immensely popular for years.

The Malla period (thirteenth–eighteenth centuries) witnessed significant development in Nepali stagecraft. Performances came out of temple precincts into open public places on *dabali*s, or raised stone platforms. Invariably they were in the form of musical and dance dramas. Malla plays were mostly written in the Newari and *Maithili languages. Kati Pyakham ('Kartik *ritual drama'), which ran for the whole month of Kartik (October–November), came into vogue. The modern proscenium stage made its appearance in the Shah period (1767 onwards) followed by the Rana period (1846 onwards), which abounded in entertaining Urdu and *Hindi theatre.

However, *dabali* performances continued to be popular and creative. The Jyapu Natak of peasant Jyapus, in the Tibeto-Burman language of Newari, evolved as a widely acclaimed genre; Dhintamai was yet another celebrated variant of Jyapu popular theatre. Attempts have been made to present modern Nepali plays in the traditional folk Jyapu styles.

Sanskrit plays were translated into Nepali ever since Shaktivallabh Aryal's version of *Hasyakadamba* ('Comic *kadamba* Tree', 1798). But a play written wholly in Nepali was first staged in Darjiling, north Bengal, in 1909 by Dhanbir Mukhia and his pioneering Gorkha National Theatrical Party: Pahalman Singh Swar's *Atalbahadur*, published from Varanasi in 1906. Worthy followers were the Himalayan and Children's Amusement Association, a club known for the popular reformist actor-dramatist Bhaiya Singh Gazmer (1898–1968), and the Gorkha Dukha Niwarak Sammelan, a social organization. Balkrishna Sama (1902–81) wrote the first modern Nepali play, the social tragedy *Mutuko byatha* ('Heart's Pangs'), in 1926. A consistently successful author, he penned as many as eighteen full-length and fourteen one-act plays. *Prahlad* (1929) is regarded as his masterpiece. A verse allegory, it reflects Gandhian principles and predicts Hitlerian methods. Gopalprasad Rimal and the Malla brothers, Govind and Vijay, ushered in realism, both social and psychological.

Contemporary Nepali dramatists, specially the front-ranking, transcend matter-of-fact realism. Their plays concretize thoughts and awareness in suitably new forms to embody the contents. Mohanraj Sharma's *Baikuntha Express* ('Paradise Express', 1985) presents the perilous journey the world has to undertake driven by the compulsive desire to reach a land of affluence and pleasure. We have all boarded the express to meet a tragic end. Sharad Chetri in *Khub nachyo kathaputali* ('Merrily Danced the Puppet', 1993) diagnoses the nothingness of all existence, which lies at the heart of all reality. Avinash Shrestha's *Ashvatthama hatshatah* ('Ashvatthama Is Dead', 1994) asserts that Yudhisthira's damnable half-truth uttered in the battle of Kurukshetra has proliferated and half-truths have come to rule the earth, mankind living an accursed life. Saroo Bhakta's *Malamiharu* ('Funereal Procession', 1995) vividly depicts all people as attendants at the funeral of our humanism. Nanda Hangkhim in his *Abhishek* ('Consecration', 1995) picks up the thread of Oedipus' tragedy to ask: could not the child born of incestuous and sinful wedlock be consecrated and crowned? Therein lies the existential test of the modern world to accept hard reality. Existence is surely more stubborn and greater too than moralistic considerations. These five writers represent the phase of high modernism in Nepali drama.   IBR

Luther G. Jerstad, *Mani-rimdu: Sherpa Dance-Drama* (Calcutta: Oxford & IBH, 1969); Kumar Pradhan, *History of Nepali Literature* (New Delhi: Sahitya Akademi, 1984).

O

ORIYA THEATRE

The eastern state of Orissa boasts a rich variety of traditional performance, from *puppetry (*Kundhei Nata, *Sakhi-kundhei Nata, *Ravana Chhaya) to balladry (*Pala), devotional ritual (*Danda Nata, *Bandi Nata), diverse forms of *Lila (*Yatra, *Dhanu Yatra, *Rahasa, *Bharat Lila), mythological presentations (*Prahlada Nataka, *Suanga), masked dance-drama (*Chhau, *Desia Nata), folk dance (*Chaiti Ghoda Nata), and satire (*Mughal Tamsha). Processionals like Sahi Yatra dedicated to Rama, as well as *Ramlila, are staged with much pomp and ceremony during Ram Navami. The above categories often overlap; no simple classification is possible. However, all these forms are fast receding owing to rapid urbanization and the traditional elements in them are disappearing. Young audiences are no longer interested in them, though some dramatists now reintroduce them to make their own work more colourful.

In 1872, students of the Catholic Mission School in Cuttack, then headquarters of Orissa Division, enacted an English play, perhaps by Oliver Goldsmith, on a temporary proscenium stage. The first of its kind in the region, it was well received by the audience. But it took another three years for Oriya drama to reach the proscenium proper. The establishment of a permanent stage in 1875 by Jagan Mohan Lala (1838–1913) in Mahanga village, Cuttack district, gave birth to modern Oriya theatre. The remains of this stage, where productions took place at regular intervals for quite some time, still stand. Lala also wrote the first Oriya social drama, *Babaji* (*The Holy Man*, 1877). The first play by Ramshankar Ray (1857–1931), *Kanchi-Kaveri*, was presented in 1881 by an amateur group in Cuttack. Other early mythological and historical dramatists included Kampal Mishra (1875–1927), Bhikari Charan Patnaik (1877–1962), and Godavarish Mishra (1886–1956). Gradually, interest for this kind of show grew among people, but Cuttack's first purpose-built theatre, Basanti Pandal, arose only in 1910. Meanwhile, permanent stages were erected by two feudal chiefs: Bikram Theatre (1895) by Bira Bikram Dev (1875–1911), himself an actor, writer, and director at Khariar (Nawapara district), and Padmanav Rangalay (1898) at Paralakhemundi (Gajapati district).

Professional troupes had emerged—like the one owned by the zamindar Banamali Pati (1876–1928), doing plays by the prolific Aswini Kumar Ghose (1892–1962)—but mostly as touring parties and without any permanent theatres. This state of affairs continued till the 1940s, when almost simultaneously two professional theatres came up in Cuttack and a third in Puri. Kali Charan Patnaik (1899–1978), an eminent dramatist, already headed a touring group that he converted into a company under a new name, Orissa Theatre, and housed in a permanent building (1942) at Banka Bazar, Cuttack. Also sensing the changing tastes of the time, he switched to realistic social plays. Similarly, a musical-drama troupe owned by Somnath Das turned into Annapurna Theatre, with branches in Puri and Cuttack. The companies in Cuttack competed to win over audiences. Memorable plays like Patnaik's *Girls' School* (1942), *Chumban* ('Kiss', 1942), and *Bhata* ('Rice', 1944), and *Mulia* ('Labourer', 1946) by Ramchandra Mishra (1921–92), were the outcome of this competition.

Bharati Theatre, another professional party, appeared in Cuttack in the early 1940s, resulting briefly in three-way rivalry. Besides, there were two touring troupes, led by Govinda Chandra Surdeo and Mohansundar Deva Goswami, which contributed substantially to Oriya theatre. After a decade of successful and regular productions Orissa Theatre closed down in 1949, but both branches of Annapurna Theatre continued. The short-lived Rupashri Theatre emerged in Cuttack in 1951, followed by Janata Theatre (1953) and Kalasri Theatre (1966), which put on daily shows, barring Mondays, alongside those of Annapurna-B—perhaps the only example of its kind in India.

All these professional companies needed a regular supply of good drama. Hence new plays were written, playwrights encouraged, and a rich

Manoranjan Das's *Sabdalipi* (1976) staged in Bhubaneswar

and healthy tradition of staged drama created. This movement was alive for almost two decades, for which critics identify this period as the 'golden age' of modern Oriya drama. A group of talented dramatists like Gopal Chhotray (1916–2003), Ramchandra Mishra, Bhanja Kishore Patnaik (1922–99), Ananda Sankar Das, and Kamal Lochan Mohanty were associated with these parties. Their plays dealt with universal values: exploring human qualities and follies, various social questions, political issues, the impact of economic and industrial revolutions, and many other contemporary problems. However, being commercial, the theatres did not give much scope for experimentation—they had to cater mainly to the demands of their middle-class viewership which, like its counterparts elsewhere, expected entertainment from the stage.

Gradually, remarkable changes in the tastes and attitudes of the audience due to social transformations alienated it from theatre. Unfortunately, neither the dramatists nor the proprietors noted this phenomenon. When changes in the dramatic style, theme, and presentation seemed necessary, these were ignored. As a result, deterioration crept into the professional stage, which also failed to attract the younger population away from the glamorous world of the silver screen. Some leading actors like Babi (1918–) successfully negotiated both the worlds of theatre and cinema. But by the beginning of the 1970s, all commercial companies had closed down, putting an end to an extraordinary dramatic tradition in this region. No professional theatre has come up in Orissa since then.

Only Manoranjan Das (1921–), an excellent dramatist, visualized the changing atmosphere during the heyday of professionalism. Although he started his dramatic career writing for professional parties, he constituted a group called United Artists in 1950 to stage his first experimental play, *Agami* ('Advent'), which brought him applause both inside and outside Orissa. For the first time the local audience noticed an Ibsenian style on stage and a novel theme based on psychological realism. This impressed the elite and the idiom was accepted. Afterwards, Das always depended on amateur groups to perform his provocative works, such as *Sagara manthan* ('Churning of the Ocean', 1964), *Banahamsi* ('Wild Goose', 1968), and *Amritasya putrah* ('Immortal Son', 1971). He started the *group-theatre movement in Orissa, which soon occupied the prominent place in Oriya theatre.

Srujani, a distinguished group in Cuttack, created history by staging a number of experimental plays during its short life (1964–71), including the above three by Das, well received by theatregoers. Biswajeet Das (1936–) wrote *Pratapgadhare didin* ('Two Days in Pratapgarh', 1967), adapted from Gogol's *Inspector General*, for them. Srujani is credited with changing the taste of audiences. Encouraged by the success of group theatre and the altering style of drama, young writers grew interested in the new movement. Their plays reflected the changing lifestyle and its agony, the hypocrisy, self-centredness, and possessiveness due to insecurity. For the first time, Oriya theatre established a direct, distinct, and strong bridge with Western drama, and characters, situations, and incidents alien to traditional Oriya society crept in. The new authors totally discarded the rural background that had prevailed in Oriya drama so far.

Among the other group theatres was Sanket, in the state capital, Bhubaneswar, who staged Biswajeet Das's existential *Mrigaya* ('Hunt', 1970) and *Samrat* ('Emperor', 1972); Friends' Union in Cuttack, who premiered *Sababahakamane* ('Pall Bearers', 1968) by the radical Bijay Mishra (1936–) and Manoranjan Das's *Aranya phasala* (*Wild Harvest*, 1969); and Ebam Ame in Bhubaneswar, performing J.P. Das's *Sabashesha loka* ('Last Person', 1978), Manoranjan Das's *Klanta prajapati* ('Tired Butterfly', 1978), Ratnakar Chaini's *Athacha Chanakya* ('Although Chanakya', 1982), and Bijay Mishra's *Tata Niranjana* ('Banks of Niranjana', 1978), *Jane raja thile* ('Once There Was a Raja', 1982), and *Badshah* ('Sovereign', 1983)—all remarkable additions to Oriya experimental drama. Independently, Gopal Chhotray had staged his one-set drama *Ardhangini* ('Better Half') as early as 1956 and Pranabandhu Kar had staged *Sweta padma* ('White Lotus', 1958), adjudged the best at an All-India competition in Calcutta, and *Ashanta* ('Restless', 1960).

For the last three decades Cultural Academy, an amateur club in Raurkela, has organized annual drama competitions. One notable product was Ramesh Das, who wrote two beautiful plays, *Baram nivasa bhala rana kshetrare* ('Better to Live in a Battlefield', 1976) and *Ajhala udei de* ('Raise the Sail', 1977). Groups like Shrasta (in Baleshwar), Silpi (Dhenkanal), Ame (Baripada), Natyam (Angul), and Kasandra (Kendujhar) organize regular competitions. More than 400 such clubs exist in different parts of Orissa, among them Satabdir Kalakar, Sabuja Natya Sangha, Kachhap, Abhinay, Jatni, and Ame Kalakar (in Bhubaneswar), Life And Rhythm and Kalinga Kala Parishad (Raurkela), Swara and Sambalpur Kala Kendra (Sambalpur), Utkal Yuva Samskrutika Sangha and Smruti (Cuttack), Trend Setter (Jajpur), Chandrabhaga (Baleshwar), Maitree (Kendujhar), and Adhuna (Koraput). The alternative group Natya Chetana (Bhubaneswar) works on a commune.

In the absence of professional theatre in Orissa, such amateur groups formed the only source of hope for theatre lovers. But they are not free from problems, the primary one being monetary. Despite continuous efforts, audiences remain infatuated with the world of electronic media and movies. Even free theatre does not attract sufficient crowds. The organizers finance their shows mainly from their own pockets. It is because of these dedicated souls that the art not only exists but also proceeds ahead, though in chequered steps. Another difficulty is that most groups fail to cross the borders of their own locality, as a result of which they never come to the state limelight.

Meanwhile, contemporary Oriya 'opera' claims to be the progeny of Yatra, once popularized by pioneers like Baishnab Pani (1882–1956) and Balakrishna Mohanty. Presently these entertainments, originating mostly in coastal Orissa, run day after day to packed houses and do roaring business. A good number of 'opera parties' such as Tulasi Gananatya, Janata Opera, Sibani Opera, Uttarkul Opera, Uttarayani Opera, Parbati Gananatya, Banirampur Opera, Orissa Opera, and Tarini Opera tour throughout the state and Oriya-dominated parts of neighbouring states. Owning an opera has become like the proverbial hen laying golden eggs. Crores of rupees are invested with alluring returns. Gone are the days when Pani had to die a pauper. Artists are hired with the assurance of good remuneration; actresses have been introduced. Modern theatre techniques are used and multi-stage systems have replaced single stages. To attract crowds, explicit scenes of violence, rape, and murder in the style of commercial films are performed so commonly that at times it becomes impossible to watch the show with one's family. Gradually, opera crossed all limits of decency, leading to calls for censorship. As the proprietors pay sumptuously, famous dramatists like Bhanja Kishore Patnaik, Bijay Mishra, Kartik Rath, and Ramesh Panigrahi (1943–) write for them. No doubt these operas solve unemployment problems to some extent, employing large numbers of artists and workers, but at the heavy cost of cultural pollution, according to critics.

The proscenium stage was increasingly occupied by opera. Occasionally a traditional play was performed on an improvised platform in rural areas. Otherwise few appeared to seek live drama, even in towns, while formal study of Oriya theatre lay neglected. Modern dramatists had severed their ties with the common mass, which proved detrimental for them. Their dependence upon the West gradually widened the gap between the people and themselves. The numerous theatrical experiments had proved very expensive, for which audiences rejected them. Consequently, some dramatists during the 1980s returned to their roots through various folk forms. They reintroduced music, dance, earthy humour, and emotional outbursts—once considered unnecessary. Myth, legend, and history are used to add colour to plays. Manoranjan Das, who once departed from the conventional path, adjusted to the trend and wrote *Nandika Keshari* (1980), a musical packed with song, dance, and melodrama.

For newer authors who experimented with form and content, like Harihara Mishra (*Nindita gajapati*, 'Censured King', 1972), Kartik Rath (*Mansara phulla*, 'Flower of Flesh', 1975), Subodh Pattanaik (*Ho bhagate*, 'Hey Devotees', 1982), Pramod Tripathy (*Suna Parikshya*

Natya Chetana's *Katha*, written and directed by Subodh Pattanaik (Bhubaneswar, 2002)

dandadhari, 'Listen, Sceptre-wielder Parikshya', 1983), Prasanna Mishra (*Jana sevak*, 'Public Worker', 1984), Shankar Tripathy (*Gandhi bhumikare*, 'In Gandhi's Role', 1996), Chinmay Das Patnaik (*Mun Similipal kahuchi*, 'Similipal Speaking', 1996), and Panchanan Patra (*Pratidwandi*, 'Rival', 1996), group theatres remained the only hope, although struggling hard for their existence. Taking the cue from these predecessors and others like Akshaya Mohanty and Ramesh Panigrahi (*Jatiya sankat*, 'National Crisis', 2002), younger playwrights led by Rati Ranjan Mishra (1952–2005), Bijoy Satpathy, Hemendra Mahapatra, Rabindranath Das, Narayan Sahu, and Ranjit Patnaik sought a new identity for contemporary drama. Instead of community, they placed a greater focus on the individual's hope and despair, happiness and sorrow.

Rati Mishra, gifted with poetic ability and a great supporter of the 'back to the roots' movement, interwove myth, history, and classical tradition with present conditions to bring to the surface the exploitation and subjugation of indigenous people, to attack the foundation on which corrupt society stands. The socio-economic aspects of human development fascinated him. He documented his own time and history in twenty plays, popular among them *Dekha barsha asuchhi* ('Look, Rain Is Coming', 1980), *Sital huana surya* ('Sun, Don't Grow Cold,' 1993), *Machha kandara swara* ('Sound of Fish Weeping', 1996), and *Avatar* (1999). While dramatizing contemporary situations or events, he maintained a distancing that helped viewers to experience something and at the same time, think about the problem dispassionately. He used the onstage fictional space to tackle the disturbing abstractions of society. Rejecting modernism, he swung towards exploratory post-modernistic form, towards spontaneity and irrationality, freedom and anarchy. A new radical theatre was born, soon appreciated by the audience. Most of his colleagues accepted his techniques and post-modern Oriya theatre emerged.   HKD

Dhiren Dash, *Puppetry in Orissa* (Bhubaneswar: Padmini Dash, 1983); Mayadhara Mansingh, *History of Oriya Literature* (New Delhi: Sahitya Akademi, 1962).

P

PARSI THEATRE

Highly influential movement between the 1850s and 1930s. An aggregate of European techniques, pageantry, and local forms, enormously successful in the subcontinent and beyond, it may be seen as India's first modern commercial theatre. As the name indicates, it was subsidized to a great extent by Parsis, the Zoroastrian community of Persian origin that had migrated to western India over the centuries. Engaged in trading and shipbuilding, the Parsis became an important business force on the west coast by the early nineteenth century, and began to cultivate the arts and philanthropy. A Parsi, Sir Jamsetjee Jeejeebhoy, bought the colonial Bombay Theatre (built 1776) in 1835. In 1846 the Grant Road Theatre in Bombay, constructed by Jagannath Sunkersett, a prosperous merchant, began hosting plays in English, then in Marathi, Gujarati, and Urdu/Hindi.

The first Parsi production is normally dated to October 1853, by the Parsee Stage Players at Grant Road Theatre. Beginning as amateur groups that soon turned professional, many new troupes were launched in this period of rapid expansion when audiences grew large, made up mostly of Bombay's middle class. Major ones included the Parsee Stage Players, Victoria Theatrical Company, Elphinstone Dramatic Club, Zoroastrian Theatrical Club, Alfred Theatrical Company, Madan Theatres in Calcutta,

Empress Victoria Theatrical Company (1876–8, partly owned in Delhi), and Shakespeare Natak Mandali (1876–8). By the 1890s, they employed salaried dramatists and actors, built their own playhouses, and printed their scripts. They may have had many Parsi financiers, managers, performers, and patrons, but the personnel were by no means exclusively Parsi. Considerable cross-regional and cross-linguistic movement of artists and writers led to a heterogeneous mix at a broadly national level, with the result that Parsi companies not only worked in Gujarati, Urdu, Hindi, and even English, but inspired theatres in virtually every corner of India.

This created perhaps the largest ticket-buying audience in Indian stage history. By 1900, troupes had started in Karachi (New Shining Star), Lahore, Jodhpur, Agra, Aligarh, Meerut, Lucknow, and Hyderabad. Although Parsi theatre survived till the 1940s and beyond, notably with Fida Hussain (1899–1999) in Calcutta, after the 1920s a majority of the companies transformed into movie studios once the Indian cinema industry was inaugurated. Later, with the coming of the talkies (*Alam Ara*, 1931), most of them either closed down or grew into larger units; but one way or another, Parsi capital sustained at least three major studios (Imperial Film, Minerva Movietone, Wadia Movietone) and one distribution network, the Madan Theatres.

The form was highly eclectic and of unlike parts, taking stories from the Persian legendary *Shahnama*, the Sanskrit epic *Mahabharata*, the fabulous Arabic *Arabian Nights*, Shakespeare's tragedies and comedies, and Victorian melodrama. Its style came from all of the above as well as English amateur theatricals, British touring repertories, European realistic narrative structures, the singing and performing traditions of nineteenth-century Indian courtesans, and the visual regime of Indian painter Raja Ravi Varma (1848–1906). The combination of simple plot, clearly delineated characters, strong emotional values, spectacle, and moral tone made the plays enormously popular.

The mythological genre principally implied Hindu myths, and might therefore be called Puranic as well. It became a heavily complicated ideological site, marking off linguistic territorialities, for example Hindi from Urdu/Hindustani, and partitioning the cultural apparatus of one language from another, especially as in the drama of Radheshyam Kathavachak (1890–1963) and Narayan Prasad Betab (1872–1945). The *mythological drama, still in use elsewhere, can also be read as a familiar and resilient inventory of figures in shorthand adopted to reflect urgent concerns. According to Ashish Rajadhyaksha and Paul Willemen, the 'invocation of myths is less important than the way the stories are treated as a genre, modified as narratives or formally deployed as allegorical relays', dovetailing the mythological with the 'conservatively constructed notion of the social'.

The social drama was equally popular. It shaded into melodrama when propelled less by story and more by emotional effects, but its issues were mostly elaborated within the family—problems about equality, sexuality, education, and inheritance enacted within domestic terms. It might also be seen as melodrama in a twentieth-century milieu, extending melodrama by introducing pressures of modernization. In telling stories with reformist concerns such as the rehabilitation of young widows, alcohol abuse, female literacy, sectarianism, polygamy, Westernization, and the anxiety of determining national and regional identities, writers like Agha Hashr Kashmiri (1879–1935), Betab, and Kathavachak depicted a broader landscape than just a domestic one.

Famous Parsi plays, covering the range from romance to mythological and social, include *Indarsabha* ('Indra's Court'), *Gul Bakavali* ('Bakavali's Flower'), *Laila-Majnun* ('Laila and Majnun'), and *Shirin-Farhad* ('Shirin and Farhad') in numerous versions, Hashr's *Yahudi ki ladki* ('Jew's Daughter', 1913) and *Rustam aur Sohrab* ('Rustam and Sohrab', 1929), Betab's *Mahabharat* (1913), *Ramayan* (1915), *Kumari Kinnari* ('Kinnari Girl', 1928), and *Hamari bhul* ('Our Mistake', 1937), and Kathavachak's *Vir Abhimanyu* ('Heroic Abhimanyu', 1914), *Shravan Kumar* (1916), and *Bharatmata* ('Mother India', 1918). The several Shakespearean adaptations included Ahsan's *Khun-e-nahaq* ('Unjustified Murder', 1898, from *Hamlet*), *Shahid-e-wafa* ('Martyr to Constancy', 1898, from *Othello*), and *Dilfarosh* ('Merchant of Hearts', 1900, from *Merchant of Venice*), Hashr's *Safed khun* ('White Blood', 1906, from *King Lear*), and Betab's *Gorakhdhanda* ('Labyrinth', 1909, from *Comedy of Errors*).

The performing conditions of the new configuration marked a significant change in viewing habits, enduringly because the proscenium arch, brought to India by the British in the 1750s and elaborated afterwards, replaced the open arena that had been the most prevalent site up to this time. The closed space that supplanted it was often roughly made with tin and bamboo or architecturally constructed with brick and mortar. Inside, seating was put in (wooden benches and sofas, for instance), and because of the elaborate stage tricks incorporated into the performance, the proscenium was pushed back a fair distance from the spectators, with an orchestra pit, usually dug into the earth where the platform ended, between it and the audience. The time of performance was generally late evening. Plays ran for weeks, even years depending on their popularity, and went on tour sometimes for months together covering India, but also Burma, Ceylon, Malaya, Indonesia, and parts of Africa.

Because it encouraged new mimetic prospects, connected to the picture frame, and to the possibilities of reproducing perspectival space, the proscenium arch was by far the most significant adaptation of Western conventions that the Parsi theatre appropriated. It achieved mimesis, or verisimilitude, through backcloths painted on the principles of optical convergence or perspectival illusion. Images receded into the distant upstage and created a fiction of reality since the paintings were governed by the notion of the central vanishing point. The 'locations' appeared more real than anything produced previously. Generalized backdrops included forest, garden, street, palace, and sometimes heaven; besides, each company had its specific curtain, its legend of sorts. The Zoroastrian Club displayed King Ushtaspa's court, with Zarathustra holding the mythical ball of fire. At first, Europeans (specially Italians) created the 'drops'; later, Indian painters trained at art colleges. The Painter brothers (Anandrao, d. 1916, and Baburao, 1890–1954) were the best-known backdrop artists.

Parsi theatre as well as *Sangitnatak and early movies employed Ravi Varma's mise-en-scène. He drew historical, mythological, and modern figures in the foreground, and a dense environment behind contextualized or provided the attendant conditions or given circumstances for their behaviour. Scene designers imitated this way of describing locale, of demarcating background from foreground, accommodating the actors' postures and gestures into it. The backdrops manifested locations analogous to those summoned by the text, and therefore interpolated the performers into physically defined, almost tangible space wherein tableaux, the *effect* of these locations, might be composed; but they also offered a spectacular and fantastic space beyond the illusionistic one. While the narrative was grounded in the atmosphere produced by the materiality of the paintings and the architecture that enclosed them, paradoxically the world of romance and dream was also revealed and made possible through this very tangibility.

Since the backcloths were framed in the proscenium arch as in a window, there appeared to be, for the viewer, a continuity of space and time. Some sort of space, or the preceding part of the locale—the palace,

Master Fida Hussain at left in *Turki hur* (Moradabad, 1987)

forest, street—existed before it came into sight; one portion existed in the arch and another beyond the arch. This continuum resembled the way we experience time and space in ordinary life. Events follow one another, the arrow of time flies toward the future. This was new for the spectators, or at least unlike what they encountered in pre-modern theatrical forms. Thus the curtains allowed new means to tell a story, perceive dramatic continuity, create character formations. Hafiz *Abdullah's *Sakhawat Khudadost Badshah* ('Generous and Godly Emperor', 1890) for the Indian Imperial Theatrical Company had fourteen backdrops. The scenes delineated became increasingly more 'real' or illusionistic.

The Parsi theatre appropriated other Western presentational modes that produced formal and experiential mutations. It assimilated the five-act structure, related by extension to the proscenium that put the chronological narrative into place in the first instance. It rearranged the cognizance of stage time and space by intervening in the conventions of frontality in Indian theatric and visual traditions. The mechanical devices to operate flying figures and furniture, imported directly from melodramas in London, shaped the textual scenarios. The melodramatic style occasioned by stage machinery became so popular that, in a sense, conventional storytelling was redrafted. By definition, melodrama integrates spoken text with music; the category now also came to be applied to romantic plots that act on the audience's emotions without considering character elaboration or logic. An economically workable commercial stage in most urban centres fitted folk performance to the European proscenium, creating technical models and unexpected marvels; eventually, and paradoxically, these were put in the service of realism as being assembled at this time. Architectural and stage technologies allowed for vampire pits, flying beds, miraculous appearances and disappearances, best suited for romances and mythological tales.

Among the most popular actors of the Parsi stage were Dadabhai Patel (1840?–76), K.N. Kabraji, Jehangir Khambata, Cowasji Khatao, C.S. Nazir, Khurshedji Balliwala, Framji Appu, Sohrabji Oghra, Abdul Rahman Kabali, Sohrab Modi, Amrit Keshav Nayak, and Fida Hussain. Among the famous actresses, Mary Fenton or Mehrbai was the daughter of an English officer in the British Indian army, Gohar (Kayoum Mamajiwala) debuted as a child, and Patience Cooper and Seeta Devi (stage name of Renee Smith) performed with Madan Theatres in Calcutta. The light-classical musical vocabulary of Parsi theatre included ghazal, qawwali, *thumri*, *dadra*, and *hori*; the common instruments were harmonium or 'organ', clarinet, sarangi, tabla, and *nakkara* drums.   AK

Somnath Gupt, *The Parsi Theatre: Its Origins and Development* (Calcutta: Seagull, 2005).

PUNJABI THEATRE

The northern state of Punjab (which, prior to Partition, stretched from west Punjab in modern Pakistan eastward to Delhi, and even after 1947 encompassed the present Indian state of Haryana as well as parts of Himachal Pradesh) has a social and political history quite distinct from other states. Its folk traditions, in particular, have not had a rational historical continuity for complex reasons. As invaders found Punjab the easiest point of entry into India, political instability through the centuries made the most inroads into old social orders. Independence in 1947 fragmented Punjab, stimulating changes that created contradictions in the values and aesthetics of the populace. The division of Punjab between Pakistan and India disrupted the people's identity. A shattered psyche hovered tentatively between an articulation of dead chauvinism and an aspiration towards urbanization; it could neither create native art nor prosper culturally.

Commercialization, affected by popular cinema, pushed the arts in directions that had no resemblance to their origins. Inner compulsions of tradition that had always supported conventional forms of theatre were submerged under mass consumerist entertainment. This led folk forms to float, with no sustaining life force to anchor them. In another significant development, the Punjabi language began to be associated with the Sikh religion, influencing non-Sikh rural performers to switch over to Hindi, which had not been part of their creative expression. Consequently the folk actor was severed not only from language but also memory, emotions, sound, images, and history. Because of all these factors, Punjabi traditional forms—*Naqal, *Swang, Dhadi, Jangam, Gatka—raise the problematic question of garnering the essential from currently superficial, vague, and faceless idioms.   NMSC

Female impersonators in a Swang troupe

Drama meant for theatrical presentation came to be written in Punjabi only from the second decade of the twentieth century. Earlier, *kissa*s (love stories), *var*s (heroic tales), and *jangnama*s (battle narratives) formed the most popular oral literature. Gripping incidents, engaging encounters, tantalizing challenges, dramatic dialogue marked them in abundance, but they were not composed with performance in mind. Thus, *Bachittar natak* ('Unique Drama'), the seventeenth-century autobiography of Guru Gobind Singh, was so only in name. Yet the Sikh Gurus clearly knew of theatre: Guru Arjan wrote in the sixteenth century, 'We hear the *nat* (performer) sing on stage of the *natik* (drama), but our mind attains no peace.' Colonial rule in the late nineteenth century brought a literary and reformist resurgence, and the emergence of new forms. Giani Dit Singh's *Raj prabodh natak* ('Drama of Royal Enlightenment', 1890) was the first literary piece in dramatic mode. But the Khalsa Temperance Society's drama committee actually staged Makhmoor Chand's *Sharab Kaur* (1895) in Lahore and Amritsar, its personification of alcohol deriding the evil of intoxication.

Yet as late as 1910, Bhai Vir Singh's *Raja Lakhdata Singh* did not fulfil the basic conditions of theatre. Meant to exalt the Sikh doctrine by example rather than precept, it ended up as an allegory for reading aloud to gatherings at a religious site. No different dispensation awaited such plays aimed at Sikh reform and development of the Punjabi language as Arur Singh Taib's *Sukka samundar* ('Dry Sea', 1911) or Barrister Gurbakhsh Singh's *Natak Manmohan* ('Manmohan's Drama', 1913), written to draw attention to the problems of prostitution, alcoholism, and English education. Paradoxically enough, this education had by then prepared the terrain for Westernized theatre in Punjabi. The incentive came from Norah Richards (1876–1971), an Irish lady whose husband Philip Ernest Richards taught English in a Lahore college. She organized his students' cultural activities and, in a competition of indigenous plays in 1913, the one-act *Suhag* or *Dulhan* ('Bride') was adjudged the best, initiating Western-type drama in Punjabi. It was written by Ishwar Chander Nanda (1892–1961) in the realistic mode that thereafter became the chief mark of Punjabi theatre for at least four decades.

Parallel to the realistic form animated with reformist zeal, there also developed a more traditional dramaturgy. Chronicle plays, which Lala Kirpa Sagar (1875–1939) wrote to glorify Maharaja Ranjit Singh's rule, employed court intrigues, grandiose scenery, and spectacular characters much in the way in which *Parsi theatre presented hybrid versions of Shakespeare. Bawa

Budh Singh (1878–1931) composed sprawling satirical plays in which village buffoons ridiculed social taboos, obscurantist habits, and puritanical beliefs. Brij Lal Shastri (1894–1988) dramatized ancient myths and legends, in the process drawing amply upon the well-wrought conventions of *Sanskrit theatre. However, none of these modes dominated Punjabi playwriting; they remained residual, allowing more space for realism to grow with candour and resilience.

The second generation of Punjabi playwrights claimed to be progressive in technique and ideology. Sant Singh Sekhon (1908–97) was the most dexterous. Imbibing the influence as much of Marxist philosophy as of Freudian psychology, his plays drew their subject matter from Indian mythology, Sikh history, and contemporary society. Rather than stop at the depiction of class character, conflict, and exploitation, he represented consciousness, true or false, that covered experiences, relationships, feelings, and beliefs. An impression lingers that Sekhon's plays were marked by theatrical inadequacy. Actually, his aversion to prevalent stage conditions constrained their performance. His prolific but prolix contemporary, Gurdial Singh Phul (1911–84), veered from reformist realism to Sikh hagiography. Phul's historical *Sant sipahi* ('Saint Soldier'), directed by Sardarjit Bawa, ran for 500 performances.

As against Sekhon, Harcharan Singh (1914–2006) was able to coordinate his playwriting with the theatre to the best possible extent for two reasons: his attention remained focused on human foibles, and he took active interest in the staging of his own works. His wife, Dharam Kaur, was perhaps the first actress on the Punjabi stage. Although less versatile than Harcharan Singh, Gurdial Singh Khosla (1912–95) established Punjabi theatre in Delhi and used social comedy to criticize the worn-out marital system, religious bigotry, and political corruption. The pioneering director Sheila Bhatia (1916–2008), more than anybody else, aroused theatrical interest among Punjabi women in Delhi and invented Punjabi 'opera' with as many as fifty *sangitnat* (musicals), while Kartar Singh Duggal (1917–) contributed significantly to radio drama. The most theatrical in this corpus were the plays of Balwant Gargi (1916–2003), with his multiple influences of Sanskrit dramaturgy, folklore, Brechtian epic theatre, and Artaudian theatre of cruelty, shifting from the realistic to the mythopoeic. For Gargi, social taboos, sex, violence, and death became the new preoccupations.

In this respect, Gargi remains the peer of major dramatists of the next generation, comprising two recognizable trends. The first, of Paritosh Gargi

(1923–78) and Harsaran Singh (1929–94), used realism for psychological probing. Harsaran Singh was conspicuous for thematic boldness. The second, of Kapur Singh Ghuman (1927–86) and Surjit Singh Sethi (1928–95), took a surfeit of anti-illusionistic methods from Strindberg to Beckett: Ghuman's *Jiondi lash* ('Living Corpse', 1958) reflects Partition symbolically; Sethi's *King, mirza te sapera* ('King, Hero and Snake Charmer', 1965) reworks *Waiting for Godot*. Paritosh Gargi's first play, *Parchhaven* ('Shadows', 1956), mercilessly exposed religious bigotry and social obscurantism; his next, *Chhaleda* ('Will-o'-the-wisp', 1958), subjected a person with a wavering mind to microscopic scrutiny. Later, he contented himself with topical drama, so the early promise faded into the background. Something similar happened with Gurcharan Singh Jasuja (1925–), whose *Gaumukha shermukha* ('Cow-faced or Lion-faced', 1955) highlighted the oddities of daily reality, but whose subsequent plays do not leave any trace of development.

Punjabi drama's fourth generation, appearing on the scene in the 1970s, did not slacken interest in European drama. Rather, with Ajaib Kamal (1932–) and Ravinder Ravi (1938–), both domiciled abroad, it turned into an obsession. In Kamal's *Ghar vich baghiad* ('Wolf at Home', 1967) and *Langra asman* ('Lame Sky', 1978), sexual orgies, drinking bouts, mass suicide, frenzied escapades, and star wars figure to the amazement and discomfiture of audiences. Some argue that television impels him to indulge in this sort of experimentation. Ravi's *Bimar sadi* ('Sick Century', 1974), *Adhi rat dopehr* ('Midnight at Midday', 1983), *Ruh Panjab di* ('Spirit of Punjab', 1984), and *Cipher natak* ('Cipher Drama', 1987) are noteworthy. He brings together characters from many countries, does away with the fourth wall, includes revolving stages as thematic metaphors, and employs props from film, television, and video.

Their colleagues in India are less indiscriminate, more discreet. As a representative of one category, C.D. Sidhu (1938–) eschews Western borrowings. More interested in the native traditions of *Raslila, Naqal, akhara* (arena), and *chaukian* (hymn-singing sessions), he has authored over thirty plays ranging from *Bhajno* (1979), *Swami-ji* ('Swami, Sir', 1984), and *Kal college band ravega* (*The College Will Remain Closed Tomorrow*, 1984), to *Shakespeare di dhi* (*Shakespeare's Daughter*, 1986), *Ikkiewin manzil* ('Twenty-first Storey', 1999), and the award-winning trilogy *Bhagat Singh Shahid* ('Martyr Bhagat Singh', 2003). Ajmer Singh Aulakh (1942–) writes on life in the countryside, highlighting problems of small farmers. However, his presentation is so circumspect that his limited area does not project him as provincial. Maturing like Aulakh through youth theatre festivals but more innovative in technique, Atamjit Singh (1950–) nevertheless does not get carried away by novelty for its own sake and has succeeded abroad. Manjit Pal Kaur (1948–) is the only woman dramatist of importance. By feminizing patriarchal legends she subverts authoritarian customs and beliefs. The few younger writers of note include Swarajbir (1958–), Jagdish Sachdeva (1958–), and Pali Bhupinder Singh (1965–).

Theatre is presently in poor shape: active groups do stage plays but on an ad hoc basis, only when they manage to get financial support. Although apparently unlike in attitude and approach, the activist Gursharan Singh (1929–) who aims at radical, albeit provocative, messages through improvisation, and the director Neelam Man Singh Chowdhry (1949–) who has mainly presented sophisticated but hybridized adaptations of European masterpieces, are similar in bringing the rural and urban together. Gursharan conducts theatre for social change in short travelling enactments deriding politics, police, corruption, and communalism alike. Chowdhry has won national and international laurels with her Naqqal female impersonators in richly colourful proscenium productions. Only when Punjabi theatre also creates a thriving middle ground between the two poles will it come into its own.

The relationship between dramatist and audience, performance and reception, has not seen much experimentation of late apart from the work of Gurcharan Singh Chani (1951–) in participatory community theatre. Successful younger producers include Kewal Dhaliwal (1964–) with over 1500 performances of 150 productions, Sahib Singh, Hansa Singh, and

Neelam Man Singh Chowdhry's production of *Hir-Ranjha* (The Company, Chandigarh, 1985)

Satish Verma, who raise hopes for the future. The director-actor couples Harpal and Nina Tiwana, Pran and Sunita Sabharwal, and Devinder and Jaswant Daman have contributed significantly, and the engineer-playwright Jatinder Brar has established a regular theatre hub in Amritsar.   TSG/KU

J.S. Grewal, *The Emergence of Punjabi Drama* (Amritsar: Guru Nanak Dev University, 1986); Surjit Singh Sethi, *The Theatre of Ibsenites in Punjab: A Critical Study* (Patiala: Madaan, 1976); Pankaj K. Singh, *Re-presenting Woman: Tradition, Legend and Panjabi Drama* (Shimla: Indian Institute of Advanced Study, 2000); Kamlesh Uppal, *Generative Impact of Absurdism on Punjabi Theatre* (Patiala: Punjabi University, 1987).

r

RAJASTHANI THEATRE

Although Rajasthani, spoken in the north-western state of Rajasthan, is an ancient language originating supposedly in the eighth century, under feudal patronage it curiously did not develop any theatrical traditions apart from folk styles away from the courts, such as *Khyal, *Rasdhari, or *Tamasa, and *puppetry famous as *Kathputli. Only as late as 1900, under the influence of *Parsi theatre, did drama come to be written in Rajasthani.

The beginning of the twentieth century brought in the era of social reforms and the national movement; many social and historical plays written for the Parsi theatre became very popular. Some were banned and the playwrights imprisoned by the British government. Taking the cue from Parsi theatre, authors writing novels and short stories in Rajasthani also took to theatre, as they thought it a powerful weapon of propaganda against social and political evils. Through their plays, they tried to force society to react and eradicate these problems.

Shiv Charan Bhartiya (1854–1919), the first Rajasthani dramatist, published *Kesarvilas* in 1900, followed by *Budhapa ki sagai* ('Old-age Betrothal', 1906) and *Phataka janjal* ('Snare of Future Trade', 1907). In his introduction to *Phataka janjal*, Bhartiya wrote that his main aim was to show social evils to the Rajasthani people. Bhagwati Prasad Daruka wrote *Vriddh vivah natak* ('Play of Elders' Marriage', 1903), dealing with old men wedding young girls, and *Bal vivah natak* ('Play of Child Marriage', 1918). Other notable plays included Gulab Chand Nagauri's *Marwadi mausar aur sagai janjal* ('Rituals of the Dead and Snares of Betrothal', 1923) and Balkrishna Lahoti's *Kanya bikri* ('Sale of Girls', 1938).

Narayandas Agarwal made an interesting experiment in *Maharana Pratap* (1924), where different characters delivered their dialogue in their own languages: Maharaja Prithviraj spoke the dialect of Bikaner, Akbar spoke in Persianized Urdu, Maharana Pratap and his courtiers in Mewari, and the Bhils (who formed the core of Pratap's army) used their tribal language. We can well presume that the work may have remained unstaged because in those days it was difficult to find actors speaking so many tongues.

However, these playwrights neither could achieve their purpose of social reform nor could they develop a Rajasthani theatre, because most of them were not closely associated with theatre and were ignorant about the needs of the stage. Almost all their plays are unstageable, with too many small scenes and occasionally very long speeches. In *Phataka janjal*, one character expounds for eleven pages. The Parsi theatre did not take up these plays because, first, they were unsuitable for professional theatre and, second, it was a national theatre movement that gave importance to Hindi and Urdu. It did not cater to drama in regional languages, although it influenced most regional theatres and later the films.

Thus most Rajasthani plays were just staged sporadically by amateur groups and failed to reach the masses. They remained in published form to be read. Today, several young dramatists are writing in Rajasthani, notable among them Arjun Dev Charan, and directors like Bhanu Bharti (1947–) have conducted research into such local forms as the Gavari, performed by the Bhils, but as yet the efforts to develop a Rajasthani theatre have not met with much success.   RS

Hiralal Maheshwari, *History of Rajasthani Literature* (New Delhi: Sahitya Akademi, 1980).

S

SANSKRIT THEATRE

Indian tradition preserved in the *Natyasastra* offers a mythical account of theatre's origin and its religious roots. According to the myth, dharma prevailed in *satyayuga* ('age of truth'; metaphorically, the golden age), therefore people were ignorant of pain and sorrow. In *tretayuga* (the silver age), dharma weakened and suffering arose in their lives. The gods, worried about human welfare, approached Brahma, the Creator, under the leadership of Indra and prayed to him to produce an object of sport (*kridaniyaka*) to give pleasure to people's eyes and ears. Brahma took recourse to yoga, selected the text (*pathya*) from the *Rig Veda*, song and music (*gita* and *atodya*) from the *Sama Veda*, acting (*abhinaya*) from the *Yajur Veda*, and aesthetic sentiment (*rasa*) from the *Atharva Veda* to create a fifth Veda, the *natyaveda* ('theatre knowledge'). He also created tradition in the form of *itihasa*, describing the exploits of gods, demigods, demons, and humans, on the basis of which dramatic scripts could be written. Brahma invited the gods to receive this unique creation, but they declined. The learned commentator on the *Natyasastra*, Abhinavagupta (950–1025), explains that they did so because they only knew happiness, whereas drama is the saga of happiness as well as suffering.

The gods called the sage Bharata, practising penance (*tapas*) and surrounded by his hundred sons and disciples, to receive this sacred art of theatre. Brahma commanded him to stage a play celebrating the victory of gods over demons. Bharata, along with his sons and pupils, rehearsed the play based on the legendary battle between gods and demons. Angry, the demons created trouble and obstacles, for example, causing the loss of the performers' memory. The show failed. Then Brahma bade Visvakarman, the divine architect, to build an auditorium (*prekshagriha*) presided over by the gods, demigods, and even demons, thus a symbolic replica of the entire universe. The demons accepted this neutrality and the gods were overjoyed by the new creation. Siva contributed to theatre with the *tandava* dance expressing vigorous emotion, his spouse Parvati gave the tender and sensuous *lasya* dance, while Vishnu was responsible for creating four styles or characteristics (*vritti*) essential to the effect of drama. Bharata then brought this celestial art to earth.

F.B.J. Kuiper reveals some interesting aspects in the structure of Sanskrit theatre. He draws attention to the cosmogonic battle between the gods and demons during which they not only employed normal weapons but also verbal combat. He refers to the use of *vivac* (literally, mutual verbal dispute), positing a connection between this cosmic fight and the preliminaries (*purvaranga*) of Indian performance. Kuiper and Christopher Byrski view Sanskrit drama as the re-enactment of cosmic creation and trace the structure of Sanskrit theatre to the re-enactment of that cosmic event. After all, theoretical treatises constantly mention *trailokya* ('triple universe', meaning heaven, sky, and earth) in defining the nature of *natya*.

Unmistakably, all the essential elements of theatre are present in the Vedas, obviously derived from ancient Indian life. A number of hymns in the form of dialogue (*samvada sukta*) exist in the *Rig Veda* itself, expressively recognized as such by early Indian tradition. The eminent German Indologist, Max Mueller, conjectured that they were possibly acted by two parties, an idea approved by the French scholar Sylvain Levi. Von Schroeder presented an elaborate theory showing the close relation between *music, *dance, and theatre. J. Hertel opined that the sung Vedic hymns represent the beginnings of a dramatic art, and A.B. Keith viewed them as dramatic. Attempts have also been made to relate the origins of Indian theatre to sacrificial *ritual and fertility drama. The dialogue hymns have been understood in this context. Richard Pischel even explained the combination of prose and verse in Sanskrit theatre as a relic of this early form of literature.

Scholars have speculated on the presence of the germ of theatrical performance in Vedic rituals, especially in the purchase of *soma* (a creeper that was pressed for its juice, served as an offering in the *soma* sacrifice). The *mahavrata* ('great vow') was another such rite intended to strengthen the sun at winter solstice, so that it may resume its vigour and make the earth fruitful. It involved a struggle between a Vaisya, whose colour had to be white, and a Sudra, black in complexion. However, Alfred Hillebrandt and Sten Konow maintain that it is an error to look to religious ceremonies for the origin of Indian theatre. They admit that these rituals have a share in its development, but suggest that the ceremonies themselves are deeply rooted in popular *mime which, with the epic, lie at the root of Sanskrit theatre.

Recitation of the epics, *gatha* (paeans to the gods), and *narasamsi* (legends honouring great men and women) had a long continuity and popularity, attested in literature. *Suta*s, *kusilava*s, and *gathaka*s comprised the community of reciters. Patanjali's *Mahabhashya* ('Great Discourse', second century BC) mentions a powerful tradition of *granthika*s and *sobhanika*s who not only recited the legends of binding Bali and killing Kamsa, but enacted them too. Albrecht Weber views this as a reference to mime. The Sitabenga cave inscriptions in Chhattisgarh suggest public poetic or dramatic presentations by the second century BC. The subjects of recitative and histrionic performances, like Krishna's exploits mentioned in the *Mahabhashya* and *Harivamsa* ('Hari's Dynasty', *c.* second century AD), indicate the religious nature of ancient theatre. The close connection of religion with performance still survives in the innumerable forms of temple theatre scattered throughout India.

Heinrich von Lueders saw the origin of Sanskrit plays in *shadow theatre, apparently referred to in Asoka's fourth rock edict (260 BC) and in the *Therigatha* Buddhist canon. Critics rejected his theory. However, Pischel held that *puppetry was the source of Sanskrit theatre and, moreover, its home was India, whence it spread all over Asia. From puppet theatre, he suggested, the words *sutradhara* (literally 'string-holder', the troupe leader) and *sthapaka* ('establisher', the director) passed over to legitimate drama. In Pischel's view, the *vidushaka* or clown also owed his origin to the puppet play. Admittedly, puppetry originated in India and has been referred to in the *Mahabharata* and many other literary works, but it presumes the existence of drama, on which it must be based. According to Hillebrandt, early dates for puppet theatre prove the even earlier existence of drama.

A few Western scholars argue that the impetus for the creation of Sanskrit theatre as an independent form might have come from Indian contact with Greeks between the third century BC and first century AD, especially through the presentation of Greek plays at royal courts in Bactria,

Punjab, and Gujarat. Weber generated this theory, repudiated by Pischel but strengthened by Ernst Windisch. Levi refuted this view, for there is no evidence of Greek drama performed in India at that time, and Keith acknowledged the lack of such proof. Plutarch (*c.* 46–120 AD) described a theatre production at the Parthian court, and similar performances might have taken place in other provinces that formed the empire of Alexander (reigned 336–323 BC), but Plutarch is silent about such activities in India. Therefore, any speculation on Greek influence is far-fetched.

The argument based on the use of *yavanika* (from *yavana*, primarily applied to Ionians, or Greeks, and secondarily applied to men from the Hellenistic empire, like Egyptians, Syrians, and Bactrians) for the curtain on the Sanskrit stage is also extremely weak. In fact, Greek theatre did not have any curtain from which the concept could have been borrowed. Considering the basically different natures of Sanskrit and Greek drama, and the extant references by the grammarian Panini (fifth or sixth century BC) to a tradition of *natasutra* ('actors' sutra'), the theory of the emergence of Sanskrit theatre under the foreign influence of Greeks or Sakas (as advanced by Levi) stands rejected. The vibrant history of theatre *theory and practice presupposes not only a gradual and systematic emergence of Sanskrit drama, but also the complete codification of performance and deep thinking on the nature of theatre and aesthetic experience.

The earliest available Sanskrit plays are the thirteen ascribed to Bhasa (between second century BC and second century AD). None of them states explicitly either in the prologue or the colophon—the usual conventions in

Bhasa's *Madhyamavyayoga* directed by K.N. Panikkar (Sopanam, Thiruvananthapuram, 1978)

Sanskrit drama—that it is Bhasa's work. In fact, their discovery and attribution to him at the beginning of the twentieth century created a controversy. However, striking thematic and technical similarities in them and the certain identification of *Svapna-Vasavadatta* ('Vasavadatta in the Dream') with Bhasa established their authorship. The plays embrace tales derived from the *Ramayana, Mahabharata*, Krishna lore, popular history, and love stories. They are marked by significant possibilities of performatory elaboration, as evident to this day from their presence in the traditional repertoire of *Kutiyattam.

*Kalidasa, the greatest Indian dramatist, remembers Bhasa with reverence. He drew inspiration from Bhasa, but himself became the paramount influence on future generations. Regarded as the supreme poet of love with the highest possible refinement and insight, he attained the culmination of genius in the world-renowned *Abhijnana-Sakuntala* ('Sakuntala Recognized'). If Bhasa sometimes appears to rebel against the conventions laid down by Bharata, Kalidasa offers the model of the Natyasastric tradition of playwriting. Asvaghosha, a Buddhist author adorning the court of Kanishka (first–second century AD), represents another ideology in Sanskrit drama. From available fragments of his work, we gather that his subject matter was conversion to Buddhism.

Sudraka (*c*. second century AD) in *Mricchakatika* (*The Little Clay Cart*) achieves astonishing heights of treatment given to contemporary social realities. His vibrant masterpiece offers a refreshing and subversive notion of love between a generous but poor Brahman and a delicate courtesan inspired by romantic ideals. In the background we see a cruel ruler, the struggling common people, the air of revolt, gamblers, monks, helpless judiciary, and prevailing fraud. On the other hand, Visakhadatta (*c*. fifth century AD) derived material from history in *Mudra-Rakshasa* ('Rakshasa's Signet Ring'), an unusual play of political intrigue between Chandragupta Maurya's minister Kautilya and Rakshasa, minister of the ousted king.

The three plays of Harsha (reigned 606–48) have been said to reveal Buddhist compassion and introduce models of romantic drama neatly structured in keeping with the plot technique taught in the *Natyasastra*. In addition, traces of folk music and dance in his *Ratnavali* mark the beginning of a new era in Sanskrit theatre. Bhatta Narayana (*c*. seventh century) develops the tragic character of Asvatthama in *Venisamhara* ('Tying of the Braid'), based on the story in the *Mahabharata*. The powerful Bhavabhuti (seventh–eighth century) is often considered Kalidasa's equal, and his play *Uttara-Ramacarita* ('Rama's Later Exploits') also contains strong evocation of *karuna rasa* (pathos). Replete with epic qualities, it presents life in diverse dimensions.

At about the same time in south India, Bodhayana and Mahendravikrama were unmatched in the established comic form of **prahasana*, incorporating realistically woven wit, humour, and satire. Bodhayana's *Bhagavadajjukiya* ('The Sage and the Courtesan') is a unique farce of situation, where a sadhu exchanges souls with a lovelorn hetaera and each begins to behave like the other. Mahendravikrama's *Mattavilasa* ('Intoxicated Delights') satirizes the perverse lives of mendicants, male and female. It is a vocal commentary on the hollowness of 'holy' people of different sects contemporaneous to the author.

Rajasekhara (ninth–tenth century) is credited with introducing the new Prakrit genre of **sattaka*, as well as setting the trend of the minor forms called *uparupaka*s, which developed in later centuries. It is generally held that after the tenth century, no significant plays were written in Sanskrit. In fact, they began to assume other forms in the hands of Murari (eighth–ninth century), Kshemisvara (tenth century), Krishna Misra (eleventh century), Jayadeva and Vatsaraja (twelfth century), Rupa Gosvamin and Kavikarnapura (sixteenth century), Anandaraya Makhin (seventeenth–eighteenth century), and Gokulanath Sharman (eighteenth century). However, creative innovations slowed down in the medieval period. Sanskrit theatre still survives, in the shape of the Kutiyattam and *Krishnattam traditional genres in Kerala.

Sanskrit drama was divided into *rupaka*s, the ten major forms, and *uparupaka*s. The *rupaka*s comprised **nataka*, **samavakara*, **vyayoga*, **dima*, **ihamriga*, **utsrishtikamka*, **prakarana*, *prahasana*, **bhana*, and **vithi*. Their plots were broadly classified as those known from tradition, which the playwright derived from myths, legends, and history, or as those newly

Ravana in a Kutiyattam performance

created by his imagination. The former category included *nataka*, *samavakara*, *vyayoga*, *dima*, and *ihamriga*; in the latter figured *prakarana*, *prahasana*, and *bhana*. *Utsrishtikamka* sometimes was sourced from tradition, sometimes from invention. *Vithi* was a class in itself, and many forms took elements from it. *Uparupaka* forms included the *natika* and *sattaka*.

Vrittis (characteristic styles of speech, mind, and body) also played an important role in determining the structure of Sanskrit drama. For instance, *nataka* and *prakarana* had all the *vrittis*, while the rest varied. *Dima* had only two *vrittis* whereas *utsrishtikamka* primarily used *bharati* (spoken) *vritti*. The number of acts was the next common distinction. *Vyayoga*, *ihamriga*, *bhana*, *vithi*, and *utsrishtikamka* were one-act plays. *Samavakara* was in three acts and *dima* (some authorities add *ihamriga*) in four. *Nataka* and *prakarana* had five to ten acts. Abhinavagupta maintains that 'pure' *prahasana* was one-act, whereas 'mixed' *prahasana* consisted of many acts. The types of heroes, namely *dhirodatta* ('firm and noble'), *dhiralalita* ('firm and playful'), *dhiroddhata* ('firm and haughty'), and *dhirasanta* ('firm and peaceful'), together with the types of heroines and accompanying characters, were also important in determining the categories.

Sanskrit theatre stressed the delineation or portrayal of *bhava (emotive state). Performers evoked to the audience these *bhavas* which, through powerful *abhinaya* (acting), were transformed into the ideal, central aesthetic experience of *rasa*. The *Natyasastra* also laid down two modes of theatrical representation. The first, *lokadharmi*, was nearer to the way things are seen in ordinary life, more natural. The second, *natyadharmi*, was more conventional. However, a dialogue between them always existed; they were not completely opposite modes, but shared some complementarity. *Lokadharmi* may be seen as having survived in innumerable Indian folk forms, whereas *natyadharmi* is viewed in classical dance or dance-drama.

The whole concept of the playhouse and *architecture of theatre space was related to cosmogony. A host of gods, goddesses, as well as demigods (Asuras, Rakshasas, Yakshas, Gandharvas, Kinnaras, Apsaras, Nagas) were given place in the auditorium and worshipped in order to protect it and the performance. An elaborate scheme of preliminaries titled *purvaranga* consisted of elements that were *paramarthika* ('supreme aims'), such as the *nandi* (invocation), and others with a definite theatrical purpose. Just as Brahma occupies the central place on stage, so did the *sutradhara* in the preliminaries, accompanied by his *pariparsvikas* (assistants), who represented the Vedic gods Indra and Varuna, whereas in the text the *nayaka* (hero) represented Indra, the *vidushaka* Varuna, and the heroine goddess Sarasvati.

The *sutradhara*, *vidushaka*, and *nayaka* formed the basic cast of Sanskrit theatre. Their evolution determined the development of traditional Indian theatre itself. The *sutradhara* survived mostly in temple theatre, while in forms enacted outside temples, the *vidushaka* took the dominant place, especially when they came to deal with changing social reality.

The linguistic structure of Sanskrit drama is also very significant, as well as the highly refined aesthetic theory of *dhvani*, or literary suggestion. From the very beginning, multilingualism provided a unique theatricality to the script. The simultaneous presence of Sanskrit (spoken by upper-class characters), the commoners' Prakrit (spoken by women and lower classes), and even Apabhramsa (later regional forms of Prakrit) infused textual strength. This feature survives in Kutiyattam, where the *vidushaka* elaborates his Prakrit dialogue into Malayalam, a modern Indian language.

Music was an integral part of theatre from the start—in order to provide pleasure (*ranjana*) in the recitation of the text (*pathya*). The *Natyasastra*, Kalidasa, and some later dramatists speak of the employment of *dhruva* songs. Certainly, musical integration began with the introduction of *gita* (song) and *atodya* (music), which served not only to determine the pace and rhythm of movement, gait, exits, and entrances, but also to incorporate *lasyanga*s (the feminine component of dance) into the play. The change in Sanskrit theatre from *rupaka*s to *uparupaka*s is marked by the increasing use of music. The tendency was already present in the period of Kalidasa and *Harivamsa*, and gathered momentum with the passage of time. Music became more essential and *uparupaka*s were often called *sangitaka*s ('song works'). Dance, too, acquired a more dominant place in the dramatic and theatrical structure. References in Abhinavagupta's *Abhinavabharati* ('Abhinava Speaks', tenth–eleventh century), Saradatanaya's *Bhavaprakasana* ('*Bhava*-expression', twelfth–thirteenth century), and other texts verify this conclusion.

The connection between 'folk' forms and Sanskrit performance is also old. The detailed stage directions in Kalidasa's *Vikramorvasiya* ('Urvasi Won by Valour'), a unique play from this point of view, reveal extensive employment of music and dance in production. Many of the terms are not traceable either to the *Natyasastra* or later treatises. They appear to have been taken from the popular theatre of the early medieval age, and prove that Kalidasa's script had an unbroken tradition of performance up to that period. A reference to the staging of Harsha's *Ratnavali* in Damodaragupta's *Kuttanimatam* ('Thoughts on Bawds', eighth century) supports the rationale for a continuous theatre history. Abhinavagupta's intimate and deep understanding of the practical aspect of the *Natyasastra* also proves the undiluted growth of that tradition as late as the tenth century. Kallinatha's elaborate choreographical account of the *nandi* in *Vikramorvasiya* makes it clear that not only Sanskrit drama in general, but that play in particular continued to be staged in his time (sixteenth century) and the style was highly dance-oriented.

Sanskrit theatre was holistic, consisting of a highly evolved text, pre-written as well as orally circulating among the community of artists. Although the manuscript tradition persisted (for example, the eighteenth century saw the emergence of Sanskrit *Kuravanji texts in Tamil Nadu), and Sanskrit plays were written sporadically right up to the present, the floating oral version easily grasped by an audience fully familiar with its story, if not content, gradually strengthened and became popular over time. It turned into the main vehicle for performance by traditional artists in different languages from the medieval period onward. In the nineteenth century, classic Sanskrit plays again offered models of structure and style for dramatists in the nascent regional literatures. The rediscovery of the *Natyasastra* and Bhasa excited scholars and artists in Sanskrit dramatic performance, nearly extinct in the twentieth century. The search for an identity in Indian theatre after Independence also resulted in a serious inquiry into both traditional forms and classical Sanskrit sources. As a result, revivals of Sanskrit plays took place under directors like K.N. Panikkar (1928–)in Kerala and actors like Daji Bhatawadekar (1921–) in Maharashtra. KDT

Robert Antoine, *Greek Tragedy and Sanskrit Drama* (Calcutta: Writers Workshop, 1985); G.K. Bhat, *Sanskrit Drama* (New Delhi: Ajanta, 1985); G.K. Bhat, *Theatrical Aspects of Sanskrit Drama* (Pune: Bhandarkar Oriental Research Institute, 1983); G.K. Bhat,

D.G. Godse's *Natyasastra*-inspired set for Kalidasa's *Sakuntala* (director Vijaya Mehta, Bombay, 1979)

Tragedy and Sanskrit Drama (Bombay: Popular Prakashan, 1974); S.C. Bhatt, *Drama in Ancient India* (New Delhi: Amrit, 1961); V.G. Bhatta (ed.), *Studies in the Sanskrit Drama* (Dharwar: Students Own Book Depot, 1927); Biswanath Bhattacharya, *Sanskrit Drama and Dramaturgy* (Delhi: Sharada, 1994); M. Christopher Byrski, *Concept of Ancient Indian Theatre* (New Delhi: Munshiram Manoharlal, 1974); Rita Chattopadhyay, *Modern Sanskrit Dramas of Bengal* (Calcutta: Sanskrit Pustak Bhandar, 1992); Siddheswar Chattopadhyay, *Theatre in Ancient India* (New Delhi: Manohar, 1993); Michael Coulson (ed.), *Three Sanskrit Plays* (Harmondsworth: Penguin, 1981); Minakshi Dalal, *Conflict in Sanskrit Drama* (Bombay: Somaiya, 1973); S.A. Dange and S.S. Dange, *Critiques on Sanskrit Dramas* (New Delhi: Aryan Books, 1994); Ratnamayidevi Dikshit, *Women in Sanskrit Dramas* (Delhi: Meharchand Lachhmandas, 1964); S.N. Ghosal, *The Inception of the Sanskrit Drama* (Calcutta: Calcutta Book House, 1977); Robert E. Goodwin, *The Playworld of Sanskrit Drama* (Delhi: Motilal Banarsidass, 1998); E.P. Horrwitz, *The Indian Theatre: A Brief Survey of the Sanskrit Drama* (London: Blackie, 1912); S. Subramonia Iyer, *Sanskrit Dramas* (Delhi: Sundeep, 1984); A.B. Keith, *The Sanskrit Drama* (Oxford: Clarendon, 1924); Sten Konow, *The Indian Drama* (Calcutta: General Printers, 1969); F.B.J. Kuiper, *Varuna and Vidusaka: On the Origin of the Sanskrit Drama* (Amsterdam: North-Holland, 1979); P. Lal (ed.), *Great Sanskrit Plays* (New York: New Directions, 1964); Sylvain Levi, *The Theatre of India* (Calcutta: Writers Workshop, 1978); Michael Lockwood and A. Vishnu Bhat (eds), *Meta-theater and Sanskrit Drama* (Madras: Tambaram, 1994); Anjala Maharishi, *A Comparative Study of Brechtian and Classical Indian Theatre* (New Delhi: National School of Drama, 2000); E.W. Marasinghe, *The Sanskrit Theatre and Stagecraft* (Delhi: Sri Satguru, 1989); Tarla Mehta, *Sanskrit Play Production in Ancient India* (Delhi: Motilal Banarsidass, 1995); Madhusudan Pati, *Sanskrit Drama* (Delhi: Amar, 1991); V. Raghavan, *The Social Play in Sanskrit* (Bangalore: Indian Institute of World Culture, 1966); V. Raghavan, *Some Old Lost Rama Plays* (Annamalainagar: Annamalai University, 1961); Adya Rangacharya, *Drama in Sanskrit Literature* (Bombay: Popular Prakashan, 1967); S. Ranganath, *Post Independence Sanskrit Drama* (Bangalore: Payonidhi, 1994); Montgomery Schuyler, *A Bibliography of the Sanskrit Drama* (New York: AMS, 1965); Indu Shekhar, *Sanskrit Drama: Its Origin and Decline* (Leiden: E.J. Brill, 1960); Kamalesh Datta Tripathi, *Sanskrit Theatre* (New Delhi: Shri Ram Centre for Performing Arts, 1998); J.A.B. Van Buitenen (ed.), *Two Plays of Ancient India* (New York: Columbia University Press, 1968); Rachel Van M. Baumer and James R. Brandon (eds), *Sanskrit Drama in Performance* (Honolulu: University of Hawaii, 1981); M.L. Varadpande, *Ancient Indian and Indo-Greek Theatre* (New Delhi: Abhinav, 1981); Henry Wells, *The Classical Drama of India* (London: Asia, 1963); Henry Wells, *Sanskrit Plays from Epic Sources* (Baroda: M.S. University, 1968); Henry Wells (ed.), *Six Sanskrit Plays* (New York: Asia, 1964); H.H. Wilson, *A Complete Account of the Dramatic Literature of Hindus* (Varanasi: Chowkhamba, 1962); H.H. Wilson, *Select Specimens of the Theatre of the Hindus* (London: Parbury, Allen, 1835); H.H. Wilson, et al., *The Theatre of the Hindus* (Calcutta: Susil Gupta, 1955).

SINDHI THEATRE

In the absence of internal or external evidence, it is difficult to determine the precise antiquity of folk theatre in Sindh, the western province surrounding the lower Indus river that became part of Pakistan in 1947. We can date only those forms that existed in the eighteenth century and those about the beginnings of which we have some acceptable evidence.

The Arabs conquered Sindh in AD 712 and remained in power up to 1032, when the local Sumra chieftains drove them out. The Arab objectives were to ransack the invaded country, to spread Islam at the point of the sword, and to destroy completely the local culture. This is what happened in Sindh, too, and the literature of the Hindu period has perished beyond recall. However, we can safely surmise that Sindh followed the same earlier cultural traditions as other areas of India. Theatrical forms must have been there, just as we know that a Sindhi *Mahabharata* existed prior to the Arab occupation, though texts are not extant to support this view.

The first performatory style that we find in Sindh is Chheja, a group dance with sticks and music, akin to Gujarati Dandia. It goes back to the twelfth century when the originators apparently toured villages urging people to fight for their rights. In time, the purpose changed and Chheja is now associated with the Sindhi New Year, weddings, and festivals. Another old form, practised since at least the sixteenth century, is Lorau, meaning desert performance. The eastern part of Sindh is desert, where the mode of transport was and still is a camel. Even in western Sindh no other means of communication was available during those times. The cameleers performed Lorau on camelback, carrying their passengers in caravans. Lorau involved reciting *dohiro*, a Sindhi verse medium, following the storylines of familiar folk legends.

*Galihyun, or tales with ballads, comprise the oldest form of Sindhi theatre, dating to the fourteenth century, if not earlier. *Munaziro or Jhero, and *Bhagati, date from the eighteenth century at the latest. While Hindus participated in *Sanga, Muslims patronized *Tamasho. Eight folk romances of Sindh—the stories of Koel and Dipak, Sorath and Rai Dyach, Mumal and Rano, Lila and Chanesar, Nuri and Jam Tamachi, Umar and Marui, Suhini and Mehar, Sasui and Punhu—gave birth to a formidable oral literature, especially during the medieval period. These tales form the core of the folk theatre performed by the *bhagats*, *bhatts*, and *charans*, minstrel bards, in the village streets of Sindh.

The tradition of folk drama continued in the modern period. *Mumal-Mendhro* ('Mumal and Mendhro', 1922) by Khanchand Daryani (1898–1965) was staged by Sindh College, Karachi, in 1928. *Umar-Marui* by Lalchand Amardinomal Jagtiani (1884–1954) was produced in 1925 by Rabindranath Literary and Dramatic Club in Hyderabad (Sindh). A play based on the Suhini-Mehar story, composed by Dingomal Thadhani in 1926, was never performed. Others inspired by folklore included Mangalsingh Ramchandani's *Sasui-Punhu* (1932), staged by College Students Dramatic Club, Karachi; Lilaram Pherwani's *Hikri rat* ('One Night', 1936); and *Mumal-Rano* (1941) and *Pakhe mein Padmini* ('Padmini in a Hut', 1943) by Ram Panjwani (1911–87). Nanikram Mirchandani (1890–1946) wrote his *Suhini-Mehar* in 1946, but it did not appear on stage. Panjwani came out with capsule versions of seven popular tales in 1952; all appeared in Bombay theatres and had repeat performances elsewhere.

Some critics believe that Haji Imam Bux 'Khadim' composed the first original Sindhi drama, *Hira-Ranjho* ('Hira and Ranjho'), in 1879, but others raise doubts about its date. Therefore, *Laila-Majnu* ('Laila and Majnu', 1880) by Mirza Qalich Beg (1853–1929) is acknowledged as the first modern Sindhi play; 1980 was celebrated as the centenary year of Sindhi drama in India and Pakistan, and Qalich Beg, who wrote thirty-six plays, is acclaimed as the father of Sindhi drama. The first staged work was his *Gul Bakavali* ('Bakavali's Flower', 1894), translated from one of the hits of the Parsi and *Gujarati theatre companies that had started visiting Sindh to perform their mythological productions, which provided an impetus to Sindhi theatre. Indeed, up to the 1930s, Sindhi drama seemed to be under the impact of *Parsi theatre, at least from the technical point of view, if not thematically.

Several dramatic societies were responsible for the growth and development of modern drama in Sindh. The pioneering D.J. Sindh College Amateur Dramatic Society, founded in 1894, brought on stage Lilaramsingh Lalwani (1867–1941), Qalich Beg, and other dramatists; in its twenty-year existence, it performed and published fifteen plays, a major achievement. During this period, Sindhi writers were afflicted by theatre fever and many other societies mushroomed in various parts of Sindh. The Dharam Upkar Amateur Dramatic Society, established in 1897 in Shikarpur, had as its main writer the founder himself, Thakurdas Nagrani, who also composed the music. The first play produced by this society was

Gangaramsingh Atmasingh's *Shakuntla-Dushyanta* ('Shakuntala and Dushyanta', published 1898). During its life of eighteen years, it staged over twenty works, the last being Gagansingh's *Dr Shyam Narain* (1915).

Qalich Beg's *Khurshid* was the first script presented by the Hyderabad Pleaders Club (established 1905), which did not remain actively involved in production but still put on a few popular plays. The Chandika Amateur Dramatic Society, founded in 1907 in Larkana by the well-known poet Kishinchand Tirthdas Khatri 'Bevas' (1885–1947), premiered all his plays. The first, *Khubsurat bala* ('Beautiful Trouble'), adapted Agha Hashr's Urdu drama of the same title. *Shaka jo shikar* ('Victim of Doubt') was the last, staged in 1931. Seven of Bevas's socially relevant one-act scripts were collected in *Indalathi* ('Rainbow', 1931).

With the establishment of the Hyderabad Amateur Dramatic Society in 1912, the change in theme of Sindhi drama became evident. The society's mainstay, Nanikram Mirchandani, introduced social realism. It staged his first play, *Farebi fitno* ('Deceitful Brawl'), in 1914, followed by many socially aware works, including four by the eminent Khanchand Daryani, closing down after his *Insan kina shaitan* ('Man or Devil', 1930, performed 1931). In 1917 Chandumal Khatri founded the Saraswat Brahmin Dramatic Society, which produced his plays *Manohar mohini* ('Attractive Enchantress', 1917), *Vahimi vikar* ('Whimsical Disease', 1918), and *Nala-Damayanti* ('Nala and Damayanti', 1919) consecutively. It presented Harumal Premchand's *Naval Lakshmi* (1918) in 1922.

Daryani started the Detileti (dowry) Committee in 1920 to bring before audiences a drama of social consciousness. His first play on dowry, *Gulaba jo gul* ('Rose Flower'), appeared the same year. *Motie ji mukhri* ('Jasmine Bud'), on the conflict between mother-in-law and daughter-in-law, was staged in 1923. Detileti Committee produced a number of well-received works. Another important dramatic club, Young Citizen Society, established in 1920 by Lilaram Tharumal Makhijani (1897–1937), also presented mostly social drama. Makhijani wrote all their scripts.

Yet another renowned group that gave a boost to the development of Sindhi drama, specially the one-act variety, was the Rabindranath Literary and Dramatic Club, established in Hyderabad by Daryani and the equally famous Mangharam Udharam Malkani (1896–1980) in 1923. It staged only drama of social reform: sixteen full-length and a few short plays in eight years. Realism in Sindhi theatre peaked with its productions. The Hyderabad National College Dramatic Society, founded in 1924, chose

Qalich Beg's *Mohini* for its debut, followed by Bhagsingh Advani's *Gumani ghamsan* ('Doubtful Furore') in 1925. Other plays included Tejumal Shahani's *Rano Pratapsingh* (1926) and Motumal Gidwani's *Vasant-Lakshmi* (1927).

Apart from the societies, many small dramatic clubs surfaced in the district towns of Sindh during the period 1880–1935. Besides, every big village with a high school had an auditorium attached, used as examination hall as well as theatre. To stage an annual show was a must.

Malkani became known as the father of Sindhi one-act drama and for his charged sexual themes. A few years before Independence, Usman Deeplai emerged as a worthy successor, but did not fulfil his early promise. One-act drama of this period (like that of Lekhraj Mirchandani, 1897–1971) was original rather than adapted, rooted in the soil, with identifiable characters, and dealing with local problems. In 1939, Muhammad Ismail Ursani's slightly lengthy *Badnasib Thari* ('Unfortunate Tharis') created ripples. It depicted how a poor Thari (resident of the Thar desert) suffered at the hands of corrupt officials. Written in Thari dialect, its staging went down well with Tharis. Most full-length plays, however, were tragedies that moved the highly emotional spectators to tears. As an antidote, directors presented rib-tickling short farces after the main drama ended in order to send the audience home in good cheer. Moreover, farce came in handy to expose the evils in society. During the 1940s, Jethanand Nagrani introduced the fast-moving slick comedy in a series of *Gamtu* plays, like *Gamtu doctor* ('Quack Doctor').

In the beginning, the duration of performances used to be five to six hours, reduced to four hours by the Rabindranath Literary and Dramatic Club, and further cut to three hours later. Up to 1920 sets did not exist in Sindhi theatre, nor was there any permanent stage. Tables would be joined together for a platform and scenes would be changed with the help of bedsheets used as curtains and backdrops. Wings and regular curtains with painted visuals came into existence on stage only after 1920.

Sindhi theatre reached its loftiest heights during the period 1920–47. It suffered a temporary setback after Independence, when Sindhi Hindus migrated to various parts of India, mainly concentrating in Maharashtra, Gujarat, Rajasthan, Delhi, Uttar Pradesh, and Madhya Pradesh. Their final rehabilitation in these areas took them several years, followed by a struggle for economic stability. However, social organizations came up almost everywhere to keep alive their language and culture. Despite many odds, Sindhi dramatists and artists made efforts to revitalize the stage at all places where Sindhis had settled in sizeable numbers. They began with one-act plays on the theme of Sindhis coming to terms with the changed socio-economic conditions: school-going children hawking goods on pavements in their spare time, young men taking up manual labour, women coming out of their one-room tenements to join their menfolk in facing the crisis and making life worth living. These efforts bore fruit shortly after the establishment of educational institutions, cultural organizations, and dramatic societies.

The Sindhi theatre found its reincarnation in India under the patronage of the Sindhi Sahit Mandal founded by Malkani in Bombay, the first Sindhi literary society in India, which started its activities in the 1950s. The first of its nine productions was Bevas's *Podhe jo parno* ('Old Man's Wedding', written in the 1930s), staged simultaneously in Bombay and Delhi in 1952. Two notable playwrights responsible for reviving Sindhi theatre in India were Das Talib and Gobind Malhi (1921–), both of whom joined the *Indian People's Theatre Association (IPTA). While Malhi came back to Sindhi theatre, Talib preferred to move on to the Hindi stage.

The tireless Ram Panjwani had already used the compound of Jai Hind College, Bombay, as a stage in 1949. Over the next twenty years, the college produced eight full-length plays, seventeen one-act plays, and two operas titled *Rai Dyach* and *Umar-Marui*, directed by Panjwani or Arjan Mirchandani. Ram Raseela presented shows for the Sindh Model High School, which has produced over fifty plays, the most important aspect of which was the life of refugees in the camps, depicted for the first time.

In 1953, Harumal Rajpal established the Sindhu Natak Mandal, which brought on stage twenty-one plays. Progressive authors founded the Sindhi Kalakar Mandal in 1958, supported by eminent artists in the field like Geeta Raj, Madan Jumani, Bhagwanti Navani (from IPTA), Ramesh Janjani, and Anand Matai (both products of *National School of Drama). They produced twenty-five plays, all written and directed by Gobind Malhi.

The Lok Sar Mandli surfaced in 1960, presenting nine shadow plays and three operas written and directed by Mohan Chhabra. Sindhu Kala Mandir, established the same year by Moti Prakash, Bhudo Advani, and S.P. Menghani, renewed the tradition of long dramatic works. Their first venture was *Under Secretary*, directed by Advani. The group still exists, and has so far produced twenty-one full-length (all but one, adaptations) and many more one-act plays. Sindhu Art Theatre, launched in 1966 by Ramesh Janjani, has done over twenty full-scale productions. Although Janjani himself wrote many one-act scripts collected in *Nirman* ('Creation') and *Samarpan* ('Surrender'), they have not been staged. Other notable

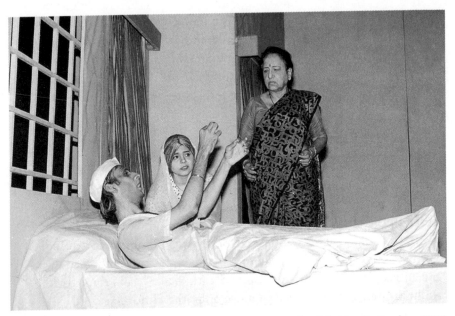

Diso paise ja ranga, written and directed by S.P. Menghani (Sindhu Kala Mandir, Bombay, 1997)

contributors to drama include Vasdev Nirmal, Madan Jumani, Arjan Mirchandani, Moti Prakash, and Popati Hiranandani. By 1965, Sindhi theatre was in full swing in Bombay and of some excellence.

The Delhi College Sindhi Sahitya Sabha came into existence in 1950, under the patronage of H.I. Sadarangani, and till 1952, had staged eight plays directed by the well-known Jivan Gursahani. The Jor Baugh Sindhi School put on Bevas's *Podhe jo parno* in 1952 and went on to produce over fifty plays, all directed by Lekhraj Hans. Among many groups that present theatre regularly, one outstanding organization is Sindhu Kala Sangam, co-founded by Gursahani and the great performer, Hemraj Nagwani. Established in 1961, it has produced nearly thirty one-act plays of the highest standard, winning popular accolades as well as critical acclaim throughout India. Another notable Delhi group, Mehran, founded by writer-director Gopal Panjwani in 1975, has also contributed to Sindhi theatre with nearly twenty productions.

In 1952, the Garbe Group initiated Sindhi theatre in Ahmadabad (Gujarat) with a few humorous plays. Afterwards, many dramatic societies surfaced but ebbed away owing to fading enthusiasm or lack of funds. The Sindhu Kalakar Mandal started by Gordhan Tanwani in 1962 had the support of many patrons, but closed after about twenty productions.

The Sindhi Drama Workshop is the main club for Ahmadabad Sindhis involved in theatre. It emerged in 1974 through the hard and elaborate efforts of Prem Prakash, a leading dramatist-director. Its activities include around fifty stage improvisations, many subsequently dramatized and published; the composition and theatricalization of mimes; a magazine, *Stage*, devoted to drama; seminars and workshops every year; recitation by poets of long poems, a few of which are dramatized in their presence; and encouragement of scriptwriters to turn directors. It has staged more than sixty works.

Prakash has so far written thirty experimental plays like the absurdist *Picnic* (1974) and *Morchabandi* ('Barricade', 1979). He has always posed a challenge to actors because of the limited possibilities of action and the burden of an entire philosophy; hence *Picnic* has not yet been performed. The main characters are in a kind of torpor, too weary to talk, too tired to move. Prakash distils the quintessential ennui of our times. He focuses on small, insignificant things, making the point that ordinary people are helplessly unable to influence events. The plot forms the backbone, as hard-edged as a cartoon strip and as plausible as tomorrow's headlines. *Morchabandi* is a political satire in which the author combines a dilution of the complicated infrastructure of the 'new drama' with the all-popular phenomenon of speed, making the artwork an excellent achievement.

By one count, over 500 Sindhi plays have been staged in India since Independence, many of them by various theatre groups in Vadodara, Adipur (Kachchh, Gujarat), Ajmer, Jaipur, Bhopal, Nagpur, Agra, Lucknow, Calcutta, and other towns, for local Sindhi audiences. Annual drama competitions are held under the auspices of the Sindhi Boli and Sahit Sabha in cities where Sindhis live. The first took place at Calcutta in 1973. Ten to twelve organizations from different places in India always participate. Sindhi theatre is still in fine form at the three main centres of theatrical activities—Mumbai, Delhi, and Ahmadabad—where productions occur at regular intervals. PA

L.H. Ajwani, *History of Sindhi Literature* (New Delhi: Sahitya Akademi, 1995).

t

TAMIL THEATRE

Theatre in the Tamil language is at least 2000 years old, probably the longest linguistic continuity in Indian, if not world theatre, unless we count the insulated pockets of *Sanskrit theatre surviving in Kerala. With no romanticization of its ancient origins, one can safely say that remnants and deviations of past traditions find their place in Tamil theatre in different forms. It has roots in highly localized, but still practised, community rituals; based on them, one can actually define cultural zones in the southern state of Tamil Nadu by geographical features, occupational aspects, and linguistic clusters. Indeed, ancient Tamil texts classified their land into five regions—mountainous (*kurinji*), forested (*mullai*), agricultural (*marutam*), coastal (*neital*), arid (*palai*)—and differentiated life, culture, and art forms in each according to these categories.

The ballad traditions have a storyline to offer, the abstract dances have no oral narratives to accompany them, and the narrative forms combine story with performance. Villuppattu and Udukkadippattu are examples of the first, from southern and western Tamil Nadu respectively. In them, local heroes survive and local deities are sung; they contain features that remain on the fringes, not absorbed by any homogenized religious system. Tappattam, Devarattam, Oyilattam, Karagattam, Poykkal Kudhirai, and Kummi belong to the second kind, some with only rhythm and instrumental music, some with supporting singers. They belong to specific communities following strict feudal orders. The most important among the third category, the thriving *Terukkuttu widely prevalent in the northern districts, combines dance, music, plot, dialogue, acting, and costume. Variations can be found in other parts. It is professional in the sense that troupes organize and remobilize each year.

The energy, theatrical potential, variety, and versatility of these forms are immense, but most do not allow women to participate or castes to mix. Although their stories deal with mythical and Puranic tales, the performance styles provide great scope to subvert, modernize, and critically interpret. Their inherent parodic features are of value in following the tradition while simultaneously inverting it. Minor forms like *Bommalattam, *Kuravanji Natakam, *Nondi Natakam, *Pallu, *Kirttanai, *Vilasam, and Katha Kalakshepam date from the seventeenth, eighteenth, and nineteenth centuries. Not all survive today. An isolated genre of Telugu dance-drama, *Bhagavata Mela, continues to exist in a few villages of central Tamil Nadu.

Tamil literature contains many references to performing traditions, modes, and theories. The *Tolkappiyam* grammar (first century BC) lists communicable emotions as *meyppattu* (literally 'physicalizations of feelings'). The *Kuttanul* treatise (date contested, first millennium AD) mentions aesthetic emotions too. Sangam works (first century BC to second century AD) refer to communities of minstrels called Panars and Viraliyars, who were local chieftains' emissaries to citizens and vice versa. The epic *Cilappatikaram* (second century AD) records performance styles in different parts of Tamil Nadu, distinguishes between classical and popular forms, and refers to stage measurements, varieties of screens, and other technical details. Its section titled *Arangetrra katai* ('chapter on the debut') can be considered a monograph on performatory norms, and reveals an advanced theatrical sensibility.

The arrival of the British introduced new forms along with the proscenium. By the end of the nineteenth century, Sankaradas Swamigal (1867–1922) explored the possibilities of professionalizing theatre. He retained the singing and (comic) dancing traditions, and the Puranic stories, but took scenic devices and stage structure from the West. He also initiated the concept of *boys' companies, which became very popular in villages. Important later leaders included 'Nawab' Rajamanikkam (1906–74), a strict actor-manager, and C. Kanniah, a wizard of set design. After the famous T.K.S. Brothers' company (established 1925) introduced actresses, women began to participate in theatre. Initially they were trained while young and grew up in the theatres. However, a few enterprising all-women troupes had already arisen by the early 1920s, such as Balamani Ammal's. There are instances of actresses cross-dressing in rajas' parts even now.

With Swamigal's texts as the central link, these musicals continue as 'Special drama', since they have unique organizational principles. The artists register in *sangam*s (associations). Each has agents who keep track of his/her call sheets. If a village invites a play, the agent through the *sangam* arranges a team that assembles on the day of the performance with prior information about the cast, and enacts an all-night show. Since the team does not present a regular production, each performance comes up with improvisation. In any case, the story is already well known, including lyrics, tunes, and sequence, so the surprise lies in these improvisations. Actors have to constantly update their literary references, contemporary views, and philosophic discourses.

Meanwhile, the advent of British rule and its attendant emergence of government jobs, Westernization, and a middle class with English education manifested itself in urban theatre in Madras. Although P. Sundaram Pillai (1855–97) wrote the first Western-style Tamil drama (*Manonmaniyam*, 1891), Pammal Sambandha Mudaliar (1873–1964) heralded this new form. A person who once detested theatre as obscene and

vulgar, he got converted on seeing literate high officials from Andhra performing in Telugu. His Suguna Vilasa Sabha (1892) started staging three-hour-long plays in fluent modern prose, the first time that prose had a legitimate part in the narrative. He also translated classic English drama into Tamil. He prioritized acting above singing but could only get men to do female roles. Many similar amateur *sabha*s (groups) sprang up in smaller cities. A new brand of educated actors evolved. Characterization and novelty of plot became important in this genre, which thrived in most towns till the 1950s, as in the patriotic plays of S.D. Sundaram (1920–79).

A scene from a *sabha* drama by P. Sambandha Mudaliar

This *sabha natakam* (drama) must be differentiated from what came to be known as *sabha*s later: urban societies formed by paid enrolment to patronize music, dance, and theatre. The new system assured performers of middle-class audiences. These *sabha*s grew into powerful agencies, determining the character of cultural life by choosing what to sponsor or not. Since more members brought better financial returns, they set dubious trends by deciding what can pass as art. However, the theatre groups were not commercial in the sense of surviving by ticket sales. Most artists were amateurs with other options for their livelihoods. Drama became an evening activity for them. The modernist S.V. Sahasranamam (1913–88), the comic Poornam Viswanathan (1920–), the popular K. Balachander (1930–), and the Marxist Komal Swaminathan (1935–95) were among the few writer-directors to practise this form seriously. Cho Ramaswamy (1934–) used it to convey political satire, almost journalistic in quality. S.V. Sekhar, 'Crazy' Mohan, and smaller upstart groups attempted this mode for entertainment, Sekhar proving extremely successful in procuring shows. This theatrical trend has almost vanished or shifted to television drama and serials for its sustenance.

On the other hand, the mass popularity of *Sangita Natakam (musical drama) continued unabated. The stellar performers in this genre were the unequalled romantic duo of S.G. Kittappa (1906–33) and K.B. Sundarambal (1906–80), and the near-classical singer M.K. Thyagaraja Bhagavathar (1910–59). Other famous actors included the specialist in villainous roles, R.S. Manohar (1929–2006), and the comedian N.S. Krishnan (1908–57). When Tamil cinema started in the 1930s, theatre provided the acting and singing talents that the talkies needed. No fundamental difference existed between the two arts: the earliest movies were just filmed prints of stage productions.

Political parties and their cultural agenda need separate study. The *Indian People's Theatre Association never had a noticeable presence in the state, whereas the *Dravidian movement especially had its own artists. Two of them became Chief Ministers of Tamil Nadu: C.N. Annadurai (1909– 69), whose revolutionary plays were the major campaign pieces of their ideology, and M. Karunanidhi (1924–), who continued that tradition of rhetoric intimately familiar to Tamils as Dravidian. This political theatre went on to have a powerful say in Tamil films. A deep relationship exists between stage/screen status and political power in Tamil Nadu, where star actors and actresses have an unquestioned mass (hence electoral) appeal. The role of leftist parties is not big, but they have been consistent in their activities. Chennai Kalai Kuzhu, ideologically Marxist, is a major force in both proscenium and *street theatre.

In Tamil, words like modern, experimental, and contemporary refer interchangeably to serious theatre in the last quarter of the twentieth century. Whatever the adjective, it certainly does not qualify as popular. Most of these efforts depend on some source of subsidy. Several groups consider theatre part of their political commitment and survive by sheer involvement of members. But their varied modes of expression make it difficult to classify them. A basic mapping of events, groups, and personalities is attempted here.

One can trace the beginning of 'modern theatre' to a workshop in Gandhigram (Dindigul district) by S.P. Srinivasan and director S. Ramanujam (1935–) in 1977. A month-long *National School of Drama (NSD) workshop followed in 1978, which consolidated the practitioners' commitment. Bansi Kaul's *Pinam tinnum satirankal* ('Corpse-devouring Customs', 1978), dealing with Duryodhana's disrobing of Draupadi, was a milestone production. In 1980, the group Veedhi in Madras invited Badal Sircar to conduct a workshop at the Artists Village. These three workshops started new trends in Tamil theatre.

Two important Madras groups, Koothu-p-pattarai led by Na. Muthuswamy (1936–) and Pareeksha led by Gnani Sankaran, began in 1977. By 1988, Koothu-p-pattarai grew into the only repertory in Tamil

Chennai Kalai Kuzhu in performance, directed by Pralayan

Nadu. Emphasis on actor's training based on traditional local forms of theatre, dance, and *martial arts is its major strength, which rubs off on its acclaimed productions. Pareeksha started with the aim of appealing to the new urban middle-class sensibility. Its members regarded theatre as a cultural movement, therefore shared all the work related to performance. They sold tickets for a flat nominal price, stuck posters, publicized and organized discussions. The introduction of Badal Sircar's plays in Tamil was its contribution. It also staged Prabanjan's *Muttai* ('Egg', 1990), Jeyanthan's *Manusha manusha* ('Humans', 2000), and short mimes on topical issues. Sircar's influence was obvious in Gnani's ideas rather than style.

In 1978, Nija Nataka Iyakkam led by M. Ramasamy of the Tamil department of Madurai University made a mark in Madurai and neighbouring areas. It originally performed mainly street plays. Highly physical and energetic, the group left an indelible mark in the southern region. *Turkira avalam* ('Turkira's Tragedy'), its major production, was an adaptation of *Antigone*. It also enacted Sircar's *Spartacus* in the round, an event that toured many places in Tamil Nadu, as did its play *Kalagakkarar thozhar Periyar* ('Radical Comrade Periyar', 2003). At a time when Periyar's contributions are questioned critically, Ramasamy tries to historically construct his unassailable role, highlighting the socialist aspects, though not his pioneering work on gender. Ramasamy now heads the Department of Drama in Tamil University, Thanjavur, and directs *children's theatre. Other than at Tamil University and the School of Performing Arts in Pondicherry University, *theatre education is non-existent, though the Folklore Resources and Research Centre in Palayankottai (Tirunelveli district) initiated theatre training, and the University of Madras encourages theatre research.

Along with Na. Muthuswamy, Indira Parthasarathy (1930–) is a major playwright, revealing a modern sensibility and knowledge of Tamil literary and philosophic traditions. Aswaghosh, Parambai Selvan, K.A. Gunasekaran, K.S. Rajendran, Jeyanthan, Rengarajan, Amshan Kumar, and 'Vizhippu' Natarajan became involved in theatre during the 1980s. A number of new groups formed, like the Chennai Kalai Kuzhu, Palkalai Arangam, Arangam, Thalai-k-kol, Adukalam, Aikya, and Aroopam, not all of them equally consistent. Many youngsters took to theatre seriously, and debates and discussions grew among theatre people. S. Ramanujam's *Veriyattam* ('Frenzied Dance', 1990), *Karunchuzhi* ('Black Whirlpool', 1990) by V. Arumugham (1955–), Pralayan's *Puratchikkav* ('Revolutionary Poet', 1991), and Parthasarathy's *Nandan kathai* (*The Legend of Nandan*) directed by R. Raju in 1997, were noteworthy productions.

In the 1990s, variety blossomed. Velu Saravanan evolved as a children's-theatre specialist and formed Azhi. Mangai focused on gender issues through Voicing Silence. Jeeva combined her gender and Dalit concerns through the APTIST group. Gunasekaran's *Baliyadukal* ('Scapegoats', 1998) spoke of a Dalit theatre. Magic Lantern established itself, performing both in English and Tamil, working closely with Alliance Française, Chennai, and organizing regular events. It is interested in aesthetics rather than ideology, and staging translations, but also dramatized Kalki's historical novel *Ponniyin Selvan* (1999) to popular nostalgia. Prasanna Ramaswami and Pritham Chakravarthi actively engaged in theatre; Pritham developed her solo shows as a powerful medium to address issues like domestic violence, child sexual abuse, and health concerns. Gandhi Mary regularly conducted workshops in schools and published plays. Ramalingam worked in a school in Hosur (Dharmapuri district). Sister Clare and Father Britto, taught by Sircar, trained several groups. Many voluntary agencies added theatre to their agenda.

The turn of the century brought a fresh breeze. K.S.K. Prasad and Jaya Rao, products of Koothu-p-pattarai, formed Mooram Arangu ('*third theatre') and Theatre Lab respectively, working on theatre training and new productions. Another Koothu-p-pattarai trainee, Chandra, concentrates on involving children and women. Graduates from the NSD, Shanmuga Raja directs in Madurai and Balakrishnan in Tamil and English through his group Theatre Nisha.

Among playwrights, the Marxist-Leninist poet Inquilab entered theatre quite late in his literary career. His *Avvai* (1998), *Manimekalai* (2001), and *Kurinji pattu* ('Mountain Song', 2005, all directed by Mangai) are based on Sangam poetry and the epic *Manimekalai*. They opened up an unexplored terrain of classical sources, connecting them to contemporary society and politics. Many of his texts have already entered various curricula. In the south, Muruga Bhoopathy builds his plays (collected as *Kundal nagaram*, 'A Town of Hair', referring to female impersonation, 2003) upon the soil and environment, keen on making theatre reclaim its ritual characteristics.

The role of various festivals deserves mention. Chief among them was the *Subhamangala* festival, organized on the initiative of Komal Swaminathan, which provided a platform for different kinds of theatre to meet in one place. A Badal Sircar festival in Tiruchchirappalli consolidated his influence on Tamil theatre. A major activity of Nija Nataka Iyakkam was to hold annual festivals. On its tenth anniversary in 1988, it started hosting modern-theatre festivals, which served as a major forum until 1992. The Sangeet Natak Akademi's regional festivals gave exposure otherwise difficult to dream of in Tamil Nadu. Purisai Nataka Vizha was another important space for traditional and modern theatre to meet. The annual Kattaikkuttu festivals of Terukkuttu in Kanchipuram enabled many theatre lovers to get to know this living art.

Nataka Veli, a journal, was a primary resource on Tamil theatre in the mid-1990s, edited by Rangarajan, of late a director. *Kattiyam*, an international theatre journal begun in 2002 as a joint venture by Sri Lankan and Indian Tamils, is a major effort in documentation, research, and discussion on theatre.   VP

Nanditha Krishna, *Folk Arts of Tamilnadu: The Performing Arts* (Madras: C.P. Ramaswami Aiyar Foundation, 1996); A.N. Perumal, *Tamil Drama: Origin and Development* (Madras: International Institute of Tamil Studies, 1981); Susan Seizer, *Stigmas of the Tamil Stage: An Ethnography of Special Drama Artists in South India* (Durham: Duke University Press, 2005); Karthigesu Sivathamby, *Drama in Ancient Tamil Society* (Madras: New Century Book House, 1981).

TELUGU THEATRE

Evidence from sculpture and inscriptions indicates that theatrical activities flourished in the present south-eastern state of Andhra Pradesh as early as the second century BC. The Nagarjunakonda excavations, in Nalgonda district, laid bare an amphitheatre dated by researchers to the second or third century AD. However, the first definite word of theatre in the Telugu language appears in Palkuriki Somanatha's poetical texts, *Basava puranamu* and *Panditaradhya charitramu* (early thirteenth century). He mentions a play, *Siriyalu charitra* ('Siriyalu's Story'), presented with appropriate prelude, correct speech and diction, and proper action during the Sivaratri festival at Srisailam (Kurnool district). The only surviving medieval script is *Kridabhiramamu* ('Graceful Sport') by Vinukonda Vallabharayudu, who translated it from a Sanskrit drama, *Premabhirama*. Written in the fourteenth century, it belongs to the genre of *vithi, one of the ten *rupakas*.

Sanskrit plays translated later were done in poetic (*kavya*), not dramatic, form. However, folk theatre entertained the rural public. During the reign of the Nayaka (1565–1673) and Maratha (1674–1855) kings based in Thanjavur, Tamil Nadu, Telugu received a boost as their court language. Thus *Yakshaganam, also called Vithi Natakam or Bhagavatam, reached its artistic zenith. *Tolu Bommalata shadow puppetry, *Kuchipudi and *Kalapam (Yakshaganam in much more codified dance forms), *Voggukatha and *Burrakatha narrative troupes, *Pagativeshalu (solo role-playing), *Kuravanji dance-drama, Harikatha solo narratives—all these folk forms remained popular for over eight centuries. After the introduction of English education in the nineteenth century, Telugu drama emerged as a distinct literary genre.

Kichaka in *Kichakavadha* by Sri Krishna Devaraya Nataka Samajam (Kuppam, Chittor district), a Yakshaganam troupe

It is commonly believed that the first modern Telugu play was Korada Ramachandra Sastry's *Manjari-Madhukariyam* ('Tale of Manjari and Madhukara', 1860?), a short work with a romantic plot and Sanskritized diction. But no authentic proof exists to validate this claim. The first play may have been Varanasi Dharma Suri's *Narakasura vijaya vyayogamu* ('Narakasura's Victory', 1871) in the *vyayoga* genre, translated into Telugu by Kokkonda Venkataratnam Pantulu (1842–1915). The following year saw partial translations of *Kalidasa's *Abhijnana-Sakuntala* by both Paravastu Rangacharyulu (1822–1900) and Kandukuri Veeresalingam (1848–1919). Translations from English soon followed, beginning with Vavilala Vasudeva Sastry's *Sizaru charitramu* ('Caesar's Story', 1875), from Shakespeare's *Julius Caesar*. A trendsetter, Sastry also wrote the first original Telugu social drama, *Nandaka rajyamu* ('Nandaka's Kingdom', 1880), a biting satire on feuds between two Brahman sects. These pioneers ushered in the three distinct dramatic directions which continued for the next half-century: translations from Sanskrit, translations from English, and original works which combined both traditions.

Between 1860 and 1880, drama was considered only as texts for reading. Veeresalingam initiated proscenium theatre by staging his *Vyavahara dharmabodhini* ('Manual on Legal Practice') in 1880 with his students and friends as actors. In that year, a travelling company, Tantipurastha Nataka Samajam, popularly called Dharwada Nataka Samajam, toured Andhra's northern coastal towns presenting a series of plays in Hindi. Its well-performed productions created a sensation and, as a result, several writers and actors there took to theatre seriously: Kondubhotla Subramanya Sastry (1853–97) in Guntur, Nadella Purushothama Kavi (1863–1938) in Machilipatnam, Vaddadi Subbarayudu (1854–1938) in Rajahmundry.

Kondubhotla founded Hindu Nataka Samajam (1881), which staged thirty of his plays not only in Guntur, but in neighbouring towns as well. Nadella's National Theatrical Society (1882), with Eemani Laxmana Swamy as the main actor, produced drama in Hindi, following the Dharwada company's practice. Vaddadi not only translated Bhatta Narayana's *Venisamhara* from Sanskrit but also acted in it creditably as Aswatthama. Other troupes like Jaganmitra Samajam of Visakhapatnam (1882) and Hindu Nataka Samajam of Kakinada (1884) soon followed suit.

Hitherto, Telugu dramatic poetry was recited, not sung. In 1887, the emergence of *padya natakam* (verse drama), in which the metrical stanzas were sung to ragas, achieved a landmark. Inspired by the musical productions of *Parsi theatre companies, the pioneering Dharmavaram Ramakrishnamacharyulu (1853–1912) started this trend in Bellary (Karnataka) with *Chitra Naliyam* ('Nala's Curious Tale', 1887). The rendition of lyrics musically was not new, but delivering verse stanzas in the same way was. This kind of stage music became immediately popular not only in Bellary, but all over Andhra. Through *padya natakam*, actor-singers turned stars overnight. To meet the audience's overwhelming response, several amateur groups performed musical theatre. New authors, basically poets, began writing plays that contained good poetry, though not necessarily good drama.

Govindarajula Subba Rao as Yugandhara in Vedam Venkataraya Sastry's *Prataparudriya natakam* (Rama Vilasa Sabha, Tenali, 1932)

Dharmavaram's contemporary and professional rival from Bellary was Kolachalam Srinivasa Rao (1854–1919), better known for his historical plays, among which *Ramaraju charitramu* or *Fall of Vijayanagar* (1907) is considered a masterpiece. He founded the Sumanorama Sabha, a theatre association that became famous owing to its lead actor, Bellary Raghava (1880–1946), who also directed in social-realistic style. Rao was perhaps the first Indian theatre historian to write a book in English on world drama: *A History of World Drama* (1907).

Two other significant contributions to dramatic literature make this era noteworthy. The classic *Kanyasulkam* ('Bride Price', 1892) by Gurazada Appa Rao (1862–1915), a social reformer and dramaturgical savant, is a full-length comedy dealing with contemporary evils such as selling brides and prohibiting widows from remarrying. *Prataparudriya natakam* ('Prataparudra's Play', 1897) by the literary commentator and translator Vedam Venkataraya Sastry (1853–1929) is the other play, still popular because it created memorable semi-historical characters and dramatized incidents from Telugu history, though often imaginary.

Padya natakam brought to the forefront many poet-dramatists active during the next twenty-five years. *Gayopakhyanamu* ('The Gaya Episode', 1889) by Chilakamarthi Lakshminarasimham (1867–1946) achieved great success mainly because of its mellifluous poems. Panuganti Lakshminarasimha Rao (1865–1940), known as the Andhra Shakespeare, wrote over thirty plays with stanzas intended for 'musical recitation', though not in elaborate ragas. The Tirupati Venkata Kavulu duo (Divakarla Tirupati Sastry, 1872–1920, and Chellapilla Venkata

Sastry, 1870–1950) perfected *padya natakam* to its aesthetic heights
in their *Mahabharata* plays. Sripada Krishna Murthy Sastry's *Bobbili
yuddham* ('Bobbili War', 1908) and Balijepalli Lakshmikantham's
Harishchandra (1912) were other important plays favoured both by
performers and audiences.

The illustrious Surabhi Theatres originated in the last decade of the
nineteenth century. Vanarasa Govinda Rao, its founder, started this
professional family company in Surabhi village, Cuddapah district, which
later grew into a consortium of commercial troupes. It is the only professional
theatre still active in Andhra. Other significant touring companies arose.
Shows by two Hindu Nataka Samajams (Rajahmundry, 1889, and Guntur,
1890), National Theatre (Rajahmundry, 1898), and the Andhra
Bhashabhivardhini Samajam (Nellore, 1899) reached all corners of the
state. Similarly, actors like Immaneni Hanumantha Rao Naidu and
Tanguturi Prakasam Pantulu (the first Chief Minister of Andhra Pradesh) in
Rajahmundry, Hari Prasada Rao and Balijepalli Lakshmikantham in
Guntur, and Kandadai Srinivasan in Nellore became prominent.

These associations and actors made possible a sustainable professional
theatre, which led to the establishment of more commercial companies in
the next decade. Men still played female roles, except in Surabhi, and the
best among them were in great demand. The frequent visits of Parsi troupes
to Andhra, 1890–1900, brought changes in lighting and music—
harmonium and tabla replacing violin, vina, and *mridangam* drums. Each
sabha (company) employed a *sutradhari* (stage manager) to introduce the
play and *hasyagadu* (comedian) to provide humour during intervals. Actors
worked under the strict supervision of director-playwrights. Discipline was
the keyword.

The first three decades of the twentieth century witnessed the birth and
death of the commercial theatre and with its passing the decline of the
musical. Three ventures need special mention, for they tried to keep up the
tradition. The Hindu Nataka Samajam, Rajahmundry, started as an
amateur association, came into the hands of two enterprising theatre lovers
in 1908: Satyavolu Gunneswara Rao, producer, and Krithiventi Nageswara
Rao, director. They entrusted each branch of production to a master
(Papatla Kanthaiah for music, A.S. Ram for costume), hired talented actors
on high salaries, and drew up regular rehearsal schedules. Their performances
were so successful that spectators had to book tickets in advance.

Bala Bharathi Nataka Samajam (1913), popularly called Mylavaram
Company, also began on the same lines. Many actors from Rajahmundry

migrated to it after it shifted from the remote village of Mylavaram in Krishna district to Vijayawada, a central town in the same district. Resident dramatists wrote plays to suit the employed actors. Yadavalli Suryanarayana and Uppuluri Sanjeeva Rao joined as leads, the famous Vemuri Gaggaiah (1895–1955) as the villain, and Daita Gopalam and Addanki Sriram Murthy played character roles. Music based on Hindustani ragas, trick scenes, and glittering costumes and ornaments made them popular. The Seetharamanjaneya Nataka Samajam (1921) at Eluru, known as Mote Vari Company after its founder Mote Narayan Rao, also practised the earlier traditions.

Whereas these three companies stationed themselves at one home base, other amateur associations toured with professional zeal, like the Rama Vilasa Sabhas at Chittoor (1920) and Tenali (Guntur district, 1921) respectively. While the former had the talented singer-actor V. Nagaiah as its leading man, the latter had many illustrious performers who brought it recognition across the region: Govindarajula Subba Rao, Linga Murthy, Madhavapeddi Venkataramaiah, the celebrated female impersonator Sthanam Narasimha Rao (1902–74), and scores of others produced classics under the stewardship of Tripuraribhatla Veeraraghava Swamy.

Notable plays served up by these theatres include Chandala Kesava Das's *Kanaka-Tara* ('Kanaka and Tara', 1911), Pandit K. Subramanya Sastry's *Sri Krishna lilalu* ('Sri Krishna's *Lila', 1914), Sriramula Sachidananda Sastry's *Savitri* (1915), Malladi Achyutarama Sastry's *Draupadi vastrapaharanam* ('Disrobing of Draupadi', 1927), and Somaraju Ramanuja Rao's *Rangoon Rowdy* (1929). The year 1920–1 saw particularly big hits on stage: Kopparapu Subba Rao's *Roshanara*, Muttaraju Subba Rao's *Srikrishna tulabharam* ('The Weighing of Sri Krishna'), Dharmavaram Gopalacharyulu's *Ramdas*, and Kallakuri Narayan Rao's *Chintamani*.

However, the commercial theatres became victims of their extravagance. The advent of cinema and economic recession after World War I added to their woes. Between 1928 and 1935 the popular verse-drama went into the hands of 'contractors' who worked as middlemen to fix places of performance and assembled musically proficient actors from different towns for unrehearsed shows. With this decline, ventures into new avenues started. The nationalist movement brought into focus patriotic drama by amateurs and enthusiastically staged historical plays featuring patriotic protagonists. Damaraju Pundareekakshudu and Sripada Krishna Murthy Sastry were the foremost among these popular writers. Sripada Kameswara Rao, Jandhyala Sivanna Sastry, Jonnalagadda Satyanarayana Murthy, and Pingali Nagendra Rao translated *historical drama from Marathi, Bengali, and Hindi.

Translations of European drama, especially of Ibsen and Molière, though infrequent, found a favourable reading public. Molière's *The Doctor in Spite of Himself* was translated several times and always succeeded on stage. Bhamidipati Kameswara Rao (1897–1958) adapted Molière and wrote original plays such as *Bagu bagu* ('Good, Good', 1923) and *Tappanisari* ('The Inevitable', 1939), favourites of college clubs and amateur groups for their humour and easy presentability. The talented actor-director, D.V. Subba Rao of Machilipatnam, popularized Pingali Nagendra Rao's *Vindhya Rani* ('Queen of Vindhya', 1928), adapted from Oscar Wilde's *The Duchess of Padua*.

Although the impact of the Romantic Age in Telugu literature during the 1920s fell most on poetry, a handful of poets showed their mettle in drama as well. Viswanatha Satyanarayana (1895–1976) composed highly imaginative plays: *Nartanasala* ('Dancing Hall') and *Anarkali* (1924–25) reveal a mastery of verse idiom and a perfect sense of characterization. Chinta Deekshitulu's symbolic *Sabari* (1925), Abburi Ramakrishna Rao's poetic *Nadi sundari* ('River Damsel', 1932), and the lyrical plays of Devulapalli Krishna Sastry (1897–1980) express a poetic sensibility rare in dramatic literature. Gudipati Venkata Chalam (1894–1979), a romantic rebel, wrote drama in which he tried to reinterpret myths and question blind age-old beliefs—the earliest Telugu plays to deal with the suffering of women in society. The rationalist movement, which interrogated the traditional value system, influenced Tripuraneni Ramaswamy Chaudari (1886–1943) to write *Sambuka vadha* ('Killing of Sambuka', 1920) and *Khuni* ('Murder', 1935).

The years between 1930 and 1943, crucial in the development of Telugu theatre, sowed the seeds of realistic drama. Ibsen's centenary in 1928, celebrated in Madras, and Bellary Raghava's plea regarding the immediate relevance of the social problem play in prose enthused new authors. P.V. Rajamannar's *Tappevaridi* ('Whose Fault Is It?', 1930), about the urban generation gap on the issues of love and marriage, spearheaded this trend. The emergence of one-act drama was the most notable event, evolving in the 1930s from mere entertainment to its present position of an intellectual and emotional medium for dramatizing contemporary problems. Viswanatha Kaviraju (1893–1947), Nori Narasimha Sastry (1900–78), and Narla Venkateswara Rao (1908–85) shaped its destiny during the initial days. Radio drama and musicals in the hands of Aaravi, Gora Sastry, Devulapalli Krishna Sastry, and Rajaneekantha Rao grew into fine artistic media.

The realistic drama started a new chapter in theatre history as well. The plays of Raghava, Rajamannar, Narla, and many others had concentrated, though mildly, on the status of women, the sensitivities of the 'kept woman', and day-to-day life in urban and rural areas. But after 1943 urgent social problems came to the fore in drama. Class struggle, economic inequality, conflicts between landlords and labourers became the themes. Theatre turned a crusader for social justice. Three different organizations were responsible for ushering in the age of realism: the Andhra Nataka Kala Parishath (ANKP), Praja Natya Mandali (PNM), and Andhra University Experimental Theatre (AUET, a wing of the Department of Theatre Arts, Andhra University).

Although founded in 1929 to provide a platform for writers and actors to discuss matters of common interest, the ANKP in its second phase stood as a pioneer championing the cause of the realistic problem play in prose. Major dramatists emerged from the annual competitions it organized: Acharya Atreya (1921–89), Pinisetti Srirama Murthy, D.V. Narasa Raju, and many others wrote for these competitions which consolidated the realistic theatre. Atreya, an actor-director who turned to playwriting, became synonymous with the movement after introducing protest drama in *N.G.O.* (1948). Pinisetti came out with *Palle paduchu* ('Young Village Woman', 1950) and *Anna-chellelu* ('Brother and Sister', 1953), both on the conflicts between rich and poor in a rural milieu. Plays on women, specially fallen women, received laurels, such as Bellamkonda Ramdas's *Punarjanma* ('Rebirth', 1956) and Avasarala Surya Rao's *Panjaram* ('Cage', 1958).

The PNM—the Andhra branch of the *Indian People's Theatre Association—catered to the tastes and needs of village audiences by modernizing old Burrakatha narratives and presenting plays on the class divide. *Mundadugu* ('A Step Forward', 1946) and *Ma bhumi* ('Our Land', 1947) are renowned examples. Ideologue, director, actor, and dancer Garikapati Raja Rao (1915–63) energized and participated in most PNM productions. *Asami* ('Landlord', 1954) by the popular Burrakatha singer Shaik Nazar (1920–) depicted the protagonist's exploiting tactics and the villagers' revolt against him. Others outside the PNM, like Pinisetti, also composed drama on rural subjects. Boyi Bheemanna wrote on the fate of farm labour in *Paleru* ('Agricultural Servant', 1942).

The AUET (1944), under K.V. Gopalaswamy's stewardship, nurtured the aspirations of college and university students by holding annual theatre competitions. It is no exaggeration to say that the next generation of playwrights, actors, and directors emerged from amongst them. The Telugu

Little Theatre (1946) helped all theatre artists with technical needs and worked as a forum for them. This movement continued under the Andhra Pradesh Natya Sangh (1954) steered by A.R. Krishna (1926–92). It started an acting school and repertory under the guidance of Abburi Ramakrishna Rao (1896–1979), dramatist, director, and actor with the AUET. The repertory staged Telugu classics like *Kanyasulkam* and *Prataparudriyamu*, Sanskrit classics like *Mricchakatika*, and translations from modern Indian drama such as Karnad's *Hayavadana* and Sircar's *Evam Indrajit*. Krishna imaginatively directed Unnava Lakshminarayana's *Mala palli* ('Untouchables' Locality', 1973), one of the best Telugu novels, dramatized by Nagna Muni, with simultaneous staging in eight different open-air acting areas.

Contemporary theatre is mostly experimental, with a strong realistic sense. Bhamidipati Radhakrishna, whose one-act comedies won recognition, wrote *Kirti seshulu* ('Noble Dead', 1960) on an actor's frustrations. Rachakonda Viswanatha Sastry's *Nijam* ('Truth', 1962) portrayed the evils of power and contained scathing attacks on the legal and police systems. Gollapudi Maruthi Rao's *Lavalo erra gulabi* ('Red Rose in a Volcano', 1963) and *Karuninchani devathalu* ('Merciless Gods', 1968) explored people's psyche in testing moments. N.R. Nandi's *Maro Mohenjodaro* ('Another Mohenjodaro', 1964) set a trend by using symbolism effectively to lay bare the exploitation of the poor and helpless.

Over 100 societies used to organize annual theatre competitions in the early 1970s, nurturing many writers. Drama gradually took up a wide

A.R. Krishna's production of Unnava Lakshminarayana's *Mala palli* adapted by Nagna Muni (Andhra Pradesh Natya Sangh, Hyderabad, 1972)

variety of socially relevant subjects. Ganesh Patro's plays and playlets, exploiting the north coastal Andhra dialect, grew popular. Korrapati Gangadhara Rao, who wrote about 100 scripts, was known for light comedies. His *Yadha praja tadha raja* ('Like Subjects, Like King', 1972) deals with power politics in villages. Attili Krishna Rao's *Turpu rekhalu* ('Eastern Sunrays', 1978) and K. Chiranjeevi's *Nili dipalu* ('Blue Lights', 1982) powerfully depicted the injustices meted out to the depressed classes. Yandamuri Veerendranath, Divya Prabhakar, Isukapalli Mohan Rao, Patibandla Ananda Rao, Pavani, and Sesi Mohan were important dramatists whose works reveal their sense of theatre.

In the realm of one-act drama, Telugu experiments were noteworthy. Patro's *Koduku puttala* ('Let a Son Be Born', 1970) and *Pavala* ('Four Annas', 1971), Veerendranath's *Rudravina* ('Rudra Vina', 1976) and *Kukka* ('Dog', 1978), Maruthi Rao's *Kallu* ('Eyes', 1979), Diwakar Babu's *Kundeti kommu* ('Hare's Horn', 1985), and Gopala Raju's *Rayi* ('Stone', 1989) were memorable both for content and mastery of technique. *Street theatre gained currency. Akella Satyanarayana Murthy's *Pedda bala siksha* ('The First Primer', 1982), A. Krishna Rao's *Tomy ... Tomy* (1984), and Tanikella Bharani's *Go grahanam* ('Captured Cow', 1986) were received with great enthusiasm.

Along with eminent playwrights came worthy directors. Atreya, Narasa Raju, J.V. Ramana Murthy, K. Venkateswara Rao (1923–73), and A.R. Krishna belonged to the first generation of realists during the 1940s and 1950s. Among their juniors, Chatla Sreeramulu (1931–), Desiraju Hanumantha Rao, M. Nagabhushana Sarma, and A. Krishna Rao established themselves with imaginative directorial work. In the next generation, one may mention Raoji, D.S.N. Murthy, Tallavajjhula Sundaram, L. Satyanand, Misro, Krishna Chaitanya, Deekshit, Prasada Reddy, and Ayyalasomayajula Gopalakrishna. Important senior actors included the educationist Banda Kanakalingeswara Rao (1907–68), the singer Kalyanam Raghuramaiah (1901–75), and the recitalist Peesapati Narasimha Murty (1920–). The next generation comprises Vemuri Ramaiah, B. Subrahmanya Sastry, P. Ramasubba Reddy, and G. Savitri.

Telugu theatre in the 1990s presented a mixed bag. Verse drama drew a niche audience, whereas the realistic prose play, though popular with urban spectators, did not find approval from rural people. Street and university theatre remained peripheral. Lack of proper auditoriums in the districts, government apathy, distraction of actors' commitment, and dwindling audience interest due to the thrust of electronic media became detrimental to the healthy growth of theatre. However, a resurgence came with the dawn of the new millennium as public response grew positive and encouraging to a spurt of all-round activity.

Firstly, the university departments of theatre, though uneven, often stress experiment either in the choice of play or in style: A. Krishna Rao's use of folk idioms, bold environmental theatre by C. Sreeramulu and Nagabhushana Sarma embedded in the folk and tribal narrative traditions, productions of contemporary classics and new plays by D.S.N. Murthy and others. Their graduates continued the good work.

Secondly, the consolidated and thoughtful efforts of Rasaranjani, since its inception in 1993, started paying dividends. It has a monthly scheme of presenting plays of high artistic merit, either its own or by other groups, at a nominal charge of Rs 10, notching up over 1100 performances of more than 200 old and modern classics, contemporary problem plays, and translations. Its annual festivals of 'Yesterday's Plays for Today's Audience' have proved a great success.

The third factor lies in the state government's annual competitions in three categories: *padya natakam*, prose drama and one-act play. Old groups and *padya natakam* were revived, new ones started, and new scripts of diverse kinds appeared. Finally, the Praja Natya Mandali remains active with its street theatre addressing social problems and its annual Safdar Hashmi Festival.   MNS

Music, Dance and Drama in Andhra Pradesh (Hyderabad: Andhra Pradesh Sangeeta Nataka Akademi, 1960); M. Nagabhushana Sarma, *Folk Performing Arts of Andhra Pradesh* (Hyderabad: Telugu University, 1995).

u

URDU THEATRE

Urdu is one of the few languages spoken across India (and Pakistan) without a clearly demarcated regional home. It developed alongside modern Hindi, with which it shares a substantial vocabulary. Although it borrows more from Persian and Arabic whereas Hindi draws from Sanskrit, and they have separate scripts, these differences are academic and facile because the colloquial overlap is considerable. The folk form of *Nautanki, for instance, uses a mixed Hindustani idiom of Hindi and Urdu, understood by speakers of both tongues.

Strictly 'Urdu' theatre begins with a number of musical compositions in the mid-nineteenth century. The earliest, called *rahas* (literally 'mystery'), were written, directed, and designed by the Avadh prince, Wajid Ali Shah (1823–87), in Lucknow. Glowing descriptions of this royal entertainment inspired Amanat Lakhnawi (1817–59) to compose his famous musical *Indarsabha* ('Indra's Court', 1853), later staged in an open public space and, probably, also in the palace compound at Lucknow. It was an immediate and immense success both in performance and in print. With *Indarsabha*, the nascent drama in the Urdu language came out of the exclusive precincts of the court and made its debut on the public stage. Such was its popular

impact that it inspired dozens of
imitations elsewhere, causing a
veritable tradition of *sabha* plays
to emerge. Amanat's work
continued to be performed by
commercial companies well into the
twentieth century.

A more evolved phase started with
the rise of *Parsi theatre in Bombay. From
1854, these groups usually concluded their
main Gujarati plays with farcical Urdu
afterpieces. In terms of the quantum written
and produced, Parsi theatre's heyday
(1880–1920s) was the most productive

The Sabaj Pari in Amanat's
Indarsabha (performer Ram Dulari,
Calcutta, year unknown)

period in the history of Urdu drama. Soon after the emergence of the first
professional companies, the commercial potential of the language was
recognized and the managers developed their Urdu activities. In the
beginning, they made do with scripts written or translated (from Gujarati)
by local Urdu speakers, of whom Raunaq Banarasi (1825–86) and Aram (fl.
1870s), who composed many plays and 'operas' for the Victoria and Alfred
troupes, are best known. Later, with growing possibilities for touring, the
owners started recruiting 'genuine' Urdu writers mainly from the United
Provinces (now Uttar Pradesh) and Delhi, like Karimuddin Murad (1842–
?) and Amanatulla Hubab (d. 1911).

As scriptwriting became a lucrative career option, many who could
write and versify in Urdu took to drama. A few stayed on in north India,
like Hafiz Abdullah (d. 1922) and Nazir Akbarabadi (fl. 1888–1913), to
become popular there. Although a majority of these new playwrights were
mechanical run-of-the-mill wordsmiths (and even plagiarists, like the
mysterious Husaini Miyan Zarif), some, such as Talib Banarasi (1855–
1922), Syed Mehdi Hasan Ahsan (fl. 1897–1905), and Agha Hashr
Kashmiri (1879–1935), had genuine talent and creativity. Hashr, in
particular, displayed outstanding merit; his work had a freshness and
originality of imagination rare in the theatre of the time. A serious author,
he tried to raise the literary and intellectual standard of drama and
introduced contemporary social and moral concerns in plays like *Khubsurat
bala* ('Beautiful Trouble', 1909), *Yahudi ki ladki* ('Jew's Daughter', 1913),
and *Rustam aur Sohrab* ('Rustam and Sohrab', 1929).

These major playwrights, employed full-time by the important companies, invented the distinct style recognizable as the standard recipe of Parsi theatre. They were often well versed in several languages and familiar with the forms and traditions of Hindustani classical music. The directors, with whom they worked closely, were college-educated and had a degree of familiarity with European literature. Under their influence, Urdu drama became technically better constructed and acquired a significantly greater sense of the theatrical than the *rahas* and *sabha* compositions. The plays were mostly based on fantastic stories of erotic love and heroic adventure, derived from diverse traditional sources such as Indian folklore, Hindu mythology, popular history, Firdausi's *Shahnama*, and the *Arabian Nights*. This preoccupation with old, unrealistic tales held the Parsi stage until its very end. However, at the behest of the managers and with their active collaboration, a number of free and highly melodramatic Urdu adaptations of Shakespeare were made around the turn of the century. Afterwards, as nationalist sentiment against colonial domination intensified, original drama of religious, social, and sometimes patriotic import also appeared.

The musical tradition continued to dominate. No opportunity was ever missed of introducing songs, dances, or rhymed verse. The Shakespearean adaptations (more precisely appropriations) also followed the standard commercial strategies. Even distinguished writers like Ahsan and Hashr were obliged to interpolate not only comic subplots and the mandatory happy ending, but an abundance of songs and dances into the plots derived from the Bard. Possibly the north Indian Urdu poets who, beginning from the 1880s, were hired as resident authors, brought over this tradition, for the kind of plays they wrote is significantly different from the kind that Parsi theatre presented in its early years. For example, in Aram's translations of Edulji Khorey's Gujarati originals, songs and verses are woven into the fabric of the plot and seldom function as autonomous musical interludes, which they usually do in the drama of subsequent decades. Another stylistic element that the Urdu writers contributed was *nasr-e-muquaffa* (rhymed prose), the lineage of which goes back to early *dastan* (narrative) literature. Although it made the dialogue stilted and artificial, it did enhance the aural quality and immediate impact in performance.

Thus, one might say that from Wajid Ali Shah down to much of the Parsi output, Urdu theatre, despite all its technical polish and literary excellence, remained trapped in more or less mindless entertainment. Disconcerted by the commercialism, a sensitive dramatist like Ahsan retired early and publicly vowed never to write plays again. Hashr, too, felt thwarted by the demands of a cognitively debased stage.

In contrast, post-Parsi Urdu drama distinguishes itself by its serious social and moral concern, and realism of form and style. Theatre was no longer merely a source of recreation but also of meaningful experience. New authors wrote plays that, directly or parabolically, dealt with contemporary reality and problems. They tended to use colloquial speech and eschewed the practice of arbitrarily superimposing songs and dances. However, there was no commercial Urdu stage any longer, therefore no professional Urdu playwriting. As in several other Indian languages, it came virtually to a halt when, following the introduction of sound, cinema became the main medium of public entertainment and caused a large-scale exodus of artists and writers from the stage to the screen. Only the actor-manager Fida Hussain (1899–1999) kept his company alive till 1968, in Calcutta. Normal growth of Urdu theatre was also disrupted by the rise of linguistic communalism, which wrongly identified Urdu and Hindi with Islam and Hinduism respectively, causing the former's popular base to shrink drastically during the middle decades of the twentieth century.

In the absence of a durable and financially viable Urdu stage, plays were written only sporadically, by litterateurs who in most cases were not primarily dramatists. Their composing of texts was separated from the theatre and the results were often unstageable, producing a literary drama of more interest in reading than in performance. Although this tradition goes back to the turn of the century (for instance Mirza Hadi Ruswa's *Laila-Majnun*, 'Laila and Majnun', 1900), it became a major phenomenon only after the death of commercial theatre. Many eminent writers—such as Imtiaz Ali Taj (1900–70), Mohammed Mujib (1902–85), Upendra Nath Ashk (1910–96), Saadat Hasan Manto (1912–55), Ali Sardar Jafri, Majnun Gorakhpuri, Rajinder Singh Bedi, Abid Husain, Zahida Zaidi, Mohammad Hasan (1926–), Rifat Sarosh—contributed to this relatively large and varied corpus of literature.

Urdu drama re-established its connection to practical staging during the 1940s with Prithvi Theatres' productions from Bombay. These works, by Lal Chand Bismil, Inder Raj Anand, and Prithviraj Kapoor (1906–72) himself, were written in Hindustani. Prithvi introduced eminent actresses to

Habib Tanvir's *Agra bazar* revived by Naya Theatre (Delhi, 1989)

the Urdu stage, like the sisters Zohra Segal (1912–) and Uzra Butt (1917–). Certain chapters of the *Indian People's Theatre Association (IPTA) also performed Urdu plays and adaptations by, among the better-known authors, Khwaja Ahmad Abbas, Sardar Jafri, Ismat Chughtai, Ashk, and Habib Tanvir (1923–). Prithvi and IPTA advanced the cause of socially committed Urdu theatre. During the 1950s, Qudsia Zaidi and her Hindustani Theatre further intensified the element of modernity by presenting serious and skilful adaptations of major European dramatists. Another major patron was Mohammed Mujib who, as Vice-Chancellor of Jamia Millia Islamia University (Delhi), provided crucial support to Tanvir, leading to the writing and production of his famous play *Agra bazar* ('Bazaar in Agra', 1954).

Tanvir's theatricalization of the eighteenth-century environment in which the poet Nazir Akbarabadi lived and wrote, was truly significant as a contemporary musical. It combined dramatic interest and music with remarkable skill and meaningfulness. His other notable Urdu contributions were *Shatranj ke mohre* ('Chess Pieces', 1951), based on Premchand, and *Mere bad* ('After Me', 1969), making him the main personality in Urdu theatre since Independence. For a period Urdu also witnessed a revival of the musical form, mainly associated with Sheila Bhatia (1916–2008) and her Delhi

Art Theatre. Between 1969 and 1990, she wrote or commissioned scripts dramatizing celebrated Urdu poets and verse, and directed them emphasizing musical rendering of poems. Her productions of *Ghalib kaun hai* ('Who Is Ghalib?', 1969, by S.M. Mehndi), *Dard ayega dabe paon* ('Pain Will Creep in Quietly', 1979), *Yeh ishq nahin asan* ('This Love Isn't Easy', 1980), and *Amir Khusro* (1987) proved highly popular with lovers of Urdu poetry, though dramatically weak. Meanwhile, stageworthy translations from Indian and foreign languages by eminent Urdu writers (Sajjad Zaheer, Majnun Gorakhpuri) continued.

In recent years a new generation of Urdu playwrights has emerged. Still struggling to make a mark, they work with little-known amateur groups in different parts of India, including Mumbai, Pune, Hyderabad, Delhi, Patna, and Kolkata. However, they do not add up to a sustained dramatic tradition. Despite their zeal and effort, the future of Urdu theatre, linked as it is to the fate of the language, continues to be problematic. There are several reasons for this: a narrowing of Urdu's social base, lack of recognition, and inadequate official support for the language and its rich cultural heritage. Another is the changed social status of theatre in general, for a marginalized art form that survives largely on government subsidy, corporate sponsorship, or patronage of a small though culturally enlightened minority, does not attract professionals. Among the notable playwrights are Javed Siddiqui and Aslam Parvez (Mumbai), Shahid Anwar and Anis Azmi (Delhi), and Zaheer Anwar (Kolkata). In some states such as Bihar, Karnataka, Maharashtra, and Delhi, government-run Urdu academies have endeavoured to promote dramatic writing and performance in Urdu.

Yet another factor that makes it difficult to speak of Urdu theatre as a distinct entity is the rise of realism itself, an important feature of which is that dramatic speech corresponds to the nature of the subject and social background of the character. This often has the effect of blurring the lines between Urdu and Hindi, a difficult distinction at all times. Apart from a few relatively minor authors and small groups dedicated to the cause of promoting Urdu drama, there are no major playwrights who write exclusively in Urdu, nor an exclusively Urdu (or, for that matter, exclusively Hindi) stage. For example, the Hindi dramatist Surendra Verma used Urdu in his play on Ghalib, *Qaid-e-hayat* ('Imprisonment of Life', 1983); B.V. Karanth employed a Persianized form of Urdu in translating Girish Karnad's *Tughlaq* because the subject demanded it; Safdar Hashmi wrote his street plays in Hindi-cum-Urdu; Habib Tanvir mostly uses a mixed naturalistic idiom in which Urdu coexists with colloquial Hindustani and Chhattisgarhi dialects; Reotisaran Sharma scripts radio and television drama in both Hindi and Urdu.   JM

Gopi Chand Narang, *Urdu Language and Literature* (New Delhi: Sterling, 1991); Muhammad Sadiq, *A History of Urdu Literature* (Karachi: Oxford University Press, 1964); Ram Babu Saksena, *A History of Urdu Literature* (Allahabad: Rama Narain Lal, 1940); Ali Jawad Zaidi, *History of Urdu Literature* (New Delhi: Sahitya Akademi, 1993).

FORMS,
GENRES,
TRADITIONS

Abhinaya (from *abhi* + *ni*, 'to carry toward'): acting, or the medium of 'carrying' the meaning of a dramatic text to the spectator. It covers all histrionic activity: the physical, verbal, mental, and decorative. Traditionally, Indian theatre classifies *abhinaya* as fourfold: *angika* (physical), *vacika* (verbal), *sattvika* (internal or emotional/mental), and *aharya* (external or 'added', of costumes, props, make-up, as well as decor). The *Natyasastra* by Bharata, followed by Nandikesvara's *Abhinayadarpana* ('Mirror of Acting', c. sixth–seventh century), provide the most detailed and systematized guidelines on *abhinaya*. They emphasize that actors must convey the *bhavas*, emotive states, to others by outward expressions called *anubhavas* ('that which follows *bhava*'). *Vibhavas* (the determinants and stimulants of *bhavas*) can also get across through *citrabhinaya* ('pictured *abhinaya*'): actors can 'picture' to the audience the persons and objects with reference to which the emotive states are evoked.

The visual aspect of performance created by actors' bodies occupies a prominent place in traditional Indian theatre, hence the *Natyasastra* offers a codification of body language based on movements of different limbs and sign language based on their usage and applicability. This *abhinaya* is called *angika* (literally, pertaining to physical parts). Gestures and movements are categorized as *mukhaja* (facial), *sarira* (bodily), and *ceshtakrita* (of the whole organism), related respectively to the anatomical classification of *upanga* (minor physical parts), *anga* (major physical parts), and *sakha* (literally 'branch', the arms and legs). The six major *anga*s comprise the head, arms, chest, sides, waist, and legs. *Upanga*s include the eyes, eyebrows, nose, lower lip, cheeks, and chin. Although parts of the head, they are the vehicles for *mukhaja*. The *Natyasastra* describes these facial expressions as the very basis of *bhava*. It codifies movements of the head together with the *upanga*s in an amazingly elaborate way.

In the *sarira* division, movements of the remaining five *anga*s find equally detailed treatment. However, the motions of the entire body in *nyaya*s (fighting sequences related to *martial arts and exercises) come under *ceshtakrita*, for the *sakha*s (striking, graceful movements of arms and legs) together with the *sthanaka*s (basic standing positions) may be observed as varying from one theatre or dance form to another, thereby lying at the root of the specificity of particular forms. The *sakha*, *ankura* (literally 'sprout', signifying imaginative and improvisational representation, or suggestive ways of evoking objects and emotive states), and *nritta* ('pure dance', or graceful poses drawn from it) constitute important aspects of *angikabhinaya*. While most of the postures have been derived from nature and ordinary life on the basis of correspondences, some have roots in *ritual.

Hand gestures, known as *abhinaya hasta*s (literally 'hands'), are also extremely useful in developing a complete semiology: their common name, mudra, actually means 'sign'. Therefore, the *Natyasastra* offers a detailed account of single as well as combined hand gestures and their implementation in *angikabhinaya*, to signify specific objects and the meaning of a work. In contrast, *nritta hasta*s are hand postures used primarily in pure dance contexts.

Movements of the chest, sides, belly, waist, thighs, shanks, and feet have also been codified in the same measure. *Cari*s (motions below the hips) are given an important place in order to represent walking, or ground motion (*bhumicari*), as well as 'aerial motion' (*akasacari*). *Cari* refers to the movement of one foot, accompanied by the shank, thigh, and waist. When both feet move together, it is termed *karana*. A combination of three *karana*s is called *khanda*, and three

A *karana* pose sculpted on the walls of the Chidambaram temple, Tamil Nadu

khandas combined make up a *mandala*. Single *caris* related to others form *vyayama* or the system of exercise used in martial arts. The *Natyasastra* defines a number of *gatis* (gaits) too, in order to impart the varied walks of superior, middle-class, and inferior male as well as female characters, such as the hero, heroine, clown, the old, the young, and the insane. It also describes a number of *asanas* or sitting postures. The general notion of performatory units of movement emerges from body control in sitting, standing, and reclining positions. *Asanas*, *sthanakas*, and *mandalas* form the basic static stylized positions from which a variety of possibilities arise.

Bharata's chapter 17, on *vacika*, brilliantly discusses the principles of recitation and rendering of dialogue. They include usage of specific musical notes for particular moods or sentiments and identification of the three voice registers in the chest, throat, and head, and the four accents or pitches of *udatta* (high), *anudatta* (low), *svarita* (circumflex), and *kampita* (quivering). Illuminating treatment is given to six *alamkaras* ('ornaments') of delivery—high or low, excited or grave, and fast or slow— taking into account the voice in terms of degree, raising or lowering it on the one hand (a spatial attribute), and in terms of speed on the other (the temporal aspect).

Six *angas* ('physical parts') further investigate the voice in its aspects of inner body space and temporal sequentiality. *Viccheda* is the suspension within a subdivision of a given syntactical unit. *Visarga* is the stop at the completion of sentence. *Arpana* is a rendering in a rich, refined, and resounding voice, as if filling the entire space. *Anubandha* is non-stop rendering without pausing for breath. *Dipana* is the heightening of the voice, starting with the lowest register and gradually rising to higher levels, whereas *prasamana* is just the opposite. Thus *angas* explore the use of voice from other angles, of vocal or verbal continuity and silence, gradual thickening of the voice and thinning it down. Bharata discusses another aspect as well, intonation, developed further by Abhinavagupta (950–1025). The chapter concludes with references to threefold rhythm and tempo, as well as the significance of pauses and stops.

Sattvika, or communication through *sattva* ('essence', of the mind), is considered to be the soul of *abhinaya*, as in the *Natyasastra*, chapter 22. Delineation of the *sthayi* (stable, permanent) *bhava* with corresponding *vibhavas*, *anubhavas*, and *vyabhicari* (fleeting) *bhavas* is further strengthened by the portrayal and enactment of *sattvika bhavas* (pure involuntary impulses), which have corporeal as well as psychic aspects and cannot be performed without purity and concentration of mind. Therefore, *sattvika abhinaya* may be viewed, on the one hand, in terms of emotional acting and, on the other, in terms of the *sattvika bhavas*, the eight external indications of internal feelings.

Since these three aspects of *abhinaya* are inherent in the performer's body, mind, and soul respectively, they may be viewed as intrinsic to his being, whereas make-up, dress, and properties are added on. Thus these are called *aharya* ('added' or external) *abhinaya* and consist of *angaracana* ('physical painting' or make-up), *vesa* (clothes), *alamkara* (ornaments), *pratisirshaka* ('on the head', *masks, headdresses, and crowns), and *pushta* (properties and decor). The *Natyasastra* gives a detailed account of the fourfold ornaments, hair styles, and basic and mixed colours, and offers guidelines for making up and costuming men and women of different classes, regions, and even universes. *Pushta* is threefold: *sandhima* ('joined') made of birch, bamboo, hide, cloth; *vyajima* (mechanically devised); and *veshtima* (wrapped). It includes such set pieces as models of hills, trees, and carriages. The *Natyasastra* instructs pragmatically that they should be light and made from articles readily available in the locality. It also lays down the principles of make-up, manufacturing the costumes, and so on.

Chapter 22 also stipulates the procedure to integrate the different components of *abhinaya* harmoniously. This general approach to performance is called *samanyabhinaya*, explained by Abhinavagupta through a remarkable image comparing the performer to a perfumer. The latter, having bought sweet-smelling substances from a merchant, concocts them into a homogeneous mixture that makes a wonderful perfume. In the same way a performer combines his acquired skills, blending all the elements learnt to give an excellent and balanced performance. The image underlines the process in which an artist freely creates according to his life experience of people (*loka*), acquisition of the shastric tradition (Veda), and inner choice (*adhyatma*), out of the various norms laid down for communicating a particular emotion or situation. It also emphasizes the freedom of the artist's innovations and experimentation underlying his judgement in selecting conventional techniques on the one hand and creating ever-fresh methods on the other.

The chapter's treatment of *samanya* (common) *abhinaya*, compared to the specific ways of using limbs or voice in previous chapters, forms the very foundation of *Sanskrit theatre. It discusses *vakya* (vocal rendering of the theatrical text), *suca* (physicalization indicating the meaning of words to come), *ankura* ('sprouting' imaginative elaborations of the *bhava* one after another to unfold the levels of textual meaning), *nivrithyankura* (responsive imaginative enactment when listening to another's dialogue), and *natyayita* (metatheatre, to present different levels of time or space simultaneously and performance during *dhruva* songs at entry or exit). It also deals with *vacika* elements like *alapa* (conversing), *pralapa* (prattling), and *vilapa* (crying) as very common items of verbal behaviour.

Samanyabhinaya constructs a syntax for acting based on these *angika* and *vacika* elements, together with such involuntary emotive *sattvika* manifestations as *romanca* (thrill, horripilation), *vaivarnya* (change of complexion or colour of face and body), *vepathu* (trembling), and the *alamkaras* (ornamentation) of female grace like *bhava* (feelings of love), *hava* (expression of feelings), and *hela* (delicate expressions arising from such feelings). Chapter 22 describes *sattvika* on the basis of the most pervasive sentiment, love (*kama*), as a model for understanding other emotive states too.

Traditional Indian actors still follow the *Natyasastra*'s recommendations regarding diet, physical honing as in massages and specific training exercises, and lessons in grammar, literature, music, dance, and aesthetics, over many years, until considered ready to appear before the public.

Often apprenticed as young children, they must learn the whole repertoire before they debut, typically in their late teens (as in *Kathakali). Even then, actors are not supposed to reach their prime until they have substantial performatory experience, maturing only after the age of forty, and only then can they make their own innovative contributions to the form.

In conclusion, reference must be made to the two practices of representation in traditional Indian performance: *natyadharmi* (conventional and stylized) and *lokadharmi* (less conventional, based on ordinary life). However, the latter should not be confused with naturalistic or realistic modes of modern theatre; even *lokadharmi* maintains a certain degree of stylization. Thus the concept of *abhinaya* is not only much wider than the notion of acting in its modern sense, it is also fundamentally different from naturalistic or realistic acting which aims at producing an illusion of reality. *Abhinaya* is basically a suggestive mode of representation, which may be defined more in terms of conveying the *bhava* than 'acting'. Its doctrines and continuity remain vibrantly present in Indian traditional forms, whether theatre or dance, classical or folk.   KDT

Iravati, *Performing Artistes in Ancient India* (New Delhi: DK Printworld, 2003); Nandikesvara, *Abhinayadarpanam*, translated by Manomohan Ghosh (Calcutta: Manisha Granthalaya, 1992); Nandikesvara, *The Mirror of Gesture*, translated by Ananda Coomaraswamy and Gopala Kristnayya Duggirala (Cambridge: Harvard University Press, 1917); Nandikeswara, *Abhinaya Darpanam*, translated by P.S.R. Appa Rao (Hyderabad: Natyamala, 1997); Shveni Pandya, *A Study of the Technique of Abhinaya in Relation to Sanskrit Drama* (Bombay: Somaiya, 1990); Rakesagupta, *Studies in Nayaka-Nayka-Bheda* (Aligarh: Granthayan, 1967).

Alkap (possibly from *al*, Arabic for 'the', and *kap*, meaning any impersonation with suitable costumes): rural performance popular in undivided Bengal, especially in Rajshahi, Maldah, and Murshidabad districts, and the Rajmahal Hills in Jharkhand state, associated with the Gajan festival of Siva around the middle of April. *Kap* also refers to *Gambhira and the *Bahurupi impersonators; several opinions exist about the origin of the word, but all place the beginnings of this form in the late nineteenth century. It has no written script but scenarios based on popular love stories, which the actors elaborate with extempore dialogues, breaking up for songs, dances, and comic or satirical sketches called *kap*. Leaning totally on improvisation, it remains open-ended and can continue for days.

Early Alkap (1890–1920) resembled Gambhira in invoking Siva at the *asar bandana* (benediction to the session) and referring to him in the *kap*s. The preliminaries included a prayer to the goddess Saraswati and were succeeded with a dance by gaudily dressed women or cross-dressed males. Dhols, cymbals, and flutes provided accompaniment and a 'concert' before the performance to gather an audience, who sat around a makeshift acting area, often marked by two posts from which hung lanterns or Petromax pressure lamps. There were no green rooms or even a passage for entrances, so no scope of changing costumes or make-up during the show; the female characters who took part in the first dance wore those same dresses throughout. The cast, adept at physical acting, marked entries and exits just by getting up and sitting down respectively. The troupes had up to a dozen personnel.

Alkap broke away from religious festivals early in its history to become a poor rural cousin of city-bred *Jatra. It has almost merged with the Pancharas—recent productions by professional companies aimed solely at entertainment using proscenium stages, electronic gadgets at village fairs, and, unlike Jatra, extemporaneous conversations while following a storyline based on popular romantic tales (often a take-off from commercial Bengali or Hindi films).   KG

Ankiya Nat ('*anka* play')/**Bhaona** ('acting'): Bhaona, the neo-Vaishnava *Assamese theatre form, is intimately connected with the distinctive genre of vernacular drama created by Sankaradeva in the sixteenth century, which had originally been variously called Yatra (processional), *nata* (play), and *anka* (a single act), but later came to be designated as Ankiya Nat. Bhaona represents the applied aspect of plays written on the Ankiya Nat model. Although the tradition of writing such scripts has continued since the days of Sankaradeva and Madhavadeva, who followed in his footsteps, normally only plays written by this duo are accepted as Ankiya Nat proper. The presentation of such drama in the orthodox style is called Ankiya Bhaona, whereas that of any other play written in the same format and staged in near-identical fashion is called simply Bhaona. The language of the typical Ankiya Nat is Brajabuli (locally called Brajawali). Nowadays, however, plays are often written in contemporary standard Assamese and their production popularly termed *matribhashar* (of the mother tongue) or *asamiya* (Assamese) Bhaona.

Scholars like Kaliram Medhi, Birinchi Kumar Barua, and Maheswar Neog have convincingly averred that in formulating the Ankiya Nat genre, Sankaradeva must have drawn elements from indigenous theatrical and semi-theatrical institutions like *Dhuliya and Oja-Pali, and integrated them with classical Sanskrit dramatic ideals—in which he must have been steeped, as an erudite Sanskrit scholar. The plays, however, exclusively deal with mythological or legendary stories connected to the various avatars of Vishnu, since Sankaradeva's express purpose was to propagate Vaishnavism.

Ankiya Nat is a dance-drama in which vernacular songs and dialogue are interspersed with slokas and other pieces in Sanskrit. There are no act or scene divisions; the various components are strung together through the activities of the *sutradhara*, who plays a pivotal role throughout—introducing the theme, announcing entrances and exits of the characters, explaining the different situations, leading the benedictory singing, and so on. The characters enter and exit with typical dance steps; dialogues are delivered in a conventional stylized manner along with dance-like movements. Previously, it was customary for young boys to take women's roles. While benedictory pieces occur at the beginning and end, songs (*git*)

The Ankiya Bhaona *Rama-vijaya*, written by Sankaradeva (Uttar Kamalabari Satra, Majuli, 1986)

set to specific ragas and talas come at frequent intervals.

The orchestra, known as *gayan-bayan* ('singers and instrumentalists'), not only provides musical accompaniment and effects but also is responsible for the elaborate preliminaries (*dhemali*). Lighting used to be provided by chandeliers (*gasa*), torches (*ariya, mahala*), and pyrotechnic devices (*mahata/mata*), but Petromax pressure lamps and electric lights are freely available today. While the use of masks (*mukha*) for demons and animals is very common, often elaborately crafted effigies and accessories (*cho*) are utilized, so the green room is called *cho-ghar*. According to some hagiographic biographies, Sankaradeva staged his first drama, *Chihna-yatra* ('Scene Yatra'), against the backdrop of painted

scenery depicting the heavens (*vaikuntha*). However, the text has never been found, and scholars believe that the presentation was more like a tableau, without any written text. In any case, painted scenes have not been a feature of Bhaona in the remembered past.

The venue for Bhaona is usually the *nam-ghar* or occasionally a temporary structure (*rabha*). Regular rehearsals (*akhara*), sometimes extending to over one month, begin with a formal ceremony called *nat mela* ('opening of the play'). In some villages of Sonitpur and Nagaon districts there is an unusual vogue of organizing Bhaona on a grand scale. A number of troupes—sometimes over twenty—present separate performances simultaneously in different arenas under a single huge canopy specially erected for the purpose. Known as *Baresahariya* ('from various towns') or *Hejari* Bhaona, such occasions offer a grand spectacle put up by the collective efforts of a cluster of villages, and also serve as big fairs. Although in the orthodox neo-Vaishnava circle Bhaona is a ritual and act of piety, it is seen more and more as an art form, and adapted for the proscenium theatre and modern audiovisual media. Gahan Chandra Goswami was a leading performer, winning the Sangeet Natak Akademi award in 1969.   BD

B.K. Barua, *Ankiya Nats* (Gauhati: Department of Historical and Antiquarian Studies, 1954); Maheswar Neog, *Bhaona: The Ritual Play of Assam* (New Delhi: Sangeet Natak Akademi, n.d.).

Architecture: The sources for theatre architecture in India include treatises on music, dance, theatre, literature, and architecture (*vastusilpa*, literally 'art of matter'), Sanskrit plays, inscriptions, extant auditoriums, and dance halls in temples and palaces—some well preserved, a few in ruins. Although theatre possibly goes beyond the sixth century BC, as we learn from the *Natasutras* ('Actors' Sutras') of Silalin and Krishashva cited by Panini in his *Ashtadhyayi*, a work on grammar, there is no reference to playhouses. The oldest existing performance space is the Sitabenga cave, perhaps from the third century BC.

The *Natyasastra by Bharata, the earliest text mentioning theatre architecture, gives detailed descriptions of three types of auditoriums—*vikrishta* (rectangular), *caturasra* (square), and *tryasra* (triangular)—each having three sizes: *jyeshtha* (large), *madhyama* (medium), and *kaniyasa* (small). Bharata considered the *vikrishta-madhyama* (rectangular medium-sized) theatre the best, measuring 64 *hasta*s (cubits) by 32 *hasta*s, 'neither too large nor too small'. It had good acoustics and sight lines, with excellent actor–spectator relationship, vital in *Sanskrit theatre. Its length was halved into two parts of 32 *hasta*s square, the *ranga-mandapa* (stage pavilion) and *prekshaka-nivesana* (audience accommodation). The *ranga-mandapa* was again divided into two halves, *ranga* (stage) and *nepathya* (behind the scenes), each 16 *hasta*s by 32 *hasta*s. The *ranga* was further separated into front and back portions, each 8 by 32 *hasta*s. The front consisted of the *rangapitha* (literally 'stage seat', 8 by 16 *hasta*s, the central acting area facing the audience), and two subsidiary acting areas on either side called *mattavaranis* (each eight *hasta*s square and demarcated by four pillars at their corners). Behind was the *rangasirsha* ('stage top'), with the

1. MAIN ENTRANCE
2. PASSAGES
3. TIERS
4. RANGAPITHA
5. KUTAPA-VEDIKA
6. MATTAVARANIS
7. RANGASIRSHA
8. NEPATHYA

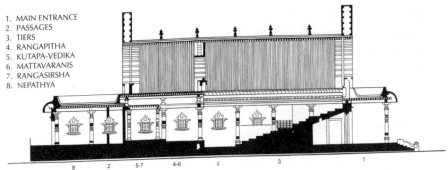

Side cross-section of medium rectangular auditorium as stipulated in the *Natyasastra*

kutapa-vedika ('orchestra platform') occupying eight *hasta*s squared in the centre.

The *ranga* was backed by a brick wall behind which was the *nepathya*. In the wall were two doors, one on either side of the *kutapa-vedika*. Each door was curtained by a *pati* or *apati* (cloth) dramatically used by actors while entering 'in anger, deep sorrow or great joy'. Stage directions in some plays indicate, 'Enter with a fling of the *pati*.' Another curtain, the *yavanika*, between the *rangapitha* and *rangasirsha*, concealed the first eight *purvaranga* preliminaries, not for viewing by the audience. Again, stage directions suggest that a single person 'draws the *yavanika* aside'. A third, flexible curtain, the *citra* ('pictured') *yavanika*, was held by two persons and lowered to reveal a character 'entering seated'. Descendants of this third variety of curtain can be seen in *Kathakali or *Yakshagana, but they normally hide standing characters.

The stage had no other equipment, as it was a theatre of the imagination. Owing to several acting areas, the action flowed smoothly from one zone (*kakshya*) to another; the locale changed by performers just walking out of it. The auditorium had tiered arrangements (*sopanakriti*) to seat spectators in public theatres and two levels (*duibhumi*) in a court theatre. The main entrance was in the east. The first tier was raised by 1 *hasta* from the floor, while the stage was raised by $1^{1}/_{2}$ *hasta*s. The shape of the auditorium was *sailaguhakara* ('like a mountain cave') for reasons of constructional necessity. The brick and wood used enhanced its acoustics. The *caturasra* and *tryasra* theatres were smaller, measuring 32 *hasta*s on each side. However, dance texts double this size for forms like the *rasaka*.

In Andhra Pradesh there exists a ruined open-air rectangular arena at Nagarjunakonda (Nalgonda district), dating from the second or third century AD. It has tiers for seating on all four sides. On one side central steps went up to the dressing room, beside which there was a shrine to the Buddhist goddess Haritti. Opposite it, the tiers were interrupted to cut out a passage through which the audience entered. The music, dance, or acting took place on the floor flush with the lowest sitting level. Several Buddhist Jataka tales mention theatre and *natasangha*s (actors' associations), who may have played at such amphitheatres.

In medieval times, the Sanskrit dramatic tradition underwent a change and acquired regional characteristics. The surviving Sanskrit genre of *Kutiyattam is staged inside *kuttampalam*s in Kerala. While these were purpose-built for theatre, other traditional forms use existing general structures. In Assam, *Ankiya Bhaona is performed in the long rectangular *nam-ghar*, or congregational prayer room, of a monastery, at one end of which is placed the sacred *Bhagavata* scripture on a high ornate pedestal. Plays are enacted facing it, in the central passage of the hall; on such occasions, a cloth is stretched on the opposite side from wall to wall, creating a dressing room from where the actors enter. In some *nam-ghar*s there is an area here especially reserved for storing costumes and props, also used as a green room (*cho-ghar*). Interestingly, women are not permitted inside *nam-ghar*s because the celibate monks who perform are not allowed to look at women, who must watch from outside the hall through a perforated wall.

In many Hindu temple complexes, the *nritya mandapa* ('dance pavilion') without walls was an obligatory architectural feature, constructed for ritual dances by devadasis as part of ceremonies or to entertain the deity. Some of the spaces are rectangular, as in the eleventh-

Ancient open theatre at Nagarjunakonda, arena in the centre

century Brihadeswara temple at Thanjavur (Tamil Nadu). In some temples of Gujarat, the octagonal dance hall is bound by eight pillars supporting the ceiling. In others (like the twelfth-century Belur temple in Hassan district, Karnataka), a square space for dance was placed in the centre of the *mandapa* with a slightly raised platform, superimposed by another circular platform, and bounded by highly ornate pillars at the corners. Theatre is still staged in *mandap*s in Manipur.

The Rajput maharaja Mansingh Tomar (reigned 1486–1516) built a unique circular *rachh* amphitheatre for dance and music, now in ruins, at Barai in Gwalior (Madhya Pradesh). It had rooms all around, while the roof above them used to seat spectators; the performances took place open-air on a central platform. A tall tower with a huge lamp inside it provided the lighting.

A few palace theatres still survive in Tamil Nadu. The *sangit-mahal* ('music hall') in the Thanjavur palace, possibly built by the ruler Accutapa Nayak (1560–1600), is a long hall with a gallery meant for the court ladies. It has a raised stage with huge square pillars at the back. Spectators seem to have sat on the floor. The Madurai palace theatre, built by Thirumal Nayak (1627–59), also has a long hall and upper gallery. Massive pillars with ornate brackets support the roof and

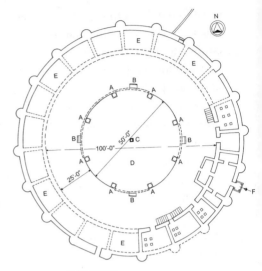

A. EIGHT LEANING TOWERS
B. FOUR PLATFORMS
C. THE CENTRAL STONE PILLAR
D. STAGE
E. ROOF ABOVE THE ROOMS
F. MAIN ENTRANCE

Floor plan of *rachh* amphitheatre at Barai, Gwalior

gallery. The rectangular stage is sunk below audience level, with steps at both ends. The king sat on its west. Opposite the stage is a large space on two levels where the audience squatted. A gauze curtain, behind which sat the queen and harem ladies, screened the gallery during performances. The Padmanabhapuram theatre (Kanniyakumari district) was erected in the eighteenth century in the Travancore palace. It has a rectangular hall with a polished black stage in the middle, sunk about a foot below floor level. Surrounding it on four sides are two tiers; courtiers sat on the upper one. The queen watched from the trellised window of a wooden box in one corner, and other harem ladies from a trellised gallery. The king sat near her, with a Saraswati shrine to his side.

Colonial times brought the curtained proscenium arch, imported from the West. Temporary private theatres combining indigenous and modern styles were constructed in such diverse locations as Wajid Ali Shah's durbar in Lucknow and zamindar mansions in Calcutta, like that of the *Tagore family. The public stage in the nineteenth century copied proscenium models fully (for example the long-lived Grant Road Theatre, Bombay, and the majestic Museum Theatre, Madras), but after the arrival of cinema and the decline of *Parsi theatre, most of them were converted into movie halls. Even in Calcutta, where the professional theatre had a residential character at such famous venues as the Great National, Star, and Minerva, the number had plummeted by the close of the twentieth century. Serious amateur groups across India after 1947 were forced to hire cinema halls in the morning, perform at ill-equipped venues, or share the few newly-built multipurpose proscenium auditoriums like the one at the Academy of Fine Arts (Calcutta).

This shortage of premises led to the opening of alternative centres for theatre. In Calcutta, for instance, many groups turned to the small Mukta Angan (1960), even though it was not well appointed.

Surprisingly, the Bengali commercial theatre gave birth to the first arena stage in the country, the Circarina, in 1976. During the 1950s in Bombay, Ebrahim Alkazi converted the terrace of his house into a tiny rooftop playhouse overlooking the sea. When he went to New Delhi, he designed two small spaces in Rabindra Bhavan: a sixty-seat studio theatre and the Meghdoot open-air theatre, both of which became legendary venues. The Chhabildas movement in *Marathi theatre grew in the hall of the Chhabildas Boys School. Newer auditoria for flexible work in Bombay are the Prithvi Theatre and the experimental theatre at the National Centre for the Performing Arts. In Delhi, such spaces include the small basement of the Shri Ram Centre and the 200-seat studio theatre at the *National School of Drama.

Contemporary theatres with an indigenous feel include the Kalakshetra and Sittrarangam,

Interior of Sittrarangam, Chennai

both in Chennai, and the Kerala Kalamandalam theatre in Cheruthuruthi (Thrissur district), Kerala. The Kalakshetra is enclosed by bars in Kerala temple style, but has a proscenium stage with a wide semicircular apron, wings, and borders. The circular Sittrarangam (literally 'small stage') has a thatched roof and trellised enclosure also in Kerala style. Its arced stage takes almost half the space; the other half has a few broad tiers for the viewers. A chamber theatre, it provides an intimate actor–audience relationship. The Kalamandalam auditorium is based on Kerala architecture, too, and used for traditional forms like Kathakali and Kutiyattam. However, modern spaces are ritually sanctified before use for devotional performances. Appukuttan Nair designed the Kalakshetra and Kalamandalam, while the Sittrarangam was designed by an Iranian architect, Shahriar Dehghan, in collaboration with Ludwig Pesch, a German musicologist.

From time immemorial, most folk forms have normally taken place outdoors, often in makeshift structures built with bamboo

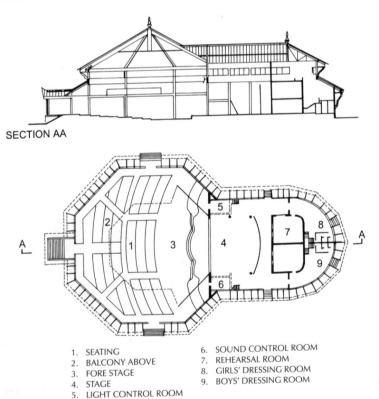

SECTION AA

1. SEATING
2. BALCONY ABOVE
3. FORE STAGE
4. STAGE
5. LIGHT CONTROL ROOM
6. SOUND CONTROL ROOM
7. REHEARSAL ROOM
8. GIRLS' DRESSING ROOM
9. BOYS' DRESSING ROOM

Cross-section and floor plan of Kalakshetra, Chennai

scaffolding, wooden platforms for a stage, cloth partitions screening the dressing rooms, and overhead canvas canopies for protection from the elements. Spectators are free to enter or leave the sitting area as and when they please. Many traditional forms now play inside proscenium halls if invited to do so. Early commercial companies, down to R.S. Manohar's National Theatres, used to erect their own improvised stages for performances on tour, but portable, prefabricated auditoria were perfected by the mobile *Bhramyaman companies of Assam. Most Indian actors still treat the stage, whether permanent or temporary, as a sacred space; even those who do not believe in religion may touch the floor or ground with their hand and then touch their forehead or chest, before entrance, as the time-honoured gesture of asking for blessings and uplifting (if not spiritually dedicating) their own performance.   GP

Dhiren Dash, *Catara, Jathara, Jatra—The Theatre* (Bhubaneswar: Padmini Dash, 1976); D.R. Mankad, *Ancient Indian Theatre: An Interpretation of Bharata's Second Adhyaya* (Anand: Charutar, 1950); Goverdhan Panchal, *The Theatres of Bharata and Some Aspects of Sanskrit Play-production* (New Delhi: Munshiram Manoharlal, 1996); Ludwig Pesch, *A Theatre for All: Sittrarangam, The Small Theatre* (Madras, Ekagrata, 2002); H.V. Sharma, *Caturasra madhyama natyamandapa* (New Delhi: National School of Drama, 2001).

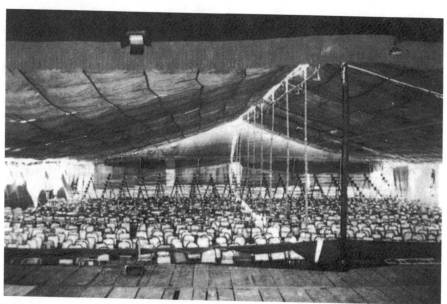

A Bhramyaman Mancha auditorium seen from the stage

Bahurupi (literally 'multi-formed'): quick-change artists across India who physically metamorphose into many characters. They transform instantly before the eyes of spectators, by just turning around. Contrary to their popular image, these impersonators require great skill in order to change both dress and personality so fast. References to such itinerant mimics or actors occur as early as the Buddhist Jataka tales (fourth century BC), and continue in the *Charyapadas* (tenth–twelfth centuries) and Abul Fazl's *Ain-e-Akbari* (sixteenth century). Society, however, labelled them as deceivers, not to be trusted, no doubt because of their ability to assume various disguises. In Bengal, children grow up with the belief that the Bahurupi is a bogeyman.

Their repertoire ranges from gods (Krishna, Rama, Kali) and

A Bahurupi

demons (Ravana, Taraka) to caricatures (sadhu, policeman, thief) and animals (tiger, bear, langur). The half-male, half-female deity, Ardhanariswara, strikingly exemplifies their virtuosic prowess, for the soloist sometimes also enacts the religious myth of Siva and Parvati or secular romances such as that of Laila and Majnun through this simultaneous double role of man and woman. Among social impersonations, Bahurupis commonly satirize the nouveau-riche but uncultured and penny-pinching babu, with straw-filled fake legs shod in new footwear made to dangle ludicrously as if from a chair.   PAg

Bandi Nata (literally 'widow dance'): an adjunct of *Danda Nata prevalent among lower-caste Hindus and tribals in Dhenkanal district and some parts of Sambalpur, Sundargarh, and Balangir in north-western Orissa. It takes its name from Bandi, which locally means 'widow', since the central character is Kutila, the widowed sister of Chandrasena, husband of Radha. Kutila plays a villainous role in the immortal love story of Radha and Krishna, but her unflinching devotion to and sacrifice for Krishna are given importance. Although Bandi Nata is Vaishnava to the core, the invocation is dedicated to Siva

and his consort Parvati, who also appear as figures at the beginning.

There are three characters: Kutila, Radha, and Krishna. Each sings a stanza, cast in the form of dialogue, and then dances to the accompaniment of a huge dhol and the wind instrument, *mahuri*. The refrains are repeated by a band of chorus singers, who occupy one side of the temporary covered structure. The drummer, dhol hung round his neck, controls the whole performance; often he shouts the beats and dances with the actors. The dramatic form is largely influenced by Danda Nata. Bandi Nata is not a written text; still in the oral tradition, it passes from one group to another. Action and humour are freely mixed with the dances and songs to keep spectators entertained. The technique is essentially folk, both in dance and music, though traditional tunes have been inserted of late.   DNP

Bandi Pethir ('clown play'), previously spelt as Bhand Pather: a distinct Kashmiri performing art combining mimicry, buffoonery, music, and dance, which emerged some 2000 years ago and reached its culmination in the tenth century. The Sanskrit aesthetician Abhinavagupta, said to have lived in Kashmir, refers to it in his *Abhinavabharati* (tenth century) as *bhanda-natya* ('clown-theatre'). It has remained the most popular folk form of *Kashmiri theatre for the last thousand years because its scope blends several arts to entertain, inform, and persuade.

Certain features have been present in every Bandi Pethir over the centuries. Typically it starts with a musical performance which, besides attracting spectators, creates an emotional mood that accords with the intended drama. The three essential components of Bandi music are the oboe-like *swarnai*, a small one-sided stick-drum (*nagari*), and a big dhol. At the end of the musical prelude, called *catusak*, the performers sing hymns and pray for the well-being of the audience. This is followed by a prologue to the

Pethir, in the form of a brief conversation among the three main actors who intimate the theme and plot. The principal actors are the *magun* (the leader), *sutardhar* (the commentator), *vidushak* or *maskhari* (the jester), and *pariparsok* or *kurivol* (the lasher). The *magun* produces the play and prays for the people, the *sutardhar* comments on the action, the *maskhari* delights the spectators with his silly tricks and taunts, and the *kurivol* lashes the jester whenever he goes beyond control.

Bandi Pethir today has deviated from many of the norms of the classical Pethir known as *banditsok* ('*bands'* clan'), but in spite of the vicissitudes of the centuries, its rudiments have remained intact. It continues as a full-blown dramatic

A Bandi Pethir troupe in performance

form in which several arts like
*masks, *mime, music, and dance
converge. Although it reflected the
changing milieus, its minimal stage
fixtures did not require fundamental
alteration. The repertoire of available
Pethirs is reminiscent of the middle
ages, as far back as the eleventh
century. The performers are tutored
to adhere to the stories and dialogue
they inherited from their ancestors:

FOOL: When did this Pethir of
yours start?

COBBLER: Harsha was the king,
Varsha was his minister, Bahur was
his fool, and Daydut his *magun*.

[From *Vatal pethir*, 'Cobblers' Play']

The main reason for Bandi
Pethir's repetitious character is the
absence of any parallel theatrical
tradition in Kashmir, particularly
since the fourteenth century. Yet it
enjoyed enormous popularity in
villages and towns as it expressed, on
the one hand, the covert protest of
the suppressed populace against the
forces of exploitation, and reflected,
on the other hand, Kashmiris'
patriotic reaction to unending alien
rule. The villainy of local landlords,
in their spaniel loyalty to the
changing foreign rulers who did not
know the language and customs of
the people, is the target of satire in
Razi pethir ('Kings' Play'). Similarly,
in *Derzi pethir* ('Dards' Play'), the
hard-hearted arrogance of the Dard
kings is exposed by reducing them
to brainless fools and jesting about
their haughtiness. Even common
men and classes living a miserable
life, like the scavengers, are ridiculed
for their incongruities; if in *Vatal
pethir* scavengers are lacerated for
their filthiness, in *Gwaseny pethir*
('Sadhus' Play'), cloistered hermits
are lampooned for their
incontinence and hypocrisy.

These well-liked plays were
performed faithfully by strolling
professionals called Bhagats or Bands
through the centuries. At some
permanent settlements of Bands in
Kashmir, they persevered to defend
the legacy of Pethir from unfriendly
conditions. The most important
centres of these entertainers are
Akingam, Takiya Imam Sahib,
Wahthor, Drwagimul, Bwamay,
Balapur, Pakharpur, Swayibug,
Palhalan, Lolapur, Gulgam, and
Kerihom. Each adheres to the style
of performance established by its
legendary founders, and allegiance
to tradition forms the basis of
distinction of the group. Some
names of antiquarian interest in the
field are Guly Muhar, Swadi Muhar,
Madhav Muhar, Karim Shala,
Mwakhti Long, Subhan Khend
(Akingam), Sidiq Joo (Shangas),
Razaq Wony (Imam Sahib), Karam
Baland (Wahthor), and Usman Batt
(Lolapur). The genre persisted despite
unfavourable political climate and
devastating calamity: most of the
Bands died in the famine of 1877,
as witnessed by Walter Lawrence.

Soon after 1947, when politics needed an effective and direct rapport with the masses, there was a sudden revival of Bandi Pethir; political and economic programmes found expression in various Pethirs which, besides providing pure entertainment to the people, disseminated the messages of family welfare, universal education, adult literacy, flood control, modernized agriculture, and so on. The state government instituted awards, organized festivals, built town halls, and established the Jammu and Kashmir Academy of Art, Culture and Languages in 1958, considerably encouraging folk theatre. Mohammad Subhan Bhagat and Moti Lal Kemmu played the most significant roles in revivifying the flagging tradition: they not only wrote about the theory of Bandi Pethir, but also composed new Pethirs with contemporary features. Inspired by Subhan Bhagat's work, the time-honoured centres of Bandi Pethir reorganized themselves under new groups like the Kashmir Bhagat Theatre, Kashmir Bandi Theatre, National Bandi Theatre, Alamdar Theatre, Baba Rishi Folk Theatre, Gulmarg Folk Theatre, and Shah Wali Luki Pethir Centre.   SS

Bayalata ('outdoor theatre') of north Karnataka: as its etymology indicates (*bayalu* means open-air

field, *ata* means theatre), Bayalata refers to virtually all forms of traditional *Kannada theatre. In southern Karnataka, both the eastern and western varieties of *Yakshagana are termed Bayalata, whereas in the north several other distinct genres are also included under the name. The most prominent of these are Dasarata and Radhanata; Parijata, popularly known as Srikrishnaparijata; Doddata, also called the *Mudalapaya* style of Yakshagana; and various others grouped collectively as *Sannata, which emerged from the lively coexistence of many Bayalata forms in the nineteenth century.

Dasarata is perhaps the earliest of them all, traced back to the Dasas—saint-poets and singers of the twelfth-century Bhakti tradition. However, it has adapted and localized the Krishna legend so much that in the prefatory episode of every performance, Krishna appears as a cowherd, extracting toll from the milkmaids. Then enters Chimana, the heroine, who confronts Goddibhimanna, the hero. They engage in a long and lively duel of wits, by turns attacking mankind and womankind, through songs and dialogue replete with Puranic allusions and contemporary references. Interludes (*sogu*) bring variety into the narrative. According to scholars, Dasarata, which appears to have been popular in the eighteenth century, was taken to Maharashtra where it influenced the formation of *Tamasha. In the nineteenth century, the influence of Tamasha flowed back to Karnataka to shape Radhanata, which looks like a distant cousin of Dasarata.

Around the same time, in the eastern district of Raichur, a poet named Aparala Timmana wrote a play based on the Telugu *Bhama-*kalapam* of Andhra Pradesh. This variation soon spread all over north Karnataka, becoming known as *Srikrishnaparijata* ('Krishna and the *parijata*'). The key performer (Dute) coordinates the songs, improvised dialogue, and continuous interaction with each character. This form, too, begins with the Krishna-and-milkmaids episode but the main plot concerns the rivalry between Rukmini and Satyabhama, Krishna's two wives, over acquiring the coveted celestial *parijata* tree. Narada's meddling in the affair turns it into a complicated battle of egos. With vigorous, high-pitched songs, energetic percussion, and witty verbal exchanges, Parijata combines the mundane and the philosophical in an extraordinary manner.

Meanwhile Doddata, the northern variant of Yakshagana, also became popular in several parts of the state. As its name suggests (literally 'big, or large, theatre'), almost everything in Doddata is larger than life—the themes belong entirely to the epic world, the dance is stylized, the speech patterned, and the costume and make-up predominantly non-realistic. Like regular Yakshagana, Doddata blends songs and speech in a fast-paced narrative, the only difference being that it uses scripted dialogue. The Bhagavata (sometimes called *sutradhara*) remains the central performer and his companion, Sarathi, provides the humour. Doddata employs varied themes, always excelling in capturing heroic sentiments, climactic combat, and supernatural elements.

Female impersonator as a Bayalata Doddata queen

Demon in Bayalata Yakshagana

All these varieties of Bayalata are enacted during village fairs and community festivals on a raised wooden platform, about 5 m by 4 m in the case of Doddata and 3 sq. m in the others. A back curtain separates the stage from the green room and in front a large harmonium placed in the middle of the stage has the troupe's name written on it. The other instrumentalists—tabla, horn, and cymbal players—sit or stand around while the main singer and his companion keep changing their places during the performance. In Doddata, men do the female roles, while in some genres like the Parijata, women take part. The costumes and make-up in Doddata are slightly simpler versions of those in Yakshagana, but in most other Bayalata forms costumes are simpler still, with almost no make-up. AKV

Basavaraj S. Naikar, *The Folk-Theatre of North-Karnataka* (Dharwad: Karnatak University, 1996).

Bhagat ('devotee', colloquially derived from *bhakta*, 'one who feels bhakti'): originally anyone in north India who acted episodes from Krishna's life, but now applied to their performances. It is related to the more popular *Raslila and *Nautanki or *Swang. In earlier times, Bhagats used to enact various characters as a devotional counterpart to the lighter tradition of Bhand entertainers. They developed their own distinctive features: a serious approach, limited jokes, and stronger singing and dancing. Bhagat's present phase started in the nineteenth century, centred in Agra, Vrindavan, and Mathura in Uttar Pradesh, where troupes or schools (*akhadas*) formed that did not restrict themselves to religious themes. Dance and music became very important, the use of various and constantly changing metres making the performance lively. Often Bhagat is staged on a high, long platform in the marketplace, with the audience sitting on two sides.   PAg

Bhagati (from Bhagatu, 'minstrel'): Sindhi folk form. The antiquity of this style of open-air theatre cannot be dated precisely. However, it appears from external evidence that Bhagati was in vogue in the eighteenth century.

A Bhagati band comprises the leading Bhagatu (plural Bhagata), one or two supporting companions (*jhelis* or *bolryas*), and a few disciples of the leader. The accompanists consist of a harmonium player, a sarangi player, and two percussionists—a *dhokri* (on tablas) and a *dholaki* (drummer). Some troupes also include one jester. When performing, the Bhagata are dressed in flowing white *jamo* or *peshwaz* (gown) reaching the ankles and red *bochhan* (sash) draped round the shoulders, flowing down to the knees and loosely held at the waist by a cummerband. They don a red *pagri* (turban), and are adorned with *kundhals* (earrings), *tilak* (mark) on their foreheads, and *chher* (anklets of small bells).

The venue is an open village street, but after Independence and the migration of Sindhi Hindus to India, Bhagati has been staged in regular theatres in cities before invited audiences. It is traditionally performed in the calm of the night.

The spectators sit on carpets spread in the street; latecomers have to watch standing. The arena, and a pathway about 30 m long, are reserved for the troupe's easy movement. The leading Bhagatu takes position at one end of the pathway, surrounded by the accompanists. The supporting Bhagata place themselves on the pathway at appropriate distances but keep changing their positions while performing.

The troupes present shows on specific invitations from a village panchayat or religious institution on the festive occasions of Holi, Baisakhi, Diwali, or the anniversaries of saints. The performance starts with an invocation to the Lord followed by a couple of devotional songs. The leading Bhagatu then starts narrating a popular folktale in dialogues, interspersed with songs, music, dance, and anecdotes. The supporting Bhagata repeat whatever he says. The Sindhi folk romances normally enacted in Bhagati are those of Dodo and Chanesar, Sorath and Rai Dyach, Umar and Marui, Mumal and Rano, Lila and Chanesar, Rup and Basant.

The specialty of Bhagati is its dancing peculiar only to Sindhi minstrels. It has vigorous, rhythmic footwork, and the *pheri* (pirouette) holds the audience in complete thrall. The dance goes on and on, ending when the music reaches a crescendo. The music is based on classical ragas like Kohiyari, Jog, Rano, Asa, Prabhati, Sindhu Bhairavi, Tilang, Manjh, and Sindhu Sorath (or Maru Vihag). Bhagati concludes in the early hours of the morning and, if the story has not reached its end, continues the next evening.   PA

Bhagavata Mela (literally, 'worshippers' ensemble'): Telugu dance-dramas presented in Thanjavur district, Tamil Nadu, as part of the festival of Narasimha Jayanti (the avatar Narasimha's birth, celebrated around the first week of June). Although Melattur is the village commonly associated with Bhagavata Mela, the nearby villages of Sulamangalam, Uthukkadu, Nallur, and Saliyamangalam also have similar performances. However, only in Melattur is it staged regularly, outside the Sri Varadaraja Perumal temple. It is perhaps the only traditional form enacted by Brahmans in Tamil Nadu. The performers are devotees of Narasimha, the presiding deity of Melattur. Although many of their families have spread to different

Hiranyakasipu and Lilavati in a Bhagavata Mela performance of *Prahlada charitram*

places across the world, they invariably arrive two days before the event, rehearse, and perform.

Narayana Tirtha (*c.* 1650–1750), a yogi, migrated from Andhra to Tamil Nadu and settled in Varagur (Thanjavur district). He composed *kritis* (works) and songs in Telugu and Sanskrit, set to dance. *Parijatapaharanam* ('Stealing the *parijata* Tree') and *Rukmangada* are his two most popular texts, written to spread devotion for Krishna. Those committed to propagate Krishna worship were called Bhagavatas, thus the dance-dramas composed by them were named Bhagavata Mela. Gopalakrishna Sastri, a disciple of Narayana Tirtha, kept alive this tradition and his son Venkatarama Sastri (eighteenth century), the best-known Bhagavata Mela dramatist, authored twelve dance-dramas in Telugu (six of them discovered recently in Melattur). The most commonly staged, *Prahlada charitram* ('Prahlada's Story'), tells the tale of Narasimha's triumph over the demonic Hiranyakasipu.

In the 1930s, a group of pandits in Melattur sought to revive *Prahlada charitram*, as Bhagavata Mela had fallen into decline since the mid-nineteenth century. The village munshi, V. Ganesa Iyer, offered to supervise these efforts and became the chief preceptor, saving the relatively unknown form from extinction. Leading performers included Balu Bhagavatar and Iyer's son, G. Swaminathan. Later, scholars like E. Krishna Iyer (who had revived Bharatanatyam) and Mohan Khokar brought it to national recognition, while Rukmini Devi-Arundale staged modernized productions based on Bhagavata Mela between 1959 and 1971, all leading to its greater acceptance as part of classical performatory heritage.

The shows, in front of the village temple, always begin with the entry of Konagi the clown, followed by Ganesha wearing an elephant mask, while all other characters enter from behind half-curtains. Men play the female roles. It is claimed that the performance is executed in keeping with the grammar explicated in the *Natyasastra. One can find strong traces of classical Bharatanatyam in the way the performers express themselves. Explanations for the songs are given through dialogue, mudras, and *bhavas*. The music, based on Carnatic traditions, adds to the impact. Most often the dancers sing as well. The accompanying instruments are tambura, flute, violin, *mridangam* drum, and *talam* (cymbals).   CA

Bhana (perhaps from *bhand*, 'to mock', 'to deride'): solo form of *Sanskrit theatre presenting the exploits of a rogue (*dhurta*) in one act comprising a variety of incidents not progressively developed. Typically, a learned and expert *vita* (a parasitic companion of a dissolute young man or of a courtesan, skilled in singing, music, and poetry, on familiar terms with his associate whom he virtually serves as a *vidushaka*) described his own or others' experiences. He suggested the *sringara* (erotic) and *vira* (heroic) *rasas*, but evoked laughter and satire. The playwright had to invent the theme and generally employed the *bharati* (spoken) *vritti*, sometimes the *kaisiki* (graceful) too. Consequently, *bhana* texts abounded in verbal description, improvised further by the performer. They contained all ten *lasyangas* (feminine components of dance), described by G.H. Tarlekar on the basis of the *Natyasastra* as follows:

Geyapada—song by the vocalist, seated, and accompanied by instrumental music.

Sthitapathya—a woman separated from her lover and suffering pangs of love recites in Prakrit, full of sentiment.

Asina—song of sorrow and anxiety rendered in a seated posture without instrumental accompaniment.

Pushpagandika—songs and dances performed by a woman but accompanied by male movements.

Pracchedaka—a woman who, afflicted by moonlight and thus excited by passion, clings to her lover even if he has done wrong.

Trimudhaka—even metres full of manly states and composed of delicate diction.

Saindhavaka—representation, using Prakrit, of a lover who failed to keep an appointment.

Dvimudhaka—song of *caturasrapada* (in four lines, each repeating the same tala pattern), full of sentiment and emotive states, used for striking effect. Afterwards, according to Abhinavagupta (950–1025), the performer steps in four directions.

Uttamottamaka—composition in various metres with many sentiments of *hela* and *hava* (the delicate expressions of feminine love).

Uktapratyukta—combination of speech and counter-speech due to pleasure or anger, containing censure, set to music.

The actor wore make-up only once (*ekaharya*) and performed many roles. He used the ingenious device of *akasabhashita* ('aerial discourse'): to accost, speak, and reply as if addressing one actually present, making rejoinders, and quoting the supposed speech of another. Thus *bhana* presented a challenge to perform various characters and incidents singly, because its nature as a monodrama could have rendered it monotonous. Only a performer fully trained in *abhinaya*, music, and dance could have succeeded in it. Moticandra's edition of very old texts titled *Caturbhani* ('Four *Bhanas*', *c.* fourth century) may best illustrate this form.

KDT

Bhaoriya ('actor' in the Assamese dialect of upper, or eastern, Assam; 'clown' in the dialects of lower, or western, Assam): The word comes from *bhao*, which has such connotations as role-playing as well as imitating, pretending, or masquerading. The Bhaona of *Ankiya Nat also has the same etymological root, which in turn derives from the Sanskrit *bhava*.

In the Kamrup region of lower Assam anybody who has a flair for wit and humour, particularly one who entertains people with funny antics, is called a Bhaoriya; but true Bhaoriyas are mostly performers of traditional and folk forms, like the *Dhuliya, of that region, in which clowning and witty repartee are integral to the performance. In many such troupes the virtuosity of a master Bhaoriya is the tour de force, and their fame and popularity rest largely on him. However, some Bhaoriyas have individually earned a name through their jesting, pranks, and other out-of-the-ordinary acts. Ningni Bhaoriya of the Barpeta area was such a figure in recent memory; many stories about him, some akin to those of Tenali Rama in south India, are popular even now. Mohan Chandra Barman of the Nalbari area, a Bhaoriya par excellence, was a living legend.

The term Bhaoriya is also attached to some traditional performing arts. A sub-variety of Oja-Pali is known as Bhaoriya Oja-Pali because it leans heavily on play-acting. Similarly, there is a folk-drama form in the south Goalpara district called Bhari-gan (*gan* means song) where *bhari* seems to be a corruption of *bhaoriya*. In the eastern Goalpara region a class of songs termed Bhaoriyar Gan also has humorous overtones.

BD

Birendranath Datta, *A Study of the Folk Culture of the Goalpara Region of Assam* (Guwahati: Gauhati University, 1990); Birendranath Datta (ed.), *Traditional Performing Arts of North-east India* (Guwahati: Assam Academy, 1990).

Bharat Lila ('*Lila from the Mahabharata*'), also known as Dwari Lila after its pivotal character: a form of musical folk theatre prevalent in the southern district of Ganjam in Orissa. The episode it depicts concerns the love and marriage of the hero Arjuna and Subhadra. In the play, Subhadra visits Arjuna and expresses her love. But Arjuna declines as she, being Krishna's sister, is like a sister to him. Then the Dwari (sentry) enters and counters all his arguments, quoting incidents from different epics and other religious texts. At last Arjuna is defeated and agrees to marry Subhadra.

There are only four characters: Krishna's wife Satyabhama, Arjuna, Subhadra, and the Dwari. Bharat Lila is not a written script but continues in the oral tradition. All the characters sing and dance. In between, improvised prose dialogues are spoken to explain the scenes and situations. The refrains of the songs are sung in chorus. The Dwari's acting and dancing provide humour. About fifty professional troupes perform Bharat Lila in and around Ganjam.   DNP

Bharud (possibly from the mythical bird with two faces): Marathi dramatic song with a humorous story which has two meanings—material at the surface level and spiritual at the deeper—to entertain and provide moral or ethical instruction respectively. A very old poetic form employed mainly by the saint poets like Eknath (1528–99), who wrote 300 Bharuds on 125 subjects, it is quite unique and very popular. Under the guise of comedy, it criticizes inhuman practices in different cults, and hypocritical or fraudulent behaviour. The characters depicted include the Joshi (fortune-teller), sadhus, housewives, and Gondhalis (Gondhal performers). The description of common situations, such as quarrels between husband and wife, scorpion bites, and exorcisms of ghosts, exposes silly customs, superstitions, and duping of ignorant people by sadhus.

Bharud may be merely sung as part of a bhajan, or sung and enacted, often within a *Lalit. The actor-singer dresses as a Gondhali, Daur (an actor), Vaghya (male worshipper of Khandoba), or Vasudev (performer with peacock feathers in his cap) and uses traditional tunes, and movements and rhythms from games like kabaddi. His companions (*sampadani*) remain in their usual clothes. Verisimilitude is added with a prop, such as a basket or a baby tied to the back. Not much make-up is applied. Dance consists of rhythmic steps and rapid spinning movements, anklets enhancing the effect. *Angik* (physical) *abhinaya* is important. Several interpolations occur in the form of dialogues between the leader and his companions. Generally the first stanzas depict the material situation and later stanzas elaborate upon the theme, before reaching the spiritual conclusion. In modern times, performers like Shahir Sabale have become crowd-pullers.   MP

Bhava (feeling, mood): theoretically, the emotive states expressed in a performance towards the evocation of *rasa. They are classified into *sthayin*, *sancarin* or *vyabhicarin*, and *sattvika*. An emotion is recognized as *rasa* if it is a sufficiently permanent and major human instinct, capable of being delineated and developed to its climax with its attendant and accessory feelings, and if there are persons of that temperament to feel imaginative sympathy at its presentation. Thus *bhavas* may be viewed first as the *sthayin* (stable, permanent) emotions, those that have the inherent potentiality of transformation into *rasa*, as follows:

Bhava	Rasa
Rati (love)	*Sringara*
Hasa (laughter)	*Hasya*
Soka (sorrow)	*Karuna*
Krodha (anger)	*Raudra*
Utsaha (energy)	*Vira*
Bhaya (fear)	*Bhayanaka*
Jugupsa (disgust)	*Bibhatsa*
Vismaya (amazement)	*Adbhuta*

A ninth, *sama* (tranquility), is also admitted as the *sthayibhava* of *santa rasa*. These durable *bhavas* are defined as the conditions that neither those akin to them, nor those opposed to them, can overpower. Such a *bhava*, when delineated in a play, poem, or any other art form, pervades the heart of the sympathetic spectator, reader, or connoisseur.

The thirty-three *vyabhicarins* or *sancarins* are relatively fleeting, the feelings and states accessory to and accompanying their respective *sthayins*. Every *sthayin* is complemented by a few relevant fleeting psychological states:

Nirveda (indifference, despondency)
Avega (agitation, excitement)
Dainya (misery)
Srama (fatigue)
Mada (intoxication)
Jadata (stupor)
Ugrata (cruelty)
Moha (distraction, delusion)
Vibodha (awakening)
Supta (dreaming)
Apasmara (dementedness, epilepsy)
Garva (pride)
Marana (death)
Alasya (indolence)
Amarsha (indignation)
Nidra (sleep)
Avahittha (dissimulation)
Autsukya (impatience)
Unmada (insanity)
Sanka (apprehension)
Smriti (recollection)

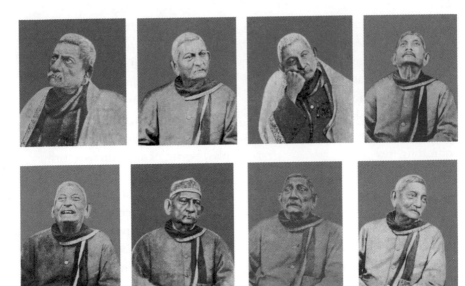

Girish Chandra Ghosh demonstrating eight *bhavas*, with bilingual captions as in the original printing in 1909: diabolic purpose (*durabhisandhi*), disgust (*ghrina o birakti*), deep cogitation (*gabhir chinta*), meditation (*dhyan*), in high glee (*ahlade atkhana*), deliberation (*samkalpa-bikalpa*), fright (*bibhishika*), smitten by beauty (*rupamugdha*)

Vyadhi (sickness)
Santrasa (alarm)
Vrida (shame)
Harsha (joy)
Asuya (envy)
Vishada (despair)
Dhriti (equanimity, endurance)
Capalata (restlessness)
Glani (weakness)
Cinta (anxiety)
Vitarka (deliberation)
Mati (resolve)

*Sattvika*s are involuntary expressions of feelings, on the one hand physical and on the other rooted deeply in the psychic state. Their involuntary nature betrays their emotive and psychic basis. Therefore they cannot be enacted mechanically and always need the performer's emotional involvement:

Stambha (paralysis)
Sveda (perspiration)
Romanca (horripilation)
Svarabhanga (disturbance of speech)
Vepathu (trembling)
Vaivarnya (change of colour)
Asru (tears)
Pralaya (fainting)

Additionally, Bharata and his commentators emphasize that when all the components of theatre beginning with *vibhava* (the stimuli of the *bhava*s and the environment in which they take place) are presented, *rasa* manifests itself in the spectator. Thus *alambana vibhava* (the determinant person or thing with reference to which a sentiment arises), *uddipana vibhava* (the attendant objects and circumstances which stimulate or enhance *bhava*), and *anubhava* (the consequent appropriate expressions on the face and external symptoms of the body indicating the rise of a *bhava*) are essential for the realization of *rasa*.

KDT

Rasa-bhaava Darshan (Delhi: Clarion, 1997).

Bhavai (perhaps derived from *bhav*, 'world', or *bhava*, 'emotion'): Gujarati folk theatre. In the fourteenth century, an excommunicated Brahman named Asaita Thakar, who was a *kathakara* (narrator of Puranic stories) familiar with dance and music, began writing plays with prose dialogue, perhaps inspired by one of the medieval Sanskrit *uparupaka* forms, enacted in the open. He is said to have written 360 scripts called *vesha* (literally 'dress'), which later came to be known as Bhavai, along with other similar plays written after him.

Bhavai is staged open-air in front of temples as a community *ritual honouring the goddess Amba. Before the actors begin, they gather near a large earthen lamp and a drawing of a *trishula* (trident) symbolizing the goddess, sing *garbi* (religious songs) in her praise, and invoke blessings for the success of the performance. The *nayaka* (leader)

A Bhavai performance, with female impersonators

then enters from the makeshift dressing room and marks a large circle called the *chachara* or *podha*, considered a sacred place of pilgrimage and inside which the performance takes place. A barber comes with a torch and oil to feed the flame that remains the central lighting source throughout the show. Next, the actors enter from a distance, providing their own light with small torches in their hands, weaving dance patterns in the air.

Members of the orchestra, comprising two *bhungala*s (long thin copper pipes), tablas, *jhanjha* (large cymbals), and harmonium, then take their place near the edge of the *chachara*. In Asaita Thakar's time the *pakhavaja* (double-ended drum) and *ravaja* (a sarangi-like string instrument) were played instead of tablas and harmonium respectively. Vocal music provides the opportunity to sing local melodies, ragas, *garbi*s, marriage songs, and other familiar folk tunes. A musical prelude is delivered addressed to Amba. The audience gathers and sits around the *chachara*, leaving a passage for actors' arrival from the dressing room to the arena. For entrances, the *avanun* (entry song) is sung and the *bhungala* played loudly to inform the actor of his cue.

First enters Ganapati, god of benevolence, holding in front of his face a bronze plate on which is drawn the auspicious swastika, and the musicians sing praising him. After

him comes the goddess Kali, dancing with two lit torches in her hands. (A man plays her role, as women do not take part in Bhavai.) She blesses the villagers and their cattle wealth. Then enters Juthana or Ranglo, the comic character, whose antics make people laugh but also have philosophical layers. He acts as the conscience, satirizing, criticizing, lampooning the doings of authority figures, and pinpointing social evils. Major plays begin around midnight and continue till early morning. Some favourites are *Jhanda Jhulan* (about the love between a Muslim youth and a Hindu merchant's wife), *Chhela Batau* (a heroic romance), and the mythological *Kana-Gopi* ('Krishna and the Gopis'). They depict social, political, or religious themes, educate the people, and try to raise the moral, ethical, and cultural life of their society. The satire takes shape through both verbal and physical humour. The entire cast wears colourful costumes.

Famous twentieth-century Bhavai entertainers included Muljibhai Nayak, Pransukh Nayak, and Chimanlal Naik. But the village environment has radically changed owing to cinema and television, and Bhavai has lost its charm and is decaying. Some workers of modern *Gujarati theatre attempted to write new plays to suit the times, though hardly any concerted effort was made in this direction.

However, two pioneering endeavours acquired all-India fame: Rasiklal Parikh's *Mena Gurjari* ('Mena of Gujarat', 1953), using elements of Bhavai dance and music, and C.C. Mehta's *Hoholika* (1956), incorporating typical Bhavai clowning.   GP

Asaita Thaker, *'Vanio' and 'Zanda Zulan'*, translated by Harish Trivedi (Calcutta: Writers Workshop, 1971); S.R. Desai, *Bhavai* (Ahmedabad: Gujarat University, 1972); Goverdhan Panchal, *Bhavai and Its Typical Aharya* (Ahmedabad: Darpana Academy, 1983).

Bhramyaman Mancha ('mobile theatre'): a phenomenon in contemporary *Assamese theatre. Touring repertories with a difference, they visit towns and remote villages in trucks carrying their own stages, equipment, generators, and even auditoria. Fully self-contained, they pitch their tents in open spaces and erect a makeshift auditorium with a seating capacity of 2000. For quick change of scenes, two stages are placed side by side, which in no time can be converted to a single stage. Three stages and stages on rails were also once used. Companies normally have two sets of twin stages. While the troupe performs at one place, an advance party erects the other set at the next venue. The average stay at each venue is four days. A company consists of 75–125 personnel (cast and crew, including musicians, electricians, and even cooks). Everyone is paid, and star artistes receive handsome salaries. It is a full-time occupation. Usually, after rehearsing for about two months, troupes go on the road around the end of August, performing every night till mid-April the following year.

Although Assamese companies had toured since the 1920s, the mobile-theatre concept was the brainchild of the young theatre worker Achyut Lahkar (1930–). Along with his brother, Sada Lahkar, he launched the Nataraj Theatre on this model in 1963. It was an instant success. Now there are thirty such companies; the movement has become big business. Usually, each has a repertoire of four plays (chosen from translations, adaptations, classics, or originals) and about an equal number of short *nritya-natya* (dance-dramas) presented as curtain-raisers. Every evening a new bill is offered. It is not that a production cannot be repeated the following season, but generally new plays are put up. There are some dozen playwrights who specialize in writing for the mobile theatre. Themes, though varied, follow a pattern that depends on popular taste and the dominant socio-political issues. Subjects cover everything from Hindu myths to the latest hit films, such as *Bandit Queen* (enacted on stage by Assamese actress Seema Biswas, reprising her on-screen role) and *Titanic*, on the S.S. Titanic disaster. High drama, extravaganza, and visual stunts are the main features.   KKB

Bhutaradhane ('spirit-propitiation'): collective name for a range of *ritual performances found in coastal Karnataka. Field studies in the area of Tulu Nadu (Dakshin Kannad district and parts of northern Kerala) reveal the cults of hundreds of Bhutas, each with its own distinct lore and form of worship. Some scholars trace the origins of Bhutaradhane to prehistoric times, but available evidence indicates that it became prominent in the socio-cultural context of medieval Tulu Nadu. In that feudal system, the purpose of the ritual was manifold: it was a religious ceremony, a medium of communication, a folk judiciary, a social therapy, as well as a kind of entertainment. In present times,

many of these forms retain their sway over their communities.

Some common Bhutaradhane include Kola, Nema, Kendaseve, Jalata, and Dakkebali. Other ceremonies like Nagamandala ('snake-mandala') show similarities with the above, but do not come under the Bhuta category. Excepting individual variations, Bhuta worship shares the same general format. Each Bhuta, for instance, has a specific *sthana* (location) where festivals are held normally once a year. This is the site where the rituals begin, sometimes with long preliminaries like the preparation of the costume, consecration, and procession, through which rites the *patri* (mediator) passes. Then, to the accompaniment of drums and horns, and the recital of *paddanas* (epic verses narrating the life history of the particular Bhuta), the mediator gets possessed and performs extraordinary deeds

Scene from *Titanic*, a popular Bhramyaman Mancha production (Kohinoor Theatre, 1998)

like walking on burning coal, as in Kendaseve. Finally comes the most utilitarian part of the ritual: the declaration of vows and submission of entreaties by devotees, and the Bhuta's reply in a vigorous formalized speech pattern.

Social functions apart, the aspects of performance and entertainment cannot be underestimated. These forms display a rich repertoire of theatrical elements—elaborate costumes made from local materials; musical pieces rising to a crescendo; gestures, postures, and dances intent on lending the Invisible a manifest form; and the controversial subject of how far *possession constitutes personification in the role-playing sense. Not surprisingly, Bhutaradhane has influenced *Kannada theatre genres like the *Yakshagana.   AKV

Sita K. Nambiar, *The Ritual Art of Teyyam and Bhutaradhane* (New Delhi: Indira Gandhi National Centre for the Arts and Navrang, 1996); Valentina Stache-Rosen, *Bhutas and Teyyams* (Bangalore: Max Mueller Bhavan, 1978); Uliyar Padmanabha Upadhyaya and Susheela P. Upadhyaya, *Bhuta Worship: Aspects of a Ritualistic Theatre* (Udupi: Regional Resources Centre for Folk Performing Arts, 1984).

Bidesiya (literally 'of the foreign'): folk form in Bhojpuri, the language of western Bihar. Probably started by a certain Guddarrai, it acquired widespread popularity and recognition owing to the talent and charisma of the legendary writer-actor Bhikhari Thakur (1887–1971), born in Qutubpur, Saran district. He had originally performed a play in 1917 about the pain, suffering, and endless wait of a newly-wed village bride, whose husband goes off to another land (often the city of Calcutta) to earn money, leaving her behind yearning for him. It took audiences through the journey of passing time with the moods of the lonely wife in response to the various seasons. The theme found such an immediate echo in social reality that, coupled with Bhikhari Thakur's histrionic and musical prowess, the play became a huge success, so much so that it acquired the status of an independent form. Several works around the same story, with minor variations, reached spectators as Bidesiya.

Primarily musical theatre, with most of the exchanges taking place through music based on existing Bhojpuri folk songs and tunes, Bidesiya stands out for the evocativeness, humour, and wit of its regional dialect. Performed very simply with everyday costumes in any available space, it requires no more than three or four actors, who double up for several roles. Dance steps are introduced for variety and fun to go along with the songs.

Bidesiya continues to be popular in Bihari villages, as its theme remains relevant, reflecting a reality of rural life where men have to migrate to the cities to earn their livelihood, leaving their families behind.   KJ

Bommalattam ('puppet dance'): Tamil *puppetry. In Tamil Nadu, marionettes are found in Salem, Kumbakonam and Mayiladuthurai (both in Thanjavur district), most often at temple festivals and exhibitions. Sometimes puppeteers perform in a tent and charge an entrance fee. Even though it is the least expensive form in terms of mobility and quantum of weight, it faces extinction from lack of patronage. The Mangala Gana Bommalatta Sabha, Sri Gana Natar Sabha, and Sri Murugan Bommalatta Sabha operate from Kumbakonam, while the Sri Rama Vilasa Kattabommu Nataka Sabha functions from Chinna Siragapatti in Salem district. In Kumbakonam, only Brahmans and, curiously, migrants from Saurashtra (Gujarat) practise Bommalattam. In Salem, the Vanniyar community takes part.

Five to seven people form a troupe, but a single artist presents the whole show. An assistant helps by picking up the right puppet, and musicians repeat the songs after the leader. Bommalattam continues almost as a family tradition, and all the members are involved in making the puppets, maintaining them, and performing. Raised platforms are built, the front hidden in such a way to reveal only the puppets. The large, 1 m-tall puppets are made of lightweight *kalyana murungai* wood (from the *Moringa oleifera* tree), painted, and decked with rich costumes, ornaments, and lovely headdresses. Their hands are attached to two rods, the other joints controlled by strings.

Valli kalyanam ('Valli's Wedding'), *Sita kalyanam* ('Sita's Wedding'), *Harishchandra*, *Lavakusa* ('Lava and Kusa'), *Nallatangal kathai* ('Nallatangal's Story'), and *Markandeyan kathai* ('Markandeya's Story') are the famous traditional tales found in Bommalattam. Of late, family planning and AIDS awareness programmes have been conducted in this form. The show begins with homage to God and continues with humorous and narrative sections. The buffoon is an extremely powerful role, displaying no limits to his fun and frolic. Through him, mythological figures gain contemporary currency.

Bommalattam refers to string puppets, but southern Tamil Nadu also has *shadow theatre, called Tolu Bommalattam ('leather puppet dance'). According to some experts, only one puppeteer still performs in this traditional style, which throws beautiful coloured shadows. However, since leather is costly and requires a complicated process of treatment and transformation, he has started using cardboard and coloured cellophane.   CA

Boys' companies: a vital component in the history of *Tamil theatre. Most famous Tamil actors (even in cinema) owe their entry and training to these companies of young boys, which mushroomed throughout Tamil Nadu in the first half of the twentieth century and from which they graduated. Samarasa Sanmarga Sabha, started by Sankaradas Swamigal in 1910, pioneered the trend. It is said that the behaviour of adult actors led him to take this move. He gave the boys rigorous training, among them the famous T.K.S. Brothers, S.G. Kittappa, and Mariappa Swamy. Swamigal wrote familiar stories in simple language for them. He then formed the Tattuva Minalochani Vidya Balasabha (1918) in Madurai. Although he had direct contact only with two or three such *sabha*s (groups), many other troupes trained themselves through his scripts. Girls were not allowed till his former pupils, the T.K.S. Brothers, took the bold step of accepting a single girl as actress.

The companies seem to have run as modern, secular versions of the ancient *gurukula* tradition where a guru looks after his disciples.   CA

Burrakatha (literally 'tambura tales'): modern variation of the old narrative form in Andhra Pradesh called Jangam Katha. While the latter served as a campaigning platform for Virasaivism since the twelfth century, the Communist movement reinvented Burrakatha in the 1940s. Both versions remain in vogue, featuring a *burra* (abbreviation of tambura) and *gummetas*, two small one-sided earthen drums, as the basic instruments to accompany the singing.

In Jangam Katha, a husband and wife sat down to sing stories in the houses of agricultural families but never in Brahman localities. Apart from the original Saiva repertoire, they gradually adopted packages of *vira gathalu* (heroes' ballads) and *perantallu*, tales of virtuous women who died as sati or for various dramatic reasons. Even though the Jangam community followed the Virasaiva cult, it later accepted many tales from such sects as Vaishnavism and the early Shaktism of matriarchal goddesses. Most Jangam Katha of the post-Virasaiva age were taken from Andhra history, like the 'War of

Burrakatha performers

Palnadu', the 'War of Katamaraju and Nallasiddi', and the 'War of Bobbili'. These set up the beginning of a genuine non-Brahmanic Telugu literature. Jangam Katha thus initiated an Andhra literature based on Andhra content.

Other performing communities later adapted it under the name of Burrakatha and, as the form was capable of projecting heroism powerfully and because of tremendous acceptance by the ordinary people, the Communists found it the most suitable vehicle for their own content of socialist heroes and martyrs. Generally, traditions appropriated for political propaganda tend to lose their charm and strength, but in this case the early Communist artists did a fine job. They improved Burrakatha's power by having the performers stand, and dance. Jangam Katha portrayed only the *karuna* (pathetic) and *vira* (heroic) *rasas*. The

Communists added *raudra* (furious) *rasa* to 'revolutionize' the material. The Praja Natya Mandali and *Indian People's Theatre Association (Andhra) depicted the valour of Communist heroes against the ruling Nizam's tyranny.

They did not change the original metre, *manjari dwipada*, one of the oldest in Telugu, but by cleverly halving each couplet, they created a *chalti* (fast-tempo) effect, which marvellously doubled the theatrical quality, particularly for scenes of anger, upsurge, and war. They standardized a three-member team instead of the earlier pairs. Besides providing the conventional echo after each couplet, one of the support singers exclusively inserted comic interludes and the other introduced topical political situations. These worked as 'alienation' devices to stop the high-flown dramatic narration by the main storyteller and make the content contemporary, whether Puranic, historical, or social. This stopping came in terms of a vital question, either as a comical or serious interruption, to facilitate interpretation by the narrator in the socio-political context for the audience's benefit.

Answerability to the illiterate viewer was Burrakatha's real strength, so the people willingly turned into an audience. Some nationalistic Burrakathas, which took the lead from the Communists, were banned by the British; *Gandhi mahatwam* ('Gandhi's Greatness') and *Guntur goppa* ('Grandeur of Guntur') were the most popular. Sunkara Satyanarayana, Lakshmikantha Mohan, and Shaik Nazar became outstanding performers, as did women like Kondepudi Radha and Tapi Rajamma later. After Independence, the public rejected the meaningless usage of Burrakatha for publicity by various governments and all political parties including the Communists. But the rural population is still fond of the older *virulu* and *perantallu* types by the traditional performing communities, particularly in the interior Rayalaseema districts. The average rural Andhra believes that, whatever the main story, Burrakatha always says something about his life.   PCR

Chaiti Ghoda Nata (literally 'horse dance in Chaitra'): a simple form prevalent among the fishermen of coastal Orissa, held for a whole month beginning from the full moon in Chaitra (March–April) to the full moon in Baisakh (April–May), during celebrations of the annual festival of Baseli worship. As the local goddess Baseli is believed to be horse-headed, the dummy-horse dance becomes a necessary part of invoking her. Most troupes have six members: three actors, two percussionists (on dhol and *jodi nagara*, or twin kettledrums), and a *mahuri* (wind instrument) player. All are professionals and go to different villages on invitation. While the actors belong to the fishermen's community, the musicians are Harijans.

The drama contains only two characters, the Rauta and his wife Rautani. The Rauta is the main singer and interpreter. His wife is usually played by a man and more recently by women. After the invocation they enact episodes from *Kaibarta gita* ('Fishermen's Song', a religious text on the community's origins). The Rauta, in between songs and intermittent dancing, narrates and interprets the events. Nowadays the performers also take up mythological stories to enlarge their repertoire. In between the episodes, humorous situations such as domestic quarrels provide entertainment to spectators. Sometimes the couple indulge in battles of wit in the form of questions and answers. The performance continues till late night.   DNP

Chavittunatakam (literally 'stomping-theatre'): Christian performing art in Kerala. This form of *Malayalam theatre originated when the Portuguese came to Kerala in the sixteenth century. It combines the Western stories of war heroes like Charlemagne and Napoleon or saints like St George, detailing their exploits and translated into Malayalam, with music and dance adapted from indigenous folk styles. The language of the earliest translations was mostly Tamil, and the texts (known as *chuvati*) were written and preserved on paper or palm leaves. Apart from the enacted tales, church songs used in High Mass also found expression. The name Chavittunatakam clearly indicates that varied and vigorous, even martial, footwork is the invigorating element of its artistry. Songs, dialogue, and dance communicate the story. The colourful costumes and backdrops are apparently inspired from medieval European miracle plays. The local instruments, *chenda* (drum) and *elatalam* (a pair of heavy bronze cymbals used for timing), accompany the all-night performance and provide strong support to the dance. Although once very popular, with all-male troupes featuring on makeshift stages on Catholic feast days or at weddings and actresses making their appearance in the 1960s, this art faces a crisis in the absence of proper patronage.   KNP

Chummar Choondal, *Christian Theatre in India* (Trichur: Kerala Folklore Academy, 1984).

Chhau ('shadow', 'disguise', or 'mask'): generic name for over a dozen different dance-drama styles prevalent in a contiguous area comprising north and west Orissa, south Jharkhand, and western West Bengal. The three most representative are now identified after their homes: Mayurbhanj (in Orissa), Saraikela (Singhbhum districts, Jharkhand, though nearly all the dancers are Oriya-speaking), and Puruliya (West Bengal). The Mayurbhanj and Saraikela styles are more evolved and sophisticated because they developed in these two princely states whose rulers extended enthusiastic patronage, so that like any classical dance, they have well-structured grammars of their own. Puruliya Chhau, on the other hand, is powerfully theatrical. Another distinction is that while Saraikela and Puruliya Chhau use *masks, Mayurbhanj Chhau does not. All three blend elements of classical, folk, and tribal performance.

Although the performers—by vocation, mostly farmers—practise throughout the year except during the monsoon, they formally present their shows to audiences on the last two days of Chaitra, in mid-April, as Chhau is an integral part of

Chaitraparva, the festival celebrated by both tribal and non-tribal communities to bid farewell to the old year. Many rituals form part of the festival, loosely associated with the performances.

Chhau has an unmistakable martial strain. The Mayurbhanj variety emerged from a martial dance called *Ruk-mar-nacha* ('defence-and-attack dance'). Saraikela Chhau, in its formative phase, was known as *Pari-khanda-khela* ('shield-and-swordplay'). In Puruliya Chhau, virtually all the dances follow the conventional pattern of build-up in three stages: encounter, challenge, and combat, culminating in the victory of the forces representing good. It seems logical to surmise that Chhau evolved from *martial arts and practices. In all the styles the legs are more eloquent than the arms, perhaps because during the formative period the dancers held shields and weapons in their hands. A number of basic steps and gaits, comprising highly stylized motions involving leg extensions, form the foundation that may differ from style to style. Some are borrowed from the typical movements of wild animals.

The element of theatre is pronounced in Chhau. Each production presents a tale usually drawn from Puranic literature such as the *Ramayana, Mahabharata*, and *Bhagavata Purana*. In the enactment, however, there is practically no verbal content. It is through stylized mimetic movements that the dancers relate the story. Therefore Chhau is a kind of non-verbal dance theatre, somewhat like Western ballet. Important modern practitioners include Chandra Sekhar Bhanj, Madan Mohan Lenka, Ananta Charan Sai, Krishna Chandra Naik, and Srihari Nayak (Mayurbhanj), Suddhendra Singh Deo, Bikram Kumbhakar, and Kedar Nath Sahoo (Saraikela), and Gambhir Sing Mura (Puruliya). A Chhau orchestra must have one or more dhols, a *dhamsa* or *dhak* (huge bowl-shaped drums with one face), and *mahuri* (a double-reed woodwind like the *shahnai*). The accompanying music played in the various Chhau styles is similar.

Mayurbhanj Chhau sparkles with fascinating choreography, especially in group numbers, and broad vigorous movements. It developed from two dances that still survive in a few remote villages in Orissa. The first, a folk form called *Amdalia-jamdalia nacha* ('mango-branch and black plum-branch dance'), was so named because the dancers decorated themselves with small branches from those trees. The other, *Paikali* ('soldier's art'), was a martial dance with shield and sword, in which *Ruk-mar-nacha* played an important part. In the repertoire of Mayurbhanj Chhau, it is performed with much greater sophistication.

The rich and extensive repertoire of Mayurbhanj Chhau includes three categories of dance: *phut* (solo), *judi* (duet), and *mela* (group). The basic gait is called *topka* and the thirty-six kinds of leg extensions *ufli*, a number of them, interestingly enough, inspired by the daily chores of Oriya housewives—such as *basana-maja* ('utensil-washing'), *chuncha-dia* ('floor-mopping'), *haladi-bata* ('turmeric-grinding'), *sindura-pindha* ('vermilion-wearing'). The images suggested by the names are evoked by stylized leg movements and the feminine grace of the actual activities is transformed into elegant masculine dance. More conventionally male characteristics are found in portrayals of the *shabar* (hunter).

In Saraikela Chhau the use of masks not only determined the line of growth but also remained its focal point even after the form crystallized fully. The mask has to be the quintessence of the character portrayed. Therefore, a very gifted artist must visualize the mask and give it shape and substance. Most of the masks require suitably ornate and symbolic headgear, which imparts a resplendent touch with coloured beads, artificial pearls, and *zari* (gold or silver brocade), also artistically balancing the face when worn. The uniqueness of Saraikela Chhau is that the masks' neutral expressions come alive during performance. Through different stances, gestures,

and positioning of the body in relation to the audience, the same mask may at one time convey great anguish or, at another, joy and happiness.

These masks come in three types. One presents mythological, historical, or social characters such as Krishna, Radha, the Rani of Jhansi, or a boatman. The second is poetic, representing abstractions conceived as having human faces, such as Marumaya (mirage), Ratri (night), Aleya (will-o'-the-wisp). The third includes masks of wildlife like the peacock, swan, deer, and butterfly. The performer does not imitate the creatures, which serve as symbols; for instance the Mayura (peacock) symbolizes a showy, narcissistic personality, deep within whom stalks the shadow of an undefined disappointment.

The former rulers of Saraikela not only patronized Chhau but also actively participated in it; Prince Subhendra Singh Deo was a great dancer. When their troupe visited Europe in 1937–8, he was acclaimed as a master performer. The dance critic of *The Sketch* wrote on 15 June 1938, 'The star dancer is Subhendra, and I am not going to compare him to Uday Shankar as they are both equally fine in their different ways.' Nearly all the numbers in the present repertoire of Saraikela Chhau were choreographed by Bijoy Pratap Singh Deo, his uncle and brother of the then ruler. Owing to the deep involvement of talented members of the royal family, Saraikela Chhau accentuated the classical elements inherent in the form. It is therefore full of dances with highly symbolic and poetic themes. The basic units of technique, called *chali* (walk) and *uphlei* (actions), bear great similarity to the *topla* and *ufli* of Mayurbhanj, and are equally marked by their stylized leg extensions. However, a sensitive spectator will experience that, with its distilled lyricism and aesthetically crafted masks, Saraikela

Suddhendra Singh Deo as Nabik, the boatman (Saraikela, 1992)

Chhau takes fantasy to the summit of poetry.

Puruliya Chhau applies masks for a different function. They are not as sophisticated as in Saraikela but vibrate with an earthiness, and effectively stylize mythological characters or enhance the theatricality of the presentation. Craftsmen, who prepare clay images of gods and goddesses in the style of modelling originating from Krishnanagar in West Bengal, make these masks as well, and Chhau groups purchase them. The main centre of mask-making is Chorda village near Bagmundi town in Puruliya district. The masks are papier-mache, integrated with towering and glittering headgear. The use of masks in Puruliya Chhau is believed to be an influence of the ritualistic Bengali *Gambhira dance. But the dramatic vigour of Puruliya Chhau and its resplendent costumes with ornate *zari*-work bear the unmistakable influence of *Jatra, the very robust Bengali folk theatre.

Puruliya was under the administrative control of zamindars who patronized Chhau, perhaps not as enthusiastically as elsewhere. Therefore it emphasizes acrobatic theatricality more than enhancement of classical elements. A few varieties of stylized walk and broad jumps and leaps are all that a performer has to master. Even though Puruliya Chhau does not have an elaborate

Kartik (left) and Parasuram in Puruliya Chhau

grammar or extensive dance phrases, it is the most virile and dramatic of all the styles. The repertoire consists of group compositions drawing upon the *Ramayana* and *Mahabharata* for themes. Each episode develops in three distinct stages. The first depicts the confrontation of benevolent and malevolent forces; the second presents the fight between them; in the conclusion, one of them triumphs. If benevolence is defeated it is a tragedy, as in *Abhimanyu badh* ('Abhimanyu's Killing'). In most cases, however, evil succumbs as in a straight morality play. Puruliya Chhau imparts to myths palpability in a charged atmosphere.   JP

Asutosh Bhattacharyya, *Chhau Dance of Purulia* (Calcutta: Rabindra Bharati University, 1972); Asutosh Bhattacharyya, *The Ramayana in Indian Chhau Dance* (Calcutta: Research Institute of Folk-Culture, 1971); Dhiren Dash, *A Brief Survey on Chhau Dance of Dhenkanal* (Bhubaneswar: Orissa Sangeet Natak Akademi); Sunil Kothari (ed.), *Chhau Dances of India* (Bombay: Marg, 1968); Sitakanta Mahapatra (ed.), *Chhau Dance of Mayurbhanj* (Cuttack: Vidyapuri, 1993); Jiwan Pani, *Purulia Chhau* (New Delhi: Centre for Cultural Resources and Training); Jugabhanu Singh Deo, *Chau Dance of Seraikella* (Cuttack: Srimati Jayashree Devi, 1973); Kapila Vatsyayan, *A Study of Some Traditions of Performing Arts in Eastern India* (Gauhati: University of Gauhati, 1981);

Theodore Vestal, *The Chhau Dance of India* (New Delhi: Educational Resources Centre, 1970).

Children's theatre: Children have always formed part of rural audiences for traditional Indian theatre. They watch performances along with their families indiscriminately, imbibing whatever they can, receiving education-in-theatre on their own mythological stories, crying in discomfort, or falling asleep whenever they feel tired at the usually overnight shows. Video recordings of *Kathakali or *Yakshagana often capture young spectators viewing the larger-than-life demons and heroes with awe, sometimes fear, and laughing gleefully when the clowns come on. As in other cultures, children particularly love *puppetry, though the various puppet forms are not intended exclusively for them, but for general consumption.

Traditionally, children have constituted another aspect of Indian theatre, as actors. Young boys born into performing families, or independently showing talent, are apprenticed to senior gurus, both in devotional temple genres and in secular folk forms. Over years of rigorous training, they pick up the tricks of the trade and act in small parts, eventually graduating into adult roles, often after spending their early teens playing the parts of women. Some are handpicked to continue female impersonation in their careers. In several religious performances, children actually assume central figures, such as the *swarup*s ('incarnations') in *Ramlila or *Raslila, whose main function is to represent deities like Rama and Sita or Krishna and Radha, receiving the worship of devotees as part of the production. They virtually 'become' 'live' gods for that period of time. More conventional acting by children as lead characters occurs in forms like *Prahlada Nataka, where the boy Prahlada can be considered the protagonist.

Possibly because the concept of theatre as an art meant only for adult viewers does not exist in Indian tradition, there are very few folk forms specifically oriented to young people. Two of these survive in Manipur. The open-air *Sansenba or Gostha Lila originated in the mid-eighteenth century, describing Krishna's experiences as a cowherd and his killing of demons (in full-body *masks) in the forest with the help of his brother Balaram. It includes fun and games, nature and adventure, the young Krishna's popular deeds, and typically children's dialogue. *Gaura Lila, a courtly operatic derivative of Sansenba, was created in the early twentieth century. It details the religious journeys of the saint Chaitanya, as part of Vaishnava proselytism.

The earliest modern experiment with drama for children came under Rabindranath *Tagore, after he founded his ashram for boys at Santiniketan in Bengal. He made theatre productions at the end of each term part of the curriculum, and himself supervised rehearsals, which he insisted should be open for all students to witness for their educational value. In 1908 he began writing new scripts for them, starting with *Sharadotsab* (*Autumn-Festival*), the first of his plays about the seasons, emphasizing man in harmony with nature. The only drama he wrote originally in English, *King and Rebel* (1913), was meant as a pedagogical exercise to improve the boys' fluency in that language. He also had his later serious, even philosophical plays premiered in the school, and often deliberately added groups of young people to the cast so as to allow maximum student participation in acting. When more girls began to enrol, he changed his dramatis personae accordingly to give them adequate scope. He advised that theatre be made a compulsory subject, arguing, 'If our schools were run on the right lines, boys and girls would never lose their natural gifts of bodily expression.'

Other pioneers in children's theatre include Sankaradas Swamigal, who initiated the popular Tamil movement of *boys' companies by forming the Samarasa Sanmarga Sabha (1910) and Tattuva Minalochani Vidya Balasabha (1918), teaching young boys to act and touring with them. He supposedly said that they were far more cooperative than adults. The T.K.S. Brothers, S.G. Kittappa, and many others trained under him. However, his productions were by children, not for them. In Karnataka, Gubbi Veeranna's company started a travelling children's theatre in 1925, while Shivarama Karanth conceived of children's operas. In 1926, the technician G.R. Shirgoppikar (1885–1956) assembled rural Marathi children into the Anand Sangit Mandali, employing his own expertise in trick scenes, sound effects, and slides. The eminent Kannada author Kuvempu wrote two children's plays, *Nanna Gopala* ('My Gopala') and *Modannana tamma* ('The Cloud's Little Brother', 1930–1); B.V. Karanth made his debut in the lead role of the former, at the age of 7. Original *Dogri theatre began with Vishwanath Khajuria's *Achut* ('Untouchable', 1935), staged by schoolchildren, followed later by his brother Narender's scripts for children.

After Independence, the *National School of Drama (NSD) in New Delhi commenced as the Asian Theatre Institute in 1958 with two courses, one of them on children's theatre, conducted by UNESCO experts. In Bombay, Sudha Karmarkar's Bal Rangbhumi started staging Marathi plays for young people in 1959 with adult actors. Associated with them, Ratnakar Matkari later directed his own scripts for Balnatya, jointly headed by his wife Pratibha. Social themes and imaginative design distinguished them from commonplace fairy stories. Many Marathi dramatists (like P.L. Deshpande) tried their hand at children's plays when radio drama for young audiences became popular; some of the printed scripts even made it to school syllabi. Vijay Tendulkar has six anthologies of drama for young people. In Gujarati, Pragji Dossa composed over a hundred children's plays. Other important children's dramatists include Satya Prasad Barua (Assamese), K.V. Subbanna (Kannada), G. Sankara Pillai (Malayalam), Safdar Hashmi (Urdu/Hindi), and Pundalik Naik (Konkani).

Meanwhile, Prime Minister Jawaharlal Nehru, particularly fond of children, had initiated the policy of constructing purpose-built auditoria for them in the major cities. The very active Children's Little Theatre in Calcutta shifted into its own premises in 1974. Simultaneously, one noticed theatre entering formal schools under the supervision of trained instructors appointed to teach it, even if at first as an extra-curricular activity. Between the years 1969 and 1973, both B. V. Karanth and Ram Gopal Bajaj taught drama at different schools in New Delhi. Bajaj staged around fifty student productions. Karanth carried on his almost magical work at his open-air amphitheatre for children in Mysore.

In Marathi, Arvind and Sulabha Deshpande floated the children's wing of their group Awishkar in 1975, named Chandrashala, under whose auspices they produced the enchanting dance-drama *Durga jhali Gauri* ('Durga Becomes Gauri', 1982), featuring over fifty young performers. Chandrashala trains children in theatre, *mime, puppetry, dance, and music, and holds annual workshops that scout for talent. Sai Paranjpye also contributed significantly to children's theatre in Bombay. She wrote several children's comedies, set apart by her characteristic humour and joie-de-vivre. At the other pole, Mohan Agashe introduced the Grips project from Germany to Pune. Instead of fantasy, Grips authors deal with the realistic urban life of children and teenagers. They do not necessarily solve problems, but try to get young people to ask the right questions. Adults and, often, professional actors portray the characters of children. This approach also caught on in Calcutta and New Delhi.

In recent years, many troupes have helped children with special needs. Barry John's Theatre Action Group (1973) worked with the

Rangakarmee's *Nanhi udan,* staged in the open with underprivileged children (Kolkata, 2002)

disabled and disadvantaged to make valuable contributions to remedial theatre. These productions develop out of workshops with the children. John became the first director (1989–92) of the NSD's Theatre-in-Education company, applying theatre for educational purposes. The NSD also conducts workshops to train teachers to use theatre techniques. The traditional Gujarati actor Pransukh Nayak set up his own group in the 1980s to stage educational drama for schoolchildren. In Tamil Nadu, M. Ramasamy and Velu Saravanan became well known as children's-theatre specialists. In 1991–3, Ninasam in Karnataka undertook its theatre-in-education project, Shalaranga, to create cultural awareness in Kannada schools with a series of workshops. *Theatre for development often involves street kids: in Calcutta, Nandikar has an ongoing programme with slum-dwelling children. Also in Calcutta, Zarin Chaudhuri runs an internationally acclaimed company of speech- and hearing-impaired youth, while a group of blind children has now grown up into accomplished adult performers calling themselves Blind Opera. More and more organizations working with children welcome theatre as a means of playful learning and expression. AL

Swatilekha Sengupta, *Theatre Games for School Children* (Calcutta: Dasgupta, 2000).

Cinema: At least four conduits, not mutually distinct, confirm the symbiotic links between theatre and film in India. The formal points to the fact that the earliest cinema in most Indian languages was straightforward filmed theatre, followed by a more complicated phase when cinema drew conventions from stage practice. The second path, of individual employment opportunities, began with the late silent movies and early years of sound, when practically every major Indian theatre practitioner worked in films, including numerous front-ranking dramatists who adapted their plays to the screen (notably Agha Hashr Kashmiri). Next, the economic or industrial channel highlights the way in which commercial theatre from the late nineteenth century to the 1930s provided both a financial as well as infrastructural context for the founding of the film industry in practically every language that has one. The fourth involves a specifically political practice, when numerous theatre personnel from the *Indian People's Theatre Association (IPTA) and allied initiatives moved into cinema partly through programmatic considerations, but also partly following local variations of the long twentieth-century history of radical fascination with popular cultural forms.

The earliest Indian movies were often filmed versions of stage plays. The 'first-ever' film, *Pundalik* (1912), was by one account a twelve-minute recording by a Bourne and Shepherd cameraman of Ramrao Kirtikar's drama on the saint-poet's life, staged by the Shripad Sangeet Mandali of Nashik (Maharashtra) and presumably commissioned by that company. A more spectacular career is that of Hiralal Sen, apparently apprenticed to a Professor Stevenson who was filming productions at the Star Theatre, Calcutta, and subsequently contracted to Amarendra Dutta's Classic Theatre, where he is supposed to have shot scenes from *Bhramar*, *Sitaram*, *Sarala*, *Alibaba*, *Buddhadeb*, *Hariraj*, and *Dol Lila* ('Holi *Lila', all 1901), *Sonar swapan* ('Golden Dream'), *Maner matan* ('What You Will'), and, perhaps his only full-length movie, *Alibaba and the Forty Thieves* in its entirety (all 1903). However, none of these theatre-films—screened, it is said, during intermissions at the Classic—survive.

Pre-histories of the cinema, in their obsession with all the 'firsts' that mark the birth of an independent art form, generally fail to account for the possibility that such instances of filmed theatre were far more widespread (there may have been many examples of the *Pundalik* variety, unfortunately lost) and that this entire sphere of activity was a free-flowing convergence between three established industries: theatre, undoubtedly the biggest mass-entertainment sector in turn-of-the-century urban India; photography as represented by agencies such as Bourne and Shepherd (Calcutta), Clifton (Bombay), or Madras Photography Stores (all of whom provided crews on hire to film plays, court events, tea parties by Parsi magnates, and other such occasions); and recorded music, after the coming of talkies. The superficial continuity marks a far more fundamental transition in which a nascent cine industry borrows a range of narrative and performatory conventions from theatre, and eventually replaces it as the prime purveyor of these practices.

It may be necessary, as a retrospective reconstruction, to emphasize a longer period that starts with the earliest films and comes down to contemporary times, demonstrating great fluidity of the boundaries dividing stage and screen. This fluidity is found in folk forms like the *Jatra, *Nautanki, *Raslila, *Tamasha, *Yakshagana, *Tolu Bommalata, the heroic folklore tradition or that of social reform in the vein of Gurazada Appa Rao's hugely influential *Kanyasulkam* ('Bride Price', 1892), and numerous other musical and theatrical idioms that cinema received wholesale and invoked in lighting, design, backdrops, special effects, and emotion-underscoring music, among the more attractive of film techniques. In fact,

*Ramlila, *Parsi theatre, *Sangitnatak, *Company Nataka, and troupes such as the T.K.S. Brothers might be seen as intermediate: theatrical genres admittedly, but on the verge of their own cinematization. Anuradha Kapur has consistently theorized this phenomenon of theatre-in-transition, about to spill over into something else. On the other hand, much recent film theory in India concentrates on concepts such as filmic performance, frontal address, the role of the frame, the tableau, and looking practices, all of which reiterate the primacy of theatrical space—or at least theatrically defined space—in cinema, countering every new technology that the moving image underwent through the last century.

A similar crossover is also in evidence in the careers of theatre practitioners from the 1920s well into the 1960s. They seemed able to move seamlessly from the stage to film and back to the stage, all the while adapting the conventions and technical possibilities of each to the other. Such theatre people included Sisir Bhaduri, Ahindra Choudhury, Durgadas Banerjee, Modhu Bose, and Utpal Dutt (Bengali); Hashr Kashmiri, Narayan Betab, Prithviraj Kapoor, and Sohrab Modi (Hindi); Bellary Raghava, Chittor Nagaiah, the Surabhi Theatres, K. Jaggaiah, and numerous film performers like Relangi or Gummadi (Telugu). In both Kannada and Marathi, where the stage industries dominated cinema for decades, two periods display this most innovative and important interface.

In Kannada, during the 1940s and 1950s, celebrated theatre manager Gubbi Veeranna, the single most famous figure in Company Nataka, made such hit films as *Bedara Kannappa* ('Hunter Kannappa', 1954), originally a play written for him by dramatist G.V. Iyer (who went on to become one of Kannada cinema's best-known film directors), and also the screen debut of his company's actor (and later movie superstar) Rajkumar. The second period was in the 1970s, when the experimental theatre movement threw up a range of artists who migrated en masse to the cinema: playwrights and filmmakers P. Lankesh and Chandrasekhar Kambar, composer-director B.V. Karanth, and actor, dramatist, and filmmaker Girish Karnad. Some, like Karnad, continued in this industry, while most others returned, after a brief foray, to their previous occupations.

Theatre controlled Marathi cinema from Sangitnatak well into the 1970s, as most film performers were borrowed from the stage, where they had separate, more intensive careers: Keshavrao Date down to Shreeram Lagoo, Neelu Phule, Nana Patekar. The vanguard group

Still from the film of Vijay Tendulkar's *Shantata! Court chalu ahe* (1971), directed by Satyadev Dubey, with Sulabha Deshpande in the foreground

Natyamanwantar, introducing modernist prose drama with *Andhalyanchi shala* ('School for the Blind', 1933), provided Prabhat Studio with many of its most creative actors (like Date), directors (K. Narayan Kale), and composers (Keshavrao Bhole). Practically all the major theatre companies contributed to cinema, especially Lalitkaladarsha, Gandharva, and Shivraj (run by future film star and composer Govindrao Tembe) Natak Mandalis. They loaned plots, actors, and equipment, and some even went into movie production— such as Balwant Sangit Natak Mandali, with *Krishnarjun yuddha* ('Krishna and Arjuna's Fight', 1934) by playwright and filmmaker Vishram Bedekar. This dominance of *Marathi theatre continued, as the 'new' Marathi cinema of the 1970s–1990s drew nearly all its talent (like Lagoo, Jabbar Patel, Vijaya Mehta, and Amol Palekar) as well as narrative practices (for example Mehta's *Rao Saheb*, 1986, adapting her stage version of Jaywant Dalvi's *Barrister*, 1977) from the experimental theatre.

Many global film histories have established that the major economic investment needed by the industry in order to found itself was in the area of exhibition—far more than production costs, the expenditure on making halls available in sufficient numbers, fitting them for projection, and wiring them for sound. It speaks a great deal for the stage industry in the period 1880–1940 that, in providing virtually in its entirety a readymade distribution context for cinema, it staved off a potential crisis in the film industry during the inter-War years, which might well have seen radically different possibilities for institutional ownership and control.

The most conspicuous case of theatre supplying a distribution infrastructure for cinema was the Madan Theatres chain. A leading Bombay-based Parsi family of theatre enthusiasts and entrepreneurs that moved to Calcutta, where it ran two prominent companies, the Elphinstone and Khatau Alfred, the Madans had fully converted their enterprise into a film network by the early 1920s. By 1927, they famously owned around half the movie halls in India, distributing Hollywood imports as well. They transformed their theatre holdings (which included entire troupes as well as copyrights for hit Parsi plays) to film numerous blockbusters—for example *Nala Damayanti* ('Nala and Damayanti', 1920), directed by the Italian Eugenio de Liguoro, advertised sequences of 'Narada's Ascent of Mount Meru to Swarga, the Heaven of Indra, the Transformation in the Clouds of the Four Gods into impersonations of King Nala, Swan Messengers of Love, the Transformation of Kali, the Demon of Evil, into a

Serpent, the Meeting of Kali and Dwapor and the Four Gods amidst the Blue Air'.

What remains largely unknown is how the theatre industry raised the kind of capital that permitted what seems to have been a reasonably smooth transition into the era of film distribution, though many historians show that by 1935—four years after the coming of sound—nearly all the major metropolitan playhouses in India had been acoustically wired and converted into movie halls. The only area on which any such research has been done is Lahore (now in Pakistan), where theatre flourished between 1900 and 1910, and it is argued that much of the money flowing into the entertainment industry came from a rural surplus caused by a Land Alienation act in 1901 and by a spurt in real estate that made owning theatre premises a profitable business, which eventually led to several owners producing films to feed their networks (such as ex-distributor Ardeshir Irani, who produced and directed the first Indian talkie, *Alam Ara*, in 1931).

A strong connection can also be made between the radical theatre movements of the early 1940s and the Bombay-based commercial film industry, particularly through such former members of the Indian People's Theatre Association as general secretary K.A. Abbas, dancer Uday Shankar, composer Salil Choudhury, and actor Balraj Sahni. Abbas, later screenwriter for Raj Kapoor, scripted and directed IPTA's *Dharti ke lal* (*Children of the Earth*, 1946), adapted from IPTA's landmark Bengali play *Nabanna* ('New Harvest', 1944), written by future scenarist-actor Bijon Bhattacharya and co-directed by stage and film actor-director Sombhu Mitra. Shankar directed *Kalpana* (*Imagination*, 1948), the most consistent moving-image record of his work. According to Sudhi Pradhan, 'With a handful of devoted Marxist cultural workers and trainers like Harindranath Chattopadhyaya, Santi Kumar Bardhan, Abani Das Gupta, Ravi Shankar, and Sombhu Mitra, we were able to make an impact on almost all the forms of the performing arts in India. ... [Another] very important contribution of our movement was to unite artists and technicians into two trade unions in Bengal through which they began to improve their working and living conditions in Stage, Screen, Radio, Gramophone and private profitmaking institutions.'

They were joined by allied groups like Prithvi Theatres, owned by theatre and film actor, director, and writer Prithviraj Kapoor, who recruited for his stage activities people such as dramatist Inder Raj Anand, co-author of the protest plays *Diwar* ('Wall', 1945), *Pathan* (1945), and *Gaddar* ('Traitor', 1948), composers

Shankar-Jaikishen, future directors Ram Ganguly (Anand's *Ag*, or *Fire*, 1948) and Ramanand Sagar (co-writer of the Prithvi drama *Kalakar*, 'Artist', 1952), and, not least, the young Raj Kapoor. Many of these theatre personnel secured employment initially in Bombay studios such as Filmistan, with some of the Bengalis finding a local supporter in producer-director Bimal Roy. Notably, ex-IPTA actor-director Ritwik Ghatak worked for both, and alongside Hrishikesh Mukherjee and Salil Choudhury on Roy's all-time hit *Madhumati* (1958), but unlike them, he did not stay on in Hindi cinema.

The impact of the revolutionary theatre in founding film industries where none existed forms one of the more striking instances of the progressives' fascination with popular culture. In Assam, for example, the leftist dramatist Jyoti Prasad Agarwala inaugurated Assamese cinema with Lakshminath Bezbaroa's militant play *Jaymati Kunwari* ('Princess Jaymati', 1915), filmed as *Jaymati* (1935). More spectacular, perhaps, are the roles in Malayalam culture of director, lyricist, and poet P. Bhaskaran; scenarist-director Thoppil Bhasi, who cinematized *Ningalenne Communist akki* (*You Made Me a Communist*, 1970) from his trailblazing 1952 drama; and indeed an entire team of stage writers, composers, and actors from the IPTA-affiliated Kerala Peoples Arts Club who virtually invented Malayalam cinema from scratch with films such as Ramu Kariat's *Nilakuyil* (*Blue Koel*, 1954) and *Muttiyanaya putran* (*Prodigal Son*, 1961, from Bhasi's play).

We could end by mentioning stage and screen director M.S. Sathyu, who continues to do plays for IPTA; for instance *Safed kundali* ('White Circle', 1980), adapted from Brecht's *Caucasian Chalk Circle*, starred film actress Shabana Azmi. He began as a young apprentice in cinema, later joining an IPTA offshoot in Bombay called the Juhu Art Theatre, headed in the 1960s mainly by Balraj Sahni, by then a prominent movie star. In 1969 he directed Kaifi Azmi's *Akhri shama* ('Last Light'), a biography of Mirza Ghalib with Sahni in the lead. This production is remembered for the fact that it initiated the trio's plans for the classic film *Garam hawa* (*Hot Winds*, 1973), stamping the theatrical origin of perhaps their best cinematic work.   AR

Company Nataka ('Company drama'): a popular term referring to two entities of *Kannada theatre: the commercial movement that won huge popularity in the first half of the twentieth century, and the genre that was created and refined during the same movement. Generically,

Company Nataka is an interesting hybrid of *Parsi theatre, Marathi *Sangitnatak, and several local performance traditions. From Parsi theatre it took perspective scenery (normally five sets of painted curtains, wings, and frills depicting five typical locales) and a range of special effects. From Marathi musicals, it learnt how to blend dialogue with song—often smoothly and naturally, but sometimes in strange ways—creating unique narrative patterns. Local traditions like the comic *vidushaka*, the subplots from folk forms, and the method of singing in Carnatic music were also picked up and adapted. The resulting mix continuously catered to a wide variety of audiences, on tour at all-night performances in tents, where the idiom was perfected.

Between 1880 and 1900, there were several short-lived attempts to build companies but success came afterwards. Three troupes that made important breakthroughs in the 1900s were the Kadasiddeshwara Sangita Nataka Mandali (founded 1901) of Konnurkar, the Mahalakshmi Prasadika Nataka Mandali (1903) of Shirahatti Venkobrao, and A.V. Varadachar's Ratnavali Theatrical Company (1904). The actor-manager Gubbi Veeranna led the famous Gubbi Channabasaveswara Nataka Sangha from 1917, with which the form reached its climactic years. Other companies which contributed significantly to the movement before Independence were Halageri Company (1912), Garuda Sadasivarao's Dattatreya Sangita Nataka Mandali (1916), Amba Prasadita Nataka Mandali (1919), Mohammed Peer's Chandrakala Nataka Mandali (1930), Vamanrao Master's Vishwagunadarsha Nataka Mandali (1931), and K. Hirannaiah's Hirannaiah Mitra Mandali (1942).

The plays were mainly mythological, sprinkled with Urdu and Hindi vocabulary, and relied heavily on improvised dialogue and music. During the 1940s the movement faded owing to the arrival of the talkies and the migration of personnel to Kannada cinema (whose early films reworked Company Nataka hits), but a few old troupes survived. Some new companies like Balappa Yenagi's Kalavaibhava Natya Sangha and KBR Drama Company came into existence later, but the decline continued, only at a faster pace after Independence. Several companies continue to operate even to this day, specially in pockets of north Karnataka, but with extremely limited influence.   AKV

Dance: According to Bharata's *Natyasastra*, the manual and source book for the various forms of performance in ancient India, the art of dance has three main divisions—*nritta* (pure dance), *nritya* (expressive dance), and *natya* (drama). The dancer, like the actor, follows the *rasa* theory as expounded in the *Natyasastra*. Both augment the *rasa*, or aesthetic emotion, by employing all the four types of *abhinaya* (acting) to cover all the nine *rasa*s experienced universally. While performing, both actor and dancer use these principles to evoke *rasa* among the spectators. Another striking aspect of Indian classical performers is the use of mudras or *hasta*s, the hand gestures and equivalent facial expressions to convey the import of the songs danced or text rendered. A distinct language of *hasta*s was codified with meticulous care and survives as a part of Indian classical dance. Among

the 'neoclassical' dance forms—Bharatanatyam, Kathak, Manipuri, *Kathakali, Odissi, *Kuchipudi, Mohiniattam, and Sattriya—

Actor-singer-dancer in the folk form of Kakkarissa Kali, from Kerala

Kathakali and Kuchipudi equally qualify as theatre by virtue of their dramatic content and collective choreography.

Dance is an integral feature of traditional *natya*. The *Sanskrit theatre as envisaged by Bharata was more like dance-drama. By the tenth century, we notice the evolution of musical dance-drama with Rajasekhara's *Karpuramanjari*, a *sattaka*, one of the theatrical genres. When the *uparupakas*—'minor' dance-drama forms in the regional languages—developed, they retained the element of dance as an inevitable component. The *Gitagovinda*, Jayadeva's twelfth-century Sanskrit poetic work, exercised a far-reaching influence on a variety of dance-dramas. As a living tradition, dance and *music play important roles in devotional forms like the mythology-based *Ankiya Bhaona of Assam, *Ras Lila of Manipur, *Chhau of Orissa, *Bhagavata Mela of Tamil Nadu, Kuchipudi of Andhra Pradesh, *Yakshagana of Karnataka, *Krishnattam and Kathakali of Kerala, *Raslila and *Ramlila of Uttar Pradesh, as well as more secularized genres like the *Tamasha of Maharashtra, *Bhavai of Gujarat, *Terukkuttu of Tamil Nadu, and *Jatra of Bengal. *Angikabhinaya*, or acting through body movement, is such an inseparable part of Indian theatre that if one removed it, indigenous theatre would lose one

of its most characteristic elements.

Although classical Indian dance and theatre separated with the passage of time, the principles of the *Natyasastra* still emerge, with varying degree of emphasis, in a dance exposition as well as a traditional theatre performance. However, in the colonial and post-colonial urban drama, we see less and less of dance or *hastas* interpreting the text with one-to-one correspondence, as elucidated in the *Natyasastra*. The influences of Western realism and its reliance on dialogue practically eliminated dance from modern

Nandita Kripalani and Mrinalini Sarabhai in Rabindranath Tagore's dance-drama *Chandalika* (Calcutta, 1938)

Indian theatre. Dance returned in the pioneering productions of *Tagore, followed after Independence by the work of dramatist-directors like K.N. Panikkar and contemporary directors like Ratan Thiyam and B. Jayashree who use classical and folk dance forms, which appear integrated and seamless in their specific theatrical contexts. But by and large the arts of dance and theatre have now acquired independent identities. SK

Richard Emmert et al. (eds), *Dance and Music in South Asian Drama* (Tokyo: Japan Foundation, 1983); *Invitation to the Dance: Bhagavata Mela, Yakshagana, Kuchipudi, Krishnattam* (Bombay: Marg, 1966); C.R. Srinivasa Iyengar, *Indian Dance: Natya and Nritya* (Madras: Blaze, 1958); K. Bharatha Iyer, *Dance Dramas of India and the East* (Bombay: Taraporevala, 1980); K.M. Verma, *Natya, Nrtta and Nrtya: Their Meaning and Relation* (Bombay: Orient Longmans, 1957).

Danda Nata (literally 'staff dance'): thought to be one of the oldest folk forms of *Oriya theatre, prevalent mostly among lower-caste Hindus in interior Orissa. It has always been part of mass religious culture in Orissa: deeply connected with worship of Siva and his consort Gauri, it is held over the month of Chaitra (March–April). Danda, the staff, represents Siva; Siva and Gauri are propitiated with a series of complex rituals.

The performance begins in the late evening and continues till daybreak. A number of characters, both mythological and social, sing their dialogue and dance intermittently, accompanied by the popular dhol and the wind instrument *mahuri*. Although deeply devotional in intent, the dances and typical songs cast in the form of dialogue present a vivid picture of rural society. The songs not only bring out stories or events from mythology and legend, but concerns of ideal family and social life. Prayer, religious messages, moral lessons, social correctives are reinforced by them. Sometimes rhythmic word-combat and song-duels cast as questions and answers occur, lasting for several consecutive nights. This variety of dramatization raises the pitch and tempo, and in the process both sentiments and artistic skills are clearly brought out. Villagers watch enthusiastically, reacting off and on with loud appreciative cheers.

The rich and varied repertoire includes *Gauri beta vandana* (obeisance to the rod representing Gauri), *Jhuna khela* (a dance in which glowing fire is created with resin powder), *Parava* ('Radiance', of Gauri), *Siva-Parvati* (Parvati is another name of Gauri), *Chadaya-chadayani* (a bird-catcher couple), *Patara saura-sauruni* (a tribal couple), *Kela-keluni* (snake charmer and wife), *Fakira-fakirani* (fakir and wife), *Kandha-Kandhuni* (Kandh tribal couple), *Vinakara-karuani* (vina-player and wife), and *Baidhana* (religious preacher). Excepting Parava and Baidhana, all characters appear in pairs. The Vinakara and Baidhana recite theological riddles in the closing item. For the character of Kutila, see *Bandi Nata.   DNP

Dhiren Dash, *Danda Nata of Orissa* (Bhubaneswar: Orissa Sangeet Natak Akademi, 1982).

Dasavatar ('Ten avatars'): Marathi and *Konkani theatre form depicting the story of any one of Vishnu's ten avatars. The origins of *Marathi theatre are traced to this folk tradition, which developed in the seventeenth century. The extant Dasavatar plays combine mummery, masquerade, pageant, and entertainment, exhibiting generic mixtures. It is believed that Shyamji Naik Kale first staged them at Adivare village, imitating *Yakshagana. Generally the itinerant actors, all male, belong to the Devali, Lingayat, or Gurav caste groups and are known as Dasavatari or Khelye ('players').

The structure of Dasavatar, which retains some features of *Sanskrit theatre, consists of two parts: *purvaranga* (prologue) and *uttarranga* (the latter performance). It takes place at night on any temporary open stage where the *sutradhara* sits in front of a small curtain with his orchestra of musicians playing harmonium, drums, and cymbals. The troupe worships its deities and masks before beginning. The play opens with a song in praise of Ganesh, the elephant-headed god, and Saraswati, goddess of learning, both impersonated by actors. A priest performs puja; the dialogues between him and the *sutradhara* are very comic. Although different troupes follow different conventions, they do not use written texts. The *sutradhara*, known as Naik ('leader') or Hardas ('devotee'), sings the invocatory *arati* slokas, while a Brahman chants mantras. After this benedictory scene, Sarada (Saraswati) and Gajanan (Ganesh) exit with stylized dancing steps. The *purvaranga* songs allude to local

The *Ganesh vandana*, or invocation to Ganesh, in Dasavatar

deities, praise patrons, and preach morals as well.

The *uttarranga* deals first with the mythological comic episode of killing Sankhasur, a demon who had stolen the Vedas. Hardas introduces Sankhasur, dressed in black, in rustic style. The fights between Sankhasur and Vishnu's Matsya (fish) avatar provide great entertainment. This episode also satirizes contemporary socio-political life. The farcical scenes are performed in stylized dance-drama form. The play proper presents an instructive dramatization of an avatar's story: the most esteemed are those of Narasimha (the man-lion), Rama, and Krishna; those of Buddha and Kalki (the celestial horse) are the least popular. The *ovi*, a song by Hardas, ends the show at dawn. Some performances conclude with references to other incarnations and even to artistes. The rich tradition of Dasavatar awaits revitalization, although performers like Babi Nalang draw crowds.   ABP

D.G. Nayak, *Rise and Decline of Dashawatar* (Bombay: Konkan Marathi Dialects Research Institute, 1962).

Desia Nata (literally 'country dance'): musical folk form prevalent in Koraput district of southern Orissa. Tribals generally perform it during their Chaitraparva celebrations in the month of Chaitra (March–April). The script is written in local dialect by the Nata Guru, who combines in himself the qualities of playwright, director, and musician. Although he is a professional, the actors are amateurs. The actions and dancing are near-mime as the performers use *masks locally prepared by traditional craftsmen. Female roles are played by men. The narratives and song-dialogues are sung either by the Nata Guru or a lead singer. The chorus, the main ingredient of supporting music, repeats them accompanied by a pair of cymbals and *mridanga* (double-ended drum).

All the plays are based on mythological episodes, the most popular among them being *Ganda badha* ('Killing of Ganda'), *Subhadra haran* ('Subhadra's Abduction'), *Taranisena badha* ('Killing of Taranisena'), *Niladri haran* ('Niladri's Abduction'), *Shashirekha haran* ('Shashirekha's Abduction'), *Bhramarabara*, *Liti Kumara*, *Brindabati*, and *Kumbhasura badha* ('Killing of Kumbhasura').   DNP

Dhanu Yatra (literally 'Bow Yatra', as in archery): a form of Krishna *Lila peculiar to western Orissa. Conceived by the chiefs of Bargarh and Ambapali villages (in Bargarh district) during the mid-nineteenth century, it is held open-air at

different locations in a wide area over twelve days. Ambapali becomes Gopapura and Bargarh, the Mathura of Krishna myths. The river Jira dividing the villages becomes the river Jamuna. Formerly Dhanu Yatra occurred in *mime, as background singers in chorus delivered episodes from the medieval Oriya epic, *Mathura mangala* ('Panegyric of Mathura'). Now prose dialogue has been introduced. All performers are amateurs belonging to both villages. Villagers gather in thousands to witness the performance. The mode of presentation provides scope for mass participation as well.

The *Balya lila* (childhood play) of Krishna, from the killing of the demoness Putana to the subduing of the snake-monster Kaliya, is performed in Ambapali. In Bargarh a spectacular procession takes place of the tyrant king Kamsa mounted on an elephant. Accompanied by drummers and dancers, the procession winds its way through the streets. Kamsa behaves like a real king, stopping and fining anybody coming in front of him by car or motorcycle. Then he is led to an elaborately decorated temporary pavilion. Krishna and his brother Balarama, escorted by Kamsa's courtier Akrura, arrive from Ambapali in a chariot drawn by horses. The fight ensues and the event ends with Kamsa's slaying.   DNP

Dhuliya ('dhol-player'): in ceremonial contexts in Assam, either an expert professional drummer or a band that includes not only the drummers (one or more) but also the cymbalist and often the fifer, providing auspicious music for rituals and social occasions. In upper (eastern) Assam master drummers (Oja Dhuliya), with the help of one or more assistants, show their wizardry on the instrument and also sing narrative and other songs. A legendary Oja Dhuliya of recent times, Maghai Oja, earned national and international fame. In lower (western) Assam there are Dhuliya troupes with various designations, such as *Bar* ('big') Dhuliya, *Dhepa* ('flat') Dhuliya, and *Jai* ('victory') Dhuliya, depending on the type of dhol and the nature of performance.

In the context of *Assamese theatre, Dhuliya is associated with a peculiar institution of lower Assam, particularly of the Kamrup region, which combines three different kinds of performance within its ambit—an elaborate system of drumming accompanied by songs and dance-like movements; peculiar acrobatic feats which call for great skill and courage; and short skits (called *sang*) replete with humour, clowning, and horseplay. Many of these plays, though rather crude and often verging on the bawdy, contain heavy doses of social criticism or contemporary social messages.

Normally there is no written text: action and dialogue are presented more or less impromptu on the basis of an oral scenario devised and agreed upon by the performers, the bulk of the responsibility shouldered by a veteran humorist-actor. Nowadays some troupes rely heavily on scripts written for them by specialist playwrights. Masks and crude stage props are freely used. Although the form has undergone various changes over the years, the changes being more striking in recent times, as an institution it has been a very popular and powerful means of mass entertainment in rural Assam for several centuries.   BD

Birendranath Datta (ed.), *Traditional Performing Arts of North-east India* (Guwahati: Assam Academy, 1990).

Dima (perhaps from the root 'to hurt', 'to injure'): form of *Sanskrit theatre. It had a celebrated story for its plot, and used representations of magic, conjuration, war, rage, bewilderment, and eclipses of sun and moon. It comprised four acts and did not employ the *pravesaka* or *vishkambhaka* introductory or linking scenes. The characters were sixteen in number and extremely haughty, encompassing gods, Gandharvas (celestial musicians), Yakshas (demigods), Daityas (demons), serpents, ghosts, *pretas*

(spirits), and *pisacas* (ghouls). *Raudra* (furious) *rasa* was the principal *rasa*, others being subservient, but avoiding the *santa* (peaceful), *hasya* (comic), and *sringara* (erotic). *Dima* prominently utilized the *kaisiki* (graceful) *vritti*. Vatsaraja's *Tripuradaha* ('Burning of the Three Cities', twelfth century) is an example. The *Natyasastra* also refers to the performance of this episode by Bharata, his pupils, and his sons, in the presence of Siva.   KDT

Dramatic Performances Act (DPA): British legislation to 'better control' subversive Indian theatre. The birth of professional *Bengali theatre with the National Theatre's *Nildarpan* (1872) brought anti-British subject matter to the general public, showing colonial planters ruthlessly oppressing poor peasants, though Dinabandhu Mitra had written it in 1860 and the publisher of the English translation, Rev. James Long, had been fined and imprisoned in 1861. In 1875, the same production created a furore on tour in Lucknow, where incensed British soldiers in the audience stopped the performance. The administration followed such incidents closely, realizing that the public stage (as opposed to the limited reach of the private stage) could prove a veritable tinderbox.

In 1876, soon after Edward, the Prince of Wales, visited Calcutta, the Great National Theatre presented a blatant persiflage titled *Gajadananda o jubaraj* ('Gajadananda and Crown Prince'), targeting a lawyer, Jagadananda Mookerjee, who had obsequiously invited the prince into his family zenana (unheard of in upper-class Bengali circles). The police proscribed the play, but the company repeated it the following week under another name, only to meet the same fate. The Governor-General promulgated an ordinance prohibiting performances 'prejudicial to the public interest'. The next day, the theatre responded in kind, flagrantly violating the order by staging Upendranath Das's earlier inflammatory *Surendra-Binodini* ('Surendra and Binodini'), in which the hero thrashes a British magistrate who attempts to rape a Bengali woman, on a joint bill with *The Police of Pig and Sheep*, burlesquing Calcutta Police Commissioner Hogg and Superintendent Lamb. Predictably, the police rounded up the culprits, on a charge of obscenity in *Surendra-Binodini*. However, the High Court threw out the case.

Although prominent citizens and the press protested a proposed bill to prevent provocative theatre, the government passed the DPA on 16 December 1876, empowering it 'to prohibit Native plays which are

Cartoon on the Dramatic Performances Act: the Bengali caption translated into English reads, 'A cannon to kill a mosquito'; the drawing of the playhouse on which the mosquito sits is a recognizable likeness of the National Theatre

scandalous, defamatory, seditious or obscene'. The police could 'enter, arrest, and seize scenery, dresses, etc'. Also, public dramatic performances 'in specified localities' had to receive a licence, so 'a copy of the piece, if written, or a sufficient account of its purport, if it be in pantomime, shall be previously furnished to the proper authorities'. As a result, scripts had to be deposited in advance with the police in many parts of India, ironically turning some police offices into archives of Indian drama. Since political plays were effectively stifled, authors exploited the loopholes in the Act and took recourse to subtler methods, commonly addressing nationalistic passions by dramatizing stories of subjugation and rebellion from mythology or history. Even these sometimes became too obvious, for the British banned many works— among them, in 1910 K.P. Khadilkar's *Kichakavadh* ('Killing of Kichaka'), in which Bhima slays the tyrant, and in 1911 Girish Ghosh's *Sirajuddaula*, about Bengal's last independent Nawab.

Curiously, after Independence in 1947 the DPA remained in effect, most states introducing their own amended versions, some of which, like the Bombay DPA (1950), actually gave more power to the administration. In 1953, the Calcutta Police served a notice on the *Indian People's Theatre Association (West Bengal) to submit manuscripts of over fifty plays, including *Nildarpan* and *Nabanna* (1944)! The same year, Kerala banned Thoppil Bhasi's *Ningalenne Communist akki* ('You Made Me a Communist', 1952) and members of his group were arrested for defying it. After an appeal, the ban was lifted, and the DPA locally replaced by the Madras DPA (1954). In Tamil Nadu, political parties in power invariably blocked pro-opposition drama. The Punjab DPA was modified in 1964. Only in West Bengal was the DPA repealed, in 1962, under persistent lobbying from artists, and the proposed state bill dropped, though theatre workers like Utpal Dutt faced prosecution under other laws, such as Section 124A (sedition) for *Duhswapner*

nagari ('Nightmare City', 1974).

In more recent times, P. Antony's award-winning *The Sixth Holy Wound of Christ* (1986), an adaptation of Nikos Kazantzakis's *The Last Temptation of Christ*, was prohibited from performance invoking the Kerala DPA (1962), for showing Christ as manic-depressive. The Supreme Court upheld the ban. When Antony received life imprisonment on an unrelated murder charge in 1989, the church reportedly claimed it was 'God's wrath'. The India Code Compilation of Unrepealed Central Acts (1993) considered the DPA one of the 'obsolete laws'. Bangladesh, whose theatre community regarded it as notorious, finally repealed it in 2001.

AL

Prabhat Kumar Bhattacharya, *Shadow over Stage* (Calcutta: Barnali, 1989); Pulin Das, *Persecution of Drama and Stage: Chronicles and Documents* (Calcutta: M.C. Sarkar, 1986); Pramila Pandhe (ed.), *Suppression of Drama in Nineteenth Century India* (Calcutta: India Book Exchange, 1978).

Dravidian movement: ideology that influenced Tamil culture after India's independence. It originated in several successive social and political formations. The earliest, the South India Welfare Association, was established in 1916 by maharajas and zamindars to counter the growing power of Brahmans in politics and society, and to agitate for their share in office proportionate to their population. Loosely called the Non-Brahman Association, it published a journal, *Justice*, which later gave it the name Justice Party. E.V. Ramaswamy Naicker (popularly known as Periyar, 1879–1973), disillusioned with the Congress Party that he believed was dominated by Brahmans, founded his Self-Respect Movement in 1925 to assert the dignity of non-Brahmans, and joined hands with the Justice Party only to take over its leadership. In 1944 he rechristened it Dravida Kazhagam and crystallized its objectives: rejection of Brahman domination in all spheres of life; rejection of Aryan and northern domination over the south; rejection of all things associated with Brahmans and the north, such as Hindi, Sanskrit, Hinduism, and the paraphernalia of worship; creation of an independent Dravidanadu (Dravidian land); reversion to Tamil culture and ethos as reflected in the old Sangam literature; and regaining the glory of Tamil history and language.

This ideological baggage appealed to a large segment of Tamil society, kindling in them a Tamil pride and dreams. The leaders of the Dravidian movement in general were powerful speakers and particularly C.N. Annadurai (founder of the breakaway Dravida Munnetra Kazhagam in 1949) an excellent orator, the like of whom Tamils had not known in their living memory. They were distinct from other political outfits in that they used an ornate, alliterative Tamil, which the masses loved for its rhythmic flow. The flowery allusions in their speeches fascinated, whether one agreed with their views or not. Annadurai also had a great love for theatre and cultivated all those connected with the stage and, later, with cinema. He was a loved and adored figure in theatrical circles, whatever anyone's persuasion, and the only politician of stature with whom theatre people felt close; otherwise they felt a discarded lot, because others spurned them.

Annadurai set the ball rolling in *Tamil theatre with propagandist drama, which had all the Dravidian rhetoric, spiced with biting satire. M. Karunanidhi joined him. Both gave the Dravidian propaganda juggernaut a long repertoire of plays, which had a tremendous impact on the public with their fiery speeches. Bharatidasan (1891–1964), virtually the poet laureate of the movement, was a very early entrant in theatre and cinema, though not all his plays and films were intended for propaganda. In his most talked-about drama, *Iraniyan* (1934), he subverted received mythology by presenting the demon Hiranyakasipu as hero and Prahlada as a Brahman stooge. It bristled with the most heated diatribe against all he chose to condemn. Several authors also constructed Dravidian versions of the *Ramayana*, glorifying Ravana as their hero and debunking Rama, the Aryan king from the north invading the south.

By the 1940s, the movement had established itself with powerful productions. Its troupes moved from town to town, village to village, creating a sensation, the police ever watchful. The principal actor and producer, M.R. Radha, director of the group that specialized in the movement's drama, possessed a peculiar style of dialogue delivery and speech-making, a kind of screechy nasal distortion, which was a characteristic blend of spite, humour, and bitterness. He also developed a knack for evading governmental bans. In course of time, the plays gained acceptability among the public and started figuring in the repertoire of reputed companies as well.

Once their acceptability and crowd-drawing potentialities were proved, their conversion into films towards the end of the decade was easy and inevitable, beginning with Annadurai's *Velaikkari* and

Nallatambi (both 1949). The response was unprecedented. The moment his name appeared on the title credits, halls resounded with thunderous spontaneous applause. This opened the floodgates of cinema for the movement. Like the political leadership in Nazi Germany and Soviet Russia, the ideologues of the Dravidian movement were quick to realize the power and penetration of the stage and screen, and talented enough to exploit it. Tamil theatre and cinema also were pliant enough to welcome this verbal onslaught, as their artistic concepts privileged the spoken word anyway.

The Dravida Munnetra Kazhagam finally won the Tamil Nadu elections in 1967 and no counter-ideology could thereafter recapture the state. The movement owed its success in a significant measure to its work in plays and movies. Once it attained power, its leadership lost the raison d'être of their formerly passionate involvement in performing arts, but their formal association continues. Of course, the movement has had uneven success in achieving its declared goals; Tamil religious faith, for example, has only taken more obsessive forms.   VS

Galihyun ('tales', singular 'Galih'): Sindhi folk form composed in Gahun ('ballads'), narrative verse glorifying the legendary heroic deeds and romances of rulers and chieftains. The oldest Sindhi theatrical form, its origin is traced to the Sumra period (1032–1352), and it developed further in the Samma period (1352–1520), under native kings who were great patrons of culture.

The earlier Sumra Galihyun were in *champu* format, where prose narration was interspersed with Gahun. Not composed in any particular metre, their main features were rhyming and rhythm which aided melody in singing. The subject matter in the Samma age gave place to the romances of common people rather than the heroic exploits of rulers. This period of Gahun, till the fifteenth century, is called the age of the literary ballad, for the earlier anonymous poets were not as skilled. The new compositions were wrought in the *kabat* metre and the ragas Hamir, Kedaro, and Sorath, which can be easily sung. Although simple, they were based on the principles of musical *rasa. Their *sughar* (skilled) poets included Sumang Charan, Hussain Aplani, Pir Patho Dabeli, and Makhdum Noah Hathiani.

The first epic Gahun may have been *Dodo ain Chanesar* ('Dodo and Chanesar', also called *Dodal-raso*, 1272), by the Sumra court-poet, Bhagu Bhan. It is not imaginary, but based on real happenings. In fact, it is a history of the Sumra period, describing the political conditions, social milieu, and economic situation. It also depicts a fraternal power struggle, ending in a great tragedy. The tale was preserved through oral tradition by the *charan* and *bhatt* bards, who travelled from village to village, singing and enacting the characters before huge gatherings on open streets, to the accompaniment of the *yaktaro* (single-stringed instrument), and at the end sought alms for their livelihood.

The composition trickled down through the centuries, until recorded by Munshi Udharam Thanwardas Mirchandani (1833–83) after listening to the performances of some *charan*s. We also get glimpses of the tale in Persian translation in the histories *Tarikh Tahiri* (1621) and *Tuhfatul Kiram* (1767). So far fourteen recensions of the Dodo-Chanesar Galih have been discovered, composed by different *charan*s based on Bhagu Bhan's epic. While they maintain the storyline, they have made changes and interpolations in certain situations and dialogue.

Some Galihyun are of short length and can be performed within three or four hours, but many continue for three or more nights, holding large assemblies of villagers enthralled. The tradition is said to be still in vogue in Sindh. All the Galihyun were recorded through fieldwork by the Sindhi Adabi Board, Hyderabad (Sindh), and published.   PA

Gambhira (from the term often used to describe the inner sanctum or outer courtyard of a Siva temple):

folk musical theatre in Bengal, part of the Gambhira festival dedicated to Siva from April to June in and around Maldah district. The festival features a large body of rituals, ceremonial processions, and masked dances as in the other variations of Gajan, the Siva festival celebrated in mid-April all over Bengal. Growing out of its earlier form, Bolbahi or Bolbai, which centred more directly on local characters and scandals, and often faced resistance from its targets, Gambhira underwent a transformation with nationalist intervention in the early twentieth century.

The new style, often performed before an image of Siva installed in a hut open on three sides, begins with a chorus, usually of four singers, invoking him. Siva appears in his popular manifestation, bare-bodied with matted hair and tiger skin around his waist, to listen to complaints, frequently presented through a series of satiric skits illustrating situations of denial and deprivation, and accusing the authorities, both local and national. Siva, a sympathetic listener, sometimes visits the authorities to plead the villagers' cases, albeit with little effect. The performers represent several vocations, classes, and castes, projecting what a British administrator-surveyor described officially in 1918 as an 'annual review of the acts of the year and penance for misdeeds'. Siva remains essentially a friend of the common people and a wise guardian, addressed familiarly as *nana* ('grandfather'). Several Gambhira troupes operate during the season, and even beyond at folk festivals sponsored by the state government or other organizations, the strong topicality of their themes and the subjects of their songs helping them to retain their popularity.   KG

Gaura Lila ('*Lila from Gaur', an ancient name for West Bengal): operatic form of *Manipuri theatre. Regarded as a court-supported continuation of the older tradition of *Sansenba, it originated in the early twentieth century using the Bengali language. Linguistic nationalism soon effected a switch to the Manipuri medium. It dramatizes the religious missions of Gaurchandra (Chaitanya), particularly the encounter of two Muslim brothers, Jogai and Madhai, with him and his associates, culminating in their conversion to Gauriya Vaishnavism. Comic interludes of the boat journey and other incidents were included; acting and theatrical aspects were given greater prominence than dance. It gradually became extremely popular in rural and peripheral areas, which led to looser construction and lack of codification. It survives, but with

far fewer performances than before. T. Kunjakishore was an award-winning exponent.   LA

Gitabhinay (literally 'lyric-acting'): hybrid of the indigenous *Jatra and Western opera in nineteenth-century Calcutta. Growing out of the new Jatra patronized by the nouveau riche, this genre with songs almost replacing dialogue became greatly influenced by popular theatre. Devoid of Jatra's religious overtones, it was more lyrical than dramatic, closer to the musical. It had scene-shifts like those in a play, but no act divisions or use of flat or drop scenes. It was certainly much less expensive than a theatre production, yet free from the gross or low taste germane to the then popular Jatra.

Harimohan Ray's *Janaki-bilap* ('Janaki's Laments', 1867) may be said to have set the fashion, though Kalidas Sanyal's *Nala-Damayanti gitabhinay* ('Gitabhinay of Nala and Damayanti', 1868) is perhaps the earliest specimen bearing *gitabhinay* in its title. Rajkrishna Ray (*Patibrata natyagiti*, 'Opera of the Husband-server', 1875) and Manomohan Basu (*Partha-parajay*, 'Partha's Defeat', 1878) were the two main contributors to this genre. The *Tagore family efforts, including those of Swarnakumari Devi

(*Basanta-utsab*, 'Spring Festival', 1879), Jyotirindranath (*Manamayi*, 1880), and of course Rabindranath (*Balmiki-pratibha*, 'Valmiki's Genius', 1881), enriched Gitabhinay and brought it to fruition.

Because of its economy in costs and popularity due to musical extravaganza, Gitabhinay enjoyed immense appeal over a considerable period in *Bengali theatre, overwhelming Jatra. Some plays already popular on the proscenium stage were turned into Gitabhinay, such as *Ramabhishek* ('Rama's Coronation', 1868), *Harishchandra* (1874), and *Sati natak* ('Sati's Play', 1874), all done by Basu, Ramnarayan Tarkaratna's *Ratnabali*, and Michael Madhusudan Dutt's *Sharmishtha* and *Padmabati*. Girish Ghosh's adoption of *Sharmishtha* for production by the Baghbazar Amateur Jatra Party (1867) was in a way responsible for crystallizing the group that ushered in the professional National Theatre. The performance of *Padmabati* at Rajendra Mitra's residence, attended by aristocrats like Jatindramohan Tagore, Kaliprasanna Sinha, and Satyacharan Ghoshal, reveals that this form won the approval of the Bengali elite. The rise of prosaic realism in the theatre dealt a death-blow to this short-lived yet brilliant genre.   SM

Gombeyata ('puppet theatre'): the name for all varieties of *puppetry in Karnataka. Researchers have identified seven such forms, of which only two—*sutrada* (string) and *togalu* (leather)—still survive.

The string puppets are 35–50 cm in height and made of soft wood, sometimes with rags stuffed inside. Each marionette is manipulated with six strings attached to a rod. A performance needs at least twenty puppets, and special ones with moveable jaws and multiple heads are added attractions. Normally two or three persons manipulate the puppets, accompanied by one helper and three or four musicians. The stage is a box closed on three sides with an opening of 1m by 6 m in front. The show, usually lit by oil lamps (now with electric bulbs), lasts the whole night. The general mode of performance is based on the predominant theatrical form in the area. Thus Gombeyata of the western districts closely follows *Yakshagana, hence is called Yakshagana Gombeyata. The respective conventions, stagecraft, and scripts of these dominant forms are followed, with minor adaptations. In the late twentieth century, U. Kogga Devanna Kamath and M.R. Ranganatha Rao contributed significantly to string puppetry.

Leather puppetry is scattered in several pockets, almost exclusively performed by the Killekyata tribe, for whom it is both a ritual duty and partly a means of livelihood. A typical troupe is a Killekyata family itself, each member assigned a playing, speaking, or singing role. The puppets come in two sizes: about 2 m in height and about 1m or less. They are two-dimensional cut-outs of translucent goatskin, meticulously carved with designs and brightly coloured with herbal pigments, containing several moveable parts operated by thin bamboo sticks. They move behind a 1m-by-2 m white screen spread out by bamboo poles, with an oil lamp projecting their shadows. Each overnight show employs at least fifty puppets—some representing entire groups like Rama's monkey army—creating a magical shadow play embellished with music and witty speech. Themes and conventions closely resemble those in Doddata/*Mudalapaya* *Bayalata, with some interesting variations: a stock character, the coarse Killekyata, keeps intervening at several points with rough and earthy humour. This earthiness is one main reason for the relative popularity of leather puppetry in Karnataka. T. Hombaiah is the best-known recent practitioner. AKV

S.A. Krishnaiah, *Karnataka Puppetry* (Udupi: Regional Resources Centre for Folk Performing Arts, 1988).

Group theatre: amateur troupes in post-Independence India, which produced the great majority of important urban theatre work, are classified as groups. Although professional companies in cities ruled the roost for nearly a hundred years, between 1870 and 1950, they gradually lost audiences to *cinema and disappeared from most regions by 2000. Only a handful of such commercially-run repertories exist. In their place, the number of groups increased rapidly after 1947, catering to an educated clientele with mainly serious and socially committed material, and disdaining pure entertainment. Since their themes precluded box-office success, groups could not hope to pay their members, who typically hold full-

Puppet of a demon in Togalu Gombeyata

time day jobs in other professions and rehearse in the evenings.

Making a virtue of their poverty, groups register as non-profit organizations, which fall within the purview of the Registration of Societies Act. Societies can engage in any legal activity, but are defined by their declared aim of not working to make any profits. As such, they qualify for public funding, corporate sponsorship and private donations, tax exemptions, and, for theatre, waiver of the high entertainment tax on tickets. Some groups have become eligible for regular but limited government grants. A few, able to muster money from diverse sources, find themselves in a position to disburse small stipends to members, but most have a hand-to-mouth existence, scraping together tiny budgets from one production to the next. In these circumstances, only the most dedicated survive. Of late, membership has grown flexible, many groups relying on a common pool of actors. Folk and traditional troupes also function under this Act nowadays.   AL

Kuntal Mukhopadhyay, *Theatre and Politics: A Study of Group Theatre Movement of Bengal* (Calcutta: Bibhasa, 1999).

Historical drama: With the sole exception of Visakhadatta's remarkable *Mudra-Rakshasa* ('Rakshasa's Signet Ring', *c.* fifth century AD), the historical play is a nineteenth-century phenomenon in Indian theatre. *Mudra-Rakshasa* revolves round the political upheaval destroying the Nanda dynasty and the installation of Chandragupta Maurya on the throne of Magadha in the third century BC. The intensity of action and vividness of characters, particularly Chanakya, Chandragupta's minister prefiguring Machiavelli, distinguish this classic from the rest of Sanskrit drama.

The growth of historical plays in various languages coincided with the growth of interest in history in general and the Indian past in particular. It was further accelerated by Indian writers' warm response to European historical romances and drama. The initial motivation was mainly the romanticization of the past as a means of escape from the harsher present, but the Indian dramatist soon realized the genre's potential, making it an effective instrument for the propagation of socio-political ideals. Historical plays followed a parallel line of development to historical novels and poems, based on well-known episodes and exploiting, more or less, identical ideas projecting a new vision of national history. However, compared to drama dealing with contemporary social problems or interpreting myths, which revealed a remarkable unity of themes, the historical plays presented a widely divergent world of subjects and characters.

*Mythological drama derived inspiration mainly from pan-Indian Hindu sources, whereas historical drama accorded greater importance to regional sources. The Assamese authors Padmanath Gohain Barooah and Lakshminath Bezbaroa, for example, chose the tragic life of the princess Jaymati, who bravely suffered at the hands of an Ahom king, for *Jaymati* (1900) and *Jaymati Kunwari* ('Princess Jaymati', 1915) respectively. Similarly, *Kanchi-Kaveri* (1880) by Ramshankar Ray and *Engrez kartrika Kataka vijaya* ('Conquest of Cuttack by the British', 1901) by Bhikari Charan Patnaik drew upon the history of Orissa. Venkataraya Sastry's *Prataparudriya natakam* ('Prataparudra's Play', 1897) in Telugu portrayed the glories of ancient Andhra, E.V. Krishna Pillai's Malayalam *Sitalakshmi* (1932) dealt with the time of Martanda Varma, several Marathi writers projected Shivaji with great pride, and Bengali dramatists discovered new icons like Pratapaditya and Sirajuddaula. The celebration of regional heroes and heroines contributed significantly to the growth of patriotism as well as towards the search for identities of different cultural and linguistic groups.

Curiously, ancient India provided subject matter only occasionally (D.L. Roy's *Chandragupta*, 1911, is one of the most popular plays based on ancient history), whereas medieval India fired the imagination of dramatists more significantly. The palace intrigues, heroism, romance, lust for political power, treachery, and self-sacrifice formed the stuff of which most Indian historical plays were made.

The most important role that the genre played till Independence was the creation of secular national heroes and heroines. Political theatre had its beginnings in historical drama. Among the distinguished writers was Girish Chandra Ghosh, whose *Sirajuddaula* (1905), *Mirkasim* (1906)—both lionizing protagonists who died protecting the freedom of India—and *Chhatrapati* ('Sovereign', 1907), valorizing the Marathi icon Shivaji, left a tremendous impression on the public. D.L. Roy achieved an even greater impact by his strong patriotic fervour, flamboyant style, and wide range of human problems. His *Shah Jahan* (1909), dramatizing the tragic life of the Mughal emperor, is one of the best-known historical plays. Roy's influence dominated Indian historical drama for a long time and reached a new high in the works of Jaishankar Prasad, the most famous of Hindi playwrights during the nationalist period.

A lull in the development followed Independence, but from the mid-1960s many dramatists again showed serious interest in history.

The new historical plays written since that time broke from earlier traditions of romanticizing the past or construction of national heroes. Girish Karnad's *Tughlaq* (1964) interrogated Prime Minister Nehru's policies; Utpal Dutt's *Kallol* ('Waves', 1965), based on the Naval mutiny of 1946, had a revolutionary agenda; Vijay Tendulkar's *Ghashiram Kotwal* (1972), though slenderly connected with Maratha history of the Peshwa age, satirized the corruption of people in power. Such texts opened new possibilities for the genre.   SKD

Ihamriga (literally 'seeking a deer'): form of *Sanskrit theatre so named because the hero seeks a woman as difficult to obtain as a deer. It consists of four acts founded on a mixed story, partly popular and partly invented. The hero and his rival are mortals or gods. Both are illustrious, 'firm and haughty' (*dhiroddhata*), but the rival covertly commits improper acts. The play exhibits a semblance of love (*rasabhasa*) in the rival, as he endeavours to win a divine lady against her will by violent means. The protagonists of the *pataka* (subsidiary plot) conventionally numbered ten and were arrogant characters. The enemy's wrath was provoked, but by some pretext, war was avoided. Magnanimous persons who may have died in the original story could not be so represented here. Some opinions declare *ihamriga* to be in one act and to have a divinity for its hero; others hold that it had six heroes battling over a celestial woman. Vatsaraja's *Rukminiharana* ('Rukmini's Abduction', twelfth century) exemplifies this form.

KDT

Indian People's Theatre Association (IPTA): pre-eminent activist institution formed as an all-India organization in Bombay in 1943, borrowing its name from Romain Rolland's book titled *People's Theatre*, but stressing 'our people's struggle for freedom, cultural progress and economic justice'. At the conferences held at the time of its formation, units from different parts of the country, some of which had begun functioning

Bijon Bhattacharya's *Nabanna* (Indian People's Theatre Association, Calcutta, 1944)

earlier (Bangalore, 1941; Bombay, 1942), participated and generated considerable enthusiasm among theatre workers, writers, musicians, and the politically-conscious intelligentsia in general. It soon became the premier forum for young people devoted to the performing arts.

Other bodies like the Progressive Writers Association (1936), Youth Cultural Institute (1940), and Anti-Fascist Writers and Artists Association (1942) prepared the ground for the emergence of IPTA. They were concerned about the lack of awareness of social and political realities, the threat of fascism, and India's colonization. Their aim was to make people conscious, through writing and other modes of communication, of the nature of problems in India and abroad. The Communist Party of India, which supported the Allies after Germany's invasion of the USSR in 1941, extended its base in many ways and built 'front' organizations in cultural and other fields. IPTA was one of them. Realism and folk idioms formed its preferred styles.

The Bengal unit of IPTA proved among the most active. By 1944, after it produced Bijon Bhattacharya's stunning *Nabanna* ('New Harvest') about impoverished peasants, its reputation spread far and wide. Apart from marking a milestone in *Bengali theatre, *Nabanna* reflected IPTA's declaration in its first bulletin of 1943 that people's theatre stars the people. All the units attracted established actors and youth who, besides having talent and dedication, espoused leftist views and ideals. Offshoots in Andhra Pradesh (Praja Natya Mandali) and Kerala (Kerala Peoples Arts Club) most successfully applied local folk forms as mediums for the message of armed struggle. Names of those who joined IPTA read like a roster of celebrities who became famous later in theatre and performance, from Jyoti Prasad Agarwala in Assam to Prithviraj Kapoor in Bombay.

IPTA produced its only film in 1946 in Hindi, the realistic classic *Dharti ke lal* (*Children of the Earth*), partly based on *Nabanna*. However, ideological differences among members, mostly centred on the question of art and politics, led to a decline in IPTA's influence from the late 1940s. The debates became increasingly strident and many disassociated themselves to form groups of their own. In Bengal those who departed, like Sombhu Mitra and Utpal Dutt, initiated *group theatre and the 'new drama movement'. Despite the depletion of a large number of its front-ranking members, IPTA did not become inactive, but lost the creative elan it began with. Nevertheless, it clung to its core creed that theatre was primarily a weapon for the masses to struggle against oppression and exploitation. In different parts of India it still produces intermittently

plays and other forms of art to spread the message.   KR

Annual Report: The All India People's Theatre Association (Bombay: Vakil and Sons, 1946); Sudhi Pradhan (ed.), *Marxist Cultural Movement in India: Chronicles and Documents*, 3 vols. (Calcutta: National Book Agency, Navana, and Mrs Santi Pradhan, 1979–85).

Interculturalism: hotly debated international trend of the late twentieth century. Broadly defined, it signifies artistic process and production through cultural exchange, but in its narrow applications in recent theatre discourse, it has come to mean Western (more accurately, Northern) appropriation of forms native to the East (or South) through what some commentators ironically term 'glocalization'. Most writers on this subject tend to forget that, first, theatre has always been intercultural in nature and, second, the influence of Southern performance on Northern practitioners has a long history predating post-colonial times. It is easy to prove the first point: Roman theatre could not have developed without Greek imports; European Renaissance drama arose on the foundations of classical theory, sometimes misinterpreted; the growth of German theatre owes much to Shakespeare; modern realism looks to the Norwegian, Ibsen, and the

Theophile Gautier's ballet-pantomime of Kalidasa's *Sakuntala* (Paris, 1858)

Russian, Stanislavsky, for inspiration; and so on. The progress of theatre itself constitutes a continuum of intercultural appropriation. To suspect or disallow it is not just ahistorical but impractical.

Some critics argue that interculturalism extends orientalism, by which the imperial West found its 'other' in the Orient, to idealize or condemn. The first major dramatic representation of India came in John Dryden's popular heroic tragedy *Aureng-zebe* (1675), written in Aurangzeb's lifetime and set in Agra in 1660. After Sir William Jones translated *Kalidasa's *Sakuntala* into English in 1789, followed rapidly by translations into other languages, successive generations of European theatre workers used this classic to suit their agenda. In 1791 Goethe composed a four-line apostrophe extolling it as the paragon of all dramatic virtues, a model of aesthetic beauty; in 1797 he wrote the prelude to *Faust* inspired by the device of poet, *sutradhara,* and actress introducing Kalidasa's play, but replaced the actress with a jester. The romancing of India continued through Mery and Gerald de Nerval's French version of Sudraka's *Mricchakatika* (1850) and peaked in Theophile Gautier's lush ballet-pantomime of *Sakuntala* (Paris, 1858). Fin-de-siecle French art brought another perspective. The avant-garde director Aurelien-Marie Lugne-Poe staged an anarchist *Mricchakatika* (1895) with programme and décor by Henri Toulouse-Lautrec, then a symbolist *Sakuntala* (1896), the very year that he premiered Alfred Jarry's radical *Ubu Roi*.

An early theoretical dialogue on the differences between Indian and Western acting took place in the art periodical *The Mask* in 1913, involving designer-director Edward Gordon Craig and scholar-curator Ananda Coomaraswamy. Meanwhile, W.B. Yeats (who had met Rabindranath *Tagore in 1912) convinced the Abbey Theatre, Dublin, to present Tagore's *The Post Office* in English translation—the world premiere of that play (May 1913), four years before its Bengali production. It received good notices when it travelled to London. Later

English performers as Kunti and Karna in Rabindranath Tagore's *The Deserted Mother* (Union of East and West, London, 1924)

that year, Tagore became the first non-European to win the Nobel Prize for Literature. This event, the first major instance of the 'empire writing back', turned more than a few sensitive readers to the literature of the East. Amateur performances of translated Indian plays, many by Tagore, sprouted across Europe and America, especially under the aegis of a group of India aficionados named the Union of East and West. In Moscow, Alexander Tairov again chose *Sakuntala* to inaugurate his Kamerny Theatre (1914) and his individualistic vision of 'universal art'. During the 1930s, the two trailblazers of contemporary world theatre, Antonin Artaud and Bertolt Brecht, formulated their theories after watching Balinese dance-drama in Paris and Beijing Opera in Moscow respectively. Both referred to India in their writings, albeit secondarily.

In 1960, the visionary Polish director Jerzy Grotowski subverted *Sakuntala* in Warsaw, debunking oriental stereotypes, cutting and interpolating the text (even with erotic passages from the *Kamasutra*), making Dushyanta stand on his head while soliloquizing. On the other hand, the production of Tagore's *The King of the Dark Chamber* in New York (1961), using an interracial cast,

Indian dance, and mudras, made critics like Robert Brustein recognize it as 'a necessary antidote to the cliches of an exhausted realism', its conventions 'liberating devices rather than restrictions, freeing his imagination to an extent almost unequalled in modern Western tradition'. But only after 1960 did European directors actually visit India to experience traditional theatre and its practices first-hand. Eugenio Barba, perhaps the first to study *Kathakali, came to Kerala in 1963 and reported back to his mentor Grotowski, who in turn arrived in 1968. Both initially took exercises from yoga and Kathakali for their own actor-training programmes (Grotowski rejected them later as an 'alien' aesthetic), after which yoga became a component in many Western regimens of performance praxis. In Barba's 'barter system', he sought the artistic commonalities among cultures, which cynics dismissed as essentialist.

The American director, professor, and India specialist, Richard Schechner, theorized interculturalism as a welcome phenomenon, allowing 'cultures of choice' in a theatre not dominated by the West. This was evidently a naïve, even if idealistic thought, for all cultures are not represented equally in the global cafeteria. In the early 1980s, French director Ariane Mnouchkine introduced Indian stage conventions into her cycle of Shakespeare's

histories. This line of development culminated in Peter Brook's nine-hour *Mahabharata* (1985), regarded by some as the theatrical event of the century. Brook researched the epic in India for about a year before starting on his eclectic, spectacular, yet inspirational masterpiece about the human race, with an international cast featuring Mallika Sarabhai as Draupadi. Nevertheless, he faced intellectual flak for decontextualizing a work of faith, exoticizing it to suit cultural tourism, packaging it neatly for Western audiences, appropriating indigenous forms, and, most damagingly, underpaying Indians whose help he had taken. Soon after, Mnouchkine completed *L'Indiade, or The India of Their Dreams* (1987), on India's nationhood after Independence, co-written by Helene Cixous.

While the charges against North–South interculturalism exemplified by Brook's *Mahabharata* may be justified, they should not become a convenient scapegoat for Indian commentators to overlook intrana-tional interculturalism. Just as foreign directors sample Indian styles, so do urban Indian directors with their traditional forms. Geographical or linguistic borders do not exclusively demarcate cultures, for the culture of a metropolis is quite different from that of its hinterland. In their own variety of cultural colonialism, city-based directors appropriated open-air folk performances for modern drama on proscenium stages. This happened in two waves: during the 1970s, when official incentives to encourage directors working on traditional theatre led to a back-to-the-roots movement in every Indian state that rapidly degenerated into a formula of inserting rural styles or performers for colour; and since the late 1980s, when government-sponsored Festivals of India abroad resulted in many local forms changing their performatory circumstances (devotionally, conceptually, temporally, and spatially) to fit the reduced format on a foreign junket. Hegemonic cultures exploit less powerful cultures within the same country, perhaps a more insidious and invidious process because less obvious.

We could just as well question absolutist definitions of traditional forms. These developed in various parts of India as the consequence of historical acculturation, for example, the Aryan domination over the Dravidians, Vaishnava reform spreading from kingdom to kingdom, or Islamic contributions in vocabulary, music, and dance. No theatre genres emerged in a vacuum, and they lasted through the centuries only by way of encountering new forces and adjusting, reinventing themselves. To defend the purity of any form is to argue on the dangerous basis of racial purity, and ignore the ground reality that theatre has grown out of syncretic hybridization. Indeed, virtually all of modern Indian drama was motivated by the emulation of Anglo-European models in its quest for progressive literature. One could even contend that Indian authors plagiarized Western originals, for many of their plays were unacknowledged cross-cultural adaptations. To bemoan now that 'cultural heritage is replaced by cultural choice' is to grant artificial valorization to heritage—after all, who created that heritage, if not by choice?

Two other little-explored areas need attention: India's own history of colonizing, and the Indian diaspora. Long before Indian theatre reached the West, it had reached south-east Asia. The Wayang Kulit *shadow theatre and Wayang Wong dance-drama of predominantly Muslim Indonesia tell the stories of the *Ramayana* and *Mahabharata*, using puppets and mudras that may have originated on India's east coast, later assimilated and transformed. Buddhist Jatakas turned into Zat texts of dance theatre in Myanmar and Lhamo opera in Tibet. Hindu kingdoms flourished in Thailand, Kampuchea, and Vietnam, influencing the evolution of genres there clearly demonstrating Indian sources, besides retelling versions of the *Ramayana*. In Malaya, touring *Parsi theatre (itself an intercultural child) gave birth to the urban professional Bangsawan companies by 1885. People of Indian

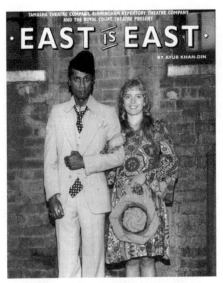

Poster for Ayub Khan-Din's *East Is East*
(Tamasha Theatre Company, Birmingham
Repertory and The Royal Court, London, 1995)

descent in other countries have also
served theatre. In Mauritius, Hindi
Natak exists as a separate form, while
dramatists like Dev Virahsawmy write
in Creole (*Dropadi*, 1982; *Toufann*,
from Shakespeare's *Tempest*, 1991).
Singapore has Tamil theatre and
South African Indians perform in
English too. In London, the Tara
Arts Group (founded in 1976 after
the murder of a Sikh in the Southall
riots) specifically addresses cross-cultural
experiences through intercultural
techniques, interpreting Sanskrit
and European classics, Tagore and
contemporary drama.

Anti-interculturalism taken to
rigid extremes would demonize
many of these creations and fetishize
nativism into near-jingoism. By this
logic, Indians should not stage

Shakespearean drama nor follow the
doctrines of Epic Theatre, both
invented in specific historical and
geographical contexts that they may
not fully comprehend; neither
should a Tamil director sample
Manipuri *martial arts, nor an Urdu
group attempt a classical Sanskrit
play. Ultimately, we must consider
only two questions in assessing
intercultural work: has the artist
exploited anyone in its making (this
applies equally to Indians lifting
copyrighted foreign material for
profit), or appropriated an exotic
form for sensation, spectacle, or
plain difference, without fully
understanding or respecting it? The
answers should be negative.   AL

Rustom Bharucha, *The Politics of Cultural
    Practice: Thinking through Theatre in an
    Age of Globalization* (New Delhi:
    Oxford University Press, 2001);
    Rustom Bharucha, *Theatre and the
    World* (New Delhi: Manohar, 1990);
    Jean-Claude Carrière, *The Mahabharata*,
    translated by Peter Brook (New York:
    Harper and Row, 1987); Chummar
    Choondal, *Christian Theatre in India*
    (Trichur: Kerala Folklore Academy,
    1984); Dorothy Figuera, *Translating the
    Orient: The Reception of 'Sakuntala' in
    Nineteenth-Century Europe* (Albany:
    State University of New York Press, 1991);
    Manomohan Ghosh, *Contributions to
    the History of the Hindu Drama*
    (Calcutta: Firma K.L. Mukhopadhyay,
    1958); David Williams (ed.), *Peter
    Brook and 'The Mahabharata'* (London:
    Routledge, 1991).

Jatra (or Yatra, 'journey'): best-known form of travelling *Bengali theatre. In older times, a procession at a religious festival where a community of devotees danced and sang in several voices, perhaps while carrying idols, was such a specialized 'journey'. The procession enveloped a wider sphere of action when it dramatically presented incidents in the life of popular avatars like Krishna or Rama. The most prevalent early Jatra, Krishnajatra, rendered such events in songs and dances woven together by dialogue, often extempore. One episode in Krishna's childhood, *Kaliya-daman* ('Defeat of Kaliya'), was so common as to lend its name to all Krishnajatra, but stories from the epics and Puranas surfaced on relevant occasions too. These theatrical representations were also called *jatra pala* (literally 'Jatra chapter', of well-known tales) and *Palagan* (*gan* meaning 'song') for their operatic character.

The earliest mentions of performance approximating Jatra come in the sixteenth century, when biographers of the saint Chaitanya, like Krishnadas Kabiraj, Paramananda Sen, and Brindaban Das, draw attention to the association of Vaishnava devotion with the medium of song and dance, not confined to *namsankirtan* (chanting God's name), to popularize a priestless adoration based on bhakti. The performances became part of the Vaishnava way to ecstasy through identification with a character under a strong emotional empathy or charge. Chaitanya's influence on Jatra as well as other Bengali folk forms can also be gauged by the fact that episodes from his life, sometimes as an introduction, sometimes a whole Pala, were added to the repertoire.

Jatra shared with Kathakata, *Kabigan, and Panchali the patronage of either the rich or the village community at large on various festive occasions. The courtyard of a wealthy patron or an open space in the village slightly cordoned off, covered by mats or carpets and lit by oil lamps (later, Petromax pressure lamps) for the all-night performance, provided the acting area. Musicians sat on one side mainly with percussion instruments like dhol or *pakhoyaj* (a two-sided drum) and *kansi* (bell-metal plate) or cymbals, complemented later by harmonium, violin, clarinet, or flute. A prompter accompanied them, covering the action with his script. The audience, usually in thousands, sat tightly packed around the acting space, leaving for the performers a narrow passage that sometimes served as extension of the acting area. Songs drawing on kirtan and based on ragas dominated the show. Dances which kept the beat, highly evocative texts making up for the lack of scenery, speeches rising to a crescendo and bursting into song, and words evoking the appropriate *rasa had enough cumulative impact to offset the garish costumes, crude make-up, exaggerated diction, sing-song delivery, and the adolescent boys impersonating women.

The Jatra easily became the most popular performing art and an integral part of village life in greater Bengal (including Bihar, Orissa, and Assam). Gradually, myths with pronounced human interest like *Harishchandra* and *Nala-Damayanti* ('Nala and Damayanti') joined the purely rural Krishna, Rama, and Manasa Jatras, to be secularized further with the addition of *Vidya-Sundar* ('Vidya and Sundar', 1752) by Bharatchandra (1712–60), court poet of Raja Krishnachandra of Nabadwip, Nadia district. Although *Vidya-Sundar* (or *Annada mangal*, 'Propitiation of Annada') belonged to the medieval Mangal-kavya (propitiatory verse) tradition, its valorization of romance and sexuality sought only an ultimate sanctification through the adoration of Annada. Its success coincided with Jatra's spatial shift to the newly growing city of Calcutta for easy accessibility, turning professional under the guidance of owner-managers who booked actors for the 'season', from Durga Puja in autumn to the start of the next monsoon. The nouveau riche in Calcutta, too, formed amateur Jatra groups mainly for *Vidya-Sundar* shows which revelled in the *khemta*, a light dance accompanied by loud gestures and swinging steps, and in extensive wordplay, riddles, and sexual innuendoes of which Gopal Ure was the best-known exponent.

The old form of Jatragan remained with such masters as Krishna Kamal Goswami (1810–88) and Motilal Roy (1843–1919) who creatively recast it into *Gitabhinay, as the musical, lyrical, and highly emotive Palas were then called. Later, the heroic efforts of Mukunda Das (1878–1934) at Barisal in east Bengal proved how powerful a medium it could become in evoking social consciousness. His Swadeshi (nationalistic) Jatra did not leave any legacy to the theatrical world but his political commitment remained an inspiration for the *Indian People's Theatre Association's *Rahu-mukta* ('Freed from Eclipse', 1954) and, later, Utpal Dutt.

After the 1920s Jatra went through major changes, the most important being its institutional settlement in the metropolis. In its quest for respectability and acceptance in urban culture, it pursued the modes and trends of Calcutta's commercial theatre, curtailing performance time to three or four hours and laying greater emphasis on plots, characterization, and social problems. Exceptional actors like Prabhat Basu, Phani Bhusan Vidyabinode (1894–1968), Phanibhushan Matilal (1910–72), and Panchu Sen (1914–72) drew consciously on the realistic tradition of Sisir Bhaduri, Nirmalendu Lahiri, Durgadas Banerjee, and Ahindra Choudhury, but worked within the stereotypes of Jatra characters: kings, princes, villains, humiliated elder queens, and selfish younger queens. The Bibek, singing incarnation of conscience, offered rich variations in individual acting styles, while still holding on to a huge vocal range and more elaborate facial expressions and hand gestures. The first generation of actresses such as Jyotsna Dutta also entered professional Jatra and gradually eased out the last generation of female

Jatra performance of the Bengali legend of *Khana*; the heroine, Khana, lies on the ground (Puruliya, 1973)

impersonators (including Chapal Bhaduri and Shatadal, alias Sunil Kumar Maiti), who at this point tried both male and female roles and totally different methods of acting.

In the 1960s a spate of annual Jatra festivals, widely and spectacularly publicized, institutionalized Jatra and its mechanism for booking long tours. Advertisements, seminars, newspaper articles on various aspects of Jatra made Calcutta aware of its presence, while the Sangeet Natak Akademi awards to Vidyabinode (1968) and Surjya Kumar Dutta (1976) went far to legitimize its existence. The *palakar*s (scriptwriters) came up with innovations that brought it closer to theatre—dialogue in conformity with character, comic personae perfectly accommodated to particular Palas, Palas on historical personalities, and mythological Palas with generous doses of sophisticated humour.

Utpal Dutt's involvement as playwright-director in the early 1970s led to a minor revolution with the introduction of political spectacle in the Jatra repertoire, more complex use of the arena space with levels, platforms, and simple but significant props, sensitive application of histrionic conventions and skills for new ends and effects, chiselling and economizing of acting, and, above everything else, the organizational and rehearsal discipline that he brought. But he fought a losing battle against a growing star system of ageing film stars coming to Jatra and proprietors exploiting their live presence to attract a rural clientele ready to be seduced by their glamour, and a new band of writer-managers setting different norms drawn from popular cinema. With textual melodrama and sensationalism becoming the main selling point, traditional Jatra is on its way out, but the logistics of touring (caravans of cars, buses, and vans on the circuit to villages and towns, stopping at each gig for a night or two) has reached foolproof efficiency and still draws 5000–10,000-strong audiences at every performance.   KG

Nisikanta Chattopadhyay, *The Yatras* (London: Trubner, 1882).

Kabigan (literally 'poets' songs'): once very popular form of dramatized singing in rural *Bengali theatre. Its merit lies in simplicity of content and delivery, and its theatrical distinctiveness in the extempore debates that the singers initiate and develop. Originally characterized by Vaishnava devotion since its inception in the mid-eighteenth century, its central themes related to Krishna and Radha. More than their love, however, the focus gradually shifted to the elements of *kalanka* (taint) and *chhalana* (deception) in the myths. As the passage of time brought marked changes in social and economic conditions, the patronage of sophisticated zamindars gave way to that of commercial merchants, and the performers succumbed to fun and alliteration for momentary pleasure and entertainment. The Radha–Krishna dialogues evolved and were secularized into Kabi *larai* (duel) involving two troupes of contesting poet-singers and their accompanists. They alternated arguments on a chosen topic of disputation, such as tradition against modernity or capitalism versus communism. Now in decline, very few performers survive. Past masters included Gonjla Guin, Haru Thakur (eighteenth century), Ram Basu, Bhola Mayra, Jajneswari, and the Portuguese-Indian Antonio Cabral (all nineteenth century)—the last-named popularly known as Antony Phiringi ('Antony the Foreigner'), and the subject of Bidhayak Bhattacharya's *Antony kabiyal* ('Antony the Poet-duellist', 1966) and the film *Antony Phiringi* (1967).   DB

Kakkarissa Kali ('nomads' drama'), also pronounced Kakkarichi, Kakkarassi, and Kakkarasa: a traditional Malayalam form of southern Kerala, much like the *Porattu Natakam. The Kakkan (and his woman, Kakkatti) belong to a class of nomads who roam the villages. They believe their ancestors were born to Siva and Parvati who once wandered as gypsies. Their main profession is fortune-telling; the men are also snake charmers and the women experts in stitching. They speak a mixture of Malayalam and Tamil. However, now mainly the Nayar community performs Kakkarissa Kali, an art almost on the verge of extinction.

Kakkan and Kakkatti are the main characters. The experiences of Kakkan, who travels from place to place with his two wives, form the major theme. In the beginning a Komali (jester) sings to entertain the audience. Another character, Kausiki, enters and renders songs in praise of Siva and Parvati. When Siva and Parvati appear, she requests Siva to save the world from wicked people. Then Kakkan arrives, introducing himself to the audience through song. A stagehand asks him about his wife. He replies that he has two, Kali and Nili, followed by the entry of the two Kakkattis.

In one of the stories depicting their experiences, Kakkan gets bitten by a poisonous snake while wandering through the forest, and dies. From the audience, a mendicant steps forward with a knapsack supposed to contain herbs and medicines to cure certain diseases, and offers to bring him back to life provided the Kakkattis give him whatever he demands. They agree, and by administering rare herbs he revives Kakkan. Then he demands that one of the Kakkattis should accept him as her husband; but Kakkan with his wives drives him away.

The Tampuran (landlord), King, minister, and hunter are other characters in these plays. Stories from Hindu epics like *Kiratam* ('Hunter's Tale') and *Harishchandra charitam* ('Harishchandra's Life') are also performed. The actors themselves sing while dancing and delivering dialogues. As in Porattu Natakam, questions are put to them by other characters or stagehands from behind, and answers elicited in the process of enactment. Men perform female roles. The musicians support the cast by singing and playing *maddalam* (drum) and *kaimani* (cymbals).   KNP

Kalapam (literally 'conflict', 'dialogue'): variant of *Yakshaganam in Andhra Pradesh, some of its forms made famous by *Kuchipudi dancers. While Yakshaganam is a generic name for various indigenous

or non-Sanskritic theatre genres in south India enacted by groups, Kalapam always centres on a prominent heroine, supported by one or two secondary characters, mostly stereotypes like a Brahman or maidservant. Kalapam is true dance-drama containing special musical compositions called *daruvu*, regular poetic metres (*padyams*), and connecting prose pieces (*vachanams*). Scholars cite four Kalapam texts, but two dominate: *Bhama-kalapam* and *Golla-kalapam*. *Radha-Madhavam* ('Radha and Madhava') and *Kshirasagara madhanam* ('Churning the Ocean of Cream') are virtually extinct.

Bhama-kalapam (from Bhama, abbreviation of Satyabhama), also known as *Bhagavatam* ('Worship') and *Parijatam* (after the crucial celestial tree in the text), was devised to facilitate portrayal of *astavidha nayikas* (the classical models of heroines in eight true emotions) in terms of specified *rasas and *bhavas according to Indian aesthetics. It brings out the protagonist's psychological and thematic complexity, despite its apparently simple and single characterization. Certainly a late form, it evolved as a specialization, of presenting Satyabhama, one of Krishna's wives, confiding to her maid

Satyabhama
(Vedantam Satyam)
and the Sutradhara in
Bhama-kalapam

about her sorrow. Thus it cannot predate the advent of Vaishnavism in Andhra, that too the cult of Krishna bhakti.

Tradition says that the founder of Kuchipudi, Siddhendra Yogi (sixteenth century), composed the play *Parijatapaharanam* ('Stealing the *parijata* Tree'), set to the best music and dance of those times. The theme is Krishna caught between his wives, Rukmini and Satyabhama, over gifting away the most precious flower from heaven. He gives it to Rukmini, resulting in trouble and drama involving the jealous Satyabhama. The latter's persona in this episode grew so popular with audiences that the sub-genre *Bhama-kalapam* came into existence, to portray her exclusively. Over a period of time Kuchipudi etched her character into one of the finest dramatic models, employing many psychological and aesthetic elements of the classical eight heroines. Thus she metamorphoses into *swadhinapatika* ('one with an independent husband'), *kalaharantarita* ('one who quarrels and repents'), *virahotkanthita* ('one languishing in separation'), *vipralabdha* ('one suspicious of her own messenger'), *khandita* ('aggressive one'), and so on.

In earlier Yakshaganam forms Krishna used to make an appearance, but not at all in Kalapam. The outstanding feature of *Bhama-kalapam* is that men perfected the art of female impersonation by religiously enacting Satyabhama. Kuchipudi artistes became inseparable from her character; the Brahman village by that name stipulated that each family must contribute at least one son to play Satyabhama. The Kuchipudi tradition thus produced great female impersonators: Chinta Venkataramayya, Vedantam Lakshminarayana Sastri, Chinta Krishnamurthy, and the legendary Vedantam Satyam. Kuchipudi men developed a practice of daring spectators to test their talent by tossing their long plait called *jada* over a small screen. If anybody won the challenge by improving on the same role, the *jada* would be submitted to be cut off.

Temple dancers in East Godavari district brought in another dimension by introducing women. Some etched into the form a super-speciality called *Nava-Janardanam* ('Nine Janardanas', Janardana being Krishna) through which nine variations of Satyabhama were performed on nine consecutive nights as a temple *ritual. Pendyela Satyabhama of Pithapuram and Manikyam of Mandapeta were outstanding exponents. The former's family members and disciple, Nataraj Ramakrishna, continued the tradition as gurus.

The 'Eastern Kalapam' or Turpu Bhagavatam of Visakhapatnam, Vizianagaram, and Srikakulam districts is more music- than dance-oriented, probably retaining the original elements of early Yakshaganam. This *Bhama-kalapam* features female impersonation too, but by non-Brahmans. The ancient musical style of *Dhruva ganam* remains intact, patronized by local zamindars and temple authorities. The performers are independently trained and have nothing to do with Kuchipudi. The most prominent in the recent past were Bonthalapati Jagannatham and Gudavalli Sankaraiah.

Apart from Siddhendra's text, other readings exist authored by various people, famous by their surnames: Vankayalapati, Chintalapati, Kasimkota, Mangu, Dasu, Narasingapalli, Nagarikanti, Nellimara. From the linguistic viewpoint, none seems to be of very old origin, including that ascribed to Siddhendra. The real age of *Golla-kalapam* is much more confusing, because some pandits claim it is the oldest. Also according to them, *Bhama-kalapam* revolves around erotic love (*sringara*) and *Golla-kalapam* around devotion (*bhakti*), but if we carefully study the latter, it sounds more socio-political.

In *Golla-kalapam*, a milkmaid of the Golla (*gowala* or Yadava) caste, generally associated with Krishna legends, becomes the heroine. The play does not deal with Krishna at all. Neither does the milkmaid fit in any frame of classical *nayikas*, although she is the main and only female character. The only male is a Brahman. They typify their castes and related sociology. She turns out to be a hard-core activist of an obscure Yogic cult, apparently Advaitic (non-dualistic), but not that of Adi Sankara, because her mission is to demolish Brahmanism and its related Vedic rituals. An Advaitic in terms of *sunyavada* (nihilistic philosophy), she defeats the Brahman despite his desperate attempts to save his beliefs.

The strength of the play lies in its extraordinary wit and sarcasm while challenging false Brahmanic superiority. At every step the milkmaid proves that her knowledge in Vedic ritual is much higher and intellectually sharper than that of an average Brahman. The tone of *Golla-kalapam* certainly relates to many religious reform movements of Saivism and Yogic cults that travelled into Andhra in various phases of history. Many non-Brahmanic literary and performing traditions, mostly oral, developed the archetype of a rustic illiterate man or woman to counter Brahmanism and Vedic authority. This commoner suddenly turned intellectually larger than life in dramatic representation.

The original author, Tarikonda Venkamamba, herself a Yogini, probably lived 300–400 years ago in Tirupati (Chittoor district), which used to have a large Golla population who may have been the first performers. Later, the text was given to touring professional Kuchipudi Bhagavatars, not adherent to any specific religious ideology. Their liberalism could have been endorsed by their own mythical founder Siddhendra and his successor, Narayana Tirtha. Kuchipudi Brahmans used to enact a textual variant, possibly rewritten or edited by Bhagavatula Ramaiah, son of Kakkaiah. Recently they stopped, perhaps sensing the real meaning.

Now only some female temple dancers perform *Golla-kalapam*, whose own tradition goes back a few hundred years under the patronage of zamindars who probably were never keen on Yogic philosophy, but might have enjoyed a dig at the Brahman caste. Later its spirit was reduced to ritualistic shows on the occasion of nuptial nights of newly-weds belonging to well-to-do families in the Godavari districts, the centre of temple dancers. This extraordinary transformation had a reason: in a portion of the text called *Pindotpati* ('Foetus-growth'), we can trace the representation of this intimate and complex scene beyond this particular play and form, to the most primitive birth rites enacted by many matriarchal cults throughout the world.

Golla-kalapam demands sizeable knowledge of Sanskrit, because the text accommodates a number of Sanskrit slokas and complicated Telugu *vrithas* (poetic metres) apart from the regular *daruvu* or typical songs of Yakshaganam. The form requires dancers to enact each poem or song twice, once in its original verse, then repeated in prose translation for commoners' understanding. Compared to others, the temple dancers with their perfect discipline, utmost precision, and social responsibility excelled in *Golla-kalapam*. Of the earlier generation, Annabattula Buli Venkata Ratnam and the Marempalli sisters (Vaidehi and Induvadana) proved to be experts. Later exponents include Maddula Lakshmi Narayana and Annabattula Mangatayaru.   PCR

Kalidasa: the most eminent Sanskrit poet and playwright. A few legends about him are told in late sources, but we have no reliable account of his life. His date is one of the most discussed problems in Indian literary history. It is clear that he came after Agnimitra Sunga (second century BC), about whom he writes, and before Vatsabhatti (fifth century AD) and Harisena (seventh century AD), authors of two inscriptions mentioning him. Hence the most plausible time frame, according to Indian tradition and modern scholars, may be the first century BC. However, Western Indologists place him in the Gupta period, in the fourth century AD.

Apocryphal sources say that he

was illiterate, but blessed with learning by goddess Kali (Kalidasa means 'Kali's servant'), and became court poet of Vikramaditya in Ujjain (however, many Indian kings assumed the honorific name of Vikramaditya). Inferring from his works, he appears to have been deeply imbued with his heritage, highly learned, and travelled throughout the length and breadth of India. He had a comprehensive knowledge of human nature, was intensely sensitive to sorrow, loved the natural world, and upheld high idealism. He wrote two epics, *Kumarasambhava* ('Birth of Kumara') and *Raghuvamsa* ('Dynasty of Raghu'), two shorter lyrical poems, *Meghaduta* ('Cloud Messenger') and *Ritusamhara* ('Cycle of Seasons'), and three plays.

Malavikagnimitra ('Malavika and Agnimitra') is a five-act drama of love set in the Sunga period. Agnimitra is the hero and the heroine, Malavika, a Vidarbha princess. Through plot complications, she reaches and seeks refuge in the palace of Dharini, Agnimitra's queen. Happening to see her portrait, Agnimitra falls in love with her and Malavika reciprocates. Although at first violently opposed both by Dharini and Iravati, Agnimitra's younger wife, the two are finally united, with the consent of the queens. The play corroborates important historical events. Pusyamitra Sunga, Agnimitra's father, overthrew the Maurya king Brihadratha, whom

he served as commander of the army. Kalidasa alludes to Pusyamitra and his grandson, Vasumitra, fighting the Greek invaders on the banks of the Sindhu (the present Indus). He also refers to the conflict between Vidarbha and Vidisa, the Sunga capital. As a romantic comedy, *Malavikagnimitra* features three delicate feminine characterizations and an active *vidushaka* jester who helps the hero in his amorous exploits but, at the same time, wittily criticizes all affairs. Well-structured and theatrically strong, it seems to be the earliest among Kalidasa's three surviving plays.

His masterpieces, also dramas of love, are *Vikramorvasiya* and *Abhijnana-Sakuntala*. *Vikramorvasiya* ('Urvasi Won by Valour') depicts the unshakeable passion of the king Pururavas for the celestial nymph Urvasi. Pururavas saves Urvasi from abduction by a demon, thereby gaining her love as indicated by the title. Kalidasa draws on the story in the *Rig Veda* (x. 95), but leaves his creative mark on the development of the plot and characters. The fourth act uniquely contains numerous *dhruva* songs, full of metaphoric images, conventionally sung by performers to strengthen not only the entries and exits of dramatis personae but also transitions from one emotive state to another. This presence in the play of *dhruva*s in Sanskrit and Apabhramsa proves its popularity in the theatre from the fourth or fifth century to the eleventh century and even later, supported by Kallinatha's sixteenth-century commentary on the musical treatise *Sangitaratnakara*, offering a detailed choreography of the *nandi* verse in *Vikramorvasiya*. The elaborate stage directions in Act Four pertaining to dance may reflect medieval interpolations, again suggesting an unbroken tradition of performance.

Abhijnana-Sakuntala ('Sakuntala Recognized'), a *nataka, describes the mythological love story of King Dushyanta and Sakuntala, daughter of the sage Visvamitra. Kalidasa builds the plot around the motif of Dushyanta's ring, gifted to Sakuntala, lost and rediscovered, symbolizing his loss and regaining of her as well as of his memory—hence the title. The Indian tradition of literary criticism gives the play pre-eminent position among all classical texts, and maintains that its fourth act and four verses in that act (the slokas when Sakuntala leaves the ashram) provide the most beautiful example of the relationship between father and daughter as well as man and nature, considered by some authorities as specific to the Indian view of life and the universe.

Europe discovered Indian literature through this play, translated into English by William Jones in 1789. Soon translated into German (1791), Russian (1792), Danish (1793), French (1803), and Italian (1815), it led to a complete revaluation and elevation of Sanskrit classics to levels previously reserved for the Greek and Latin canon. Deeply inspired and influenced by the play, Goethe apostrophized in 1791:

Would'st thou the young year's blossoms and the fruits of its decline,
And all by which the soul is charmed, enraptured, feasted, fed,
Would'st thou the earth and heav'n itself in one sole name combine?
I name thee, O Sakuntala! and all at once is said.

Kalidasa excels over others in delineating the soft, delicate, and finer aspects of love and pathos. His deep understanding of the human heart is reflected in the vast panorama of life presented in his plays not only through his heroes and heroines, but carefully crafted minor characters as well. Most of all, he is the author par excellence of *sringara* (erotic or romantic) *rasa. His mastery over the poetic rendering of the tenderest emotions, sensitive handling of situations, powerful portrayal of sentient nature, highly refined humour, and insight into Indian ideals and values gave him his acknowledged place as the acme of *Sanskrit theatre and the model for writers in all Indian languages.   KDT

Abhijnana-Sakuntala, translated by
    M.B. Emeneau (Berkeley: University
    of California, 1962); *Abhijnana-
    Sakuntalam*, translated by

B.P. Kirloskar's
Shakuntal (Bombay,
year not known)

C.R. Devadhar and N.G. Suru
(Delhi: Motilal Banarsidass, 1972);
Abhijnanasakuntala, translated by
T.R. Ratnam Ayyar (Madras: Star of
India, 1896); *Abhijnanasakuntala*,
translated by K. Bandopadhyaya
(Calcutta: Harasamudra Machine
Press, 1901); *Abhijnanasakuntala*,
translated by Bidhubhusan Goswamin
(Calcutta: Kedarnath Bose, 1903);
Abhijnanasakuntala, translated by B. Jain
and M.G. Shastri (Lahore: Mercantile
Press, 1932); *Abhijnanasakuntala*,
translated by a Master of Arts (Madras:
V. R. Sastrulu, 1930); *Abhijnanasakuntala*,
translated by G.N. Patankar (Poona:
Shiralkar, 1902); *Abhijnanasakuntala*,
translated by Brahmadatta Shastri
(Agra: Santi, 1924); *Abhijnanasakuntala*,
translated by Nobinachandra
Vidyaratna (Calcutta: Ratna, 1901);
Abhijnanasakuntalam, translated by
Saradaranjan Ray (Calcutta: S. Ray,
1946); *Abhijnanasakuntalam*, translated
by B.S. Vyas (Bombay: A.R. Sheth,
1962); *The Dramas of Kalidasa*,
translated by Bela Bose (Allahabad:
Kitabistan); *The Hero and the Nymph*,
translated by Sri Aurobindo (Pondicherry:
Sri Aurobindo Ashram, 1952); *The
Loom of Time*, translated by Chandra
Rajan (Harmondsworth: Penguin,
1990); *Malavikagnimitra*, translated
by V.S. Apte (Poona: Vrttaprasaraka,
1897); *Malavikagnimitra*, translated
by S. Seshadri Ayyar (Poona: Dyan
Prakash, 1896); *Malavikagnimitra*,
translated by M.R. Kale (Bombay:
Standard, 1933); *Malavikagnimitra*,
translated by G.R. Nandargikar (Poona:
Shivaji Press, 1879); *Malavikagnimitra*,
translated by A.S. Krishna Rao (Madras:
V.R. Sastrulu, 1930); *Malavikagnimitra*,
translated by C.H. Tawney (Calcutta:
Thacker Spink, 1891); *Malavikagnimitram*,
translated by C.R. Devadhar (Delhi:
Motilal Banarsidass, 1980); *Sacontala,
or The Fatal Ring*, translated by
Sir William Jones (Calcutta: Joseph
Copper, 1789); *Sakoontala, or The Lost
Ring*, translated by Monier Monier-
Williams (London: George Routledge,

1895); *Sakuntala*, translated by Laurence Binyon and Kedarnath Dasgupta (London: Macmillan, 1920); *Sakuntala and Her Keepsake*, translated by Roby Datta (Calcutta: Das Gupta, 1915); *Sakuntala or The Fatal Ring*, translated by J. Holme (London: Walter Scott, 1902); *Sakuntala or The Idyll of the Lost Ring*, translated by C.R. Vasudeva Row (Madras: Colonial Press, 1918); *Shakuntala and Other Writings*, translated by Arthur W. Ryder (New York: Dutton, 1912); *Vikrama and Urvashi*, translated by P. Lal (Calcutta: Writers Workshop, 1985); *Vikramorvasi*, translated by Ananda Acharya (London: Francis Griffiths, 1914); *Vikramorvasi*, translated by E.R. Cowell (Hertford: Stephen Austin, 1851); *Vikramorvasiya*, translated by M.R. Kale (Delhi: Motilal Banarsidass, 1967); *Vikramorvasiya*, translated by K.B. Paranjpe (Bombay: Native Press, 1898); *Vikramorvasiya*, translated by C.D. Shastri (Lahore: Shamsher Singh, 1929); *Vikramorvasiya*, translated by G.B. Vaidya (Bombay: Tattvavivechaka, 1894); *Vikramorvasiyam*, translated by C.R. Devadhar (Delhi: Motilal Banarsidass, 1979); P.B. Acharya, *Tragicomedies of Shakespeare, Kalidasa and Bhavabhuti* (New Delhi: Meherchand Lachhmandas, 1978); P. Balakrishnan, *Glimpses of Kalidas* (Bombay: Bharatiya, 1971); S.C. Banerjee, *Kalidasa Apocrypha* (Varanasi: Chowkhamba, 1990); G.K. Bhat, *Appointment with Kalidasa* (Ahmedabad: L.D. Institute of Indology, 1982); Mandakranta Bose, *Supernatural Intervention in The Tempest and Sakuntala* (Salzburg: Institut für Anglistik and Amerikanistik, 1980); R.M. Bose, *Kalidasa: 'Abhijnana Sakuntalam', A Synthetic Study*

(Calcutta: Modern Book Agency, 1970); H.C. Chakladar, *Geography of Kalidasa* (New Delhi: PPH, 1970); S.C. Dey, *Kalidasa and Vikramaditya* (Calcutta: 1928); Dorothy Figuera, *Translating the Orient: The Reception of 'Sakuntala' in Nineteenth-Century Europe* (Albany: State University of New York Press, 1991); S.N. Ghosal, *The Apabhramsa Verses of the Vikramorvasiya from the Linguistic Standpoint* (Calcutta: World Press, 1972); Sri Aurobindo Ghose, *Kalidasa* (Calcutta: Arya Sahitya, 1929); G.C. Jhala, *Kalidasa* (Bombay: Padma, 1943); Lacchmidhar Kalla, *The Birthplace of Kalidasa* (Delhi: 1926); V.Y. Kantak and S.S. Bhave, *Comparative Study of Theatre and Drama with Reference to Shakespeare, Sophocles, Ibsen, Kalidasa and Bhavabhuti* (Baroda: M.S. University, 1960); R.D. Karmarkar, *Kalidasa* (Dharwar: Karnatak University, 1960); K. Krishnamoorthy, *Kalidasa* (New York: Twayne, 1972); Jagdish Kumar, *Sarasvata Home of Kalidasa* (Delhi: Eastern Book Linkers, 1985); C. Kunhan Raja, *Kalidasa* (Waltair: Andhra University, 1956); T.G. Mainkar, *Kalidasa* (Poona: Deshmukh, 1962); Mayadhara Mansingha, *Kalidasa and Shakespeare* (Delhi: Motilal Banarsidass, 1969); Barbara Stoler Miller (ed.), *Theater of Memory* (New York: Columbia University Press, 1984); Satya Pal Narang, *Kalidasa Bibliography* (New Delhi: Heritage, 1976); Gangadhar Panda, *Dramas of Kalidasa: The Treatment of the Supernatural* (Orissa: S.S.K. Sanskrit Vidyapeetha, 1983); V. Raghavan, *Love in the Poems and Plays of Kalidasa* (Bangalore: Indian Institute of Culture, 1955); Walter Ruben, *Kalidasa* (Berlin: Akademie-Verlag, 1957); S.A. Sabnis, *Kalidasa* (Bombay: N.M. Tripathi, 1966); Dimbeswar Sarma, *Kalidasa*

(Author, 1968); K.S. Ramaswami Sastri, *Kalidasa* (Srirangam: Sri Vani Vilas, 1960); S.V. Sastri, *Kalidasa in Modern Sanskrit Literature* (Delhi: Eastern Book Linkers, 1991); S.V. Sastri, *Kalidasa Studies* (Delhi: Eastern Book Linkers, 1994); S.V. Sastri, *New Experiments in Kalidasa* (Delhi: Eastern Book Linkers, 1994); B.K. Shivaramaiah, *Kalidasa's Sakuntala: A Study* (Mysore: Ramya, 1994); C. Sivaramamurti, *Epigraphical Echoes of Kalidasa* (Madras: Thompson, 1944); N.R. Subbanna, *Kalidasa Citations* (Delhi: Meharchand Lachhmandas, 1973); K.V.K. Sundaram, *Plays of Kalidasa* (New Delhi: Patriot, 1988); B.K. Thakur, *Text of the Sakuntala* (Bombay: Taraporevala, 1922); Romila Thapar, *Sakuntala: Texts, Renderings, Histories* (New Delhi: Kali for Women, 1999); B.S. Upadhyaya, *India in Kalidasa* (Allahabad: Kitabistan, 1947).

Kalsutri Bahulya (literally 'string puppets'): Marathi folk form, immensely popular till the early twentieth century. References to these puppets abound in ancient texts and saint poetry. Vishnudas Bhave, the pioneer of modern *Marathi theatre, is known to have begun his career with puppet shows that he called *Yamapuri* ('City of Yama', after the god of death). Today they have become almost obsolete, found only among some tribes like the Thakar, in pockets of Maharashtra.

The puppets are made of clay or carved from the light wood of the *pangara* (coral tree), according to the character represented. Their height varies from 20 to 45 cm. Each figure is divided into two sections: the upper contains the head and torso, and the lower is draped in colourful cloth. Three strings are attached, one to the head and two to the hands. Dancers have two more strings tied to their legs, and demons, the tallest, have a string attached to their lower jaw, manipulated to open the mouth wide and shut it with a bang.

The show requires a specially prepared stage for which a 9-by-1m wooden frame is raised on a 1 m-high platform; the sides are covered and a 1 m-wide space is kept open for viewing. The puppets move downstage and the *sutradhara* stands at the back with the strings in his fingers, unseen by the audience. At a time, four puppets can be made to perform. An assistant sings the story, often from the epics, to the accompaniment of various instruments such as *tal* (cymbals), the stringed *tuntune*, and dholak.

Some puppets, the *kal bahulya*, do not have long strings. They are carved hollow, with head and arms loosely attached by wooden sticks to the body, small strings tied to these limbs and gathered inside the back. The puppeteer puts his hand inside and manipulates the strings to move the arms and neck. These figures are beautifully decorated with ornaments, costumes, and flowers. Very often, this is a one-man show, in which the performer uses his left hand for the puppet and narrates or sings the tale to *tal* accompaniment in his right hand.   MP

Karaga (literally 'earthen pot'): popular theatrical *ritual of southeastern Karnataka, named after the pot carried on the head by the worshipper-performer. Legends trace Karaga to several episodes in the *Ramayana* and *Mahabharata*, but currently the form is prevalent as a mode of worship to the mother goddess Adishakti, also known as Karagadamma ('Karaga's mother'). Variations of it are found in parts of Tamil Nadu; its present popularity in Kolar and Bangalore districts of Karnataka suggests that it may have travelled from Tamil Nadu to these areas, possibly during the fourteenth century.

The Karaga festival runs over nine days in the first month of the lunar calendar. It begins with the sanctification of the pot and the ritualistic preparation of the Karaga *gudda* (carrier). The climax occurs on the fourth day, when the carrier takes the pot on his head and the devotees move around the village in a ceremonial procession. The rites are interspersed with semi-theatrical events comprising recitals and presentations of situations from the

Mahabharata. Meanwhile, the carrier gets possessed and performs vigorous dances as well as acrobatic acts. These features indicate that, like other Indian paratheatrical rituals, Karaga stands somewhere between religious worship and theatrical performance; indeed, it belongs to a community that does not distinguish between them. Karaga remains alive as a vibrant form, with local variations.   AKV

Karyala (possibly from *karola* or *karaula*, 'teasing' or 'having fun'): prominent folk form of Himachal Pradesh performed in the dialect of Sirmaur district. There is no clear research on its origin; some claim for it continuity from classical *Sanskrit theatre, while others believe it began in the eighteenth century. It is normally performed around the Dussehra festival, in October–November. Traditionally it used to play continuously for sixteen nights, but now it can be presented on any number of days and any occasion, like village fairs or on invitation by individuals as part of a promise to the gods for fulfilment of a wish.

The open-air acting space measures about 3 m by 4 m, where the essential accessories are two *dyut*s (lamps fixed on tripods made of forked branches) placed on two sides and a *ghiyana* (stack of lighted sticks) used to keep people warm and also as an object of worship. Drums announce the start of the performance. Like most rural forms it goes on overnight, and consists of several small playlets imitating and ridiculing various characters that villagers come across in everyday life. The first two obligatory acts are those of *Chandravali* and the *Bairagi*. The former opens any Karyala event, serving the function of consecrating the arena; the latter contains humorous yet uplifting exchanges between different types of mendicants, some knowledgeable and some fraudulent.

The other scenes follow, full of fun, satire, buffoonery, and double-entendre dialogue in verse. They are unscripted, passed on orally, and kept alive through the performers' improvisatory skill and ready wit. The lines, even if spontaneous, rhyme poetically, though they have very little musical and dance accompaniment. The music is based on familiar regional melodies and rhythms, and dance occurs only in one or two specific episodes like the *Chandravali*, otherwise only in interludes between sequences. The chief instruments in use comprise the dhol, *nagara* drums, *naphiri*, and *karnal* (both wind instruments). Karyala's strength is its close link to the lives of the people. Apart from the original fifteen-odd scenarios, several new ones have been written on contemporary local issues, which remain popular.   KJ

Open-air performance of Karyala in Delhi, 1979

Kailash Ahluwalia, *Karyala* (New Delhi: Reliance, 1995); Ashok Hans, *Karyala* (Delhi: Sahitya Sahakar, 1987); S.S.S. Thakur, *Karyala* (New Delhi: Sangeet Natak Akademi, n.d.).

Kathakali (from *katha*, story, and *kali*, drama): celebrated dance-theatre tradition of Kerala, believed to have originated in the small principality of Kottarakkara in erstwhile Travancore (south Kerala). In 1661, the ruler dramatized the *Ramayana* in eight parts for staging in a style that assimilated elements from the folk performing arts of the region and combined them into a total theatre form, originally known as Ramanattam ('Rama enactment'). He wanted a more populist idiom than the elite *Kutiyattam tradition of Sanskrit plays, so he wrote in Malayalam, allowed all castes to perform, and took it outside temples. Still, the stylized acting and visual representation of Kutiyattam and the ritualistic proto-theatrical *Mutiyettu largely influenced Kathakali during its formative period. Its texts were called *attakkatha*, 'stories for acting'. Over a hundred *attakkathas* survive and about fifty remain popular, written by many authors, among whom the Raja of Kottayam (late seventeenth century), Unnayi Variyar (mid-eighteenth century), and Irayimman Tampi (1783–1856) deserve special mention, diversifying their sources to include the *Mahabharata* and other myths. They composed poetic narratives in organic plots consisting of a sequence of scenes.

In course of time the art evolved through a process of sophistication at the hands of creative connoisseurs like the Raja of Vettattunatu, Kallatikkotu Nambudiri, and Kaplingatu Nambudiri, who gave their names to the three geographical schools that developed: northern (Vettattunatu), central (Kallatikkotu or Kalluvazhi), and southern (Kaplingatu). They embellished the language of gestures, enriched the footwork and *kalasam*s (rhythmic phrases for dances punctuating the text), and improved the balance between singing and choreography. In the case of make-up and costumes, too, a steady change occurred from naïve origins to varied and empirically aesthetic levels. Thus the headgear made of areca sheaths was replaced by wooden frames differentiated by character type, decorated with shells of wasps' nests, shafts of peacock feathers, broken pieces of glass, and other objects. It is believed that in the early stages the actors themselves sang. Later the vocalization was given to two singers, the leading *ponnani* and the supporting *sankiti*, who occupy the back portion of the performance space along with the drummers. The entire sung text is interpreted and physicalized by non-speaking actors.

Elaborate preliminaries precede a performance. The *keli*, a percussion ensemble, plays to the public in the evening to announce the ensuing show, which begins late at night and continues till the small hours of the morning. At the *arangu keli*, a tall bell-metal oil lamp is ceremoniously lit in front of the acting area, behind which the ensemble starts with the *maddalam* drum as lead instrument. During *totayam*, two female characters enter behind a hand-held moving curtain, called *tirassila*, and dance to musical accompaniment. This invocatory *ritual includes salutation to the space and the instruments. *Purappat* follows, a prologue danced by a male and a female character. The *chenda* drum is introduced at this stage. The *manjutara* comes next, another technical item in which a passage from an *ashtapadi* ('eight-verse' song from Jayadeva's *Gitagovinda*) is sung to the accompaniment of all instruments—an occasion to exhibit the musicians' talents before the audience. This concludes the preliminaries, and the enactment commences.

The *tirassila* is of prime importance in the presentation. Its use for the entry of *rajasik* (majestic) and *tamasik* (wicked) characters registers dramatic projection as they touch it from behind and move it up and down to rhythm accompaniment. At one point, the *tiranottam* ('cur-

tain look'), the character shows his face, introducing his basic emotion (*sthayi *bhava*) with all its embellished nuances in front of the oil lamp, which has two wicks, one toward the actors and the other toward the audience. This lighting system creates an added dimension to the epic atmosphere. The actors' gestures are based on the ancient Sanskrit manual, *Hastalakshana dipika* ('Light on Hand Gestures'), which lays down twenty-four basic mudras, of one hand (*asamyuta*) and both hands (*samyuta*). Subtle facial and eye movements and dance steps are just as important; trainees must spend years learning them. For effective theatrical thrust in certain situations another level is provided for characters to sit on or climb.

Kathakali characters are broadly divided into five categories based on the mind's qualitative attributes. *Paccha* ('green') represents the *sattvik* or morally good heroes like Arjuna, Bhima, and Nala; they do not open their mouths. Certain characters like Siva have light red make-up called *pazhukka*. *Minukku* ('shining face') includes women, sages, and messengers of *sattvik* virtue. *Katti* ('knife') is *rajasik* in quality—valour with a tint of arrogance, as found in Ravana, Kichaka, Duryodhana— sporting a shade of red bordering the green on the face and a small white globular ball, *katesam*, pasted on the tip of the nose. The fourth

The lowering of the *tirassila*, or half-curtain, in Kathakali

group, *tati* ('beard', usually red), is *tamasik*, manifesting evil or ignorance, typically of demons and wicked humans. *Tati* can have black or white beards too, denoting brave primitives and divine animals respectively. *Kari* ('black') comprises demonesses and woodsmen. *Katti*, *tati*, and *kari* characters often make grotesque sounds.

The music is sung in the Sopanam temple style of Kerala, which assumes an applied form by the method of elaboration required. Each line is repeated many times to enable the actor to convert the meaning of each word and feeling into action through gestural language, bodily movement, and facial expression. The *chenda* and *maddalam* drums bring out the *tandava* (vigorous) and *lasya* (gentle) aspects respectively. The *ponnani* singer marks time on the *chengila* (bronze gong) with a stick, and the *sankiti*, while repeating the song's lines, does the same with cymbals. The *chenda* is the main instrument, cylindrical in shape, made of wood covered with hide on both sides; on one side the hide is tightly fastened to create high tones. It hangs from the shoulder with the high-strung side facing the player who uses two sticks on it. The *sudha maddalam*, added later, is also cylindrical, hung from the waist and played on both sides with palms. Its left side has a thick coating of black gum mixed with rice pasted on to give tonal quality, and the hide on the right is highly strung to create sharp notes. A third drum, the *edakka*, has an hourglass shape, covered on both sides with hide, hung from the shoulders, played with a stick in the right hand, and tonally varied by manipulating the wooden frame with the left hand.

Vallathol Narayana Menon (1878–1958), Malayalam poet laureate, was responsible for giving new life to

Kathakali and popularizing it by establishing Kerala Kalamandalam, a centre for its study at Cheruthuruthi village in Thrissur district, in 1930. Rabindranath *Tagore sent a student there to learn the form and teach it at his school in Santiniketan, and later termed Kathakali a 'supreme form of art ... where drama, song, rhythm, and movement are combined in a highly stylized triumph of grace and technique'. Through individual dedication, government patronage, and international exposure, Kathakali flourished in the twentieth century like never before, producing a host of exceptional performers with distinctive individual styles of interpreting episodes. The family tree of its three branches presents an interesting study in continuity.

The Vettattunatu school is the least known among them, Chandu Panikkar being the main guru, while M. Vishnu Namboodiri and K. Karunakaran Nair became experts in it though they had mixed training. The now most-popular Kalluvazhi tradition developed under Pattikkantodi Ramunni Menon, who taught a host of famous disciples like T. Ramunni Nair, M. Madhava Panicker, K. Sankarankutty Panicker, V. Kunchu Nair, V. Nanu Nayar, K. Kumaran Nair, K. Chathunni Panicker, T. T. Ramankutty Nair, K. Padmanabhan Nair, K. Krishnan Kutty Nair, Kalamandalam Gopi, and Kottakkal Sivaraman. The Kaplingatu school grew with Kunchu Kurup, Chengannur Raman Pillai, and students such as M. Sivasankara Pillai, C. Chellappan Pillai, and M. Vasudevan Nair. Many Kaplingatu specialists like K. Kunjan Panicker also learnt the Kalluvazhi style, especially later at modern institutions like the Kalamandalam; such versatile exponents include C. Pachu Pillai, Gopi Nath, K. Krishnan Nair, and O. Kochugovinda Pillai. KNP

The Art of Kathakali (Trivandrum: Department of Archaeology, Travancore State, 1933); Kathakali Plays in English, translated by Agatha Jane Pilaar (Kottayam: the author, 1993); David Bolland, A Guide to Kathakali: With the Stories of 35 Plays (New Delhi: Sterling, 1996); Alice Boner, On Kathakali (Varanasi and Zurich: Alice Boner Foundation, 1996); K. Bharatha Iyer, Kathakali (London: Luzac, 1955); Clifford Jones and Betty True Jones, Kathakali (New York: Theatre Arts, 1970); Kathakali (Bombay: Marg, 1958); P. Narayana Kurup, Unnayi Warrier (New Delhi: Sahitya Akademi, 1997); Kalamandalam Govindan Kutty, Kathakali (Calcutta: Asiatic Society, 1999); K.P.S. Menon, A Dictionary of Kathakali (Madras: Orient Longman, 1979); D.A. Nair and K.A. Paniker, Kathakali: The Art of the Non-Worldly (Bombay: Marg, 1993); Avinash C. Pandeya, The Art of Kathakali (Allahabad: Kitabistan, 1961); Vasudeva Poduval, Diagrams of Hand Poses in Kathakali (Trivandrum: Government Press, 1930); Premakumar, The Language of Kathakali: A Guide to

Mudras (Allahabad: Kitabistan, 1948); Vidya Bhavani Suresh, *Understanding Kathakali* (Chennai: Skanda, 2004); K.P. Padmanabhan Tampy, *Kathakali* (Calcutta: Indian Publications, 1963); Unnayi Varier, *Nalacaritam*, translated by Sudha Gopalakrishnan (Bangalore: Sahitya Akademi, 2001); Unnayi Variyar, *Nala Caritam*, translated by V. Subramania Iyer (Trichur: Kerala Sahitya Akademi, 1977); G. Venu, *Mudras in Kathakali* (Irinjalakuda, Trichur: Natana Kairali, 1984); Phillip Zarrilli, *The Kathakali Complex: Actor, Performance & Structure* (New Delhi: Abhinav, 1984); Phillip Zarrilli, *Kathakali: Where Gods and Demons Come to Play* (London: Routledge, 1999).

Kathputli (literally 'wooden doll'): Rajasthani form of string *puppetry, a hereditary profession for the nomadic Bhat community from western Rajasthan. Although most of the puppets (made of painted wooden heads and cloth-stuffed bodies wrapped in skirts) are articulated with only three strings attached to the puppeteer's fingers, they are manipulated with great dexterity and imagination. A few, like the court dancers required to perform very complicated movements, have five to seven strings. Trick puppets—a juggler throwing up balls, a horse rider, the Bhand (clown) from Jaipur, a snake charmer with snakes—fascinate audiences. A mask-maker with two faces, one of a man and the other of a woman, is very popular because the faces are changed skilfully in an instant. The faces are carved at opposite ends or neck-to-neck. If the former, the marionette is so draped that one face remains hidden under its skirt; when the puppeteer deftly inverts the figure, the skirt exposes that face and covers the other. If the latter, the manipulator gives it a swift turn so

Kathputli performance, horse rider in foreground (Delhi, 1990)

that in the twinkling of an eye the male puppet becomes a female one.

As it survives now, Kathputli theatre is not particularly dramatic since its text proper has shrunk to a minimum, but it never fails to entertain with characters like a kettle-drummer who refuses to die and rises from a lifeless heap each time he is struck down. The main 'play' in the repertoire comprises ballads about the brave deeds of Amar Singh Rathor, legendary seventeenth-century Rajput prince of Nagaur (Rajasthan), allowing for long battle scenes. The other items comprise acrobatic song and dance numbers. The improvised stage has a backcloth behind which the puppeteer stands; besides him, a typical troupe consists of a singer and percussionist. Kathputli music draws heavily from the rich and varied folk forms of the region. While delivering dialogue, the puppeteers use the *boli*, a kind of whistle made by stretching a thin rubber tape between two bamboo strips tied firmly at both ends. When blown, it acts like a reed, producing a shrill note. Lines spoken through it acquire a weirdly interesting tone. At times it is used to create a trilling sound that helps in establishing an otherworldly atmosphere.   JP

Khyal (possibly derived from *khel*, 'to play', in the sense of 'playing' drama): popular folk form of *Rajasthani theatre influenced by *Parsi theatre. Not very ancient, only about a hundred years old, the three varieties of Khyal (Alibuxi, Shekhawati, and Kuchamani) are associated with three playwrights— Alibux, Nainuram (1823–1905), and Lacchiram respectively—who were near-contemporaries and great frequenters of Parsi companies. As they wrote for troupes travelling to villages, where halls were not available, they changed what they saw to suit their purpose, dispensing with the elaborate settings and other heavy trappings of Parsi theatre to make Khyal relatively simple.

The plays are performed in open spaces using wooden platforms (*takhat*, easily available in every village) about 1 m high, with spectators sitting on three sides. In more elaborate multi-level shows, separate *mahal* (palace) or *jharokha* (window) platforms are erected, up to 6 m off the ground, representing different locales. There are no curtains, the actors enter in full view of the audience and, having performed their part, sit down beside the musicians; subsequent entries are made from that very spot. Women's roles are played by men, one of the foremost female impersonators being Ugamraj Khilari. Music is extremely important. The dialogue, written in verse, is sung by the characters to the main accompaniment of *nagarra* (kettledrum) and harmonium. The style of singing differs: Alibuxi

Khyal mixes classical and folk, in Shekhawati the music is pure classical, and in Kuchamani it is folk.

Nearly all the plays have the same themes as those of Parsi theatre, such as the lives of Amar Singh Rathor, Raja Harishchandra, Jaidev Kankali, and Gopichand Bharathari. In Parsi theatre the dialogue was in a special metre and the last words of songs or speeches were emphasized, and often repeated by audience members, prompting the interaction of spectators and actors. Khyal is composed in similar style, except that it is in Rajasthani and there is very little use of prose— as in the prototypical Parsi Urdu play, Amanat's *Indarsabha*, where all the lines were in verse. In Khyal, too, the audience joins in on the last words, establishing interaction with the performers.

The patronage to Khyal came from the people. When the troupe reached a village, the people took responsibility of its board and lodging, and gave money as appreciation to the artists in the course of the performance. Typically, a member of the audience raises his hand and shows a currency note. The actor steps out of his character, walks down to the person, takes the money, asks his name, and, coming back on stage, announces the person's name and places the money on the harmonium.

Alibuxi Khyal was founded by Alibux, Nawab of Mandawar in Mewat (Alwar). He was also a poet who wrote several plays, but his favourite was *Krishna-lila* ('Krishna's *Lila*'), depicting Krishna's life. As a religious form, Alibuxi Khyal wonderfully exemplifies India's secular culture: the poet and the singers were Muslims, yet great devotees of the Hindu deity, Krishna. Today, it is nearly extinct, with only some singers keeping up the musical traditions. Vulgarity has crept into Khyal, influenced by the electronic media and industry sponsorship of the performers as entertainers for tourists. Kuchamani Khyal, being rooted in folk music, remains popular (with star actors like Pukhraj Gaud) but Shekhawati Khyal is dying a slow death due to its highly classical base. Unfortunately, both the Shekhawati and Kuchamani varieties do not have any playwright to write on modern themes for present-day rural audiences.   RS

Kirtaniya (from 'kirtan'): form of *Maithili theatre that prevailed in Mithila, north Bihar, from the fourteenth to the early twentieth century. It evolved when Jyotiriswara (1280–1360), in his farce *Dhurtasamagam* ('Confluence of Knaves', c. 1325), infused indigenous Maithili music into classical *Sanskrit theatre, by inserting Maithili conversational songs, entrance songs, and narrative songs to suit regional taste. The great poet Vidyapati (1360–1440) further improved this trend in his play *Gorakshavijay* ('Goraksha's Victory', c. 1415). The historian Abul Fazl in *Ain-i-Akbari* (1596–7) referred to Kirtaniya as 'a dramatic performance of the acts of Lord Krishna, a devotional drama organized on auspicious occasions'.

Troupes, called *jamati*, contained between three and eleven members. They consisted of the *nayak* (hero), *nayika* (heroine), *sakhis* (female friends), *vipta* (clown), and an orchestra. Actors had to be versatile in playing women and singing traditional folk songs like Maheshvani, Nachari, Tirhuti, Mana Sohar, and Samdauni. *Vipta* was a stock character and accomplished dancer; he acted the Ghatak (marriage negotiator) or mimicked an astrologer, performed ethnic stereotypes like a Muslim enjoying the hookah and ridiculed current social follies.

Plays started with the *nandi-git* (benedictory song). The *sutradhara* (director, always a *nayak*) entered and called for the *nandi-git* to stop. He invited the *nati* (dancer) to come on stage. Together they gave detailed information on the occasion, patron of the performance, and the names of the play, dramatist, and characters. They created the situation for development of the action. The *sutradhara* urged the *nati* to perform a *sangitak* (song with dance). After this, the drama began and every character was introduced to the audience in a *pravesh-git* (entrance song), of which there were three kinds:

one sung from the background, another delivered by the character himself, and a third in which one character introduced another. The play ended with the *bharatvakya* (concluding speech), sung either in Sanskrit or Maithili.

Shows took place both in the day and at night on a simple platform. Performers held a *pati* or *jamanika* (curtain) in their hands before scenes started. Wooden structures of the mythological Garuda, Mayura, and Airavat were used as properties. Dialogue was delivered in Sanskrit, Prakrit, and Maithili, and in various metrical forms such as *doha* (couplet) and *choupai* (quatrains). In regular Kirtaniya, male characters spoke Sanskrit, female and lower characters Prakrit, while all sang songs in Maithili. This trend quickly disappeared in irregular Kirtaniya, where Maithili became the only language.

Barring a few, most plays had Puranic themes of Krishna, Siva, Nala, and other legends. The leading plays were Umapati's *Parijat-haran* ('Lost *parijat* Tree', c. 1650), Ramdas's *Anand-vijay* ('Anand's Victory', c. 1650), Ramapati's *Rukmini-parinay* ('Rukmini's Wedding', c. 1750), Nandipati's *Srikrishna-kelimala* ('Krishna's Garland of Games', c. 1800), Lalakavi's *Gauri-swayambar* ('Gauri's Choice of Groom', c. 1750), and Ratnapani's *Usha-haran* ('Usha Lost', c. 1850). Socio-cultural changes and the invasion of *Parsi theatre and *Ramlila caused the virtual disappearance of Kirtaniya. Today it exists partially in Lagma (Darbhanga district). Traces can also be found in Maithili folk dances like Vidapat-Nach and Choupara-Nach.   RJ

Kirttanai (from 'kirtan'): hybrid Tamil form. Since the thirteenth century, Tamil culture faced extensive artistic and linguistic influences from other parts of India. Their impact was obvious in theatre as well. The significant two-way transactions between Telugu and Tamil resulted in Kirttanai.

Rendering a story through musical narration is called Kirttanai, different from balladeering traditions in its dramatic aspects. The first part involves invocation and *kappu* (prayer), as in the case of most written forms. The mid-section relates the tale and the last section concludes it. Among the most famous composers, Arunachala Kavirayar (1711–88) abridged the whole *Ramayana* into *Rama nataka kirttanai* ('Kirttanai of Rama's Drama'), and Gopalakrishna Bharati (1810–81) used Hindustani, Carnatic, and folk melodies in *Nandanar charittira kirttanai* ('Kirttanai of Nandan's Life'), staged by various groups at the end of the nineteenth and beginning of the twentieth centuries. The latter became a favourite source for films as well, starring such popular singers as Sundarambal.

Interestingly, the gods praised in Kirttanai are mostly worshipped by the upper strata of society. Very few folk deities find a place in this form.

Kirttanai is written in the *sindu* poetic tradition, closely related to folk music. It can thus illustrate how folk forms merged into evolving Carnatic classical music. It is also an important resource to study the link between Carnatic music and *Tamil theatre. Its major songs are called *viruttam, taru,* and *tibatai. Taru,* in particular, contains all the elements of theatre. Kirttanai also employs *katka, tandaham, nondi sindu, lavani, kannigal, kummi, tukkada, esal, ananda kalippu, agaval,* and *javali* varieties of song.   VA

Kotamuri (corrupt form of *godavari,* which signifies a cow): village art performed by the Malayan caste in Kannur district, Kerala. The Malayan community is professionally known for practising exorcism, singing their traditional song called *kannerupattu.* Many of the men are *Teyyam dancers, specializing in the spirits of Vishnu Murti, Kutti Chathan, Bhairavan, Pottan, Chamundi, and Gulikan.

They enact Kotamuri during the time of harvest as a fertility rite. The main performer is a boy in the guise of a cow, his face painted elegantly and wearing a small headdress, with a cow's mask tied to a frame attached to his waist. He dances to the songs of accompanying musicians and the rhythms of the *chenda* drum. Two interesting characters called Paniyan, wearing painted *masks made of areca spathes, play with the cow, making jokes of contemporary social relevance. The performers visit every house, receiving paddy and other gifts. The villagers believe they are harbingers of prosperity.

The songs accompanying the dance generally deal with stories of the beautiful mother goddess of Cherukunnu temple who reached the village from the Arya country by sea in an open canoe. Siva, the principal deity of the nearby temple at Taliparamba, came to see her and fell in love. She started demanding gifts from him; he readily complied, giving her even his own belongings, and in the end had to run away bereft of everything. She is considered the mother of fertility. Many songs about the cow of fertility are delivered which include the following line: 'Let the houses that the Kotamuri visits thrive with abundance of paddy and money.'   KNP

Krishnattam or Krishnanattam ('Krishna enactment'): unique, exquisitely-designed *Sanskrit theatre form in Kerala. Its forerunner was the Ashtapadiyattam dance-drama in which local dance and music had established a happy blending, based on the Krishna lore and *ashtapadis* ('eight-verse' songs) of Jayadeva's Sanskrit *Gitagovinda* (twelfth century). This form became extinct, transfiguring its legacy into the new Krishnattam. In 1653, Manaveda Samutiri, the Zamorin (ruler) of Kozhikode, composed *Krishnagiti* ('Krishna Lyrics') in Sanskrit, inspired by Jayadeva, depicting Krishna's whole story in eight parts, with many more characters. The stage rendition of this poem became known as Krishnattam.

The eight stories on Krishna's life—*Avataram* (his birth as an avatar), *Kaliyamardanam* ('Kaliya Crushed'), *Rasakrida* ('Ras Sport'), *Kamsavadham* ('Slaying of Kamsa'), *Svayamvaram* ('Choice of Groom'), *Banayuddham* ('War with Bana'), *Vividavadham* ('Slaying of Vivida'), *Svargarohanam* ('Ascent to Heaven')—are each presented over several hours on eight nights in the precincts of the famous Srikrishna temple at Guruvayur, Malappuram district, as a votive offering to the presiding deity by pilgrims. Rich devotees may sponsor performances, considered a means to attain their prayers. The troupe engaged in this art is the only one of its kind, and maintained by the temple, which gives the actors systematic training from a young age. Only men can take part. C. Sankaran Nair exposed this rare art to the rest of India after Independence by taking it on tour outside Kerala.

A Krishnattam performance in Guruvayur, 1994

More sophisticated and differentiated compared to *Kutiyattam, Krishnattam's make-up, costumes, and ornaments look similar to those of *Kathakali, with striking variations especially in the case of the painted wooden *masks used by certain characters. The dance is lyrical and the story communicated through beautiful choreography, using a few hand gestures and facial expressions. Intimate minimalism is the core of the performance, including the simple treatment of vocal music with restrained use of melodic patterns. The meaning of each word in the text is not interpreted in action as in Kathakali, but the total meaning of a passage is conveyed mainly through dance. The graceful

coordination, precision, and elegance with which a group of characters moves cannot be seen in any other form of Kerala. This is well illustrated in the story of *Rasakrida* where Krishna revels with the Gopis: *mullappuchuttal* (literally 'going in a circle like jasmine flowers') is a brilliant dance in which the performers move with intricate footwork, creating a sense of the flowers being fastened into a garland.

As in Kathakali, two singers stand behind the acting area and the percussionists share space with them. The main vocalist has a gong-like *chengila* in his hand on which he keeps time with a stick. The *chengila* is a round alloy of brass, copper, and lead, specially combined to create the sound. The second vocalist uses the *elatalam* (a pair of heavy metal cymbals for timing). The accompanying percussion instruments are *maddalams* and *edakka*, drums that provide attractive patterns of rhythmic support to the flow of dance. KNP

Martha Bush Ashton-Sikora and Robert Sikora, *Krishnattam* (New Delhi: Oxford and IBH, 1993); M.T. Dhoopad, *Krishnattom* (Bangalore: Vidya, 1982).

Kuchipudi: all-male dance-drama tradition that takes its name from Kuchipudi village in Krishna district, Andhra Pradesh. It developed with the popularity of the Bhakti cult in the seventeenth century. Legend has it that Siddhendra Yogi (*c.* sixteenth century), while crossing a river in spate, prayed to Krishna to save his life. Thankful when he survived, he wrote a play in praise of Krishna, *Parijatapaharanam* ('Stealing the *parijata* Tree'), gathered Brahman boys of Kuchipudi, and told them to perform it with dance and song regularly. Their descendants continue the tradition to this day in Kuchipudi.

However, historical evidence suggests that the form flourished in the sixteenth century: a mention of similar dance-drama before the ruler of Vijayanagar occurs in the Macchupalli Kaifiyat (1502), a revenue record. A deed on a copper plate in the seventeenth century testifies that the Nawab of Golconda, pleased on seeing a performance, granted the village of Kuchipudi to perpetuate the tradition. Eventually, the actor-dancer Chinta Venkataramayya (1886–1945) formed a professional troupe there, the Venkatarama

The Sutradhara and Madhava in a Kuchipudi dance-drama

Natya Mandali, which toured all over India popularizing the form under his son Chinta Krishnamurthy. In this school, the actors spoke and sang themselves. Vedantam Lakshminarayana Sastri (1886–1956) introduced solo novelty items like *tarangam*s ('waves') as divertissements within dance-dramas: the performer dances on a brass plate while balancing a full pitcher on the head. *Abhinaya* to compositions by traditional poets like Khettrayya and Annamacharya also became common. Finally, Vempati established solo Kuchipudi for women, on the lines of Bharatanatyam; his students include Sobha Naidu.

The regular large-cast plays—*Parijataparanam*, *Bhama-kalapam* and *Golla-kalapam* (see *Kalapam), *Rukmini-kalyanam* ('Rukmini's Nuptials'), *Sasirekha parinayam* ('Sasirekha's Wedding'), and so on—dwell on mythological stories. The most renowned female impersonator is Vedantam Satyam; other family members included Vedantam Parvateesam and Vedantam Prahlada Sarma. Disciples of Vedantam Lakshminarayana Sastri and his school include Chilakamari Rama Acharya, Josyula Seetharamaiah, P. Venu Gopala Krishna Sarma, Nataraj Ramakrishna, and Raja and Radha Reddy. Shri Siddhendra Kalakshetram, Kuchipudi, is the premier institution offering Kuchipudi training. Several film stars, like Hema Malini, know Kuchipudi dance very well.   SK

C.R. Acharya and Mallika Sarabhai, *Understanding Kuchipudi* (New Delhi: Indira Gandhi National Centre for the Arts and Darpana, 1992); Anuradha Jonnalgadda, *Kuchipudi Dance: Who Is Who* (Hyderabad: 1993); Sunil Kothari and Avinash Pasricha, *Kuchipudi: Indian Classical Dance Art* (New Delhi: Abhinav, 2001); Rama Rao and K. Uma, *Kuchipudi Bharatam or Kuchipudi Dance* (Delhi: Sri Satguru, 1992); Vidya Bhavani Suresh, *What Is Kuchipudi?* (Chennai: Skanda, 2003).

Kundhei Nata (literally 'doll dance'): the traditional glove/hand *puppetry in Orissa. It uses only two figures representing Krishna and his love Radha, nowadays so humanized that at times they act like any rural boy and girl.

In the twelfth century, when the poet Jayadeva wrote the *Gitagovinda*, the Krishna-Radha theme grew extremely popular in Orissa for dramatic presentation. Krishna worship became more and more extensive and reached its peak in the sixteenth century when it influenced not only theatre but also all branches of art and literature. During this period, it is likely that both glove and string puppet traditions of Orissa adopted Krishna legends as their exclusive thematic content. Many lyrics, short poems, and long narrative verse (*kavya*) written between the sixteenth and nineteenth centuries were inspired by Krishna; others had human heroes and heroines. The glove puppeteers use these poems, mainly devotional but sometimes secular.

Kundhei Nata comprises only two persons, the lead puppeteer and a drummer-cum-puppeteer. They require no stage to present their performance, neither do they hide behind a screen. They sit on a mat or level ground and manipulate the puppets in full view of the audience. At times, the drummer (who plays the barrel-shaped dholak) holds one of the two puppets. While manipulating the figure, he occasionally beats one face of the drum with the hand that wears the puppet: it appears as if the puppet is playing the drum. This act immensely amuses viewers. There is not much drama in a Kundhei Nata show, nor is the technique in any way complicated though, at times, it is quite imaginative. Its main attraction lies in the singing and the literary quality of the songs. Interspersed humorous sequences enhance the appeal.   JP

Kurattiyattam ('Kuratti enactment', from Kuratti, the womenfolk of the Kuravas, an aboriginal Dravidian tribe): Malayalam dance theatre performed in village temples. The Kuravas inhabit the hill regions of interior Kerala and contiguous Tamil Nadu and Karnataka. However, the form is presented not by them but mostly the Nayar community.

Kuratti, Kuravan (a tribal man), and Muttiyamma (grandmother) are the main characters, hence the name. Men appear in the roles of women. Kurattiyattam takes place in the open courtyard of temples, in front of a lit traditional oil lamp.

The instrumentalists and vocalists who support the actors sit at the rear with *mridangam* drums and *kaimani* (small cymbals). They commence by singing in praise of the god Ganesha and goddess Saraswati, followed by the entrance of two Kurattis who assume the characters of the spouses of Vishnu and Siva. They engage in a wordy duel, dramatized through singing and dancing. In their quarrel they find fault with each other's husbands. In the end a third Kuratti impersonating Saraswati comes to the rescue and strikes a compromise. Then comes the Kuravan, who exhibits many acrobatic feats including rope dancing to musical accompaniment. Finally his old mother dances, which provides a lot of fun to the audience.   KNP

Kuravanji (literally 'Kurava woman'): possibly ancient south Indian dance-drama. Kurava and Erukala are two names of the same tribe in Andhra Pradesh and Tamil Nadu (see *Kuravanji Natakam) that specializes in soothsaying. Kuravanji centres on the act of soothsaying, by a tribal

woman who predicts the marriage of a princess or a goddess with her chosen lover (who does not appear in the play).

Supposedly one of the most ancient theatre traditions in the south, it does not figure in the list of eleven primitive Tamil forms. We can trace it only to the reign of the Telugu Nayak kings (1565–1673) in Thanjavur and Madurai (in Tamil Nadu). Many Kuravanji scripts started appearing in Telugu during the Nayak period, fusing its original folk elements with a new classicism. Each text is full of kirtans, *padam*s (dance lyrics), and *jati*s (syllabics) facilitating dance, connected by prose parts. The art flourished under the Marathi rulers of Thanjavur (1674–1855) who patronized Telugu Kuravanjis on par with *Yakshaganam. Kuravanjis also appeared in Kannada and Marathi during this time.

Like *Kalapam, Kuravanji is a woman-centric form. The main enactment takes place between the heroine and soothsayer, supported by one or two maidservants. *Viraha* (separation from a lover) characterizes all Kuravanji heroines. As with the tradition of *sabdam* dance items, Kuravanjis were also specially written to sing and dance in praise of kings. Well-known Kuravanjis of *rakti* (pleasure) are named after Vadaya, Sarabendra, Bhupala, Shahaji, and Rajagopala, while Kuchimanchi Jaggakavi's *Jnana Erukala kuravanji*

('Wise Erukala Maid's Kuravanji') became famous for bhakti.

A few Telugu temple dancers continued to perform *Jiva Erukala kuravanji* ('Lively Erukala Maid's Kuravanji') till recently. Similarly in Tamil Nadu, Rukmini Devi-Arundale staged Kuravanjis and, in Gujarat, Mrinalini Sarabhai adopted a few in her repertoire. Nobody seems interested in performing Kuravanji these days as an independent form, but its soothsaying component still appears in Yakshaganam and Tamil *Terukkuttu.   PCR

Kuravanji Natakam ('Drama of Kuravanji'): Tamil folk dance-drama that evolved around the eighteenth century. Kuram, Kuravanji, and Kuluvam are more or less synonymous. Kuravan and Kuravanji (or Kuratti) are respectively the male and female gypsies who appear in ancient Tamil literature, sculpture, ballads, stories, and Bharatanatyam dances. The form deals with the relationship of these hill tribes with their landscape. The narrative rests on the dialogue between the two characters.

In the eighteenth century, writing Kuravanji as a literary genre came into vogue. The authors also elevated the gypsy couple into god and goddess. We have evidence proving that Kuravanji was performed in the court of the Maratha kings ruling

Thanjavur (1674–1855), from a reference in Sivakkozhundu Desikar's *Tanjai Sarabendra pubala kuravanji* ('Kuravanji Praising Sarabendra of Tanjai'). This text has the Maratha king Sarabendra as its hero and is said to have been staged as a musical dance. The famous Thanjavur brothers Chinnaiah (born 1802), Ponnaiah (born 1804), Sivanandam (born 1808), and Vadivelu (1810–45) composed its music; their family retains this tradition of performance. Rukmini Devi-Arundale (1904–86) choreographed some Kuravanji plays as ballets, reviving old texts like Rajappa Kavirayar's eighteenth-century *Kurrala kuravanji* ('Kuravanji of Kurrala'), in 1944. P. R. Thilagam was an innovative recent exponent.

At least sixty Kuravanji scripts survive, some in print and some in palm-leaf manuscripts. The plays start with a princess who falls in love with a prince while he passes by in the street during his *nagar valam* ('tour of the city'). She pines for his love and her parents seek the help of the gypsy to prophesy her future. The gypsy reads the princess's palm, identifies the source of her worries, and predicts a happy future. Meanwhile the gypsy's partner comes in search of her and they unite after playful dalliance. The gypsy woman comes across as a powerful character with knowledge, skills, mobility, and selfhood. Kuravanji must be seen in the broader context of minor literature like *Pallu, which attempted to represent the voice of marginalized communities in society.   VA

Kutiyattam and **Kuttu**: ancient form of *Sanskrit theatre still extant in Kerala. Kuttu (play) is the generic name for these two varieties of Sanskrit drama performed in *kuttampalams* (playhouses attached to temples). Kuttu proper involves solo storytelling; Kutiyattam ('collective enactment'), the full-fledged staging. A reference to Kutiyattam in *Cilappatikaram*, the famous Tamil poem dated between the second century BC and fifth century AD, provides valid evidence that it came into existence about 2000 years ago. Certainly by the seventh century it had become quite popular. Two kings of the Chera dynasty in the tenth century, Kulasekhara Perumal and Cheraman Perumal, actively patronized its development.

In Kuttu, the actor presents tales from the epics, enlivening the narrative by impersonation through mime and gesture. The Chakkiyar caste was traditionally engaged in this profession; hence it is also known as Chakkiyarkuttu. The soloist brings into his performance numerous references in Malayalam to contemporary social and political events, and criticizes satirically people's shortcomings. Dramatic in word and action, he represents the

Usha Nangiyar performing in Kutiyattam

Edakka (an hourglass-shaped drum), *kuzhal* (double-reed pipe), and *sankhu* (conch) are also added at times, giving the ensemble the name of *panchavadyam* ('five instruments').

Men (Chakkiyars) and women (Nangiyars) act Kutiyattam, in *kuttampalam* theatres constructed in accordance with the prescriptions set down by the *Natyasastra*. The raised stage, not fully enclosed, without curtains or sets, is decorated with fruit-bearing plantains, bunches of tender coconuts, a measure full of paddy, among other things. A tall bronze oil lamp is ceremoniously lit in front. In the beginning the Nambiyar plays and recites the invocation, followed by *arangutali*, the sprinkling of water on the stage as a purificatory ritual by the *sutradhara* (stage manager). Then the main character is introduced. Kutiyattam presents only certain *anka*s (acts) from classics by famous Sanskrit playwrights like Bhasa, *Kalidasa, Sudraka, Harsha, and Bodhayana. It is believed that the first Sanskrit play in Kerala was written by Saktibhadra in the ninth century; the Chakkiyars perform many acts from his *Ascaryacudamani* (*Wondrous Crest-Jewel*), based on the *Ramayana*. Other important plays in the repertoire include *Subhadra-Dhananjaya* ('Subhadra and Dhananjaya') and *Tapati-Samvarana* ('Tapati and Samvarana'), both by the king Kulasekhara.

The acting preserves the fourfold conventional aspects of *abhinaya*:

suta (storyteller) of ancient times and appears in special outfits with headgear and make-up. A Nambiyar man plays the all-important *mizhavu* and a Nangiyar (woman of the Nambiyar caste) the *kuzhitalam* (bronze cymbals). The *mizhavu* is a unique instrument, a big 1 m-high copper pot, its mouth covered tightly with hide, fixed on a wooden stand called the *mizhavana* placed at the rear of the acting area, behind which the Nambiyar sits on a stool and plays the *mizhavu* with his palms.

vacika (vocal), *angika* (physical), *sattvika* (psychological), and *aharya* (decorative). Footwork and choreography are rhythmic, to the beat of percussion. Unlike Kuttu, the language is exclusively Sanskrit and the enactment a prolonged process over a number of nights, taking several hours each night through extensive physical elaboration of single words and lines—the most important part of acting Kutiyattam. For the vocal delivery of the text, the Chakkiyar actors evolved a stylized method using tonal variations to express emotions, indebted to the traditional rendering of the Vedas by the Nambudiri Brahmans in developing their dramatic articulation. Verse is delivered in musical modes suited to the respective sentiments. The elaborate make-up, along with flowery crown and various ornaments, uses a colour scheme symbolizing the characters' basic qualities.

The Chakkiyars preserve detailed *attaprakara*s (acting manuals) and *kramadipika*s (literally 'light on procedure', or production guides) for their scripts, evidently of considerable age. Before their first stage appearance, the actors undergo years of long and rigorous training in precise techniques of subtle physical movements fully utilizing the body's expressive potential. The *vidushaka* has a prominent role, entrusted with the responsibility of adding rich humour through improvisation and contemporary allusion. Despite cultural pressures in the twentieth century, the community produced exemplary hereditary actors who kept the tradition alive, including the legendary Ammannur Chachu Chakyar, Painkulam (Koyappa) Rama Chakyar, Mani Madhava Chakiar, Ammannur Madhava Chakyar, and Moozhikulam Kochukuttan Chakyar. Of late, performers from other castes have also learnt the art.   KNP

Clifford Reis Jones (ed.), *The 'Wondrous Crest-Jewel' in Performance* (Delhi: Oxford University Press, 1984); Goverdhan Panchal, *Kuttampalam and Kutiyattam: A Study of the Traditional Theatre for the Sanskrit Drama of Kerala* (New Delhi: Sangeet Natak Akademi, 1984); Nirmala Paniker, *Nangiar Koothu: The Classical Dance-Theatre of the Nangiars* (Irinjalakuda, Trichur: Natana Kairali, 1992); K.G. Paulose (ed.), *'Natankusa': A Critique on Dramaturgy* (Tripunithura: Government Sanskrit College Committee, 1993); K. Kunjunni Raja, *Kutiyattam: An Introduction* (New Delhi: Sangeet Natak Akademi, 1964); L.S. Rajagopalan, *Kudiyattam: Preliminaries and Performance* Chennai: Kuppuswami Sastri Research Institute, 2000); L.S. Rajagopalan, *Women's Role in Kudiyattam* (Madras: 1997); Saktibhadra, *The Wonderful Crest Jewel*, translated by C. Sankararama Sastri (Madras: Balamanorama, 1926); Saktibhadra, *The Wonderful Crest Jewel*, translated by R.V. Vasudeva Sarma (Trichinopoly: 1927); G. Venu, *Production of a Play in Kutiyattam* (Irinjalakuda, Trichur: Natanakairali, 1989).

Lai Haraoba (literally 'pleasing the deity'): ancient Manipuri fertility rite celebrating cosmic union between male and female principles, later enlarged to incorporate cosmological and ideological categories of the Meitei nation, assuming an intense and complicated *ritual theatre structure. Mediated through the ritual functionaries of the Yoirel (priest), Amai (priestess), and Pena (minstrel), representing the primal elements in creation, of fire, wind, and water, it is performed by the entire community during the pre-agricultural season (February–June) and, in some villages, the pre-harvest winter months. The ritual lasts normally seven or nine days in the lunar calendar; the Moirang principality (in Bishnupur district) celebrates it for a month, in May.

Four varieties of Lai Haraoba emerged, corresponding to ethnic and geographical distribution of constituent Meitei communities: Kanglei (the core Meitei culture based in Imphal and surrounding areas), Moirang (including Loktak Lake), Kakching (the Loi tributary of the Meitei, at Kakching in Thoubal district), and Chakpa (village tributaries, with the Andro on the eastern foothills of Nongamijing hills and other peripherally spread Chakpa villages to the north, west, and south). The Kanglei Lai Haraoba is regarded as the core ritual, reflecting the Meitiei belief systems and philosophy.

Deeply inlaid principles of the creation of the universe and its existence through the balancing factors of male and female union, of the sky-father and earth-mother, their copulation sustaining equilibrium and strength, and the interaction between ancestral energy and humankind, are enacted with dance, music, sports, theatre, and ritual. The human acts as priest to effect this cosmic drama. The cult of the placenta takes on a metaphysical character to enunciate the origin, life force, and creative energy of deities appeased during the celebrations: creation of the universe by Atiya the sky-father, creation of the world and mankind by Asiba the creator-son, and organization of human affairs in the conduct of Pakhangba, the father-knowing figure. The eternal father and mother assume a dynamic, vital position in the centre of the temple precincts, the spirits of clan or lineage

deities are drawn out through Maibis (female mediums), and the guardian spirits and other community gods invited to participate.

At each annual cycle, the lineage or clan ancestral deities are given life; they assume habits normally associated with humankind. The initial ritual is connected with the drawing-up of the life spirit by a female medium in a trance, via specially prepared raw thread hung through a pot on the necks of the lineage males. She draws the deities' spirit up from the life-giving water, taken in a simulated boat journey to the temple precincts. The participants cross the ancestral space in the compound where fertility-giving materials are kept. The Maibi then restores the deities' life spirit. The

Lai Haraoba in October 1976

ritual enactment is termed *lai ikouba* (drawing the deity from the water).

The next day, the slumbering Lai is awakened by the Pena's songs and bathed. The Lai then relates to worshippers through the female medium who gets possessed and, in trance, provides messages for healing the sick and infirm. In the afternoon, traditionally attired members of the community take out an elaborate processional ritual, enacting the beginning of the universe, stars, sky, sun, moon, and the creation of men, through the giant sexual act of the primal forces. This is termed *laipou* (imaging the deities). *Laiching*, the medium's symbolic institutionalized dance to draw the Lai to the ancestral space of celebration, depicts micro-level gestures of the creation act, while *laipou* enacts at macro level the creation of the gods and goddesses and their fulfilment in union. Embryological events in conception and birth are danced out to Pena music and termed *hakchang sagatpa* (formation of the body). The father's seeding and its acceptance by the mother is mimed in *khayom jagoi* ('cosmic-bud dance') to the '*Hoirou hoya*' Pena song addressed to the male and female principles. The action starts after moments of stillness: the earth's motion begins and the human moves. The procession takes the shape of the ancestral serpent dragon, as the Maibi and Pena form the head, the Lai bearers with the maidens the jaws and teeth, and the men, women, and children its body.

After prolonged chants and simultaneous movements and hand gestures depicting the sequence of the Lai's birth, growth, settlement, and clothing, the action goes on to the sexualization and romanticization of phallic energy heightened by mellifluous dance and archaic erotic lyrics. The Maibis' *paton jagoi*, where their dance steps simulate the straight but wavelike movements of Nachan, the centipede, energizes the sexuality, and the playful remarks between the lead and the response group, of catching fish with a phallic character, begin the symbolic foreplay for sex. The *Panthoibi jagoi* (*jagoi* means dance), with romantic overtones to sexual congress between the creative forces Nongpok Ningthou and Panthoibi, represents the union of male and female principles. Finally, the universe begins to throb with the orgasm of creation, as a white cloth spread in the centre takes the form of the expanse of the universe, fixed on four lineage males acting as pillars, and two Maibis holding thread balls dance the sexual act.

Next, the community led by the Maibis moves around the yard, confirming the fixation of *nonglon* (sky), *leirol* (earth), and *nunglon* (underworld). The *paphal* (dragon's spread) also signifies the balanced order of the universe. The semen or vital energy is now absorbed into the earth-mother's womb for future procreative acts: the father is present in the mother. Each day, these rituals are performed, and the Pena lulls the deities to sleep through the *naosumlol* (king's lullaby). Two days before the close, the gods and their consorts are taken out in a palanquin for a hunt and feast in a natural environment. The daily rituals continue, but sports and races are organized. At the end, the Maibis dance the *thang thaba* (cleansing by sword) to ease out bad and foul elements in the body polity, and scrap and consign them to the flames. Health, longevity, and the necessity of energy to flow again seem to be emphasized.

On the penultimate day, a new ritual is added, the enactment of human concerns to secure the world's life and society's health through a dramatic performance of *Saram Pakhangba* (another name for Nongpok Ningthou). Here Panthoibi as Nurabi, a plains tribal woman, clears the jungle with her colleagues played by women in the audience. They meet a hill man who disputes their possession of the land; they quarrel, but are united through an elder's mediation. This signifies maintenance of the body polity through manipulation of the earth and cleansing of rivers and waterways, just as the body's nerves and veins are kept in proper order through healthy activity, with morality,

discipline, and love. Jokes, fun, wit, and sexual banter reverberate in this ritual drama. Earlier, perhaps in the twelfth century when these characters are mentioned in royal texts for distribution of tasks, the performance was antiphonally sung; prose and dialogue could have been added later when crosstalk became a feature of south-east Asian theatre. Another ritual, of seeking the Lai's marriage, is not compulsorily attached.

The last day is one of serene, intense oath-keeping engagement between the gods and the worshippers-enactors of their revelry. The community performs another ritual, of songs of cutting down trees, and finally *ougri hangen* ('song of creation', the chant of *thengou*, the ultimate 'summoning of the spirit'), which perhaps symbolizes the gathering-up of souls after the straying of elements during the festivities. It is also a vow of the deities when, after being appeased and celebrated for the past few days, the continuity of the universe and liberation of the minds and bodies of the human group is the efficacious result. Lai Haraoba patterns human interaction with the gods and elements for the benefit of the future.   LA

Saroj N. Arambam and John Parratt, *The Pleasing of the Gods: Meitei Lai Haraoba* (New Delhi: Vikas, 1997).

Lalit (literally 'pleasure'): very old Marathi folk form combining devotion and entertainment, performed as part of the concluding ceremony at functions like the Navaratri festival, a Vaishnava processional yatra, Kirtan or *namsaptaha* (public reading of holy texts), and resembling the *Raslila of Bengal, Braj, and Mathura. It is presented by a *sutradhara*, his companions, and a *vidushaka*, dressed as different deities and twenty-five to thirty castes or social types such as *bhaldar* or *chopdar* guards, Vaghya-murali worshippers, or those impaired of speech, sight, and hearing. They act out scenes from the Puranas and epics, or humorous anecdotes and incidents involving common people. Lalit can continue from midnight to dawn.

It has a loose structure and changing form. In the Lalit performed after Kirtan, actors impersonating deities dramatically present the event described. Some *Bharuds are sung as well. The Lalit at the end of folk festivals is staged on a 4 m-by-6 m platform built with wooden planks. The accompanists sit at one side with their musical instruments and the assistants at the back. The other side is used for entrances and exits. The costumes of the *sutradhara* and *nati* (actress) are not very characteristic, but the *vidushaka* generally wears a black robe with salwar and jingling anklets, and holds a mirror.

First the men sing classical *dhrupad*, followed by the *sutradhara* and his companions singing an invocation to Ganesha. Sometimes the *sutradhara* entreats his wife to duet with him. Then Ganesha enters, and sometimes Saraswati. They dance and converse with the *sutradhara*; the *vidushaka* keeps interrupting with his jocular quips, often vulgar and coarse. They bless the *sutradhara* and the second part begins, containing comic episodes between two contrasting pairs of people who vastly differ from each other in language, costumes, customs, and status. Humour is a basic element in Lalit, signifying the conflict between the ideologies and customs of the elite and proletariat. It thus encodes artistic expression of perceptive social criticism.   MP

Lila: technical term in Hindu theology that signifies, among other things, sport, dalliance, play, the playful deeds of gods, as also performance that chronicles such deeds. For instance, *Ramlila means 'Rama's playful deeds'. The need to describe the 'acts' of gods as play derives from the need to explain why gods, axiomatically perfect, act at all, inasmuch as they require nothing and desire nothing. Gods are not obliged to act, but as they still do, their actions must be understood within the terms of the only relatively free and non-utilitarian activity we know of: play. By extension, *lila* means action not defined by any goal but brought about for pleasure. Thus the universe, and everything in it, is a manifestation of God's play, of God's pleasure.   AK

William Sax and John Carman (ed.), *God's Play: Lila in South Asia* (New York: Oxford University Press, 1994).

Mach (from *manch*, 'stage'): traditional *Hindi theatre of Malwa, in Madhya Pradesh. A comparatively young form said to have originated around the end of the eighteenth and early nineteenth centuries, it shares the secular nature and characteristics of other north Indian genres like *Nautanki and *Khyal. Based on religious, historical, romantic, or social themes, it was invented and developed by prominent artists like Guru Gopalji, Guru Balmukund, Kaluram Ustad, and Radhakrishan Ustad, who not only penned the scripts but also acted and managed the performances. Siddheshwar Sen is the most acclaimed recent exponent. About 125 manuscripts survive, including a few printed ones.

The open-air theatre consists of a platform nearly 4 m high and a canopy, simply but tastefully decorated. It is known to have been three-storeyed (*tin khan ka khel*) previously, with specific actions assigned for different levels. Single and double stages exist now. The stage pole (*khamb*) is put up about fifteen days before the performance with elaborate rituals to ensure success. Musicians sit at the rear and a special place is assigned for the initiated, who also prompt the actors when they miss out words or actions. The show commences with an equivalent of the *purvaranga*, where characters like the *bhishti* (water carrier) and *farrasa* (carpet spreader) enact humorous pieces, followed by *vandana* (invocation) to several deities, chief among them Ganesh and Bhairav. All the actors move around in somewhat stylized gait to suitable introductions, and the main *khel* (play) begins.

Apart from its delicate and evocative verse, the attraction of

Mach lies in a highly evolved and theatrical musical structure combining the classical and folk melodies of the region, that is the primary mode by which the narrative unfolds through the night. A systematic pattern exists in which certain tunes are used in certain situations known as *rangat*s, of which there is a large variety. The two major accompanying instruments, dholak and sarangi, with well-defined rhythms and inventiveness respectively, play an equal part in evoking the magic. While the stories involve heroes, a character called Sher Khan also acts the *vidushak* (jester), creating humour while linking up the tales to topical incidents within the community.

Costumes and jewellery are borrowed from the villagers and returned afterwards; in earlier days Mach performers, particularly actors playing female roles, were known to wear extremely heavy and genuine jewellery, according to their characters and arranged by the community. Previously light came from torches, then from Petromax pressure lamps, and now through electricity. Today, the themes of Mach have become more social than mythological, but as with most traditional forms, it faces an acute struggle for survival from exposure to newer and more glamorous media of entertainment.   KJ

Siddheshwar Sen and group in the Mach production of *Rajyogi Bharthari*, 1984

Martial arts: Experiments with the body as a source of theatrical expression formed part of the general movement in post-colonial Indian arts under the modernity project. These innovations were followed up by the next generation, aware of the artistic and philosophic discourses on theatre language and the body by such theorists as Antonin Artaud and Maurice Merlau-Ponty. The *interculturalism initiated by Jerzy Grotowski's visit to Kerala in 1968, and subsequent activities by Eugenio Barba in his International School of Theatre Anthropology and the general interest in Indian traditional performances among Euro-American practitioners, caused a silent movement in contemporary Indian theatre to research its ancient performing arts.

The richness of gestural language in martial arts like Kalarippayattu (in Kerala), Huyen-Lallong (popularly known as Thang-Ta, in Manipur), or Gatka (Punjab), and their obvious influence on forms like *Kathakali, *Terukkuttu, or *Chhau, enamoured a host of theatre workers. The opening-up of these resources through the government-sponsored international Festivals of India accelerated the movement to rethink theatre productions by grafting folk and ethnic traditions. The adoption by American universities of actor training systems based on such principles (as those of Kalari by Phillip Zarrilli) also encouraged Indian directors to look into the martial arts for theatrical purposes. Adapting the physical, realistic, and natural orientations of the body's movement through extra-daily techniques and behaviour became a feature in urban Indian theatre processes during the 1980s.

Thang-Ta performance

The first group of enthusiastic artists in Kerala, Manipur, and Karnataka usurped the martial art of their respective regions as part of their theatrical idiom, simply lifting motifs onto their productions. The coded vocabularies, choreographic patterns, and combat principles were incorporated physically in, for instance, adaptations from Sanskrit classics like Ratan Thiyam's *Chakravyuha* (1984), and the precision of execution, the skills of the performers, and the tension of the action created exotic images which often dazzled audiences, specially those at festivals on the international circuit. But unthinking exploitation of the techniques without changing their structure smacked of utilitarian necessities.

Later innovators, however, entered the interior of the body's resources to imbibe its energy, eliminating superficial borrowing of external forms while stressing the pre-expressive levels of creativity. The vital energy of chi was sought, as by Vinapani Chawla, which could inflect bodily movements into various kinaesthetic dimensions. This effort had better scope for subtle intervention, since the gestural and postural traditions that had become codified through the work of the ancients had evolved meanings in their own contexts, and to use them in contemporary experiments necessitated deconstruction of those genres and recreation of new principles inspired by them. Creative practitioners in Asia and Europe, therefore, utilize the martial energy, not the form, in performatory circumstances.

The postmodern discourse on martial arts in India has not yet assumed critical and scientific dimension as in the West, where analysis of physical energy had become visible through post-Grotowskian paradigms. Although the heritage of martial arts remains upfront in the public domain,

imaginative use of its potential in theatre has yet to develop.   LA

Masks: Anything that covers the face is a mask; it has always been a way of defying human vulnerability. It not only protects but transforms, disguises, and enhances the face. Born of mankind's myth-creating faculty that transposes experiences from the subconscious into images, the mask has ever been the unfailing companion of the face as its mysterious double—the alter ego. It seems probable that deep in the prehistoric past each primitive society developed its own masks to minimize the feeling of helplessness and exposure to the forces of nature. Their myth-making imagination suggested that the good forces that help in sustaining life are gods, and the evil forces that destroy life are demons or evil spirits. They devised rituals, which are but enactments of myths, to please the gods and appease the evil spirits. From myth and *ritual, therefore, were born many idols, images, and icons. Masks are a special kind of icon.

If theatre is defined as the enactment of a series of situations through assumption of one or more characters, the person who shaped the first mask unknowingly gave birth simultaneously to theatre (if theatre had not already existed previously). Masked rituals are but a kind of theatre and to distinguish them from other kinds, epithets like 'religious' or 'bizarre' are used. But it is now generally accepted that theatre began as ritual and aesthetic considerations came later. Many Indian theatre traditions still have ritualistic overtones and some of them decorate the actor's face either with masks or mask-like make-up.

Masks are generally used in three ways. When the wearer totally identifies with the mask, its magic power seizes him and what he performs is more or less a ritual, sometimes classed as *possession. Here the mask serves the purpose of an instrument to re-enact some elemental experience by projecting and reflecting supernatural powers. But when the wearer realizes that by putting on the mask he has only changed his outward appearance and not his true self, ritual gives way to human drama. The mask is then a means of treating the actor's face. Of course, when the mask is stripped of its symbolic character and used as a protective covering, such as the masks worn by astronauts and surgeons, the purpose is entirely utilitarian.

In India masks have been used for centuries either as ritual objects or to cover actors' faces and, sometimes, for both purposes: in such a traditional form as *Prahlada Nataka, the mask of Narasimha, Vishnu's fourth avatar, is worshipped in a temple when it is not donned by the actor in a performance. When used in a ritual, the mask is like an antenna of some supernatural power. The wearer experiences the force flowing through the mask to his body to possess it. A kind of double metamorphosis takes place: the mask psychologically elevates him to

Mask of Mayura, the peacock, in Saraikela Chhau

influence the supernatural power to whom he appeals and at the same time permits the power to transfigure him. He then acquires psychic substance from the power and passes this on to the passive participants of the ritual. The magic spell is not limited to the wearer of the mask; all participants in the ceremony feel the presence of the supernatural power summoned by the magic force of the mask.

Most Indian mask rituals are dances. Quite a few tribal communities, such as the Sherdukpens and Monpas living in the north-east, perform ritual mask dances, especially in a festival called Torgyap. It is believed that the performance of these dances drives away evil spirits and ensures prosperity, good harvest, and favourable weather throughout the year. Ritualistic masked dances are also performed by lamas of Himalayan monasteries in Ladakh (Jammu and Kashmir), Kinnaur and Dharamsala (Himachal Pradesh), and Sikkim. Their themes centre on the legend of the Buddha and depict his victory over evil to attain enlightenment. Among mask dances that give their audience entertainment as well, some styles of *Chhau, especially that from Saraikela (Jharkhand), deserve mention because they have pronounced theatrical elements.

Many traditional theatre forms employ masks. Very few, such as Sahi *Yatra of Orissa, mask all the dramatic personae. Most mask only some characters: see *Krishnattam, *Ramlila, *Ankiya Nat, *Bhagavata Mela, *Terukkuttu, *Desia Nata. In the repertoire of *Bandi Pethir, only the play named *Shikarga* features several characters who wear masks. Another variety, the pliant mask, comprises highly stylized make-up that gives the face a mask-like appearance. Its theatrical function is the same—a device for imparting impersonality to an actor so that the spectator is discouraged from identifying with the character in favour of a more intense dramatic experience. Some major forms utilizing this kind of mask are *Kutiyattam, *Kathakali, *Teyyam, *Mutiyettu, *Patayani, and *Yakshagana.   JP

Jiwan Pani, *World of Other Faces: Indian Masks* (New Delhi: Publications Division, Ministry of Information and Broadcasting, 1986); Sabita Ranjan Sarkar, *Masks of West Bengal* (Calcutta: Indian Museum).

Mime: acting without words. The roots of mime go back to prehistory, before man developed spoken languages, when, presumably, he used gestures to communicate his thoughts. In India, the classical concept of *abhinaya* (acting) constitutes four aspects, of which the *angika* (physical) pertains to mime. It stresses the systematic coordination of facial and body muscles. Thus, in most traditional Indian theatre and dance forms—like *Kathakali—every hand signal, movement, or facial expression has specific meaning. Their language of mudras resulted from ordinary gestures refined and codified into a sophisticated semiotics. However, they do not qualify as pure mime because they normally feature verbal narratives or supporting singers. They also employ elaborate and significant costumes and make-up. European mime is simpler, derived exclusively from human gestures, which are then honed and stylized, but not according to a predetermined grammar.

Mime and pantomime are often confused. Originally classical Greek and Roman forms, they both utilized

Jogesh Dutta

language. Popular modern mimic entertainment, invented in eighteenth-century France, omitted words completely, as did the spectacular nineteenth-century pantomimes of Jean-Gaspard Deburau. Mime now refers to the style formulated in France by Etienne Decroux in the twentieth century, and spread worldwide by his most famous pupil Marcel Marceau, who inspired many Indians on his tour in 1960. In English-speaking countries, however, pantomime defines a particular genre of musical performances for children during the Christmas season.

In a mime show, the actor wears a basic costume, conventionally black, without any changes. No props or sets are required, though recorded music is a common ancillary. The performer suggests different objects and spaces, even if staying in one spot, through his gift of creating illusions so believable that he can virtually make the audience 'see' the prop or place. Therefore, he must cultivate his powers of observation and imagination in order to enlighten viewers. Frequently solo, a mime traditionally acts many roles in the course of a presentation, but group mime is equally effective. Marceau popularized the stock mime make-up, of a white mask with darkened eyes and lips, but not all artistes apply it now.

As early as 1924, Rabindranath *Tagore experimented with a mime production of his play *Arup ratan* (*Formless Jewel*), but it contained songs by a seated chorus and recitation of the text by readers. The most renowned Indian mime, Jogesh Dutta, started performing in the 1960s influenced by Marceau, and established the Jogesh Mime Academy in Calcutta. Other disciples of the Marceau school included Irshad Panjatan, a soloist with a large repertoire of items; Bunty Paintal, who acted in Hindi movies; Awanti Chawla in Vadodara; and Janardan in Hyderabad. In Delhi, Alok Roy and Irfan Asgari used mime as a tool of social propaganda, the latter for the government's Song and Drama Division.

Niranjan Goswami, a student of Dutta who founded the Indian Mime Theatre (Calcutta) in 1976, evolved a training method and an 'Indian mime' idiom based on the *Natyasastra*. His experiments drew from Kathakali and classical dance forms. Zarin Chaudhuri began on duets with Panjatan in Delhi, Bombay, and Pune (1967–71), then initiated The Action Players (1973), the only company of deaf mime artists in India. Based in Calcutta, The Action Players has performed in the USA, Japan, and Taiwan, and incorporated sign language and contemporary dance in their shows. Mime groups exist now in many towns, among them Mime Academy (Guwahati), Kanglei Mime Theatre (Imphal), Kaladhar Mime Academy (Warangal, Andhra Pradesh), Vasant Kala Mandir (Udaipur, Rajasthan), The Mimers (Thiruvananthapuram), Coochbihar Mime Centre (Koch Bihar, West Bengal), Samoohan Kala Sansthan (Azamgarh, Uttar Pradesh), and The Talent (Delhi).   ZC

Moirang Parva ('Moirang chapters'): Regarded as a true embodiment of ethnic *Manipuri theatre, Moirang Parva began in the early twentieth century and lasted some seventy years. It belonged to the *Shumang Lila genre. Moirang, on the banks of the Loktak Lake in Bishnupur district, was a powerful, independent lacustrine principality ruled by the Moirang clan, which had a proud history and genealogies traced back to the first century BC. The last clan to integrate with the nation-forming Meitei state in the eighteenth century, Moirang had a peculiar relationship with the Meiteis, who needed to appease and appropriate its pride, independence, and richness of lore into the corpus of Meitei civilization. The epic story of the love between Khamba and princess Thoibi of Moirang in the twelfth century was divided into episodes; the Moirang chapters formed the last of the seven tragedies in the Langon cycle of lovers manifested by the deity Thangjing.

Itinerant players took up this rich repertoire of stories in the early twentieth century, though according to one tradition there was a late nineteenth-century 'environmental' production at Wahengbam Leikai, on Thoibi's return from exile in Kabow and escape from the rich noble Nongban. Thoibi rode a real horse as Nongban chased her in this performance. The event impressed the public as well as the palace, for the British regent banned future enactment with the warrant that it was tantamount to establishment of a parallel kingship in the state.

Probably in 1914 in Kongpal, an extended household concentration in the eastern valley of non-Hindu Meiteis who specialized in handloom products, a few elders under Kshetri Kanhai Singh built up a troupe of ten performers and inaugurated what is termed Ariba (old) Moirang Parva. They acted the episode of the punishment meted out to Khamba by Nongban's henchmen, followed by Thoibi chasing away the villains, and some incidents of fun and laughter. In 1920, the Anouba (new) Moirang Parva arose, led by Phurailatpam Nilkrishna Sharma, based in central Imphal with a mixed cast of Brahmans and Meiteis, and larger representation of newly invented clown characters. The latter's presence, mutual recriminations, and crosstalk became typical features of this genre.

These groups shared an intense rivalry during the 1930s, presenting many choice episodes from the love story in an operatic manner. The actors sang in the archaic, related languages of the Moirang and Meitei, and delivered falsetto prose dialogues, often transforming them into ethnic songs. Exchanges amidst the king and his retinue were in chaste court language, while the clown spoke vernacular slang. The indigenization of themes, performance, and language was perhaps not patronized by royalty, but emerged as part of the general trend of linguistic nationalism that swept colonized Manipur between 1910 and 1930. The aristocrats, typically Nongban, epitomized decadent, narcissistic, self-destructive nobility, given to manipulation and blackmail. One clown, Shoura, dependent on Nongban, loved him for his foibles, but sided with the lovers in times of real crisis, as the representative conscience of the justice-desirous public.

Moirang Parva reached a high level of grace and novelty. Body-size masks of tigers and elephants, wooden horses tucked under the armpits, large bent phallic cane sticks, beautifully-coloured costumes in ethnic types, and the style of turbans imported by nobles, were utilized. In common with other Indian forms, scenic unfolding was dramatized through song, and circular movements on stage signified long travels. But static tableaux of seated courtiers were placed in the background while other scenes were enacted in front. Improvisatory materials were used in plenty: a chair could double as a tree, a handkerchief as fan or sword. The female impersonator playing Thoibi sported a native hairstyle of moon-shaped cuts, and wore gold *kajenglei* (the traditional headwear of a goddess) and striped sarong with a full blue-velvet bodice imported from Burma. Her soft body movements, sensuous facial expressions, the look in her eyes, the mellifluence of her dances, and gentle sexual allusions made this form one of the highlights of Manipuri theatre.

The rivalries between the groups enforced contrasted visualization of the episodes. What one did, the other did not. Once an extended household invited both troupes to perform on the same night, as a sort of unofficial competition. Generally, Anouba Moirang Parva was more modern in approach, in the sense that it catered to diverse tastes in action—more aware of changing demands—and therefore managed to be subtle and varied, while Ariba Moirang Parva conservatively stuck to the traditional delineation of the original lore. Anouba Moirang Parva had more performers and, besides the clowns, Nilkrishna Sharma's suave bull-like arrogance and Loitam Yaima's appealing ignorance

as Nongban were additional feathers in its cap. Naturally, it lasted longer on the circuit.

However, in the 1930s, the new literati and educated Imphal elite reacted adversely to the plays. They objected to the depiction of the poor young Khamba and his sister seeking clothes and shelter late at night. The middle class pressurized extended households not to invite Moirang Parva. Reactions were divided, and there were disputes among local populations due to the shows' popularity. By the 1970s, the passing away of veteran performers, the transformation in audience behaviour and tastes, the advent of films and shifting of public allegiance to other forms of entertainment, and the gradual decline of the subject of Khamba and Thoibi as eternal lovers effected its demise. The managers of art tried to revive it but it survived only in the repertoire of all-women troupes. The new middle class reads the story in publication, as in *Khamba Thoibi seireng* ('Poem on Khamba and Thoibi') by Hijam Angahal.   LA

Mughal Tamsha ('Mughal entertainment'), also known as Chaiti Tamsha since it was performed in the month of Chaitra (March–April): satirical folk play prevalent in Bhadrak and a few surrounding villages of northern

Mirza and the Chopdars in a Mughal Tamsha performance (Sahapur Bhadrak, 1996)

coastal Orissa. Most probably it was created during the early part of the eighteenth century when the Marathas wrested power from the Mughals locally. Though the author, Bansi Ballav Goswami, wrote a number of Tamshas, this one is the most popular for its pure entertainment. It is a multilingual improvised play with songs and dialogue in Persian, Urdu, Hindi, Bengali, and Oriya.

It satirizes Mirza, a Mughal administrator who exploited the local people. The play does not have a definite story. Mirza, the pivotal character, remains on stage right through. Each of the other characters—Chopdar (guard), Zamindar, Vestiwala (water bearer), Hukawala (hookah bearer), Pankhawala (fan bearer), Bhat (panegyrist), Daptari (clerk), Bhandari (storekeeper), and Guwalon (milk-maid)—has only one scene in which

to sing and act. The Chopdar summons them one by one as desired by Mirza, and they introduce themselves through mostly farcical songs. Each couplet is repeated by a chorus. After the performance they ask for baksheesh from Mirza and, while leaving the stage, ask the chorus leader, 'What is happening here?' He replies, 'The festival of Siva is being celebrated,' then sings in praise of Siva and exits. The play is customarily performed in the precincts of a Siva temple.   DNP

Munaziro or Jhero (synonyms for 'contention'): Sindhi folk form in verse, depicting disputation in dialogues between two parties who, for the sake of entertainment, compete with each other for superiority. The audience includes an arbiter. Enacted in places like courtyards, Munaziro

has all the features of short drama featuring three characters.

The opponents become abstract ideas personified, such as Love and Reason, Youth and Age, or husband and wife, two birds or beasts of different species, or two characters from the romantic tales of Sindh. The drama unfolds with a prologue in praise of God, followed by mention of the two parties concerned and the circumstances that led to the argument between them. Very interesting and convincing dialogue is the basic technique. The composer must be a keen observer and natural critic. Through his treatment of the theme, he could depict the conflict's trifling nature, the contenders' aggressive behaviour, or the arbiter's impartial attitude.

For example, one Munaziro by folk poet Chhato Sangi (eighteenth century) describes a dispute between Kaunro (earthen water vessel) and Chilama (hubble-bubble) set against a village court in which other earthen vessels comprise an audience. Witnesses are produced, who depose against Chilama. Then, Chilama files an appeal in the court of a pitcher where the scene of a physical fight is created and averted by other vessels. At this point, a third character, a bowl, is introduced to act as arbiter, who explains that all vessels are important in their own ways, and the differences among them are due to different shapes and names. Thus everyone goes away satisfied and the drama ends.   PA

Music: Indian theatre is a composite art that seamlessly blends music, *dance, and drama. Music enhances the impact, for it can coordinate all the elements of scenic presentation into a harmonious whole in a way utterly beyond rational understanding. Thus music and the stage enjoy a symbiotic relationship, perhaps never greater than in Indian culture, evident from the earliest records. Bharata's *Natyasastra* states that the musicians sat on the *rangasirsha* (upstage) and that the *kutapa* (orchestra) served definite dramatic purposes. The *gayaka* (singer) and *gayika* (songstress) sang from *nepathya* (behind the scenes) on the actors' behalf. Music, both vocal and instrumental, was an indispensable adjunct of *Sanskrit theatre, used to entertain the audience from the *purvaranga* (preliminaries) to the *bharatavakya* (valedictory blessing). Songs remained an integral part of the Indian stage; through them, dramatic themes and grand conflicts have always been expressed and reconciled.

Enough proof exists in Sanskrit drama to support this contention. In Sudraka's *Mricchakatika* (*The Little Clay Cart*), the hero explains the beauty of a song he heard at a concert to his *vidushaka*. In *Kalidasa's *Malavikagnimitra* ('Malavika and Agnimitra'), the heroine sings; in his *Vikramorvasiya* ('Urvasi Won by Valour'), one whole act consists of songs. In Harsha's *Ratnavali*, two maids sing before the king. According to Rajasekhara, '*dhruva hi natyasa prathame pranah*' ('*dhruva*s are the primary life of theatre'). Dramatic songs pre-eminently were *dhruva*s, of five classes: *pravesiki* (for entrance), *akshepiki* (for turning aside), *prasadiki* (for countenance), *antara* (for transition), and *nishkramiki* (for exit), in the course of the plot's development. *Dhruva*s therefore served as a background score based on their content, metre, language, tempo, and tala, suggesting the acts and moods of different characters. The *Natyasastra* devotes considerable space to music in chapters 28–34. The ancient, extant temple theatre of *Kutiyattam also displays the importance of music.

Parallel to the courtly Sanskrit plays, folk drama developed in different regions of India, also richly based on song. Sarngadeva (1175–1247), the famous Maharashtri musicologist, mentioned the musicians of the coastal Konkan area, who accompanied theatre performances. Forms classified under *sangitaka* ('song work', or musical) grew between the tenth and fifteenth centuries, though the

Natyasastra or subsequent dramaturgical works do not use the term. A collection of *Caturbhani* ('Four *Bhanas*', *c.* fourth century) first refers to it as performed by courtesans. Bana's *Harshacarita* (seventh century) and Yadava Prakasha's *Vaijayanti* (eleventh century) also cite it. The play *Goraksha-vijaya* ('Goraksha's Victory', fifteenth century), attributed to Vidyapati, applies it to a song along with dances by two characters from Tailanga Desh, or modern Andhra. Finally, a sloka in Subhankara's *Sangit damodara* (fifteenth century) describes the *sangitaka* as having five elements: vocal music, instrumental music, dance, a stage, and the performers.

Historically, song began to dominate popular art all over the country following the success of Vaishnava reform movements—as a medium of devotion and for propagation of the faith. Jayadeva's *Gitagovinda* (twelfth century) was frequently dramatized in virtually all languages, its songs containing its essential appeal. Between 1485 and 1550 different Vaishnava theatrical forms evolved, like *Raslila in north India, or were invented by such saints as Sankaradeva in Assam (*Ankiya Nat), Chaitanya in Bengal (*Jatra), and Narayana Tirtha in Andhra (*Kalapam). Much later, secular forms arose like *Tamasha in Maharashtra and *Nautanki in Uttar Pradesh. The common feature in all traditional genres of theatre, even now, is that their performances are embedded with songs and music.

Significantly, when Western drama came to India, the first play in an Indian language staged inside a proscenium-arch auditorium was presented in Calcutta by a Russian musician, Herasim Lebedeff, on 27 November 1795. He adapted into Bengali an obscure English script, *The Disguise*, using the songs of a famous eighteenth-century Bengali poet, Bharatchandra Ray. Thus the twin heritage of Sanskrit theatre and folk Jatra persisted. Henceforth, educated Indian dramatists skilfully adapted British models, but retained the indigenous passion for music by frequent insertion of songs. In 1835, Nabin Chandra Basu edited and dramatized Bharatchandra's romance *Vidya-Sundar* ('Vidya and Sundar'), its songs the mainstay of his production. The play became a cult favourite and Vidya-Sundar groups proliferated all over Calcutta.

In the 1850s, the chief Bengali playwrights were Ramnarayan Tarkaratna and Michael Madhusudan Dutt. A Sanskrit scholar, the former followed classical convention to make the characters of the *nat* and *nati* (actor and actress) introduce the drama with songs. Dutt was inspired by European literature, but in plays like *Sharmishtha*, *Padmabati*, and *Krishnakumari*, even in his satire *Ekei ki bale sabhyata? (Is This Called Civilization?*, all 1859–61),

he added songs of classical and semi-classical Indian origin. Both authors received help from specialist composers like Jatindramohan Tagore and Kshetromohan Goswami on their music. During the 1870s Manomohan Basu (1831–1912), a poet, produced many plays based on Hindu mythology blended into the socio-political scenario, as *Gitabhinay (literally 'lyric-acting'), in which songs were the prime factor.

Nagendranath Banerjee's *Sati ki kalankini* ('Chaste or Fallen Woman', 1874), scored by Madanmohan Burman, played a vital role in developing Bengali stage music. This so-called opera, with an orchestra, was emulated by Jyotirindranath Tagore, who always used music as his main dramatic prop. An adept both in Indian and Western styles, he effortlessly melded them. He created a hybrid raga, 'Italian Jhinjhit', in *Ashrumati* (1880). Nationalist sentiment, against the colonial backdrop, took the form of stage songs on his *Puru-bikram* ('Puru's Valour', 1874) and *Sarojini* (1876). The same passion permeated Amritalal Basu's *Hirakchurna* ('Diamond Dust') and Upendranath Das's *Surendra-Binodini* ('Surendra and Binodini') in 1875. The songs evoked patriotic aspirations and fervour, ultimately prompting the infamous *Dramatic Performances Act. The language of lyrics had begun to change. In 1883, *Vande* *mataram* ('Hail Mother', from Bankimchandra Chatterjee's novel, *Anandamath*), later to become the national song, was set to music by Devkantha Bagchi for Kedar Chowdhury's dramatization.

The musical background of the great pathfinders of *Bengali theatre needs mention. Girish Chandra Ghosh, 'the father of Bengali theatre', was originally a composer. After turning dramatist and director, he produced social, religious, political, and philosophical scripts having music as their crucial component. D.L. Roy, too, started his playwriting career as a musician. Owing to his versatility in Indian and Western music, his works were enriched by songs, very popular for their uplifting, emotional quality: *Dhana-dhanya-pushpa-bhara* ('Full of riches, food and flowers') in *Shah Jahan* (1909) became Bengal's de facto anthem at the time. Rabindranath *Tagore stood alone. Classically trained but with a sensitivity to folk music, he brought an individualistic style transcending fashions that eventually turned into a separate genre, Rabindrasangit. His compositions, many of which he sang on stage himself, gave his plays their distinctive quality.

The music director Krishna Chandra Dey (1893–1962, also a well-known singer) and actress-singers Niharbala, Indubala, and Angurbala were the trendsetters of the next generation. Kazi Nazrul Islam (1898–1976), a major poet and composer, helped playwrights like Manmatha Ray and Sachindranath Sengupta. His music set a new trend, different from Tagore's, by incorporating nationalistic aspirations in classical and semi-classical forms. After the *Indian People's Theatre Association appropriated folk song radically to fit its political agenda, starting with *Nabanna* ('New Harvest', 1944), stage music changed across the country. A parallel theatre with socialistic ideas emerged, beside the no-longer-political commercial theatre. In Bengal, Sabitabrata Dutta gained fame as actor, singer, composer, and director, followed by Ajitesh Bandopadhyay, who based his adaptations of Brecht on folk tunes.

Urban *Marathi theatre and musical drama both date to 1843, when the first proscenium performance took place: *Sita swayamvar* ('Sita's Choice of Groom') by scriptwriter-composer Vishnudas Bhave. He may have borrowed the concept from traditional forms that he had seen. The real beginning came with *Shakuntal*, produced in 1880 by Annasaheb Kirloskar, who created the institution of Marathi *Sangitnatak ('music-drama'). Educated and with a highly cultivated taste for music, he invented the formula of stanzas in popular metres, ranging from folk tunes, simple attractive women's songs, to musical discourses on religious subjects. The Kirloskar pattern improved the taste of theatre audiences, till Khadilkar's plays ushered in the golden age of Marathi stage music after 1910.

Music direction was now turned over to an expert. From its inception, Marathi theatre used music principally as a vehicle for the flow of narrative. Govindrao Tembe introduced an original idea, heightening the impact by sharpening the songs' emotive content. Music and song became more stylized and fashioned into independent highlights. Tembe composed both literary and musical texts of grand operas or fully musical plays. Meanwhile, Bal Gandharva turned into a legendary actor-singer; his inspired, almost celestial voice combined with superb female impersonation to make him a national icon. In contrast, Keshavrao Bhonsle was known for his volume, and manly, even aggressive vocal style.

By the 1930s, a definite trend grew to curb music on stage. A show's average duration (inflated by innumerable encores of songs) was brought down from five or six hours to three hours. The composer who set this trend was music critic Keshavrao Bhole (1896–1967), whose wife, Jyotsna Bhole, was the foremost singer-actress of the time. Still, Dinanath Mangeshkar, whose short and meteoric career left a tremendous impact on the Marathi

stage, Sawai Gandharva, Vinayakrao Patwardhan, Mirashibuwa, Bhatebuwa, Hirabai Barodekar, and many others were chosen for their roles mainly on account of their singing abilities. Most had classical gurus as teachers. Up to Vidyadhar Gokhale's *Panditraj Jagannath* (1960), music by Chhota Gandharva and Vasant Desai (1912–75), or *Mandarmala* (1963), music by Ram Marathe, productions in which songs dominated proved remarkably successful. Desai, experienced in cinema, used

Portrait of Bal Gandharva as Rukmini in K.P. Khadilkar's *Swayamvar* (Gandharva Natak Mandali, Bombay, 1916)

instrumentation and background songs prominently in plays like *Panditraj Jagannath*.

Meanwhile Jitendra Abhisheki (1932–98), a highly trained vocalist, created his own idealism, from traditional music for Vasant Kanetkar's *Matsyagandha* (1964) and Purushottam Darwhekar's *Katyar kaljat ghusli* ('Dagger Pierced the Heart', 1967), to phrasing from popular Goan melodies for Kanetkar's *Lekure udand jali* ('Too Many Brats', 1966). The eminent classical singer Vasantrao Deshpande (1923–83), deeply influenced by Mangeshkar's ebullience, caused a sensation as one of the feuding vocalists in *Katyar kaljat ghusli*. As a group, Theatre Academy attained fame for musical productions: in Vijay Tendulkar's satirical *Ghashiram Kotwal* (1972), composer Bhaskar Chandavarkar drew melodies from rural and classical traditions of Maharashtra; *Tin paishacha tamasha* (Brecht's *Threepenny Opera* adapted by P.L. Deshpande, 1978) mixed folk with popular music; Satish Alekar's *Begum Barve* (1979) was an innovative musical about Sangitnatak.

Between the fifteenth and nineteenth centuries a court theatre had flourished in Hindi-speaking regions, based on the Vaishnava movement. It owed its poetic beauty to the Sanskrit tradition, its inspiration to the devotional songs of Vidyapati and Chandidas, and its

flexibility to folk festivals, thereby continuing as a living institution. In 1853, *Urdu theatre commenced with Amanat's *Indarsabha* ('Indra's Court') staged at the Lucknow palace of Wajid Ali Shah, inspired by his *rahas* shows. This production, too, was operatic, in verse and comprising a rich variety of music and songs. The founder of modern *Hindi theatre, Bharatendu Harishchandra, adopted features of Vaishnava performance that had survived in Bengali Jatra, perceptible in his version of *Vidya-Sundar* (1868) and other plays, where raga-based songs received an important place.

From the late nineteenth century to the twentieth century, *Parsi theatre in Hindi and Urdu held sway across many parts of India, influencing countless spectators with its spectacular romantic musical extravaganzas. Born in Bombay, and originally in Gujarati, its immediate commercial success enthused the companies to turn professional, and go on tours over the length and breadth of the country, even abroad. Some of the performers recorded their songs on disc, which became bestsellers. Early derivatives include the *padya natakam* (verse drama) of *Telugu theatre, invented in 1887 and surviving much after Independence through the Surabhi Theatres chain.

After 1947, Hindi directors applied music creatively by exploiting folk forms like *Bhavai (from Gujarat)

Actress-singers of Surabhi Theatres

and Nautanki in such plays as Shanta Gandhi's *Jasma Odan* (1968) and Sarveshwar Saxena's *Bakri* ('She-goat', 1973) respectively. However, Habib Tanvir, who used the lively dialectal songs of his Chhattisgarhi actors in his productions, had already pioneered this technique. Similar back-to-roots methods soon became a fashion, from Bhanu Bharti interacting with Bhil tribal performers in Rajasthan to the west, to Satish Anand working with *Bidesiya in Bihar to the east. The *National School of Drama also encouraged musicals in its repertory, commissioning renowned music directors like Mohan Upreti.

In modern *Gujarati theatre, Raghunath Brahmbhatt achieved fame as a young poet-lyricist upon his debut, *Buddhadev* ('The God Buddha', 1914). He wrote songs for other dramatists too. Shayada (1892–1962), known as *ghazal samrat* ('Emperor of Ghazals'), made his name as a playwright with *Sansar nauka* ('The Boat of Life') at the age of 25. After Independence, the production of Rasiklal Parikh's *Mena Gurjari* ('Mena of Gujarat', 1953) combined Bhavai with Beijing Opera into a major cultural event. Around the same time, Sheila Bhatia created the musical in *Punjabi theatre, while Dina Nath Nadim introduced 'operas' in *Kashmiri theatre.

The oldest theatrical expression in Assam is the sung narrative Oja-Pali, formulated along with Ankiya Nat by Sankaradeva. In *Manipuri theatre, similar Vaishnava performances coexist with ancient tribal proto-theatrical rituals incorporating song. The trailblazer of modern *Assamese theatre, Jyoti Prasad Agarwala, had a natural aptitude for blending different types of melodies, to create a world of romance and beauty. In recent years, young playwrights and directors, searching for a theatre indigenous in character, took over elements from Oja-Pali and Ankiya Nat, including their musical traditions.

Various music-dominated *Lilas, *Palas, and *Yatras flourished as the most popular entertainment in Orissa over the past three centuries. In the mid-eighteenth century, an

Oriya drama called *Gauri harana* ('Gauri's Abduction') was staged in Puri during the reign of Birakishor Deb I. The playwright inserted Hindi songs, obviously to please the Marathas, then the overlords of Orissa. Modern *Oriya theatre dates from the 1870s, but the musical component remained. In the first half of the twentieth century, Baishnab Pani revolutionized Yatra into a strong operatic form. Current Oriya drama looks back to Kali Charan Patnaik, who began his career as the manager of a *Rahasa party and composer of lyrical plays and music. Manoranjan Das, the most respected contemporary dramatist, wrote *Nandika Keshari* (1980), a love story packed with songs.

The primary factors in all Karnataka folk forms—*Yakshagana, *Bayalata, *Sannata, even *Gombeyata puppetry—are music and dance. The songs are delivered mainly by the lead Bhagavata, sometimes with an accompanying chorus. The arrival of B.V. Karanth in 1972 was of great importance to *Kannada theatre. Music and dance became integral parts of the directorial idiom forged by him. Using familiar compositions by such saint-poets as Purandaradasa (sixteenth century), mixed with folk and classical music, he created an altogether new style. B. Jayashree followed suit in the next generation, becoming extremely popular. Among dramatists, Chandrasekhar Kambar and H.S. Shiva Prakash write plays studded with energetic songs in traditional modes.

In the Tamil folk form of *Terukkuttu, men play all roles and the female impersonators must have high-pitched feminine voices, but all actors are well versed in music and dance. Sankaradas Swamigal introduced intensely poetic dialogue and music that inspired the birth of amateur as well as professional groups in the early twentieth century. However, *Tamil theatre also has a tradition of *Sangita Natakam that became commercially viable owing to its popularity and gave widespread exposure to classical Carnatic vocals. In Swamigal's *Valli tirumanam* ('Valli's Marriage'), a song by Valli symbolically opposed the British. Several such plays underwent censorship and many actors were arrested, but the songs propagating freedom won over the stage completely. In more recent times, in T. Janakiraman's *Nalu veli nilam* ('Four Measures of Land') and K. Alagirisamy's *Kavichakravarti*, based on the life of Kamban, music played a substantial role.

While music features significantly in all *Malayalam theatre traditions like *Kathakali, Kerala also has a history of *Sangitanataka, influenced by touring Tamil companies. As in Tamil Nadu and Maharashtra, the singing overpowered the acting. The parallel amateur groups, which initially shunned music, came to grips with it after the concept of indigenous *Tanatu Natakavedi arose. Moreover, the tradition-based dramas of K.N. Panikkar inspired many theatre artists. He also directed three Sanskrit plays of Bhasa in a style evolved by the recreation of stage practices defined in the *Natyasastra* on the model of those found in the regional forms of Kerala. These productions gained wide recognition as valuable contributions to contemporary 'total theatre', encompassing local music and songs.

DB

Richard Emmert et al. (eds), *Dance and Music in South Asian Drama* (Tokyo: Japan Foundation, 1983); Ashok Ranade, *Music and Drama* (New Delhi: Shri Ram Centre for the Performing Arts, n.d.).

Mutiyettu (literally 'wearing of the crown'): ritualistic prototype of theatre, one of the earliest known representing the fertility cult in Kerala. Kali, the goddess of shakti, is the protagonist and Darika the demon antagonist. The slaying of evil forces, represented by Darika and his elder brother Danava, by Kali and her retinue, the Kulis and Koimpidar (also called Koimpida Nayar, a warrior who interjects with comical comments and dance), forms the storyline. The leading twentieth-century exponent was Pazhoor Kunjan Marar.

The musical prelude, called *kalampattu* or *kalamezhutupattu*, sometimes takes place by itself, not followed by the play. It occurs within the building in front of a temple sanctum. When organized at people's residences, a special *pandal* (thatched shed) is erected in an open space in front of the house, decorated with fresh coconut leaves, flower garlands, and so on. The figure of Kali is drawn (*kalam*) on the floor with five colours—white (rice powder), black (charred rice husk), yellow (turmeric), green (leaves), and red (lime and turmeric combined)—by two or three members of the community of temple artists known as Kurup. The consecrated floor has a central point from which Kali's figure assumes shape slowly, through the spreading colours representing the energized cosmic presence. Her size varies according to the number of her hands, normally four to eight. On special occasions they may increase to sixty-four, in which case the *kalam* occupies the large temple courtyard covered by a special *pandal*. Kali holds different weapons. Her breasts are represented by heaps of paddy and rice dotted with coloured powder.

Kalampattu (*pattu* means ballad or poem) commences by dusk with rituals at the *kalam*. Drummers sit on the side of the *kalam* and sing the *tottam*, the musical benediction narrating Kali's story, also called *nirampadal* ('singing of colours') because it poetically describes the goddess from head to toe. It concludes with the ritualistic erasure of the *kalam*, using a bunch of tender coconut leaves. The figure becomes a muddle of colours with only the breasts intact, presumably symbolizing continuing fertility. The coloured powder is distributed to devotees as *prasadam* (holy gift).

The play begins in the open courtyard around the temple, in the localized light of oil torches, the acting area changing from place to place as Kali and Darika shift their area of interaction. The audience also moves along with them, as active participants in the event. The atmosphere gets charged with the combatants' battle cries and the crowd's enthusiasm. The story has it that Darika, by undergoing strict penance, managed to get a boon from Brahma, lord of creation, that he would never be killed by anyone other than a woman and if a drop of his blood fell, a thousand Darikas would emerge from it. Thus protected, he set out with his brother and the demons to oppress virtuous humans. The drama starts with the sage Narada reporting their misdeeds to Siva, lord of destruction. Kali, born from Siva's third eye, is deputed to save the world from the evil. Darika makes his entrance behind a hand-held curtain and enacts his indomitable

A Mutiyettu performance

prowess. Likewise, the conventional 'curtain-look' by Kali follows. Then the other characters enter.

Since the theme is conflict, the fight between Kali and Darika assumes prime importance, happening at different places; each time, Kali grows furious and chases Darika, who flees. Stagehands tightly hold Kali so that she cannot wriggle out. Every battle is fought with renewed vigour, creating a crescendo of frenzied drumming and dancing; the performance goes on till midnight or later. There are also verbal duels. The opposing forces create a hue and cry and come to loggerheads, at the end of which Darika disappears from the arena and Kali's headgear, at the height of her fury, is snatched away by the stagehands. In the middle of battle sequences, Koimpidar's entry provides comic relief. The last fight culminates in the possessed Kali slicing a bunch of plantain fruit, ritualistically representing the slaying of Darika. She makes her final appearance dancing with Darika's headgear, followed by *guruti*, the concluding ceremony of offering blood (a mixture of turmeric paste and lime) at the goddess's altar.

In southern Kerala the *ritual connected with Kali worship is called Parnettu or Kaliyuttu ('feeding of Kali'), enacting the same theme with certain striking differences from Mutiyettu in execution and other details. The playing area is much bigger, accommodating 10,000 or even more, on the side of the temple, not around as in the case of Mutiyettu. At the two ends of the rectangular field high platforms are built with stairs to climb onto them. One, Kali's seat, is made of trunks of coconut trees, higher than the other, Darika's seat, made of areca trunks. These platforms are known as *parna*, hence the name Parnettu ('climbing on the *parna*'). The battles take place in the arena, around which huge crowds congregate. The performance begins about 4 p.m., the descending sun providing spectacular scenic brilliance, and goes on through the night. Darika runs out of the temple precincts pursued by Kali; they shout war cries from their respective platforms. At regular intervals they descend and taunt and chase each other, sometimes fighting pitched battles. The double-reed *nagaswaram* and *tavil* (double-faced drum) are the accompanying instruments. The ritual ends with a sacrifice at the sanctum in the small hours of the morning. KNP

Mythological drama: Most Indian languages witnessed an abundant growth of plays based on themes taken from the Sanskrit epics and Hindu or Buddhist mythology in the later part of the nineteenth century when modern theatre and

drama were in their formative stage. Popularly known as mythological plays, by the end of the century they became accepted as a critical category. Paradoxically, since most of *Sanskrit theatre had derived its thematic content from those very sources, Sanskrit criticism had not used any such classificatory term. However, it was useful for the modern Indian critic to differentiate the corpus of drama based on mythological episodes and characters from that based on history or contemporary life, the criterion being the employment of time in the dramatic action. Mythological plays, operating within mythic time, dealt with characters and situations recorded in ancient stories, particularly in the two Sanskrit epics, the *Ramayana* and the *Mahabharata* (or their various transcreations in different Indian languages), and in the Puranas.

Another distinguishing feature of the majority of these plays is the dominance of devotion. They also incorporated several elements of traditional religious performances, particularly the music, which played an extremely important role in the emergence and popularization of this genre. In these respects they relate to traditional forms such as the varieties of *Lila dealing with the lives of Rama and Krishna. For instance, the *Ankiya Nat can be called mythological drama. However, the nineteenth-century plays based on myths did not grow purely out of such ancient traditions. They were constructed on European or Sanskrit dramaturgical principles, like the *historical drama or social plays of the period.

A considerably large number of the scripts contained full-blooded projection of human characters and predicaments, despite the presence of the supernatural. They centred on interesting episodes in the lives of famous mythical heroes and heroines, such as Rama, Bhishma, Arjuna, Karna, Sita, Savitri, or Damayanti, who had attained archetypal dimensions in the Indian consciousness. In this respect Indian mythological theatre resembled Greek tragedy, in which playwrights constructed and interpreted myths in their own ways. However, it showed remarkable uniformity in approaches to themes and characters. The most popular stories were those of romance and love (such as the marriage of Subhadra, or of Usha and Aniruddha), moral questions (the game of dice in the *Mahabharata*, young Abhimanyu's death in an unfair battle, or Karna's struggle against destiny), and the trials of women (the stripping of Draupadi or Sita's banishment). The sufferings of Harishchandra for his allegiance to truth inspired many authors, including Bharatendu Harishchandra in Hindi, Veeresalingam in Telugu, and Lilaramsingh Lalwani in Sindhi.

Nearly all the major Indian dramatists experimented with mythological themes and achieved popularity in varying degrees. Girish Chandra Ghosh, Rabindranath *Tagore, and Kshirod Prasad Vidyavinod in Bengali, K.P. Khadilkar, R.G. Gadkari, and N.C. Kelkar (1872–1947) in Marathi, are notable examples. Chilakamarthi Lakshminarasimham's *Gayopakhyanamu* ('The Gaya Episode', 1889), in Telugu, sold in thousands. The potentiality of the genre was fully utilized by twentieth-century writers, who infused in it topical meanings and new significance. Khadilkar's *Kichakavadh* ('Killing of Kichaka', 1907) was a landmark, the first successful attempt towards the politicization of mythological drama, which led to a ban by the British authorities. He identified Draupadi with India and Lord Curzon with the villain Kichaka who tried to molest her. Manmatha Ray's *Karagar* ('Prison', 1930), in Bengali, also used myth as political allegory, associating Krishna's evil uncle, Kamsa, with the British rulers.

The Bengali play *Sita*, by Jogesh Chaudhuri (1886–1941), created stage history in 1924 because of the portrayal of Rama by legendary actor Sisir Bhaduri. Denuding Rama of his divinity but still clothed in epic attire, Bhaduri represented the psychological state of the mortal lover. In 1929 B.M. Srikantiah (1884–1946) based *Asvatthaman*, considered a milestone in Kannada literature, on Asvatthama's tragic life, but took its subtext from Sophocles's *Ajax*. This highly controversial play was not only a fine instance of bold appropriation of both Hindu and Greek mythology but also of the total secularization of mythological drama.

The genre did not fade away after India's independence. On the contrary, important playwrights applied it to interpret contemporary concerns. Dharamvir Bharati's powerful Hindi verse drama *Andha yug* (*Blind Age*, 1954), based on the Kurukshetra war and the moral degeneration it brought about, and *Tapaswi o Tarangini* ('Tarangini and the Ascetic', 1966) by the Bengali poet Buddhadeva Bose (1908–74), using an episode from the *Ramayana* celebrating the power and beauty of sex, are two eloquent examples.   SKD

R.G. Joshi, *Myth in Indian Drama* (New Delhi: B.R., 1994).

Nacha ('dance'): traditional *Hindi-theatre form of Chhattisgarh in which, as the name suggests, dance constitutes an important part. Performed all night, without any written script, it combines dance, music, acrobatics, and improvised dialogues to tell the story in the form of small playlets. The themes are drawn from the daily life of the artists, mostly semi-literate or illiterate farm workers: Nacha has responded from time to time to the issues, problems, and contradictions plaguing rural society. Therefore plays like *Jamadarin* ('Scavenger Woman') highlight untouchability, *Munshi munshin* ('Munshi and Wife') young widowhood, and others present child marriage or class exploitation. These topics are dealt with satirically and the texts are full of proverbs and witty repartee.

Clearly the performers create a close relationship with their audience through innovativeness blending entertainment and education. Nacha depends entirely on their ingenuity. Without any formal training, all are adept at singing, dancing, acting, improvising, and musicianship. Most urban artists would find it difficult to match their energy and versatility. Men play female roles. Two regular and attractive characters, the Pari (fairy) and Jokkar (from 'joker', or clown), are the life of this form. The actor impersonating the Pari captures the imaginary celestial being's sensuality and delicate beauty, while the Jokkar comments on the situations and uses all kinds of tricks to keep viewers in splits.

Nacha is very informal, performed in everyday attire and in any space available in the village. Wherever possible a small platform is reserved for the instrumentalists, and the audience sits surrounding the site on three sides. Originally, musicians standing up played the *chikara* (a string instrument), *manjira* (small cymbals), and tablas tied to the waist; now harmoniums and dholaks are also used. Lighting came from flaming torches, gradually replaced by Petromax pressure lamps and now floodlights. Nacha underwent a survival crisis like most traditional forms till some local initiatives and particularly Habib Tanvir's interest in artists like Fida Bai Markam gave it a new lease of life, and it is now nationally recognized.   KJ

Naqal (from the Persian, 'to imitate'): enacted by Naqqals, also known as Bhands ('clowns'), rural itinerant actors in Punjab and Haryana, performing in Punjabi or Haryanvi Hindi. They originally came from the low *bazigar* (acrobat) caste, patronized by local lords, to whom they ritually apologize before starting. Naqal is normally presented by two men who, through a series of jokes, improvisations, and horseplay, make sharp, satirical comments on society and politics. One carries in his hand a leather strap, the size of a folded newspaper, which he wields as a weapon to hit his partner to underscore the witty punch lines. They wear a costume of *tehemat* (wraparound lower garment), short kurta, and dunce cap. As jesters, they are the symbols of the common man who relates to issues of tradition, progress, and modernity in a light-hearted, frivolous, yet incisive manner through the power of their repartee. By exposing the hypocrisy of old and new alike, Naqqals function as both social critic and popular psychiatrist through their verbal gymnastics on such topics as dowry or usury.

Their repertoire includes cliched relationships of mother-in-law and daughter-in-law, father and son, servant and master, law and citizenry, explored in ways that are hilarious, caustic, and close to the people's heart. A monologue on declining moral standards that have led to hunger

Mehar Chand, a Naqal artiste

and unemployment expresses social truths which, though painful reminders to the audience, immediately communicate and create empathy through humour and laughter. The energy level is frenzied and combines dialogue with songs that tend to border on the risqué. Innuendoes, double entendres, fantastically absurd remarks, and gags have spectators participating in ways that sometimes create the flow of the entertainment. The female impersonators' seductive wiles, accentuated by pelvic thrusts and provocative pouts, leave the crowd screaming for more.

The Naqqal's other function is to provide the comic interludes offering counterpoint and softening the impact during serious moments in the performance of a full-length *Swang. Larger bands of Naqqals, such as a family troupe comprising actors, clowns, singers, musicians, and dancers, often put on Swang. During the festival season or at weddings the female impersonators, in loud costumes, can be seen gyrating furiously to the latest musical hits. At *Ramlila time, they manage to earn a tidy packet, dancing to disco beats while the singers may soulfully render lyrics pertaining to the epic *Ramayana*. The ballads in their repertoire may belong to the narrative tradition or include popular film songs, depending upon the occasion.   NMSC

Nataka (literally 'drama'): the most important and popular form of *Sanskrit theatre, in five to ten acts. It had a celebrated story for its plot, the quality of vivacity, characters contributing to the hero's prosperity, and abundant sentiments of pleasure and pain as clearly exhibited in the narratives of Rama and Yudhishthira. Thus it portrayed life on a panoramic canvas. The plot was drawn from such sources as the epics, Puranas, or historical events. The hero was high-spirited, powerful, and virtuous, a god, demigod, royal sage, or Kshatriya from a renowned family. He could be *dhirodatta* ('firm and noble') like Rama, *dhiralalita* ('firm and playful') like Udayana, *dhiroddhata* ('firm and haughty') like Bhima, or *dhiraprasanta* ('firm and serene') like the Buddha. Four or five characters engaged in assisting the task undertaken by him. The principal *rasa was either *sringara* (erotic) or *vira* (heroic); the *adbhuta* (marvellous) *rasa* could arise in the fulfilment at the end.

Theorists write that *nataka* must be so composed as to end like a cow's tail. Some explain this statement to mean that each act is gradually made shorter than the preceding one, while others maintain that as cows' tails have short and long hairs, so in *nataka*s, important incidents are distributed among acts without trying to make them equal in length or number. Bhasa's *Pratimanataka*

('Statue *Nataka*'), *Svapna-Vasavadatta* ('Vasavadatta in the Dream'), and *Pratijna-Yaugandharayana* ('Yaugandharayana's Pledge'), *Kalidasa's *Abhijnana-Sakuntala* ('Sakuntala Recognized'), Bhavabhuti's *Uttara-Ramacarita* ('Rama's Later Exploits'), Harsha's *Nagananda* ('Bliss of the Serpent'), Visakhadatta's *Mudra-Rakshasa* ('Rakshasa's Signet Ring'), and Bhatta Narayana's *Venisamhara* ('Tying of the Braid') are the best examples of this form.

KDT

Natika (literally 'small *nataka*'): minor form of *Sanskrit theatre founded on an invented story, consisting of four acts, and abounding with female characters. The hero is an illustrious king, *dhiralalita* ('firm and playful') of nature. The heroine is a maid of the royal family, newly in love, either belonging to the hero's household as an attendant to the queen, or employed as a musical performer. The king, who loves her, conducts himself with restraint for fear of the queen. The queen, older than her rival, is bold and indignant, and the union of hero and young heroine occurs under her control. Her *kaisiki* (graceful) *vritti* must employ action. As the premier form of *uparupaka*, the *natika* offered a model for the minor plays in Indian tradition. The *Natyasastra* notes

that it was replete with songs and dance, *lalita* (playful) *abhinaya*, and love in union. Harsha's *Ratnavali* (seventh century) and Rajasekhara's *Viddhasalabhanjika* ('The Resembling Image', tenth century) are well-known examples. KDT

Parvati Tandon, *Sanskrit Natikas* (New Delhi: Munshiram Manoharlal, 1986).

National School of Drama (NSD): India's premier training institution for theatre. It started as the Asian Theatre Institute (ATI) in January 1958 under the joint aegis of UNESCO and the Bharatiya Natya Sangh with courses in *children's theatre and rural theatre conducted by UNESCO experts, and headed by Nihar Ranjan Ray and M.M. Bhalla. In July, the ATI was taken over by Sangeet Natak Akademi and merged with the NSD, the concept of which had been proposed by the Akademi's board. The NSD-ATI formally began in April 1959, to provide a diploma in dramatics at the end of a two-year integrated course under its first Director, Satu Sen, and the Akademi's Officer on Special Duty, Nemichandra Jain. Several eminent theatre practitioners were inducted as faculty in different disciplines.

In July 1962, Ebrahim Alkazi took charge as Director, extending the course to three years and introducing specializations in acting, stagecraft, and direction. The school became an autonomous registered society in 1975, funded by the Government of India, and 'Asian Theatre Institute' was dropped. Meanwhile the idea of an in-house professional repertory had taken shape in 1968, with the recruitment of four members, and it turned into a full-fledged repertory in 1976. In 1989 a Theatre-in-Education company was established to use theatre for educational purposes, primarily for children. In 1994, the NSD set up its first Regional Research-cum-Resource Centre, in Bangalore, as a step towards decentralization and opening of regional drama schools.

The primary objectives in the NSD's charter were to impart training to theatre practitioners from all over the country; create a sound technical, theoretical, and practical base for these expected leaders; and set high standards of theatre production in India. These aims gradually underwent subtle shifts over the years as theatre itself changed. In the absence of existing formal education in modern urban theatre, the NSD followed the European model for the first eighteen years. Around 1977, after B.V. Karanth became Director, the

Shakespeare's *Macbeth* adapted as *Barnam vana*, directed by B.V. Karanth (National School of Drama Repertory Company, New Delhi, 1979)

emphasis moved toward indigenous traditions, greater attempts to relate to Indian reality, exposure to a wider range of approaches and styles through visiting experts, and stretching the overall canvas through outreach programmes to hold workshops in different regions. A deliberate link was forged with traditional forms by mandatory exposure of students to at least one such form and organization of traditional theatre festivals. In the 1990s, the NSD made an intervention in the school system with its Theatre-in-Education company, started a systematic documentation and publication programme to benefit students and researchers, prepared training methodology for theatre teachers, and asserted its intention to decentralize and network through extension workshops and regional centres.

By 2000, the NSD had trained 620 theatre artists through its diploma course and approximately 2500 in short-term workshops. Its 200 productions by established directors, Indian and foreign, and an equal number staged by students as exercises, covered the gamut of world drama from the classics to contemporary avant-garde plays by young Indian writers. By commissioning translations of Indian and foreign plays it made available a treasury of dramatic literature in Hindi. Through its

sustained work, the NSD encouraged a spirit of experimentation in all areas—space, design, direction, acting—and moulded many outstanding personalities who contributed significantly to Indian theatre and even films. Its alumni include Karanth, Om Shivpuri, Mohan Maharishi, Uttara Baokar, Surekha Sikri, Manohar Singh, Ratan Thiyam, Bansi Kaul, Naseeruddin Shah, Om Puri, Seema Biswas, and many others.

However, as a national institute and the only one of its kind in a culturally diverse nation like India, the NSD has its share of disadvantages, most apparent in its actor training. Its pedagogy privileges Hindi- or English-speaking students, though it cannot afford to be rooted to the cultural ethos of one language or region. While it provides the essential education based on different traditions to students from all parts of India, it is unable to explore or evolve a definitive theatre language that could be termed Indian. Additionally, though it provides rigorous training, there is virtually no professional theatre afterwards where graduates can employ it or hone their potential further. It cannot focus its education to suit any one kind of theatre, as it has to equip students for the wide range of approaches and styles prevalent in the country; hence, its attempt to encourage variety in the training programme has advantages, but can also be read as absence of direction.   KJ

J.N. Kaushal (ed.), *Rang Yatra: 25 Years of the National School of Drama Repertory Company* (New Delhi: National School of Drama, 1992).

Natyasastra (literally 'Theatre Shastra'): most important single source for understanding the character of classical and *Sanskrit theatre, poetics, aesthetics, dance, and music. Apart from its religious denotation, shastra can refer to any authoritative and systematic discipline—normative as well as prescriptive—code, manual, treatise, text, as well as science. According to Indian tradition, every shastra was first composed in sutra ('thread') or aphoristic style couched in cryptic language marked by brevity and precision. It later developed through *vartika* and *bhashya*. *Vartika* is a text explaining what is unsaid or imperfectly said and supplying omissions. *Bhashya* is a further investigation of both sutra and *vartika* almost word by word, offering comments of its own and unfolding implicit concepts. Tradition grows further in commentaries and sub-commentaries explicating abstruse ideas, expanding and updating the text, if need be.

In theatre, poetics, and aesthetics, Bharata is regarded as the author of the sutra (*Natyasastra*), Harsha of the *vartika* (since lost), and Abhinavagupta (950–1025), a scholar from Kashmir, of the only available *bhashya* (titled *Abhinavabharati*, 'Abhinava Speaks'). Bharata's date is much debated (second century BC to fourth century AD), but the *Natyasastra* is the oldest extant work on the *theory and practice of ancient Indian performance. It offers the fundamentals of theories developed later, especially those of *rasa and *dhvani*. An encyclopaedic compendium, it also contains elements of architecture, painting, prosody, language, grammar, phonetics, and other aspects as related to theatre, and draws on disciplines as diverse as philosophy, psychology, mythology, *ritual, and geography. A few scholars have raised the question of the text's heterogeneity, though tradition regards it as homogeneous. As the history of theatre was vibrant, the updating, growth, and expansion of the text cannot be ruled out. This may explain the variations, but inner consistency and coherence is amply present in the text and demonstrated by Abhinavagupta.

We know of commentaries on the *Natyasastra* dating from the sixth or seventh centuries, and the earliest surviving one by Abhinavagupta was followed by works of writers such as Saradatanaya (twelfth–thirteenth century), Sarngadeva (thirteenth century), and Kallinatha (sixteenth century). Abhinavagupta provides not only his own illuminating interpretation of the *Natyasastra*, but wide information about pre-Bharata traditions as well as varied interpretations of the text offered by his predecessors.

In modern times, the *Natyasastra* was known to H.H. Wilson as a lost work in 1826, before Fitzedward Hall chanced upon a copy and printed four chapters in 1865. In 1874, the German scholar Heymann described its contents on the basis of a single manuscript available to him. Paul Regnaud, a French scholar, found another manuscript and published chapters 15–16 in 1884, following this with chapters 6–7 in the same year under the title *La Rhétorique sanskrite* ('Sanskrit Rhetoric'). A pupil of his, J. Grosset, published chapter 28 in 1888. The eminent Indologist Sylvain Levi wrote an important book based on the *Natyasastra*, titled *Théâtre indien* (*The Theatre of India*), in 1890. Grosset brought out a critical edition of chapters 1–14 in 1898.

Meanwhile, Pandit Shivadatta and Kashinath Pandurang Parab had printed the full text for the first time in 1894 from Bombay. An important point of departure was the publication from Baroda in 1926 of the first volume of a critical edition, by Ramakrishna Kavi, on the basis of several manuscripts procured from different parts of India, together with the *Abhinavabharati* based on a single manuscript of the commentary discovered in Kerala. However, later volumes took time and the work was completed only in 1964. It opened a new era in the understanding and interpretation of the text. Another edition had appeared in 1929 from Varanasi, edited by Batukanath Sharma and Baladeva Upadhyaya. Manomohan Ghosh prepared a text (1956) and translated it into English. Many more editions and translations in Hindi, Marathi, Gujarati, Telugu, Malayalam, and Nepali have appeared since then.

The *Natyasastra* has been divided into 36 chapters, sometimes into 37 or 38 due to further bifurcation of a chapter or chapters. A vast treatise, it contains about 6000 verses. It begins with the origin of theatre, opening with inquiries made by Bharata's pupils, which he answers by narrating the myth of its source in Brahma. He also explains the very nature, objective, and expanse of *natya* as a Veda through this unique myth. We may interpret it in many ways, but can draw certain obvious characteristics of Sanskrit theatre, as follows. It consists of four elements—*pathya* (text, including the art of recitation and rendition in performance) taken from the *Rig Veda*, *gita* (songs, including instrumental music) from the *Sama Veda*, *abhinaya (acting, the technique of expressing the poetic meaning of the text and communicating it to the spectator) from the *Yajur Veda*, and *rasa* (aesthetic experience) from the *Atharva Veda*. It is, at the outset, the *anukarana* ('re-doing') of the triple universe and life in its entirety, but ultimately it is the '*anukirtana* of *bhava*' ('re-telling' of emotive states) in order to create a new world of 'imagination'.

As an audio-visual form, it mirrors all the arts and crafts, higher knowledge, learning, sciences, yoga, and conduct. Its purpose is to entertain as well as educate. An ideal theatre artist is one who, like Bharata, has experienced pleasure as well as pain in life, and is gifted with restraint as well as vision. Performance is a collective activity that requires a group of trained people knit in a familial bond, just as Bharata had a family of one hundred pupils and sons. The company comprises both men and women, bound to each other in a family-like relationship. The spectators come from all classes of society without any distinction, but are expected to be at least minimally initiated into the appreciation of theatre, so that they may respond properly to the art as an empathetic *sahridaya* (literally 'same heart', or connoisseur). Theatre flourishes in a peaceful environment and requires a state free from hindrances. The first chapter ends emphasizing the significance and importance of drama in attaining the joy, peace, and goals of life, and recommending the worship of the presiding deities of theatre and the auditorium.

The second chapter lays down the norms for theatre *architecture or the *prekshagriha* (auditorium), which also protects the performance from all obstacles caused by adverse nature, malevolent spirits, animals, and men. It describes the medium-sized rectangular space as ideal for audibility and visibility, apparently holding about 400 spectators. Bharata also prescribes smaller and larger structures, respectively half and double this size, and square and triangular halls. Saradatanaya speaks of a circular space too. Bharata's model was an ideal intimate theatre, considering the subtle *abhinaya* of the eyes and other facial expressions he prescribed. It was not a proscenium stage, and there is no reference to anything like a proscenium curtain in the *Natyasastra*. The tradition of the *Natyasastra* auditorium survived in *kuttampalam*s built for the performance of *Kutiyattam in temples of Kerala, and some of its principles may be seen in folk

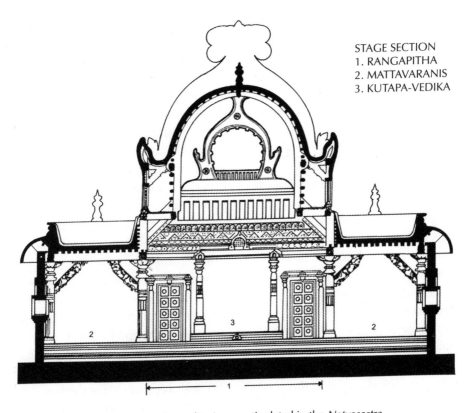

STAGE SECTION
1. RANGAPITHA
2. MATTAVARANIS
3. KUTAPA-VEDIKA

Front view of medium rectangular auditorium as stipulated in the *Natyasastra*

forms or the *Ankiya Bhaona of Assam.

The third chapter describes an elaborate puja for the gods and goddesses protecting the auditorium, and prescribes rituals to consecrate the space. The entire hall appears to be a replica of the cosmos presided over by gods, goddesses, demigods, as well as demons, presenting the triple universe according to theatrical needs. Chapter 4 begins with the story of a production of *Amritamanthana* ('Churning of the Nectar'), a

samavakara performed according to Brahma's instructions on the peaks of Kailasa, witnessed by Siva. After some time, a *dima* titled *Tripuradaha* ('Burning of the Three Cities') is staged, relating Siva's exploits. Siva asks Bharata to incorporate *tandava* dance in the *purvaranga* preliminaries and directs his attendant Tandu to teach Bharata. Tandu explains the components of *tandava*, the categories of its movements, and their composition in choreographical patterns. These form the pure dance movements required for the worship of the gods and the rituals. This chapter also lays the foundation of *angika abhinaya* (physical acting) developed in later chapters. The fifth chapter details the elements of *purvaranga*. Thus the first five chapters are structurally integrated to the rest of the text, but some scholars hold the view that they are later interpolations.

The sixth and seventh chapters deal with the fundamental emotional notions and aesthetics of *rasa* and *bhava*. The *bhava*s, which include the *vibhava*s, are communicated to spectators through *abhinaya*, especially *angika*, which therefore receives elaborate treatment in chapters 8–12. These codify body language based on a definite semiology. Movement requires well-defined blocking, so immediately afterwards the *Natyasastra* lays down the principle of *kakshyavibhaga* (zonal division) in the thirteenth chapter. The extremely flexible and easy principle of establishing space on stage and altering it through *parikramana* (circumambulation) is a unique characteristic of traditional Indian theatre and dance. In the same chapter we read of *vritti*, or characteristic styles of activity. It closes with the discussion of the two modes of performance, *natyadharmi* and *lokadharmi*, the former more conventional, stylized, and refined,

and the latter more natural, nearer to behaviour seen in people's ordinary lives, thus spontaneous and simpler.

Poetic text is considered the very embodiment of drama; therefore, the *Natyasastra* elaborately articulates the structure and metres to be employed, in chapter 14. The next two chapters discuss the metres and distinctive poetic form and diction of the performance script. The seventeenth chapter examines several levels of language, such as Sanskrit and the Prakrits present in Sanskrit plays. It analyses dramatic language deeply in order to enrich the understanding of playwright and artist, so that a good text for performance is created and better comprehension of verbal delivery attained. Bharata shows the broader principles of phonetic change from Sanskrit to Prakrit and explores the dialects for characters hailing from different regions or belonging to various classes. He enumerates the appellations and epithets occurring in Sanskrit drama, offering insights on the use of nomenclature. The chapter then discusses *vacika* (verbal) *abhinaya* in detail.

Chapter 18 discusses the ten major *rupaka*s (forms of drama) and **natika*, a variety of *uparupaka*. The next chapter analyses the structure of drama as well as the inclusion of *lasyanga*s (components of feminine dance derived from popular dance and recitative forms) in theatre. Chapter 20 gives an elaborate account of the *vritti*s.

Chapter 21 deals with *aharya* ('added') *abhinaya*, which covers make-up, costume, properties, *masks, and minimal stage decor. Chapter 22 begins with *samanya* ('common') *abhinaya*, which compounds the four elements of *abhinaya* harmoniously. It discusses other aspects of production too, which may be viewed as 'inner', adhering to prescribed norms and systematic training, and 'outer' or done freely outside such a regimen. This chapter ends with an analysis of women's dispositions, particularly pertaining to love and terms of address, while the following chapter deals with male qualities and patterns of sexual behaviour, as well as classification and stages of feminine youth. Chapter 24 enumerates the types of characters in Sanskrit drama. Chapter 25 deals with *citrabhinaya* ('pictured acting'), especially meant for delineating the environment occurring as a stimulant (*uddipana vibhava*) of different *bhava*s. It also defines the specific ways of expressing different objects and states, and the use of gestures, postures, gaits, walking, and theatrical conventions. The next two chapters present the nature of dramatis personae, the principles of make-up, and speak about the success and philosophy of performance.

Seven chapters deal with music employed in theatre. Chapter 28 covers *jati* (melodic types or matrices), *sruti* (micro-intervals), *svara* (notes), *grama* (scales), and *murcchana* (modes, now ragas). Chapter 29 describes stringed instruments like the vina and distinguishes between vocal and instrumental music, further dividing vocal into two types, *varna* ('colour', only syllabics) and *giti* ('song', with lyrics). Chapter 30 describes wind instruments like the flute and ways of playing it. Chapter 31 deals with cymbals, and tala, rhythm, and metrical cycles. Chapter 32 defines *dhruva* songs, their specific employment, forms, and illustrations. Chapter 33 lists the qualities and defects of vocalists and instrumentalists. Chapter 34 relates the origin and nature of drums.

The concluding chapters lay down the principles for distributing roles and the qualifications for members of the troupe. Bharata narrates the story of his sons, who ridiculed the sages and were cursed. He instructs them to expiate their sin, so that they attain their lost glory again. He returns to the performance in heaven where Indra enacts Nahusha, and finally to the descent of theatre on earth. Bharata ends by stating the glory of theatre and of its Veda.

For about 2000 years the *Natyasastra* has inspired new texts and various regional traditions of theatre. Kutiyattam in Kerala is an extant Sanskrit form that imbibed and developed the theory and practice originating from the *Natyasastra*. A number of other forms all over India, and preserved in Bali (Indonesia), are directly connected with the *Natyasastra*. Moreover, in the 1950s and 1960s a movement started among urban theatre workers to search for the identity of Indian theatre. In course of this quest the attention of scholars and theatre practitioners was drawn towards folk and classical forms, as well as the *Natyasastra*. As a result of this movement, a dialogue between *Natyasastra* experts and contemporary theatre people took place.   KDT

The Natyasastra, translated by Manomohan Ghosh (Calcutta: Manisha Granthalaya and Asiatic Society, 1961–67); *The Natyasastra*, translated by Adya Rangacharya (New Delhi: Munshiram Manoharlal, 1996); *The Natya Sastra*, translated by a board of scholars (Delhi: Sri Satguru, 1981); Pramod Kale, *The Theatric Universe: A Study of the Natyasastra* (Bombay: Popular Prakashan, 1974); R.P. Kulkarni, *Theatre According to the Natyasastra of Bharata* (Delhi: Kanishka, 1993); G. Maralusiddayya (ed.), *Bharata Natyasastra: Alankar Bhaga* (Mysore: Institute of Kannada Studies, 1973); Anupa Pande, *A Historical and Cultural Study of the Natyasastra of Bharata* (Jodhpur: Kusumanjali Prakashan, 1991); Anupa Pande, *The Natyasastra Tradition and Ancient Indian Society* (Jodhpur: Kusumanjali Prakashan, 1993); C. Rajendran (ed.), *Living Traditions of Natyasastra* (Delhi: New Bharatiya, 2002); Adya Rangacharya, *Introduction to Bharata's 'Natya-Sastra'* (Bombay: Popular Prakashan, 1966); P.S.R. Appa Rao, *A Monograph on Bharata's Naatya Saastra* (Hyderabad: Naatya Maalaa, 1967); P.S.R. Appa Rao, *Special Aspects of Natya Sastra* (New Delhi: National School of Drama, 2001); Sudha Rastogi, *Natyasastra of Bharat Muni* (Varanasi: Chowkhamba, 1990); S.A. Srinivasan, *On the Composition of the Natyasastra* (Reinbek: Verlag fur Orientalische Fachpublicationen, 1980); Padma Subrahmanyam, *Bharata's Art* (Madras: Nrityodaya, 1979); Padma Subrahmanyam, *Natya Sastra and National Unity* (Tripunithura: S.R.G. Sanskrit College, 1997); G.H. Tarlekar, *Studies in the Natyasastra: With Special Reference to the Sanskrit Drama in Performance* (Delhi: Motilal Banarsidass, 1991); Radhavallabh Tripathi, *Lectures on the Natyashastra* (Pune: University of Poona, 1991); K.M. Varma, *Seven Words in Bharata: What Do They Signify?* (Calcutta: Orient Longmans, 1958); Kapila Vatsyayan, *Bharata: 'The Natyasastra'* (New Delhi: Sahitya Akademi, 1996).

Nautanki, originally called Sangit ('music') or *Swang: major musical *Hindi-theatre form of north India, encompassing Uttar Pradesh, Bihar, Madhya Pradesh, Haryana,

Himachal Pradesh, and, partly, Punjab and Rajasthan. A nineteenth-century development of the medieval *rahas*, *Bhagat, and *Khyal, it originated in enacted devotional music and storytelling or ballad singing. The name Nautanki may have come from a popular play on a certain princess Nautanki.

Unlike many other traditional theatres, Nautanki preserves complete written texts, a kind of libretto, for all characters including the Ranga, the director-narrator who links the episodes, describes the locale, or comments on the action. The language eclectically mixes Hindi, Urdu, Brajbhasha, and Avadhi, and the stories may come from mythology (*Harishchandra*), history (*Amar Singh Rathor*), romances (*Laila-Majnun*), folklore (*Sultana*), or even the deeds of contemporary popular icons (dacoit queen Phulan Devi). The structure is simple and the treatment, though melodramatic and more or less one-dimensional, has tremendous popular appeal with its mix of love, valour, pathos, and humour, accounting for the repeated printing of these plays, sold in hundreds of thousands of copies. Each unit of the script is composed in metres like *doha*, *chaubola*, and *daud*, occasionally varied by introducing *langdi daud*, *lavani*, *bahar-e-tabil*, and *chhanda*. There is very little prose dialogue or narration except when

spontaneously improvised by the actors.

The major source of Nautanki's great popularity is its unique music, both vocal and instrumental, distinctively and dramatically fusing classical ragas with folk tunes. The performers sing at a very high pitch in order to reach out to large rural or semi-urban audiences, but maintain the melodic and sonorous quality of their voices. In spite of the metrical repetitiveness, they constantly modulate and vary the tempo and choice of raga or melody according to the mood, character, or situation. The performances, lasting several hours, demand unusual stamina acquired through prolonged training and practice. Nautanki singing is in no sense a folk art learnt easily. The most distinctive among the accompanying instruments is the *nakkara* or *nagada*, a two-piece drum played with sticks, providing continuous but constantly changing rhythms to the singer and highlighting or intensifying theatrical moments. Other instruments include the softer dholak played with the hands, sarangi, harmonium, and, occasionally, clarinet.

Previously, Nautanki was staged only on makeshift or existing raised platforms or any cleared ground in open fields, but now frequently occupies proscenium theatres in towns. Traditionally, the audience sits in front, or on two or three sides

The Nautanki play *Aurat-ka-pyar* directed by Gulab Bai, 1985

(actors sometimes repeat their lines to spectators in different directions). Musicians sit either at one side or at the back. Shows take place at night under available artificial light. Preceded by a long spell of inviting *nakkara*-playing called *lahara*, they begin with the *bhent*, an invocatory chorus by all performers, after which the Ranga sings a broad outline of the play. There is little 'acting', facial or physical, except for some exaggerated gestures of eyes and hands. The performers keep changing their positions from one part of the arena to another without any choreographic pattern. Hardly any dancing is used but for a sensuous dance based on Kathak or folk movements in court scenes before princes or other dignitaries, nor much make-up apart from beards and wigs. Costumes, however, are loud and colourful, based on everyday wear of different social strata or on conventional clothes of historical or mythological characters.

Presently, two schools (*akhadas*) of Nautanki exist, called Sangit or Swang in Hathras (Aligarh district) and Nautanki in Kanpur, the two Uttar Pradesh towns that became its most important centres. The original, Hathras school, nurtured by composer-performers like Inderman and his disciples Chiranjilal and Natharam Gaud, and carried on by gifted singers like Giriraj Prasad, emphasizes artistic, sophisticated singing without visual frills. The Kanpur school, started and popularized by Trimohan Lal after breaking away from Hathras, Srikrishna Pahalwan, and the famous singer-actress Gulab Bai, is more theatrical with a different singing style. It is enacted on existing or improvised proscenium stages with painted curtains, glittering properties and costumes, melodramatic acting, and catchy familiar tunes. The Kanpur Nautanki introduced women performers, who frequently became its chief attraction, rather than the uniqueness of its music.

In the late twentieth century, film music began dominating both schools and they started losing their distinctive character as well as patronage. As a result, traditional performers proceeded to migrate to other professions. Efforts to revitalize Nautanki by the Braj Kala Kendra in Hathras and Nautanki Kala Kendra in Lucknow and Kanpur did not meet with much success. However, its great aesthetic and theatrical potential was amply demonstrated in urban Hindi productions that applied Nautanki technique, like *Mitti ki gadi* ('Clay Cart', 1958, Sudraka's classic *Mricchakatika* directed by Habib Tanvir) and Mudra Rakshasa's *Ala afsar* ('Senior Officer', 1977), based on Gogol's *Inspector General* and directed by Bansi Kaul.   NJ

Kathryn Hansen, *Grounds for Play: The Nautanki Theatre of North India* (Berkeley: University of California Press, 1992).

Nondi Natakam (literally 'lame drama'): thus called because the dancers tie up one leg during performance. A popular Tamil form known for its simple language and engaging music, it is associated closely with *Terukkuttu and *Kuravanji Natakam, and was in vogue during the seventeenth and eighteenth centuries. Traditionally, it was presented as an offering to the ruling deity of a village at the temple. Hence specific varieties have prefixes like Tiruchendur, Tirupullani, Palani, and Tirumalai—indicating the places of worship. Variants such as Gnana and Sitakkatti are performed by Christians and Muslims respectively.

In villages, a stage made of coconut leaves is specifically constructed for this theatre. The texts have three sections: prayer, drama, and *mangalam* (benediction). Prayers are offered to a set of gods, for example, in Tiruchendur Nondi Natakam (Chidambaranar district), to Vinayagar, Murugan, Sivan, Siddhi Vinayakar, the Hindu trinity, and many others. The story deals with a lame thief, his love life, devotion, and conversion. Some studies link this form to the Kallar community, but no proof exists. References to prostitutes and their livelihood are a special feature. It is interesting to note that the marginalized communities of thieves and prostitutes have a performatory genre to define a space in tradition. However, they are treated in a didactic fashion. Mere representation does not seem to automatically guarantee a genuine space and voice.

CA

Pagati-veshalu (Telugu, 'daylight portrayals'), also called Bahurupalu ('many roles'): an ancient solo folk form of role playing in Andhra Pradesh, of stereotyped professions or faiths. A few enactments are performed by husband-and-wife teams. The main actor is supported by one or two others as chorus and instrumentalists. Whether individually or in pairs, Pagati-veshalus portray characters of less privileged communities positively and isolate Brahmans for ridicule and caricature.

The term Bahurupalu has been synonymous with theatre in Telugu literature since the *Basava Puranam* and *Sarveswara satakam* (thirteenth century), without any description of the form. Tradition says that kings encouraged their spies to wear disguises from every walk of life, mingling with the people in daily situations, obviously without revealing their identity. The sixteenth-century historian Ferishta corroborates this phenomenon in the Vijayanagar empire. Comedy, satire, and social comment seem to be Pagati-veshalu's main purpose during the last two centuries. But in earlier times the form engaged in door-to-door campaigns disseminating the faiths, mythologies, and messages of competing reformist religions like Virasaivism and Viravaishnavism that attacked the caste system.

The standard repertoire till 1960 comprised over sixty characters, each team choosing its favourites, among them Karanam (accountant), Somayaji and Somidevamma (Brahman and wife),

Reddy or Naidu (headmen), Komati Setti (merchant), Chitti Pantulu (Brahman accountant who cheats people to visit brothels), Bhatraju (bard earning his living by flattering the rich), Budabukkala (migrant Marathi beggar), Jangam (Saiva priest), Acharya (Vaishnava Brahman), Sathani (non-Brahman Vaishnava priest), Sode (soothsaying woman from the ancient *Kuravanji archetype), Madiga (untouchable), Dommara (gymnastic tribe), Koya (forest tribe), Gollabhama (milkmaid), Dasari (low-class Vaishnava performer), Haridasu (Harikatha performer), Avadhani (literary improviser), Bairagi (renouncer), Bhetala (talking dead), Mondi (beggar who does not leave without taking something), the traveller to Kasi, snake charmer, magician, cloth seller, drunkard, widow, troublesome wife, troublesome mother-in-law, and divinities like Ammavaru (Mother goddess) and Ardhanariswara.

Because of their institutional nature, some characters developed authorial scripts. For example, Mudumba Narasimha Charyulu's *Nambi-Nancharamma vesham* ('Portrayal of Nambi and Nancharamma'), with systematic dance and music, was given for performance to Sathanis and Dasaris. The Sathanis also conducted *Dasavataralu* ('Ten avatars'), a prototype of the later Harikatha, with songs composed in Raga Kedara. Guru Siddalingam's famous *Jangam devara* ('Divine Jangams') done by Jangams covered the entire Palnadu region at all Saiva festivals and fairs. Jangams and Gollas started enacting Somayaji and Somidevamma to censure orthodox Vedic Brahman couples, further heightened by Bhagavathula Yadavadasu's *Golla-vesham*, perfected over generations by Gollas of Palagudem village, West Godavari district, from where hailed the great actor Sunnapu Veeraiah (early nineteenth century). *Golla-vesham* of both male and female varieties developed a perfect logic and outstanding scholarship. *Golla-kalapam*, by Tarikonda Venkamamba, a Yogini of the Balija caste, also endorses the same theme. But we do not know whether *Kalapam or *Golla-vesham* came first.

In due course many underprivileged communities, oppressed by the false superiority of Brahmanism, received positive characterizations of their castes. Budabukkala, Erukala (Kuravanji), Madiga, and Koya, developed their own protagonists. We are not sure whether these roles, with exact slang and perfect costume, were created by their own castes or by the reform movements, since they were enacted not by one community but by many as a full-time profession.

Pagati-veshalu invented a unique modern character in the British era called Pittala Dora (bird shooter), with khaki uniform, hat, and wooden gun, caricaturing the image of a British officer. He boasts about his wealth, properties, and expensive food habits but constantly reveals that in fact he represents the working class, fast becoming a begging class. Like Charlie Chaplin, Pittala Dora is loved by one and all.

Certain enactments were taken for granted and villagers fell into the performers' theatrical trap. Without any actual ritual, some characters were received with reverence and fear. Bhetala and Ammavaru, especially when acted by superb performers like Sunnapu Veeraiah, turned into more than icons. Veeraiah's terrific get-up as Ammavaru, brought in on a cart, preceded by drum-beating, singing, and dancing, apparently used to frighten men in broad daylight. Children were never allowed to see it, and very few women even peeped through the windows.

Usually a troupe of ten–fifteen members came to a village to spend a month. They announced the roles a day ahead and the village got into a festive mood. The performance moved from one locality to another, covering all castes and classes with each stop. The season generally ended with *Devarapetti* ('magic box'), actually a magic show coupled with great drama. *Devarapetti* never travelled street to street. As the grand finale, it was staged in the village centre to thousands of viewers. The performer turned neem leaves into live scorpions and kumkum powder into blood without adding any liquid. He poured sand into a jar of water and took it out dry. Corn was fried in wet cloth and coconuts walked on the ground. The best groups were invited by villages, though many toured on their own, avoiding already covered sites. Much competition and rivalry resulted. Till the 1970s, the coastal districts claimed to have the best troupes, led by Narappa, Ravuri Suraiah, Vemula Bapaiah, and Anellapalli Gangadharam.

Because of quarrels and breaks in *Kuchipudi companies, individual Kalapam artistes used to join up to do Pagati-veshalu for a livelihood. Gradually, famous personalities followed suit: Chinta Chalamaiah, Vedantam Lakshminarayana, Tadepalli Peraiah, Hemadri Ven-kateswarlu, Vedantam Narasim-ham, Eleswarapu Punnaiah, Pasumarthi Seshaiah, Mahankali Satyanarayana, and Venkaiah. In Kuchipudi Pagati-veshalu three roles grew very common: Ardhanariswara, Dadinamma (grandmother), and Balintha (pregnant woman). *Balintha vesham* names the pregnant lady as Yasoda, Krishna's mother, but the enactment deals with her labour pains specifically. It is complete in itself, but least interested in Yasoda's character, and focused on a would-be mother's agonies—indeed a unique piece of literature and performance, created by the Gollas. Logically it succeeds a unique portion of *Golla-kalapam* that deals with *Pindotpati* ('Foetus-growth').

Finally, the *Indian People's Theatre Association (Andhra) also adapted Pagati-veshalu with a purpose, reinterpreting and rewriting the portrayals of Pittala Dora, Bairagi, and others for the cause of a people's movement. However, very few individuals perform the art today; it has become a form of begging, with only one or two roles like Pittala Dora still surviving.   PCR

Pala (literally 'turn'): unique form of balladry in Orissa which artistically combines elements of theatre, classical Odissi music, highly refined Oriya and Sanskrit poetry, wit, and humour. It is more sophisticated than the other Oriya ballad tradition, Daskathia. Pala is presented in three ways: *baithaki* ('seated'), in which the performers sit on the ground throughout; *thia* ('standing'), more popular and aesthetically more satisfying, in which they stand; and *badi*, a kind of *thia* in which two groups vie for excellence—the most entertaining as there is an element of competition.

Usually, there are six to seven performers in a group, which cannot present Pala traditionally with fewer than four members. The *gana* (also *gayaka*, 'singer') sings the lead, the *bana* ('drummer') plays the *mridanga* drums, and the *palias* ('Pala-player') are two to five associate singers, of whom the leader is called *sri-palia* and who strike large cymbals called *kartal*. The *palias*' role is, more or less, like that of a chorus. They sing the refrain together with the *gana* and echo the last few words of other sung lines. The *sri-palia* is of great importance as he frequently interacts with the *gana* and punctuates the show with comedy.

A loud percussion ensemble comprising *mridanga* and cymbals precedes the singing, to let the prospective audience know that the Pala is starting soon and to serve as aesthetic prelude (*purvaranga*). In rural areas, the performance begins after 8:30 in the evening. At the end of the prelude, the *gana* enters the arena, usually level ground spread with a large cotton carpet. He begins with an invocation eulogizing the presiding deity, Satyapir, worshipped by both Hindus and

Govind Chandra Panigrahi and group performing Pala, 2000

Muslims. This can be traced back to the Mughal period when there were conscious efforts to bring about amity between the two faiths. After the invocation the presentation proper commences.

As in Daskathia, so also in Pala, the *gana* structures the ballad himself, but the style differs. The major portion of Pala ballads comprises stanzas of ornate Oriya poetry written by eminent poets from the seventeenth to mid-twentieth centuries. These poems and *kavya*s (long narrative verse) were meant not only to be read but also sung in the traditional Chhanda classical form. While composing a particular ballad, the *gana* follows the same pattern as of classical Oriya *kavya*, which narrates the birth of the hero and heroine, after which different cantos depict their growing up through infancy, adolescence, and youth. They meet and fall in love; finally they marry. One or more cantos describe the beauty of the hero and, specially, the heroine at each stage of growing up. The picture of the youthful heroine's beauty from head to toe occurs in great detail with wonderful similes.

Pala has the same structure. The *gana* does not himself compose the descriptions of the aspects of beauty but takes them directly from *kavya*s. For instance, if the Pala compiler wants to relate the beauty of the young heroine's eyes, he can extract different relevant stanzas from *kavya*s written in Oriya or Sanskrit and attribute them all to his heroine. Thus, borrowing from various poets, the account of the heroine's beautiful eyes may go on for hours.

The *gana* not only sings these stanzas in appropriate Chhanda style, but also translates the meaning of the highly difficult lines in simple language. Thus Pala popularizes sophisticated poetry among common people. If the *gana* is not talented enough to structure a ballad, he may requisition the services of a suitable literary person to compile it for him. But he must have an extraordinary memory to remember the countless stanzas and a high degree of literary sensibility so that he can properly explain the meaning as well as poetic merit to listeners. The *gana* who agrees to participate in a *badi* Pala has indeed a phenomenal memory and ready wit, because the other *gana* may challenge him on any aspect of the story.

The *gana* is also an excellent actor with multifaceted talents. While singing or explicating he brings in drama to heighten the appeal. He then uses his *chamara* (fly whisk) to suggest different properties. At one time it indicates the god Indra's thunderbolt, at another it may delineate the lyrical movement of waves or the contour of a graceful creeper. The *gana* usually wears a costume similar to the formal dress of erstwhile royal nobility. The others in the group wear clothes not so splendid.

Unfortunately, this fascinating and dignified performing art is gradually disappearing because people have become so addicted to the mass media that the number of persons who prefer Pala to a film or television serial are very few. To be a good *gana*, one has to devote years of study and practice. It is a full-time job. If one is not assured that earnings from this profession can make one a decent living, why should one be tempted to master this difficult art? The last great *gana*s were Harinath and Niranjan, in popular demand till the early 1950s. The demand decreased, but they held sporadic Palas till the mid-1960s. Those who perform Pala now show not even a shadow of the real art. They are at best amateurs, far from the excellence of a Pala professional.

JP

Palagan (from *pala*, a part, phase, chapter, or episode of a longer narrative; and *gan*, 'song'): generic Bengali term covering a wide range of oral narrative, musical, and theatrical traditions. *Pala* was added to titles describing particular episodes from myths narrated or performed in various traditional modes. The Vaishnava Lila-kirtan, celebrating Krishna's career and exploits (*Lila) in elaborate suites of songs, which became popular after the great Kheturi festival (c. 1576) convened by Narottamdas, is known as Palagan since it broke up Krishna's life into separate Lilas, each set to a musical pattern underscoring its *rasa. The Palas centred on themes like Goshtha, Ras, Danalila, Naukabilas, Jhulan, Holi, Abhisar, Mathur, from phases or incidents in the Krishna legend. Since the kirtan singers came to concentrate on the dramatic element as it evolved in the Palas, they needed more songs, and anthologies (Padabali-samhitas) offering compositions by several lyricists arranged according to the themes or needs of Palas were compiled and circulated.

A direct line of descent has been traced from the kirtan as Palagan to *Jatra, which for a long time was described as Palagan, a word that now conveys the sense of a theatrical performance predominantly through songs. Although Jatra has over the years lost a lot of its musicality and its texts have become mostly prose drama, its plays are still called Pala or Palagan, its scriptwriters palakars, and its productions gaona ('singing'). Song sequences on different narrative subjects, not necessarily mythological, and even several modern plays written in mock-archaic musical modes, carry Pala as a suffix, for example Abanindranath Tagore's Lambakarna pala ('Pala of the Long Ears', 1930s), Lila Majumdar's Bak-badh pala ('Pala of Bak's Killing', 1955), and Sombhu Mitra's Chand baniker pala ('The Merchant Chand's Pala', 1978).   KG

Pallu (from Pallar, a low caste of farmhands): Tamil genre relegated to minor status, one of ninety-six forms of composition in currency in medieval Tamil literature. Conventionally, it falls under the geographical division of marutam (belonging to agricultural life) and is defined as a folk dance-drama set to music. It is structured as exchanges between the farmhands and the landlord, and again between the farmhand and his wife, containing graphic descriptions of the varieties of farm produce, of peasant life and its pathos, studded with rustic humour. It also has a religious element intended finally to lead the audience to the presiding deity of the place or temple after which a particular Pallu takes its name, to seek divine blessings. The most famous such work, Mukkutar pallu (eighteenth century), is of unknown authorship. Originally a poetic composition, it is the most literary Pallu. Later, Ennayinar rendered it into a broader dance-drama.   VS

Pandavani ('about the Pandavas'): narrative ballad form of Chhattisgarh, sung primarily by the Pardhan and Devar castes, and based essentially on stories from the *Mahabharata*. Since the epic was read by and accessible only to upper castes, a body of folk poetry developed around it that became popular in villages and among lower castes. This literature is the source for Pandavani. It has two varieties, Kapalik (literally, from the forehead) and Vedamati (based on the Vedas). The former uses the outline of the *Mahabharata* but has Bhim as its hero, and being highly improvisatory, freely brings in local legends and myths (stored 'in the head') existing in the collective popular consciousness, whereas the latter bases itself strictly on the epic. The Kapalik performer stands and moves around, incorporating song, dance, and acting to create a solo theatrical show, while Vedamati consists of pure ballad-singing from a seated position.

The legendary Jhaduram Devangan and his family initiated Vedamati as a kind of protest against the Kapalik tradition, when he accidentally came across the *Mahabharata* rewritten by Sabal Singh Chauhan, faithful to the original and in verse. It features mostly a single performer who sings the couplets from the text, set to folk tunes. Using a rural three-stringed tambura with bells tied at one end and *kartal* (hand cymbals also with bells) both as accompaniment and as props, the actor-singer brings alive the characters, their traits, moods, and situations while sitting on his knees. Other instrumentalists usually play tablas and *manjira* (small cymbals). The performer also provides explanations of the couplets as he goes along. In some cases a companion, the *ragi*, facilitates relevance by asking questions related to the lives of the people as they connect with the story.

Pandavani is a riveting genre of storytelling in either of its varieties. Vedamati acquired recognition through imaginative and skilled rendering by Punaram Nishada, Chetan Ram, and their mentor Jhaduram Devangan, while the extremely energetic Kapalik form found its best representative in Teejan Bai, possibly its first woman practitioner and now a national celebrity.   KJ

Patayani (literally 'array of soldiers'): ancient proto-theatrical form in Kerala. The collective social

consciousness preserved myths and rituals as mediums of empirical pragmatism about nature and life. Patayani illustrates a creative resolution by which the festive involvement of the social mind enlarges and illumines its horizon. Since martial training is involved, the etymology of the name has relevance, but in a wider connotation it denotes people at large. The whole village, irrespective of cast or creed, participates from preparation to final execution. Patayani is performed in the open courtyard of certain temples to Devi in Pathanamthitta district.

References in certain Patayani songs indicate that it existed in the eighth century. Afterwards, a solo art by the name of *kolam* *Tullal ('masked dance') developed, practised by members of the Kaniyan community of professional astrologers. They used to make *masks from areca sheaths painted in natural colours with grotesque figures of different spirits. Wearing these masks, they performed dances of *possession in village homes to ward off evil spells. The spirits propitiated in this *ritual—Devata, Pisachu, Sundara Yakshi, Sukumara Yakshi—are common to Patayani. The Kaniyans contribute even now to Patayani by painting the *kolam*s (masks) for the performers.

The festival usually falls in the Malayalam month of Medam (April–May) and its duration may

Madhavan Pillai performing Patayani, 1984

vary from seven to twenty-eight days. Different territorial divisions of the village are represented by their leaders, who assemble in front of the temple on the first day with torches lit from the lamp in the sanctum. They proceed in a procession around the temple to the accompaniment of *tappu*, a special percussion instrument exclusively used in Patayani, with cymbals keeping time. The *tappu* is round and wooden, covered with very thick hide heated to the maximum to produce a high tone. On occasions when it is played without heat treatment, it is called *pacha tappu*.

From the third day of the festival, the masked dance commences with Ganapati *kolam*, painted with the god Ganapati's face. Among the many *kolam*s in the rich repertoire, Kalan (god of death or time) is prominent. Kalan appears, to take away the life of the young boy Markandeya whose death was predestined at age 16. But through strict penance and concentrated devotion, Markandeya pleased Siva, who kills Kalan when he tries to snatch the boy's life. The dancer performs all three roles. Accompanying vocal music describes the whole Puranic myth of Markandeya. The song describes graphically the consequences of the death of the god of death, and the dancer enacts the pangs of death suffered by Kalan. When the dancer in his possessed state collapses, stagehands sprinkle water on his face to wake him up after a while to resume the drama.

Another *kolam*, of Kutira (the horse), refers to the establishment of commercial relations between Kerala and Arabia in the past. Apart from the manifestation of spirits, social characters like the Brahman landlord with his valet and the Christian ferryman make for interesting dramatic sequences in performance.

KNP

Porattu Natakam (literally 'frolicsome theatre'): Malayalam folk theatre prevalent in Palakkad district, similar to *Kakkarissa Kali of southern Kerala. Unlike most traditional forms in Kerala, Porattu is secular in nature. The artists engaged in this profession belong to the Panan caste, known for their excellence in singing. The plays are performed on a stage specially erected in an open field after harvest, with a front curtain separating the performers and audience, and sometimes in temples. In earlier times Petromax pressure lamps provided lighting.

A preliminary session of music, called *keli*, in the evening announces the performance usually starting around 10 at night. An actor enters in the beginning and performs benediction by singing in praise of God and the audience. He also apologizes in advance for all shortcomings in presentation. As in *Kathakali, the two main musicians stay at the back. They ask questions of the characters, who reply. The plot unveils through these questions and answers. There are many characters, all drawn from ordinary life: Vannan and Vannatti (washerman and washerwoman), Kuravan and Kuratti (gypsies), Komali (jester), Pukkari (flower girl). The stories are woven from their rustic experiences, incorporating many situations of fun, satire, and social criticism. The main musicians control the actors by questioning, singing, directing them to enter or exit, and editing the enacted scenarios. They use the *mridangam* (double-faced drum), *kaimani* (cymbals), *sruti* box (drone), and *chaplamkatta* (two wooden pieces held by the fingers of the right hand to mark time).   KNP

Possession, in which the portrayed personality overwhelms and appropriates the performer, is a feature that theatre probably adopted and adapted from religious *ritual. In many parts of the world, theatre is believed to have developed from ritualistic practices, and possession was one of the elements taken over from ritual into ritualistic or secular

theatre. In a broad sense, however, it could be said theoretically that every actor at the moment of involved acting is possessed by the character he or she is impersonating. The sense of possession is common to ritual and theatre—it could even be argued that it is an extension of an experience that often happens in everyday life, when people get carried away by their fantasies.

Traditional cultures resort to exorcism, especially in tribal villages when manifestations of hysteria are noticed among the vulnerable. Induced possession thus becomes a means of repossessing lost identity. Such parapsychological experiences are also associated with witchcraft and black magic, ostensibly theatrical folk practices prevalent in many parts of India, whose potential has often been used in traditional theatres as well as modern theatrical experiments that draw heavily upon folk rituals. M.P. Bhattatiripad's *Ritumati* (1938), a Malayalam play, is an example of the theatrical use of exorcism.

There are documented instances of possession in folk rituals like Tumpi *Tullal in Kerala, where the girl performer loses consciousness and behaves as though possessed, or when a *velichapad* (oracle) attached to some shrines assumes the role of the deity and prophesies future events or cures diseases. Traces of it are also found in the cult of

Ayyappan and perhaps even in the mass prayers of the Christian Pentecostal sect, both in Kerala. It is believed that devotees of Murugan in south India become possessed while dancing the Kavadi; this device may have carried over into traditional street plays like the *Terukkuttu of Tamil Nadu or the *Yakshaganam of Andhra Pradesh. In many tribal dances, the crescendo of drumbeats in unison with human voices works out a kind of mass mania conducive to possession.

The most striking cases of possession in Indian theatre occur in ritual drama. Its influence may be seen to varying degrees in *Chhau (eastern India) or *Ramlila (northern India), while in *Teyyam and Tira in northern Kerala, ritualistic possession is common. One vivid example in traditional theatre is the Kalan *kolam*, discussed in *The Theatre of the Earth Is Never Dead*, edited by G. Sankara Pillai. In this important item of *Patayani, the songs, drums, flaming torches, the viewer-worshippers' wild excitement, all contribute to the creation of an otherworldly atmosphere. The performer who wears the *kolam* (mask) of Kalan, the god of death, enacts the story of the young devotee Markandeya, destined to die at 16 but able to attain immortality through his devotion to Siva, who kills Kalan. The actor impersonates Kalan,

Markandeya, and Siva. As his dance moves to a climax, he feels giddy, becomes possessed, and has to be held back by at least two people to control his vital energy released by possession.

A slightly different pattern is noticeable in the festival of Kaliyuttu ('Feeding of Kali'; see under *Mutiyettu) also in Kerala, at which, after forty-one days of fasting and penance, performers assume the roles of Kali and the demon Darika, and enact the ritual drama of Kali killing Darika. In some temples they fight pitched battles, which may last for hours. The end comes after a series of possessed dances. The devotees, who also participate in the frenzy of posses-sion, are the beneficiaries, freed from want and disease until the next performance.

Classical Indian theatre promotes impersonality and non-identification between actor and character, as also between spectator and character, hence the *natyadharmi* (theatrical) style of presentation avoids possession. On the other hand, folk influences seem to encourage at least temporary identification through *lokadharmi* (popular) devices, which may not stand in the way of possession. In *Kathakali, for instance, we come across scenes in which possession may not be completely ruled out. Anecdotes, perhaps exaggerated to prove individual performing skill, relate how actors playing Rama became possessed by his spirit and actually killed the actor impersonating his enemy, Ravana. Similar tales circulate on *Prahlada Nataka in Orissa, about Narasimha vis-a-vis Hiranyakasipu. It may be ventured that possession, and elitist resistance to it, respectively indicate acceptance and rejection of a basic feature of popular culture.   KAP

Prahasana ('farce'): comic form of *Sanskrit theatre. It represented reprobates invented by the dramatist, drawn from life, and mostly incorporated wit, humour, and satire. *Prakarana*, *bhana*, and *prahasana* formed a class in themselves, very often reflecting the social reality of their time and sometimes critiquing it through laughter. *Prahasana* resembled *bhana* in the number of *sandhi*s ('junctures' of plot) and *lasyanga* (feminine components of dance), while the elements essential in *vithi* were not obligatory. Its principal *rasa* was *hasya* (comic). When the hero was an impudent ascetic, mendicant, or Brahman, it created 'pure' *prahasana*, in one act. Bodhayana's *Bhagavadajjukiya* ('The Sage and the Courtesan') and Mahendravikrama's *Mattavilasa* ('Intoxicated Delights'), both sometimes ascribed to Mahendravikrama in the seventh or eighth century, best

exemplify this variety. When a multitude of reprobates was represented, it became a 'mixed' *prahasana* in several acts.   KDT

Mahendra-Varman, *The Farce of the Drunk Monk*, translated by P. Lal (Calcutta: Writers Workshop, 1968); S. Ramaratnam, *Prahasana in Sanskrit Literature* (Mysore: Kavyalaya, 1987); *Three Sanskrit Lighter Delights*, translated by C.C. Mehta (Baroda: M.S. University, 1969).

Prahlada Nataka ('Prahlada Drama'): highly stylized *Oriya theatre form prevalent in Ganjam district, southern Orissa. The tradition is not very old. In the late nineteenth century, Raja Ramakrishna Chhotaraya, an Oriya feudatory ruler of Jalantar (now in Srikakulam district, Andhra Pradesh), conceived the first performatory edition. The first text was written in Sanskritized Oriya by Gopinath Parichha, a poet-dramatist who received generous patronage from the Raja. As a gesture of gratitude he not only dedicated the work to the ruler but also ascribed its authorship to him. Within a few years of its birth, Prahlada Nataka became so popular that it inspired rulers of neighbouring princedoms to prepare other versions. No matter which version, the plot remains the same, based on the myth of Narasimha, Vishnu's man-lion

Young boy as Prahlada in Prahlada Nataka

avatar. Thus Prahlada Nataka has only one 'play' in its repertoire.

Similarities of make-up and costume suggest that *Terukkuttu of Tamil Nadu and *Yakshaganam of Andhra Pradesh influenced Prahlada Nataka, but the theatrical style is close enough to *Suanga and *Yatra of Orissa. It takes place as arena theatre, presented open-air and on level ground (sometimes temple precincts), but a must for performance is a five- or six-tiered wooden platform some 2 m high. The top has an area of about 2 m by 1 m, on which rests the throne of Hiranyakasipu, the demon whom Narasimha kills at the end. The platform is usually collapsible, easily erected before and dismantled after a show. The acting area of about 4 sq. m is enclosed with ropes in front of the platform. To the left, about 6 m from the platform, stands a hollow structure representing the pillar Hiranyakasipu smote.

The accompanying musicians take their places to the right of the acting area, close to the platform. The band normally comprises three instruments: a harmonium, a double-ended drum called *mardal,* and *gini* (a pair of small cymbals). A few groups have started using violin and trumpet, adding a touch of glamour, but actually enhancing the aesthetic appeal of the music, which is the life-breath of Prahlada Nataka. It not only provides the base but also determines the dramatic structure. Both vocal and instrumental music at appropriate points intensify the impact. Dialogue winged with music takes the emotive intent farther than realistic delivery. Prahlada Nataka draws heavily upon traditional Odissi music, with over 100 songs, each set to a raga and tala.

Since music dominates, the director must be a good singer. More often than not, he serves as the lead vocalist called *gahaka* ('singer'), not quite a character in the drama, yet the pivot on which the performance turns. Primarily, he leads the chorus, but acts also as interpreter, commentator, and conductor of the band. Although, usually, he does not wear make-up or formal costume, he has specific songs and dialogue. He sings eulogies of gods and narrates events preceding a dramatic situation or pertinent to the plot but not enacted. At times, he speaks a character's asides and comments on his or her mood and thoughts. He is entrusted with the responsibility of explaining to lay spectators the cryptic, pithy lines. His role resembles that of the Sanskrit *sutradhara.* Although songs predominate, there are also long prose passages, besides prose dialogue linking the sung passages.

The demonic role of Hiranyakasipu is the most demanding. The way he goes up and down the tiered platform with vigorous dance-like movements is indeed a treat for the eyes. A professional actor who excels in this part is, at times, hired by more than one group. Though Narasimha appears only in the last, climactic scene and is seen onstage for only around fifteen minutes, his is also a difficult role. The actor fasts on performance days. Putting on the lion mask and tapered nails simulating claws, he stands amazingly transformed. It is said that years ago an actor playing the part—so complete was his empathy—actually killed the one playing Hiranyakasipu. Apocryphal or true, it led to the custom of tying a rope around Narasimha's waist, held by two or three stagehands who must avert a killing should the spirit of Narasimha take charge. The choice of an actor for this role is made with much care.

In some villages like Bokagaon near Chhatrapur, Narasimha's mask is worshipped in a temple and believed to have divine powers. Hiranyakasipu wears no mask, but his face is painted bright red to suggest ferocity. His moustache consists of thick ropes of black thread twined with golden *zari* (brocade) and runs across the full expanse of the cheeks down to the nape of the neck, where it is tied in a knot. Both he and Prahlada wear colourful skirts and huge magnificently-crafted headgear embellished with glittering glass beads. The major male characters sport shoulder decorations and artificial ornaments. Apart from female and minor characters, all are costumed in such an exaggerated manner that they seem masked head to foot. In keeping with the stylized make-up and dress, the acting is choreographic, having a strong dose of dance.

Prahlada Nataka is so popular in Ganjam that there are now more than thirty troupes, though not all equally good. Simanchal Patro made a name as Hiranyakasipu, and Raghu Nath Satapathy as a singer-musician. To watch a performance by a really powerful unit is an unforgettable experience. Tuneful music, operatic songs, poetic dialogue, dramatic dance, vigorous acrobatics, stylized mime, elaborate spectacle, colourful costumes, and sumptuous decorations all combine to induce a hypnotic state of consciousness between wakefulness and dream.   JP

Prakarana (from the root 'to do perfectly'): the major form of those plays in *Sanskrit theatre in which the dramatist invented the plot. The story was human and mundane. Like the *nataka, it offered a panoramic view of life in five to ten acts. When contrasted with the *nataka*, based on tales drawn from the Vedas, epics, Puranas, or great men's exploits, the *prakarana* appears to be deeply rooted in the life of common people and social reality. Love and comedy were its principal themes or *rasas, and the hero a Brahman, minister, or merchant of the *dhirasanta* type ('firm and peaceful'), intent on meritorious deeds yet seeking with selfish motives objects of desire and wealth, which perish or bring but transitory pleasure. The heroine was sometimes a noblewoman and sometimes a courtesan, sometimes both. *Prakarana*s featured characters like the *vita*—the parasitic companion of a prince, of a dissolute young man, or of a courtesan, skilled in singing, music, and poetry, on familiar terms with his associate whom he serves as a *vidushaka*. Minor characters included gamblers, thieves, and servants. The *Natyasastra* prescribes wider use of Prakrits and dialects in *prakaranas*. Sudraka's *Mricchakatika* (*The Little Clay Cart*) and Bhavabhuti's *Malati-Madhava* (*Malati and Madhava*) are excellent examples of the form.   KDT

Puppetry: A puppet is an inanimate figure articulated by human agency. Thus puppets are different from dolls that are children's playthings and also from automata that are moved mechanically or electrically. Puppets are dramatis personae for whom the manipulators and associates provide dialogue; although not human, they are not merely the bits of wood and rags with which they are made. Just as *masks are considered the other face of human beings, so also may puppets be regarded as 'other' beings. Since puppets are endowed with such extraordinary 'life' of their own, they can carry drama to levels beyond the reach of mankind. A puppet is, in fact, the mask complete, from which the human actor has withdrawn, not to be dissociated from but united with subtler objectivity to explore yet another dimension of theatre—yet another plane of reality. Although puppets owe their life to human agency, they can surpass human performers in theatricality.

Many scholars believe that puppetry originated in India and migrated to other Asian countries along with the epic themes. Richard Pischel in *The Home of the Puppet Theatre* (1902) says, 'it is not improbable that the puppet play is in reality everywhere the most ancient form of dramatic representation. Without doubt, this is the case in India, and there, too, we must look for its home'. There is much literary evidence to prove that puppetry reached great heights in India more than two millennia ago. An unmistakable reference occurs in the Tamil classic *Cilappatikaram*, written during that time. Although the *Natyasastra* does not mention puppets, it terms the producer-cum-director of the human theatre as *sutradhara*, 'string-holder'. The word must have found its place in theatre terminology long before the *Natyasastra* was compiled; there can be little doubt that it comes from marionette theatre. This leads logically to the assumption that

Indian puppetry was established and very popular by this time.

That it was impressive and respected as an art in ancient India is evident from the way it has been referred to in poems with metaphysical content. For instance, in the *Bhagavata Purana*, God is likened to a puppeteer who with three strings—*sattva* (essence, mind, or virtue), *rajas* (action), and *tamas* (vice)—manipulates all human beings. The Sanskrit language also took a deeper view in calling puppets *puttalika* or *puttika*, both of which etymologically mean 'little son'. This meaning has sunk so deep in the minds of traditional puppeteers that they usually keep the box containing their puppets in their own bedrooms; when a puppet gets old and cannot stand any further manipulation, it is not just rejected and discarded. It is taken to a river and, to the chanting of mantras, consigned to the water.

Considering differences in design, mode of manipulation, and presentational techniques, puppets belong to basically four types: glove, rod, string, and leather (for the last-named, see *shadow theatre). All four varieties survive in different parts of India. Nearly all the themes of traditional puppet plays are drawn from the epics *Ramayana* and *Mahabharata*, the *Bhagavata Purana* and other Puranic literature, or from local legends. The accompa-

nying music is mainly inspired by the folk music of the region, at times blended with the classical.

Glove puppets, also known as hand puppets, are the simplest, but that does not mean they are less fascinating. Generally, a glove puppet is a miniature figure with movable head and arms and a long flowing skirt that the puppeteer wears like a glove. While the index finger manipulates the head, the thumb and middle finger control the arms. Traditional Indian glove puppeteers frequently squat on the ground and manipulate the puppets in full view of the audience: they do not hide behind a screen. The form survives in Orissa (*Kundhei Nata), West Bengal (*Putul Nach), Uttar Pradesh (Gulabo-Sitabo), and Kerala (Pavakuttu, 'puppet play'). The last-named has a rare variety called Pava Kathakali ('puppet *Kathakali'), saved from extinction in the 1970s by the intervention of Kamaladevi Chattopadhyaya. Two or three manipulators articulate these minia-turized wooden puppets in Kathakali dress, presenting Kathakali stories and accompanied by a percussion ensemble of drums and cymbals.

The rod puppet is an extension of the glove puppet, but often much larger, with a full-length rounded figure. The supporting and concealed base is a rectangular wooden frame with a handle.

Through two holes in the frame a rod is inserted vertically to hold the head. The hands are jointed to the two upper corners of the frame. Near the wrist of each hand is fixed a slender rod hidden inside the flowing costume. The puppeteer moves the head and hands with the rods attached to them. Usually, he hides behind a head-high screen, pushes the puppet above and manipulates it from below. The movements are limited compared to a string puppet's, but control is absolute and can attain broad gestures of rare beauty. One kind of rod puppet in Karnataka is made like string puppets, but instead of strings, rods are attached to the jointed limbs; these are manipulated from above, like string puppets. Traditional rod puppets survive in West Bengal (Putul Nach) and Orissa (Kathi-kundhei Nata, 'wooden-doll dance'). The former are much larger than the latter.

String puppetry is widespread in India, with a variety of themes and techniques. These full-figure puppets or, strictly speaking, marionettes have jointed limbs controlled by strings, which allow far greater flexibility and therefore make these the most articulate of all puppets. Originally they may have been controlled by one rod or stout wire for the head and strings for the hands. Although manipulation is more complicated, according to available evidence this

type seems to be the most ancient. Some scholars think that shadow theatre evolved earlier than string puppetry, but this belief may not hold much water. The earliest reference to shadow puppets is in Tamil Sangam literature of the first century AD, whereas the term *sutradhara* predates it and cave drawings etched millennia ago unmistakably represent string puppets. Indian marionette traditions exist in Rajasthan (*Kathputli), Orissa (*Sakhi-kundhei Nata), Maharashtra (*Kalsutri Bahulya), Karnataka (*Gombeyata), Tamil Nadu (*Bommalattam), Assam (Putla Nach, 'doll dance'), and West Bengal (Putul Nach).

Unfortunately, though India is the home of puppet theatre, at present it is perhaps the most neglected art. Many of the forms mentioned above are on the verge of extinction. The mass media of cinema and television entice audiences with so much glamour that there are few who would go to watch a puppet play. Contemporary puppet theatre has considerable aesthetic appeal, but practitioners are rare. Its main centres are Kolkata and Ahmadabad, with some in Rajasthan. Among the modern puppeteers who not only dedicated their lives to the art during the 1950s but also excelled in it were Meher Contractor (Ahmadabad), Devilal Samar (Udaipur,

A Meher Contractor puppet play using traditional shadow theatre technique (Delhi, 1990)

Rajasthan), Raghunath Goswami (Calcutta), Madhulal Master (Bombay), and Haripada Das (Tripura). Leading puppeteers who continue to be active and creative are Suresh Dutta of Kolkata and Dadi Pudumjee of Ahmadabad, now living in Delhi.   JP

Meher R. Contractor, *Creative Drama and Puppetry in Education* (New Delhi: National Book Trust, 1984); Meher R. Contractor, *Puppets of India* (Bombay: Marg, 1968); Sunil Kumar, *Puppetry: A Tool of Mass Communication* (Varanasi: National Council of Development Communication, 1989); *Our Cultural Fabric: Puppet Theatre in India* (New Delhi: Ministry of Education and Culture, 1982); Jiwan Pani, *Living Dolls: Story of Indian Puppets* (New Delhi: Publications Division, Ministry of Information and Broadcasting, 1986); Anupama Shah and Uma Joshi, *Puppetry and Folk Dramas for Non-formal Education* (New Delhi: Sterling, 1992); Tandra Devi, *Village Theatres* (Srinagar: Tandra Devi, 1938).

Putul Nach (literally, 'doll dance'): *puppetry in the Bengali-speaking region, extending from West Bengal to Tripura and Assam. The oldest form, *danger putul* (rod puppets), is found in South 24 Parganas district. The 1.5 m-tall figures, made of bamboo or hollowed wood, are jointed for easy manipulation with strings attached to various parts of their bodies. The *nachiye* (manipulator) has a wooden cup attached to a waistband in which the rod supporting the large puppet rests. The troupe includes a singer who usually plays the harmonium, and musicians on the clarinet, *sanai* (double-reed wind instrument), dhol, and *kansi* (bell-metal plate beaten with a stick). Often performed at rural fairs, the form uses an improvised proscenium and starts with the adoration of Krishna. A variation in Murshidabad district utilizes dolls made of bamboo and a round stage.

At the Sati Mela (a fair named after Siva's consort) in Kalyani,

Nadia district, 15–20 cm rod puppets known as *Yamerpuri putul* (dolls from the palace of Yama, god of death) appear on a darkened stage viewed through bamboo slats. The shows are moralistic in tone, with instructions for various rites associated with the worship of Siva and advice for women.

The *benir putul* (glove puppets) found at village festivals in Medinipur district have terracotta heads and wooden hands. They used to be played by palanquin bearers to while away their time between trips and to earn some extra money. The stories accompanying their 'dances' were normally about Krishna. The puppeteers still perform without any stage, in full view, wearing their dolls on both hands.

Putul Nach using marionettes made of pith, measuring 1 m and attached to four wires, has gone

Puppeteers manipulating
Putul Nach rod puppets

professional in Bagula, Nadia district. Brought from Bangladesh by a refugee, Jiten Haldar, who saw such puppets at home in the possession of itinerant Rajasthanis, they became the means of livelihood for residents of Panchmura colony. The group has a repertoire of fifteen or sixteen plays based on the *Mahabharata* and *Ramayana*, mythological stories like that of Harishchandra, or even comparatively modern social scripts. It tours Bengali-speaking areas, beginning from Viswakarma Puja in autumn (Viswakarma is the patron god of technicians). The master puppeteer single-handedly sings all the songs and delivers the various dialogues, accompanied by musicians. The 1-m apron stage has a second tier for the manipulators.

A variety of table puppet theatre common among the tribal Adivasis of western Bengal employs small, dark marionettes of seasoned wood and bamboo, manipulated by a combination of rods and strings to songs accompanied by flute and drums. The Santals call this form *chadar badar*.

Raghunath Goswami (1931–95) and Suresh Dutta (1934–) contributed most to modern puppetry in West Bengal. Goswami, through his work with The Puppets, founded in 1953, tried to streamline the indigenous conventions and introduced a richer literary content, but remained loyal to native roots. He made the first Indian puppet movie to win a national film award, *Hattagol vijay* (1952, in Hindi). Dutta, who trained under Russian genius Sergei Obraztsov, went for more gorgeous and illusory spectacle. In Tripura, Haripada Das invented contemporary rod puppets.

Maldah district is the home of a highly unusual form known as *manab putul* ('human dolls'), in which actors imitate marionettes. It has hardly any narrative to speak of, mainly relying on the sheer humorous novelty of the concept. The performers sing, indulge in crosstalk, and mimic puppet behaviour, jumping and moving with limp limbs and jerky motions as if pulled by strings. Men impersonate the female puppets.   KG

Rahasa (Oriya dialect for *Ras*, the love sport of Radha and Krishna): a variety of *Raslila in musical dance-drama form mostly confined to the coastal districts of Puri and Cuttack in Orissa. Many Rahasa scripts were written by Vaishnava poets as *Basanta* (spring) *rahasa* and *Sarat* (autumn) *rahasa*. Very popular for over a century, it is performed both by amateurs and professionals, by young boys and girls. The duration depends on the number of episodes. In some villages it is held for more than a week by amateur artists of the village. The performance includes elaborate singing with gestures and mild dancing. The most popular and important contributors to Rahasa were Mohansundar Deva Goswami, Govinda Chandra Surdeo, Bhakta Charan Das, and Kali Charan Patnaik. They toured all over Orissa with their professional troupes till the early 1940s. The famous Odissi dance guru Kelucharan Mahapatra initially belonged to Goswami's excellent group.

Another form of Raslila prevalent in the southern district of Ganjam is known as Radhaprem *Lila (literally 'Radha's Love Play'). Written and started by Pitambar Rajendra in the late nineteenth century, it is performed in front of a *kunja* (bower) built with wood and beautifully painted with floral designs. Radha and her companions, the Sakhis, sit there while Krishna comes in different disguises to meet her. Though fully operatic it has various acrobatic dance sequences. Both styles of Rahasa use classical Odissi dance and music.   DNP

Ramlila (literally 'Rama's *Lila'):
Hindi folk form. The *Ramayana*,
the shorter of the two great Sanskrit
epics, consists of seven books and
24,000 couplets. Written in elegant
verse, and telling the story of
Vishnu's avatar Rama, it is
traditionally ascribed to the poet
Valmiki. Scholars suggest that its
greater part was composed between
the first century BC and second
century AD, the beginning and
ending in all likelihood added later.
Besides worshipping Rama
(pronounced Ram in north India),
Hindus revere his queen Sita, his
brother Lakshmana (Lakshman),
and his follower Hanumana
(Hanuman) as ideal embodiments
of wifely devotion, fraternal duty,
and loyal service respectively.

Popular all over India, the
Ramayana is sustained widely
through translations and recensions,
of which Tulsidas's version, the
Ramcharitmanas ('Wondrous Lake of
Ram's Life'), is by far the best
known. Tulsidas (traditional dates
1532–1623) wrote in his native
Avadhi, a language whose name
originates in Ayodhya, Ram's home
town in myth, and usually classified
under the family of Hindi. The
Ramcharitmanas has so affected the
minds and emotions of north
Indians that it serves as a sort of
sentimental education for them.
Reciting it, or the *Ramayana*, is
considered a religious act. It is
related with or without commentary
in temples, homes, streets, and over
loudspeakers at maidans, ghats, and
squares; it is dramatized and enacted
in various styles throughout India
and south-east Asia. By way of such
recitation as well as through
storytelling, devotional singing,
and Lila performances, Ram's
narrative abides, most familiarly
through the presentation of Ramlila.

This annual enactment of Ram's
story, during the Dussehra festival in
September–October celebrating his
defeat of Ravana, is found in most
north Indian cities and villages,
among various castes, classes, and
even religions. Customarily organized by local committees and
sustained by community
contributions, the performances
differ greatly in style and scale, but
also share certain characteristics.
Among the latter, they are usually
not presented in a single day but go
on for a number of consecutive days
ranging between nine and thirty-
one. (However, the celebrated urban
Ramlila organized by Shri Ram
Bharatiya Kala Kendra in Delhi is
played out in a day but runs for
several months.) They are not
necessarily staged at a single location,
but move through the local
landscapes. They are based on the
Ramcharitmanas. Through the
enactment Ram, Sita, and Ram's

brothers Bharat, Lakshman, and Shatrughna are worshipped in the manner of gods.

Probably the most famous among the many hundreds of Ramlilas in north India is the one at Ramnagar, located across the Ganga from Varanasi, and the capital of the Maharajas of Banaras (Varanasi) since the mid-eighteenth century. Its unique intensity is effected by the 200-year-old patronage it has enjoyed from the Maharajas, whose very visible participation confers upon it both handsome material assistance and great religious significance. When it came into existence is a matter of conjecture and several legends developed to account for its origin. In all probability it began when a small Ramlila belonging to a nearby village, Chhota Mirzapur, was appropriated, brought to Ramnagar, and expanded by Maharaja Udit Narayan Singh in the early nineteenth century. James Prinsep's book *Benares Illustrated in a Series of Drawings* (1833) described it in considerable detail that tallies with the Lila's format even today, suggesting that it had become reasonably well developed by the 1820s.

While most Ramlilas narrate the incidents in the *Ramcharitmanas* over a series of performances lasting on average ten to twelve days, the Ramnagar Lila's scale is probably unmatched in world theatre: it goes on for a month and moves through an area of about 50 sq. km. It concludes four or five days after Dussehra, therefore lasting thirty to thirty-one days, depending on the lunar calendar. The town square, its two main temples, its lakes and tanks, the gardens, fields, and villages on its outskirts, all come within the Lila's great boundary. In other words, nearly all its important landmarks are also important landmarks in the Lila. Moving from one location to another is very much a part of the performance, and on occasion may take the better part of a day's Lila.

Because of the Lila's breadth of duration and locale, its experience of time is often very different from that of the *Ramcharitmanas*. For example, Tulsidas may describe a journey briefly, but in Ramnagar it might take hours, configured to become meaningful by the act of walking. For episodes such as *Bharat milap* ('Meeting Bharat'), huge crowds gather to occupy vantage points long before the performance, causing Ramnagar's main square to fill up four hours in advance; on account of the long tantalizing wait, desire and meaning are teased out of the moment, attenuating the emotional impact far beyond the text. The journeys, and the sites to which they are made, are chosen to maintain a certain fidelity to the story, to put in

Ramlila performance, with Ram at right

place the concept of near-verisimilitude. But as ponds are ponds and not rivers or seas, a series of transformations takes place; the presentation is composed frame within frame, from local everyday space to theatre space, metaphoric space, epic space, and finally sacred space.

The performance style is an amalgamation of wordless tableaux (*jhanki*) and processional drama, in which actors move from place to place and speak dialogues. There is not much variation in the manner of delivering the lines; most actors speak in a well-modulated, sing-song, declamatory fashion. Make-up and costuming of the *swarup*s ('incarnations') take two to four hours every day. Decorations make them both strange and fabulous:

patterns fashioned of small, coloured, glinting sequins and gems bedeck the face; lines of sandalwood paste are combed on legs, arms, foreheads; and obligatory iconographic details like jewellery, garlands, crowns, bows, arrows, swords, and lotuses produce a splendid radiance. Other characters wear minimal make-up; brass masks are used for the older monkeys and bears, and cloth masks for the monkey and demon armies comprising children of all ages.

All the players are male Brahmans, except the real boatman in the popular scene where Ram crosses the Ganga, and the small boys in the monkey and demon armies, who may belong to any caste. In July, forty to fifty

Brahman boys are brought to the Maharaja for him to pick five *swarup*s: he auditions them, and the most suitable are selected. Suitability depends on their physical attributes, height, beauty, age, and voice. A boy may begin acting at the age of 8 or 9; he may first play Shatrughna, then graduate to the roles of Bharat, Lakshman or Janaki, and, later, perhaps Ram. He can hold his position no more than three or four years at a stretch; for, according to the inexorable law of Ramlila, his career as *swarup* must end as soon as hair appears on his upper lip or his voice begins to crack. The chosen boys stay in Ramnagar for three months at the Maharaja's expense. They live with the *vyas* (director) and, under his guidance, rehearse for two months and perform for one.

Most other actors are adults, even those playing female roles. Local families have performed for five or six generations; for example Ravana has long been acted by men of one family, the tradition passed from father to son, sometimes from older brother to younger brother. Honoraria are small, ranging from 50 paise to Rs 3 per day, and not considered as remuneration; the work is voluntary and, moreover, an act of worship. Some actors also get food rations. A few incur considerable expenses travelling to Ramnagar to perform.

Customarily the Ramlila rituals begin earlier and end later than the period of actual enactment. They are heralded by a puja to Ganesh two months before the Lila starts, virtually in tandem with the choice of the *swarup*s. In that ceremony the *swarup*s are worshipped along with their crowns, the masks, the *Ramcharitmanas*, the performance script, and implements of the carpenter, tailor, painter, and others. Thereafter, preparations are formally initiated. Another Ganesh puja takes place ten days before the Ramlila, when the Ramayanis (chanters of the *Ramcharitmanas*) start reciting the opening sections of the text, which are not performed. The enactment commences with the episode of Ram's birth. The Ramlila officially closes ten days after the presentations have ended, following the *rajyabhishek* ('royal consecration') of the *swarup*s in the private courtyard of the palace, where the Maharaja and his family entertain the divinities, worship them, and finally bid them farewell, bringing to an end their annual residence in Ramnagar. The palace courtyard is not part of the acting space until this episode, which is interpolated in the performance text and does not occur in the *Ramcharitmanas*.

The Maharaja regulates the ebb and flow of the presentation on a scale quite different from the *vyas*.

The *vyas* exists primarily inside the performance, as prompter, stage manager, and director, but the Maharaja exists crucially outside it as well. During the course of the Lila, the Maharaja offers himself in several different capacities, guises, and roles: at one and the same time he is king, god, and actor. Clearly, his identity receives support from the spectacle, for his majesty is at no time spotlighted and displayed, as during the Ramlila month. He is demonstrably king: his Cadillac, horse-driven carriage, elephants, and armed constabulary band are there for all to see, part of the spectacle that thousands assemble to witness. But he is meant to be the *pratik* (symbol, pointer, representative) of Siva, patron deity of the city. Therefore, while showing himself as king, he also shows himself as God's representative. During the Lila, every time he passes on his chosen vehicle, the people call out *Har har Mahadev* ('Hail Mahadev', or Siva), just as they shout *Bol Sri Ramchandra ki jay* ('Say victory to Ramchandra') for Ram.

As king and as Siva's symbol, the Maharaja has some very special privileges. By custom, the daily performance cannot begin if he (or a member of his family) is not present. Most importantly, he has the power to interrupt the performance; when he goes for his evening prayers the Lila stops, and restarts only when he returns. In a sense, he is as important as the principal players. As an actor in the story, he misses only one event, the slaying of Ravana on Dussehra, observing the royal protocol that a king must not witness the death of another. On Dussehra, he cuts across the Lila space and goes back to his palace. Once he departs, the last battle in which Ravana dies is enacted.

Primarily a devotional narrative, with the *swarups* actually revered as deities, the Ramnagar Ramlila has a mix of codes like the interpolation of the Maharaja's presence, and rituals like the *arati* (invocation) and *jhankis* that recall popular iconographical traditions. Another aspect of this mix is the colloquial entertainment and informal fun that range from the boisterous misdeeds of the demon army to the *mela* (festival) that surrounds the performance area with food, toy shops, Ferris wheels, and bioscope machines.   AK

Norvin Hein, *The Miracle Plays of Mathura* (New Haven: Yale University Press, 1972); Anuradha Kapur, *Actors, Pilgrims, Kings and Gods: The Ramlila at Ramnagar* (Calcutta: Seagull, 1990); Richard Schechner, *Performative Circumstances from the Avant Garde to Ramlila* (Calcutta: Seagull, 1983).

Ras Lila, Manipuri (derived from the Ras dance): Manipur's contribution to court theatres of the

world. It is an ethnic version in song, dance, drama, and *ritual of Krishna's mythical divine play with the Gopis (milkmaids) of Vrindavan. The text comes from the *Ras panchadhyay* ('five chapters on Ras', or cantos 29–33) in the tenth book of the *Bhagavata Purana*. The performance was first organized for five days till the full moon of Kartik (November) in 1779. Govinda (Krishna) was crowned as God-king at an auspicious moment in the new capital Langthabal (Canchipur, in Imphal West district), and the Ras Lila was presented that evening and subsequently for five nights.

King Chingthangkhomba, alias Bhagyachandra (1763–98), had finally liberated Manipur from Burmese occupation, and had also witnessed the religious crisis of the time, involving debates on the foreign religion of Hinduism threatening to supplant native Meitei faith. Sectarian violence, conflicts on interpretations, disparate discourses in court circles continued to create an atmosphere of tension. The disturbed world of Manipur needed a healing system to dispel fears and anxieties, and Chingthangkhomba attempted to provide this spiritually satisfying polity. Although personally a convert to Gauriya Vaishnavism, he did not set aside the traditional beliefs and practices which constituted the primal religious core of the majority.

The indigenized Ras Lila embodied this grand synthesis.

He fused the oppositional Hindu and Meitei belief systems with a creative representation of the self into the other. The centre of the Meitei universe, located in the navel of the body politic represented by Kangla, seat of the serpent-dragon Pakhangba, was synthesized by placing Govinda in the centre with a close motif of Pakhangba carved in the navel of the wooden idol. The native concept of God-king was expanded with Govinda's coronation, and Chingthangkhomba symbolically reduced himself to a simple servant and arranger of the divine revelry. Vrindavanchandra (Krishna as lord of Vrindavan) was declared crown prince and Rama (of the *Ramayana*) commander-in-chief.

The presentation of the God-king amidst the Gopis in the Ras Lila was also associated with the dedication of Chingthangkhomba's daughter Vimbabati Manjari to Govinda, and the Maha (great) Ras performed on this auspicious occasion was in reality the betrothal of a princess to divinity, not simple role-playing of Raseshwari by her. It was an ingenious kinship world-view of relationship with the Lord, for He became the devotee's son-in-law, possibly blasphemous in classical Hindu mores. Vimbabati, when she played Raseshwari in the enactment, was worshipped by *arati* (sacred fire) together with Govinda's idol at the centre of the mandala, having been conceived as welded together in union in the early hours of dawn. In future representations of Radha's idol at Govinda's side, the face of Krishna's consort was carved like a mask, an indigenous identification of female energy in Meitei beliefs. Therefore it did not seem strange that a foreign god was placed at the uxorilocal centre of the native bride, marrying the indigenous virgin and becoming God of her people and kingdom.

Access to the Lord through the female principle was the sole motif of the entire *Raslila tradition. It suited the newly entering Gauriya Vaishnavism too. Here access to Govinda was through the psycho-spiritual perceptions of the Bengali religious teacher Chaitanya, himself regarded as the reincarnation of Krishna and Radha, whose sport experienced by him via female feeling (Radha *bhava*) was adopted by Manipuris as the means to enter the divine sphere. The enactment is centred at Vrindavan, a historical space, yet dehistoricized and re-enacted into the ancestral world of the deities, an imaginary cosmic realm from whose environment and sexual rites ancient Meitei kings and queens drew energy and creative strength. The whole process of entry into this realm, dramatization of sport, ritual of culmination through sexual union, and derivation of spiritual energy was an already refined practice of pre-Hindu

Ras Lila within a temporary *mandap* in Manipur

Meitei culture. A foreign text was structured into a performance system inlaid with a corpus of indigenous cultural expressions. Ras Lila was thus a spiritual production deeply ingrained with Meitei political, social, and sexual behaviour.

Raslila as depicted in the *Ras panchadhyay* delineates simply the love, union, separation, and reunion of God with His devotees. The Maha Ras enacts the unfolding of the divine play as determined in the Gopis' prayers at Katyayani Puja, to have the Lord as their husband. His flute calling them, their arrival leaving various mundane tasks, the dialogue between Him and them on the householder's principles, His beseeching them to go back to their husbands, and their refusal to do so comprise the sequence of love. The sport of union then begins, each Gopi by herself in self-actualization through the Lord, thereby developing an inner pride of possession, which is not the way of relationship with Him. Suddenly each Krishna believed to have been individually realized vanishes, and the Gopis are traumatized in their anguish of separation and search for the relationship's real meaning. The lead Gopi, Radha, suffers the same fate, and they collectively seek the Lord on the banks of the Jamuna river. Krishna reveals Himself at an

appropriate time, after the dissolution of individual egos. The final consummation of the ritual union is marked by *jugal arati*, joint worship by sacred fire at the composite image of the male and female principles.

The performance text is elaborate. The Meiteis approach the divine celebration through two autonomous components structurally united to embody the entire *yajna* (sacrifice) in the realm of the deities. An all-male prologue of song, dance, and drumming termed Nata Sankirtana (actors' kirtan procession), a Vaishnava perfor- mance motif, precedes the enactment. Sixty-four singer- dancer-drummers in a chorus, wearing white dhotis and turbans, build up the atmosphere of entry to the divine sport. Then follows the main text by *sutra*s (singers) at the north-western edge of the space, a north-Indian import with native directional beliefs. An all-women cast of Gopis in richly accoutred dress enters the mandala where Govinda's wooden idol has been ritually placed. In the palace, where the performance began, the 8-year- old Krishna is not impersonated; only Govinda's idol is in the middle, around which the Gopis dance. Later, in the sacred courtyard of Vijay Govinda (the king's uncle's residence) and in villages, a boy or girl represented Krishna. At another ritually connected precinct, Ningthoukhong, the Lord's statue is placed in the pavilion and the young Krishna's role also played.

Sankirtana, considered the *purvaranga* by the elite, has a rigid code following *Lai Haraoba traditions, as a classless, non-hierarchical journey into the ancestral world. The entire congregation of performers constitutes participants in the primal enactment of creation, *hakchang sagatpa* (formation of the body), through which all senses unfold. They imagine the formation of Gauranga (Chaitanya) in their mind's eye, and sing and dance out His experiences. All body movements are inspired by the continuous serpentine motif of renewal and fertility. Journey into the divine realm is also one into the world of the dead, hence the dancers used to show few facial expressions. Outward behaviour atmospherically represented mortuary sequences, or communion with ancestors. The professional purveyors today betray these principles. Until recently, amateurs performed and attended to Govinda's daily rituals through the *lallup* system (periodic labour for public service). They included the king, nobility, and members of the royal household. Commoners and aristocracy mixed in performance, essential to the culture since dead parents were assured a place in heaven once an individual joined Sankirtana. In 1779, Chingthangkhomba himself played the lead drum, representing Advaita, Chaitanya's companion.

In the Maha Ras, realization of the nature of God is revealed, human awareness of the absolute experientially gained through the soul, and the five elements—*sabda* (sound, ether), *sparsha* (touch, wind), *rupa* (form, fire), *rasa* (taste, water), *gandha* (smell, earth)—are articulated in the consciousness. The ultimate arrival of the union and its necessity are heralded through the true sound of the flute, the call for the play. Touch is heightened when Krishna plays with each Gopi and the sensation of the coming union is anticipated as the wind. Pain, suffering, and re-examination provide enlightenment on the nature of the relationship with the Lord, signified by form, or the fire of recognition. The dance of the final union, in conscious abandonment, creates the taste, the awareness of God, and the eternal principles of male and female energies coalesce as water. At the end of the rapturous exercise, the Gopis lay down their clothes on the sand, ask questions on love and devotion, and arrive at the eternal truth of God's place in their universe, where everything is in Him, an essence signalled by smell, the sensory principle represented by earth.

Scholars divide the genre according to the seasonal cycle of

Ras performed by Krishna: Basanta ('spring', at the vernal full moon, reflecting the play of red vermilion between Krishna and the Gopis), Kunja ('bower', in Asvin or October), Maha Ras (at the full moon in Kartik or November), Nitya or Narta ('everyday', performable any time in villages), and Divya ('daytime', not allowed in the palace, but in villages and other areas). In all of them, the celebratory nature of man's relationship with the divine is experienced through performance.

LA

Rasa (literally 'juice', 'flavour'): In traditional Indian aesthetic *theory, the creative process emerges from the *rasa* experience of the poet/artist and is concretized in the *anukirtana* (re-telling) of *bhava (emotive states) in the dramatic text or the work of art—poetry, painting, sculpture, and so on. Ancient Indian culture had an integrated view of creativity and aesthetics, based in a holistic view of the universe and a circular concept of time. Therefore, *Sanskrit theatre became a means of realizing this intense, immediate, and direct *rasa*, or aesthetic experience, also known by such synonyms as relishing (*rasana, asvadana*), mastication (*carvana*), flash of wonder (*camatkara*), immersion (*nivesa*), and enjoyment (*bhoga*).

Bharata declares in the *Natyasastra, 'Nothing proceeds on the stage without reference to *rasa*.' He and his commentators emphasize that when all the components of the drama beginning with *vibhava* (the stimulus of the *bhava* and the environment in which it takes place) and *anubhava* (the 'consequents' expressive of the *bhava*s) are presented, the realization of *rasa* manifests itself in the spectator. Conversely, when any element required for the manifestation of *rasa* is missing, the realization is rendered difficult, indirect, or incomplete. Thus theatre is viewed experientially as *rasa*. While *anukirtana* of the *bhava*s is a creative act in the sense of *kriya* (practice), *rasa* is an experience of the self—the subtlest, most intrinsic, indivisible, fundamental, fullest, and purest aspect of the consciousness.

This holistic artistic process requires music and dance as integral elements, besides theatre, in order to infuse *ranjana* (pleasure) and *sobha* (beauty). Music causes instant experience of delight, while dance instils stylized beauty through visual action and behaviour. The manner in which the performer elaborates the *bhava*s and the surroundings given in the theatrical text, through movement, gesture, facial expression, songs, and music, lies at the heart of the *rasa* system. The difference between Indian and Western modes of presentation has been analysed as follows: 'Rather than acting out on stage an important action as is usual in Western drama—the death of a character, for example—in Sanskrit practice the character is shown reacting to that action. The performer mirrors in ever more elaborate patterns the chain of emotional responses that an action triggers. Dramatic form and theatrical technique, it could be said, are designed to reveal and to express emotional states, and it is the audience response to those emotional states that is Rasa.'

Since cosmic multiplicity was created through the primordial act of sacrifice, unity may be regained through the same sacrificial act, freeing the self from its limitations of temporality and spatiality. The same creative act takes place in the sphere of aesthetic experience. Beginning with an awareness of the physical world of relationships, the *sahridaya* (literally 'same heart', or sympathetic connoisseur) of Indian art, literature, and performance attains *atmavisranti* ('repose in self') for a moment and experiences *rasa* by ultimately transcending the duality of ordinary temporal and spatial differentiations. Although it begins with the delineation of *bhavas*, the point of culmination is *sadharanikarana* ('to generalize',

depersonalization or universalization), in which these *bhavas* appear neither belonging or not belonging to the *sahridaya*, nor belonging or not belonging to others (whether enemy, friend, or someone quite indifferent), for there is neither affirmation nor negation of specific relationships at the stage of universalization. This aesthetic experience is defined as *anuvyavasaya* (re-perception). *Rasa* is, thus, awareness of the unfragmented self. Hence it is wonderful.

The *rasas* recognized in Sanskrit poetics are *sringara* (erotic), *hasya* (comic), *karuna* (pathetic), *raudra* (furious), *vira* (heroic), *bhayanaka* (terrible), *bibhatsa* (odious), and *adbhuta* (marvellous). *Santa* (peaceful) *rasa* was added later. Each corresponds to an equivalent *sthayi* (stable) *bhava*. They can appear in various permutations in individual plays, as long as the abiding *rasa* remains one and undisturbed. KDT

Raniero Gnoli, *The Aesthetic Experience According to Abhinavagupta* (Varanasi: Chowkhamba, 1968); V.M. Kulkarni (ed.), *Some Aspects of the Rasa Theory* (Delhi: Motilal Banarsidass, 1986); J.L. Masson and M.V. Patwardhan, *Aesthetic Rapture: The Rasadhyaya of the Natyasastra* (Poona: Deccan College, 1970); J.L. Masson and M.V. Patwardhan, *Santarasa and Abhinavagupta's Philosophy of Aesthetics* (Poona: Bhandarkar Oriental Research Institute, 1969); Hari Ram Mishra, *The Theory of Rasa in Sanskrit Drama* (Bhopal: Vindhyachal, 1964);

V. Raghavan, *The Number of Rasas* (Madras: Adyar Library, 1975); V. Raghavan, *Sanskrit Drama: Its Aesthetics and Production* (Madras: V. Raghavan, 1993); Rakesagupta, *Psychological Studies in 'Rasa'* (Banaras: Banaras Hindu University, 1950); *Rasa-bhaava Darshan* (Delhi: Clarion, 1997); A. Sankaran, *The Theories of Rasa and Dhvani* (Madras: University of Madras, 1973); Susan Schwartz, *Rasa: Performing the Divine in India* (New York: Columbia University Press, 2004).

Rasdhari: originally a name given to the performers of *Raslila, it now signifies a popular form that evolved when the original spread westwards to the adjoining Hadoti and Mewati regions of eastern Rajasthan. Raslila contains episodes from Krishna legend, but Rasdhari incorporated stories from Rama's life and other myths too. It occupies a geographical and artistic middle ground between Raslila and *Khyal of Rajasthan, perhaps closer to the latter with its combination of entertaining dance, song, and dialogue. Although it started as a community activity expressing devotional joy, troupes have become professional, performances serving as their livelihood. As in other north Indian forms, an open (often circular) space at ground level serves as the acting area. There is no provision for furniture; if required, one of the artists functions as a chair or stool. Spectators watch from all sides, the actors entering amidst them and the musicians sitting with the audience.

PAg

Raslila (from the Ras dance and the term *Lila): one of the most fascinating traditional theatres of north India, particularly the Braj region of western Uttar Pradesh, which speaks Brajbhasha, a variety of Hindi. Strongly devotional and ritualistic in purpose as well as form, it uniquely combines the poetic word, music, dance, and colourful tableaux. Its themes almost exclusively deal with the playful childhood and adolescent life of Krishna, incarnation of the god Vishnu, during his mythical stay in Gokul and Vrindavan, near the ancient town of Mathura in Braj.

The Ras dance is still prevalent in some parts of the country, specifically Manipur in the east (see *Ras Lila) and Saurashtra (Gujarat) in the west. With the rise of the religious Krishna Bhakti movement in and after the fifteenth century in Braj, it acquired a more dramatic character and structure and came to be called Raslila. The troupes, based in that region, perform all the year round, especially during the rainy season, throughout India, before large audiences of mainly devotees but also theatre enthusiasts. Distinctively, only young boys in their late childhood or early adolescence are recruited as performers, who have to retire as they reach puberty.

Raslila is staged both open-air and indoor, on a simple usually round platform, with viewers on three sides squatting on cotton mats and white sheets on the ground. A plain or decorative back curtain called *pichhwai* covers the fourth side, in front of which are two thrones for the main characters, Krishna and his beloved Radha (called *swarup*s or incarnations, worshipped by the devotees as actual deities), and some tiered or stepped seats for the Sakhis (Radha's companions) at their side. The performance space is generally treated as sacred, which spectators enter after removing their shoes. The actors are hidden by another curtain, hand-held or hanging from rings run on wire across the stage, before, during the performance at climactic points, and at the end. The *samaji*s (singers and instrumentalists) and Swami (producer and proprietor of the *mandali* or company, also the chief singer) remain visible throughout.

The music, though predominantly classical in earlier times, has over the years creatively blended with folk music. The traditional instruments are sarangi (and now frequently the ubiquitous harmonium), double-ended *pakhavaj* drums, dholak and/or tabla, and small cymbals. Characteristic costuming and make-up are important features and every troupe has a trained specialist named the *sringari*, who carefully makes up and dresses the *swarup*s. The facial make-up of Krishna and Radha is suggestive of the divine, and Krishna's attractive crown (*mukut*) and clothes provide a touch of fantasy, but the rest of the colourful costumes are stylized versions of the everyday garb worn in Braj.

In the beginning, as soon as all are seated, the Swami followed by the *samaji*s sing the *mangalacharan*, a benedictory prayer, concluding with another song by the Swami. Before it ends, the Sakhis stand up on both sides of the divine couple to perform and sing the *arati*, a propitiatory welcome, with a lighted oil lamp placed on a plate. The number and duration of the songs vary with the occasion. After the *arati*, the Sakhis tell Radha and Krishna that it is time to perform the Ras. The present structure of the performance, which evolved and changed in various ways since the inception, consists of two parts: *nityaras* and *lila*. The *nityaras* is a somewhat self-contained but intrinsic prologue to the *lila*. Krishna accepts the Sakhis' request and pleads with Radha to join him in a fascinating sequence of mime and song specifically composed for the purpose. Eventually Radha agrees, both get up and the *nityaras* starts with a solo or choral song followed by collective dances.

Most of the choreography—solo, duet, and group—is circular, climaxing in a vigorous, agile, and highly accomplished knee dance by Krishna alone. After this exhausting display all return to their seats for a brief interlude. Sometimes a hand-held curtain is brought in to allow them to relax while the Swami continues singing. Following this dance-oriented phase, the *pravachana* (sermon) is presented in which Krishna, through songs or in lyrical prose supported by dance, expounds the reasons for his incarnation, the importance of bhakti, or some of the basic precepts in the *Bhagavad Gita*. This exposition of faith by a charming young performer is so surcharged and lyrical that it does not seem didactic, and enchants both devotees and ordinary spectators by its theatricality.

Then begins the second phase of *nityaras*, in which the performers, including Radha and Krishna, sing alone, in duet, or together, with the *samaji*s frequently joining. Although dances also intersperse this portion, the emphasis falls on songs. The final phase of *nityaras* is the *jhanki* (tableau). The *swarup*s return to their seats behind the curtain where the *sringari*s, with only a handful of properties and costumes, prepare an eye-filling and spectacular freeze while the *samaji*s continue their lilting songs. When the curtain is removed, the sight produces great jubilation and exuberant expression of fervour and piety in spectators, who pay their respect to the divine couple and present money and gifts to the troupe. This period of appreciation over, the curtain is drawn, and the *swarup*s retire to the green room.

After a brief interval the *lila* begins. It is more dramatic, enacting situations using straightforward or rhythmic dialogue, song, movement, dance, and spectacle. The most popular episodes include Krishna's birth in a prison in Mathura where his uncle Kamsa holds his parents captive; his father, Vasudev, secretly carrying him to Gokul for protection, to stay with the local chieftain Nanda and his wife Yashoda; Krishna's childhood pranks with his foster parents and their boundless love for the precocious boy; his quietly eating butter and curd, and pretended innocence when caught; his slaying of demons like Kaliya and Putana, and lifting of Govardhan hill on his finger to protect the villagers from the fury of the rain god Indra; his popularity with village boys and Gopis (milkmaids), and innocently amorous dalliance with the latter, particularly concealing their clothes while they bathe in the river Yamuna, teasing them in various ways, or dancing with them in the Vrinda forest meadows; his eventual return to Mathura and, after killing Kamsa, enthroning his father; and the Gopis' pangs of separation.

A number of devotee-poets have written on these themes. While many important Brajbhasha poets, such as the great Surdas and Nandadas, composed mainly lyrics on various aspects of Krishna's childhood and adolescence, quite a few also wrote *lila*s intended for performance. They include Hita Harivansha (1502–52), Hariram Vyas (1510–98), Hita Dhruvadas (1573–1643), Brijavasidas (1703–63), Chacha Vrindavanadas (*c.* 1708–93), Narayana Swami (1828–1900), Swami Meghashyam (1900–62), Swami Ladlisharan Goswami (1891–1978), and, among contemporary artists, Harigovind Sharma, Ram Swarup Sharma, and Shriram and Fatehkrishna Sharma, who also run their own troupes. In recent decades, besides imaginary or unexplored incidents from the life of Radha and Krishna, *lila*s related hagiographies of many well-known mythical *bhakta*s (devotees) like Sudama, Krishna's poor friend of his adolescent years, Dhruva, and Prahlad.

The plays, like ancient *Sanskrit theatre, are *rasa-oriented and present quite a wide gamut of the generalized emotions such as faith, love, valour, and humour. They imaginatively and theatrically fuse the narrative and the lyrical, the ritualistic and the aesthetic, everyday reality and fantasy, devotional ecstasy and common sentiments. That is possibly the secret of Raslila's survival as a performance tradition and its popularity among large sections of people.   NJ

John Hawley, *At Play with Krishna: Pilgrimage Dramas from Brindavan* (Princeton: Princeton University Press, 1981); Norvin Hein, *The Miracle Plays of Mathura* (Delhi: Oxford University Press, 1972); David Kinsley, *The Divine Player: A Study of Krsna Lila* (Delhi: Motilal Banarsidass, 1979); Selina Thielemann, *Rasalila* (New Delhi: APH, 1998); M.L. Varadpande, *Krishna Theatre in India* (New Delhi: Abhinav, 1982).

Ravana Chhaya ('Ravana's shadow'): the traditional *shadow-theatre form of *puppetry in Orissa. It is noteworthy that though this style draws exclusively upon the Rama legend, its name comes from Ravana, his adversary. The usual explanation is that Rama, a god, hence a luminous being, cannot have a shadow. Therefore this shadow theatre is named after Ravana. We may question the plausibility of this explanation since Rama's figure does cast a shadow in Ravana Chhaya. Moreover, it is not designed in any special manner, whereas Ravana's figure towers in comparison and looks much more bold and dramatic.

This has led to the surmise that Ravana's importance over Rama could reflect the influence of Buddhism and Jainism, the two religions that held sway over Kalinga (ancient Orissa) 2000 years ago. It is not known what version of Rama's story Ravana Chhaya followed earlier, but for the last hundred years or so it has delivered the text of *Vichitra Ramayana* by Vishvanath Khuntia, a medieval Oriya poet.

The puppets are made of opaque deerskin and cast black and white shadows in bold dramatic poses. To keep them straight, split bamboo sticks are attached vertically, which have a handle at the lower end. Many props such as trees, mountains, chariots, are also used to create appropriate 'sets'. Ravana Chhaya figures are quite simple. Off screen they look neither artistic nor attractive, but their shadows formed by shimmering golden lamplight acquire a breathtaking beauty. Although small in size—the largest no more than a metre in height—and without jointed limbs, they create very powerful yet lyrical shadows, especially when manipulated in the puppeteers' peculiar jerky movement.

A bowl-shaped earthen lamp, filled with castor oil and lit with two thick wicks made of cotton rags soaked in oil, forms the light source. The lamp is placed on a stand made of a bamboo stick with a small wooden plank fixed to one side. The height of the stand is so adjusted that the lamp is about 30–37 cm from the bottom of the screen at the central line. The distance between light and screen is at most 30 cm; the manipulators raise the puppets in between while sitting on the ground.

The leader stands on the other side of the screen in full view of the audience, singing and playing a *khanjani* (a small frame drum) held in his hands. A vocalist often assists him from behind the screen. All of them deliver the impromptu prose dialogue for the puppets, but the soul of the performance is music. The songs admirably blend both folk and classical Odissi, specially the traditional Chhanda form in which all the poems of the *Vichitra Ramayana* are composed. Besides *khanjani*, a pair of wooden castanets called *daskathi* provides percussive accompaniment to the singing.

Kathinanda Das, born into a village family of hereditary Ravana Chhaya puppeteers in 1909, single-handedly kept the form alive in modern times. He crafted as well as manipulated his puppets, and handed the technique down to Kolha Charan Sahoo (1936–), president and guru of the Ravana

Chhaya Sansad since 1986, and author of a book on the form, who took his puppets on performances all over India.   JP

Jiwan Pani, *Ravana Chhaya* (New Delhi: Sangeet Natak Akademi, 1983).

Ritual: Traditional theatre in India is deeply embedded in ritual, a characteristic collectivist activity generated by religion and faith. Societal ties with ancestral spirits or supernatural forces are institutionalized in procedures of repetitive action believed to be efficacious. Blessings of deities are sought, that the community is protected from sickness, calamity or death, that living possessions in domestic animals do not fall prey to disease or epidemic, that plentiful harvests or bountiful rains follow, and that harmony with nature prevails. Mourners undergoing social oblivion in mortuary rites become reinstated to communal equilibrium through rites of passage. When people searched for association with the divine, special mediums developed professionally to facilitate the relationship. Their intense practices imbibed non-corporeal, spiritual faculties or characters (see *possession) to help ease the subjects' transcendence. These phenomena were possible only through ritual.

Cyclical community performances incorporating dance, music, formalized movement, feasts, appeasement of malignant spirits, offerings of food, vegetables, fruits, flowers or aromas, processional and celebratory events, pervade ancient agricultural civilizations. Fertility, abundance, peace, and avoidance of evil concerned warring or martial societies, too, where ritualistic life brought order and sanity to an otherwise relentless world habitually engaged with insecurity and survival. The religious and intellectual elite developed deep philosophies to sustain the world view, manifested by the masses in physical enactment of the cosmic order. Subterranean forces were eased by the repeated action and routine of ritual participants in free and creative abandon, giving them the self-belief necessary to face oncoming disasters or danger. Ritual, therefore, was not simply a culture of primitive, non-rationalist, pre-modern societies. Highly advanced spirituality, non-materialism, and universality of thought and wisdom were associated with it.

Indian theatre automatically reflected such attitudes, though such ancient proto-theatre as the Manipuri *Lai Haraoba epitomizes ritual performance. Both classical and popular forms presented stories of ancestral heroes, narratives of

The Nagamandala ritual in Karnataka

mythic lore and legends as communicative acts to link the mundane with the world of special forces. In *theory, the whole production formed a ritual, founded on the Hindu philosophical premise that life is *Lila, a divine play. In addition, *Sanskrit theatre specified elaborate preliminaries (*purvaranga*) that connected the performance with an act of worship. The citizens were disciplined through the enactment of familiar movements and procedures, volitional acts, mantras, and chants that could effect beneficial changes in the course of nature. Even now, the *sutradhara* explicitly voices a benedictory *nandi* to invoke blessings of gods and goddesses. To this day, an urban performer may ritualistically touch the stage floor before entry as a symbolic act of personal faith and to elicit good fortune.

Ritual was consciously studied and became part of the larger intercultural research in the twentieth-century quest for theatrical experimentation. After Antonin Artaud identified Asian theatre as an inexhaustible source of ritual practices, Euro-American scholars and directors led such ventures, resulting not only in academic discourse, but also in productions by Jerzy Grotowski, Peter Brook, Richard Schechner, and Eugenio Barba in the 1970s and 1980s that knowledgeably derived ritualistic elements from Indian theatre.

Efforts by contemporary Indian artists to use aspects of ritual were noticed mainly in Kerala, Tamil Nadu, Karnataka, and Manipur, where ancient theatrical ritual remained strongly embedded in tradition. Western practitioners, confronting an angst of lost community severed (since the European Renaissance, when religious drama began to decline) by secularism, industrialization, and capitalism, produced new social ceremonials innovatively bringing spectators into a rediscovery of the modern community. On the other hand, Indian directors vibrantly explored the living nuances of an ongoing culture, creating imagery and patterns evoking subtle effects and aesthetic novelties based on previously undiscovered motifs (as by S. Ramanujam), but helping to reinforce conventional spiritual expressions. The world of ritual in theatre and theatre in ritual has substantive potential for deeper insights into human communication and exchange.   LA

Carl Georg Bohne, *Primitive Stage* (Calcutta: Firma K.L. Mukhopadhyay, 1971); J. Gonda, *Vedic Ritual* (Leiden: Brill, 1980); Natalia Lidova, *Drama and Ritual of Early Hinduism* (Delhi: Motilal Banarsidass, 1994); Fritz Staal, *Agni—The Vedic Ritual of the Fire Altar* (Berkeley: University of California, 1983).

Sakhi-kundhei Nata (literally 'woman-companion doll dance'): the traditional string *puppetry still extant in Orissa. So far only a few troupes of this fascinating form have been located in remote rural areas. It is not clear why the epithet *sakhi* is used to designate their puppets. Some surmise that the name arose because the form earlier used to present shows based exclusively on Krishna legends, which feature Radha's *sakhi*s (female companions). According to another opinion, *sakhi* is often used as a term of endearment; since the puppets are cute dolls and acquire a kind of life when manipulated, they were endearingly called *sakhi-kundhei*.

The puppets are made of light wood and, like the *Kathputli of Rajasthan, have no legs but long flowing skirts. However, they have more joints as the hands and torso are also made of wood. Figures representing major characters have joints at their neck, shoulders, and elbows as well. Five to seven strings attached to the puppet are usually tied to a triangular wooden prop. Orissa temple sculptures and *pothi chitra*s (drawings in palm-leaf manuscripts) have inspired the conception of most puppets. The costumes, music, and style of presentation are somewhat similar to those of the *Yatra, operatic in character, where singing dominates over prose dialogue. The puppeteers' prose dialogues are often impromptu. The music admirably blends folk with sophisticated Odissi, the singing style close to that of the traditional Chhanda form.   JP

Samavakara (from the root 'to disperse'): form of *Sanskrit theatre in which a multitude of things huddled together. The story, pertaining to gods and demons, was well known and presented in three acts. It had twelve high-spirited characters, all famous divinities and demons. It had to represent the triple doctrine of dharma, *artha* (material gains such as property, kingdom, wealth), and *kama* (sensual desire, voluptuousness), the threefold circumvention of delusion (caused by nature, an enemy, and fate), and the three *vidrava*s of confusion (caused by inanimate things, animals, and human beings). Composed in a variety of metres, principally the *gayatri* and *ushnih*, it stressed the *vira* (heroic) *rasa, seldom employed the *kaisiki* (graceful) *vritti*, and used the thirteen elements of *vithi as needed. Vatsaraja's *Samudramanthana* ('Churning of the Ocean', twelfth century) is a rare extant play of this variety. Significantly, the *Natyasastra refers to this mythical episode as the first drama ever performed— *Amritamanthana* ('Churning of the Nectar') in the presence of Siva—but that text has not survived.   KDT

Sanga (literally 'impersonation'): Sindhi folk form in which the actors (Sangi) were presented in the guise of Hindu mythological characters. Sanga used to be performed during the religious festivals of Dussehra, Janmashtami, and Holi. During Dussehra (celebrating Rama's victory) and Janmashtami (Krishna's birth), the Sangis impersonated Rama, Sita, Hanuman, Krishna, Kamsa, and others, gathering at one place to enact, but not necessarily adhere to, episodes from the *Ramayana* and *Bhagavata Purana*. At Holi, they wore the get-up and make-up of eerie characters who formed part of a procession followed by *shernai* (the double-reed *shahnai*) players and drum beaters. In village streets, they performed absurd stories with unconnected scenes composed by them, often not in decent language. After the Partition in 1947, when Sindhi Hindus migrated to India, Sanga lost its lustre and is no more in vogue.   PA

Sanghakali (literally 'group drama'), also known as Chattirankam, Sastrankam, Yatrakali, and Panenkali: socio-religious entertainment of the Nambudiri Brahmans in Kerala. In the context of this art *sangham* has the added connotation of a group engaged in gymnastic practice. Significantly, *chattiran* means 'warrior' and *ankam*, 'action'.

No authentic evidence survives to precisely fix the period when it evolved. Scholars think that the Nambudiris reached Kerala between the sixth and eighth centuries. However, the Sanghakali songs available now, in the mix of Malayalam and Sanskrit known as Manipravalam, can only claim an antiquity of about 600 years.

Oral history says that Sanghakali originated at a time when the Nambudiris commonly practised animal sacrifice in their rituals, considered taboo by believers of Buddhism. Cheraman Perumal, Buddhist ruler of the Chera dynasty in the tenth century, forbade animal sacrifice and persecuted the Brahmans, who took refuge in a temple at Trikkariyur village. An unknown ascetic (supposedly the epic sage Parasurama, believed to have rehabilitated the Nambudiris) visited them and advised them to form a congregation to recite the *nalupadam* mantra representing the quintessence of the four Vedas, for fulfilment of their mission. The Nambudiris who assembled at the conclave finally organized themselves into a militia to fight the ruler.

Sanghakali has ritualistic as well as artistic implications. The performance is called *satram*, which denotes a holy sacrifice of long duration. This *ritual used to be conducted as a family function in connection with marriages and other ceremonies such as feeding children

their first meal, naming them, or investing a Brahman boy with the sacred thread. On the night before the *satram*, the frontage of the house where the ritual takes place is decorated with a lit bell-metal lamp, betel leaves, areca nuts, coconuts, and flowers. The participants, in martial outfits, reach the gate to the accompaniment of drums. They offer salutations to the lamp, ceremoniously arm themselves with sword and shield, and sing the *pukkulamala* ('garland of flower clusters') in praise of the presiding deity of the village.

In the morning a percussion ensemble plays; at a music session in the afternoon, the participants provide rhythm to their own vocals on big copper vessels (*chembu*) turned upside down. After the evening bath and prayer the *nalupadam* hymn is ceremoniously rendered in front of the lamp—the most significant part of the ritual. During dinner the group recites passages (*kari* slokas) describing the delicious dishes served. The *titturam vayana*, or reading of the decree, comes next: a pronouncement on an epic or contemporary situation that enlivens the dramatic effect for the ensuing performance. Then the troupe sings *vanchippattu* (boat ballads) recalling a historical *chattiran* exodus by sea.

The all-night performance before the lamp commences with *pana*, an auspicious musical prelude.

Many interesting characters appear, having the flavour of life. Kaimal, also known as Ittikkandappan, is a comic representative of decadent aristocracy, made fun of for his disreputable stand of siding with the ruler in persecuting the Nambudiris. Other characters like Muttiyamma (old woman), Kallukudiyan (drunkard), and Kuratti (gypsy) enter, fascinating the audience through dance, music, and dialogue. The performance has the nature of a variety show because it reflects, as if in a mirror, many popular arts and hence has a loosely-knit structure. The main appeal is its contemporaneity of social satire and rich humour, besides artistic agility and gusto.   KNP

Sangita Natakam (musical drama): From ancient times, the Tamil language was classified under three distinct categories, *iyal* (prose), *icai* (lyric), and *natakam* (drama). We also discover in the Sangam works (second century) the widespread tradition of Panars (minstrels) who, playing musical instruments, used to criss-cross the Tamil country singing lyrics of love and panegyrics praising kings and feudal chiefs, in dramatized form. On more formal stages, however, dance performances giving expression to songs passed for theatre. From commentaries on the *Cilappatikaram*, we learn that numerous texts on *natakam* dealt with the grammar of *music and *dance.

Epigraphic evidence testifies that one *Rajarajesvara natakam* ('Drama of Lord Rajaraja') was performed in the Brihadeswara temple precincts at Thanjavur during the reign of Rajendra Chola (1014–44) eulogizing his father, Rajaraja Chola (985–1014). It seems to have been a story presented by a dancer to musical accompaniment. During the time of the Telugu Nayak chieftains who ruled Tamil Nadu in the seventeenth and eighteenth centuries, the *Yakshaganam of Andhra was introduced, and many such librettos composed. Some survive in palm-leaf manuscripts at the Madras Oriental Library and Saraswati Mahal Library, Thanjavur, such as *Nili yakshaganam* ('Nili's Yakshaganam'), *Sarangadeva yakshaganam* ('Sarangadeva's Yakshaganam'), *Sirutonda yakshaganam* ('Sirutonda's Yakshaganam'), and *Narasimha vijaya yakshaganam* ('Yakshaganam of Narasimha's Victory'). *Vattala Rajan yakshaganam* ('Vattala Raja's Yakshaganam'), *Madana Sundara vilasam* ('Madana Sundara's *Vilasam'), *Pandiya Keli vilasa natakam* ('Vilasam Drama of Pandiya Keli'), and *Pururava natakam*

('Pururava's Drama') have been published. These, as distinct from Kannada *Yakshagana, can be classed as operatic, since their stories unfold in the form of dramatized songs. *Bhagavata Mela uses similar Telugu texts.

These apart, all popular commercial *Tamil theatre till the time it was chased out by the craze for the talkies comprised operatic work to which the term Sangita Natakam strictly applies. All discourse was in classical Carnatic music, there were hardly any prose dialogues, and the actors vied with one another in exhibiting their singing prowess. Cinema lifted this musical form of presentation lock, stock, and barrel while succeeding and replacing theatre as favoured entertainment. Hit productions were made into films and singing stars of the stage became film stars. But the theatrical trend continued till the late 1940s. To its credit, Sangita Natakam gave a platform to legendary exponents of Carnatic classical, in turn making that music not the exclusive preserve of elites and connoisseurs, but popular among the untutored masses. It threw up names like S.G. Kittappa, K.B. Sundarambal, M.K. Thyagaraja Bhagavathar, and P.U. Chinappa, and employed giants of the classical concert establishment like Maharajapuram Vishwanatha Iyer, Rajaratnam Pillai, M.S. Subbulakshmi,

Dandapani Desikar, N.C. Vasantaka Kokilam, and G.N. Balasubramaniam, creating a golden era for classical music. VS

S.A.K. Durga, *The Opera in South India* (Delhi: B.R., 1979); Thulasi Ramasamy, *Tamil Yaksagaanas* (Madurai: Vizhikal, 1987).

Sangitanataka ('musical theatre'): popular genre of *Malayalam theatre, also the first (after *Kathakali) for which original scripts began to be written in Malayalam. Earlier drama, mostly translations of Sanskrit texts, was generally meant for reading. Sangitanataka was composed specifically for staging, inspired by the success of similar Tamil *Sangita Natakam, presented throughout Kerala by commercial troupes coming from the east. *Music was its most essential component. Leading actors were expected to sing classical music on specified occasions in the course of performance. Their main qualification was their ability to sing. The necessary accompanists sat on stage. Even though such passages meant a serious deviation from the theme and structure of the play, they happened to be the most popular aspects of Sangitanataka. Apart from music, introduction of jesters at regular intervals and incorporation of irrelevant humorous interludes solely for entertainment became common features. The acting involved exaggerated expression of emotions.

The first Sangitanataka, T.C. Achyuta Menon's *Sangita Naishadham* ('Musical on Naishadha', 1892), depicted the myth of Nala and Damayanti. It was followed by K.C. Kesava Pillai's *Sadarama* (1903), which dealt with the story of a Tamil drama bearing the same name. Both proved extremely successful, resulting in shows at a large number of places. Their popularity prompted other poets and artists to write and produce similar plays; thus started the first theatre movement in Kerala led by professional troupes organized on commercial lines. In the initial period, Sanskrit drama was adapted and even poetical works recast to suit the requirements of this form. Later, plays with social themes also were written and presented as Sangitanataka. But in course of time, the formula-based structure became a subject of severe criticism and, gradually, Sangitanataka disappeared from the scene. Yet the songs and humorous episodes had become so popular that those practices came to stay in the professional Malayalam theatre.   KSNP

Sangitnatak (literally 'music-drama'): glorious phenomenon in *Marathi theatre during the early decades of the twentieth century, representing an amalgam of two parallel structures—singing of lyrics (*pada*s) and theatrical acting. If we do not count folk performance, or the court theatre in Thanjavur (1684–1855), the tradition of using songs in Marathi plays dates to 1843 with Vishnudas Bhave, the first dramatist. But 'Annasaheb' Kirloskar is credited with the parentage of Sangitnatak because of his artistically perfect blend of *music and drama.

In a sense, Sangitnatak was a response to colonial domination. With the advent of the British, the systems of cultural production in native society had received a setback. Classical music, for example, was losing royal patronage in the durbars, whereas the popular rural form of *Tamasha, which employed folk music, was also on the decline in urban areas like Pune and Bombay. Besides, the newly-educated middle class, which had imbibed Victorian values of morality from the British, looked down upon Tamasha's horseplay and open sexual jokes as cheap and vulgar entertainment. This had created a vacuum in the cultural life of the region, which the new literate sought to fill with translations and adaptations of plays by Shakespeare,

Molière, and others. Although these created a taste for well-knit drama, their unfamiliar form and alien themes, significantly different from traditional theatre, could not fire the imagination of the general public. At the same time, translations from Sanskrit playwrights gained popularity among readers owing to the regeneration of interest in the indigenous literary and mythological heritage. Artists felt the need to invent an authentic cultural form to express suppressed creative energies and establish a meaningful relationship with tradition for their audience.

Influenced by *Yakshagana, Bhave incorporated music as an important formal element. The songs in his plays were set to tunes from classical ragas as well as folk forms such as *saki*, *ovi*, *dindi*, and *katav*, and sung by the *sutradhara* to express the various characters' feelings. After Bhave, Datar Shastri developed the 'Vishnudasi' plays further. He started preparing written scripts on the lines of the 'bookish', or translated English and Sanskrit drama, composed verse dialogue, and also used Kannada and Hindi in the lyrics. At the same time, interesting developments took place in Bombay's emerging *Parsi theatre. It catered to the tastes of a new cosmopolitan audience and evolved a genre of entertainment that presented well-made plots based on tales of fantasy interspersed with beautiful dances and melodious music.

In the 1880s, Kirloskar combined various elements borrowed from all these predecessors, and modified and recast them to create Sangitnatak. He perceived the importance of classical and folk music, the organized structure of Sanskrit and English drama, and the romantic and comic aspects of *Sanskrit theatre. It is said that the performance of *Indarsabha* by Sorabji Patel of the Parsi theatre greatly impressed him, for the actors themselves sang, unlike in Bhave's plays where the *sutradhara* used to sing all the songs. Kirloskar's *Shakuntal*, adapted from *Kalidasa's *Abhijnana-Sakuntala*, firmly established Sangitnatak in 1880. It had a close-knit form, and the romantic tale was well known to his audiences and conducive to music.

The characters delivered songs, as in the Parsi theatre, set to lilting melodies from classical, semi-classical, and folk music. Kirloskar employed Hindustani ragas such as Yaman Kalyan, Kafi, Deskar, Hindol, and Sohini, as well as Carnatic ragas like Lilambari, Arabhi, Sankarabharanam, and Ananda Bhairavi. Lesser-known Hindustani ragas like Lalitagauri, Marva, and Jhinjhoti were also used. Thus the play was like a concert of sorts. The *padas* were not external to the story but part of the dialogues (which were mostly in prose). They offered a lot of scope for actors to display their histrionic and singing

Bal Gandharva as Bhamini
in K.P. Khadilkar's
Manapaman, with
Narayanrao Joglekar as
Dhairyadhar (Kirloskar
Natak Mandali, Bombay,
1911)

abilities. Kirloskar was ably assisted
in this endeavour by some of the
best singer-actors of his time, like
Balkoba Natekar and Moropant
Waghulikar, who mesmerized
audiences with their electrifying
rendering of the *pada*s. Kirloskar
made his musicians sit in the
orchestra pit, as in Western theatre,
rather than in the wings, as in
Bhave's plays. The middle-class
spectators were enthralled.

After Kirloskar, G.B. Deval
further refined Sangitnatak. He
blended the *pada*s more organically
with the text, the diction became
more lucid, elegant, and, at
times, poetic and intense. His play
Sharada (1899) was a landmark.
S.K. Kolhatkar's *Viratanaya* ('Hero's
Son', 1896) experimented with
musical forms borrowed from Parsi
theatre. B.V. Warerkar added a new
dimension with *Kunjavihari*
('Wanderer in Gardens', 1908), and
R.G. Gadkari's plays (1912–19)
proved eminently successful. But Bal
Gandharva's Gandharva Natak

Mandali and Keshavrao Bhonsle's Lalitkaladarsha Natak Mandali took Sangitnatak to its highest pinnacle. Their productions were instant hits, like *Manapaman* ('Honour and Dishonour', originally for Kirloskar, 1911) and *Swayamvar* ('Choice of Groom', 1916) written by K.P. Khadilkar, the first author who did not compose the music himself.

These plays made use of tunes picked up from the newly available records of such popular singers as Gauharjan, Johrabai, and Moujudin Khan, skilfully adapted by gifted 'music directors' like Govindrao Tembe (the first of this breed), Bhaskarbuwa Bakhle, and Ramkrishnabuwa Vaze, to provide a theatrical structure. They innovated on conventions of classical music to suit the dramatic situation, for instance the time for singing specific ragas, or the moods they could evoke. Some verse forms and their traditional melodies, like *katav* or *dindi*, even lent themselves easily to rhythmic rendering of prose dialogues and prose-like *padas*, thus adding an astonishingly easy flow to the language. Various changes in instrumentation took place. Previously only harmonium and tabla were used. Later, the Gandharva Natak Mandali introduced organ and two sarangis, which enhanced musical quality greatly.

After the 1930s, Sangitnatak began to slide. With the emergence of realist social themes from the mid-1920s, music and plot had already started to separate, because music could not be cast into the form that the new topics required. Sangitnatak remained in the straitjacket of traditional, classical, and similar styles of presentation. Music did not integrate with the narrative; on the contrary, it dominated, far exceeding the limits set by the context. Soon, people went to hear a play only as a recital. Moreover, it catered to the taste of limited sections of the middle class. The use of exclusively classical music, not exploring the links with bhakti or folk, rendered attempts to develop this genre futile. Besides, on stage, the singer-actors ignored their roles and utilized the space to project themselves only as vocalists. Bal Gandharva popularized singing to such an extent that the play was virtually thrown backstage when he came forward to sing. *Alap* (introduction), *tankari* (embellishment), and *swaravilas* (elaboration) were profusely utilized and productions went on for over six hours because of the demand for encores.

A general feeling that Sangitnatak was irrelevant, unnatural, or an appendage grew among playwrights and the discerning public. Eventually, texts without songs, or prose drama, usurped the stage. The appearance of films in the 1930s as a medium of entertainment contributed substantially to Sangitnatak's decline in popularity. Cinema offered a lot of scope to artistes for narrative experimentation as well as compositions from various Indian musical traditions, therefore it could chart out ways left unexplored by Sangitnatak. However, playwrights like P.K. Atre and M.G. Rangnekar attempted to breathe life into Sangitnatak; producers like A.N. Bhalerao, through Mumbai Marathi Sahitya Sangh, staged the old plays more systematically.

After Independence, Vidyadhar Gokhale's Ranga Sharada Pratishthan tried to sustain the form in *Suvarna tula* ('Weighed in Gold', 1960), *Panditraj Jagannath* (1960), *Mandarmala* (1963), and *Madanachi manjiri* ('Madan's Playmate', 1965), with very talented singer-actors like Ram Marathe, Ashalata Wabgaonkar, Arvind Pilgaonkar, and Jyotsna Mohile. Experimentation by the Goa Hindu Association through Vasant Kanetkar's plays such as *Matsyagandha* (1964) and *Lekure udand jali* ('Too Many Brats', 1966), inserting songs more organically into

Ram Marathe as Krishna and Daji Bhatawadekar as Balaram in Kirloskar's *Sangit Saubhadra,* revived by Ganesh Bodas (Mumbai Marathi Sahitya Sangh, Bombay)

the texture of the script, briefly rejuvenated the form. The Shiledar family also contributed to attempts at revival in the 1960s, as did Purushottam Darwhekar and his Ranjan Kala Mandir with productions such as *Abol jhali satar* ('The Sitar Has Become Mute', 1969) and *Chandra nabhicha dhalala* ('The Moon Is Down', 1972).

Music directors like Yashwant Dev, Bhaskar Chandavarkar, and Jitendra Abhisheki brought a spirit of experimentation to the conception and presentation of song structures but it was short-lived. Chandavarkar and Anand Modak evolved a completely different idiom for Theatre Academy, Pune, in Vijay Tendulkar's *Ghashiram Kotwal* (1972), Satish Alekar's *Mahanirvan* (1973) and *Begum Barve* (1979), and P.L. Deshpande's *Tin paishacha tamasha* (1978, adapted from Brecht's *Threepenny Opera*). These may not qualify as Sangitnatak, yet they represent significant attempts to integrate various, including Western, musical forms in Marathi theatre.

The history of Sangitnatak illustrates how it evolved as a cultural strategy, but also reveals how an imperfect and inadequate understanding of the traditions of music and theatre language resulted in a stilted genre that became a curiosity. It remained imprisoned in the narrow classical confines of middle-class Brahman sensibility, and few attempted to explore the music available in various native traditions.   MP

Ashok D. Ranade, *Stage Music of Maharashtra* (New Delhi: Sangeet Natak Akademi, 1986).

Sannata ('small/little theatre'): an umbrella term for various small-scale *Kannada theatre forms of north Karnataka; the adjective refers to the relative scope and the degree of stylization. Previously called Dappinata after the *dappu*, a small drum used in performances, Sannata got its present name as a contrastive coinage to Doddata, the 'large-scale' *Bayalata variant of eastern *Yakshagana, whose nomenclature reflected its larger-than-life portrayals. In the second half of the nineteenth century, the arrival of the British and the synthesis of Hindu and Sufi traditions in north Karnataka prompted a cultural shift. As a part of this process, theatre forms began to lean towards popular entertainment, themes moved towards the worldly, and performances became less stylized. This trend crystallized into the Sannata, which became as popular as earlier Bayalata forms like the Dasarata and Radhanata.

Sannata is mainly played by non-professional villagers who bring from outside their fold some professional singers and actresses for certain roles. It conveniently allows amateurish performance, as the stage is a simple 3-sq. m space, the dance steps minimal, and the costumes of an ordinary kind. A Bhagavata called Mummela, helped by his companion Himmela, weaves the episodes, works the interludes, and keeps providing background support to the performers, thus building up the narrative. Scholars have identified at least three kinds of Sannata plays according to themes used—Vishnu legends, Siva legends, and contemporary issues. In terms of treatment, however, all varieties show a basic similarity in that archetypal characters are made to appear like normal human beings.

The best example is *Sangya-Balya* ('Sangya and Balya'), the most popular Sannata text. Based on a real-life incident, it depicts the extramarital relationship between Sangya and Gangi, leading to Sangya's tragic murder by Gangi's husband. Banned by the British authorities of the day, the play is now considered a landmark in Kannada drama. On the one hand, it continues to deal with the archetypal themes of forms like the Radhanata, sticking completely to conventional modes of narration; on the other, it suggests the turmoil of its times that introduced new values of money and love, and new institutions or pursuits like the judicial court and non-traditional commerce. The play is remarkably modern in its attitude to this conflict, concluding with an open ending, unlike older works. Later, with many more plays modelled upon *Sangya-Balya*, Sannata moved towards the idiom of the newly arrived *Company Nataka, and the passage from the premodern to the modern phase becomes blurred.   AKV

Basavaraj S. Naikar, *The Folk-Theatre of North-Karnataka* (Dharwad: Karnatak University, 1996); M. Shankar, *Sannata: Minor Folk-Plays of North Karnataka* (Udupi: Regional Resources Centre for Folk Performing Arts, 1986).

Sansenba (literally 'tending the cows') or Gostha Lila: traditional Manipuri *children's theatre, normally falling on Gostha Ashtami (the eighth lunar day of Hiyangei or November). It developed in the mid-eighteenth century, though the origins of the play and its creator remain unrecorded. Oral traditions, however, allude to King Chingthangkhomba, alias Bhagyachandra (1763–98), who introduced *Ras Lila in Manipur. The royal chronicles mention an event in 1803, when during an outing, the wooden bridge on the Imphal river broke and a troupe member died in the accident.

Brajabuli and Sanskrit were often the medium of communication, which changed to Manipuri in the early twentieth century.

The form depicts Krishna's experiences as a cowherd—his becoming ready to tend cows at the age of 5, Narada's advent at Gokul, and Krishna beseeching his foster-father to let him look after the cows with his friends. After much argument and feasting, the children go out to a forest where Krishna and his elder brother Balaram kill the demons Bakasur and Dhenukasur respectively. They return when the cows go back to their sheds. The story is taken from cantos eleven and fifteen in the tenth book of the *Bhagavata Purana*. A clown, Balabasu, attached to Narada, was incorporated to provide bland jokes and improvised humour. Similar to the Bahua in the *Ankiya Bhaona of Assam, Balabasu however was outspoken and adamant, not usually silent as his Assamese counterpart. Sansenba combines fun, frolic, adventure, and environmental enactment, with demons in body-size *masks and *ritual worship at the end in the evening. The young Krishna's exploits are very popular, and games, theatrics, and children's linguistic interplay entertain. The mother's role provides real scope to actresses. LA

Sattaka: a form of *uparupaka* in Prakrit. Scholars explain its etymology differently. A.N. Upadhye derives it from *sa* + *atta* ('drama' or 'dance', a word of Dravidian origin) + *ka*. Thus he understands it as 'a dramatic representation accompanied by dance'. On the contrary, N.G. Guru interprets the word from the Sanskrit root *sat*, meaning to show, display, manifest. Thus it means 'a kind of spectacle, a show, a display', wherein dancing predominated rather than dialogue as in a *nataka. Both agree on the nature of *sattaka* as a minor play abounding in dance and music. Visvanatha's *Sahityadarpana* ('Mirror of Literature', fourteenth century) defines it as drama with a Prakrit text and without *pravesaka* or *vishkambhaka* (the introductory or linking scenes). *Adbhuta* (marvellous) *rasa prevails in it. Rajasekhara's *Karpuramanjari* ('Camphor Blossoms', tenth century) is the best-known example. KDT

Chandramouli Naikar, *Sattaka Literature: A Study* (Dharwad: Medha, 1993).

Scenography: In the context of Indian theatre, stage design needs assessment by parameters different from Western standards or ideas. In classical *Sanskrit theatre and the folk forms, the need to physically show the environment or

'background' did not exist because Indian traditions were non-realistic, non-representational, and ritualistic in content and form. Being openly presentational in expression, they were highly stylized, predominantly using elements of dance and gesture to suggest or describe a locale. Often the text was recited or sung by members of a visible chorus consisting of musicians and singers, rather than by the actor, additionally creating a set of conventions that together gave the performances a codified structure.

Sanskrit drama was staged in buildings, within temple or palace complexes, constructed according to the principles outlined in the *Natyasastra*, with auditory and performing spaces clearly demarcated by measurements (some sets by theatre *architecture scholar Goverdhan Panchal recreate those plans). The raised platform had four elaborately designed pillars (often adorned with flowers) at the corners, leaving a strip in front in the foreground. Stools or simple pieces of furniture may have indicated thrones, chariots, or other such seating. A change in locale was suggested by a circumambulation around the stage, and the new environment described by gestures and words. In the back wall stood two doors for entrances, and a hand-held curtain hid new actors on stage in a manner that was dramatic as

well as a process of revealing the character in phases. Similar stages are presently used for the highly codified *Kutiyattam, performed in *kuttampalams*. Similar half-curtains survive in such forms as *Kathakali, where two stagehands bring on a 3 m-by-2 m cloth behind which an actor stands in character, 'entering' in medias res when they lower it in full view, and sometimes even 'exiting' when they raise it to conceal him again.

Folk theatre normally takes place in neutral, fluid spaces, in the village centre or other such prominent open-air venues. The performing area is at ground level or sometimes raised, the audience seated in about three-quarters of a circle around it. Occasionally, the troupe erects a temporary makeshift structure of wood and bamboo covered with canvas, and a 'backstage' cordoned off with cloth. These genres depend strongly for their visual art on elaborate *masks, costumes, and make-up, their characters and themes often from mythology or local folklore. The style varies from region to region, the design elements derived from regional iconography. Here again there is generally no attempt to reproduce locales realistically, and only a few props symbolically represent the status of characters or places of action.

During the late eighteenth century in Bengal and Maharashtra,

S. Ebotombi's design for Kalidasa's *Sakuntala* (Rangmandal, Bhopal 1990), inspired by the traditional Manipuri *mandap*

a new urban theatre originated. To host their entertainments in India, the British constructed formal proscenium-arch playhouses in growing cities like Calcutta, Bombay, and Madras. Interested natives evolved a new concept of theatre, based on Western idioms of performance. A number of indigenous companies came into existence in the mid-nineteenth century, influenced by reading Shakespeare and other European playwrights, presenting texts inspired by their stagecraft but soon incorporating Indian mythological stories, Sanskrit drama in translation, and, later, social themes sourced from local milieus.

The Renaissance Italianate style of painted perspective scenery—still fashionable in nineteenth-century Western theatre—became Indianized, offering a simple solution to the production of vast visual extravaganzas, recreating on stage such locales as palaces, forts, jungles, or streets. In Calcutta, an English artist, David Garrick, formerly principal of an art college, painted four 'tasteful sceneries' at the Great National Theatre, of a court, garden, forest, and interior, for *Kamyakanan* ('Desirable Garden', 1873), a fairy tale by Amritalal Basu and Nagendranath Banerjee. Dharmadas Sur (1852–1910), the first known Indian scene painter, followed suit, using portable rolled-up scenes on canvas. In Bombay, too, painted sets grew popular during this time; the Painter brothers, who got their name from their trade, later supplied scenery for the theatre as well as silent films.

Initially, single painted curtains depicted different places, hence between four and six curtains in a production pictured all locations. This technique soon underwent further elaboration. By the turn of the century, a scene was represented by two or three curtains cut in various shapes and placed one in front of another, to create a feeling of enhanced depth. These were known as 'cut scenery', the cut-out portions held together by means of transparent gauze-like material to form the entire curtain. The scrim allowed spectators to see through into the depth, from the curtains placed in the foreground to those in the background. This pattern also affected the lighting plan, so that separate sets of lamps used to highlight the different curtains one behind the other. Sometimes the wings were also camouflaged by strips of painted scenery continuing the artwork, to make the illusion complete.

Spectacular devices or 'trick scenes', such as miniaturized railway trains colliding to explosions on stage, fairies emerging from rose petals, and beheadings of characters, comprised some of the special effects and quick changes creating high points of scenic splendour. The management of Kshirod Prasad Vidyavinod's *Alibaba* (Calcutta, 1897) proudly advertised that its 'Grand Cave Scene is worth seeing'. Soon this style of design became popular all over India, adopted by Gujarati and especially *Parsi theatre companies, which toured everywhere. Rabindranath *Tagore, irritated by this literalism and 'the costly rubbish ... clogging the stage',

Painted backdrop used by Kasi Nagari Natak Mandali, Varanasi

advocated a return to the symbolism and stylization of the *Natyasastra* in his revolutionary essay *Rangamancha* (*The Stage*, 1902), and encouraged his artist nephews, Abanindranath and Gaganendranath Tagore, to cultivate an impressionistic approach for his plays. Ultimately entrusting his sets to the famous painter Nandalal Bose, he mounted productions in open-air natural surroundings at Santiniketan, or specified suggestive minimalism and simplification indoors.

The use of painted scenery continued till the late 1920s and early 1930s—under talented artists like P.S. Kale in Bombay, surviving even till the end of the century in such commercial companies as R.S. Manohar's National Theatres, Madras—while a new movement began to take shape. Ibsenian realism became important, coinciding with new plays written on social issues. Painted curtains gave way to painted flats (the box set) and multiple levels on stage, with realistic furniture and properties. Along with levels came the wagon stage and the revolving stage (introduced by the visionary Satu Sen) as early as 1933 in Calcutta, designers like Charu Roy, Ramen Chatterjee, and Manindranath Das (on lights) becoming the forerunners of the new style. The changing shape of theatre was evident from Sisir Bhaduri's production of *Jibanranga* ('The Stage of Life', 1941) and Bijon Bhattacharya's *Nabanna* ('New Harvest', 1944). The *Indian People's Theatre Association and Prithvi Theatres began focusing on socialistic drama presented realistically.

In 1953, a revival in *Marathi theatre gave birth to yet another phase of innovation on Bombay's professional stage. This rejuvenation led to the emergence of a large number of artists experimenting with ideas of design using abstract forms and symbolic settings suggestive of locales, rather than replicating them in entirety. To some extent reminiscent of the stylized realism or expressionism of Max Reinhardt, designers like D.G. Godse, Damu Kenkre, Raghuvir Talashilkar, Mohan Wagh, and Shyam Adarkar transformed sets into a new instrument in the theatre. In Calcutta, Khaled Choudhury made his own statements in designing productions, which he felt must remain true to the essence and style of a play. An illustrator as well, he gave his scenes a graphic quality, plus strong structural features that communicated the mood through formal elements like line, colour, and shape. His set for Tagore's *Raktakarabi* (*Red Oleander*, 1954) became a milestone in symbolism.

Also in Bengal, Utpal Dutt's *Angar* ('Coal', 1959) and *Kallol* ('Waves', 1965), with Tapas Sen's

Khaled Choudhury's set model for Bohurupee's production of Tagore's *Rakta-karabi* (director Sombhu Mitra, Calcutta, 1954)

pioneering special effects, offered integrated technical teamwork, not seen earlier on the Indian stage. The use of lighting to create plastic forms in space marked a breakthrough in this era. Traditional Indian theatre relied on torches or fixed oil lamps for lighting—still visible in Kutiyattam and Kathakali, where actors often come nearer the tall brass lamp to convey important facial expressions better. Gradually, kerosene and Petromax pressure lamps, gaslight, and electric lights had arrived, the last two in urban auditoria during the late nineteenth century. Developments in the new theatre movement of the 1930s and 1940s had influenced practitioners employing painted scenery, who began their own innovations in lighting, throwing out footlights,

illuminating multiple curtains in a manner that created highlights accentuating the illusion of depth, while avoiding actors' shadows on the painted curtains. Following Tapas Sen, other contemporary light designers included V. Ramamurthy (Bangalore), Kanishka Sen (Calcutta), and G.N. Dasgupta (Delhi). The recent son-et-lumiere works of N. Krishnamoorthy in Kerala show the further consolidation of lighting in stage design.

The last four decades of the twentieth century brought many further changes. While it is not possible within the scope of this article to detail every significant theatre designer or all the modern and contemporary trends in design, certain important ones merit mention. The *National School of

Drama for the first time formalized theatre training in all its specialities, including stagecraft. Its director, Ebrahim Alkazi, himself designed many unusual sets applying the doctrine of interpreting the text, as well as mounted plays at different sites in Delhi, such as the ruins of Ferozeshah Kotla and the old Fort, incorporating the natural surroundings as the setting. My own work in Delhi started by juxtaposing three-dimensional form with the painted image, focusing on the perception of the image suspended in space. This led to experimentation in different environments, rearranging the relationship between audience and performer, breaking the linearity and continuity of image and sound in space.

The 1960s also gave birth to a search for roots in contemporary urban theatre, under the influence of folk forms, evolving a new idiom both modern yet based on indigenous tradition. While this style re-examined the nature of performance, exploring the use of space in the essentially bare picture-frame of an indoor auditorium, the process of evolving an Indian scenography in this mode remains very much at a formative stage. However, some designers like M.S. Sathyu did attain consistent aesthetic success.   NA

Shadow theatre: unique performing art related to *puppetry. While in puppet theatre the audience directly sees the puppets, in shadow theatre it sees only their moving shadows cast by light on a screen. The audience sits in front of the screen, while the puppeteers operate behind it. Thus the spectators and actor-manipulators are placed as if in different rooms separated by the all-important screen, which filters and modifies the action—almost like a primitive motion picture. The actor-manipulator is isolated from his audience, unlike the performer's experience in live theatre. He must present a projection of his thoughts and expect the viewer to reassemble and interpret them, for it is not the figure in his hands but its shadow on the screen's other side that constitutes the dramatic image. The audience retranslates these moving pictures into actions and incidents in this fascinating and exciting experience.

Backstage, between a light source and the screen, the puppeteers insert flat figures, lightly pressing them on the screen so that the shadows are sharp. If they are not pressed on the screen their shadows become hazy. Normally, the puppet figures in shadow theatre are made of leather. Of course, they can be made from any opaque material like cardboard, but leather can be used many more times without damage. The leather is carefully stencilled so that the shadows suggest the puppets' clothing, jewellery, and other accoutrements. Some figures have jointed limbs which, when manipulated, show the audience beautiful moving shadows.

India has a very long and rich tradition of shadow theatre. According to many scholars, the art originated here two millennia ago. The earliest reference appears in *Cilappatikaram*, a Tamil classic written during that time. Many Western Indologists, such as Pischel, Lueders, and Winternitz, think that the well-known Sanskrit drama *Mahanataka* ('Great Drama') was originally a text for shadow theatre. Although its exact date cannot be fixed, it was written before AD 850. Subhata's *Dutangada* ('Angada the Messenger'), a play from the thirteenth century, is expressly designated as *chayanataka* (shadow drama). These documents indicate that India has a continuous history of shadow theatre for about 2000 years. Possibly the form reached south-east Asia, where it now flourishes, thanks to maritime and cultural relations originating from India's eastern seaboard.

Fortunately, shadow theatre traditions still exist in varying styles in peninsular India: Orissa (*Ravana Chhaya), Andhra Pradesh (*Tolu Bommalata), Tamil Nadu (Tolu *Bommalattam), Kerala (*Tolpavakuttu), Karnataka (Togalu *Gombeyata), and Maharashtra (Chamdyacha Bahulye, 'leather puppets'). While the puppets of Orissa, Kerala, and Maharashtra cast shadows in black and white, and draw exclusively upon Rama myths for their stories, those of the other three states throw spectacular multicoloured shadows. To make them coloured, the leather is first treated into translucency, then different dyes are applied. These colour forms derive narrative material from the epic *Ramayana* and *Mahabharata*, as also other Puranic literature.

The Maharashtrian form barely survives in the hands of one troupe in Kudal village (Ratnagiri district), which knows how to present its plays with the old figures handed down by its forefathers, but has lost the art of making these delicately-coloured group puppets and single characters with highly stylized settings. In contrast, Andhra Pradesh now has the strongest activity in shadow theatre, with more than a hundred puppeteers. Their puppets are very large, ranging from 1 to 2 m. Karnataka, too, uses similar figures as well as other much smaller ones.

All the styles have stock characters, many known for wit and humour. Music, heavily dependent

Tolu Bommalata artists
manipulating puppets
behind the screen

on local folk instrumentation, plays a
very important role. Traditionally, oil
lamps with thick wicks provide the
light source, which conveys colour
shadows beautifully. Their lyricism
melts in the fixed glare of gaslight or
electric bulbs. Similarly, the vegetable
dyes used for colouring have given
way to chemicals, which have not
proved as satisfying aesthetically.
Shadow theatres are dying slowly
because people prefer 'modern'
entertainment like movies and
television. Governments provide
financial incentive for their survival,
but it is too meagre. Besides, no art
can thrive under doles. Unless society
becomes genuinely interested in the
continuation of these rare forms,
they are destined to vanish sooner
or later.   JP

Stuart Blackburn, *Inside the Drama-
    House: Rama Stories and Shadow
    Puppets in South India* (Berkeley:
    University of California, 1996);
    Meher R. Contractor, *The Shadow*

Puppets of India (Ahmedabad:
Darpana Academy of the Performing
Arts, 1984); M.V. Ramana Murthy,
The Art and Science of Leather Puppetry
(Madras, 1976); T. Ramaswamy, *The
Shadow Theatre in India* (Madras:
International Institute of Tamil
Studies, 1982).

Shumang Lila (literally 'courtyard
*Lila'): term given to Manipuri
courtyard theatre by the elite only in
1976, though it evolved through
various stages from the Phagi (clown
plays) of the nineteenth century.
The genre denotes the contemporary popular and itinerant dramatic
performances held in open spaces,
especially in the courtyards of
extended households, fields in front
of public schools, precincts of native
spirit deities (*umanglais*), or river-
sides with embankments designed
for all-round viewing. Female
characters are still enacted by men,

which gives its distinctive identity and taste, along with the Phagi-puba (clown), an essential element. The latter has changed his role, since in the scripted plays beginning from 1950, he was assimilated within the narrative, and situational and character interactions were given prominence, instead of having an independent presence for the sake of humour alone. Although the dramatists tried hard to retain the same elements of fun and laughter, there was a gradual decline in the art of the traditional clown.

In Imphal there are some twenty professional troupes that receive invitations to tour villages or towns, where three to four shows can be arranged in a day. The season begins in early February, ritually associated in the traditional calendar with the start of the agricultural cycle.

Directors and scriptwriters are able to live comfortably. The Nupi-shabi (female impersonator) charges extremely high fees; he is coveted by various groups and bought over as in football transfers (the rate in 2000 was Rs 25,000, apart from his share of the proceeds). A troupe normally consists of ten to twelve members, and when it travels, it carries music and sound equipment since the song sequences call for sophistication. Playback singing, like in Hindi films, has become part of the technique, the singer and musicians sitting on one side, while the heroine lip-syncs on stage.

The Manipur State Kala Akademi, an autonomous cultural body sponsored by the government, organizes annual festivals with prizes for the top three plays judged by scholars and literati. Huge pavilions

Three female impersonators in Shumang Lila: Ranjit Ningthouja's *Refugee* directed by Naba Wareppa (Naharol Khongthang Artistes Association, 2002)

are constructed in fields, with a raised square stage in the middle, and viewing arrangements all round. Some fifteen all-male troupes and six or seven amateur all-women ones vie in different categories (women have separate competitions). Large audiences follow the fate of popular groups, and sometimes the enclosing fences are broken by enthusiastic youths. The prize-winning male groups have solid runs of their plays for a year or two; new scripts are written and fresh productions mounted the next season. The female groups comprise mostly market women, who cross-dress for male roles. Their subjects are essentially folk legends and semi-historical drama. They get some invitation shows, but poverty and lack of motivation haunt these enterprises.

Shumang Lila has perhaps the longest history in *Manipuri theatre, believed to have started as comic skits by the jesters of feudal royalty in the nineteenth century, ridiculing the snobbish nobility and exposing their foibles and weaknesses. Ancient Manipur utilized slavery as a mode of production, and each noble's household had one or two slaves termed *phunganai*. In the fifteenth and sixteenth centuries, the *phunganai* did lots of acrobatics and boisterous animal imitations in drinking bouts with hill chieftains at their ritual receptions in October.

Later, princesses and court ladies had female retinues who almost became conscience-keepers, whose roles in folk theatre were extremely popular and drew sympathy. The slaves developed a piece-de-resistance in their characterization, and their jokes, puns, and equilibrium-destroying antics targeted the masters themselves, who enjoyed the jests at their own expense. The feudal system often needed subversion and creative reproduction, the energy of sexual urges recharging it through fun and humour. The clown provided this original function of social revitalization through destruction and renewal.

Elders narrate stories of how Maharaja Chandrakirti (1850–86) possessed excellent wits, the more famous ones being Oina Bijando and Thengbai Mera. Other jesters like Abujamba Shaiton and Khari Laisuba were reported to have invented the comic skits. One day they improvised the discovery of large footmarks in the palace verandah, which they suspected to be those of an elephant. They mimed the digging of pits for its capture, watched by the king and court, including a noble, Thokchao, who possessed an extra-large heel. The clowns discovered that the footmarks belonged to none other than him. The incident had everyone laughing uproariously, except Thokchao who vigorously objected to the personal insult. The Maharaja effected a compromise and ordered the start of Phagi Lila. The offended noble also dined the funsters and requested them not to play jokes against him again.

There is enough indication that by the 1870s these originally impromptu improvisations became regular exhibitory features, and larger audiences were incorporated in their enactment. British officials were often exposed to such entertainment. Mrs Grimwood, wife of the political agent, had witnessed a performance of three clowns in 1891, and left a vivid impression: 'The Manipuri specimens were very funny indeed. Their heads were shaved like the back of a poodle, with little tufts of hair left here and there; and their faces were painted with streaks of different-coloured paints, and their eyebrows whitened. They wore very few clothes, but what they had were striped red and green and a variety of shades.' It is easy to deduce the Manipuri court's awareness of other clown plays in different parts of India, Burma, and Indochina, and the participants' awareness of their own exhibitory skills.

The vibrancy, vitality, and continuance of this itinerant form were in fact conditioned by the resilience of peasant society and its general attitude to life. Crosstalk, an Asian theatrical possession of rapid exchange of phrases and wit,

was called *chin-kangjei* ('word-hockey') in native parlance, though the date of its migration from either China or south-east Asia is uncertain. Manipuri clowns were adept at this art, and by the end of the nineteenth century, personal competition in antiphonal repartee, fluency of diction, innovation in rhythm and declamation, and richness of vocabulary and thematic content all became part of the developing stylistics of performance. Enactment of imaginary bouts and confrontations, and temporary destruction of equilibrium became cornerstones of humour.

The clowns in the early twentieth century gradually got rid of painted faces, and more down-to-earth crosstalk, distortion of limbs and facial muscles, utilization of nonsense syllables, and narration of humorous tales came into currency. The plays were short, but in between were plenty of impromptu performances, and digs at the nobility, social oppression, human foibles, and sexual peccadilloes. Strings of brief narratives linked together made one full presentation. Normally six to seven actors toured the countryside, and the most attractive members were the Nupi-shabi and Phagi-puba, who became the troupe leaders. The plays came to be named after the clown: thus, *Yotshubi Phagi, Amuthoi Phagi, Chengba Phagi.*

The advent of these clowns transformed annual religious celebrations. The Durga Puja at the palace was a great event, where many enactments, operas, dances, and Phagis were held on each day of the ten-day festival. Various performing groups came from the villages, stayed at adjacent noblemen's houses, were fed and taken care of by court ladies and generous families, and watched by large audiences. Extended households and other adjacent populations also called them to present their shows after community feasts; such invitations became so overcrowded that competitiveness, quarrels, and fights ensued. The court was often pressed to issue notices to regulate such shows, and aristocratic circles lobbied furiously in the 1930s to suppress rival groups.

By 1918, the nature of performances was embellished by regular stories in a proper dramatic structure from texts outside Manipur; *Raja Harishchandra* was the first Hindu mythological play done in the itinerant manner. The plot of a pious king's suffering and the Brahman's oppressive presence were symbolic of the social context of that period. Later, the discrete coexistence of long narratives with improvised skits was compromised by clown episodes presented between the two halves of a play, though some Phagis remained more famous than the drama that sandwiched them. Such proliferation of performance reached unprecedented dimensions with the creation of many forms of Pala (opera) and the ethnic theatre of *Moirang Parva; the first half of the twentieth century could be regarded as the golden period of Shumang Lila. However, the loss of Manipur's freedom in 1891 and the cultural transformation that took place under colonial aegis led to a change in its nomenclature, as being derived from the *Jatra of Bengal. Itinerant groups came to be known as Jatrawalis and, when the Theatre Centre organized their first festival in 1967, they named it the All Manipur Jatra Festival.

Shumang Lila now presents an entirely changed syndrome of survival in the midst of changing laws of the market. It became the purveyor of popular drama, with directors controlling the texture, sequence, and structure of scripted narratives, rather than clowns spontaneously embellishing on the vivacity of their improvisatory tradition. Cosmopolitan theatre added choreographic organization in movement and scenic unfolding. Enactment of contemporary violence, clashes between the police and insurgents, stories of manipulation, intrigue, and revenge turned into major themes. More sophistication of skills and techniques in presenting physical violence and bloodshed was demanded, due to competition from television in villages. The intrusion of an overwhelmingly dominant filmic culture effected transformations in behaviour, spectacle, and acting methods. The art of crosstalk vanished, replaced by large-scale melodramatic rhetoric. Social disquiet during the counter-insurgency operations also resulted in loss of young audiences.   LA

Street theatre: Although most Indian rural performances take place in open-air public spaces, and *Terukkuttu in fact literally translates as 'street theatre', the term refers now to mainly left-wing theatre at street corners and in open spaces, which Safdar Hashmi defined as 'a militant political theatre of protest [whose] function is to agitate the people and to mobilize them behind fighting organizations.' Its beginnings are unrecorded, possibly originating in the anti-British and anti-fascist struggles of the late 1930s. While it is certain that street theatre did take place in the 1940s, we have no precise information on actual productions until the Praja Natya Mandali, formed in 1943 in Andhra Pradesh, quickly proliferated into hundreds of village-based units all over the state. Members used traditional forms like *Burrakatha

and Harikatha to sing, among other things, of the glorious peasant struggle of Telengana and to exhort people to rise against exploitation. In 1948, Habib Tanvir did one of the first street plays, strictly speaking—*Shantidut kamgar* ('The Labourer, Messenger of Peace')—for the *Indian People's Theatre Association (IPTA).

Chargesheet (1949) was among the earliest street plays in Calcutta. Utpal Dutt recalls that it happened at the instance of Panu Pal, who interrupted an IPTA rehearsal and urged those present to do a quick, short improvisation on the imprisonment of Communist leaders. The very next day, at 5 p.m., *Chargesheet* was performed at Hazra Park to an audience of thousands of workers, and later repeated many times across West Bengal. The experience impressed the young Dutt with the robust, rough theatricality of the *pathanatika* (literally 'street playlet'), its immediacy, and its political sharpness. Parallel to his proscenium career, he worked in this genre—which he called the 'poster play'—till the end of his life, mostly during election campaigns. In terms of form, though, early street theatre seems to have mimicked the stage, with the action often taking place in front of a wall or some other backdrop, and actors entering from and exiting into makeshift wings. A few plays like Dutt's *Din badaler pala* ('*Pala of Changing Times', 1967) were more elaborate, stretching to three hours. Even so, further formal innovations had to await a new generation of artist-activists.

The broken and sporadic history of the movement in India coincided with periods of political unrest. During the turbulent 1970s, Calcutta saw hundreds of such performances by radical outfits. With the Emergency declared by the central government, repression unleashed against Communists, and the revolutionary Naxalbari uprising in Bengal, street theatre entered a new and potentially dangerous phase. Performers were attacked, often by the police, which resulted in the death of at least two activists, Ashis Chatterjee of Theatre Unit in 1972 and Prabir Datta of Silhouette in 1974. Many others were arrested,

beaten up, tortured. In terms of form, Badal Sircar's work had great influence. Abandoning mainstream drama, he took to open-air performance, communicating with the dissatisfied and uprooted urban working class in an intensely physical style. Although he does not see himself as part of the movement, many street theatre groups benefited from the workshops he held all over the country. Bengal continues to have a vibrant tradition with regular shows performed by such veterans as Probir Guha.

In north India, Safdar Hashmi's Jana Natya Manch (or Janam), formed in 1973, led the movement. Till 2002, it had notched up about 7000 performances of fifty-eight street plays, many of them later translated or adapted by groups

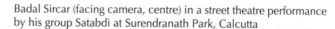

Badal Sircar (facing camera, centre) in a street theatre performance by his group Satabdi at Surendranath Park, Calcutta

across south Asia. Its first such play, *Machine* (1978), is a classic; *Aurat* ('Woman', 1979), *Halla bol* ('Attack!', 1988), and *Artanad* ('Scream', 1996, on sexual abuse of children) exemplify a popular political theatre that features direct confrontation and energy as well as artistry. Theatre Union (1983–9, in Delhi), counting among its members Anuradha Kapur, Maya Rao, and Rati Bartholomew, did some excellent street productions, such as *Toba Tek Singh* based on Saadat Hasan Manto's short story. Another Delhi group, Nishant, is led by Shamsul Islam and his wife Neelima. In Punjab, Gursharan Singh persevered with street theatre advocating social change and civil rights for over two decades, through the years of militancy (1980s), braving threats to his life, and inspiring a whole generation of young theatre workers. In Gujarat, the groups Samvedan, Garage, Lok Kala Manch (all in Ahmadabad), and Parivartan (in Vadodara) perform street plays.

South India has some of the best exponents, starting with Samudaya (formed 1975) and its many units in Karnataka, while among Kannada dramatists, Chandrashekhar Patil used the form to satirize social evils and human follies. Although Samudaya enacted *Belchi* (1978), on the true story of a Dalit massacre in Bihar,

around 2500 times, its productivity decreased over the years. However, 1989 marked a turning point for street theatre after Hashmi's shocking murder during a show: 30,000 performances paid tribute on his birthday, 12 April, now observed across India as National Street Theatre Day. Among the groups that took to street theatre as a direct response to Hashmi's death was the revitalized Praja Natya Mandali in Andhra Pradesh. Nija Nataka Iyakkam (formed 1978 in Madurai) performs very physical and energetic Tamil street theatre, while the Marxist Chennai Kalai Kuzhu (formed 1984 in Madras) skilfully employs a lot of colour, delightful slapstick, as well as sheer poignancy. Kerala also has considerable street theatre.

The movement has now spread to all states; in Orissa, for instance, Natya Chetana sets an example. Feminists, both of the left and non-left, produced high-quality street plays from the 1980s. The most notable among these are *Om swaha* (1979), originally performed for Stree Sangharsh and then taken up by Theatre Union, and *Mulgi jhali ho* ('A Girl Is Born', 1983) written by Jyoti Mhapsekar of Stree Mukti Sangathana, Bombay. In 1984, the shocking death of thousands after a poison gas leak from the Union Carbide plant in Bhopal sparked off protest theatre at street corners in many towns, some groups mobilizing support and donations for survivors. During the 1990s, non-governmental organizations (NGOs) used street theatre to promote ecological consciousness, AIDS awareness, and family planning. Didactic in purpose, most of this work is of indifferent theatrical quality. Whereas leftist street groups solicit voluntary audience donations to cover costs after concluding their shows, NGO *theatre for development is normally financed by donor agencies, often foreign.   SD

Sudhanva Deshpande (ed.), *Theatre of the Streets: The Jana Natya Manch Experience* (Delhi: LeftWord, 2007); Sudhi Pradhan (ed.), *Marxist Cultural Movement in India: Chronicles and Documents*, 3 vols. (Calcutta: National Book Agency, Navana, and Mrs Santi Pradhan, 1979–85); Shirin, *Beyond the Stage: Street Theatre against Communalism* (Delhi: Media House, 2002); Jacob Srampickal, *Voice to the Voiceless: The Power of People's Theatre in India* (New York: St Martin's Press, 1994).

Suanga (literally 'masque, farce'): a form of musical folk theatre most popular in coastal Orissa till the early part of the twentieth century. Although it has become extinct there, it is still prevalent in Kalahandi and Balangir districts of western Orissa. The technique of Suanga also informs the spectacular *Prahlada Nataka. Suanga playwrights who dominated *Oriya theatre with their performing troupes were Jagannath Pani, Gopal Das, Bandhu Nayak, Dayanidhi Swain, Baishnab Pani, and Balakrishna Mohanty. All later converted to *Yatra because of popular demand.

The themes of Suanga plays are always mythological. The actors are required to sing their own dialogue, the refrain repeated by a chorus of singers. All the characters introduce themselves through songs. For example, when Siva enters he sings, 'I am Siva, God of three worlds; Ganga is in my matted locks, I live in Kailash.' While the choruses are sung the actors dance gently. *Gini* (cymbals) and *mardala* or *mridanga* (double-ended drums) are the only accompanying instruments. Enough humour is provided by minor characters such as the Dwari (sentry) and Vaidya (village doctor). They sing and gesticulate according to the mood and meaning of the songs. Their portions of sung dialogue are written in common colloquial language.   DNP

Swang (literally 'masquerade'): Punjabi or Haryanvi Hindi folk-theatre style in Punjab and Haryana, closely related to *Naqal; also a synonym in *Hindi theatre for the

north Indian form known as *Nautanki. We may distinguish between the comic duos of Naqqals (also known as Bhands) and full-fledged dramatic performances by a troupe, better classified as Swang; the former has exclusively satirical content, the latter heroic romance interspersed with comic prologue and interludes. The term Swang appears with theatrical associations in Punjabi as early as the religious writings of Guru Nanak (1469–1538): 'The great Actor started masquerading (*swang*) in this playground called the world,' and 'When He winds up this great masquerade (*swang*) of multiplicity, He becomes one again.'

The main Swang play after the mandatory introductory Naqal is based on the legends that are part of Punjabi folklore: *Hir-Ranjha* ('Hir and Ranjha'), *Sassi-Punnu* ('Sassi and Punnu'), *Sohni-Mahiwal* ('Sohni and Mahiwal'), *Puran Bhagat*, *Raja Bharathari*. Sometimes a troupe also stages works based on famous *gathas* (lyrical narratives) like *Prithviraj Chauhan*, *Puran Bhagat*, or *Guga Pir*. The leader is director/playwright/actor all rolled into one. The texts that he evolves are totally uninhibited by any rules of syntax or dramatic structure. Mad mixtures of tragedy and comedy, they swing from the esoteric to the ridiculous.

The mesmeric performance uses a vast repertoire of songs and dances, with musical patterns based on classical ragas and movements that combine Kathak dance and folk forms. The style of presentation is totally non-realistic, as when the protagonist pats his horse and sings adieu to his mother but his charger, unsatisfied with the rendering, starts singing and repeats the lines in a more mellifluous voice. A character breaks into a dance measure set to a tune, even if receiving bad news. No scenery appears: a couple of transversely poised sticks suggest an army camp; colourfully wrapped bamboos, held by actors, form pillars; cloth raised aloft creates diverse majestic gates. After playing a part a performer (still in costume) could either join the singers or sit in a corner smoking a cigarette, becoming 'invisible' on stage by letting go, almost metaphysically, of his presence.

Men enact the female roles. In fact, all training of Swang and Naqal actors involves female impersonation, because the entire process of transforming an actor to a character becomes more complex when he also has to change gender. With over-powdered faces, seductively-drawn eyes, blood-red lipstick, cascading wigs, and accentuated false breasts, performers with names like Miss Rosy and Miss Lilly are the real stars of the show. They serve an imperative function in a conservative society by depicting behavioural patterns that are more open and sexual, their provocative pouts and pelvic thrusts thus feeding the fantasy of the male audience.

The actors have never heard of Brechtian alienation effects, but they continuously urge the audience away from being passive spectators to participating in the social activity. Their ability to detach themselves from the action of the play and comment on the situation creates immediate rapport with viewers.

Total performers, they sing, dance, act, compose, and improvise in ways that always infuse new life and vigour in their art form. The most accomplished among them include Tule Ram and Lakhmi Chand.

NMSC

Krishan Chander Sharma, *The Luminous Bard of Haryana: Lakhmi Chand* (New Delhi: Siddharth, 1990); R.C. Temple, *The Legends of the Punjab* (London: Trubner, 1883).

Tagore, Rabindranath (1861–1941): Bengali dramatist, director, actor, choreographer, composer, educator, theorist, and literary guru of modern India. Born into the aristocratic Tagore family, one of the most important households in the so-called 'Bengal Renaissance' of nineteenth-century Calcutta, he received an enlightened upbringing and education at home. Among other things, the large extended family regularly organized a variety of in-house cultural activities in their improvised courtyard theatre. Here he made his acting debut, at the age of 16, in elder brother Jyotirindranath Tagore's adaptation of Molière's *Le Bourgeois Gentilhomme*. In 1881 he published his first three plays, of which the *Gitabhinay Balmiki-pratibha ('Valmiki's Genius', on the legendary author of the *Ramayana*) created an immediate public impact: he acted the lead and composed the elaborate score, boldly refashioning classical ragas and even adapting a few British folk melodies. For another of his musicals, *Mayar khela* ('The Game of Maya', 1888), the women of the family acted all the roles, including those of men—an unusual event for its time.

Over the next few years Tagore wrote heightened verse drama and a number of skits subtitled 'riddle plays'. *Prakritir pratishodh* ('Nature's Revenge', 1884) presented an ascetic who finds truth not in renunciation but in affection for an ostracized orphan girl. *Raja o rani* ('Raja and Rani', 1889) and *Bisarjan* ('Immersion', 1890) were somewhat melodramatic five-act tragedies modelled after Shakespeare, a style he rejected later as 'exaggeration', though *Bisarjan* still carries a powerful message against idol worship. Significantly, *Raja o rani* was the one Tagore play repeatedly revived on Calcutta's commercial stage. In *Chitrangada* (1892), he created a more original, lyrical form for his thesis on the chimera of physical attractiveness and the true nature of love and human beauty. In *Malini* (1896), he first dramatized his deep respect for Buddhist principles. He also produced two full-length farces of social satire during this period: *Goray galad* ('Error at the Outset', 1892) and *Baikunther khata* ('Baikuntha's Notebook', 1897).

In 1901, Tagore moved to Santiniketan in the Bengal countryside, which his father used as a religious retreat, and where he founded a boys' ashram that grew into an experimental school and ultimately into the university, Visva-Bharati. He rethought his approach to theatre, attacking foreign influences in a revolutionary essay, *The Stage* (1902): 'The cost which is incurred for mere accessories on the stage in Europe would swamp the whole of histrionic art in famine-stricken India ... the creative richness of poet and player are overshadowed by the wealth of the capitalist.' Instead he supported the suggestive imagination found in *Sanskrit theatre and the free

interaction in Indian folk forms. This theory heralded completely new dramatic vistas for him, starting with *Sharadotsab* (*Autumn-Festival*, 1908), possibly reinforced by the

Rabindranath Tagore as Valmiki in his *Balmiki-pratibha* (Calcutta, 1890 revival?)

fact that he now composed and directed plays specifically for the students in his school, thus pioneering *children's theatre as a curricular activity. These productions often took place in the open, under the trees; it stands to reason that *Sharadotsab* sang a paean to autumn, as a season of fulfilment. It was the first of several plays about the seasons, stressing the immanent bond between nature and humanity. Also, he turned to prose as his preferred medium, interspersed liberally with songs.

A very productive period in Tagore's dramatic career followed. *Prayashchitta* ('Penance', 1909) introduced a character prefiguring Mahatma Gandhi and propagating the political doctrine of satyagraha, years before Gandhi arrived in India. The masterpiece *Raja* (1910) allegorized man's realization of the true nature of divinity. *Achalayatan* ('Immovable Institution', 1911) parodied the rigid, frequently unjust beliefs of orthodox Hinduism, and in turn faced denunciation from conservative Bengalis. The touching *Dakghar* (*Post Office*, 1912), about a little boy's death, perhaps Tagore's best-known play internationally, received its world premiere at the Abbey Theatre, Ireland, in 1913. The announcement late in 1913 that he had won the Nobel Prize for his book of poems, *Gitanjali*, made him an instant worldwide celebrity, and all his works began appearing in translations. Sadly, the familiar English translations published by Macmillan and later reprinted by Rupa are unsatisfactory—most of them condensed, some quite inept, and one even unauthorized (*The King of the Dark Chamber*).

From this point on, typically, Tagore premiered his Bengali originals in Santiniketan and took them subsequently to Calcutta for eagerly awaited public shows. *Phalguni* (1915, translated as *The Cycle of Spring*), another season play, overwhelmed Calcutta spectators with its beauty, but also introduced dramaturgical novelties like a play within the play and generic dialogue unassigned to specific characters. However, he was unable to stage two of his finest, difficult symbolical works, *Muktadhara* (1922) and *Rakta-karabi* (*Red Oleander*, 1924). They forcefully indicted the oppression of subjugated people and exploitation of the earth's resources—*Muktadhara* on damming rivers and *Rakta-karabi* on digging mines—while embodying in their protagonists the spirit of self-sacrifice for a noble cause. *Natir puja* (1926, translated as *The Court Dancer* and released as a film, 1932) contrasted institutional Hinduism with the fundamental equality preached by

Buddhism, but also originally contained no male characters—a radical step in Indian theatre at a time when society frowned on actresses' morality.

Tagore displayed a characteristic restlessness in playwriting, frequently changing lines in the rehearsal process, reworking earlier scripts, compressing or improving them for new performances, or continuing to revise the text until he had convinced himself he had done justice to the theme. Sometimes the alterations were substantial enough to warrant new titles, virtually assuming the guise of new plays: for example *Raja* turned into *Arup ratan* (*Formless Jewel*, 1935), a much tighter rendering. In 1929 he undertook perhaps his most ambitious such project, completely recasting *Raja o rani* into *Tapati*, its heroine a powerful testament to feminism. He also dramatized his own fiction, often at the request of professional Bengali companies; the social comedy *Chirakumar sabha* ('Celibates' Club', 1925), adapted from a novel, proved quite successful and is periodically revived in *Bengali theatre.

In later life, Tagore grew fascinated with the incorporation of *dance into theatre. As with *music, his implementation of dance resulted from a drive to liberate classical styles from strict conformity and sheer virtuosity to a heterogeneous lyricism that appealed to the emotions.

Last scene of Tagore's *Dakghar* (Calcutta, 1917): seated at left, Gaganendranath Tagore; standing at right, Rabindranath Tagore and Abanindranath Tagore

Purists disapproved of his hybrid technique, but he could not be bothered with man-made regulations and emphasized the expression of aesthetic values without any formal rigidity. Inspired by the dance-dramas he had seen on trips to south-east Asia, he applied mixed choreography to fully musical texts. Testing the ground with *Taser desh* ('Land of Cards', 1933), which satirized fossilized prejudices, he perfected the art in a triptych upon the varying registers of love—*Chitrangada* (1936), *Chandalika* (1938, from his 1933 play about an untouchable girl), and *Shyama* (1939)—touring the productions to acclaim across India.

Although his repertoire consciously constituted 'art theatre', it offered a serious alternative to the frequently escapist entertainment available in Calcutta. And he remained acutely aware of its theatricality: he insisted that his plays 'be seen and heard, but not read'. This impulse also made him repeatedly rewrite them into what he called 'stageworthy' versions. It justifies the performatory importance of his songs, too, which crystallize the theatrical *rasa at critical points. As a director, though a perfectionist, he shared a wonderful understanding and easy relationship with his actors. Eyewitnesses describe his acting as natural, revealing 'an inner world of beauty and truth';

understandably, Tagore condemned the great Henry Irving's 'imitative naturalism' and exaggeration, which ruined 'inner beauty'. Progressively he broke all illusions of reality in design, culminating in aesthetic minimalism and, in his later work, openly sat in one corner downstage for all to see.

It is not within the scope of this entry to mention Tagore's enormous output of songs, poetry, fiction, essays, philosophical discourses, and paintings. Perhaps we can even rationalize this omission on the ground that they have tended to swamp appreciation of his achievement in theatre, which needs separate attention to emerge from that neglect. Most definitely, he was the leading pathfinder of modern Indian theatre.   AL

Chitra (London: India Society, 1913); *Chitrangada*, translated by B.N. Roy (Calcutta: Sribhumi, 1957); *'Chitrangada' and Other Dramatic Poems,* translated by Shailesh Parekh (New Delhi: Rupa, 2007); *'The Crown', 'King and Rebel'* (New Delhi: Rupa, 2002); *The Curse at Farewell,* translated by Edward Thompson (London: George Harrap, 1924); *The Cycle of Spring* (London: Macmillan, 1917); *The Dancing Girl's Worship* (New Delhi: Rupa, 2003); *Devouring Love,* translated by Shakuntala Rao Sastri (New York: East West Institute, 1961); *The King of the Dark Chamber* (London: Macmillan, 1914); *The Post Office*, translated by Devabrata Mukerjea (London: Macmillan, 1914);

The Post Office, translated by Krishna Dutta and Andrew Robinson (New York: St Martin's, 1996); *The Post Office*, translated by William Radice (London: Tagore Centre, 1996); *Red Oleanders* (London: Macmillan, 1925); *'Sacrifice' and Other Plays* (London: Macmillan, 1917); *Three Plays*, translated by Marjorie Sykes (Bombay: Oxford University Press, 1950); *Three Plays*, translated by Ananda Lal (New Delhi: Oxford University Press, 2001); *Three Riddle Plays*, translated by Prithvindra Chakravarti (Calcutta: Writers Workshop, 1983); *'The Trial', 'Autumn-Festival'* (New Delhi: Rupa, 2002); *Two Buddhist Plays*, translated by Shyamasree Devi (Calcutta: Writers Workshop, 1993); *The Waterfall* (New Delhi: Rupa, 2002); K.S. Appaswami Ayyar, *A Critical Study of Rabindranath's 'Chitra'* (Madras: Chandra, 1952); Bishweshwar Chakraverty, *Tagore the Dramatist* (Delhi: B.R., 2000); R.N. Roy, *Rabindranath Tagore the Dramatist* (Calcutta: A. Mukherjee, 1992); Edward Thompson, *Rabindranath Tagore: Poet and Dramatist* (London: Oxford University Press, 1948).

Talamaddale ('cymbals and drums'): variant of the *Kannada theatre form of *Yakshagana, deriving its name from *tala* (cymbal) and *maddale* (the Yakshagana drum), and quite popular in the western districts of Karnataka. Essentially it presents Yakshagana *prasanga*s (scripts) with songs and dialogue but without dances and stagecraft. Historically, it seems to have originated before Yakshagana but continued to retain a separate identity and stronghold even after the latter gained popularity. The reasons are twofold: Talamaddale provides occasion to relish exclusively the intricacies of the song and prose components of Yakshagana without the distractions of stagecraft, and it is a way of capitalizing on the enthusiasm for Yakshagana during the off-season when open-air shows are not possible. Therefore, Talamaddale sessions abound during the monsoon, from June to October. However, amateurs often continue performing throughout the year and, occasionally, professional Yakshagana artists are invited to join.

The performance takes place in any common indoor space where the singers, instrumentalists, and actors sit in a prominent spot and the audience in the rest of the area. These shows are not ticketed, the modest expenses being shared by the patrons or the local community. As in Yakshagana, the Bhagavata (the main singer) is the key person. He introduces the plot, beginning with an invocation and minimal preliminaries. Then the actors, all in a squatting posture, one by one assume their respective roles, each giving a long introduction to his character, contextualizing it in the Puranic panorama and locating it in the episode of the day. Through extempore dialogue and rhetorical speech, the performance develops into a lively battle of wits where the actors interrogate one another, extensively quoting from the epics, and take the plot to its climax.

The structure juxtaposes two seemingly disparate matrices, the mythic-epic and the contemporary: the songs tell of epic events while the dialogues are free-floating, often venturing into contemporary socio-political allusions. As Talamaddale relies solely on songs and dialogue, every actor (significantly called an *arthadhari*, 'one who conveys meaning') needs to have a good voice, a capacity to blend musical delivery with witty speech, and a thorough knowledge of the epics and the specific episodes. These qualifications combined with an impressive stage presence make a star performer. Talamaddale's wide popularity complements that of Yakshagana, both forms influencing and sustaining each other.   AKV

Tamasa (literally 'entertainment'): the youngest form of *Rajasthani theatre, invented by the Bhatt family hailing from Telengana in Andhra Pradesh. They were Kirtankars (Kirtan singers) there and came to Jaipur along with Kanwar Ram Singh, son of Mirza Raja Jai Singh, who as a Mughal

commander in the reign of Aurangzeb (1618–1707) had gone south to capture Shivaji. Many confuse the origin of Rajasthani Tamasa with that of the *Tamasha of Maharashtra, but this is a fallacy.

Maharaja Ram Singh II (1835–81) of Jaipur was a great patron of music and theatre, who founded the Gunijan Khana where musicians and dancers were permanently employed. In 1876 he built Ram Prakash Theatre, on the lines of the Victorian auditoria constructed in those days all over India, and established a company like those of the *Parsi theatre, which used to tour Jaipur regularly. The Bhatts, singers at the Gunijan Khana, were assigned to the Ram Prakash company. In the later part of Ram Singh's life and especially after his death, the theatre virtually came to an end and the company was disbanded. It was then that the Bhatts, who were enamoured by Parsi theatre, adopted that style of performance and started putting up plays in Brahmapuri, where they lived, and at Amber in Jaipur district.

The texts of Tamasa are almost all from Parsi theatre, such as *Hir-Ranjha* ('Hir and Ranjha'), *Gopichand*, and *Laila-Majnu* ('Laila and Majnu'). There is also the same mixture of prose and poetry in the dialogue, spoken or sung in the Parsi style. The only difference is the language, Rajasthani, having the flavour of the dialect spoken in Jaipur. Yet the influence of Parsi theatre is so great that a lot of Urdu is judiciously mixed with the Rajasthani. The music has a classical touch, and shows take place in the open and in the round.

Although Tamasa performances are not very frequent, young members of the Bhatt family who are involved in urban theatre have started writing new Tamasa plays with modern content. It is an interesting experiment and a genuine effort at continuity, yet the danger is that most of the younger generation have not learnt music professionally and very few can sing. Without the music it will be very difficult to keep the tradition of Tamasa alive.   RS

Tamasha (from Arabic, 'fun', 'playful entertainment'): most popular folk form of *Marathi theatre. Renowned for its elasticity and versatility, Tamasha evolved as a composite, borrowing elements from *Dasavatar, Gondhal, Kirtan, and Vaghya-murali (worshippers of the folk god Khandoba). Yet the concoction became a unique blend with comedy, eroticism, and music as integral parts. Tamasha subverts the established ideologies of social power by presenting them in an inverted and outrageously funny manner through typical characters and situations, affording people a release for their suppressed anger against hegemonic hierarchies. It bears some resemblance to *Nautanki and *Swang in northern India.

Although the precise date of origin remains unknown, Tamasha existed in the eighteenth century and prospered during the later Peshwa period. Yet the word was used since the twelfth century and came to signify amusing performance, such as the *Kalsutri puppet show and acrobatics to entertain Mughal armies. In the nineteenth century, the term covered plays as well. It is argued that Tamasha bears a resemblance to the Sanskrit *prahasana* and *bhana*, but structural dissimilarities and lack of any significant evidence render this hypothesis untenable.

There are two main types of Tamasha, *dholkibari* ('dholak's turn': public and outdoors) and *sangitbari* ('music's turn': private and indoors). *Dholkibari* has many performers, of whom the main Shahir (poet-singer), Nachi ('dancer', a cross-dressed boy in the past, or a young woman today), and Songadya (clown) are the most important. Often they belong to family troupes, as in the case of the renowned Bapurao Narayangaonkar and his daughter Vithabai. The Shahir and male accompanists begin with a *gana* (song) vigorously rendered. The style is similar to Gondhal but the open-air theatre space here is not believed to be charged with divine presence. Then the Nachi enters dancing, back to the audience, her sari's *pallav* (end) held high like a mast and, after straining the viewers' curiosity and suspense to the limit, shows them her face.

The *gaulan* follows, presenting a humorous dramatic encounter between Krishna and his *vidushaka*

friend and the milkmaids of Gokula. The Songadya enters in the form of the milkmaids' elderly aunt. The dialogues have double meanings, often the source of ribald and raucous humour, verging on the obscene for elite tastes. This part, called *rangabaji* (erotic performance), also contains *lavanis* or amorous songs, danced to the accompaniment of several instruments such as the stringed *tuntune*, *kade* (metal triangle), *daph* (tambourine), small *sambal* and *dimdi* drums, and dholak. The style of dances resembles the spinning movements

Vithabai Narayangaonkar performing in Tamasha, 1980

and *abhinaya of Kathak. *Bhedik lavani*s, with philosophical riddles, and encounters between Shahirs belonging to Siva and Shakti cults, called Turewale and Kalgiwale, grew popular.

A *batavani* (a typical humorous event, joke, or anecdote) is presented in which politicians, higher-caste people, merchants, rulers, and even gods are subjected to extremely comic or scurrilous treatment. Then the *vag* (scenario) begins, an enactment of a mythological or purely imaginative tale. The Shahir first delivers an introductory song and the performance proceeds through music, songs, narration, and dialogue, all laced with racy fun, satire, and slapstick. The *vag*, introduced in the nineteenth century, probably indicates the influence of the new tradition of drama. A *mujra* dance comes last, paying homage to great Shahirs and holy persons, and the Tamasha is over.

Sangitbari, also called *baithakicha* ('seated-style') Tamasha, is performed in rooms or private places. It consists of *lavani*s without the *batavani* and *vag*. Women sing and act out *lavani*s, but do not dance, and the Songadya creates humour. Satyabhamabai Pandharpurkar is one of the most noted exponents. However, some researchers do not consider it true Tamasha. Regional variations of Tamasha exist, such as Khandeshi, Waideshi, Khadi Gammat, Jalsas, and Kolhatinicha. In all forms, the Songadya is an essential component, whose farce, mimicry, double-edged dialogues, and impromptu comments and interpolations create a distinctive brand of comedy.

Although Tamasha has had artists from different communities, it has been associated with the lower castes of Mahars, Mangs, and Kolhatis, hence with low prestige. Female dancers contributed greatly to its development, yet, often treated as prostitutes, they were blatantly used both sexually and economically through customs like *daulatjada*, where a spectator offered the woman money not only to sing and dance a song of his choice, but also as a price to touch her. Most performers are illiterate and this exacerbates their exploitation by several people, including the *thekedar*s (Tamasha contractors). The Government of Bombay established the Tamasha Sudharak in 1958, which did considerable work for their organization and upliftment.

Tamasha influenced both theatre and films. Writers like Vijay Tendulkar (*Ghashiram Kotwal*) and P.L. Deshpande (*Tin paishacha tamasha*, adapted from Brecht's *Threepenny Opera*), and directors like Vijaya Mehta (*Ajab nyaya vartulacha*, from Brecht's *Caucasian Chalk Circle*) adopted it successfully. Dadu Indurikar, Ram Nagarkar, and Dada Kondke invented Loknatya ('folk theatre'), an 'improved' version of Tamasha without the bawdy elements, which played a useful role in social reform and political movements in Maharashtra. During the 1950s and 1960s, Tamasha inspired Marathi cinema eventually to Tamasha's own detriment, as its spectators began to want film-style songs and dances. At the end of the twentieth century around 360 *phads* (groups) performed for an audience of over six lakh—not exactly a dying art, but still in need of protection.   MP

Tamasho ('entertainment'): rural form of *Sindhi theatre, essentially a prerogative of Muslim feudal lords in Sindh. Although an erotic idiom like the Marathi *Tamasha, it is quite different. Tamasho performers are called by Vaderas (landlords) to present a show in an open place before the invited audience, mostly on such occasions as weddings or the circumcision of Muslim boys. The Tamasho party consists of one or two songstresses, accompanied by their own instrumentalists and a jester. The witty dialogue between the women, or between jester and singer, is followed by romantic lyrics generally based on the ragas Pilu, Sindhu Kafi, and Bhairavi. The music normally uses *changu* (Jew's harp), sarangi, tabla, dholak, and *duhilu* drums. Tamasho goes on for hours and ends with lavish payments to the participants and a feast for the audience.   PA

Tanatu Natakavedi ('indigenous theatre'): important development in contemporary *Malayalam theatre. The idea, vague to begin with, came up at a theatre camp or Kalari held in Sasthankotta, Kollam district, in 1967. Those who conceived it felt that the theatre of Kerala could become creative and strong only if it had an identity of its own and, to achieve that, it had to be rooted in the native culture and associated with the artistic tradition of the land. Soon, playwrights and directors undertook the task of translating this concept into reality, their efforts encouraged by similar attempts in other parts of India to evolve an 'Indian theatre'.

C.N. Srikanthan Nair, an ingenious dramatist, took up the challenge of writing a play indigenous in form as well as content: *Kali* (1968) dealt with a semi-mythical narrative expressed through a sequence of similar images. Although its production did not succeed, it induced others like G. Sankara Pillai and K.N. Panikkar to mould their own models. Pillai adopted modern dramatic concepts to suit the Indian outlook, incorporating characters and images from the native tradition. Many of his plays, especially *Karutta daivatte tedi* ('In Search of the Black God', 1980), represent this theory. Some were effectively staged, and well received even outside the state. A number of young directors followed his example. Unfortunately, some of their works tended to become odd combinations of Western and Indian ideas, failing to appeal to playgoers in general. A few attempted to adapt traditional forms like *Kathakali to dramatize new themes, but the approach invited criticism from advocates of conventional proscenium theatre as well as those who opposed any distortion of traditional performing arts.

Panikkar conceived the narrative in a mythical form as in traditional theatre but relied on its underlying aesthetic concepts and not on borrowed foreign techniques to give expression to that content. Some young artists came forward to add variety to this type of performance, thereby giving it an undeniable place in contemporary Malayalam theatre. However, the success of this approach depended on a sound knowledge of the basic elements of the tradition, the absence of which limited its wider application, because many did not have the in-depth knowledge of the aesthetic aspects of Kerala's performing arts, the indigenous system of music, and the principles of the *Natyasastra* that Panikkar possessed.   KSNP

Terukkuttu (literally, 'street theatre'), Kuttu for short: 500-year-old folk form mainly of the northern districts in Tamil Nadu, comparable to *Kathakali or *Yakshagana. Its southern style has less sophistication in costumes and many imaginary tales in the repertoire. Over 200 professional companies perform, each for about 200 days a year, from March till mid-September. Harvested land is the performance space, normally as part of Draupadi Amman festivals (from March to August) for ten to sixteen days at a stretch. Sometimes single shows are staged in individual households at funeral ceremonies.

During the day, the mythological story may be narrated in the temples and at night, the same story enacted. The play begins around 10 p.m. and goes on till 5 a.m. Sometimes the whole village takes part: in *Arjuna tapas* ('Arjuna's Austerities'), *Bakasuran*, and *Padukalam* ('Prostrate on the Field', about Duryodhana's death), the village becomes an arena and all the villagers participate. The same happens at the eighteen-day enactment of the Kurukshetra war in Purisai village

(Tiruvannamalai district), the best-known centre of Terukkuttu.

At these all-night shows, the performers sing, dance, speak, and act. They adorn themselves with colourful costumes and heavy ornaments, since the tales are drawn from the Puranas and epics. The headgear and winged ornament on the shoulders, called *bujakirti*, and chest shield are wooden, together easily weighing 40 kg. The costumes are designed to go with these accoutrements. On the waist is worn a multilayered, well-pleated, jutting-out dress called *vittuduppu*. Jingling metal anklets accentuate the vigorous, suggestive, and vibrating dance movements. The speciality of the steps is to finish by doing the spinning *kirukki* (literally 'rotation'). There are *kirukki*s performed on the knees as well.

A small tent functions as the green room in front of which a bench serves as the seat for musicians and also as the throne, chariot, terrace, or whatever location in which the play takes place. The instruments used are *mukhavina* (a smaller, high-pitched version of the double-reed *nagaswaram*), harmonium, *mridangam* drums, and *talam* (cymbals). Those standing next to the musicians repeat all the songs.

Each character enters from behind a screen, announcing his name, lineage, and history. Men act women's roles. Kattiyakkaran (literally 'announcer'), a combination of *vidushaka* and *sutradhara*, dances in first, welcomes the spectators, propitiates the deities, leads the narrative, introduces the characters, explains the world of the story, takes on many roles, links the past to current society, and speaks the audience's mind. He bridges the

Terukkuttu actor of the Erankur Narayanasamy Nataka Mandram

sensibilities of the actors and viewers. He can relax and tighten the narrative depending on the need of the hour. He even asks children to participate. The tales may be old, but the artists amaze by their ability to infuse contemporary references and opinions, particularly through Kattiyakkaran's improvised colloquial jibes at gods and humans.

The Thambirans (literally, 'respected masters') of Purisai produced three famous twentieth-century performers: Natesa Thambiran, Kannappa Thambiran, and N. Subramaniya Thambiran. Terukkuttu faced penury and near extinction in the mid-century, until national recognition lifted it to a sustainable activity, supported by grants and government trips to foreign festivals. In recent times, interesting experiments have taken place. With the interaction of Na. Muthuswamy's Koothu-p-pattarai, the Purisai Terukkuttu Company adapted Garcia Marquez's short story *The Old Man with Huge Wings* into their form. They also performed Brecht's *Caucasian Chalk Circle* as an all-night show. V. Arumugham's Thalai-k-kol group staged Molière's *George Dandin* as a Terukkuttu. The juncture at which traditional Terukkuttu and modern theatre stand seems very promising.   CA

Hanne M. de Bruin, *Kattaikkuttu: The Flexibility of a South Indian Theatre Tradition* (Groningen: Egbert Forsten, 1999); Richard Armando Frasca, *The Theater of the 'Mahabharata': 'Terukkuttu' Performances in South India* (Honolulu: University of Hawaii, 1990).

Teyyam (literally 'spirit', of a deity): ritualistic form in the north Kerala districts of Kannur and Kasaragod, performed in shrines (known by different names like Kavu, Mundiya, Palliyara), houses, ancestral homes, and public places, as a worshipful offering of the community, intended for its common welfare. The person who transforms into a Teyyam acquired the right to officiate through family lineage; the major communities engaged in this religious practice are the Malayan, Vannan, Velan, Pulayan, Mavilon, and Koppalam. Generally an annual festival, its periodicity varies in certain temples to once in several years. When the *ritual comes after several decades, widespread cooperation of many villages in the vicinity ensues and such an event is termed *perumkaliyattam* (grand festive enactment). In some cases it is conducted as an individual's offering for attainment of material prosperity, warding off evil spells, or curing of diseases.

A large variety of Teyyams exists, belonging to gods and goddesses, war heroes, ancestors, animals, serpents, trees, and even devils. After their death, war heroes and ancestors are socially accepted as deified spirits. Godly spirits fall into three major categories: Saiva, Vaishnava, and Shakta. Vettakkorumakan (the son born to Siva and Parvati during a hunt), Vayanat Kulavan, Bhairavan, and Pottan are Saiva, dedicated to Siva. Vishnu Murti and Palottu Teyyam come under the Vaishnava group, dedicated to Vishnu. Bhagavati and Chamundi are of Shakta denomination, for Shakti. The prominent Kathivanur Viran belongs to the warrior class. Animals include Pullikkarimkali, Puliyurkali, Pulimarutan, and Bali. Ilanjikkal Bhagavati represents tree worship. Each is noted for specific make-up and outfits, designed on the basis of traditional colour

A Teyyam with accompanying percussionist

concepts presenting the sentiments of the concerned spirit. They are gorgeous and mostly made of natural materials. The headgear (upon a wooden frame) can have several sizes and shapes—round, triangular, tower-like, fish-like—elaborately decorated to add to the Teyyam's visual brilliance.

The process of deification sometimes gives a mythic dimension to a local event; ultimately this lower myth gets dissolved in an already existing popular higher myth. In Palemthayi Kannan, for example, an individual experience assumed mythicization and merged in the larger myth of Vishnu Murti, representing Vishnu's Narasimha avatar. In Kathivanur Viran, based on a highly emotional village tale of love, after the lover was martyred in war with a neighbouring state, his spirit became glorified as a Teyyam. Pottan is another noteworthy Teyyam in this context. The saint Sankaracharya once came across an untouchable Chandala (or Pottan). Upper-caste Hindus believed in untouchability, and did not allow Chandalas to walk on the main road. When Sankaracharya saw him treading it, for fear of pollution he commanded him to move away. This led to argumentation between them on the soul's inviolability and the evil practice of untouchability. Sankaracharya accepted defeat and fell at the feet of the Chandala, who enlightened him on non-dualistic Advaita philosophy and, to Sankaracharya's great surprise, revealed himself as none other than Siva.

The Teyyam repertoire, with its rich variety of stories rendered as *tottam* (narrative songs describing the myth) and its enactment, provides the ethnic, religious, and socio-political experience of the people's uninterrupted culture. The *tottam* details the exhaustive background against which the impersonator brings out the subtle feel of the Teyyam. The enactment does not literally convey the narrative, but highlights the emotional content through body movements, gestures, vocal articulation, costumes, and *possession. The performer gets transformed into the spirit through several stages. While he and his associates sing the *tottam*, he continues in a possessed dance. The instruments accompanying the dance are *chenda* (double-faced drum), cymbals, and sometimes *kurumkuzhal* (a small double-reed pipe). Each Teyyam showers blessings in his peculiar way to devotees and distributes *prasadam* (holy gifts), mostly turmeric powder and in some cases ash, flowers, or rice. Some Shakti Teyyams give toddy and alcohol as their favourite *prasadam*.   KNP

K.K.N. Kurup, *The Cult of Teyyam and Hero Worship in Kerala* (Calcutta: Indian Publications, 1973); K.K.N. Kurup,

Teyyam: A Ritual Dance of Kerala (Trivandrum: Department of Public Relations, Government of Kerala, 1986); Sita K. Nambiar, *The Ritual Art of Teyyam and Bhutaradhane* (New Delhi: Indira Gandhi National Centre for the Arts and Navrang, 1996); J.J. Pallath, *Theyyam: An Analytical Study of the Folk Culture, Wisdom and Personality* (New Delhi: Indian Social Institute, 1995); Valentina Stache-Rosen, *Bhutas and Teyyams* (Bangalore: Max Mueller Bhavan, 1978).

Theatre education: India's 2500-year theatre tradition implies equally ancient modes of actor training. From the *Natyasastra*, which indicates a high degree of stylization, it is obvious that the sophisticated elite *Sanskrit theatre must have required a rigorous regimen. Subsequently, the traditional forms found in different regions also show varying degrees of stylization, including gestural language, and complex dance and music, imparted by the *guru-sishya parampara* ('guru-disciple relationship') over a period of many years, or through observation and participation from childhood within hereditary performing families. In the more formal of such systems, theoretical studies include the reading of classical texts, a single mudra, eye movement, or posture may take weeks to perfect, and gurus may not even allow their students to perform publicly until several years have elapsed.

After 1850, along with British influence due to colonial rule, a new form of entertainment resulting from imitation of *English theatre came to exist in the urban centres. Broadly called the 'company theatre' because of its overall organization, it had unfamiliar elements such as the auditorium, and technical or visual aspects that demanded coordination and actors adjusting to them. Theatre enthusiasts assimilated the art by first copying the British and then learning on the job, under the supervision of their seniors, often the actor-managers. Some companies had specific music and dance teachers who taught the artistes under strict discipline.

When ideologically modernist, more purposeful theatre activity was generated in the mid-twentieth century, many young people got involved and pioneers tried to initiate them through discussions and workshops. Institutional education in theatre began at the M.S. University (Vadodara) in 1950 with a diploma course. In independent India, the need was felt to provide training in various components of theatre to enable pupils to undertake this art form with greater awareness and confidence. The Sangeet Natak Akademi articulated this perception at a national theatre seminar in 1956, and the *National School of Drama (NSD) was set up in 1959 under its umbrella.

This was the beginning of grappling with the problem of devising an institutionalized education for a theatre whose acting had no base in Indian tradition and which had considerable new technology. The pattern had to be derived from the European model, which Indians were emulating, and had an evolved methodology. The NSD's first syllabus therefore attempted basic familiarization with set and costume design, make-up, lighting, acting, and production, along with Western and Indian theatre history. The instructors had no formal training but had developed expertise and methods for teaching their respective subjects through experience. While

the NSD underwent several changes of syllabus, the basic structure of the course remained more or less the same, with shifts only in emphases and approaches in keeping with changes in theatre. It runs a three-year diploma course, with two years' specialization in acting or production, preparing graduates to work as professionals in their specializations and also generally, if necessary.

Only one such institution in India was obviously not enough to answer the requirement all over the country. Besides, the NSD concentrated on performance in Hindi. Hence local academicians interested in theatre in their own languages opened departments of drama or theatre at their universities. Around thirty universities teach the subject, some offering a part-time or

Rooster stance practised inside a traditional Kalari

one-year certificate, others a two- or three-year diploma, some a three-year bachelor's degree and others a master's or research options for those wanting to pursue advanced studies. The syllabi consist of nearly the same curriculum as found at the NSD, with some theoretical inputs specific to the concerned state where the university is located. However, the faculty in these departments largely constitutes academics from different disciplines and with little or no experience of theatre, often unable to do justice either to the practical aspects or the theory.

Trained or seasoned theatre workers run a few of these departments, like those at M.S. University, Rabindra Bharati (Calcutta), Calicut School of Drama (Thrissur), Punjab (Chandigarh), and Rajasthan (Jaipur), but problems of funding, rigidity of the academic system, and lack of understanding on the part of authorities about the needs of such courses come in the way of satisfactory education. Despite the constraints, these departments have created a whole cadre of informed enthusiasts, imparted knowledge about dramatic literature, and generated theatre activity on their respective campuses involving many more students as spectators. More facilities, finances, and vision could achieve greater rigour and

commitment, producing serious theatre scholars and fulfilling region-specific demands.

Some other institutes, government and private, provide theatre training alongside repertory companies, like Bhartendu Natya Akademi (Lucknow) which offers a two-year diploma; Ninasam (Heggodu) which has a one-year acting course combining traditional forms of Karnataka and modern theatre; and Shri Ram Centre (New Delhi) which runs a two-year part-time acting programme. Several smaller outfits give short-term courses in different parts of India. Another mode of training, though elementary, comprises workshops conducted by eminent practitioners. These create an awareness of the various aspects of theatre and how they need to be creatively coordinated towards a production, and give a temporary fillip to theatre in the area where the workshop is held.

The primary crises facing theatre education at the turn of the twenty-first century were the absence of a professional theatre that could absorb the trained personnel, rising costs of production and infrastructure facilities, and the prospect of careers in cinema and television which weans both actors and technicians away from their chosen specialization in theatre.   KJ

Theatre for development:
term encompassing diverse
practices and movements using
theatre for social progress and
change. Activist and grass-roots
bodies, government and non-
government organizations (NGOs),
as well as socially-aware theatre
groups or individuals, working
with Dalits, women, children, sex
workers, and other marginalized
populations, all qualify as
practising theatre for development.

The conscious use of
performance for these reasons as an
all-India phenomenon can be traced
to the *Indian People's Theatre
Association (IPTA), which sought
to raise social and political
awareness through theatre and
other art forms. Reacting to the
fascism and imperialism of the
1940s, the artists and intellectuals
of IPTA saw themselves as a socialist
vanguard, which would 'make of
our arts the expression and the
organizer of our people's struggles'
and enlighten 'the [oppressed]
masses about the causes and
solution of the problems facing
them'. IPTA productions, involving
proscenium and street or open-air
performances, never really became
grass-roots theatre; however, they
were the first to include traditional
forms and enlist folk artists,
realizing that the 'masses' already
had performance idioms used for
effective communication.

Following IPTA, official agencies
were among the earliest to pick up
on the advantages of theatre for
consciousness-raising and information dissemination; in a country
with low literacy and high population, theatre, especially *street
theatre, provided a low-cost and
immediate means of reaching the
illiterate. Whereas IPTA included
rural performers in its fold, the
Indian government encouraged folk
artists, often monetarily or through
other forms of patronage, to include
given social messages in their
particular repertoires. The
government's model of development was certainly not about
people's struggle in the revolutionary sense, but focused instead on
education, family planning, hy-
giene, building of pit latrines, and
other such national concerns. Other
organizations also took up similar
themes: the mobilization of theatre
for science literacy by the Kerala
Sahitya Sangharsh Parishad is a
notable example.

In the 1980s and 1990s, NGOs,
non-partisan activist societies, and
grass-roots groups all over the
country increasingly began to use
street theatre as a means of
addressing issues and working
towards social change. Theatre for
development now covers subjects as
diverse as sexual health, female
infanticide, gender, and Dalit
concerns; the ideology remains

social progress, but the idea of what constitutes progress has evolved. It reflects the historical shift in the notion of development, where earlier agendas of people's struggle and nation building are now joined by a focus on human and individual rights.

However, theatre practice in the interests of development has not shown much change. The majority continues as crude examples of street theatre, thematically and stylistically; the late Safdar Hashmi's Jana Natya Manch (Delhi), Praja Natya Mandali (Hyderabad), and Natya Chetana (Orissa) are refreshing exceptions to this rule. Much theatre for development also retains the IPTA logic of a leadership speaking to the oppressed, taking up their problems, and providing solutions. The advent of organizations at the grass-roots level wrought some change in this dynamic; the person on stage now also belongs to the group whose difficulties are being addressed. However, this person is invariably seen as a social activist, and thus holds to a large extent the exalted position given to the vanguard in the earlier IPTA scenario. Moreover, the activists, grass-roots or not, continue to take on the entire responsibility of choosing, analysing, and solving an issue *before* presenting it—the audience plays the role of passive consumers.

Some individuals and organizations reacted to the passive nature of such 'theatre *for* the oppressed' (a term coined by Brazilian theorist-artist Augusto Boal), and opted to experiment with theatre in ways that include and involve the target groups. Boal's *Theatre of the Oppressed*, particularly the technique of 'forum theatre', was adopted by workers in different parts of India. In forum theatre, actors present a pressing problem, but instead of providing answers, invite the audience to enact possible solutions, which are then resisted by the actors in socially realistic ways, giving rise to discussion and exploration of the issue through theatre. The goal is two-fold—to look for practicable solutions and, more importantly, to encourage spectators to act, to become 'spect-actors', as a step toward becoming active participants in their own struggles. Jana Sanskriti, based in rural West Bengal, is specially innovative and successful in its practice of forum theatre, setting up over forty units (some all-female) across the state as well as elsewhere, mobilizing such movements as anti-arrack, anti-dowry, and demand for health care. They pay particular attention to gender, collaborating with women's NGOs to sensitize audiences while simultaneously empowering women to come forward and seek their own answers through theatre.

An attention to process rather than product is yet another way in which theatre is harnessed for active participation. Organizations working with children welcome theatre as a means of play and expression; theatre people are also invited to conduct workshops with other groups. There seems to be a small but growing recognition in the development sector that theatre process—the exercises and techniques used by actors and directors—can make unique and powerful contributions to individual self-awareness and growth, as also to building collective trust and collaborative endeavour. While none of these factors create empowerment or development in and of themselves, they are being understood as necessary prerequisites to enable and sustain development. As of now, most of these workshops last only a few days, and the need to see a result or finished product—usually a play with a message—still overrides the newer concept of the benefits of the process. Those working with women, particularly, accept these benefits. Jana Sanskriti's female units, Mahila Samakhya (Karnataka), and Voicing Silence (Chennai), an NGO whose credo is 'women's theatre for women's empowerment', see theatre process as central to their activities.

Throughout the history of Indian theatre for development, there has been a belief that folk forms are uniquely suited to communicate to the multitudes. In contrast to the governmental approach of providing messages for distribution, the collaboration of Alarippu (Delhi) with *Pandavani performer Shanti Bai Chelak in Pirda (Chhattisgarh) instructively engages the rural artist herself. Chelak incorporates powerful gynocentric performances, reflecting her own sophisticated understanding of gender, in her repertoire. Grass-roots troupes also draw on

Jana Sanskriti performing at a village in Bokaro district, Jharkhand

traditional forms and include village actors; groups dealing with Dalit problems, such as Chennai Kalai Kuzhu (Chennai), Chemmani (Tirunelveli), and the feminist theatre of M. Jeeva (all in Tamil Nadu), claim to use Dalit folk expression as a conscious political stance. Furthermore, some traditional performers themselves have taken up issues relating to development: theatre on the environment by *Terukkuttu artist P. Rajagopal of Tamil Nadu Kattaikkuttu Kalai Valarchi Munnetra Sangam (Kanchipuram) offers one such example.   SI

Sudhi Pradhan (ed.), *Marxist Cultural Movement in India: Chronicles and Documents*, 3 vols. (Calcutta: National Book Agency, Navana, and Mrs Santi Pradhan, 1979–85); *Theatre for Change* (*Seagull Theatre Quarterly*, Special Issue, December 1998–March 1999).

Theory: Indian theatre offers the most extensive, if not the oldest, theoretical analysis of performance among classical traditions in the world. The myth of theatre's origin in Brahma and the story of the first dramatic performance, occurring in the first chapter of Bharata's *Natyasastra*, are important from this angle. In particular, the failure of the first show, whose theme was the defeat of the Daityas (demons), has deep implications. Angry, they created trouble during the play. They told Brahma, 'This knowledge of theatre, which your Lordship has created at the behest of the gods, has humiliated us.' The performance took the form of *anukriti* or *anukarana* ('redoing', or imitation) and it is apparent that the Daityas took *anukriti* too literally. Brahma tried to remove their misgivings by describing theatre as 'the glorious *anukirtana* (retelling) of the *bhavas* (emotive states) of the entire triple universe (heaven, sky, and earth)'.

Although Bharata also defines the nature of theatre as *anukarana*, Abhinavagupta (950–1025) emphasizes that it is essentially *anukirtana*. His *Abhinavabharati* ('Abhinava Speaks') raises deeper ontological and aesthetic options, asking whether we comprehend theatre as reality (*tattva*), as similar (*sadrisya*) to it like a twin, or as an error (*bhranti*) like silver mistakenly identified in mother of pearl. It questions whether theatrical reality is superimposition (*aropa*), like viewing a beloved's face as the moon, or identification (*adhyavasaya*), like saying, 'This man from the land of Vahika is a bull.' Abhinavagupta rationalizes his objections from the perspectives of the playwright, actor, and aesthetic experience of the spectator or connoisseur. He singles out the concept of *anukarana* for repudiation, since it appears to be the basis for all other hypotheses, and argues that it (imitation) amounts to a farcical copy of the 'real', a *vikarana* ('undoing', or distortion). It makes the indifferent simply laugh and may cause indignation in those who belong to the side of the imitated.

Moreover, the reproduction of figures like Rama that belong to a mythical past is simply impossible. Neither can someone similar to Rama be presented, because no one exists at the time of performance who can be supposed to have seen Rama, nor can the actor replicate his own sorrow as Rama's because the original is absolutely absent in him. Indeed, if it were actually present in him, his performance would not be a reproduction. Thus the theory of *anukarana* stands totally rejected and, if that happens to the prima facie view of *anukarana*, all similar views are automatically rejected. Theatre is, rather, an *anukirtana* of the *bhava*s, a 'retelling'. However, this retelling is not that of an actual event, but the re-presentation of the *bhava*s underlying that event.

Abhinavagupta does not elaborate the concept of *anukirtana*. We have no option except to understand it through the etymology of *kirtana*, which means firstly 'telling' or 'narrating', rather than 'imitating', 'making', or 'reproducing'. It is in no way an exercise at creating an illusion of the real. The creative aspect of retelling the *bhava*s entails endless ways of narrating life and the world, for *kirtana* connotes repeated telling, reciting, and describing. Second, the act of presenting *bhava*s, *lokasvabhava* ('people's behaviour', or the internal and external nature and behaviour of all beings), and *trailokya* ('triple universe') belongs to the order of extolling them. It not merely restates the real, but retells the real in order to glorify it. Thus *anukirtana* captures the essential meaning of the original more powerfully than an imitation. Third, it is a creative act of the dramatist and performer, who exercise their freedom to avoid whatever they deem fit to avoid and incorporate what has to be adopted.

Kirtana etymologically includes all three meanings but the most important is the idea that it is not imitational reproduction, but reverberative representation. An artist does not recreate reality; he retells it in a glorious way. In course of time, *kirtana* acquired another, more specific, meaning of 'raising a temple or monument' to celebrate an auspicious or favourable occasion. *Anukirtana* is deeply rooted in Vedic ideas of *yajna*, or *ritual and sacrifice. Theatre is sacred as well as secular, but essentially its nature is that of a sacrifice. It must be performed on consecrated ground. Thus it sublimates human action through 'universalization', and pleases the gods. This sense of celebration is abundantly present in the meaning of *anukirtana*. Although *anukirtana* may be rendered simply as re-presentation, imaging, or mimicking, we must carefully qualify it to realize the immense underlying difference with the Aristotelian concept of mimesis.

Theatre is further defined as the *abhinaya (acting) of *rasa and *bhava*. Sarngadeva, a thirteenth-century exponent of *dance and *music, explains it in consonance with the doctrines of Bharata and Abhinavagupta primarily as *rasa* and secondarily as *abhinaya*. Thus Sanskrit drama has all along been viewed in terms of *prayoga* (performance) and *kriya* (practice). Moreover, whatever is extrinsically *abhinaya* is intrinsically *rasa*. Theatre is ultimately *rasa*. In order to make the *sahridaya* (literally 'same heart', or sympathetic connoisseur) experience the *rasa* through *bhava*, the *prayokta* (performer) is required to delineate *bhava*s through *vibhava*s (stimuli). This is why, in the *Natyasastra*, the exposition of *abhinaya* takes place after that of *rasa* and *bhava*.

Since acting is primarily body language, *angika* (physical) *abhinaya* comes first and receives substantial treatment. It is loaded with several layers of contextual meaning that can be understood in terms of the whole spectrum of

Indian tradition, from the mystical and speculative to the ritualistic as well as purely corporeal. Bharata's contextual framework is an essential prerequisite for comprehending the seemingly simple and arbitrary, aphoristic classification of the body and its uses in expressing the emotions and situations. The *Natyasastra*, chapters 8–12, clearly defines the relationship of 'expressive' and 'expressed' body language, based on movement and rest, while Abhinavagupta expounds their significance in *Abhinavabharati*. Just as in life, emotive states (*bhava*) as well as their stimuli and environment (*vibhava*) are intertwined, so also in the realm of *abhinaya*.

Thus, in traditional Indian theatre, while *abhinaya* may begin as *anukarana* of the entire universe, it ultimately transcends mimetic reproduction and attempts 'metacreation' through the imagination, on the basis of conceived form and behaviour, in order to 'retell' the *bhava*. In fact, *anukarana* and *anukirtana* may be viewed as functionally parallel to *abhidha* (denotation) and *vyanjana* (revelation through suggestion) in the *dhvani* theory. Imitation is needed as the first step in performance but, if it remains too much in the likeness of the real, it appears too gross and creates, at best, an illusion of the real. Such attempts in art correspond to matter-of-fact statements in ordinary life. On the other hand, retelling of the real through gestures, colours, lines, notes, and so on parallels *vyanjana*.

The concepts of *bhavanukirtana* and *rasa* also seem to be fully captured in the idea of theatre as 'free creative activity', or an object of diversion, namely 'play'. Sometimes it has been viewed as sport (*krida*), in terms of maya, when the entire expanse of the phenomenal world is seen as an illusion, according to the Advaita Vedanta school of philosophy. It is taken as free activity when this grand expansion of plurality manifests shakti in the consciousness and *svatantrya* (freedom). The latter approach towards artistic creation occurs from as early a period as the Upanishadic. The notion of theatre as *lila* (divine play) is seminally present in the *Natyasastra*. Somewhat later, it developed into theatre as freedom (*svatantrya*) and as 'repose in one's self' (*svatmavisranti*) in the Kashmiri Saiva tradition.

Everyone embarks upon an activity with a specific objective (*karya*). Therefore action constitutes the basis of plot in *Sanskrit theatre and is divided into five temporal phases (*avastha*)—beginning of the effort, hope of attaining the fruit, frustration, certainty of attaining the fruit, and finally its attainment. The *Natyasastra* stresses that this linear sequence universally applies to every action. Yet another concept, *arthaprakriti* ('nature of aim'), describes the texture or thickness of action. According to Byrski, it takes into account that the time factor, though important, should not falsify the true character of each action, for in an action lasting five hours, it is naïve to think that the first hour is dominated by desire, the second by effort, the third by hope, and so on. Obviously, all these function simultaneously; only, at different stages, different ones come to the forefront. The nature of the aim expresses the themes more precisely.

These *arthaprakritis* number five—*bija* (seed), *bindu* (drop), *pataka* (flag), *prakari* (episode), *karya* (objective). Strictly speaking only *bija*, *bindu*, and *karya* describe the main sphere of action. The botanical image of *bija* suggests development until its fruition. *Bindu* refers to continuity of action or its uninterrupted flow. *Pataka* is the subsidiary plot and *prakari* the chain of episodes in which the hero receives assistance from others, bringing first the stage of hope and then certainty of success. The course joins with the unfolding of the dramatic action identified as the five junctures (*sandhi*): opening, progression, development, pause, and conclusion. This is the logic of plot structure in Sanskrit drama.

During the nineteenth century,

Western dramaturgy gradually infiltrated into regional literatures under the impact of colonialism, and modern Indian playwrights followed fundamentally Aristotelian or Shakespearean form. A few notable exceptions, like Rabindranath *Tagore, rebelled and created their own theories, mostly inspired by classical Sanskrit tenets. The Ibsenian model of social realism later influenced many writers. After India's independence, some activists turned to Brechtian or Artaudian guidelines and mixed them with indigenous or personal ideas to initiate concepts like the *Third Theatre of Badal Sircar. However, no major original theorist emerged.   KDT

R.H. Ahuja, *Theory of Drama in Ancient India* (Ambala: Indian Press, 1964); Bharata, *Bharata-Natya-Manjari*, translated by G.K. Bhat (Poona: Bhandarkar Oriental Research Institute, 1975); G.K. Bhat, *Natya-Manjari-Saurabha: Sanskrit Dramatic Theory* (Poona: Bhandarkar Oriental Research Institute, 1981); M. Christopher Byrski, *Methodology of the Analysis of Sanskrit Drama* (Delhi: Bharatiya Vidya Prakashan, 1997); Siddheswar Chattopadhyaya, *Nataka-Laksana-Ratna-Kosa: Perspectives of Ancient Indian Drama and Dramaturgy* (Calcutta: Punthi Pustak, 1974); Dhananjaya, *The Dasarupa: A Treatise on Hindu Dramaturgy*, translated by George Haas (New York: AMS, 1965); Bharat Gupt, *Dramatic Concepts: Greek and Indian* (New Delhi: DK Print World, 1994); Manjul Gupta, *A Study of Abhinavabharatai on Bharata's Natyasastra and Avaloka on Dhananjaya's Dasarupaka* (Delhi: Gian, 1987); T.G. Mainkar, *Sanskrit Theory of Drama and Dramaturgy* (Delhi: Ajanta, 1985); T.G. Mainkar, *Studies in Sanskrit Dramatic Criticism* (Delhi: Motilal Banarsidass, 1971); T.G. Mainkar, *The Theory of the Samdhis and Samdhyangas* (Delhi: Ajanta, 1978); R.N. Rai, *Theory of Drama: A Comparative Study of Aristotle and Bharata* (New Delhi: Classical, 1992); Sagaranandin, *The Natakalaksanaratnakosa: A Thirteenth-Century Treatise*, translated by M. Dillon, M. Fowler, and V. Raghavan (Philadelphia: American Philosophical Society, 1960); Surendra Nath Shastri, *The Laws and Practice of Sanskrit Drama* (Varanasi: Chowkhamba, 1961); R.L. Singal, *Aristotle and Bharata* (Hoshiarpur: Vishveshvaranand Vedic Research Institute, 1977); B.K. Thakkar, *On the Structuring of Sanskrit Drama* (Ahmedabad: Saraswati Pustak Bhandar, 1984); K.H. Trivedi, *The Natyadarpana of Ramacandra and Gunacandra* (Ahmedabad: L.D. Institute of Indology, 1966); Horace Hayman Wilson, *On the Dramatic System of the Hindus* (Calcutta: Sanskrit Pustak Bhandar, 1971).

Third Theatre or *anganmancha* (literally, 'courtyard stage'): the name given by Badal Sircar to a form which, he felt, would extend the horizon of *Bengali theatre and rescue it from its staleness and rusted practices and preoccupations. He proposed a combination of urban and rural styles, with socially committed themes, performed informally in found spaces, taking theatre to people everywhere. When he wrote his early comedies and major plays he did not have either misgivings about the proscenium stage or any clear idea of the Third Theatre. These evolved as he began work with his group Satabdi in the 1970s.

However, Sircar had been exposed to theatre in foreign countries, and particularly attracted by experimentation that abjured conventional auditoriums. He confirms in his book on the subject how his thinking was substantiated (though not necessarily influenced) by what he saw in various Indian folk forms like *Jatra, experimental theatre in England (1957–9), France (1963–4), the USSR (1969), and, most importantly, Jerzy Grotowski's productions in Poland (1969). In New York in 1972, his participation at Richard Schechner's Performance Group rehearsals and discussions with Julian Beck and Judith Malina of the Living Theatre helped him concretize his vision of Third Theatre, kindred to arena theatre, theatre in the round, environmental theatre, and similar innovations.

A few excerpts from Sircar's book best describe the idea and its practical exposition: 'The city theatre to-day is not a natural development. ... It is rather a new theatre having its base on Western theatre ... whereas the traditional village theatre has retained most of its indigenous characteristics. ... What we need to do is analyse both the theatre forms to find the exact points of strength and weakness and their causes and that may give us the clue for an attempt to create a Theatre of Synthesis, a Third Theatre. ... I have been trying to break through this system of "story" and "characters" and in my plays "theme" and "types" respectively began to replace them gradually. Working on the Third Theatre I began discovering new possibilities of using ... words addressed directly to spectators more than "dialogue" between stage characters, using physical "acting" more than "language". ... Third Theatre liberated from the bondages of stage, auditorium, lighting, sets, props ... is very much feasible. ... We found that *theatrical experience* rather than narration of a story is more relevant to the Third Theatre for it affords much more directness in communication than the conventional proscenium theatre'.

Satabdi performed *Spartacus* in an empty room and outdoors at a downtown Calcutta park in 1972–3. Sircar first directed his own *Michhil* (*Procession*) and *Bhoma* for village shows in 1974 and 1976 respectively, the latter written and produced collectively with the villagers. By conducting workshops all over India, Sircar inspired many a Third Theatre activist in other states; he remarks that 'slowly but surely the Third Theatre is taking

Third Theatre production of *Kalo basti*, written and directed by Probir Guha (Alternative Living Theatre, Khardah, 1992)

roots in the soils of India'. Dedicated followers with long careers of commendable work include Probir Guha in Bengal, but there is no evidence yet that Third Theatre poses a challenge to the proscenium. For all of Sircar's ideas and exemplary effort in giving shape to them, it remains a fringe phenomenon in contemporary Indian theatre.   KR

Badal Sircar, *The Third Theatre* (Calcutta: Badal Sircar, 1978).

Tiatr (from Portuguese *teatro*): a distinct form of *Konkani theatre developed by the Goans converted to Christianity since colonial contact with the Portuguese in the early

sixteenth century. It is reported that Konkani Tiatr began in Bombay as late as 1892 with the staging of *Italian Burgo*, which imitated the *English theatre of amateur companies in British Bombay. But in Goa much theatrical activity took place previously. However, as the 'Romi' (Roman script) manuscripts of the early Konkani Tiatras are not yet transcribed into Devanagari script, the process of literary acculturation cannot be explained fully. What is clear is that from Joao Agostinho in the 1890s to Lambert Mascarenhas in the 1990s, Goan Christians developed a cross-pollinated dramatic genre called Tiatr and Khel (literally 'play') Tiatr, first in Portuguese and then in more Sanskritized Konkani.

The elements of Tiatr are drama, music, comedy, and improvisation. A loose storyline is punctuated by sideshows—irrelevant and improvisational material consisting of songs (solos, duets, or choral *cantaras*), dances, skits, and monologues. It is accompanied by a steel band sitting between the audience and the performers: the Roman Catholic Church popularized Western music. Villagers, specially the Sudirs (Sudras), perform Khel (or in its Westernized pronunciation, Phel), the Zagor dance, and Contra Danca. Tiatr and Tiatrists before 1961 were pro colonial establishment politically, but since Goa's liberation Tiatr has become a popular commercial theatre. Khel Tiatr even follows the sensational action-packed formula of Hindi films. The schoolteacher-performer Tomazinho Cardozo's *Mhowal vikh, samaj seva* ('That Beehive Poison, Social Service', 1992) and *Laj nasalelo* ('Shameless') by Felicio Cardoso (1932–) are popular recent Tiatr plays. M. Boyer's contribution as actor is immense.   ABP

Tolpavakuttu (literally 'leather-puppet play'): ancient and endangered art of *shadow theatre popular in Palakkad district, Kerala. Only a few families of the Pulavar community of scholar-performers

continue the tradition, usually staged in Kali temples during the annual festival of Bhagavati or Bhadrakali. The permanent puppet theatre attached to the shrine is called *kuttumatam*. The goddess is supposed to witness it, so the playhouse faces the temple. The measurements of an ideal *kuttumatam*, as in the Kavalapara temple, are 11 m 43 cm in length, 3 m 81 cm in depth, and 1 m 53 cm in height. A thin white cloth covers the front. Behind it is a wooden stand across the length of the stage for the backlights, usually twenty-one oil lamps. Torches also are used for special effects.

Stories from the *Ramayana* are presented, commencing from Rama's birth and ending with his coronation. The text consists of twenty-one parts, so the ceremonial theatre season extends for twenty-one nights. The plays have verse and prose dialogue, in Tamil. Originally there was a script specially written for the form. Now it comes from the *Kamba Ramayana*, by the Tamil poet Kamban (twelfth century). The Pulavars add to it by improvising speeches and *vaiteri*s (meaningless syllables) to emphasize certain situations. They explain the verses and dialogues in a language mixing Tamil and Malayalam.

The opaque painted leather puppets, as in *Ravana Chhaya, are made of deer skin, carefully shaped into different characters with one or both hands jointed, and tiny holes punched through to suggest costumes and highlight the shadows projected on the white screen from the row of lamps behind them. There are 130 puppets, portraying humans as well as animals and birds. Before the show begins it is announced by the *keli* ensemble, using drums. Around 9 p.m. the *velichapad*, or oracle representing the goddess, becomes possessed and as a gesture of giving sanction, blesses the artists. The Pulavars start by singing benedictory songs of Ganapati, Saraswati, and other deities. As in *Sanskrit theatre, there is a *prastavana* (introduction) called *patta pava*.

Five puppeteers do the manipulation. They hold the figures with anklets on their own hands, which make sounds when shaken. Sometimes they have to run to cross the screen, especially when battles take place. The puppets walk, take different postures, engage in fighting. It requires utmost dexterity and skill to make their minute expressive movements match the musical rhythms. The master in this field is Krishnan Kutty Pulavar. *Ezhupara* (a percussion instrument of jackfruit wood with both ends covered with hide) and cymbals provide the accompanying music. *Chenda*

drums, pipe, conch, and gong highlight the dramatic situations.

KNP

G. Venu, *Tolpava Koothu: Shadow Puppets of Kerala* (New Delhi: Sangeet Natak Akademi, 1990).

Tolu Bommalata (Telugu, 'leather-puppet dance'): strongest tradition of *shadow theatre in India. Leather *puppetry in Andhra Pradesh is famous for its life-size images, highly intricate ornamentation, brilliant colours, rich style of singing, and adoption of *Yakshaganam texts to present full-length theatre. The first reference in Telugu literature appears in Palkuriki Somanatha's *Panditaradhya charitramu* ('Panditaradhya's Story', thirteenth century), which indicates the form was highly evolved by that time and called *chira marugula bommalata* ('puppet dance behind a sari', alluding to its screen). An inscription of 1208 found in Mukkamala village says that Gundapa Nayaka gave a puppeteer some land.

However, the present performers are not of Andhra origin; known as Are Marathi or Are Bondili, these families of Maratha or Bundel army background entered the Rayalaseema region of interior Andhra around 1850. Totally assimilated into

Andhra culture, they now speak Telugu. Madhavapatnam in East Godavari district is the leading centre with 100 such families, whose ancestors received the art 250 years ago from previous practitioners belonging to the Kamsala community in Andhra. According to them, Tolu Bommalata originated in medieval times among the Kamsala goldsmiths and accountants who, persecuted for their Jain faith, escaped into the forests, where they created a new art of image-making with the medium of leather. Because of their skills at gold crafting, the artisans retained elaborate and intricate ornamentation in every inch of each puppet.

The classic puppets stand from 2 to 3 m tall, and are brightly coloured, originally with vegetable and mineral dyes, later with chemicals. Initially deer skin was used for the characters of divinities and lamb or buffalo skin for the others. The skin is tanned to a transparently thin quality for which the Madiga community is famous, but the technique was picked up by the Marathis. It takes thirty to fifty days to make a life-size puppet. During the festivals of mother goddesses, the skins of sacrificial lambs used to be donated to puppeteers by individuals to make specific characters of their choice in their name as ritual offerings.

After tanning, artisans of three different skills collectively work on each puppet. Image drawing and cutting is the foremost, bringing out the personality. Every figure is cut into several parts: head, torso, hip, legs, hands. Each limb is sliced into three at the joints, to facilitate movements. This drawing and cutting is done by the senior craftsmen. The second skill is ornamentation and dressing, by perforating countless tiny holes that let light through to the screen in the shape and design of costumes and jewellery. The third skill is to fill in colours according to traditional patterns. Then all the parts are loosely tied, allowing free movement at each joint. Three stitched bamboo sticks make the puppet workable: one vertical from head to hip, also to hold the figure straight, and the others connected to the forearms.

The manipulation is considered secondary, because everybody in the team from children up knows how to man a puppet. But only the seniors know how to make them. The first-grade puppet-makers of the traditional style are nearly all gone. Since each puppet survives for an average 100–150 years, only one or two sets of around 100 puppets are kept by each team, good enough to serve two or three generations. Because of this longevity, very few puppeteers really

Tolu Bommalata puppet of Sita in the *ashoka* forest

used. Each puppet is held almost touching the screen from behind, keeping the manipulator's body away. Generally, each puppeteer handles one character at a time, singing and talking suitably while making special sound effects by stamping his legs rhythmically on two flat wooden planks placed one upon the other.

The Yakshaganam repertoire used is mostly based on the *Ramayana* and *Mahabharata*. The best teams are capable of staging these epics in ten parts, each part in ten days, at the rate of three hours daily. In earlier times, with overnight shows, a two-month festival could be possible for each epic, though in practice the troupes performed only a few chapters every season at the villagers' request. Apart from the regular puppet seasons (winter and summer), there is a belief that a dedicated perfor-mance, particularly *Rama natakam* ('Rama's Play'), brings rain during periods of famine.

bothered to learn puppet-making, whereas practically every child is taught the manipulation and singing in Yakshaganam style.

At a show, eight to ten members stand behind a huge white screen about 5 m wide and 2–3 m high to manipulate the figures. The screen is erected very tight, without any folds, but kept slightly slanted from top to bottom, leaning a little to the inside so that slight errors in the fall of the image can be covered. Traditionally, castor-oil torches illuminated the puppets behind the screen to give soft and red light. These days, Petromax pressure lamps or red electrical bulbs are

Before the show commences, the puppets of the god Ganesh, a Dishtibomma ('evil chaser'), and the comedian Juttupoligadu ('erect-tuft fellow') are displayed. The performance begins with a prayer to Ganesh generally in Raga Todi, followed by the *Sabha varnana*, a song praising the audience and inviting the chief guests. The actual play always starts with Raga Nata and closes with Surati. *Mridangam* drum, harmonium, and cymbals provide the music. All artistes sing at a very high pitch to reach the thousands of spectators.

The main attraction is three types of comedians who appear in all texts. The first is the husband and wife, Juttupoligadu and Bangarakka ('golden girl'), who always quarrel. Irrespective of the play, the show starts with this couple who also interrupt many times with typical jokes, sometimes connected to the story but mostly on topical issues. The second type of comedian is called Allatappa ('not an easy man'), whose wit proves superior to the first pair's. He always

provokes the wife against her husband to ignite the quarrel further. The third is known as Ketigadu ('intruder'), a tiny puppet who jumps between everybody and everything even when the screen is full with a dozen characters, making some space for himself, pushing the dramatis personae aside to comment on the text. Depending on the team's taste, the comedy turns vulgar sometimes, but tradition has designed this bunch of comedians as the integral part of the show. Since no separate scripts are written for puppetry, the creation of these jesters could be the puppeteers' special genius.

The old generation of Andhras admits that, prior to cinema, Tolu Bommalata surpassed all other kinds of theatre and entertainment in popularity. Now, the last few families of puppeteers cannot survive on this profession alone. Although Tolu puppeteers still operate in the Godavari districts and a few villages in Anantapur, Nellore, Visakhapatnam, and Guntur districts, the great tradition is fast dying.   PCR

M. Nagabhushana Sarma, *Tolu Bommalata: The Shadow Puppet Theatre of Andhra Pradesh* (New Delhi: Sangeet Natak Akademi, 1985).

Ravana in Tolu Bommalata

Tullal ('dance'): specific form of enacting a story through dance and music, which originated in the early eighteenth century at Ambalapuzha, a small principality on the coast of the erstwhile Travancore area in south Kerala. It was invented by the trendsetting Malayalam poet Kunchan Nambiyar, who rendered his poetry based on epic themes in this newly formulated visual style. He belonged to the Nambiyar community, percussionists by profession, accompanying on the instrument called *mizhavu* the traditional presentation of Sanskrit plays known as Kuttu and *Kutiyattam.

An interesting story survives of Tullal's creation. During a performance the proficient Kunchan Nambiyar dozed off for a while and did not provide percussive support to the Chakkiyar actor. The Chakkiyar made fun of his behaviour with some whimsical remark. Nambiyar took offence and walked off. In protest against the Chakkiyar's comments, he dissociated from Kutiyattam and started contemplating a different art form, thus conceiving Tullal. Leaving aside the question of credibility, the fact remains that Nambiyar, an active participant in the elitist *Sanskrit theatre, made his art more meaningful and appealing to the common people by introducing a new technique of storytelling. Apart from his own experience in Kuttu in which social criticism and satire are of prime importance, he delved deep into the popular form of *Patayani and combined indigenous narration, rhythms, dance, and costumes in the total art of Tullal.

While retelling stories from the epics, Nambiyar dealt with events and experiences in his contemporary context and made the epic characters live among the people. Social commentary, humour, satire, colloquial expressions, proverbs, gave his texts immediate appreciation from the common man. Tullal has three variations—Ottan, Sitangan, and Parayan—adopted by Nambiyar from Patayani characters and assigned specific costumes. There are differences in metrical structure and tempo in each style. He composed many stories in each of the above denominations, for a total of forty-one. Later authors also composed Tullal poems, but only a few made lasting impact. All the poems came down as oral literature, finally printed only in the early twentieth century.

The solo Tullal performer sings the entire passage, repeated by a musician from behind to the accompaniment of cymbals and *toppi maddalam*, a cylindrical drum with both sides covered with hide and played with the palms. He also translates the meaning of the sung text into action through dance,

Ottan Tullal performer
(Kerala Kalamandalam,
1986)

gestures, and facial expressions. The footwork is extensively patterned to blend with the rhythms and the gestures are simple and communicative, following the ancient Sanskrit text *Hastalakshana dipika* ('Light on Hand Gestures', a treatise on gestural language popular in Kerala). Malabar Raman Nair of Kerala Kalamandalam was the best-known exponent in the mid-twentieth century, followed by Vechoor Thankamani Pillai in recent times.   KNP

V.S. Sharma, *Thullal: An Audio-Visual Art Form of Kerala* (Madras: Higginbothams, 1982).

Utsrishtikamka: form of *Sanskrit theatre in one act. According to some scholars, it was so named to distinguish it from *amka* or *anka* ('act'), the structural divisions within drama. However, Abhinavagupta (950–1025) observed that 'the play is marked by sorrowful women whose *srishti* (creation) appears to depart from their bodies due to woe', hence the nomenclature. Devoid of celestial beings, it had ordinary people as heroes. Abounding in lamentations of women and self-disparagement, it was dominated by *karuna* (pathetic)

*rasa. The plot used a well-known story expanded by the poet's imagination. The *sandhi*s ('junctures' of the plot), *vritti*s (styles or characteristics), and *lasyanga*s (feminine components of dance) were the same as those in *bhana. War, victory, and defeat were presented and improvised in *bharati* (spoken) *vritti*. Visvanatha's *Sahityadarpana* ('Mirror of Literature', fourteenth century) cites the lost *Sarmishtha-Yayati* ('Sarmishtha and Yayati') as an example of *utsrishtikamka*.   KDT

Vilasam (literally 'pleasure'): *Tamil theatre form that evolved as a result of interactions with other cultures. It came into vogue in the nineteenth century. The Maratha rulers of Thanjavur used to invite *Parsi theatre companies to perform at their court. Folk *Terukkuttu and Parsi theatre combined to give birth to Vilasam in the tradition of Carnatic music, just as *Kirttanai grew out of Telugu influences. Soon it also became a literary genre. Not all the scripts were written with intention of staging. Dictionaries define the connotations of *vilasam* as 'dance and play', and as a suffix it is used interchangeably for dramatic literature and performance. For example, *Markandeya natakam* ('Markandeya's Drama') is also titled as *Markandeya vilasam*. In Sri Lanka, Vilasam texts are found to be close to Terukkuttu texts.   VA

Vithi (literally 'road', 'way'): solo form of *Sanskrit theatre in one act. It represented one character who, by means of *akasabhashita* ('aerial discourse', meaning performance of a supposed speech and reply as if actually spoken and heard), suggested the *sringara* (erotic) *rasa, and other *rasa*s to some degree. It extensively used *kaisiki* (graceful) *vritti* and employed thirteen essential elements, as follows:

Udghatyaka—when having heard some words and not understood their sense, the character adds some of his own to make a meaning out of them.

Avalagita—when parallel stage business (such as hinting of the hero's entry) is performed in unison.

Prapanca—a conversation exciting laughter.

Trigata—deriving more than one meaning from words, leading to laughter.

Chala—deception by words apparently friendly but inimical in reality.

Vakkeli—a passage exciting laughter by means of two or three rejoinders. According to others, it defines breaking off a speech before its sense is complete, or a single answer to a variety of questions.

Adhibala—an interlocution of high words in mutual defiance.

Ganda—a hurried or sudden speech causally connected with a matter in hand, though having a different significance (having no intended reference to what it chances to be connected with).

Avasyandita—interpretation of a speech contrary to the sense in which it was first spoken.

Nalika—enigma associated with pleasantry. Its being attended with a joke distinguishes it from *avasyandita*.

Asatpralapa—incoherent or nonsensical talk, as by a mad person or when one awakes from sleep.

Vyahara—words spoken giving rise to laughter in the hero.

Mridava—when faults turn into merit or merits into faults.

These elements occurred in *nataka*, *bhana*, and other forms, but derived from *vithi*, which proves its significance.   KDT

Voggukatha (Telugu, '*voggu* tales', from *voggu*, a small *damaru* or hand drum associated with Siva): primitive narrative form of *Telugu theatre. Not as recognized in the outside world as the popular *Burrakatha, it is one of the prides of Andhra folk art. It is performed by the pastoral Kurama community, one of the two main sheep-rearing tribes of the Deccan plateau. Each of their denominations developed its own performing art around the story of their Mulapurusha, the founder, also called Birappa or Birdev: in Maharashtra simple devotional bhajans; in Karnataka a gymnastic dance and narrative using large cymbals called Kamsale; and in interior Telengana of Andhra, the more complex and tremendously plastic Voggukatha.

The origins are as old as Deccan pastoral culture. Voggukatha's original story was composed prior to the history of Virasaivism in Telengana, initially as a simple sung narrative. The singing technique is older than that of Jangam narratives, an offshoot of Virasaivism in the twelfth century. Because of its specialized traditional style, it did not spread rapidly, though some attempts were made to appropriate it. In the process of social transformation from a nomadic pastoral lifestyle to rigid feudal society, Voggukatha also metamorphosed, acquiring elements of later *Yakshaganam, in terms of theatrical enactment of scenes. But an apparently conscious desire to retain its primitive, powerful singing saved the form from succumbing totally to the patterns of Yakshaganam. At least ten types of original tunes decide the character of Voggukatha even now.

One of the accompanying instruments is also unique—a drum called *dillem bhillem* owing to its special sound effects which silence the audience and to which the performers enter. The other instruments are *kanaka-dappu* (a small tambourine), *napira* (an iron horn), and the *voggu*, symbolic of the community's conversion to Saivism. Despite the conversion and Voggukatha's name, the Kuramas retain intact their faith in the ethnic god Birappa. They started calling him an incarnation of Virabhadra, a form of Siva. Their conversion brought several new stories into the repertoire, like that of Mallanna (deity of the Saiva pilgrimage centre, Srisailam, in Kurnool district), also utilizing earlier matriarchal cults like those of Ellamma, Nallapochamma, and Mandhata, but the prime story remained the original one of Birappa.

Contrary to other narrative forms that have one main singer or narrator, Voggukatha has two, both singers and dancers, with the same dress, who also deliver the *vachana*s (connecting prose parts). The main difference with other narratives is that Voggukatha suddenly changes into theatre for important scenes. To illustrate an episode, the narrators singing in the third person turn into characters and enter into an exchange of verse dialogue demonstrating the actor's quality of subjective involvement with the roles portrayed. If the scene requires more than two characters, the chorus, drummer, cymbalist, and other instrumentalists turn actors, though they never leave their instruments.

Voggukatha performance, 1987

During the Telengana insurrection (1940s), revolutionary artists like Suddala Hanmanthu and Tirunagari Ramanujachary took popular elements of Voggukatha to propagate their message, renaming the form 'Gollasuddulu' ('Golla Sayings', Golla being the Yadava caste). In the next phase of the Communist armed struggle (1970s), non-Kurama revolutionary singers like Gaddar started using the new version, but with the old name Voggukatha, leading to protests from the original community. Original Voggukatha is still enacted by at least fifty different troupes of Kuramas in Telengana, patronized by all communities. Present-day champions of the form are Chukka Sathaiah and Sanike Balappa, virtuoso performers. Featuring fast pace with quick changes of characters, each of their stories spreads over three days. They can also reduce their shows to a three-hour performance on one day with the same stunning impact.   PCR

Vyayoga ('intense or manifold action'): form of *Sanskrit theatre in one act. It used a well-known story for its plot, and its dramatis personae consisted mostly of males and a few females. It represented contentment, not provided by a woman. Hence it was composed without the typically feminine *kaisiki* (graceful) *vritti*. The hero was a celebrated personage—a royal ascetic (*rajarshi*) or god of the 'firm and haughty' (*dhiroddhata*) variety. Its principal *rasas* did not include the *santa* (peaceful), *hasya* (comic), and *sringara* (erotic). Bhasa's *Madhyamavyayoga* ('Vyayoga of the Middle One') is the typical example, describing the exploits of Bhima overpowering Ghatotkacha in the *Mahabharata*.   KDT

Women's theatre: Women authors in India, as elsewhere, have preferred to write fiction or poetry rather than drama. Considering their valuable contribution to the arts in general, the obvious question that begs response is why they did not choose to make better use of theatre's volatile space to highlight women's issues. What could have been particularly hostile or restrictive about writing plays? The reason lies in the requirement for drama to be performed. Theatre necessitates the breaching of the 'private space–public space' divide that most women artists seemed reluctant to initiate. Yet the voice of women expressing their experiences of life—not through female characters controlled ventriloquistically by male dramatists—needed to be heard in public arenas like the theatre and were indeed heard in greater numbers during the later decades of the twentieth century. Women's playwriting makes apparent deeper and long-suppressed dimensions of life seen through gendered lenses, manifesting women's experiences of joy, sorrow, oppression, violence, and exploitation that only they know and can write about. Their plays are candid, reflexive, often disturbing. It seems as though these texts demand articulation so that the drama of women's lives that remained subliminal and/or behind closed doors for so long could come into the open. They do not seek to resolve issues, nor end with author-defined conclusions. Rather, they invite the receptors' participation in dealing with the raw emotions evoked, the otherness of everyday beings, and the questioning of stereotypes.

Indian women contributed to theatre from the late nineteenth century, though not in a major way, reflecting the dual influence of European drama and indigenous performance traditions. Nevertheless, women's contributions ignored, trivialized or 'hidden from history' gain in significance as profoundly affecting the landscape of social inequities and rewriting of the country's cultural history. In this context one must note the trailblazing but largely forgotten efforts in the early twentieth century of Balamani Ammal, a former devadasi who led her own troupe consisting only of women who needed shelter, that travelled all over Tamil Nadu. The director and male impersonator R. Nagarathnamma (1926–) followed in her footsteps, forming an all-female Kannada company in 1958. The earliest plays by women were composed in Bengali, Urdu, and Marathi. Swarnakumari Devi (1855–1932) and Rasheed Jahan (1905–52) highlighted social evils through their Bengali and Urdu works respectively. The pioneer lawyer, Cornelia Sorabji (1866–1954), wrote the first drama in English by an Indian woman, *Gold Mohur Time* (1930), a parable play that she succeeded in publishing from London. Bharati Sarabhai's socialistic *The Well of the People* (in verse, 1943) and *Two Women* (prose, 1952) followed.

The numbers increased appreciatively after Independence.

The issues raised amaze by their range with regard to women's experiences. Important women dramatists include Mahasweta Devi, Nabaneeta Dev Sen, and Saoli Mitra (Bengali); Dhiruben Patel and Varsha Adalja (Gujarati); Mannu Bhandari, Kusum Kumar, Mridula Garg, Shanti Mehrotra, and Mrinal Pande (Hindi); Malatibai Bedekar, Mukta Dikshit, Tara Vanrase, Jyoti Mhapsekar, Sushma Deshpande, and Prema Kantak (Marathi); Manjit Pal Kaur (Punjabi); Ambai and Mangai (Tamil); Volga and Vinodini (Telugu); Jameela Nishat (Urdu). Dina Mehta is among the best known of those writing in English, addressing various themes on *Mythmakers*; *Tiger, Tiger*; *Sister Like You*; *When One plus One Makes Nine*; and the most celebrated, *Brides Are Not for Burning* and *Getting Away with Murder*. In 1989, Bilkiz Alladin dramatized the historical romance of the British Resident in Hyderabad, James Kirkpatrick, with the beautiful Khairunnissa as *For the Love of a Begum*, which revealed the interface of the Raj and harem politics. The new millennium opened with great promise. Manjula Padmanabhan shot to fame with her award-winning *Harvest*, followed by *Lights Out, Hidden Fires*, and *Mating Season*. Poile Sengupta wrote some fascinating plays, like *Mangalam* and *Keats Was a Tuber*.

Hardly a domain of life is left untouched by these playwrights, who offer a variety of analyses of the position of women, exploration of female subjectivity, and different strategies that need adoption to negotiate social change. Their work and voice ask for reformulation of conventional paradigms and meaningful social intervention, the reconsideration of historical knowledge and the re-examination of the basic premises of traditionally organized systems of knowledge about social and literary dynamics. In doing so, they shape a new dramaturgy—a womanist theory of theatre that finds unacceptable the notions of Aristotelian catharsis and Bharata's *rasa as the feelings aroused in viewers. The plays upset the equilibrium, provoke, and demand response from an audience that will not expect entertainment but will participate in the dialectics since the issues concerning women and children are of the kind that have invariably been and continue to be sidestepped and neglected by society.

Happily, the emergence of women directors as individual cultural producers with gendered perception, innovative semiotics, and sensitive treatment of social issues, has opened up the field to accommodate women's experiences and viewpoints as well as re-present, with gender-sensitive treatment, texts by male playwrights. This is of utmost importance as far as the impact and consolidation of women-centred theatre in India is concerned because theatre as a patriarchal hegemony is quite capable of absorbing female texts, nullifying their cutting edge, and even turning 'feminine concerns' into new commodities for male consumption. Dina Gandhi-Pathak, Shanta Gandhi, Sheila Bhatia, Vijaya Mehta, Rekha Jain, and Joy Michael were the pioneering directors, succeeded by such innovative creators as Kirti Jain, Anuradha Kapur, Amal Allana, Neelam Man Singh Chowdhry, Usha Ganguli, Sohag Sen, Tripurari Sharma, Anamika Haksar, Anjana Puri, B. Jayashree, Maya Rao, Rati Bartholomew, Nadira Zaheer Babbar, and Vinapani Chawla. Younger talents like Robijita Gogoi, Shailaja J., and Jayati Bose, to name a few, are forging new idioms.   TM

Body Blows: Women, Violence and Survival (Calcutta: Seagull, 2000); Tutun Mukherjee (ed.), *Staging Resistance: Plays by Women in Translation* (New Delhi: Oxford University Press, 2005); Kikkeri Narayan (ed.), *Akka: A Dialogue on Women through Theatre in India* (Mysore: Central Institute of Indian Languages, 2004); Lakshmi Subramanyam (ed.), *Muffled Voices: Women in Modern Indian Theatre* (New Delhi: Shakti, 2002).

Yakshagana ('Yaksha songs'): generic term referring mainly to a traditional form of *Kannada theatre predominant in coastal Karnataka, variants of which are found in other parts of the state as well, under names such as *Bayalata, *Dasavatar, and Bhagavatara Ata. Its early history is not well established. Yakshas form a class of demigods in Hindu mythology, but their connection to this genre remains unclear. A twelfth-century epigraphic reference to *Talamaddale suggests nothing but Yakshagana sans its dances and stagecraft. Other sources indicate that Yakshagana at that time was either a genre of music or literary composition but not a theatre form.

During the halcyon days of the Vijayanagar Empire (fifteenth to sixteenth centuries), Yakshagana seems to have developed a distinct identity under two major influences. One was the Bhakti movement that provided an ideological framework and from which common cultural matrix emerged the *Kuchipudi, *Kalapam, and *Bhagavata Mela as well. The Bhakti trait still remains conspicuous in Yakshagana as, regardless of diverse themes and plots, each performance is basically structured as a *Lila (divine play) of Krishna. The other major influence was *Bhutaradhane—*ritual forms of the Dakshin Kannad region from which Yakshagana borrowed elements of dance, costume, make-up, and conventions like *oddolaga*, the preliminary entry of main characters. But once Yakshagana absorbed these variegated influences, it began to evolve its unique style, growing into a lively medieval entertainment.

Oddalaga mass entry in Yakshagana

From the eighteenth century onwards, it changed rapidly. Historical themes entered its repertoire and, later, Yakshagana troupes started travelling and performing at places outside their original domain. One such *mela* (troupe) journeyed as far north as Pune and, incidentally, formed an impetus for the beginning of modern *Marathi theatre.

Two developments are prominent in Yakshagana in the twentieth century. First, it refined itself, shedding its 'roughness' and consequently gaining recognition as art. For this, it owes a great deal to K. Shivarama Karanth who, like Vallathol Menon in Kerala with respect to *Kathakali, conducted extensive research into the Yakshagana tradition and later created his own version of it, modelled on Western ballet. He also founded Yakshagana Kendra, a training institute, and Yaksharanga, a repertory. Second, Yakshagana moved towards a commercially viable form of organization. Around mid-century, new *mela*s sprang up with modern appurtenances like tents, chairs, power generators, transport vehicles, and started putting up itinerant, ticketed shows. Microphones, floodlights, and painted curtains also made their entry. These external changes were often accompanied by changes in the essential nature of Yakshagana—melodramatic characterization gained popularity and fairy tales were interpolated into the traditional corpus.

Variants of Yakshagana spread over Karnataka fall into two broad categories: *Mudalapaya*, the eastern variety, and *Paduvalapaya*, the western. The former is also called Doddata in parts of north Karnataka. While sharing many conventions with western Yakshagana, Doddata/*Mudalapaya* differs in several aspects: the speech is scripted; *chende*, the popular percussion, is absent; costumes are less elaborate; the singers move around the stage; and it has not yet entered the commercial arena. These features prompted some scholars to argue that this eastern variety is of earlier origin. *Paduvalapaya* itself has two distinct styles: *Badagutittu*, the northern, and *Tenkutittu*, the southern. The latter, with its beaded headdresses and longer *chende* and gong, shows a marked influence of Kathakali, while the former is based much more on local ritual forms. *Badagutittu* produced some of the most celebrated Yakshagana performers of the twentieth century: Haradi Rama Ganiga, B. Veerabhadra Naik, K. Shivarama Hegde, K. Mahabala Hegde, K. Shambhu Hegde.

Although almost every Yakshagana troupe is named after a particular deity, its performance is not exclusively attached to a temple. It can take place virtually in any open space and is financed by patrons or the village community. The theatre is erected the day before the scheduled show and, after the performance that lasts from 9 p.m. to 6 a.m. the next morning, it is dismantled. Usually a troupe consists of one or two singers (Bhagavatas), at least three instrumentalists—a *maddale* drummer, one for *chende*, and one to provide the drone on a harmonium —and ten to fifteen actors playing both male and female roles. Non-commercial Bayalata travelling companies have larger crews, while commercial companies (called Tent Ata) are the largest, with a manager at the helm.

Normally, the Yakshagana 'stage' is a 50-sq. m plot demarcated on the ground (or a raised platform in the case of commercial shows), with the green room at the back and the audience sitting around the other three sides. The musicians sit on a table at the rear of the stage and the two corners on either side of them are used for entrance and exit of the characters. There are no stage props, except a *ratha* (makeshift stool), used as a chariot or a throne or whatever else the situation demands. The absence of scenery is made up for by theatrical conventions: a small hand-held curtain (*tere*) conceals the entry of characters, who then execute an elaborate and attractive curtain dance, the *terekunita*. There are also some stock dance patterns for typical actions like war or journey, used in any performance.

In acting and stagecraft Yakshagana employs a very interesting method of juxtaposing the *lokadharmi* (natural) and *natyadharmi* (theatrical) modes. It has developed an elaborate system of metrical compositions, postures, and choreographic patterns, but unlike Kathakali it does not rely much on gesture language. It lays emphasis on the entire body rather than just the hands and face. The characters range from gods and kings to Brahmans and servants, from supernatural *rakshasas* (demons) to common people. Likewise, the speech ranges from the musical-rhetorical to normal conversational, the make-up from mask-like ornamentation to the bare minimum, and the costumes from large head-dresses and decorations to ordinary dhotis and turbans.

A typical performance opens with the Bhagavata's invocation and his duologue with the *hasyagara* (comedian), followed by ornate dance pieces by Balagopala (the child Krishna) and the female characters. Then the particular *prasanga* (script) begins with the *oddolaga* and moves from one episode to another, mingling songs and dances with improvised dialogue. The plot usually climaxes with a battle and concludes with a wedding, hence most traditional *prasanga*s are titled either as *kalaga* (battle) or *kalyana* (wedding). The present repertoire comprises about 300 such *prasanga*s, all composed before the twentieth century and handed down in the oral mode, based on the *Ramayana*, *Mahabharata*, and *Bhagavata*. Later *prasanga*s, however, incorporate fanciful and fairy tales. Yakshagana remains a very popular entertainment, patronized by tens of thousands of spectators spread mainly over the three western districts of Karnataka.   AKV

Martha Bush Ashton and Bruce Christie, *Yaksagana: A Dance Drama of India* (New Delhi: Abhinav, 1977); Guru Rao Bapat, *Semiotics of Yakshagana* (Udupi: Regional Resources Centre for Folk Performing Arts, 1998); G.S. Hegde, *Yaksagana and It's* [sic] *Sanskrit Sources* (Delhi: Parimal, 1997); K. Shivarama Karanth, *Yaksagana* (New Delhi: Indira Gandhi National Centre for the Arts and Abhinav, 1997); Thulasi Ramasamy, *Tamil Yaksagaanas* (Madurai: Vizhikal, 1987).

Yakshaganam, also called Bhagavatam ('worship'), Vithi Natakam ('street play'), and *Kalapam in Andhra Pradesh: *Yakshagana in south India started as songs (*gana*) or narratives of ethnic stories by a single person, usually a woman (Yakshi), later supported by a man (Yakshudu). Then dance and acting by many performers converted it to a theatrical genre. Yakshagana, an umbrella term, retained folk form in certain versions and in other versions turned to classical or Sanskrit heritage, absorbing the dance grammar of Bharata and later masters like Nandikesvara and Jayapa Senani. If we dig into the past of the tradition through the information available in Telugu literature, it gives the impression that Yakshagana originated on Andhra soil. However, the same kinds of stories are available all over the south.

Scholars agree that the Andhra Yakshaganam was related to a community called the Jakkulu (Sanskritized equivalent, Yakshulu, plural of Yaksha). The Jakkulus still exist in Andhra,

identified as a cluster of communities, all professional singers and dancers of Telugu performing arts, whether folk or classical. Collectively named Bhogam, which is generally dubbed the prostitute caste, their ethnic nomenclature breaks into Bhogalu, Sanulu, Jakkulu, Kurmapulu, and Nagulu or Nagavasulu. The Jakkulus and Nagulus figured prominently

Chindu Yakshaganam, by Chindu Yakshagana Kalasamiti (Arumur, Nizamabad district)

throughout known Andhra history—from the Satavahana (second century BC–third century AD) to the Buddhist and Jain periods, the medieval Kakatiya and Vijayanagar empires, the Nayak kingdoms of Madurai and Thanjavur in Tamil Nadu, and the Maratha rule ending in the early nineteenth century. This unbroken continuity was responsible for the birth of all kinds of Yakshaganam.

Group performances are called *natyamela* ('theatre troupe') and solo performances of *kelika*s ('entertainments') are called *nattuva mela* ('actor's troupe'). Under complete theatre forms of Yakshaganam, we can count the following:

1) Jakkulu-Bhogalu-Nagulu-Sanulu-Kurmapulu female traditions;

2) *Kuchipudi-Kapatrala-Korukonda-Melattur Brahman male traditions;

3) mostly non-Brahman male traditions from the coastal Vizianagaram-Visakhapatnam-Srikakulam districts;

4) non-Brahman male traditions from interior Telengana and Rayalaseema.

Among narrative and semi-theatrical forms related to the original singing Yakshaganam, we can list:

1) Jangamkatha-*Burrakatha-Jamukulakatha storytelling or narrative forms in the third person by two or three performers;

2) *Voggukatha narrative-cum-theatre form in the first person by a troupe;

3) solo Harikatha narratives in the third person;

4) Valakalu semi-theatrical form in the first person, by many performers.

With this background of typology one can understand how several Andhra performing traditions are closely or distantly connected. The art originated in Jakkulu and related communities, developing into temple and court forms of Yakshaganam. Then through various reformistic religious movements associated with Saiva, Vaishnava, and Yogic cults, they percolated into non-Brahman castes like the Jangam, Balija, Dasari, Golla, Kurma, Mala, and Madiga. A few Brahman families also practised performance and wrote scripts, but Brahman orthodoxy never approved of it till recent times.

It has not been possible to locate the oldest texts in the singing forms, but we can find some of the theatrical variety. S.V. Jogarao and Nataraj Ramakrishna identified the first text as *Soumbhari charitam* ('Soumbhari's Story') by Proluganti Chenna Souri in the fifteenth century, but it is now lost. The earliest extant scripts are Kandukuri Rudrakavi's *Sugriva vijayam* ('Sugriva's Victory') and Chakrapuri Raghava's *Vipranarayana vijayam* ('Vipranarayana's Victory'), both probably late sixteenth century. A book on Telugu poetics from the same period, *Lakshana sara sangraham* ('Collection of Poetic Features') by Chitrakavi Peddanna, gives the basic features of the Yakshaganam literary genre. If criticism on it is available from the sixteenth century, the form must be much older.

Through these literary sources one can trace the range of poetic metres in Yakshaganam that could be set to the tala-based music and dance. All of them belong to the folk tradition and suit the talas that guided the dance patterns, specifically the footwork. Probably a little later, the most characteristic element of later Yakshaganam, the *daruvu* musical composition (related to the *dhruva-gana*), made inroads to revolutionize the form by enabling greater elaboration in singing and dancing. The evolution of Yakshaganam proved that it could accommodate any range of metres for any range of talas. Complicated Telugu metres called *vritha*s and even Sanskrit slokas have been set to music and dance in this form.

The Kuchipudi tradition, even though it identifies with Kalapam as its essential texts, also gradually adopted complete Yakshaganam like *Prahlada charitra* ('Prahlada's Story'), *Sugriva vijayam*, and *Usha parinayam* ('Usha's Wedding'). But

scholars believe that Kalapam itself was an offshoot of an early Yakshaganam titled *Parijatapaharanam* ('Stealing the *parijata* Tree'). Visually the art of Kuchipudi Brahmans and Jakkulu temple dancers is more appealing than older Yakshaganam, because of the added classical dance grammar and mastery over **abhinaya* (acting) which, based on the system of facial and hand expressions, improved later Yakshaganam.

The golden period of Andhra Yakshaganam was initiated in the seventeenth century by the Nayak dynasty, Telugu by birth. Its legacy in Thanjavur started with the legendary kings Raghunatha (1613–30) and his son Vijayaraghava (1633–73). Raghunatha seems to have written only one script, *Rukmini-Srikrishna vivaha yakshaganam* ('Yakshaganam on the Marriage of Rukmini and Krishna'), but Vijayaraghava is said to have penned more than forty, of which only six are available. One of his wives, Rangajamma, authored many, of which *Mannarudasa vilasam* ('Mannarudasa's Exploits') is an excellent piece of classical Yakshaganam which, experts say, is the real test for performers. The exceptional feature of the Nayaks was that they encouraged many women of their court to write Yakshaganam.

The tradition was taken to further heights by the Maratha

rulers who not only declared Telugu as their official language, but also themselves wrote drama in Telugu. Shahaji (1684–1712) alone composed sixteen Yakshaganams, the most outstanding among them *Vishnu pallakiseva prabandham* ('Script of Court Ritual for Vishnu') and *Sankara pallakiseva prabandham* ('Script of Court Ritual for Sankara'), which are still performed. The later Maratha kings Tulajaji and Ekoji II also scripted plays and patronized dramatists. The renowned Telugu composer Tyagaraja (1767–1847) composed two famous Yakshaganams, *Nauka-charitam* ('Boat Story') and *Prahlada bhakti vijayam* ('Victory of Prahlada's Bhakti').

Historically the coastal belt, eastern Andhra, and Thanjavur, Madurai, and Melattur in Tamil Nadu happened to be the centres of Telugu Yakshaganam. But in modern times, Telengana in the interior north has dominated. Since the eighteenth century more than 100 scripts were written, the majority by the single author Chervirala Bhagayya, mostly performed by marginalized communities.   PCR

Yatra ('procession', 'journey'), pronounced Jatra: In the formative stage of this traditional *Oriya theatre, Yatra was a kind of rudimentary processional. This still survives in Puri, Orissa, performed every year at the time of Rama Navami, associated with religious ceremonies dedicated to Rama. Called Sahi ('local') Yatra, this form uses no dialogue. Actors wearing *masks represent well-known characters of the *Ramayana* and, while going in a procession with a stylized dance-like walk to the rhythm of drums, they depict through simple gestures selected familiar episodes from the epic. From this processional theatre developed a style of arena theatre known as Yatra.

J.C. Mathur and other scholars think that around the twelfth century a category of *uparupaka* evolved, called the *sangitaka* ('song work'), dominated by music and dance. According to them, Jayadeva wrote his famous *Gitagovinda* for presentation as a *sangitaka*. Arena-theatre Yatra had *sangitaka* as its model and, in the sixteenth century, Balarama Das's popular *Lakshmi Purana* was staged this way. Around the eighteenth century, some devout Vaishnavas organized Ras (called *Rahasa in colloquial Oriya) groups to perform Oriya versions of *sangitaka* exclusively drawing upon Krishna legends for their plays, along the lines of *Raslila or Krishna-yatras in Vrindavan and Mathura, Uttar Pradesh. Yatra was much influenced by Rahasa, which is why song and dance dominate it, and it is more operatic than the *Jatra of Bengal.

Present-day Yatra has lost much of its original character and, for popularity's sake, has imbibed substantially from commercial cinema. All actors in traditional Yatra were men. Now, some professional companies employ actresses. A Yatra performer must be versatile, because he has to act, sing, dance, and mime. The dialogue is either sung or delivered in a recitative manner. Of course, exchanges in humorous sequences occur in plain prose. Previously, most plays were mythological; later, all kinds of themes were admitted. As Yatra is basically stylized, melodrama and theatricality are its strong points. Realism has made gradual inroads via movies but, instead of enhancing the appeal, it has robbed Yatra of much of the theatrical vigour.

In olden days Yatra music was traditional Odissi or folk, but towards the latter part of the nineteenth century Hindustani classical music became popular in Orissa. Ragas like Yaman, Bhairavi, Kedar, Khamaj, Pilu, Kafi grew in favour with Yatra composers, and the *thumri* style of light classical singing inspired them too. A distinctive type of Yatra music emerged. Also, the harmonium, violin, trumpet, and tabla almost replaced indigenous instruments such as the *mardala* (the Odissi version of the *pakhawaj* drum), *mridanga* drums, vina, and flute. As a result, the music became louder but highly popular. In the 1930s and 1940s, before film songs spread their magic, Yatra songs were quite the rage with the masses. Yatra music nowadays is totally influenced by Hindi film music.

Conventionally, before the show proper begins, the orchestra plays a typical tune. It is both a prelude (*purvaranga*) and a sort of announcement to prospective spectators that the performance is about to start. After the orchestral flourish, a *gotipua* (teenage boy dressed as a dancing girl) dances Odissi in a curtain-raiser. The dance appeals more to popularity than adhering to sophisticated classical rules. After these preliminaries the play begins. The only property used is a chair representing, according to the dramatic situation, anything from a throne to a hiding place or bathing ghat.

The arena for presentation may be on level ground, but often is a slightly raised platform. The audience sits on three sides, sometimes four, the actors moving in such a way that no side can be considered the front. A gangway about $1^1/_2$-m wide, called the *pushpapatha* ('flower-path'), connects the arena with the green room. It not only serves as entrance, but at times also becomes an extension of the acting area, especially when the stock character Niyati (Destiny) punctuates the dramatic sequences.

Niyati's role is interesting. Invariably, whatever he says is in the form of song, almost always like an aside. He symbolizes different things in different scenes: fate, conscience, divine warning, a character's inner voice when he or she contemplates something. The stock *sutradhara*, who introduces the play, now rarely appears. Another age-old stock type, the Dwari (gatekeeper) or Bankuli-badi ('crooked stick'), has been totally omitted. Although a minor character, he used to add a good deal of humour with his typical gait, humorous songs, and dialogue. Certain actors used to specialize in this role.

There were many Yatra playwrights, Baishnab Pani the most powerful and popular among them. Now, professional companies seldom present his plays. Although these companies have drifted away from convention, a few serious amateurs at times stage old plays adhering strictly to tradition and aesthetic considerations. Some modern Oriya directors have adopted Yatra's theatrical presentational techniques.

JP

Dhiren Dash, *Jatra: The People's Theatre of Orissa* (Bhubaneswar: Padmini Dash, 1981).

General Bibliography

Source Texts

[Modern translations of the three major sources of stories and episodes most commonly encountered in traditional Indian theatre]

The Bhagavata Purana: Book X. Translated by Nandini Nopany and P. Lal. 2 vols. Calcutta: Writers Workshop, 1997.

Valmiki. *The Ramayana*. Condensed and transcreated by P. Lal. New Delhi: Vikas, 1981.

Vyasa. *The Mahabharata*. Condensed and transcreated by P. Lal. New Delhi: Vikas, 1980.

Drama Anthologies

Body Blows: Women, Violence and Survival. Calcutta: Seagull, 2000. [Contains Dina Mehta's *Getting away with Murder*; Manjula Padmanabhan's *Lights Out*; Poile Sengupta's *Mangalam*]

Coulson, Michael (trans.). *Three Sanskrit Plays*. Harmondsworth: Penguin, 1981. [Contains Bhavabhuti's *Malati and Madhava*; Kalidasa's *Sakuntala*; Visakhadatta's *Rakshasa's Ring*]

Deshpande, G.P. (ed.). *Modern Indian Drama*. New Delhi: Sahitya Akademi, 2000. [Contains Satish Alekar's *Mahapoor*; Datta Bhagat's *Whirlpool*; G.P. Deshpande's *Roads*; Utpal Dutt's *Hunting the Sun*; Chandrasekhar Kambar's *Siri Sampige*; Girish Karnad's *Hayavadana*; Mahasweta Devi's *Mother of 1084*; Arun Mukherjee's *Mareech, the Legend*; K.N. Panikkar's *The Lone*

Tusker; Indira Parthasarathy's *Aurangzeb*; Mohan Rakesh's *One Day in Ashadha*; Adya Rangacharya's *Listen, Janamejaya*; Badal Sircar's *Evam Indrajit*; Vijay Tendulkar's *The Vultures*; Surendra Verma's *From Sunset to Sunrise*]

Kambar, Chandrasekhar (ed.). *Modern Indian Plays*. 2 vols. New Delhi: National School of Drama, 2000–2001. [Vol. 1 contains Dharamvir Bharati's *The Blind Age*; Chandrasekhar Kambar's *The Mother Supreme*; Girish Karnad's *Death by Beheading*; Mohan Rakesh's *One Day in Ashadha*; Adya Rangacharya's *Listen! Oh, Janmejaya!*; Badal Sircar's *There's No End*; Rabindranath Tagore's *The River Unbound*; Vijay Tendulkar's *Ghashiram Kotwal*. Vol. 2 contains Satish Alekar's *Begum Barve*; J.P. Das's *Before the Sunset*; G.P. Deshpande's *A Man in Dark Times*; Mahesh Elkunchwar's *Old Stone Mansion*; Debasis Majumdar's *Unrhymed*; Indira Parthasarathy's *The Story of Nandan*; Bhisham Sahni's *Hanush*; Surendra Verma's *Wings in Chains*]

Lal, Ananda (ed.). *Twist in the Folktale*. Calcutta: Seagull, 2004. [Contains Chandrasekhar Kambar's *Jokumaraswami*; H. Kanhailal's *Pebet*; Habib Tanvir's *Charandas Chor*]

Lal, P. (trans.). *Great Sanskrit Plays*. New York: New Directions, 1964. [Contains Bhasa's *The Dream of Vasavadatta*; Bhavabhuti's *The Later Story of Rama*; Harsha's *Ratnavali*; Kalidasa's *Shakuntala*; Sudraka's *The Toy Cart*; Visakhadatta's *The Signet Ring of Rakshasa*]

Mee, Erin B. (ed.). *Drama Contemporary: India*. Baltimore: Johns Hopkins University, 2001. [Contains Datta Bhagat's *Routes and Escape Routes*; Mahesh Dattani's *Tara*; Usha Ganguli's *Rudali*; Girish Karnad's *The Fire and the Rain*; K.N. Panikkar's *Aramba Chekkan*; Tripurari Sharma's *The Wooden Cart*]

Mukherjee, Tutun (ed.). *Staging Resistance: Plays by Women in Translation*. New Delhi: Oxford University Press, 2005. [Contains Swarnakumari Devi's *The Wedding Tangle*; Usha Ganguli's *The Journey within*; Nabaneeta Dev Sen's *Medea*; Varsha Adalja's *Mandodari*; Tripurari Sharma's *A Tale from the Year 1857*; Kusum Kumar's *Listen Shefali*; Mamta Sagar's *The Swing of Desire*; Catherine Thankamma's *Beyond Facades*; Malatibai Bedekar's *Prey*; Muktabai Dikshit's *Gamble*; Manjit Pal Kaur's *Sundran*; Neelam Mansingh Chowdhry's *Fida*; C.S. Lakshmi's *Crossing the River*; Mangai's *Frozen Fire*; Chalam-Volga's *The Six of Them*; Vinodini's *Thirst*; Rasheed Jahan's *Woman*; Jameela Nishat's *Purdah*]

Van Buitenen, J.A.B. (trans.). *Two Plays of Ancient India*. New York: Columbia University Press, 1968. [Contains Sudraka's *The Little Clay Cart*; Visakhadatta's *The Minister's Seal*]

Wells, Henry (ed.). *Six Sanskrit Plays*. New York: Asia, 1964. [Contains Bhasa's *The Vision of Vasavadatta*; Bhavabhuti's *Rama's Later History*; Harsha's *Nagananda*; Kalidasa's *Shakuntala* and *Vikramorvacie*; Sudraka's *The Little Clay Cart*]

Wilson, H.H. (trans.). *Select Specimens of the Theatre of the Hindus*. London: Trubner, 1871. [Contains Bhavabhuti's *Malati and Madhava* and *Uttara-Rama-Charitra*; Harsha's *Ratnavali*; Kalidasa's *Vikrama and Urvasi*; Sudraka's *The Mrichchhakati*; Viskhadatta's *Mudra-Rakshasa*]

Books

Alkazi, Roshen. *Ancient Indian Costume*. New Delhi: Art Heritage, 1983.

Anand, Mulk Raj. *The Indian Theatre*. London: Dennis Dobson, 1950.

Aspects of Theatre in India Today. New Delhi: Ministry of Scientific Research and Cultural Affairs, 1960.

Awasthi, Suresh. *Drama, The Gift of Gods: Culture, Performance and Communication in India*. Tokyo: Tokyo University Institute for the Study of Languages and Cultures of Asia and Africa, 1983.

_____. *Performance Tradition in India*. New Delhi: National Book Trust, 2001.

Baskaran, S. Theodore. *The Message Bearers: The Nationalist Politics and the Entertainment Media in South India 1880–1945*. Madras: Cre-A, 1981.

Benegal, Som. *A Panorama of Theatre in India*. New Delhi: Indian Council for Cultural Relations, 1967.

Bhatia, Nandi. *Acts of Authority/Acts of Resistance: Theater and Politics in Colonial and Postcolonial India*. Ann Arbor: University of Michigan, 2004.

Chattopadhyaya, Kamaladevi. *Towards a National Theatre*. Bombay: All India Women's Conference, 1945.

Choondal, Chummar. *Christian Theatre in India*. Trichur: Kerala Folklore Academy, 1984.

Chopra, P.N. (ed.). *Folk Entertainment in India*. New Delhi: Ministry of Education and Culture, 1981.

Contemporary Playwriting and Play Production. Delhi: Bharatiya Natya Sangh, 1961.

Cousins, James H. *The Plays of Brahma: An Essay on the Drama in National Revival*. Bangalore: Amateur Dramatic Association, 1921.

Dalmia, Vasudha. *Poetics, Plays, and Performances: The Politics of Modern Indian Theatre*. New Delhi: Oxford University Press, 2006.

Das, Varsha. *Traditional Performing Arts: Potentials for Scientific Temper*. New Delhi: Wiley Eastern, 1992.

Das Gupta, Hemendranath. *The Indian Stage*. 4 vols. Calcutta: Metropolitan and M.K. Das Gupta, 1934–44. [Reprinted as *The Indian Theatre*. Delhi: Gian, 1988.]

Dass, Veena Noble. *Modern Indian Drama in English Translation*. Hyderabad: V.N. Dass, 1988.

Dharwadker, Aparna. *Theatres of Independence: Drama, Theory, and Urban Performance in India since 1947*. Iowa City: University of Iowa, 2005.

Dhingra, Baldoon. *A National Theatre for India*. Bombay: Padma, 1944.

Durga, S.A.K. *The Opera in South India*. Delhi: B.R. Publishing, 1979.

Gargi, Balwant. *Folk Theater of India*. Seattle: University of Washington, 1966.

——. *Theatre in India*. New York: Theatre Arts, 1962.

Ghosh, Manomohan. *Contributions to the History of the Hindu Drama: Its Origin, Development and Diffusion*. Calcutta: Firma K.L. Mukhopadhyay, 1958.

Ghurye, G.S. *Indian Costume*. Bombay: Popular Prakashan, 1966.

Gowda, H.H. Anniah (ed.). *Indian Drama*. Mysore: University of Mysore, 1974.

Gupta, Chandra Bhan. *The Indian Theatre*. New Delhi: Munshiram Manoharlal, 1991.

Indian Drama. New Delhi: Publications Division, Ministry of Information and Broadcasting, 1956. [Second edition, 1981.]

Iyengar, K.R. Srinivasa (ed.). *Drama in Modern India and the Writer's Responsibility in a Rapidly Changing World*. Bombay: P.E.N. All-India Centre, 1961.

Jacob, Paul (ed.). *Contemporary Indian Theatre: Interviews with Playwrights and Directors*. New Delhi: Sangeet Natak Akademi, 1989.

Jain, Nemichandra. *Indian Theatre: Tradition, Continuity and Change*. New Delhi: Vikas, 1992.

——. *Asides: Themes in Contemporary Indian Theatre*. New Delhi: National School of Drama, 2003.

Jalote, S.R. *Contemporary African American Theatre and Dalit Theatre*. Varanasi: Banaras Hindu University, 2001.

Lal, Ananda and Sukanta Chaudhuri (eds). *Shakespeare on the Calcutta Stage: A Checklist*. Calcutta: Papyrus, 2001.

Lal, Ananda and Chidananda Dasgupta (eds). *Rasa: The Indian Performing Arts in the Last Twenty-Five Years; Theatre and Cinema*. Calcutta: Anamika Kala Sangam, 1995.

Lutze, Lothar (ed.). *Drama in Contemporary South Asia*. Heidelberg: Heidelberg University, 1984.

Mathur, Jagdish Chandra. *Drama in Rural India*. New York: Asia, 1964.

Mehta, C.C. (ed.). *Bibliography of Stageable Plays in Indian Languages*. Baroda: M.S. University, 1963.

Menon, Narayana (ed.). *The Performing Arts*. Bombay: Marg, 1982.

Mukhopadhyay, Durgadas. *Lesser Known Forms of Performing Arts in India*. New Delhi: Sterling, 1975.

Nadkarni, Dnyaneshwar. *The Indian Theatre*. New Delhi: Shri Ram Centre for the Performing Arts, 1999.

Nagarajan, S. and S. Viswanathan (eds). *Shakespeare in India*. Delhi: Oxford University Press, 1987.

Narasimhaiah, C.D. (ed.). *Shakespeare Came to India*. Bombay: Popular Prakashan, 1964.

Narasimhaiah, C.D. and C.N. Srinath (eds). *Drama as Form of Art and Theatre*. Mysore: Dhvanyaloka, 1993.

Pandey, Sudhakar and Freya Taraporewala (eds). *Studies in Contemporary Indian Drama*. New Delhi: Prestige, 1990.

Pani, Jiwan. *Back to the Roots: Essays on the Performing Arts of India*. New Delhi: Manohar, 2004.

Parmar, Shyam. *Traditional Folk Media in India*. New Delhi: Research Press, 1994.

Proceedings of the 1956 Drama Seminar. New Delhi: Sangeet Natak Akademi, n.d.

Rangacharya, Adya. *Indian Theatre*. New Delhi: National Book Trust, 1984.

Reddy, K. Venkata and R.K. Dhawan (eds). *Flowering of Indian Drama*. New Delhi: Prestige, 2004.

Richmond, Farley; Darius Swann, and Phillip Zarrilli (eds). *Indian Theatre: Traditions of Performance*. Honolulu: University of Hawaii, 1990.

Sarat Babu, M. *Indian Drama Today: A Study in the Theme of Cultural Deformity*. New Delhi: Prestige, 1997.

Shah, Anupama and Uma Joshi. *Puppetry and Folk Dramas for Non-formal Education*. New Delhi: Sterling, 1992.

Shankar, D.A. (ed.). *Shakespeare in Indian Languages*. Shimla: Indian Institute of Advanced Study, 1999.

Sharma, H.V. *The Theatres of the Buddhists*. Delhi: Rajalakshmi, 1987.

Sinha, Biswajit. *Encyclopaedia of Indian Theatre*. 3 vols. Delhi: Raj, 2000 and continuing.

Sisson, C.J. *Shakespeare in India: Popular Adaptations on the Bombay Stage*. London: Oxford University Press, 1926.

Theatre in India. Paris: International Theatre Institute, n. d.

Theatre India 1977. Trichur: Kerala Sangeet Natak Akademi, 1977.

Trivedi, Poonam and Dennis Bartholomeusz (eds). *India's Shakespeare: Translation, Interpretation, and Performance*. Newark: University of Delaware, 2005.

Varadpande, M.L. *History of Indian Theatre: Loka Ranga; Panorama of Indian Folk Theatre*. New Delhi: Abhinav, 1992.

———. *Invitation to Indian Theatre*. New Delhi: Arnold Heinemann, 1987.

———. *Krishna Theatre in India*. New Delhi: Abhinav, 1982.

———. *The Mahabharata in Performance*. New Delhi: Clarion, 1990.

Varadpande, M.L. *Religion and Theatre*. New Delhi: Abhinav, 1983.

———. *Traditions of Indian Theatre*. New Delhi: Abhinav, 1978.

Varadpande, M.L. and Sunil Subhedar (eds). *The Critique of Indian Theatre*. Delhi: Unique, 1981.

Vatsyayan, Kapila. *Traditional Indian Theatre: Multiple Streams*. New Delhi: National Book Trust, 1980.

Wade, Bonnie. *Performing Arts in India: Essays on Music, Dance and Drama*. Berkeley: University of California, 1983.

Yajnik, R.K. *The Indian Theatre: Its Origin and Its Later Developments under European Influence, with Special Reference to Western India*. London: Allen and Unwin, 1933.

Yarrow, Ralph. *Indian Theatre: Theatre of Origin, Theatre of Freedom*. Richmond: Curzon, 2001.

Journals

Enact
National Centre for the Performing Arts: Quarterly Journal
Natya: Theatre Arts Journal
Rangvarta
Sangeet Natak
Seagull Theatre Quarterly
Theatre India (*Journal of the National School of Drama*)

Credits for Illustrations

We gratefully acknowledge the cooperation of Anamika Kala Sangam (AKS), Natya Shodh Sansthan (NSS), Sangeet Natak Akademi (SNA), and The Seagull Foundation for the Arts (SFA) in allowing us to print photographs from their collections or publications, and apologize to owners of any copyrighted material if we have inadvertently overlooked them.

p. 7	Photo Seagull, courtesy Nandikar	p. 68	Photo Sopanam Institute of Performing Arts and Research, courtesy AKS
p. 11,	12 Courtesy NSS		
p. 14	Courtesy Bohurupee	p. 72	Courtesy Kerala Peoples Arts Club
p. 16	Courtesy AKS		
p. 20	Photo SNA	p. 74	Courtesy AKS
p. 25	Photo Boman Irani, courtesy SFA	p. 78–9	Photo Amit Bararia, courtesy AKS
p. 27	Courtesy Anuradha Kapur	p. 83	Courtesy SFA
p. 29, 33	Courtesy Budreti Theatre and Media Centre, Ahmadabad	p. 85	Courtesy NSS
		p. 87	Photo Theatre Academy, courtesy AKS
p. 35	Photo SNA		
p. 40	Photo National School of Drama, courtesy AKS	p. 98	Courtesy AKS
		p. 101	Photo Pashupati Rudra Pal
p. 43	Photo National School of Drama Repertory Company	p. 107	Photo SNA
		p. 109	Courtesy The Company, Chandigarh
p. 44	Photo Pronab Basu, courtesy AKS		
p. 52	Courtesy NSS	p. 113	Courtesy SFA
p. 55	Photo Pronab Basu, courtesy AKS	p. 120	Courtesy AKS
p. 56	Photo Yajna, courtesy AKS	p. 122	Photo Sopanam Institute of Performing Arts and Research, courtesy AKS
p. 61	Courtesy Shafi Shauq		
p. 65	Photo Kala Academy, Goa		

p. 390   Photo Ananda Lal

p. 395   Courtesy AKS

p. 401,403 Ananda Lal collection

p. 408   Photo SNA

p. 412   Courtesy AKS

p. 414   Photo Kerala Sangeetha Nataka
            Akademi

p. 417   Courtesy SFA

p. 421   Courtesy Jana Sanskriti

p. 428   Photo Alternative Living
            Theatre, courtesy AKS

p. 432,433 Courtesy M. Nagabhushana
            Sarma

p. 435,439 Photo SNA

p. 445   Photo Regional Resource Centre
            for Performing Arts, Udupi

p. 448   Courtesy M. Nagabhushana
            Sarma